Julian; National Art Library Marshall

A catalogue of engraved national portraits in the National Art Library

I0086021

Julian; National Art Library Marshall

A catalogue of engraved national portraits in the National Art Library

ISBN/EAN: 9783741170430

Manufactured in Europe, USA, Canada, Australia, Japa

Cover: Foto ©Thomas Meinert / pixelio.de

Manufactured and distributed by brebook publishing software
(www.brebook.com)

Julian; National Art Library Marshall

A catalogue of engraved national portraits in the National Art Library

DEPARTMENT OF SCIENCE AND ART
OF THE COMMITTEE OF COUNCIL ON EDUCATION,
SOUTH KENSINGTON MUSEUM.

A

CATALOGUE

OF

ENGRAVED NATIONAL PORTRAITS

IN THE

NATIONAL ART LIBRARY,

WITH A PREFATORY NOTE

BY

JULIAN MARSHALL.

LONDON:
PRINTED FOR HER MAJESTY'S STATIONERY OFFICE
BY EYRE AND SPOTTISWOODE,
PRINTERS TO THE QUEEN'S MOST EXCELLENT MAJESTY.
AND SOLD AT THE SOUTH KENSINGTON MUSEUM.

1895.

Price Five Shillings and Threepence.

PREFATORY NOTE.

The British, Irish, and a few American portraits, described in the present Catalogue, have been collected during a period of more than forty-two years, some by gift or bequest, the rest by purchase. Among the benefactors by donation or legacy were the late Mr. J. Sheepshanks in 1857, the late Rev. Chauncy Hare Townshend in 1868, Dr. Diamond, Mr. William Smith, Mr. George Smith, and others. After a somewhat desultory beginning, as early as April 1853, the buying of portraits, and especially those of natives of the United Kingdom, was more systematically taken up and actively pursued during eight years by a Committee, appointed as advisers, December 14, 1867, and including Mr. William Smith, Chairman, Mr. S. Redgrave, Mr. G. W. Reid, and Mr. Woodward. Mr. R. Redgrave and Mr. George Smith also attended and advised. This Committee reported, in January 1876, that the portraits collected at that date exceeded 1,500 in number, and recommended that they "should be at once brought together and exhibited as a whole." A large number of the portraits were accordingly framed and shown in the galleries at South Kensington. In the Seventeenth Annual Report, 1870, it had already been mentioned that " the Collection of prints had " been largely augmented, the number acquired being 6,655," of which a good proportion consisted of portraits.

There are few Collections more interesting than one such as is here catalogued. It appeals to the eye, to memory and historical association, and to the natural regard and veneration felt by all for the heroes of Army, Navy, Law, Literature, Art, Science, Church, or State. Nor are women, distinguished by their beauty, intellect, literary fame, or heroism, absent from such a Collection. Not a few of them will be found in the present Catalogue. By their execution these prints directly illustrate to the student the qualities and limits of the engraver's art, of whatever kind it may be, and indirectly even some of the painter's skill. The last-named is eminently striking in the works of such men as Faithorne, Loggan, White, J. R. Smith, and others of our great Mezzotint School, where the engraver was himself also the painter or designer, whose picture he transferred to the copper from the paper or canvas before him.

Of this Collection, now considerable both in extent and in value, some hundreds of specimens have been from time to time circulated throughout the country, appearing for periods more or less long, according to needs and circumstances, at provincial Museums and temporary exhibitions; and so they have served a most useful purpose.

In the National Art Library, the great bulk of this Collection, preserved in portfolios, has hitherto been not easily available to the public for reference or study, partly owing to the rapid accumulation of specimens, partly to the want of a Catalogue, and partly to the arbitrary division into classes, never a very convenient system for the student who is not familiar with its principles or details. The present Catalogue aims at supplying one deficiency; while the classes have been broken up, the portraits have been arranged strictly in alphabetical order, and all duplicates have been weeded out and placed in a separate category. The result of these changes will be, it is hoped, that, in future, few minutes need be spent in finding and producing any portrait that may be asked for, if it is in the Collection.

The compiler of the Catalogue has received, throughout his labours, the most willing and courteous assistance of all the members of the official staff of the National Art Library, to whom he desires to express here his most cordial thanks; and he takes this opportunity of especially thanking Mr. Freeman M. O'Donoghue, of the Department of Prints and Drawings in the British Museum, for his frequent, generous, and valuable help, backed by his familiar acquaintance with the splendid Collection in his department, without which the identification of several of the portraits here catalogued would have been most difficult, if indeed possible.

In describing the portraits, the words " right " and " left " are used as denoting the right and left of the spectator, *not* those of the subject, except when applied directly to the person represented.

The painter's (or designer's) name is given, in each case, when known, on the left, immediately after the short biography; and the engraver's on the right.

The manner of execution is often added, after the name of the engraver, thus *etch.* or *etched, wood-cut, stipple, mez.* (for *mezzotinto*), &c. *Mixed mez.* describes a style in which etching, stipple, or other methods, have been mingled with mezzotinto in the engraving of the plate described.

Where no indication of method is given, it may be assumed that the engraving is by line, more or less pure.

Prints which have been described already by J. C. Smith in " British Mezzotinto Portraits," are not measured or described here anew, but have references to his book appended. Similar references are given, in the case of prints engraved by Faithorne, to L. Fagan's Catalogue of that artist's works; in that of Hollar's etchings, to the Catalogue by Parthey; in that of portraits of Queen Elizabeth, to " A Descriptive and Classified Catalogue of " such portraits, by F. M. O'Donoghue, 1894; and so on.

ABBREVIATIONS.

Ha. len. means *half-length.*
Sh. ha. len. means *short half-length.*
T. Q. len. means *three-quarter length.*
Wh. len. means *whole length.*
b. means *born.*
cr. means *created.*
suc. means *succeeded.*
m. means *married.*
d. means *died.*
dep. means *deposed.*
bur. means *buried.*

The dimensions of the plates are given in all cases where possible, the height first, the width next; but not in the cases of vignettes, wood cuts, or lithographs, where there are no plate-marks. Dimensions in brackets, as (10 × 8), are those of the subject, or of as much of that as may have been spared by the knife or scissors.

The prints are measured by English inches and fractions down to sixteenths.

ABBOT, CHARLES. *See* COLCHESTER.

ABBOT, GEORGE. Archbishop of Canterbury, 1562–1633, b. at Guildford, Surrey; educ. at Free School and at Balliol Coll., Oxford, 1578; a Fellow, 1593; D.D., 1597, and Principal of Univ. Coll.; Dean of Winchester, 1599; Vice-chancr, 1600, '3, '8; one of the translators of the New Test., 1604; Bishop of Lichfd. and Coventry, 1609; of London, same year; archbp. Cantuar., 1610; accidentally shot a keeper with a cross-bow shaft; author of several works. Anon., mez.

Bust, inclined to right, looking to front; wearing a ruff, dark gown, square beard, and cap on head.

$7\frac{1}{8} \times 5\frac{1}{4}$. ($6\frac{1}{2} \times 5\frac{1}{4}$). 26572.

This print has not been described before.

—— From an original picture in the possession of Mr. Kingsley.
J. Houbraken.

Sh. ha. len. to front, wearing gown, cap, &c.: oval, in frame, censer and crozier below.

$14\frac{5}{16} \times 9$. ($13\frac{3}{4} \times 8\frac{1}{2}$). 22446.

ABBOTT, CHARLES. *See* TENTERDEN.

ABBOTT, LEMUEL FRANCIS. 1760–1803, portrait painter, b. in Leicestershire, son of a clergyman; pupil of F. Hayman; settled in London, where he acquired reputation and employment; exhibited portraits at R. Academy, 1788, '89, '98, 1800; Lord Nelson sat to him several times; overwhelmed with work, worried with anxiety, and married unhappily, became insane.

L. F. Abbott. V. Green, mez.
J. C. Smith, 1, 2d state. 25764.

ABERCROMBY, JAMES. 1776–1858; Master of the Mint and Cabinet Minister, 1834; Speaker, 1835–'39; cr. Baron Dunfermline, 1839.

J. Jackson. W. Walker, mez.
Hn. len., seated; looking to right.
Engraver's proof before all letters.
$17\frac{1}{2} \times 12\frac{5}{8}$. ($11\frac{1}{2} \times 9\frac{3}{4}$) 22799.

ABERCROMBY, SIR RALPH. 1738–1801, General; b. at Tullibodie, Scotland; ent. the Army, 1756; served under the Duke of Brunswick in Seven Years' War; Comm.-in-chf., West Indies, 1795–'7, and in Ireland, 1798; comm. the Expedition to Egypt, 1800; landed at Aboukir, and defeated the French at Alexandria; d. from his wounds; bur. at Malta; K.B., &c.

J. Hoppner, R.A. F. Bartolozzi, R.A.; stipple.

O 82849. 500.--11/94. Wt. 7499. A

Ha. len., to front, in uniform, looking to left, wearing the star and ribbon of the Bath ; his right arm across his middle; Jany. 1, 1802.
($12\frac{1}{4} \times 10$). 21999.

—— wounded, at the Battle of **Aboukir.**
P. de Loutherbourg, R.A. A. Cardon, stipple.
A composition of many figures; Sir Ralph is sitting, wounded, on a chest, on the right, surrounded by his staff; the battle is raging in the distance.
Proof with skeleton letters; 1806; the title is in English and also in French.
(?) $\times 32\frac{1}{4}$. ($21\frac{1}{4} \times 30\frac{1}{4}$). 27114.

—— the Death of.
T. Stothard, R.A. F Legat, & (another name, suppressed).
A Composition of many figures; in the centre is Sir Ralph, dying, supported by several officers, of whom one kneels, on the left.
Ind. proof with open letters, 1828.
$19\frac{3}{16} \times 24\frac{1}{2}$. ($16\frac{7}{8} \times 23\frac{1}{4}$) 22949.

ABERDEEN, GEORGE HAMILTON GORDON, 4th Earl of, 1784–1860; statesman; ambassador at Vienna and Paris, 1813–'4; Sec. of State for Foreign Affairs, 1828–'30 and 1841–'6; Prime Minister, 1852–'5; K.T., F.R.S., F.S.A., &c.
Sir T. Lawrence, **P.R.A.** C Turner, mez.
Ha. len. to left, facing and looking to right, wearing a wide open collar and dark cloak with chain ; curtain behind ; title and inscription on ruled margin below.
Pubd. Nov. 12th, 1813, by Colnaghi & Co.
$13\frac{3}{4} \times 9\frac{3}{4}$. ($11\frac{3}{4} \times 9\frac{3}{4}$). 23556.

———

Sir T. Lawrence, P.R.A. S. Cousins, mixed mez.
T. Q. len. to front, looking to right, wearing the star and ribbon of the Order of the Thistle ; left hand resting on a folded paper on table, on which is the seal of the Foreign Office.
Ind. proof with skeleton letters; pubd. by Colnaghi Senr., Dom. Colnaghi, & Co., July 28, 1831.
$21\frac{1}{2} \times 16\frac{3}{8}$. ($16\frac{3}{4} \times 13\frac{1}{4}$) 22137.

ABERDEEN Cabinet, The, deciding upon the Expedition to the Crimea, 1854.
Sir J. Gilbert. W. Walker, mixed mez.
A composition of 15 figures, the name of each personage engraved beneath the subject; the Earl of Aberdeen seated, facing to front and looking slightly to left, hands clasped on knee, legs crossed.
$21\frac{7}{8} \times 30$. ($17\frac{7}{16} \times 26\frac{1}{4}$). 22950.
The members of the Cabinet were the Earl of Aberdeen, Earl Granville, Lord John (aftds. Earl) Russell, Marquess of Lansdowne, Earl of Clarendon, Duke of Argyll, Mr. Gladstone,

Sir W. Molesworth, Sir James Graham, Sir Charles Wood (aftds. Visct. Halifax), Lord Cranworth, Visct. Palmerston, Sir George Grey, Mr. Sidney Herbert (aftds. Lord Herbert of Lea), and the Duke of Newcastle.

ABERGAVENNY. *See* BERGAVENNY.

ABERNETHY, JOHN, 1764–1831, b. in London ; educ. at Wolverhampton Gr. Sch. and St. Barthol. Hospl. ; assist.-surgeon, 1787 ; suc. as full surg. to the hospl. after 28 years ; lect. on anatomy ; F.R.S., 1796 ; lect. on Anatomy and Physiology at Coll. of Surgs. ; 1814–1817 ; acquired great reputation and extensive practice ; his fame does not rest on his books, which are considered flimsy.

    C. W. Pegler.   C. Turner, mez.

    T. Q. len. to left, seated, looking to front ; right hand in breast of coat, left on arm of chair, the sides of which are caned.

    Open letter proof ; Nov. 17, 1828.

    18¼⁸ × 13.   (14¼ × 11½)   21895.

ABINGER, JAMES SCARLETT, Lord, 1769–1844, lawyer, b. in Jamaica ; M.P., 1818 ; assisted Mackintosh and Romilly in the reform of the Criminal Code ; Attorney-General, 1827 ; Chief Baron, and raised to Peerage, 1834.

    Sir M. A. Shee, P.R.A.   H. Cousins, mez.

    Ha. len. to front, looking to left ; coat buttoned over light waistcoat and white neckcloth.

    Open letter proof, March, 1837.

    17 × 13.   (11½ × 9¾).   21948.

ABINGTON, FRANCES BARTON, Mrs., 1731–1815, b. in London ; after many difficulties, appeared, Drury Lane, 1755, with success ; m. to Mr. James Abington ; became unrivalled Queen of Comedy, and favourite with the public till her retirement, about end of the century ; possessed of rare talents, elegance, taste, and piquancy, which enabled her to overcome defects of voice and feature.

    Sir J. Reynolds.   J. Watson, mez.

    J. C. Smith, 1, 3rd state.   27149.

—— speaking the Epilogue to the Tragedy of Zingis.

    Dod del.   Cook.

    Pubd. by Fielding and Walker, Novr. 10, 1779.   28187. 1.

ACADEMICIANS, THE ROYAL, assembled in their Council Chamber to adjudge the medals to the successful students in Painting, Sculpture, Architecture, and Drawing.

    H. Singleton.   C. Bestland, stipple.

    A group of many figures, seated and standing ; in the centre, seated in the chair, and wearing his hat, is the figure of B. West, P.R.A.

    (22½ × 30⅜).   22014.

ACADEMY, The Royal, of Arts, instituted by the King, in the
year 1768.
J. Zoffany. R. Earlom, mez.
J. C. Smith, 1, intermediate state between first and second,
the artists' names and publication-line, " *Publish'd August 1st*,
1773. *R. Sayer Excudit*," scratched on the plate; not described
by J. C. S.
24678.

ADAIR, Sir Robert, G.C.B., Diplomat; 1763–1855.
Julien, lith.
Ind. proof before the title, &c.
$13\frac{3}{4} \times 10\frac{1}{2}$. $(5\frac{3}{4} \times 4\frac{3}{4})$. 27196.

ADDINGTON, Henry. *See* SIDMOUTH, Visct.

ADDISON, Joseph, 1672–1719, Poet, Essayist, and Statesman,
wrote the "Campaign," in celebration of Marlborough's victory
at Blenheim; founded with Swift the "Spectator," 1711; produced his tragedy of "Cato," 1713; app. Sec. of State, 1717
Sir G. Kneller. J. Simon, mez.
J. C. Smith, 2, 2nd state. 21879.

DELAIDE, Queen, 1792–1849, eldest child of George, Duke
of Saxe Meiningen; m. to the Duke of Clarence, 1818; became
Queen Consort, on the Duke's accession to the throne as
William IV., 1830; Queen Dowager, 1837; d. at Bentley
Priory, Stanmore, Middlesex.
Sir W. Beechey, R.A. S. W. Reynolds, mixed mez.
Wh. len. to front, in black dress, with white sleeves, holding
flowers in right hand, pillar and curtain behind.
Proof before all but the artists' names, arms, and publication-
line, on a supplementary plate; Septr., 1831.
$25\frac{1}{2} \times 17\frac{2}{16}$. $(25\frac{1}{4} \times 16\frac{1}{2}$; sup. plate, $2\frac{3}{4} \times 17\frac{1}{8})$. 23151.

Sir W. Beechey. T. Lupton, mez.
Sh. ha. len. to front, wearing a ruff collar, and four rows of
pearls in her hair. Oval in frame. Open letter proof.
$15\frac{3}{8} \times 12\frac{1}{2}$. $(11 \times 9\frac{1}{2})$.
In Genealogical Chart, 553. 1. 25051.

Anon. (G. Richmond?) Anon., stipple.
Head, in a cap; on a ruled ground, on steel plate. Vignette.
Ind. proof before all letters.
$13\frac{13}{16} \times 11$. $(9\frac{1}{2} \times 7\frac{6}{10})$. 23163.

AIKIN, John, 1747–1822, physician and author, b. at Kibworth;
educ. at Warrington by his father; stud. at Edinb. and London
M.D., Leyden; settled in med. practice at Grt. Yarmouth,
1784; came to London, 1792; friend of Priestley, Pennant,
Darwin, Howard, Southey, &c.
See MEDICAL SOCIETY.

AISKEW, Clerk Assistant in the House of Commons, during Sir
Robert Walpole's Administration.
  See COMMONS.

ALAND, Sir John Fortescue.   *See* FORTESCUE, Lord.

ALBANY, John, Duke of, — — 1525, regent of Scotland,
1514; retired, 1524, to France; killed at Pavia; with Queen
Margaret, and another figure (Henry, Stuart, E. of Methven,
her third husband(?)) behind her, pointing at Albany.
  Anon.   Birrel.
  Ha. len. He is receiving from her a purse (?). Coins,
pens, and ink are on the table, on left.
  "From a picture in the possession of the Marquis of Bute."
  Pub. Feb. 7, 1798, by Edwd. Harding.
  $7\frac{2}{16} \times 10\frac{3}{8}$. $(6\frac{3}{4} \times 9\frac{7}{16})$.   24052.

ALBEMARLE, Arnold Joost Van Keppel, 1st Earl of,
1669–1718, of Dutch family; Lord of Voorst; came with
William of Orange to England, 1688, as page; cr. 1695-'6;
rose to great favour; Colonel of Guards, 1699; K.G., 1700;
resided much in Holland, and acted in several engagements in
concert with Marlborough; d. at the Hague.
  Sir G. Kneller.   J. Smith, mez.
  J. C. Smith, 2, 2nd state.   22448.

ALBEMARLE, Christopher, second Duke of, c. 1653–1688,
son of George Monck, first Duke; suc. 1670; Govr. Jamaica,
1687.
  T. Murray.   I. Beckett, mez.
  J. C. Smith, 1, 2nd state.   27629.

ALBEMARLE, George Monck, first Duke of, 1608–1670,
second son of Sir Thomas Monck, of Potheridge, Devon, great
soldier and statesman; member of Cromwell's House of Lords;
restorer of the Monarchy; K.G.; cr. Baron Monck, Earl of
Torrington, and Duke of Albemarle, 1660.
  F. Barlow.   P. Stent excud.
  Ha. len. to front, with right hand resting on helmet.
  Three lines of dedication, above; below, five lines of titles,
&c. Very rare (Evans).
  Cut $(8\frac{3}{4} \times 7\frac{1}{16})$.   27251.

—— "His Highness, George Monck, *Duke of* Albemarle and
Captaine-*general of all his Maties. land forces, &c.*"
                                                         Anon.
  Bust in oval to left, wearing scarf with medal.
  Cut $(5\frac{1}{2} \times 3\frac{7}{9})$.   20924.

—— "His Excellency, George Monck, Generall of all the
Forces in England, Scotland, and Ireland, &c."
                                     Anon. [Gaywood?]
  Ha. len. to right, looking to front; long hair, wide collar.
  Cut $(5\frac{1}{2} \times 3\frac{3}{4})$.   20925.

ALBERT, Duke of Saxe-Coburg-Gotha, Prince Consort, 1819–1861; m. 1840.

W. C. Ross, A.R.A. H. T. Ryall, Esq.
Vignette. Arms below. July 1840, Published by Messrs. Colnaghi and Puckle.
Ind. proof before the title.
$14\frac{15}{16} \times 11\frac{7}{8}$. $(6\frac{1}{2} \times 5\frac{1}{4})$. 23591.

—— (From a photograph?) J. L. Raab sc. Nuremberg
Wh. len. leaning against a pillar; below is a facs. signature.
$10\frac{1}{2} \times 7\frac{7}{8}$. $(6\frac{7}{8} \times 4\frac{9}{16})$. 22180.

—— H. Thorburn. Fr. Hanfstaengel lith. 1844.
T. Q. len. in plate armour, right hand resting on helmet by his side.
$(11\frac{5}{8} \times 9\frac{3}{8})$. 22178.

—— with his brother Ernest, Duke of Saxe-Coburg-Gotha, 1818–1893; suc., 1831.
R. Thorburn. T. H. Maguire lith., 1851.
T. Q. len.; the Prince in a Van Dyck dress, on the left; the Duke, who is in plate armour, is on the right.
$(14\frac{1}{4} \times 12\frac{8}{16})$. 22179.

—— W. C. Ross, A.R.A. F. Bacon.
T. Q. len. to left, looking to front.
Septr., 8th, 1841. Published by Colnaghi and Puckle.
$(8 \times 5\frac{1}{8})$. 25053. 2.
In Genealogical Chart, 553. 1.

—— Mayall photo., 1861. J. L. Raab sc. Nuremberg; 1865.
Sh. ha. len. profile to left. Oval in a border.
$9\frac{3}{4} \times 8\frac{3}{4}$. $(7\frac{1}{8} \times 5\frac{13}{16})$. 22181

—— Fr. Holl.
T. Q. len. seated to left, face in profile; facs. signature below
A Private plate. Jany. 10, 1862. Ind. proof.
$14\frac{1}{2} \times 12\frac{3}{8}$. $(7 \times 5\frac{7}{16})$. 25072.

—— F. Winterhalter. J. A. Vinter lith.
Bust, in uniform, to left, looking to front; facs. signature below.
An oval.
$(20\frac{7}{8} \times 16\frac{15}{16})$. 22176.

—— K. Macleay, R.S.A. J. A. Vinter lith.
Wh. len. in Highland dress.
$(26\frac{1}{8} \times 19\frac{7}{8})$. 22182.
See FIRST OF MAY.
See VICTORIA, Princess Royal, Christening of.

ALBERT EDWARD, Prince of Wales (1841–   ; m.
1863), with the Princess Royal, Prince Alfred, Princesses
Louisa, Alice, Helena, and Prince Arthur.

Smyth, woodcut.
Wh. len., the Pr. of Wales in Highland dress; Windsor Castle
in the distance.
From the Illustrated London News, 1852.
(14 × 20⅝.)   25070.
In Genealogical Chart, 553, 1.

___

A. Hunt.   Leighton Bros.
"In India;" in uniform, standing, with his right arm on the
saddle of his charger.
A coloured print (Illustrated London News).
(17¹⁸/₁₆ × 12¾).   15741.

___

J. H. Lynch, lith.
Full ha. len. to right, in uniform, with facs. signature below,
1859.
(16¼ × 12¾).   22183.

___

F. Winterhalter.   T. Fairland lith., 1852.
As a boy; in an oval.
(13¼ × 12⅜).   22190.

ALBINESS, The Beautiful.
Anon.   Anon.
See LA BELLE ASSEMBLÉE, 1816,   13867. 32.

ALDERMEN, Four of the eight (second plate); John
Barber, Francis Child, Richard Levett, Sr. John Wil-
liams, Knt.; 1725.   J. Simon, mez.
J. C. Smith, 4.   27540.

ALDERSON, Robert,   –   ; Recorder, Ipswich, Yarmouth,
and Norwich.
T. J. W., MD.   R. Cooper (Norwich), line and stipple.
Sh. ha. len. to left, in profile, seated.
Ind. open letter proof, 1828.
11⅛ × 10⅜.   (6 × 4¹⁶/₁₆).   24729.

ALDRICH, Henry, 1647–1710, b. at Westminster; educ. by Dr.
Busby, and at Oxford; Dean of Chr. Ch. Coll., 1689; had
great knowledge of Architecture and Music; designed Peck-
water; composed anthems, services, catches, &c.; collected and
preserved fine old music, and materials for a history of Music;
wrote "Artis Logicæ Compendium;" d. at Ch. Ch., Oxford.
Sir G. Kneller.   J. Smith, mez.
J. C. Smith, 3, 3rd state.   21878.

ALEXANDER, William, 1767–1816, water-colour painter, b.
at Maidstone; pupil of W. Pars and of Ibbetson; stud., R.

Academy, 1784; went with Lord Macartney's mission to China, as draftsman; profr. of drawing to R. Military Coll., Great Marlow, 1802–'8; Assist. Keeper of Antiq., Br. Musm.; later, Keeper of the prints and drawings; pubd. views in China, &c.

H. Edridge del. C. Picart, stipple.

Sh. ha. len. to front, looking to right; vignette; private plate.

$9\frac{1}{16} \times 8\frac{1}{2}$. ($4\frac{3}{4} \times 5\frac{3}{8}$). 24651.

ALFRED, "The Great," 849–c. 900; suc. to the throne of England, 871 G. Vertue.

Ha. len. slightly to right, crowned, with ermine collar to cloak; from a picture at University Coll. Oxon. and an ancient stone head.

$11\frac{1}{4} \times 7\frac{1}{2}$. ($10\frac{7}{8} \times 7\frac{1}{4}$). 27178. 2.

ALFRED, Prince. *See* **SAXE-COBURG-GOTHA.**

ALISON, Archibald, 1757–1839, son of Patrick Alison, provost of Edinburgh; educ. at Glasgow, and Balliol; matr., 1775; LL.B., 1784; took orders; pubd. "Essay on the Nature and Principles of Taste," 1790; became Prebendary of Sarum, Rector of Roddington, &c., and Senior Minister of S. Paul's Chapel, Edinb.

Sir H. Raeburn, R.A. W. Walker, stipple.

Ha. len. to left, looking to front.

Open letter proof, April, 1823, Edinb.

$16\frac{1}{2} \times 12$. ($8\frac{5}{16} \times 6\frac{7}{8}$). 23165.

ALICE MAUD MARY, Princess, 1843–1878, m. to Prince Louis of Hesse-Darmstadt, 1862.

F. Winterhalter. J. A. Vinter lith., 1861.

T. Q. len. to right, in an oval.

($18\frac{5}{8} \times 15\frac{1}{2}$). 22186.

ALLAN, Sir William, 1782–1850, Knt., P.R.S.A., and R.A., subject-and-history painter, limner to the Queen in Scotland; of humble origin, stud. in R. Academy schools; imitated Opie; exhibited first in 1803; visited Russia, Tartary, Turkey; returned, 1814; befriended by Sir Walter Scott; A.R.A., 1825; suffering from illness, went to Rome, Naples, thence to Constantinople, Asia Minor, Greece; returned, 1830; travelled again; R.A., 1835; P.R.S.A., 1838.

Anon. J. Hastin (?), woodcut.

Sh. ha. len. to right, right hand to head; vignette, in oval; facs. signature below; from an illustrated paper.

($3\frac{1}{2} \times 3$) E. 1948.–'89.

See also SCOTT, Sir Walter.

ALLEN, John, 1770–1843, b. at Colinton, near Edinburgh; librarian to Lord Holland; author of "Illustrations of Mr. Hume's Essays," a translation of Cuvier's study of the animal

Economy, 1801, "Inquiry into the Rise and Growth of the Royal Prerogative in England," 1830, &c., &c., M.D. Edinb., &c.
See HOLLAND.

ALLEN, ALAN, or ALLYN, WILLIAM, 1532–1594, Cardinal, b. at Rossal, Lanc.; educ. at Oxford; settled at Louvain; embarked in controversy; returned to England, where he published pamphlets which rendered him odious to the government; retired to Flanders, 1568; Th.D., at Douai; canon of Cambrai and, later, of Reims; suggested the invasion of England to Philip II. of Spain; Cardinal Archbishop of Mechlen; lived at Rome till his death.
W. Haines del. (from Original Picture). S. Freeman, stipple.
Ha. len. to left, looking to front, wearing cardinal's cape and cap; pubd. by Lackington & Co.
$14\frac{1}{8} \times 10\frac{7}{16}$. $(7\frac{1}{16} \times 5\frac{1}{2})$.   22447.

ALLEN, CAPTAIN WILLIAM, –1698, of the "Bonadventure," killed in action.
See NAVAL HEROES (2).

ALLEN, WILLIAM, 1779–1843, chemist and philanthropist; son of a Quaker silk manufacturer in Spitalfields; chemist in Plough Court; lecturer on Chemistry at Guy's Hospital; promoted abolition of slavery, education and improvement of condition of the poor; first presidt. of Pharmaceutical Socy.; F.R.S.
H. P. Briggs, R.A.   H. C. Shenton.
T. Q. len. slightly inclined to right, seated, looking to front; white hair, high waistcoat, right arm resting on prints on table.
Ind. proof; facs. signature; Oct. 1, 1845.
$13\frac{3}{4} \times 11\frac{1}{4}$. $(9\frac{1}{4} \times 7\frac{1}{2})$.   22948.
See also SCIENCE.

ALSOP, MRS.
R. E. Drummond.   J. Alais, stipple.
See LA BELLE ASSEMBLÉE.   13867. 1

ALTHORP, JOHN CHARLES, Viscount, and afterwards Earl Spencer, statesman, 1782–1845; educ. at Harrow and Trin. Coll. Camb; M.P. 1806–1834; suc., 1834; Chanc. of Exch.; devoted himself to the improvement of agriculture; founded the Royal Society of Agriculture.
T. Phillips, R.A.   C. Turner, A.R.A., mez.
Published, June 14, 1831, by Mr. Turner.   Mez.
Proof with open letters.
$15\frac{1}{4} \times 12$. $(11 \times 8\frac{1}{2})$.   22800.

AMELIA, SOPHIA ELEONORA, Princess, 1710–1786, second daughter of George II.; b. in Hanover; d. in Cavendish Square, unm.; bur. in Henry VII.'s Chapel, Westminster Abbey.
P. Mercier, 1728.   J. Simon, mez.
J. C. Smith, 6, 1st state.   27520.

AMELIA, PRINCESS, 1783–1810, youngest daughter, and last and fifteenth child of George III.; very delicate; after long illness, d. at the age of 27.

H. Ramberg. W. Ward, stipple.
With a bird, in oval.
Cut ($10\frac{7}{8} \times 8\frac{3}{4}$). 26725. 6.
Also, a duplicate in Genealogical Chart, 553. 1.
$11\frac{1}{1}\frac{5}{6} \times 8\frac{7}{8}$. 25068. 2.

Anon. [P W. Tomkins] stipple.
With a rosebud.
Proof before letters, except the publication-line.
Publd. as the Act directs, Aug. 25, 1790, by P. W. Tomkins.
$9\frac{3}{8} \times 7\frac{5}{16}$ ($6\frac{7}{16} \times 5\frac{3}{16}$) 23148.

Sir W. Beechey. Cheesman.
T. Q. len. front, looking right, in oval.
Published by Harding, 19 May, 1806.
$10\frac{7}{8} \times 8\frac{7}{8}$. ($7\frac{1}{4} \times 6\frac{3}{8}$). 25059. 3.
In Genealogical Chart, 553. 1.

A. Robertson. A. Cardon.
Ha. len. in hat.
Published, June 1, 1810.
$9\frac{1}{2} \times 6\frac{3}{8}$ ($5\frac{7}{8} \times 5$). E. 1062–'88.

AMHERST, SIR JEFFREY, aftds. 1st Baron, 1717–1797, entd. the army; served under Ligonier and the Duke of Cumberland; rendered brilliant services in the conquest of Canada from the French, Governor of Guernsey, 1770; cr. Baron Amherst, 1776; Field Marshal, 1796; K.C.B.; &c.

Sir J. Reynolds. J. Watson, mez.
J. C. Smith, 2, 3rd state. 21913.

AMHERST, WILLIAM PITT, 2nd Baron, 1st Earl, 1773–1857, statesman; b. at Bath; educ. at Oxf.; B.A., 1793; M.A., 1797; Ambas. Extr. to China, where he was refused admission, 1816; Gov.-Genl. of India, 1822–'8; G.C.H., P.C., cr. Visct. Holmesdale and Earl Amherst, 1826; m. Sarah, dow. Countess of Plymouth, widow of 5th Earl, 1800, and (2nd) Mary, dow Countess of Plymouth, widow of 6th Earl, 1839.

Sir T. Lawrence, P.R.A. C. Turner, mez.
Wh. len. to front, in robes, hat in right hand, left hand on papers lying on a stone pillar; view of Canton in the background; Decr. 1, 1826.
$26\frac{1}{8} \times 15$. ($24\frac{1}{4} \times 15$). 22108.

ANDERSON, MRS. LUCY, 1790–1878, dau. of John Philpot, music-seller at Bath, where she was born; received some lessons on the pianoforte from Windsor (of Bath), her cousin; became eminent in London as a player; m. to G. F. Anderson, 1820, a violinist,

who became aftds. master of the Queen's Band; she instructed
the Princess (now Queen) Victoria, and her children, and was
the first female pianist who ever played at the Philharm.
Concerts.
See FIRST READING.

ANDREWS or ANDREWES, LANCELOT, 1555–1626, b. in the
parish of All Hallows, Barking; educ. at Merchant Taylors'
School, and Pembroke Hall, Cambr.; fellow of Pembr., 1576,
and, later. of Jesus, Oxf.; took orders, 1580; presd. to the
living of St. Giles's, Cripplegate, made a prebend residy. of St.
Paul's; and master of Pembr. Hall, 1589–1605; Dean, West-
minster, 1601; Bishop of Chichester, 1605; of Ely, 1609; of
Winchester, 1619; Dean of Chapel Royal; P.C.; &c.
(G. P. Harding del.)   J. Tuck.
Ha. len. to right, in gown and cap.
Ind. proof, Aug. 1, 1822.
$8\frac{7}{16} \times 6\frac{3}{8}$. $(4\frac{7}{8} \times 4\frac{3}{10})$.   28159.

ANGLESEY, HENRY WILLIAM PAGET, 1st Marquess of, 1768–
1854; General; eld. son of the Earl of Uxbridge; disting. at
Waterloo, in command of the united British and Belgian
Cavalry; twice Lord Lieut. of Ireland; Master General of the
Ordnance; Field-Marshal; G.C.B., G.C.H., K.G., &c.
Sir T. Lawrence, P.R.A.   C. Turner, A.R.A., mez.
Wh. len., standing, inclined to left, looking to front, in
hussar uniform, holding busby in left hand.
Open letter proof; Oct. 8, 1828
$28 \times 17\frac{1}{16}$. $(24\frac{5}{8} \times 14\frac{3}{4})$.   22107.

ANNE, 1507–1536, second Queen of Henry VIII., dau. of Sir
Thomas Boleyn, aftds. Earl of Wilts. and Ormond; Maid of
Honour to Queen Catharine; privily m. to Henry VIII., 1533;
cr. at Westminster Hall, on Whitsunday; became mother of
Queen Elizabeth, 1533; tried and condemned on very doubtful
evidence, and beheaded.
H. Holbein.   J. Houbraken.
Ha. len. to left, wearing pearls in cap, on neck, and on dress;
oval in frame; Cupid, with reversed torch, &c., below. In
Birch's " Lives."
$14\frac{1}{2} \times 9$. $(14\frac{1}{5} \times 8\frac{1}{4})$.   21810.

———

                                  H. T. Ryall.
"From the original of Holbein in the Collection of ... the
Earl of Warwick."
Ha. len. wearing a peaked cap, ornamented with pearls.
Published, May 1, 1832, by Harding and Lepard.
Cut $(4\frac{3}{4} \times 3\frac{13}{16})$.   14352.

ANNE OF CLEVES, 1516–1557; Queen of Henry VIII., 1540;
divorced after six months.

"Holbein pinxit. In the Collection of Thomas Barret, Esq."
                                        J. Houbraken, 1739.
Sh. ha. len. wearing two necklaces, and a jewelled cross above
them. In Birch's " Lives."
    14½ × 9¼.   (14⅜ × 8¾).   27117   1.

----

*Adn. vander Werff.   Vermeulen.
Copied from the portrait by Holbein.
Sh. ha. len. to front, wearing two necklaces, with a cross above
them.
    12½ × 7¾.   (11½ × 6¾).   14168.
* Not the original designer. This remark applies to many other portraits
which bear his name.

ANNE (of Denmark), 1574-1619, Queen Consort of James I.,
    1589.
    "Are to be fould over against the Exchange by Comp.
Holland."   Anon.
    T. Q len. to right, looking to front, holding a kerchief in her
right, and a feather fan in her left hand : 16 verses below,
in two columns.
    A fine impression of a rare print.
    11¾ × 8⅛.   (10¼ × 8⅛).   26669.
    Query : is this the print mentioned by Bromley, with the address, " Stent
exc." ?

                                                       Anon.
    Ha. len. in an oval, to front ; below, ANNA . REGINA . SCOTORVM.
    Cut (6 × 4½)   25024.
    In Genealogical Chart, 553.   1.

ANNE, PRINCESS, c. 1636-1640, 3rd daughter of Charles I.
    See CHARLES, PRINCE OF WALES, &c.

ANNE, QUEEN, 1665-1714, second daughter of James II.; b. at
    St. James's Palace ; m. to George, Prince of Denmark, 1683 ;
    suc. William III. (the husband of her elder sister, Queen Mary
    II.), 1702 ; d. leaving no children surviving her.
    Sir G. Kneller.   J. Smith, mez.
    As Princess of Denmark.
    J. C. Smith, 4, 2nd state.   25036.
    In Genealogical Chart, 553.   1.

    Sir G. Kneller.   J Smith, mez.
    As Queen.
    J C Smith, 7, 1st (or 2nd ?) state.   26670.

ANNE, PRINCESS OF ORANGE, 1709-1759, eldest daughter of
    George II ; m. to William IV., Prince of Orange, 1734.

H. Pothoven del. J. Houbraken, 1750.

Ha. len., to left, looking to front, left hand to bosom; oval in ornamental border.

$14\frac{1}{2} \times 9\frac{1}{4}$. ($13\frac{5}{8} \times 8\frac{1}{2}$). 29717. 15.

A duplicate is in Genealogical Chart, 553. 1. 25018. 4.

Ph. Mercier, 1734. J. Faber, junr., mez.

J. C. Smith, 265, 1st state. 22474.

ANON.

A. Geddes, 1812. J. Stewart, 1819.

Bust, to right, looking to front; wide open collar; vignette; private plate. "Printed by Hayward," scratched.

Ind. proof.

$10\frac{1}{8} \times 8\frac{1}{8}$. ($4\frac{1}{2} \times 4\frac{3}{8}$). 28300. 28.

ANSON, George, Lord, 1697–1762, b. at Shugborough, Staffordshire; entd. navy, 1712; rose rapidly; commodore of expedn. against the Spanish, 1740, when he made his famous voyage round the world; took six French men-of-war off Cape Finisterre, 1747; cr. Baron; first Lord from 1751 to his death, June 6, 1762.

Sir J. Reynolds. J. McArdell, mez.

J. C. Smith, 2, second state.

From John Young's collection. 26671.

See TRIUMPH OF BRITANNIA.

ANSTEY, Christopher, 1724–1805, only son of Rev. Christopher Anstey, D.D., of Brinkley, Cambs.; educ. at Bury, Eton, and Cambr.; B.A., and fellow of King's, 1746; author of the "New Bath Guide," 1766, "Election Ball," 1776; &c.

T. Lawrence, R.A. W. Bond, stipple.

Ha. len. to front, looking to right, seated at table, holding pen in his right hand; ætat. 52.

Open letter proof (?); March 1st, 1807.

$11\frac{13}{16} \times 9\frac{3}{8}$. ($6\frac{5}{16} \times 4\frac{3}{4}$). 24053.

ANSTRUTHER, Sir John, Bart., 1753–1811, M.P., Anstruther; Recr Genl. of Bishop's rents (Scotland); Ch. Justice, Bengal, 1798; resigned, 1806; d. in Albemarle St.

G. Dance. Wm. Daniell.

Sh. ha. len. to right, seated, in profile; vignette. Feb. 1, 1809.

$10\frac{5}{8} \times 7\frac{7}{8}$. ($7\frac{3}{4} \times 5\frac{1}{4}$). 28146. 1.

ARCTIC COUNCIL, The, discussing the plan of search for Sir John Franklin; Sir Francis Beaufort (q. v.) seated in the centre.

S. Pearce. J. Scott, mixed mez.

A group of 10 figures, all standing, except Sir Francis Beaufort and, on the extreme right, one other;

Viz.—Captain Sir George Back, F.R.S.; Rear Admiral Sir
W. Edward Parry, F.R.S.; Capt. E. J. Bird; Capt. Sir James
C. Ross, F.R.S.; Rear-Admiral Sir Francis Beaufort, K.C.B.,
F.R.S.; John Barrow, Esq., F.R.S., F.S.A.; Lt.-Col. Sabine,
R.A., V.P.R.S.; Capt. W. Baillie Hamilton; Sir John Richard-
son, C.B., F.R.S.; Capt. F W. Beechey, F.R.S.; and (on the
wall) Sir J. Franklin, Capt. Fitzjames, and Sir J. Barrow.
Open letter proof (?); May 2, 1853.
(18 × 28¾). 21960.

ARGYLL, Archibald Campbell, ninth Earl of; "MacCallum
More," 1663–1685. Confederate of Monmouth; beheaded.
Wm. Derby. W. Freeman.
From the original in the Collection of His Grace the Duke of
Argyll.
Published, Dec. 1, 1826, by Harding and Lepard.
14 × 10 (cut?). (7$\frac{1}{16}$ × 5$\frac{5}{8}$). 28162.

———

J. B. de Medina. P. Vanderbanck.
In armour, in an oval; coats of arms on each side.
17½ × 12¼ (cut?). (15¼ × 12¼). 24688.

ARGYLL, Elizabeth, Duchess of Hamilton, and aftds. of Argyll,
1734–1790, second daughter of John Gunning, Esq., of Co. Roscommon; surreptitiously m. 1st, Feb. 14, 1752, to James, 6th
Duke of Hamilton (who d. Jany. 17, 1758); 2nd, March 3,
1759, to Lieut.-Colonel John Campbell, Marquess of Lorne
(who became 5th Duke of Argyll, 1770); cr. Baroness Hamilton, of Hambledon, co. Leicester, 1776; one of the two
"beautiful Miss Gunnings."
C. Read. J. Finlayson, mez.
J. C. Smith, 1, 3rd state. 22106.

ARGYLL, Sir George Douglas Campbell, 8th Duke of, 1823–
; Lord Privy Seal, 1853; Post-Master General, 1855–'8;
again Ld. Privy Seal, 1859–'66; Sec. of State for India, 1868–
'74; once more Ld. Privy Seal, 1880–'1.
See ABERDEEN Cabinet.

ARGYLL, John Campbell, 2nd Duke of, 1680–1743, son of
Archibald, 1st Duke; b. at Ham House; cr. an Engl. Peer as
Baron Chatham and Earl of Greenwich, for promoting the union
with Scotland, 1705; served under Marlborough in Flanders
with distinction; Ambassador and generalissimo in Spain, 1710;
Com.-in-Chf., in Scotland, against the Pretender's invasion,
1715; cr. Duke of Greenwich and K.G., 1719; d. at Sudbrook
House, Petersham, 1743; bur. in Westminster Abbey, with
monument by Roubilliac; *Jeenie Deans's* Duke, in the "Heart
of Midlothian;" described by Pope as—
"Argyll, the state's whole thunder born to wield,
And shake alike the senate and the field."
A. Ramsay, 1740. J. Faber, junr. mez.
J. C. Smith, 15. 24200.

ABLINGTON, HENRY BENNET, 1st Earl of, 1618–1685, Statesman; volunteer in Royalist army, in Civil War; shared exile of
Charles II., knighted by him at Bruges, 1658; Principal Sec.
of State, 1662; member of "Cabal" Cabinet, 1670; cr. Earl,
1672; K.G.; adviser of the "Test Act;" impeached, but
acquitted by the House of Commons.
Sir P. Lely.   J. Houbraken.
Sh. ha. len. to right, looking to front, wearing a patch across
his nose, long wig, and the star of the Garter; oval in ornamental border; 1739; in Birch's "Lives."
14¾ × 9¼.   (14⅛ × 8¾).   22449.

ARMSTRONG, JOHN, 1784–1829, stud. med. at Edinb.; M.D.,
1808; pubd. several medical works, and contributed to professional journals; his lectures appeared in the "Lancet," 1825.
Sir J. Reynolds.   E. Fisher, mez.
J. C. Smith, 3.   24435.

ARNE, THOMAS AUGUSTINE (the second name assumed), 1710–
1778; son of the "Political Upholsterer" in King St., Cov.
Garden; educ. at Eton; intended for the law, preferred music;
pupil of Festing; re-set Addison's "Rosamond," composed
the "Opera of Operas;" "Zara," 1734; "Comus," 1738;
"Alfred," 1740, in which "Rule Britannia" first appeared;
"Judith," "Artaxerxes," many glees, songs, catches, &c.;
Mus. Doc., 1759; he was the first to introduce female voices in
Oratorio Choruses.
Dunkarton.   Anon.
Ha. len. to right, looking to front, holding music in right
hand; oval, in frame, in Universal Magazine, May, 1784.
(5⅞ × 3 13/16; oval, 4 × 3 3/16).   E. 249.–'90.

F. Bartolozzi del.   F. Bartolozzi, stipple.
Ha. len. to right, in profile, playing on a harpsichord.
9⅝(?) × 6 13/16(?).   (8½ × 6⅔).   22293.

ARNOLD, SAMUEL, 1740–1802, b. in London, educ. at the Chapel
Royal and under Dr. Nares; Mus. Doc., Oxf., 1773; Organist
and Composer to Chapel Royal, 1783; Organist of Westminster
Abbey; composed oratorios, operas, church music, &c.; edited
the works of Handel.
T. Hardy.   T. Hardy, stipple.
Ha. len. to right, looking to front, wearing Doctor of Music's
gown and cap, and bands.
Open letter proof; Jany. 10, 1797.
10¼ × 8.   (8¾ × 6¾).   22490.

ARNOLD, THOMAS, 1795–1842, educ. at Warminster, Winchester,
Corp. Xti, Oxf.; grad. first class, 1814; fellow of Oriel, 1815;
ordained, 1818; Master of Rugby, 1827; B.D., and D.D.,
1828.
T. Phillips, R.A.   H. Cousins, mez.

T. Q. len. to front, seated, looking to left, with a large book open on his lap.
Open letter proof, May 29, 1840.
$19\frac{7}{8} \times 14\frac{1}{8}$. $(16\frac{9}{16} \times 13)$.   25815.

ARTHUR, PRINCE OF WALES, 1486–1502; Eldest son of Henry VII.
"From an Ancient Painting on Board."   Barrett.
Ha. len., wearing cap and feather, and holding hilt of sword in left hand
Published, June 29, 1795, by G. Barrett.
Cut $(3\frac{7}{8} \times 2\frac{3}{4})$.   14350.

ARTHUR, WILLIAM PATRICK ALBERT, Prince.   See CON-NAUGHT and FIRST OF MAY.

ARTISTS, "a society of, that existed about the year 1738."
Hogarth.   ·   R. Sawyer, etched.
A company of 15 wh. len. figures in a room, some seated and others standing. The following names are given, with references to eight of the persons represented, viz. :—
Rysbrack, Gibbons, Laroon, Kent, Hamilton, Dahl, Vander-banck, and Bridgman (see these names for biographical notices).
Pubd. by W. B. Tiffin, May 1, 1829, from the original sketch in his possession.
$12\frac{3}{4} \times 14$. $(11\frac{3}{8} \times 13\frac{9}{16})$.   22801.

ARUNDEL, THOMAS HOWARD, Earl of, 1585–1647; K.G., 1611; P.C.; Earl Marshal, 1621; ambassador to Germany, 1636; Lord Steward; Lord High Steward; Captain General; cr. Earl of Norfolk, 1644; &c.
A. van Dyck.   W. Sharp.
Full ha. len. to right, seated, looking to front, holding a paper in his right, and in his left hand a jewel, attached to a broad ribbon which passes round his neck.
Ind. proof; 1 July, 1823.
$18\frac{7}{16} \times 14\frac{3}{8}$. $(10\frac{1}{8} \times 7\frac{7}{8})$.   20893.
Also, a duplicate, with remark F added, in inner margin, immediately below little finger of right hand.   22489.

———

From the original of Rubens.
W. Hilton, A.R.A. del.   E. Scriven.
Ind. proof with open letters.
$14\frac{7}{8} \times 10\frac{3}{8}$ full. $(7\frac{1}{8} \times 5\frac{5}{8})$.   28154.

———, with Alathea Talbot, his Countess.
A. van Dyck.   L. Vorsterman.
T. Q. len. seated, with a terrestrial globe, compasses, &c. 4 Latin verses below.
Cut $(11\frac{3}{16} \times 16\frac{1}{8})$.   23126.

ARUNDELL OF WARDOUR, BLANCH, 1584–1649, 6th daughter of Edward Somerset, 4th Earl of Worcester; m.,

1607, to Thomas Arundell, 2d Baron Arundell of Wardour; she defended Wardour Castle against the Parliamentary forces, but (by her husband's directions) a mine was sprung, and the Castle sacrificed; d. at Winchester.

W. Hilton, R.A.   E. Scriven, stipple.

T. Q. len. to right, looking to front, wearing a triple collar of pearls, and other pearls in her hair and on her dress; holding with her left hand a book, on a cushion, and a handkerchief in her right; Decr. 25, 1820.

$14\frac{7}{8} \times 10\frac{5}{8}$. $(7 \times 5\frac{5}{8})$.   **28164.** ~

ASHBURTON, ALEXANDER BARING, Lord; Statesman, 1774–1848.

Sir Thos. Lawrence, P.R.A.   C. E. Wagstaff, mixed mez.
Published Aug. 1, 1837, by Hodgson & Graves.
Proof before the title, &c.
$12 \times 9\frac{1}{16}$. $(8\frac{1}{4} \times 6\frac{1}{2})$.   28148.

ASHBURTON, JOHN DUNNING, Lord, 1731–1783, chancellor of duchy of Lancaster, and Peer, 1782.

Sir J. Reynolds.   [Bond ?]

T. Q. len. to right, seated, in robes.
Cut $(7\frac{5}{8} \times 6\frac{1}{2})$.   28158.

ASTLE, THOMAS, 1734–1803, antiquary, settled in London, empl. in Govt. offices; became Keeper of the Public Records in the Tower; his principal work is the "Origin and Progress of Writing," 1784; F.R.S., F.S.A.; a trustee of the British Museum.

See TOWNELEY.

ASTON, WALTER, First Lord, Ambassador to Spain; 1579–1639.
From the original.
R. W. Satchwell del.   R. Cooper.
T. Q. length, with embroidered dress.
Published Dec. 1, 1815, by Lackington, Allen & Co.
$14\frac{3}{8} \times 10\frac{1}{2}$. $(7 \times 5\frac{1}{2})$.   27158.

ATHLONE, GODART DE GINKELL, first Earl of, ——1703, of Amerougen, prov. of Utrecht, Lt.-Genel. and Comdr.-in-Chf., Ireland, and, having distingd. himself by the capture of Athlone, and at battle of Aghrim, was cr., 1692, Baron of Aghrim and Earl of Athlone; Comdr.-in-Chf. of allied armies in Flanders, and Veldt-Marshal, 1702.

Sir G. Kneller.   J. Smith, mez.
J. C. Smith, 15, 2nd state.   E. 2123.–'89.

ATTERBURY, FRANCIS, 1662–1731, b. at Milton, Bucks; educ. at Westminster and Oxford; Chaplain to William and Mary and Q. Anne; Dean of Westminster and Bishop of Rochester, 1713; refused to sign the Bishops' Declaration of Allegiance to George I.; suspected of conspiring in favour of the Pretender, tried and banished, 1723; d. at Paris.

Sir G. Kneller.   M. Vander Gucht.

O 82849.   B

Ha. len. to right, looking to front; oval, in a border of oak leaves; mitre and arms below; pubd. by P. Overton.
$13\frac{13}{16} \times 10\frac{1}{8}$. ($13\frac{1}{4} \times 9\frac{3}{8}$). 22207.

ATTWOOD, THOMAS, Founder of Political Unions, –1856.
G. Sharples. C. Turner, mez.
T. Q. len. seated.
Published July 10, 1832, by Mr. Turner.
Proof with open letters.
$13\frac{7}{8} \times 9\frac{15}{16}$. ($10 \times 8\frac{1}{4}$). 24624.

AUCKLAND, GEORGE, Second Baron, First Earl of, 1784–1849; Governor-General of India, 1835–'42.
L. Dickinson. J. Thomson.
T. Q. len. standing, holding a paper in his left hand.
Published, 1850.
$24\frac{1}{2} \times 18$. ($17\frac{1}{16} \times 12\frac{3}{8}$). 25816.

AUCKLAND, WILLIAM EDEN, Baron, Statesman, Ambassador, scholar, and author, 1750–1814.
Sir T. Lawrence, R.A. W. Dickinson, mez.
J. C. Smith, 3, 2nd state.
$20\frac{1}{16} \times 14\frac{1}{8}$. ($17\frac{3}{4} \times 14\frac{1}{8}$). 22947.

AUGUSTA OF SAXE-GOTHA, 1719–1772, Consort of Frederick, Prince of Wales.
J. B. Vanloo. B. Baron.
Wh. len. to front, in a rich dress.
Cut ($20\frac{7}{8} \times 15\frac{1}{4}$). 21989.

AUGUSTA, HEREDITARY PRINCESS OF BRUNSWICK AND LUNENBURG, 1737–1813.
Sir J. Reynolds. J. McArdell, mez.
J. C. Smith, 9. 13774.

AUGUSTA SOPHIA, PRINCESS, daughter of George III., 1768–1840.
H. Ramberg. W. Ward, stipple.
Oval, with an Italian greyhound.
Cut ($11 \times 8\frac{7}{8}$). 26725. 2.
Also, a duplicate, in Genealogical Chart, 553. 1.
$13 \times 9\frac{15}{16}$. 25067. 3.

———

Sir W. Beechey. S. W. Reynolds, mez.
T. Q. len. to right, looking to front, in a hat with feathers, in a landscape.
Publd. March 8, 1824.
($10\frac{3}{4} \times 8\frac{5}{8}$). 25054.
In Genealogical Chart, 553. 1.

AYLMER, MATTHEW WHITWORTH, fifth Baron, 1775–1850, General; Govr., Canada; Adjt. Genl., Ireland; K.C.B., 1815; G.C.B., 1836.
H. W. Pickersgill, R.A. W. Ward, mez.

Ha. len. to front, looking to left, in uniform, holding cocked hat in both hands.

Open letter proof, Feb. 1, 1837.

$13\frac{7}{8} \times 10\frac{1}{2}$. $(10\frac{7}{8} \times 8\frac{1}{2})$. 27197.

BABINGTON, WILLIAM, 1756–1833, physician and mineralogist, b. at Portglenone, near Coleraine, co. Antrim; appr. at Londonderry; compl. his med. educn. at Guy's Hosp.; assist. surg., Haslar; lecturer at Guy's, and apothecary; M.D., Aberdeen, 1795; physician to Guy's; L.C.P., 1796; F.C.P., 1827; M.D., Dublin, 1831; F.R.S., &c.

See MEDICAL SOCIETY.

BACK, SIR GEORGE, 1796–1878, Admiral and Arctic explorer, b. at Stockport, Cheshire; midshipman, 1808; taken prisoner, 1809, by the French, at Deba; travelled on foot through France, 1813–'4; volunt. in the Trent under Franklin; again, 1824, with Franklin; went in search of Ross, 1833; made extensive discoveries; Capt. by order in Council, 1835; received G. S. medals; Knt., 1839; Admiral, 1857; D.C.L., F.R.S.

See ARCTIC COUNCIL.

BACON, FRANCIS, 1st Visct. St. Albans, and Baron of Verulam, 1561–1626, educ. at Cambr.; stud. Gray's Inn; barrister, 1582; M.P., 1585; M.A., 1594; Queen's Counsel Extr., 1595; King's Counsel Extr., 1603; Knt., 1603; Sol.-General, 1607; Att.-General, 1613; P.C.; Lord Keeper, 1618; Baron, 1618; Chancellor, 1619–'21; Visct., 1621; devoted rest of life to study; d. at Highgate; author of "Essays," 1597; "Advancement of Learning," 1605; "Novum Organum Scientiarum," 1620.

Anon. (in possession of Martin Foulkes).

J. Houbraken, 1738.

Sh. ha. len. to left, looking to front; wearing hat; oval, in border; in Birch's "Lives."

$(14 \times 8\frac{3}{4})$. 24650.

See also CHARLES II. (3).

BACON, JOHN, F.S.A., 1738–1816, served in Queen Anne's Bounty Office; edited Ecton's "Thesaurus"; senior clerk, 1778; receiver, 1782; d. in the manor-house of Whetstone, or Friern Barnet, which he had bought from the Dean and Chapter of St. Paul's.

J. Russell, R.A. T. Blood, stipple.

Ha. len. to left, in profile, holding a roll of paper in right hand; engraved for the European Magazine; Feb. 1, 1815.

$(4\frac{1}{4} \times 3\frac{5}{16})$. 28300. 3.

BACON, JOHN, 1740–1799, sculptor, b. in Southwark, son of a cloth-worker; apprent. to a china manufacturer in Lambeth; gained a premium, and eight more afterwards, from Socy. of Arts; stud. at R. Academy, 1768; invented a machine for transferring the design from the plaster model to the marble; gained the Academy's first gold medal; A.R.A., 1770; executed monuments to Pitt, Dr. Johnson, and others; bronze statue of George III., Somerset House, &c.; R.A., 1778.

Anon.   Anon.
Sh. ha. len. to right, looking upwards; a bust partly seen, on right, with tools, &c., on a table; oval.
$(3\frac{7}{4} \times 3\frac{1}{4})$.   28300. 4.

G. Dance.   W. Daniell, stipple.
Sh. ha. len. to right, in profile, seated; vignette.
$10\frac{3}{4} \times 7\frac{1}{8}$. $(7\frac{1}{4} \times 5)$.   28299. 1.

J. Russell, R.A.   A. Roffe.
Ha. len. to left, looking to right, holding mallet and chisel, his left hand resting on a marble head, the face of which is turned upwards; facs. signature below; Ind. proof; 1830.
$7\frac{7}{8} \times 4\frac{1}{2}$ (?). $(3\frac{1}{2} \times 2\frac{7}{16})$.   26262.

BACON, Sir Nathaniel, 1547–1615, Knt., half-brother to Lord Chancellor Bacon; stud. art in Italy; painted portraits and still life with much talent and success; some of his works, including his own wh. len. port., are at Gorhambury; he left some also at Redgrave Hall, Suff.; buried in chancel of Culford Church.

Sir N. Bacon.   W. Richardson.
T. Q. len. to right, looking to front; holding a framed paper, or canvas, in left hand, on table; Aug. 10, 1793.
$(5\frac{1}{4} \times 4\frac{1}{8})$.   28443. 1.

BACON, Sir Nicholas, 1510–1579, jurist and statesman; Lord Keeper, 1558; opposed giving up Mary, Q. of Scots, 1571, and asserted the right of the Stuarts to the Throne.

F. Zucchero.   J. Houbraken, 1738.
Sh. ha. len. to left, looking to front, in furred robe, ruff, and flat cap; oval in frame; the bag below.
In Birch's " Lives."
$14\frac{1}{2} \times 9\frac{5}{8}$ $(14 \times 8\frac{5}{8})$.   28156. 1.

Zucchero.   R. Cooper.
Ha. len. to right, looking to front, in robes.
From Lodge's Large Series.
Ind. proof before all letters.
Cut $(6\frac{7}{8} \times 5\frac{1}{16})$.   28163.
The plate was reduced for insertion in the book.

A. vander Werff,   P. à Gunst.
Sh. ha. len. to right, looking to front, in flat cap, ruff, and furred robe; circular, in frame; name and 4 French verses on a circular tablet, suspended below.
$12\frac{1}{2} \times 7\frac{1}{4}$. (Circle, $5\frac{1}{2}$ diamr.).   28147. 2.

BADDELEY, Mrs. Sophia, 1745–1801, daughter of Mr. Snow, sergeant-trumpeter to George II.; celebrated for her beauty, her intrigues, and her extravagance; a pleasing actress, with a good voice; d. in extreme poverty at Edinburgh.
See KING.

BAGOT, Miss Elizabeth, Court beauty, temp. Charles II.; *see* " Beauties of the Court of Charles II.," by Mrs. Jameson, II., 63.
Sir P. Lely.   I. Thomson, stipple.
See LA BELLE ASSEMBLÉE, 1819.   13867.   25.

BAILLIE, Matthew, 1761–1823, Physician and Anatomist: son of a clergyman, nephew of Wm. and John Hunter, and brother of Joanna and Agnes Baillie; b. in Lanarkshire; educ. at Glasgow and Oxford; Physician to St. George's Hospital and to George III.; wrote on " Morbid Anatomy," &c.; d. at Cirencester.
J. Hoppner, R.A.   C. Turner, mixed mez.
Hn. len. to front, looking to right, seated; hands clasped. Scratched letter proof (?); Decr. 25, 1809.
14 × 10.   (11¾ × 10).   22802.

BAILLIE, William, 1723–1810, amateur artist, b. at Killbride, co. Carlow; educ. at Dublin; came to London, 1741, to study law, but entd. the army; served at Culloden, and in Germany, at Minden, changed into 17th Light Dragoons; left the army; commissioner of stamps; exhibited mezzo-tints and etchings at Spring Gardens, 1774; imitated Rembrandt; etched " The Three Trees " and retouched the " Hundred Guilder " print of that master, beside executing other views, battles, and portraits.
(W. Baillie ?)   Anon. (W. Baillie ?), stipple.
Hn. len. slightly to right, looking to front, wearing broad-leafed hat, and a breast-plate under furred cloak; oval; supported on each side by a cupid holding up a curtain; the name on a label, below.
12½ × 13¼.   (9¾ × 10⅝, including border, 1).   24644.

BAILY, Edward Hodges, 1788–1867, sculptor, b. at Bristol, where he was educ. at Grammar School; entd. a merchant's office; began making portraits in wax; introduced to Flaxman, who assisted him; entd. Flaxman's studio, 1807; worked for Rundell, silversmith, stud. in Academy School; gained silver medal, 1809, and gold medal, 1811; A.R.A., 1817; produced " Eve at the fountain;" R.A., 1821; constant exhibitor; retired 1863.
T. Bridgeford del.   J. Smyth.
Hn. len. to right, seated, looking towards left; vignette; facs. signature below.
Ind. proof.
8⅞ × 4⅞.   (5⅝ × 4½).   27579.

BAILY, Francis, 1774–1844, disting. mathematician and astronomer; b. at Newbury; son of a banker, and engaged till the age of 50 as a stockbroker; active in founding the Astronomical Society, 1820; among his works were the repetition of the Cavendish experiment, improvement of Nautical Almanack, &c.; D.C.L.; Pres. Astr. Socy., contrib. to its Memoirs, and superintended the formation of its Catalogue; wrote on Life Annuities and Assurances, Astronomy, &c.; discovered "Baily's Beads;" d. in Tavistock Place.

T. Phillips, R.A. T. Lupton, mez.
Full ha. len. to front, dark figured waistcoat, with seals, left hand holding glasses and resting on papers on table.
Ind. proof with facs. signature below
$20\frac{7}{8} \times 16$. $(17\frac{1}{4} \times 13\frac{11}{16})$. 22803.
See also SCIENCE.

BAIRD, Sir David, 1757–1829, b. at Newbyth, Scotland; General, commanded in Ireland; took a disting. part in the capture of Seringapatam, 1799, and the siege of Pondicherry; assisted at the taking of Alexandria, 1801; took the Cape of Good Hope from the Dutch, 1873; succ. Sir John Moore as commander, at Corunna, 1809, and cr. Bart.; afterwards Governor of Kinsale and of Fort St. George; K.B., &c.

Sir H. Raeburn, R.A. T. Hodgetts & Son, mez.
Wh. len. to right, standing, looking to front, right arm extended, left over neck of charger.
Proof before all letters, the additional plate below having only the artist's name in skeleton letters.
$24\frac{3}{8} \times 16$. $(24\frac{1}{4} \times 15\frac{1}{4})$. 24106.

—— finding the body of Tippoo Sahib.
Sir D. Wilkie, R.A. J. Burnet, line and stipple.
A composition of many figures; Baird is in the centre, his left hand raised sword in right, lowered; Tippoo is lying in the foreground, dying, supported by two natives, who wear white turbans.
Proof before all letters, on Ind. paper.
Cut (?) $\times 23\frac{7}{8}$. $(28\frac{5}{16} \times 21\frac{1}{4})$. 22134.

BALD, Robert, –1861, mining engineer; wrote "A General View of the Coal Trade of Scotland, 1808," said to be the best work on the subject at that time; F.R.S.E.
Sir J. W. Gordon, R.S.A., A.R.A. T. Dick, stipple.
T. Q. len. slightly to left, seated, looking to front, left leg crossed over right; holding a paper between his two hands; in background is a miner's "safety lamp."
Ind. proof, October, 1856.
$18\frac{1}{4} \times 13\frac{1}{4}$. $(14\frac{7}{16} \times 11\frac{1}{4})$. 22959.

BALE, John, 1495–1563, b. at Cove, near Dunwich, Suffolk; educ. at Carmellite Convent, Norwich, and Jesus Coll., Cambr.; converted from the Rom. faith by Lord Wentworth; wrote scriptural dramas, which attracted Cromwell's notice; fled to Germany, 1540, where he continued controversial writings; returned, 1547; rector of Bishopstake; vicar of Swaffham,

1551; Bishop of Ossory, 1553; fled to Holland on accession of
Q. Mary; taken prisoner; released; went to Holland, and
Basel, till 1559; returned, and accepted stall of prebend at
Canterbury, where he died.

Anon.   H. Hondius.

Ha. len. to left, in gown and cap; name, and 4 Latin verses
below.

$6\frac{3}{4} \times 4\frac{1}{8}$. $(5\frac{3}{16} \times 4\frac{1}{13})$.   29996.

BALLANTYNE, JAMES, 1772–1833, the printer of Sir Walter
Scott's works; son of a general merchant at Kelso, where he
was born; his friendship with Scott began, 1873, at the Gr.
School at Kelso; renewed at the Teviotdale Club; Solicitor,
1795; began as a printer, 1799, and continued to print Scott's
works till the death of the author.

See SCOTT, SIR WALTER.

BANCROFT, EDWARD, 1744–1821, naturalist and chemist, M.D.,
F.R.S., a man of versatile talents, friend of Franklin and
Priestley; pubd. an able tract in defence of the liberties of the
American Colonies, 1769; wrote "Charles Wentworth," a
novel; interested in dyeing and printing calico, about which he
made some important discoveries.

See MEDICAL SOCIETY.

BANKS, SIR JOSEPH, 1743–1820, educ. at Ch. Ch., Oxf.; went
on a voyage to Labrador and Newfoundland, 1768, and with
Capt. Cook, in the Endeavour, circumnavigated the world;
Presid. R.S., 1777–1820; published various works on Agricultural, Archæological, and other scientific subjects; G.C.B.;
&c.

[G. Dance].   [W. Daniell].

Sh. ha. len. to right; hair tied at back; high coat collar.
Proof before all letters.

$10\frac{5}{8} \times 7\frac{1}{4}$. $(8 \times 6\frac{3}{4})$.   28146. 2.

T. Phillips, R.A.   N. Schiavonetti.

Ha. len. to front, wearing the star and ribbon of the Bath,
seated, as President of the Royal Society, the mace lying before
him, with inkstand, &c.

Ind. paper proof; 1812.

$20\frac{3}{16} \times 15\frac{1}{4}$. $(17\frac{1}{16} \times 13\frac{5}{8})$.   21997.

—— wearing Otaheitan mantle.

B. West.   J. R. Smith, mez.

J. C. Smith, 7, 2nd state, retouched; publication-line cut off.
                     24635.

F. Chantrey. (H. Corbould delin. from statue). S. Cousins,
mez.

Wh. len. to right, seated, looking to front, holding paper in
left hand; right hand on arm of seat; vignette.

Open letter proof.
The statue was presented to the Br. Museum.
$18\frac{7}{8} \times 13\frac{7}{8}$. ($11\frac{3}{4} \times 9\frac{7}{8}$). E. 279.-87.
See DILETTANTI SOCIETY, and see also SCIENCE.

BANKS, THOMAS, 1735 (or '38)–1805, sculptor, b. in Lambeth;
educ. at Ross; apprent. to a wood-carver in London; at the age
of 23, entd. St. Martin's Lane Academy; gained Socy. of
Arts' medal, 1763; employed under Kent, and stud. in Academy
Schools, obtaining gold medal, 1770, and travelling scholarship,
1772; returned to London, 1779, having m. a lady of some
property, and bringing several good works in marble to finish;
went to St. Petersburg; returned, 1781; R.A., 1785; executed
many fine pieces of sculpture.
J. Northcote, R.A. W. Blenkinsop, stipple.
Ha. len. to front, looking to left; left hand holding a sculptor's chisel and resting on a bust.
Proof before all letters; Jany. 16, 1802.
$10\frac{1}{2} \times 8$. ($5\frac{3}{8} \times 4\frac{3}{8}$). 27198.

————

J Northcote, R.A. W. Leney, stipple.
Sh. ha. len. to front, looking to left; oval.
$6\frac{3}{16}(?) \times 4\frac{1}{2}$. ($3\frac{3}{8} \times 2\frac{5}{8}$). 28300. 7.

————

G. Dance. W. Daniell, stipple.
Sh. ha. len. to right, in profile, seated; vignette.
$10\frac{3}{4} \times 7\frac{7}{8}$. ($7 \times 5$) 29299. 2.

————

I. Condé del. (from a model by T. Banks). I. Condé, stipple.
Bust, to left, in profile, oval; Aug. 1, 1791.
$7\frac{3}{4} \times 4\frac{5}{8}(?)$. ($4\frac{3}{16} \times 3\frac{9}{16}$). 28300. 6.

BANNISTER, JOHN, 1760–1836, admirable comedian; favoured
by Garrick, made first appearance at Drury Lane at age of 12;
permanently engaged, 1779; excelled in "Sylvester Dagger-
wood," "Lingo," "Trudge," "Bobadil," "Pangloss," &c.;
retired, 1815; known by the name of "Gentleman Jack."
G. Clint, A.R.A. G. Clint, A.R.A., mez.
T. Q. len. to front, seated, holding hat in left and stick in right
hand. Open letter proof, May 1, 1829.
$18 \times 13\frac{1}{2}$. ($16\frac{7}{8} \times 13\frac{1}{4}$). 24672.

—— as "Gradus" in "Who's the Dupe?"
S. de Wilde. E. Bell, mez.
J. C. Smith. 1, 2nd state. 21933.

————

R. A. Westall, R.A. J. Heath, A.R.A., stipple.
Wh. len. to right, with sword in right hand, protecting two
children, in the character of "Walter," against the attack of
"Oliver," in the "Children in the Wood."
($15\frac{1}{8} \times 18$) 26427.

—— and WILLIAM PARSONS (q.v.), as "Scout" and "Sheep-
face" in "The Village Lawyer."
S. de Wilde.   J. R. Smith, mez.
J. C. Smith, 11, 3rd state.   21883.

BARBAULD, ANNA LÆTITIA, 1743-1825, b. at Kibworth,
Leicestershire; only daughter and eldest child of John Aikin,
D.D., a tutor at the new academy at Warrington; she acquired
languages very quickly; in 1773 she pubd. a vol. of miscell.
poems, which were most successful; Devotional Pieces, 1775;
"Evenings at home," with her brother, &c.
From an original drawing.   H. Meyer, stipple.
Bust-size to left, in profile, wearing a cap.
March 9, 1822, vignette.
12$\frac{1}{16}$ × 9$\frac{1}{2}$ (?). (6$\frac{3}{4}$ × 6$\frac{3}{4}$).   24060.

BARBER, JOHN, Lord Mayor of London, 1733-1741.
B. Dandridge.   G. Vander Gucht.
In oval frame, with mace, sword, and roll of "The City
Petition agst. the Excise Scheme."
17 × 11. (16$\frac{1}{4}$ × 10$\frac{5}{16}$).   27599.
See also ALDERMEN.

BARETTI, JOSEPH, c. 1716-1789, b. at Turin, came to England,
1750; friend of Dr. Johnson; teacher of Italian, and author;
tried, 1769, for the murder of a man, named Morgan, whom he
stabbed, in a brawl in the Haymarket, but acquitted, as having
acted in self-defence; Secretary for Foreign Correspondence to
the Royal Academy.
Sir J. Reynolds.   J. Watts, mez.
J. C. Smith, 1, 2nd state.   23135.

——
Sir J. Reynolds.   J. Hardy, stipple.
Ha. len. to right, seated, holding a small book close to his
face, as in the preceding print.
Pubd. March 6th, 1794, by W. Richardson.
(8$\frac{5}{8}$ × 7$\frac{1}{4}$).   E. 1266.-'86.

BARHAM, SIR CHARLES MIDDLETON, Lord, 1726-1813, b. at
Leith; Lieut., R.N., 1745; Post Cap., 1758; served with distinction in W. Indies; Comptroller of Navy, 1778-'90; Bart.,
1781; M.P. for Rochester, 1784; Rear Admiral, 1787; Adm.
of Red, 1803; 1st Lord of Admiralty, and cr. Lord Barham,
1805.
I. Pocock.   C. Picart and D. Robertson, stipple.
Wh. len. slightly to right, wearing robes; papers, lettered
"Digest of the Civil Affairs of Navy," in right hand, left
resting on a plan of the battle of Trafalgar which lies on a
table; a ship in distance, on left; May 25, 1807, pubd. by D.
Robertson.
24$\frac{15}{16}$ × 16$\frac{1}{2}$. (22$\frac{1}{4}$ × 15$\frac{3}{8}$).   22008.

BARING, CHARLES, 1742–1829, brother of Sir Francis Baring, whom he assisted in founding the famous house of Baring; d. at Exmouth.

See BARING, SIR FRANCIS.

BARING, SIR FRANCIS, 1740–1810, London merchant and financier, 3rd son of John Baring, Esq., of Larkbear, near Exeter; founder of the house of Baring Brothers, with his brother, Charles; M.P., and supporter of Pitt; cr. Bart., 1793.

  Sir T. Lawrence.   J. Ward, mez.
  With his brother Charles and C. Wall.
  J. C. Smith, 2, 2nd state.   22492.

BARING, THOMAS, 1800–1873, 2d. son of Sir Thomas Baring, 2d Bart. (1772–1848); educ. at Winchester, joined banking-house of Hope and Co., Amsterdam; entd. house of Baring Bros. and Co., 1828; head of the firm till 1871; chairman of Lloyds, 1830–'68; Pres. Lond. Institution, 1835, till death; M.P. for Great Yarmouth, 1835–'37, and for Huntingdon, 1844 till death; declined Chanc. of Exchequer, 1852 and 1858; d. at Bournemouth.

  G. Richmond, A.R.A.   W. Holl, stipple.
  Bust, to left, looking to front; facs. signature below; vignette.
  Ind. proof.
  $11\frac{1}{4} \times 9$. $(5\frac{4}{8} \times 3\frac{3}{4})$.   27199.

BARKER, ROBERT, 1739–1806, inventor and painter of the Panorama; b. at Kells, Co. Meath; failed in Dublin; settled at Edinburgh, and practised portrait-painting; painted a half-circle of Edinburgh which he brought to London, 1788; afterwards completed the circle, and made one of London, and others also, exhibited at the corner of Leicester Square; d. at Lambeth.

  C. Allingham.   J. Flight, mez.
  J. C. Smith, p. 510* (appendix).   21932.

BARLOW, PETER, 1776–1862, b. at Norwich; began by keeping a school; obtained, after severe struggles, the place of assist. mathem. master, 1801, and afterwards professor, R.M.A.; Hon. Mem. I.C.E., 1820; F.R.S., 1823; corresp. mem. of several foreign academies; pubd. many scientific works.

  W. Boxall, A.R.A.   S. Cousins, A.E., mixed mez.
  Full ha. len. seated, to right, holding a paper in right hand.
  Ind. " *Subscribers Proof*," with open letters.
  $18 \times 13\frac{1}{4}$. $(13\frac{5}{16} \times 10\frac{7}{16})$.   28254.

BARNARD, SIR JOHN, 1685–1764, b. at Reading, of Quaker parents; M.P. for City, 1722–'61; Lord Mayor, 1737; opposed Walpole (who highly respected him) and the Excise Bill; was honoured with a statue, during his lifetime, which was, after his death, inscribed " Humani Generis Decus;" great-grandfather of Palmerston; of him Pope said, "Barnard in spirit, sense, and truth abounds;" d. at Clapham; bur. at Mortlake.

  A. Ramsay.   J. Faber, junr., mez.
  J. C. Smith, 24, 2nd state.   24058.

BARNARD, Thomas, 1728–1806, eldest son of Dr. W. Barnard, bishop of Derry; educ. at Westminster and Cambr.; grad. M.A., 1749; archdeacon of Derry, 1761; cr. D.D.; dean, 1769; bishop of Killaloe and Kilfenora, 1780; transl. to Limerick, 1794; F.R.S.; member of Johnson's Club, &c.

G. Dance, 1793.   W. Daniell.

Ha. len. to right, in profile; July 1, 1812. Vignette.
$10\frac{1}{16} \times 8$. $(8\frac{1}{4} \times 5\frac{3}{4})$.   28146.   3.

BARNES, Joshua, 1654–1712, educ. at Christ's Hospital, and Emmanuel Coll., Cambr.; grad. B.A., 1675; fellow, 1678; M.A., 1679; B.D., 1686; Prof. Greek, 1695.

     R. White, ad vivum.

Sh. ha. len. to right, looking front; oval in frame, supported by books in two piles; below, 3 lines of title, followed by 4 Greek hexameters, describing his career briefly, from his birth in London.

Cut $(10\frac{3}{16} \times 7\frac{1}{16}.)$ 22804.

BARNETT, John, 1802–1890, composer, b. at Bedford; his mother was Hungarian, his father Prussian, Bernhard Beer; the son showed early talent and had a good voice; articled to S. J. Arnold, and sang at Lyceum till his voice broke; instructed by C. E. Horn and Price, and later under Perez and Ferd. Ries; composed many pieces for the theatre, including "The Mountain Sylph" and "Farinelli," an oratorio, nearly 4,000 songs, - &c.; settled at Cheltenham as a singing-master.

     Baugniet, 1845, lith.

Sh. ha. len. to front, looking to left; curling hair; vignette; facs. signature below.

$(7\frac{1}{2} \times 7)$.   27676.

BARRÉ, Isaac, 1726–1802, Lt.-Colonel; son of a Dublin merchant; educ. at Trin. Coll., Dublin; ent. the army; served under Wolfe at Quebec; sat in Parliament afterwards, supporting Lord Shelburne, and became known as a vigorous speaker

C. G. Stuart, 1785.   J. Hall.

Ha. len. to left, seated, holding in left hand a roll of paper, inscribed, "Anno Dom. 1784 | XX Geo. III. | *A Bill for appointing | Commissioners to examine take | and state the Public Accounts | of the Kingdom;*" publ. April 5, 1787

Cut $(11\frac{7}{8} \times 8\frac{7}{8})$.   22021.

BARRINGTON, Samuel, 1729–1800, 5th son of John, first Viscount Barrington; entd. navy, æt. 11; lieut. 1745; posted to the Bellona, 1747; repulsed the French at St. Lucia, 1778; distinguished at relief of Gibraltar, 1782; Admiral of the Blue, 1787; died at Bath.

B. Wilson.   R. Earlom, mez.

J. C. Smith, 7, 2nd state.   27580.

BARRINGTON, Hon. Shute, 1734–1826, 6th and youngest son of John Shute, first Viscount Barrington; educ. at Eton and Merton Coll., Oxf.; grad. B.A., 1755; got fellowship and ord., 1756; M.A., 1757; Chaplain in Ordy. to George III., 1760; canon of Chr. Ch. 1762, and D.C.L.; canon of S. Paul's, 1768, at Windsor, 1776; bishop, Llandaff, 1769; transld. to Salisbury, 1782; to Durham, 1791, where he remained 35 years.

Sir T. Lawrence. C Turner, mez.
T. Q. len. seated, in robes, to left, looking right.
Proof with scratched letters, March 28, 1817.
$21\frac{7}{8} \times 16$. ($17\frac{3}{16} \times 14$). 22805.

BARRINGTON, William Wildman, Viscount, politician, 1710–1793.

T. Lawrence, R.A. C. Knight, stipple.
Æt. 75, ha. len. seated, facing front.
$8\frac{13}{16} \times 7\frac{1}{4}$. ($6\frac{3}{4} \times 5\frac{5}{8}$). 27995.

BARROW, Isaac, 1630–1677, Divine and Mathematician; b. in London; educ. at Charterhouse and Felstead, and Trin. Coll., Cambr.; Gr. Prof. Cambr., 1660; Lucas Prof. of Math., on its foundation, Cambr., 1663; Master of Trin. Coll., 1672, and founder of its Library; D.D.; bur. in Westminster Abbey.

D. Loggan "ad vivum delin." D. Loggan.
Sh. ha. len. to right, looking to front, in wig and gown; oval, in frame
Brilliant proof before the inscription below the arms; prefixed (in ordinary state) to his "Works" in English.
$10\frac{15}{16} \times 7\frac{1}{2}$. ($9\frac{1}{2} \times 7\frac{3}{16}$). 24097.

BARROW, Sir John, 1764–1848, b. near Ulverston, Lancashire; accomp. Lord Macartney to China, 1792; Sec. to Admiralty, 1804–'45; constant promoter of Arctic Voyages of discovery; cr. Bart., 1835; author of travels, biographies, articles in "Quarterly Review," "Autobiography," &c.

J. Lucas. G. T. Payne, mixed mez.
Ha. len. to front, slightly inclined to left, looking to front; right hand resting on paper, on table.
Open letter proof, May 27, 1847.
$15\frac{1}{8} \times 12$. ($11\frac{5}{8} \times 9\frac{1}{8}$). 22953.
See ARCTIC COUNCIL.

BARROW, John, F.R.S., F.S.A. (query: son of Sir John Barrow (q.v.), and aftds. Colonel, and biographer of his father?).
See ARCTIC COUNCIL.

BARRY, Sir Charles, 1795–1860, articled to an architect and surveyor; exhibited at the R.A., 1812; travelled in Italy, Greece, Palestine, and Egypt, 1816–'20; built several churches soon after his return; architect to Dulwich Coll.; rebuilt Houses of Parliament; built Reform and Travellers' Clubs, College of Surgeons, &c., R.A. 1842; Knt.

T W Harland del. T. W. Harland, stipple and line.
T. Q. len. to left, seated, looking to front, arms folded and legs crossed; facs. signature below.
Ind. proof.
13×10. ($7\frac{15}{16} \times 6\frac{5}{8}$). 25817.

BARRY, James, 1741–1806, b. at Cork; pupil of F. West, in Dublin; noticed by Burke, who introduced him in London, 1764; visited Italy, where he devoted himself to classic art, disliking the more profitable business of portraiture; R.A., 1773; Prof. of Painting, 1782; of a violent and quarrelsome temper; expelled from R. Academy, 1799.

J. Barry. Anon.
Ha. len. to right, looking to front, holding a picture with his left hand, and in his right a crayon.
Proof before all letters.
$6\frac{1}{2} \times 4\frac{3}{4}$. $(3\frac{1}{4} \times 2\frac{1}{2})$.   26261. A.

NOTE.—Another proof is in the Br. Museum, similarly wanting the engraver's name.

W. Évans del. (from a cast).   C. Picart, chalk and dot.
Ha. len. to left, coat buttoned, white neckcloth; vignette.
Open letters.
Published, Feb. 11, 1811, by T. Cadell and W. Davies.
$14\frac{7}{8} \times 12\frac{7}{8}$. (7×7).   27155.

BARRY, Mr., speaking the Prologue to the "Earl of Essex."
From a " Collection   . of English Prologues," &c., 1779
28187. 2.

BARRY, Mrs., speaking the Occasional Prologue before the Play of "Douglas."
From a " Collection . . . of English Prologues," &c., 1779.
28187. 3.

BARTLEMAN, James, 1769–1821, celebrated bass singer, b. in Westminster, educ. under Dr. Cooke in the Choristers' School; soon showed voice and talent; distinguished as a chorister; patronised by Sir John Hawkins; bass chorister at the Ancient Music Concerts, 1788–91; first solo bass at vocal concerts; principal bass singer at Ancient Concerts, 1795; made popular some of Purcell's finest but forgotten songs; left a large and valuable musical library, sold after his death.

Hargreaves.   I. Thomson.
Sh. ha. len. slightly to left, coat buttoned across chest; music on a table on left, behind him; facs. signature below.
Ind. proof, "Published by the Misses Bartleman, May 1st, 1830."
$9\frac{7}{8} \times 7\frac{3}{4}$. $(5\frac{1}{16} \times 4\frac{3}{16}$, incl. ruled border, $\frac{5}{8})$.   27201.

BARTOLOZZI, Francesco, 1727–1815, b. at Florence; pupil of Wagner; executed many plates in line; came to England, 1764; engraver to the King, rivalling Strange; original R.A.; engraved great number of plates, chiefly after Cipriani's designs, in stipple and chalk manner; went (1802) to Portugal, where he was knighted; d. at Lisbon.

Sir J. Reynolds.   T. Watson, mez.
J. C. Smith, 3, 1st state; publication-line cut off.   28771.

Sir J. Reynolds.   R. Marcuard, stipple.

Ha. len. slightly to left, looking to right, holding crayon in right hand; furred coat; oval; Jany. 1, 1788.
$(9\frac{1}{2} \times 8)$.   E. 1961.—'89.

W. Artaud.   Pastorini and P. W. Tomkins, stipple.
T. Q. len. to right, seated, facing and looking to left ; left hand on portfolio, pencil in right, which rests on a paper, lying on a shelf, near which are books and a graving-tool.
Skeleton letter proof, Feb. 1, 1803.
$20\frac{1}{4} \times 15\frac{1}{16}$. $(18\frac{1}{16} \times 13\frac{7}{8})$.   21829.

Sir J. Reynolds.   J. E. Haid, mez.
Sh. ha. len. to front, looking to right, in a circle.
$8\frac{5}{8} \times 5\frac{5}{8}$. $(5\frac{1}{4}$ diamr.$)$.   28705.

F. Bartolozzi del.   J. Romney, etched.
Wh. len. to right, seated at a table, looking at a picture on an easel, on left ; holding a crayon in right hand, resting on sheet of paper ; facs. signature below. April 1, 1817.
$(6\frac{3}{4} \times 4\frac{3}{8})$.   28300.   9

J. Vendramini del.   E. Scriven, stipple.
Sh. ha. len. slightly inclined to right, looking to left ; vignette ; engr. for the " Library of the Fine Arts," 1832.
$7\frac{3}{8} \times 5\frac{1}{2}$ $(3\frac{3}{8} \times 3\frac{1}{4})$.   28300.   8.
See also CARLINI.

BATES, Joah, 1740–1799, b. at Halifax, educ. under Dr. Ogden, stud. music under Hartley, organist of Rochdale ; stud. organ-playing at Manchester under R. Wainwright ; went to Eton, thence to Cambridge, where he became fellow and tutor of King's Coll. ; priv. sec. to Lord Sandwich, who started the Concert of Ancient Music, of which Bates was app. Conductor ; projected, with Lord Fitzwilliam and Sir W W. Wynne, the Handel Commemoration, which he conducted.
G. Dance, 1794.   W. Daniell, stipple.
Ha. len. to right in profile, seated ; July 1, 1809 ; vignette.
$10\frac{1}{16} \times 8$. (8×6) 28146.   4.

BATES, servant to Catesby, Gunpowder Plot conspirator.
See CONCILIUM.

BATESON, Sir Robert, 1st Bart., 1780–1863, only son of Thomas Bateson (1752–1811) ; sheriff of co. Down, 1809 ; cr. a Bart., 1818 ; M.P. for Londonderry, 1830–'42 ; d. at Belvoir Park, Belfast.
M. Cregan.   S. Cousins, A.R.A., mixed mez.
Ha. len. to front, looking to right, left hand on side ; trees in distance, on left ; facs. signature, below.
Ind. proof, Aug. 1, 1845.
$16\frac{13}{16} \times 12\frac{7}{8}$. $(12\frac{3}{16} \times 9\frac{1}{2})$ 23585.

BATH, WILLIAM PULTENEY, Earl of, 1682–1764, statesman ; ent. Parlt. as a supporter of Sir Robert Walpole; Sec. at War, 1714–'17; joined the opposition in consequence of a dispute with Walpole; cr. Earl, after Walpole's resignation, 1742 ; Prime Minister for two days, 1746, but failed to form an administration; P.C., Lord Lieutt.; F.R.S., &c.

A. Ramsay.   D. Martin, 1763.

Sh. ha. len. to right, looking to front, in robes, with wig ; arms below.

  13¼ × 9⅜.   (10¼ × 8¾).   E. 210.–'93.

BATHURST, HENRY, Earl, 1714–1794, second son of Allen, Lord Bathurst (cr. Earl, 1772); barrister; M.P. Cirencester, &c.; Judge of Com. Pleas, 1754; Ld. Chancr., 1771–'8 ; cr. Baron Apsley, 1771 ; suc. as Earl Bathurst, 1775 ; presided at the trial of the Duchess of Kingston, 1776 ; built Apsley House.

  D. Martin, 1776.   T. Watson, 1778, mez.

  J. C. Smith, 4, 2nd state.   22951.

BATTY, ROBERT, c. 1763–1849, b. at Kirkby Lonsdale ; M.D., St. Andrew's, 1797 ; soon settled in London, as obstet. phys.; admitted by Coll. Phys., 1800, licent. midwify.; licent. of the Coll., 1806 ; phys. to Lying-in Hospital, Brownlow St., and edit. for some years " Medical and Physl. Journal ; " d. at Fairlight Lodge, Hastings.

  G. Dance, April 8, 1799. W. Daniell, Aug. 15, 1810, stipple.

Sh. ha. len. profile to right ; vignette.

  10⅛ × 7¼.   (8 × 5).   28146.   5.

BAXTER, RICHARD, 1615–1691, b. at Rowden, Shrops. ; parish minister at Kidderminster ; chaplain in Parliamentary Army ; chaplain to Charles II. at Restoration ; ejected under Act of Uniformity, 1662 ; tried for sedition, and imprisd. by Jeffreys, 1685 ; author of the "Saints' Everlasting Rest," "Call to the Unconverted," and other pious works.

  J. C. Smith, 4, 2nd state.   J. Spilsbury, mez.
             21931.

BAYLEY, SIR JOHN, Knt., 1763–1841, Judge ; pubd " Summary of the Law of Bills of Exchange," 1789, &c. , puisne judge of King's Bench.

  Russell.   W Say, mez.

T. Q. len. slightly to right, looking to front, seated, in robes, holding in right hand a book, which rests on his right knee, his left hand resting on a table.

Scr. letter proof, March 2, 1823.

  20⅜ × 14¹³⁄₁₆.   (17¾ × 14⅛).   25767.

BAYLY, THOMAS HAYNES, 1797–1839 ; son of a solicitor ; b. near Bath ; intended for the Church, and stud. some time at Oxf.; suffered loss of fortune, 1831, and took to literature with

great industry ; in a few years he wrote 56 pieces for the stage,
several novels and tales, and "hundreds" of songs.
F. Say delin.   Thomson, stipple.
Ha. len. to front, seated, the body slightly incl. to the right ;
the hands loosely clasped ; facs. signature below.
Ind. proof ; June 1, 1831 ; vignette.
$8\frac{3}{4} \times 5\frac{5}{8}$. ($5\frac{1}{2} \times 4\frac{1}{2}$).   27581.

BAZELEY, Captain John,   –1805, commanded a ship, June
1, 1794, in Howe's Victory off Ushant ; Admiral, &c.
See COMMEMORATION (1).

BEACONSFIELD, Benjamin Disraeli, Earl of, 1804–1881 ;
author, conservative politician, Prime Minister, 1868, cr. Earl,
1876, K.G., 1878.
D'Orsay, 1834.   Anon. lith., slightly tinted.
Turned to the left, in profile. Published by J. Mitchell.
($7\frac{3}{4} \times 6\frac{6}{16}$).   23582.
See also DERBY CABINET, and COMMONS (2).

BEALE, Mrs. Mary, 1632–1697, portrait-painter, b. in Suffolk ;
daughter of Rev. Mr. Cradock, Walton-on-Thames ; painted in
oil, water-colour, and crayons ; enjoyed much encouragement,
and painted portraits of many very distinguished persons,
especially clergy ; made a good income, m. a chemist, who
prepared colours, in which he traded ; she was reputed also as
a poet ; left a son, a miniature-painter.
M. Beale.   T. Chambars.
Sh. ha. len. to right, looking to front, pearls round neck ;
oval in frame ; below, on the left, in a smaller oval, her son
Charles, slightly turned to right, looking to front ; from Walpole's "Anecdotes," iii., p. 67, 1763.
($5\frac{3}{4} \times 4\frac{1}{4}$).   25461. 9.

BEARD, John, 1716–1791 ; sang in Handel's operas ; m. Henrietta, daughter of Earl Waldegrave, and widow of Lord
Edward Herbert ; afterwards m. a daughter of Rich, patentee
of Covent Garden ; played "Macheath," with Miss Brent as
"Polly," to crowded houses for 52 successive nights, 1759 ;
retired, 1768 ; d. at Hampton.
See SHUTER.

BEARDMORE, Arthur, Attorney,   –1771, with his son.
R. E. Pine.   Jas Watson, mez.
J. C. Smith, 7, 2nd state.   28040.

BEATRICE, Mary Victoria Feodore, Princess Henry Henry-
Maurice of Battenberg ; b. 1857 ; m. 1885.
F. Winterhalter.   J. A. Vinter lith., 1859.
As a child ; in a circle.
($12\frac{1}{2}$ diamr.).   22196.

BEATTIE, James, 1735–1803, b. at Laurencekirk, Kincardine,
Scotland ; educ. at the Marischal Coll., Aberdeen ; M.A., 1753 ;

schoolmaster at Fardoun; contributed to "Scots Magazine," studied music; master at Grammar School, Aberdeen; Prof. Mor. Phil. and Logic, Marischal Coll., 1760, and lectured there 30 years; published "Original Poems," &c., 1761 ; " Essay on Truth," 1770; and the "Minstrel," 1771–4.

Sir J. Reynolds.   Jas. Watson, mez.
J. C. Smith, 9, 2nd state.   25768.

BEAUFORT, Sir Francis, 1774–1857, rear-admiral and hydrographer to the Navy; ent. Navy, 1787 ; saw much splendid service in "Phaëton," 1795 ; wounded severely, 1800, in capturing "San Josef ; " made several surveys ; Hydrographer to Navy, 1829–'55 ; influential in promoting Arctic exploration ; F.R.S., D.C.L., and Corresp. Member of the Inst. of France.

S. Pearce.   J. Scott, mixed mez.
T. Q. len. to front, facing and looking to right; spectacles in right hand, which rests on a chart lying upon a table, on which are an inkstand, with pens, ruler, &c., and a book.
Open letter proof (?) ; March 17, 1857.
$21\frac{2}{3} \times 16\frac{1}{4}$. $(16\frac{7}{8} \times 13\frac{1}{2})$.   22954.
See also ARCTIC COUNCIL.

BEAUMONT, Francis, 1584–1616, Dramatist, 3rd son of Francis Beaumont, judge of Com. Pleas; educ. at Oxford ; friend of John Fletcher, in collaboration with whom he wrote about 50 plays ; bur. in Westminster Abbey.
(From the original picture in the Duke of Dorset's Colln.)
           G. Vertue, 1729.
Sh. ba. len. to right, looking to left ; oval in frame ; arms below oval; title, 3 lines, on pedestal; dedication to Lionel, Duke of Dorset, 3 lines, below, in Latin.
$14\frac{2}{3} \times 9\frac{2}{8}$. $(13\frac{1}{8} \times 8\frac{3}{4})$.   21808.

BEAUMONT, Sir George Howland, Bart., 1753–1827, connoisseur, patron of artists, and disting. amateur painter ; only child of Sir George, 6th Bart. ; b. at Dunmow, Essex; educ. at Eton and Oxford ; promoted formation of National Gallery, to which he presented 16 pictures.
J. Hoppner, R.A.   W. Say, mez.
Ha. len. to front, facing and looking to right; coat fastened by one button across chest, white neckcloth and waistcoat; Decr. 26, 1808.
" Proof " (in lowest corner at right).
$13\frac{5}{16} \times 9\frac{5}{16}$. $(12\frac{1}{8} \times 9\frac{5}{16})$.   22109.

BECKFORD, William, 1709–1770, a wealthy merchant, b. in Jamaica; son of the Hon. Peter Beckford, speaker of the assembly in that island; educ. at Westminster ; M.P. for the City; advanced liberal, supported Wilkes; Lord Mayor, 1769; made a memorable impromptu reply to George III., after presenting an address; his reply is engr. in gilt letters on the pedestal of his monument in Guildhall.
J. Dixon del.   J. Dixon, mez.
J. C. Smith, 4, 4th state.   22110.

—— with JAMES TOWNSEND, M.P., and JOHN SAWBRIDGE, M.P.; a group, 1769.
R. Houston del. R. Houston, mez.
J. C. Smith, 9. 24061.

BEDFORD, FRANCIS RUSSELL, Earl of, 1624–1646.
A. van Dyck. G. Vertue, 1737.
Oval. From the picture at Woburn.
In Birch's "Lives."
$14\frac{1}{4} \times 9\frac{1}{8}$ (?). ($13\frac{7}{8} \times 8\frac{7}{8}$). 28155.

BEDFORD, FRANCIS RUSSELL, 5th Duke of, 1765–1802, grandson of John, 4th Duke; suc., 1771; educ. at Westminster and Cambr.; a great promoter of Agriculture; d. of the effects of a tennis-ball (or a cricket-ball), at Woburn Abbey, unmarried.
J. Hoppner, R.A. J. R. Smith, mez.
J. C. Smith, 13. 22113.

BEDFORD, JOHN PLANTAGENET, "of Lancaster," Duke of, 1389–1435. 3rd son of Henry IV.; K.B., 1399; K.G., 1399 (or 1402); Warden of East Marches, and Capt. of Berwick, 1403–'14; Constable of England, 1403; cr. Earl of Kendal and Duke of Bedford, 1414; cr. Earl of Richmond, 1414; Protector, 1422; Regent of France, &c., 1422; crowned his nephew, Henry VI., at Paris, King of France, 1432; d. at Paris.
G. Vertue.
"From a curious Limning in a (MS.) rich Prayer-book presented by himself to K. Hen. 6," &c.
$11\frac{5}{8} \times 7\frac{1}{2}$ (?). ($11\frac{1}{16} \times 7\frac{1}{8}$). 22807

BEDFORD, JOHN RUSSELL, 1st Earl of, c. 1485–1554, assisted Philip of Austria, when wrecked off Weymouth; introd. by him at Court; attended the king at taking of Therouenne and Tournay, 1513; Knt., 1522; served in Italy, Germany, France; Baron, 1537, and P.C.; Lord High Admiral, 1542; Privy Seal, 1543–'7, 1547–'53; Earl, 1550; &c.
Anon. J. Houbraken.
Oval; in Birch's "Lives;" 1739.
$14\frac{7}{8} \times 9\frac{3}{8}$. ($14\frac{1}{8} \times 8\frac{3}{4}$). 28156. 4.

BEDFORD, JOHN RUSSELL, Duke of, 1710–1771; 1st Lord of Admiralty, 1744, and P.C.; one of the Lords Justices of the Realm, 1745, and Col. in the Army; Sec. of State, 1747–'51; K.G., 1749; Maj. General, 1755; Ld. Lieut. of Ireland, 1756–'61; Lt. General, 1759; Lord High Constable, 1761; Privy Seal; Ambas. to France, Lord Pres. of Council, &c.
Sir J. Reynolds. H. Robinson.
T. Q. len. in robes; Jany., 1831.
$14\frac{11}{16} \times 10\frac{3}{8}$. ($5 \times 3\frac{7}{8}$). 27156.

BEDFORD, WILLIAM RUSSELL, Duke of, c. 1613–1700, K.B., 1626; M.P., 1640; General of Horse, 1642, when a peer, in Parl. service; did great execution at Edgehill; joined

the King, 1643 ; sat again in House of Lords, 1660, active in
effecting restoration; K.G., 1672 ; cr. Marquess of Tavistock
and Duke of Bedford, 1694 ; cr. Baron Howland of Streatham,
1695.
  Sir A. van Dyck.   J. Houbraken.
  In Birch's "Lives ;" a fine, early impression, but cut at
edges.
  (14 × 8½).   28157.   1.

BEECHEY, CAPTAIN FREDERICK WILLIAM, 1796-1856, ent. Navy,
1806 ; in action off Madagascar, 1811 ; in expedition to N.
Orleans, 1815 ; served, as Lieut., under Sir J. Franklin, in
Northern Exploration, 1818 ; under Parry, 1819 ; on a survey,
N. Coast of Africa and elsewhere, 1821 ; Post-Cap., 1827 ; pub.
a " Narrative of Voyage to the Pacific and Behring's Straits,"
&c., 1825–'8 ; made surveys of Coast of South America, Coast
of Ireland, &c.
  See ARCTIC COUNCIL.

BEECHEY, SIR WILLIAM, 1753-1839, portrait-painter, b. at
Burford, Oxfordshire ; entd. Academy Schools, 1772 ; exhibited
some small portraits, 1775 ; went to Norwich for four or five
years ; began life-size portraits,1783 ; A.R.A., 1793 ; gained Court
favour, painting portraits of the Queen, George III., &c. ; Knt.
and R.A., 1798 ; became fashionable painter ; sold his collection
of pictures, books, and prints, 1836 ; d. at Hampstead.
  Beechey.   W. Ridley, stipple.
  Sh. ha. len. to right, looking to front ; oval in rectangular
border with angles cut off ; in the " Monthly Mirror," July 31,
1798.
  6 $\frac{7}{16}$ × 4 $\frac{3}{8}$.   (3 $\frac{3}{8}$ × 2 $\frac{13}{16}$; oval, 3 $\frac{5}{16}$ × 2 $\frac{5}{8}$).   28300.   10.

  G. Dance.   W. Daniell, stipple.
  Sh. ha. len, to right, in profile, seated ; vignette.
  10 $\frac{1}{4}$ × 7 $\frac{14}{16}$.   (6 $\frac{1}{4}$ × 4 $\frac{3}{4}$).   28299.   3.

  M. A. Shee, 1830   Anon. lith. (J. Graf, printer).
  Bust-size, to left, looking to front ; vignette ; private plate. .
  (4 $\frac{3}{4}$ × 4 $\frac{3}{8}$).   26243.

  W. J. Newton   E. Scriven, stipple.
  Sh. ha. len. slightly to left, looking to front, seated ; coat buttoned up, white neckcloth, the body roughly sketched below
shoulders. In the " Library of the Fine Arts," 1832 ; vignette ;
facs. signature below.
  7 $\frac{3}{4}$ × 5 $\frac{5}{8}$ (?).   (3 $\frac{1}{4}$ × 3).   28300.   11

                                W. Skelton, lith.
  Full ha. len. to front, seated, holding crayon in right hand,
and book in left.
  Ind. proof, with open letters.
  (10 $\frac{3}{4}$ × 9).   E. 1267.   –'86.

J. Wood. G. T. Payne, mixed mez.
Ha. len. to left, white neckcloth and frill, dark coat, drapery
behind him. June 1, 1840.
$14\frac{7}{8} \times 11\frac{5}{8}$ (?) $(9\frac{1}{4} \times 7\frac{4}{8})$. 27202.

BEHN, APHRA (christened "AYFARA"), 1640–'89, b. at Wye,
Kent, the daughter of John Johnson, a barber; went, still a child,
with a relative, whom she called her father, to Surinam, where
he had been nominated Governor; returned, c. 1658; m. to a
Dutch merchant, who d. before 1666; sent to Antwerp, as a
spy; wrote and published many plays, novels, and letters, of a
lively but licentious character.
Mrs. Beale. J. Fittler, A.R.A.
Sh. ha. len. to left, looking front, wearing a collar of pearls.
The picture is at Stowe.
Ind. proof before all letters, except the engraver's name.
$8 \times 5\frac{7}{16}$. $(3\frac{3}{4} \times 2\frac{13}{16})$. 24059.

BELL, REV. ANDREW, 1753–1832, founder of the Madras system
of mutual education; son of a barber in St. Andrew's; educ. at
St. Andrew's University; went to Virginia, 1774; returned,
1781, and took orders; sailed for India, with a complimentary
degree of D.D., 1787; obtained eight army chaplaincies; app.
superintendent of Madras Male Orphan Asylum, where he
instituted his new system, which in 1798 he introduced at home.
W. Owen, R.A. C Turner, mez.
T. Q. len. seated, to left, wearing glasses and looking to front;
in gown.
Open letter proof, January 29, 1813.
$19\frac{13}{16} \times 13\frac{7}{8}$. $(17\frac{1}{8} \times 13\frac{3}{4})$. 22956.

BELL, JOHN, 1745–1831, publisher, defied the London combination
of some 40 publishing firms, self-called "the trade;" brought
out the "British Poets," 1782, in 109 vols., 18mo, illustrated;
pubd. similar edition of "Shakspear," and the "British Theatre;"
one of the original proprietors of the "Fashionable World,"
the "Oracle," "Morning Post," 1772; as a printer, was the
first to discard the long f (s).
G. Clint, A.R.A., 1825. T. Lupton, mixed mez.
T Q. len. slightly to left, looking to front; holding spectacles
in right hand, and in left his "Weekly Messenger," a Sunday
paper, which he started.
Ser. letter proof.
20×14. (16×13). 22960.

BELL, JOHN, 1764–1836, b. at Kendal; only son of Matthew
Bell; educ. at gram. sch. at Beetham, and Trin. Coll. Cambr.;
grad., 1786, first Smith's prizeman, and sen. Wrangler, and
fellow; ent. Mid. Temple, 1787, and Gray's Inn, 1790, having
taken M.A. degree, 1789; bar., 1792; K.C., 1816; had the
repute of being the best lawyer at the Equity, though, as Lord
Eldon said, he could neither read, write, walk, nor talk.
T. Stewardson. S. Cousins, mez.

Ha. len. seated, to front; hands loosely clasped, and right elbow leaning on table, on which are books.

Open letter proof.

$15\frac{7}{16} \times 12$. $(12\frac{1}{4} \times 9\frac{1}{2})$. 27203.

BENEDICT, Sir Julius, 1804–1885, composer, pianist, and teacher, b. at Stuttgardt; stud. under Hummel and Weber, conducted at Vienna, 1823; produced his first work "Giacinta ed Ernesto," at Naples; went to Paris, 1835, and to London, where he fixed his residence; produced several works, more or less successful; conducted for A. Bunn at Drury Lane; accomp. Jenny Lind in her American tour; wrote the recitatives for "Oberon;" composed the "Lily of Killarney," and other operas, 2 symphonies, 2 oratorios, &c.; knt. 1871.

See FIRST READING.

BENNETT, Sir William Sterndale, 1816–1875, the greatest and most original English composer since Purcell; b. at Sheffield; educ. at the R.A.M., of which he afterwards became Principal; pupil of Lucas, Dr. Crotch, W. H. Holmes, and C. Potter; influenced by Mendelssohn; went to Leipzig for a year, and won there general admiration, and the friendship and enthusiastic eulogies of Schumann; conducted Philharm. Concerts, 1856–'66; Mus. Doc., and Mus. Prof., Cambr., 1856; M.A., 1867; composed Concertos, Overtures, Oratorio ("Woman of Samaria,") "The May Queen," a Pastoral; P.F. pieces, songs, &c.

See FIRST READING.

BENSLEY, Robert, 1738(?)–1817(?), actor, said to have been a lieutenant of Marines, appeared at Drury Lane as Pierre in "Venice Preserved," Oct. 2, 1765; played other parts successfully; appeared at Cov. Garden, until 1775, when he returned to Drury Lane, and appeared also at Haymarket; praised highly by Charles Lamb; retired, 1796; his greatest character was "Malvolio."

G. Dance, April 20, 1795. W. Daniell, stipple.

Sh. ha. len. to right, in profile, seated; vignette; April 2, 1814.

$10\frac{3}{4} \times 7\frac{15}{16}$. $(7\frac{1}{4} \times 4\frac{7}{8})$. 27999. 1.

BENTHAM, Jeremy, 1748–1832, b. in Red Lion St., Houndsditch, grandson of a pawnbroker, son of an Attorney; precocious and forward, before going to Westminster, 1755; went to Queen's Coll., Oxf.; B.A., 1763; M.A., 1766; called to the bar, c. 1772; dabbled in chemistry, stud. phys. science, and speculated on politics and jurisprudence, to which he devoted his life, and on which he wrote many works.

H. W. Pickersgill, R.A. C. Fox.

Sh. ha. len. to front, looking to left; coat fastened with a ribbon; his hair long and white; vignette.

Ind. proof before all letters, except the artists' names.

$10\frac{13}{16} \times 8\frac{3}{8}$. $(6\frac{1}{4} \times 4\frac{7}{8})$. 24739.

BENTHAM, SIR SAMUEL, 1757–1831, naval architect and engineer, youngest son of Jeremy Bentham, an attorney, and brother of Jeremy Bentham; educ. at Westminster; appr. to the master-shipwright of Woolwich Dockyard; present at the battle off Ushant; went to Russia, 1780; settled on Potemkin's property at Kritchev, where he established a shipbuilding yard, with success; ordered to Cherson, 1787, where he organised a flotilla; returned to England, 1791; apptd. adviser to the Admiralty; resided in France, 1814–'27; returned to England, 1827.

See SCIENCE.

BENTINCK, WILLIAM GEORGE FREDERIC CAVENDISH, commonly called Lord George Bentinck, 1802–1848, fifth child and second surviving son of the 4th Duke of Portland; educ. at home; cornet in 10th Hussars, 1819; priv. sec. to Canning for 3 years; fond of sport, in which he excelled; rode at Goodwood, in a match, 1824, and occasionally, down to 1845; M.P. for King's Lynn, 1826 till death; devoted himself to racing, in which he was very successful; opposed Free Trade.

S. Lane. — S. W. Reynolds, mixed mez.

T. Q. len. slightly inclined to left, standing, facing and looking towards right, right hand on papers which lie upon a table, another roll of papers in left.

Ind. paper proof before all letters.

$20\frac{1}{8} \times 15$. $(16\frac{3}{8} \times 12\frac{13}{16})$. 23762.

Another impression, lettered; Feb. 5, 1849.

$20\frac{1}{16} \times 15\frac{1}{16}$. $(16\frac{3}{8} \times 12\frac{7}{8})$. 21958.

BENTINCK, LORD WILLIAM CAVENDISH, 1774–1839, the second son of William Henry, third Duke of Portland; ensign, Coldstr. Gds., 1791; Captn., 2d Light Dragoons, 1792; Lt.-Col. 24th Light Dragoons, 1794; served on staff of Duke of York, in Netherlands; in Italy, 1799, with Suwaroff, present at all battles till 1801; 1803–7, Govr. Madras; recalled, 1808; Maj. Gen.; served in Peninsula; envoy and Commander-in-Chf., Sicily, 1811; Govr.-Genl., Bengal, 1827–'35.

T. Phillips, R.A. — G. H. Phillips, mez.

Wh. len. to front, standing, looking to right, in uniform.

Open letter proof, Oct. 2, 1838.

$28\frac{1}{2} \times 18\frac{3}{8}$. $(25 \times 15\frac{11}{16})$. 24619.

BENTLEY, RICHARD, 1662–1742, Scholar, Critic, and Divine; b. at Oulton, near Wakefield, where he was educ., and at Cambr.; Boyle Lecturer; Keeper, Roy. Library, St. James's Palace; eng. in corresp. with Hon. Charles Boyle about the "Letters of Phalaris," in which he crushed his attacker; Master of Trin. Coll., Cambr., 1700; involved for many years in contention with the Coll. and Univ.; ultimately victorious; D.D.; pub. Boyle Lectures, Sermons, Editions of Homer, Horace, Terence, &c.; d. at Trin. Coll.

Sir J Thornhill. — G. Vertue.

Sh. ha. len. to left, facing and looking to right, wearing wig, bands, and gown ; oval in frame ; æt. XLVIII. MDCCX. (8 × 6).   22493.

BERESFORD, WILLIAM CARR BERESFORD, Viscount, 1768–1854, general ; illegit. son of 1st Marquess of Waterford ; ent. army, 1785 ; served in India, Egypt, at the Cape, and Madeira, 1799–1807 ; with the Br. Army in Portugal ; Com.-in-Chf. of Portuguese troops, 1809 ; defeated Soult at Albuera, 1811 ; cr. Baron, 1814, Viscount, 1823 ; Master-Genl. of Ordnance, G.C.H., &c.

Sir W. Beechey   C. Turner, mez.
Ha. len. to front, looking to left, in full uniform, with the collar of his Portuguese decoration (Tower and Sword). Open letter proof, Sepr. 21, 1814.
14 × 9⅞. (12 × 9⅛).   21894.

BERGAVENNY, JOANE, 1375–1435, sister and eventually (1415) co-heir to Thomas (Fitzalan), Earl of Arundel, daughter of Richard, Earl of Arundel, by Elizabeth, daughter of William (Bohun), Earl of Northampton ; m. to William Beauchamp, 1st Baron Bergavenny (later called Abergavenny) ; she held the Castle and Honour of Abergavenny, in dower, after his death (1411), until her own death.

Anon, stipple.
Ha. len. to front, looking to left ; dress cut square in front ; necklace, rings, a flower in left hand ; *"from an Original Picture at Strawberry Hill. Publish'd May* 12, 1798, *by S. Harding,"* &c.
7⁵⁄₁₆ × 5¾. (4⅞ × 3¼).   26194.

BERKELEY, GEORGE, 1684–1753, metaphysician, b. in Kilkenny co. ; educ. at Dublin ; pub. "Theory of Vision," 1709 ; "Principles of Human Knowledge," embodying his philosophy, 1710 ; came to London, 1713, and wrote for Steele's "Guardian ; " Dean of Derry, 1724 ; went to America to convert the Indians, 1728 ; failed, and returned to England ; Bishop of Cloyne, 1734 ; d. at Oxford.

J. Latham.   J. Brooks, mez.
J. C. Smith, 4.   22451.

BERKELEY, CAPTAIN the HON. GEORGE CRANFIELD, 1753–1818, son of the 4th Earl of Berkeley ; commanded a ship, June 1, 1794, in Howe's victory off Ushant ; Admiral of the White ; G.C.B. ; some time Lord High Admiral of Portugal ; d. in South Audley Street.
See COMMEMORATION (1).

BERKELEY, SIR WILLIAM. *See* NAVAL HEROES (2).

BERNAL, RALPH,   –1854, politician and art collector, descended from a Jewish family of Spain ; educ. at Chr. Coll., Cambr. ; B.A., 1806 ; M.A., 1809 ; called to the bar, 1810 ; inherited large property in W. Indies ; M.P., 1818–'52, spent 66,000*l.* on elections; Presid. Br. Arch. Socy., 1853; pubd. his inaugural address, speeches, papers of antiquities, &c.; formed a magnificent collection of china, plate, miniatures, glass, &c., which realised nearly 71,000*l*.

A. Wivell. J. Thomson, stipple.
Sh. ha. len. to right, apparently seated; coat buttoned across chest; a curtain and window behind.
Ind. proof; March 14. 1822.
$8\frac{3}{8} \times 6\frac{7}{8}$. $(3\frac{7}{8} \times 3\frac{3}{16})$.   24652.

BERNARD, Sir Thomas, 1750–1818, educ. at Harvard Coll., U.S.A.; Treasurer of Foundling Hospital; one of the founders of Royal Institution and British Gallery; established a free chapel and schools in Seven Dials, London; Chancellor of Diocese of Durham; d. at Leamington; buried in Foundl. Hospital.

J. Wright del. C. Picart, stipple.
Ha. len. to left, looking to front, seated; vignette.
Open letter proof; May 11, 1815; in Cadell's series.
$14\frac{7}{8} \times 12\frac{7}{8}$. $(8 \times 6\frac{7}{8})$.   28153. 1

BERRY, Sir Edward, 1768–1831, joined the navy as a volunteer, 1779; lieut., 1794; appointed to Nelson's ship, Agamemnon, 1796, soon distinguished himself by conspicuous bravery, and became Nelson's intimate friend; knighted, 1798; cr. Bart., 1806; Rear-Adml., 1821; died at Bath, having been paralysed for some years.

H. Singleton. G. Keating, mez.
J C. Smith, 1, 2nd state.   24201.

BERRY, Mary, 1763–1852, b. at Kirkbridge, Yorks.; almost entirely self-educ.; travelled with her father and sister, 1783, in Holland, Switzerland, and Italy; began her "Journals and Correspondence," finished 70 years later; made, 1788, the acquaintance of Horace Walpole, then aged 70, of whom she and her sister became intimate friends, and who bequeathed to them a handsome legacy; she pubd. "Comparative View of Social Life of England and France," 1828, &c.

J. R. Swinton. H. Robinson, stipple.
Bust, slightly to left, looking to front, wearing cap; facs. signature below, "æi: 86." Vignette.
Ind. proof before all letters, except the artists' names, facs. signature, and publication-line, 1850.
$22\frac{3}{4} \times 17\frac{7}{8}$. $(10 \times 9\frac{3}{8})$.   22952.

BERTIE, Sir Thomas, 1758–1825, Vice-Admiral, son of George Hoare, Esq.; ent. navy, 1773; m. Catherine Dorothy, dau. of Peregrine Bertie, whose name he took; Cap. 1790; com. a ship, June 1, 1794, in Howe's Victory; under Nelson, at Copenhagen; Adm., 1808; Knt., Vice-Adml., 1813.
See COMMEMORATION (1).

BERWICK, James Fitz-James, Duke of, 1670–1734, natural son of James II, and Arabella Churchill; served with distinction

in the French Army; became a Marshal of France; killed at
Siege of Philipsburg.
  B. Gennari.   P. Drevet.
  A. Firmin-Didot, 20, 1st state, the name of the painter being
altered by hand, with a pen and ink; see " Les Drevet," by
A. Firmin-Didot, Paris, 1876, p. 16.
  $(19\frac{7}{10} \times 16\frac{3}{8})$.   21966.

BEST, Lord Chief Justice. See WYNFORD, Lord.

BETTERTON, Thomas, " the silver-tongued," 1635-1710, b. in
Tothill-street, Westminster ; son of a cook of Charles 1. ;
apprent. to a bookseller ; became an actor ; first perf. in Rhodes's
Comp., at the Cockpit, Drury Lane, 1659 ; opened a new
theatre, 1659 ; was the most eminent player of his time,
manager, and highly respected in private life ; played Shakspere and Congreve equally well ; bur. in Westminster Abbey.
  Sir G Kneller.   R. Williams, mez.
  J. C. Smith, 7, 2nd state.   22209.

BETTY, William Henry West, 1791-1874, b. at Shrewsbury ;
first appeared at Belfast, 1803, as Osman in " Zara," and in
Dublin ; eng. at Cov. Garden for 12 nights at 50l. a night with
a clear benefit, and at Drury Lane, on same terms, 1804 ; after
3 nights, salary raised to 100l. a night ; known as the " Young
Roscius ;" returned to the stage, 1812, without success.
  J. Northcote, R.A.   J. Ward, mez.
  J. C. Smith, 4, 2d state.   21912.

  J. Northcote, R.A.   J. Heath.
  Wh. len. to front, standing on steps leading up to the bust of
Shakspere, below which his right hand rests ; his left is extended
towards the right side, on which stands a tripod with incense.
  $24(?) \times 17(?)$. $(22\frac{1}{4} \times 15\frac{7}{8})$.   27128.

BEWICK, Thomas, 1753-1828, wood-engraver ; son of a coal
miner in Northumberland ; apprent. to an engraver in Newcastle ; gained premium of Soc. of Arts for a cut of illustration
to Gay's Fables, 1775 ; became famous by designs and wood-
cuts for " History of Quadrupeds," " History of British Birds,"
&c. ; d. at Gateshead.
  J. Ramsay.   J. Burnet.
  Ha. len. to left, looking to front ; on his right are some books,
the upper one being labelled " Bewick's British Birds, Vol. II."
  Open letter proof ; Oct. 25, 1817

  J. Ramsay.   Anon., stipple.
  Ha. len. to left ; vignette.
  $11\frac{1}{2} \times 7\frac{1}{2}$. $(5 \times 4\frac{1}{4})$.   .   E. 1958.-'89.

  J. Ramsay.   F. Bacon.
  Wh. len. standing, turned towards right, leaning on stick,
held in right hand ; behind him, the Tyne and Newcastle in the

distance. Pubd. by R. Turner, Newcastle, P. & D. Colnaghi
& Co., London.
16×12. (8×6⅓). 24098.

—— Copy of the above. Anon., woodcut.
From an illustrated paper.
5¼×2⅞. (4⅝×2¹³⁄₁₆). E. 1954.-'89.

BEXLEY, Rt. Hon. Nicholas Vansittart, 1st Lord, 1766–
1851, called to the Bar, 1792; M.P., Hastings, 1796; Sec. to
Treasury, 1801–'4, 1806–'8; Chief Sec., Ireland, 1805; Chancellor of Exchequer, 1812–'23; Chancellor, Duchy of Lancaster,
1822–'8; cr. Baron Bexley, 1823; d. at Foot'scray-place, Kent.
   W. Owen, R.A.   W. Ward, A.R.A., mez.
   J. C. Smith, 85.   22062.

BIDDER, George Parker, 1806–1878, rapid calculator and
engineer, born at Moreton Hampstead, on the borders of Dartmoor; son of a stonemason; showed as a child extraordinary
power of mental calculation; educ. at Camberwell and Edinb.;
devoted himself to engineering; assoc. with R. Stephenson;
originated the Railway swing-bridge.
   See MENAI STRAITS.

BIFFIN, Miss Sarah, 1784–1850, miniature-painter, b. at East
Quantox-head, near Bridgewater, Somerset, without hands or
feet; her arms were rudimentary, pupil of Craig, miniature-
painter; when painting, she held the handle of the brush, between her lips; gained a medal, 1821, from the Society of Arts;
patronised by Royalty; fell into poverty in age; retired to
Liverpool, where an annuity was bought for her by subscription;
d. there.
   S. Biffin, min.   R. W. Sievier, line and stipple.
   Wh. len., to front, seated, wearing hat and feathers; a table
with palette, brushes in tumbler, and drawing-desk before her;
a brush is held in a ring on her right shoulder, ready for use.
   Pubd. by Miss Biffin, 33, Strand, June, 1821.
   14×11⁷⁄₁₆. (5¹⁵⁄₁₆×4⅞, excl. of ruled border, 1 in.). 26646.

BIGG, William Redmore, 1755–1828, subject-painter; pupil of
Penny, R.A., and entd. Academy schools, 1778; exhibited,
1780; A.R.A., 1787; R.A., 1814; constant exhibitor of domestic scenes and, later, some landscapes, popular at the time;
"a more amiable man never existed" (Leslie, R.A.).
   W. Fisk.   W. Barnard, mez.
   Ha. len. to right, looking to front, seated; white neckcloth,
black coat buttoned across; facs. signature below; pubd. by
W. Fisk, and W. Barnard, June 20, 1831.
   10¹¹⁄₁₆×8⁷⁄₁₆. (9¼×7¹³⁄₁₆). 24054.

BILL, Anne, 1589–1621, wife of John Bill, who, with Bonham
Norton, was printer to the King; she appears to have been an
amiable and accomplished woman.
                                        S. Pass del. et. sc.

Bust, to left, on small pedestal, in a monumental effigy; Granger (Vol. 2, p. 56) gives the inscription incorrectly; it runs thus : " Æternæ Memor. et Quiet AN. BILLæ Uxori lectiss. " | et dilectiss Io BILL Conuix mœstiss. P.P. ; " a tablet, on right, in foreground, is inscribed "TrICesIMo | tertIo ætatIs | De VIXIt.," a chronogram from which the date of her death appears ; the print is prefixed to "A Mirror of Modestie," 1621.

Cut ($5\frac{11}{16} \times 3\frac{3}{16}$).   29608.   1.

BILLINGTON, MRS. ELIZABETH, c. 1768–1818, the greatest of English singers, b. in Soho, London ; daughter of Carl Weichsel, a native of Freiberg, Saxony, princip. oboe at the King's Theatre ; her mother was a singer ; Elizabeth was a pupil of her father, and of Schroeter ; m. to James Billington, contrabassist ; appeared in Dublin ; at Cov. Garden, 1785 ; in Italy ; returned to London, 1801 ; played at Drury Lane and Cov. Garden alternately, and sang at all principal concerts ; amassed a fortune ; m. twice, and unfortunately ; secondly to a French impostor, Félissent, who was expelled this country, 1801 ; she d. in Italy.

Sir J. Reynolds, P.R.A.   J. Ward, mez.
J. C. Smith, 5, 2nd state.   25735.

BIRD, EDWARD, 1772–1819, b. at Wolverhampton, son of a carpenter ; apprent. to a tea-tray maker, whose trays he embellished with landscapes, fruit, and flowers ; started a drawing-school at Bristol ; painted miniatures and theatrical scenery ; exhibited at R. Academy, 1809 ; A.R.A., 1812 ; R.A., 1815 ; historical painter to Princess Charlotte ; d. at Bristol, in poverty.

F. L. Chantrey, R.A., 1816.   Mrs. Dawson Turner.
Bust, to right, slightly executed ; vignette ; private plate.
$9\frac{1}{4} \times 7\frac{1}{8}$.   ($6\frac{1}{8} \times 6$).   28298.   1.

"From the Original Sketch " [by Chantrey].
         Anon., chalk and dot.
A head, to left, slightly sketched ; vignette ; facs. signature below.
$7\frac{1}{4} \times 5$ (?).   ($2\frac{3}{4} \times 2\frac{3}{16}$).   28300.   13.

BIRD, CAPTAIN E. J., R.N.   See ARCTIC COUNCIL.

BIRKBECK, GEORGE, 1776–1841, son of William Birkbeck, banker and merchant at Settle, where he was b. ; stud. med. at Edinb. and London ; M.D. Edinb., 1799 ; prof. Nat. Phil., Anders. Univ., Glasgow ; estab. lectures for workmen, 1800, "Glasgow Mechanics' Institution," 1823, the first of its kind ; came to London, 1804 ; founded Mechanics' Lect.-room, 1824 ; first presidt. of "London Mechanics' Instn.," afterwards called "Birkbeck Instn."

S. Lane.   H. Dawe, mixed mez.

T. Q. len. slightly to left, looking to right, standing, with
left hand resting on book, labelled "History of Mechanics'
Institutions. MSS. 1825."
Skeleton letter proof; January, 1827.
$20\frac{5}{8} \times 15\frac{3}{4}$. $(17\frac{1}{4} \times 13\frac{1}{8})$. 22213.

BISHOP, Sir Henry Rowley, 1786–1855, musical composer;
author of many Operas, Glees, Songs, Odes, &c.; Musical
Director of Covent Garden, Director of Concerts of Ancient
Music, Prof. Music, Oxford; Knt., 1837.
T. Foster.   S. W. Reynolds, mixed mez.
T. Q. len. to right, facing and looking to left, seated, enveloped
in a cloak, holding a roll of music in right hand, left on knee;
book, lettered "National Melodies," and curtain in background;
July, 1822.
$20\frac{1}{8} \times 14$. $(17\frac{7}{16} \times 13\frac{3}{4})$. 21902.

BISHOPS, the seven, committed to the Tower, 1688, viz.:—
    CANTERBURY, William SANCROFT, (q.v.), in the
centre.
  Above, on left,
    ELY, Francis TURNER, ... –1700, bishop, Roches-
ter, 1683; transd., 1683; depr., 1691.
  Above, on right,
    ST. ASAPH, William LLOYD, 1627–1717, consecr.,
1680; bishop, Lichfield, 1692; Worcester, 1699.
  Middle, on left,
    BATH and WELLS, Thomas Kenn (q.v.);
  Middle, on right,
    CHICHESTER, John LAKE, ... –1689; bishop,
Sodor and Man, 1683; Bristol, 1684; Chichester, 1685.
  Below, on left,
    BRISTOL, Sir Jonathan TRELAWNEY. c. 1648–
1721, Bart., Bishop, Bristol, 1685; Exeter, 1688; Winchester,
1707.
  Below, on right,
    PETERBORO', Thomas WHITE, ... –1698; arch-
deacon, Northampton; consecrd., 1685; deprived, 1691.
                        Anon. [Albert Haelwegh sc. ?].
A group; ovals in a border of scrollwork, surmounted by a
cherub; below, an inscription in Latin, Dutch, and French; in
centre, in two circles, the Tower of London, and the Sun
and Moon, weighed in scales.
$16\frac{13}{16} (?) \times 11\frac{3}{8}$. $(13\frac{13}{16} \times 10\frac{1}{16})$. 26668.

BLACK, John, 1783–1855, b. near Dunse, Berwicks.; educ. at
Dunse parish sch.; articled, 1796, to a writer, with whom he
remained four years; clerk in a bank; obliged to leave the
town, on account of a practical joke; went to Edinb. as clerk;
attended classes at the Univy.; came to London, 1810; engaged as a reporter for the "Morning Chronicle," of which he

gradually became editor, 1817 ; fought a duel, 1835, with J. A.
Roebuck ; invited to resign, 1843.

W. H. Worthington.   W. H. Worthington.
  Full ha. len., slightly to right, seated, looking to front, wearing spectacles, and holding " Morning Chronicle " in left hand ;
facs. signature below ; 1835.
  $11\frac{3}{8} \times 9\frac{3}{8}$. $(8 \times 6\frac{7}{16})$.   24055.

BLACK, JOSEPH, M.D., 1728-1799, chemist ; b. in France ;
  educ. at Univ. of Glasgow and Edinb.; Prof. of Anatomy, and
  lect. on Chemistry at Glasgow, 1756 ; made the discovery of
  latent heat ; Prof. of Chemistry at Edinb., 1766 ; pub. " Ex-
  " periments upon Magnesia, Quicklime, &c." ; F.R.S.
    Sir H. Raeburn, R.A.   J. Heath, A.R.A., stipple.
  Ha. len. slightly to left, seated, looking to front, coat buttoned
with two large buttons ; oval ; March 20, 1800.
  Title in open letters.
  $10\frac{7}{8} \times 8\frac{1}{4}$ (?). $(7\frac{15}{16} \times 6\frac{11}{16})$.   22217

BLACKBURNE, LANCELOT, 1658-1743, educ. at Westminster and
  Ch. Ch., Oxf.; took orders, 1681, and went to West Indies ;
  M.A., 1683 ; attached himself to Bishop Trelawney ; prebend,
  1691 ; sub-dean, 1695 ; rector, Calstock, Cornwall, 1696 ; dean,
  Exeter, 1705 ; archdeacon, Cornwall, 1715 ; bishop, Exeter,
  1717 ; archbishop of York, 1724 till his death ; gay and witty ;
  the object of much satire and slander, which appear to have
  been ill-founded.
    I. Zeeman.   G. Vertue.   1726.
  T. Q. len. to left, looking to front, seated, in robes.
  $15\frac{1}{2} \times 11\frac{1}{2}$. $(12\frac{1}{2} \times 10\frac{1}{4})$.   23125.

BLACKMORE, SIR RICHARD, 1650(?)-1729, Kt., M.D.,
  Physician and poet ; son of an attorney ; b. at Corsham, Wilts. ;
  educ. at Westminster and St. Edm. Hall, Oxf. ; B.A., 1674 ;
  M.A., 1676 ; began as a schoolmaster ; travelled in France,
  Germany, Netherlands ; M.D. at Padua ; F.R.C.P., 1687 ;
  Physician to William III., who knighted him ; author of poems,
  " Prince Arthur," " Alfred," " Creation," &c.
    J. Vanderbanck.   G. White, mez.
    J. C. Smith, 4, 2nd state.   22690.

BLACKSTONE, SIR WILLIAM, 1723-1780, eminent lawyer ; b.
  in Cheapside ; educ. at Charterhouse ; Vinerian Professor,
  Oxford ; Recorder, Wallingford, Berks ; M.P., Hindon, Wilts ;
  Puisne Judge of King's Bench, 1770, removed in same year to
  the Com. Pleas ; published " Commentaries on the Laws of
  England," 1765-8.
    T. Gainsborough.   S. Bellin, mixed mez.
  Ha. len. to left, looking to front, in full wig and robes, holding
a document with seal in right hand.
  Proof with scratched letters.
  $15\frac{3}{8} \times 12$. $(11\frac{3}{16} \times 9)$.   22214.

BLAGROVE, HENRY GAMBLE, 1811–1872, son of a musician at
Nottingham, where he was born; played at Drury Lane, 1817;
stud. under Spagnoletti, 1821; and at the R.A.M. 1823,
where he gained a medal, 1824; a member of Queen Adelaide's
private band, 1830–'7; went to Germany, 1832–'4, studying
under Spohr; became one of the most distinguished of English
violinists, and remained at their head for 30 years.
See MUSICAL UNION.

BLAIR, HUGH, 1718–1800; son of an Edinburgh merchant;
educ. at Edinb.; M.A., 1739; licensed to preach, 1741; ordd.,
1742; appointed to the High church, 1758, where he remained
till his death; profr. of rhetoric, 1760; Reg. profr., 1762;
pubd. lectures and sermons; supported the authenticity of
Ossian.
    Sir H. Raeburn.   F. Bartolozzi, stipple.
    Ha. len. to right, looking to front, in gown, seated, with folded
hands.
    Open letter proof, July 1, 1802.
    $15\frac{1}{16} \times 12\frac{3}{4}$. $(12\frac{1}{2} \times 10)$.   24099.

BLAIR, WILLIAM, 1766–1822, surgeon, b. at Lavenham, Suff.;
stud. under Mr. J. Pearson; surgeon to Lock Hosp.; M.A.;
became eminent; surgeon to several Dispensaries, &c.; M.R.C.S.
and of the Medical Societies of London, Paris, Brussels, and
Aberdeen; pubd. several learned and useful works.
    See MEDICAL SOCIETY

BLAKE, ROBERT, 1599–1657, Republican Admiral, educ. at
Oxford; M.P., 1640; joined the army, under Sir J. Horner,
1642; held Lynne against Prince Maurice, and took Taunton,
1644, and held it till after Naseby; appointed Admiral in comd.
of fleet, 1649, and blockaded Prince Rupert at Kinsale, and in the
Tagus, and followed him to Cartagena and Toulon; compelled
the surrender of Scilly islands; fought Tromp and de Ruyter;
defeated the Turks at Porto Farina, 1655; destroyed the
Spanish fleet off Santa Cruz, 1657.
    From the picture at Wad. Coll., Oxf.   J. Mollison, stipple.
    Sh. ha. len. to left, looking to front.
    Ind. proof, with open letters.
    $11\frac{1}{4} \times 7\frac{1}{8}$. $(4\frac{5}{10} \times 3\frac{3}{18})$.   -   28160.

    Anon.   T. Preston, mez.
    J. C. Smith, 1, 1st state.   21740.

BLAKE, WILLIAM, 1757–1827, engraver, painter, and poet; b.
in London; son of a hosier; wrote verses when a boy of 12;
apprent. to James Basire; engraved book-illustrations; friend
of Flaxman; published "Poetical Sketches;" opened a print-
shop, 1784; printed his own poetry, illustrated by himself;
exhibited at Academy, 1780, '84, '85, '99, 1808.
    E. Bocourt.   J. Guillaume, woodcut.

Hu. len. to right, looking upwards to left; vignette; from an illustrated paper.
(3¾ × 3⅗) E. 1950.–'89.

T. Phillips, R.A. L. Schiavonetti, V.A.
Full ha. len. to left, facing and looking towards right, seated, holding crayon in right hand; the lower parts of the subject in outline; lettered "GUILLERMO BLAKE;" vignette.
Cut, 14⅛ (?) × 10¼. (11½ × 9¼). 22215.

BLAKENEY, WILLIAM, BARON, 1672–1761, b. in Ireland; defended Stirling Castle, 1745; and, with insufficient garrison, defended Minorca, 1756, with great bravery and talent, against the French, who allowed him to march out, when obliged to capitulate, with all the honours of war; cr. Baron, 1756; Lt.-Genl., K.B.; &c.
T. Hudson. J Faber, 1748, mez.
J. C. Smith, 35, 1st state. 25765.

BLANCHARD, MISS E. W.
R. E. Drummond. Anon., stipple.
See LA BELLE ASSEMBLÉE, 1818. 13867. 2.

BLANCHARD, WILLIAM, 1769–1835, comedian, b. at York; manager at Penrith, Cumberland; at Hexham, Northumberland; at Barnard Castle and Bishop's Castle, Durham; d. at Chelsea.
G. Clint, A.R.A. C. Cooke.
Wh. len., seated, with Mrs. Davenport and Miss M. Tree, as Peachum in the Beggar's Opera; he is on the right, holding a bottle in his left hand, resting on his knee, and pointing with his right, across Mrs. Davenport (Mrs. Peachum), to Miss Tree (Polly), who is kneeling.
Ind. proof, with open letters.
10⅛ × 12. (8¼ × 10²⁄₁₆). 27582.

BLANCHARD, WILLIAM, with LISTON and MATTHEWS, in the Farce of "Love, Law, and Physic."
G. Clint, A.R.A. T. Lupton, mez.
Wh. len. group, Blanchard on the left, as "Log;" Liston in the centre; Matthews, as "Flexible," on the right, with left hand on hip, right extended, answering Log's question,—
"Do you mean as you can prove black is white?"
Flex. "Sir, black is white: shall a timber-merchant dare "contest with me in points of Law?"
April 22, 1831.
18¾ × 15. (17⁹⁄₁₆ × 14½) 21908.

BLESSINGTON, MARGUERITE, COUNTESS OF, 1789–1849, authoress, wit, beauty, and leader of fashion, b. at Knockbrit, near Clonmel; daughter of Edmund Power, a dissolute man, whose home was a miserable one for her; educ. by a Miss Dwyer; very precocious and clever; obliged to marry, 1804, a Capt. Farmer, a violent debauchee; after his death she married

48

the Earl of Blessington, 1818; became a friend of Byron,
D'Orsay, C. Mathews, and all the most distinguished people of
the day; on the death of her second husband devoted herself to
literature.
Sir T. Lawrence, P.R.A.
S. W. Reynolds and W. Reynolds, mez.
Full ha. len., seated, to left, looking to front, in a low dress,
with flowers in her bosom; hands lightly joined in lap; inscribed
" English Lady; Dame Anglaise."
Open letter proof.
$14\frac{1}{8} \times 10\frac{5}{16}$. $(11\frac{7}{16} \times 9)$.   24649.

BLIZARD, Sir William, 1743–1835, b. at Barn Elms, 4th
child of William Blizard, auctioneer; apprent. to a surgeon at
Mortlake; stud. at Lond. Hospl. and at St. Barthol.; surg. to
the Lond. Hosp., 1780, and founded, 1785, with Dr. Maclaurin,
the Med. Sch. there; F.R.S., 1787, and twice Presid. R.C.S.
J. Opie, R.A.   S. W. Reynolds, mez.
T. Q. len. slightly to right, looking to left, seated, holding a
paper in left hand, right hand open and resting on arm of chair;
wearing robes. " London Published, 1805," and Published
(for the benefit of the London Hospital) March 1, 1810, by
Boydell & Compy., &c.
$20 \times 13\frac{1}{4}$. $(16\frac{1}{2} \times 13\frac{1}{4})$.   25704.

BLOMFIELD, Charles James, 1786–1857, son of a schoolmaster at Bury St. Edmunds; educ. at the grammar school
there, and at Trin. Coll., Cambr.; B.A., 1808; published editions of " Prometheus," " Septem," " Persæ," &c., 1810–'23;
Contrib. to Edinb. Rev. and Qly.; ordd., 1810; archdeacon, Colchester, 1822; bishop, Chester, 1824; London, 1828; cr.
" Bishop of London's Fund;" opposed the " tractarian" movement; resigned, 1856.
S. Lane.   W. Ward, mez.
As Bishop of Chester; T. Q. len. to front, looking to left,
seated, in robes, holding a roll in his left hand.
$22\frac{1}{4} \times 16\frac{1}{2}$. (18×14).   23134.

BLOOD, Thomas, c. 1618–1680, the adventurer, commonly
called Colonel; b. probably in Ireland; disbanded officer of
Cromwell's army; attempted to surprise Dublin Castle; attempted to assassinate the Duke of Ormond; nearly succeeded,
1671, in carrying off the regalia from the Tower; pardoned and
pensioned by Charles II.; imprisoned for libel on the Duke of
Buckingham; liberated on bail; d. 14 days later.
Anon. [G. White?]   G White, mez.
J. C. Smith, 5, 1st state.   22208.

BLOOMFIELD, Robert, 1766–1823, b. at Honington, Suffolk;
son of a village tailor; taught to read and write by his mother,
who kept the village school, and by a Mr. Rodwell, of Ix-
worth; worked on a farm, and afterwards at shoemaking under
his eldest brother, George, in an alley near Coleman St.,

London; studied by himself; sent verses to the "London Magazine," where they were printed; in 1790, " sold his fiddle and got a wife;" wrote his "Farmer's Boy" in a garret, pubd., 1800; appointed undersealer in Seal Office; made Æolian harps; d. in great poverty at Shefford.

P. Violet. J. Young, mez.

J. C. Smith, 8, but not exactly as described by him; the painter's name is as given above; the name of the personage in open letters; the date, Jany. 1st, 1805, &c. 24062.

BLOW, John, 1648–1708, b. at North Collingham, one of the first set of " Children of the Chapel Royal," 1660, under Capt. Henry Cooke; composed anthems while yet a chorister; stud. under J. Hingeston, and Dr. Chr. Gibbons; organist of Westminster Abbey, 1669; displaced, 1680, to make room for Purcell, on whose death, 1695, Blow was re-appointed; master of the children, 1674, and organist of the chapel; composer to the Chapel Royal, 1699; Mus. Doc., Lambeth; composed odes, anthems, services, songs, &c.

R. White, del. R. White.

Sh. ha. len. to right, looking to front; long wig; oval in border; arms below; prefixed to his " Amphion Anglicus," a collection of his songs, &c.

$9\frac{1}{4} \times 6\frac{1}{16}$. $(8\frac{1}{4} \times 5\frac{11}{16})$. 24653.

BOADEN, James, 1762–1839, b. at Whitehaven, came early to London; educ. for commerce; turned journalist; editor of the " Oracle," 1789; wrote " Fontainville Forest," 1794, and several other pieces, biographies, criticisms, &c.

1. Opie, R.A. E. Bell, mixed mez.

J. C. Smith, 3, intermediate state between 1st and 2nd, described in Appendix; "London, Published Feby. 20, 1801, by A. Beugo," &c. 24654.

BODLEY, Sir Thomas, 1545–1618, diplom. and scholar, chiefly remembered as founder of the great library at Oxford; b. at Exeter; educ. at Geneva, and Magd. Coll., Oxf.; B.A., 1563; fellow, 1565; M.A., 1565; proctor, 1569; travelled abroad, 1576–1580, and acquired several languages; was sent on a mission to Denmark, 1585; to France, 1588; married a rich widow, 1587; perm. resident at the Hague, 1589–1596; began the Bodl. Library, 1598, opened solemnly, 1603; named, 1604.

M. Burghers delin. et sculp.

T. Q. len. to right, looking to front, with lace collar and cloak; left hand on sword-hilt; in border, in each corner of which is a small portrait, head, of W Earl of Pembroke, Archbp. Laud, Ken. Digby, and J Selden; 6 lines of Latin inscription above, and 6 below.

(Cut ?) $12\frac{7}{16} \times 7\frac{3}{8}$. $(12\frac{9}{16} \times 7\frac{5}{8})$. 24202.

C. Janssens. (Drawn by T. Uwins.) E. Scriven, stipple.

O 82849. D

Similar to the portrait by M. Burghers, q.v., but shorter, only part of the sword-hilt appearing; the collar is plain, without lace, &c. The picture is in the Bodleian Library.

$14\frac{3}{4} \times 10\frac{7}{16}$. ($7\frac{1}{8} \times 5\frac{5}{8}$). 24655.

BONE, HENRY, 1755–1834, enamel-painter, son of a cabinet-maker; b. at Truro; apprent. to a china-manufacturer at Bristol; came to London, 1779; painted on enamel for jewellers; became distinguished as a miniature portrait-painter on enamel; enamel-painter to George III. and IV., and William IV.; A.R.A., 1801; R.A., 1811.

G. H. Harlow. F. C. Lewis, mez.

Sh. ha. len. to front, white neckcloth, dark waistcoat, coat buttoned; oval in rectangular border.

Proof before all letters.

$8\frac{7}{8} \times 7$. ($5\frac{15}{16} \times 5$). 22808.

—— Another impression.

Proof with scratched letters; Decr. 1, 1824.

26244.

——

Anon. J. Thomson, stipple.

A bust, to right; vignette; facs. signature below.

($4\frac{3}{4} \times 3\frac{1}{4}$) 28300. 14.

BONINGTON, RICHARD PARKES, 1801–1828, landscape and subject-painter, b. at Arnold, near Nottingham; went to Paris with his father and mother, 1816; stud. in the Louvre, and at the Institut, and in the atelier of Baron Gros; gained a gold medal for a sea-piece; went to Italy, 1822; exhibited at the Br. Institn., 1826, at Academy, 1828; excellent draftsman and colourist; highly esteemed in France; painted marine-pieces, landscapes, figures, and genre, with much originality and grace.

M. Carpenter J. P. Quilley, mez.

Ha. len. to front; dark neckcloth, light waistcoat; dark coat, buttoned.

Proof before all letters.

$12\frac{3}{8} \times 9\frac{1}{4}$. ($8\frac{11}{16} \times 7\frac{1}{8}$). 27206.

——

Anon. A. Colin, lith., 1829.

Ha. len. to front, looking rather to left; coat thrown open; vignette; facs. signature below.

Ind. proof, July, 1829.

($5\frac{1}{4} \times 6\frac{1}{2}$). E. 1956.–'89.

——

M. Carpenter. J. D. Harding, lith.

Bust, to front; coat buttoned; vignette; facs. signature below; pubd. by J. Carpenter & Son, Old Bond St., Aug. 1, 1829.

Ind. proof.

($6 \times 5\frac{1}{4}$). E. 1955.–'89.

A. Shaw delt.   E. Scriven, stipple.
Sh. bu. len. to front, looking to right; coat buttoned;
vignette; facs. signature below.
Ind. proof; for the " Library of the Fine Arts," 1832.
7¾ × 5⅞. (3¾ × 3¼).   E. 247.–'93.

A. Paquier (?).   J. Guillaume, woodcut.
Sh. ha. len. to front; coat buttoned, dark neckcloth; vignette; from an illustrated paper.
(4⅞ × 3⅜).   E. 1957.–'89.

BONOMI, JOSEPH, 1739–1808, architect, b. at Rome, where he
stud.; came to London, 1767; worked for the brothers Adam;
m. a cousin of Angelica Kauffmann, 1775; returned to Italy,
1783, for a year; A.R.A., 1789; exhibited, 1783–1806; executed many architectural works in England; hon. architect of
S. Peter's, Rome, 1804.
G. Dance.   W. Daniell.
Ha. len. to right, in profile; seated; vignette; proof.
10¾ × 7¹⁸⁄₁₆. (8¼ × 6).   E. 1959.–'89.

BOSCAWEN, EDWARD, 1711–1761, 3rd son of 1st Lord Fal-
mouth; in 1726, entd. navy; served under Vernon at Porto
Bello; M.P. for Truro; took several French ships at different
times, and defeated their fleet off Cape Lagos; Admiral of the
Blue; P.C.; &c.
A. Ramsay.   J. Faber, junr., mez.
J. C. Smith, 36, 1st state (Appendix); but *Blue* is so spelt
here, and not *Blew*, as quoted by J. C. S.

                                                 24056.

Sir J. Reynolds.   Js. McArdell, mez. 1757.
J. C. Smith, 24, 1st state.   29732.
See also TRIUMPH OF BRITANNIA.

BOSWELL, JAMES, 1740–1795, b. at Edinburgh; stud. law
there, and at Glasgow, and Utrecht; introd. to Dr. Johnson,
1763; travelling on continent, made the friendship of Paoli,
memoirs of whom he publd. 1768; issued his famous biography
of Johnson, 1791; called to Engl. bar, 1785; d. in Portland
St., London
Sir J. Reynolds, P.R.A.   J. Jones, mez.
J. C. Smith, 8, 2nd state.   21884.

BOULTER, HUGH, 1672–1742, b. in London; educ. at Oxford;
tutor to Frederick, Prince of Wales; Bishop of Bristol, 1719;
Archbishop of Armagh, 1724; devoted himself to political as
well as ecclesiastical work; ridiculed by Swift; excluded Rom.
Catholics from all offices connected with law, was liberal in his

charities to Protestant Churches; his portrait by Bindon in hall of poor-house, Dublin.

F. Bindon. J. Brooks, mez.
J. C. Smith, 5, 1st state. 22216.

BOULTON, MATTHEW, 1728–1809, mechanical inventor; founded Soho Works, near Birmingham, 1762, in which James Watt became his partner; improved construction of steam-engines; produced improved coinage, plated wares, bronzes, &c.; F.R.S., F.S.A.

Sir W. Beechey, R.A. W. Sharp.
T. Q. len. to right, seated, looking to front; legs crossed, left over right; a coin in left hand, and a magnifying glass in right.
Open letter proof, May 1, 1801.
Cut (16¼ × 13⅝). 21994.
See also SCIENCE.

BOURGEOIS, SIR PETER FRANCIS, 1756–1811, of a good Swiss family; b. in London; intended for the Army, preferred art: encouraged by Reynolds and Gainsborough; stud. under Loutherbourg; acquired, in his nineteenth year, reputation by his landscapes, battles, and sea-pieces; travelled abroad, 1776; A.R.A., 1787; R.A., 1793; landscape-painter to the King, 1794; founded and endowed Dulwich Gallery, where are eighteen of his pictures.

Colloppy. W. Ridley, stipple.
Ha. len. to right; coat buttoned; oval; pubd. by Vernor & Hood, March 31, 1804.
6⅜ × 4⅝. (3⅜ × 2⅞). 28300. 15.

———

Sir W. Beechey, R.A. (W. Evans del.).
J. Vendramini, chalk and dot.
Ha. len. to left, looking to front; wearing ribbon and medal; vignette.
Pubd. by T. Cadell & W. Davies, May 7, 1811.
Open letter proof (?).
15 × 12⅞. (7 × 8¼). 28153. 2.

BOWRING, SIR JOHN, 1792–1872, linguist, traveller, and author; b. at Exeter; educ. at private school; entd. a merchant's office, and began learning languages, French, Italian, Spanish, Portuguese, German, and Dutch, to which he added afterwards Swedish, Danish, Russian, Servian, Polish, Bohemian, Magyar, Arabic, and made good progress in Chinese; travelled abroad, 1819–20; imprisoned at Calais, 1822; went with deputation to Louis Philippe, 1830; M.P., 1835–'41; consul at Canton, 1847; plenipo., 1854; edit. works of Jer. Bentham, and published many other works; F.R.S.; &c.

H. W. Pickersgill, R.A. W. Ward, mez.
Full ha. len. to right, looking to front, seated, with left elbow on table, glasses in left hand.

Proof before all letters, except artist's name and publication-line, June 4th, 1832.

15×11. (11¼×8¾). 25818.

BOWYER, ADMIRAL, 1740(?)–1800, 3rd son of Sir William Bowyer, Bart., of Denham, Bucks, and by right of his wife, of Radley, Berks; Lieut., R.N., 1758; Commander, 1761; Capt., 1762; served under Vice-Adm. Byron in West Indies and N. America; at Grenada, 1779; M.P., 1784; Rear-Adm., 1793; hoisted his flag on the "Prince" under Howe; disting. in the victory off Ushant, June 1, 1794, when he lost a leg; mentioned in despatches; cr. Bart., received a pension of 1,000l. a year, and a chain and gold medal; Vice-Adm., 1794; suc. his elder brother, Sir William, the 4th Bart. in the older Baronetcy.

See COMMEMORATION (1).

BOWYER, WILLIAM, 1699–1777, learned printer, son of a London printer; stud. at Camb.; partner with his father, 1721; distinguished for his scholarly correction of press, adding prefaces, notes, and indexes to many books issued by him; pub. "Critical Conjectures on the New Testament," "Origin of Printing," &c.; printer of the votes of the House of Commons; printer to R. S., &c.

J. Basire. J. Basire.

Sh. ha. len., slightly to left, looking to front, wearing a wig, bushy at sides of head; oval in border; title below.

11₇⁄₁₆×9₇⁄₁₆. (9¾×7¼). 22450.

BOYCE, WILLIAM, 1710–1779, composer, b. in London, son of a cabinet-maker, beadle of the Joiners' Company; chorister at St. Paul's; pupil of Greene; organist of Oxford Chapel, Vere St.; stud. under Pepusch; became slightly deaf; organist at St. Michael's, Cornhill, 1736, and composer to the Chapel Royal; conductor, 1737, of the meetings of the "Three Choirs;" master of the King's band, 1756; organist of Chapel Royal, 1758; composer of services, anthems, entertainments, songs, odes, &c.; Mus. Doc., 1749.

J. K. Sherwin. J. K. Sherwin.

T. Q. len. to left, looking to right, holding a pen in right hand, resting left on music-paper on table, on right; Decr. 1, 1788.

Last state of the plate.

11¾×9⅞. (10¾×9₃⁄₁₆). 21834.

BOYD, SIR ROBERT, 1710–1794, General, Col. 39th foot, and Governor of Gibraltar, was (1740) storekeeper of ordnance at Port Mahon, Minorca, where he was still (a civilian), 1756, when besieged by the French and Spaniards; in recognition of his services he received a Commn. as Lt.-Col., 1758; served in Foot Gds. in Germany; Col., 1766; Lt.-Govr. Gibraltar, 1768; Maj.-Genl., 1772; Lt.-Genl., 1777; Gov. Gibraltar, 1790; Genl. 1793; buried in the wall of the King's Bastion, Gibraltar; K.B.; &c.

A. Poggi. J. Hall, 1789.

Sh. ha. len. to left, in uniform, with star, cocked hat on head; profile.
Open letter proof; arms below.
16 × 12.   (14¾ × 10¼⅞).   24203.

BOYDELL, JOHN, 1719-1804, engraver and publisher, b. at Dorington, near Ower, Shrops.; son of a land-surveyor; fancied engraving; walked to London; apprent. to Thoms, and stud. at St. Martin's Lane Academy; member of Incorp. Society of Artists; began publishing some small prints of bridges, 1750; Views in England and Wales, 1751; employed some of the best engravers on large works; "Shakespeare Gallery," 1786; Sheriff, 1785; Lord Mayor, 1790.
    A. Pope del.   J. Condé, stipple.
    Ha. len. to right, in robes of office; oval; for the "European Magazine," March 1, 1792.
    (5⅞ × 4¼)   E. 1949.-'89.

———

    Josiah Boydell.   V. Green, mez.
    J. C. Smith, 10.   21856.

BOYLE, HON. ROBERT, 1627-1691, natural philosopher; seventh son, and 14th child, of Richard Boyle, Earl of Cork; b. at Lismore; educ. at Eton; travelled on the Continent; took part in founding the Royal Society; made considerable improvements in the air-pump; pub. "Experiments upon colours," "Hydrostatical Paradoxes," &c.; founded the "Boyle Lectures."
    J. Kersseboom.   G. Vertue, 1739.
    Sh. ha. len. to right, facing and looking to front, wearing long wig, white neckerchief, and loose gown; oval in border; books, compasses, air-pump, and other instruments below; in Birch's "Lives."
    14½ × 9½.   (13⅞ × 8⅛⅜).   21821

BRADFORD, JOHN, 1510(?)-1555, b. at Manchester, educ. at Cath. Hall, Cambr., and Temple; preb. of St. Paul's Cath.; opposed Romanism on accession of Mary; burnt at Smithfield.
    See REFORMERS, a group.

BRADLEY, JAMES, 1693-1762, astronomer; b. at Sherbourn, Gloucestershire; educ. at Balliol Coll., Oxf.; Savilian Prof. of Astronomy, Oxf., 1721; Astronomer-Royal, 1742; his two great astron. discoveries were "Aberration" and "Nutation;" d. at Chalford, Gloucest.; bur. at Minchinhampton.
    T. Hudson.   J. Faber, junr., mez.
    J. C. Smith, 41   24647.

BRADLEY, THOMAS, 1751-1813, physician, b. at Worcester, where for some time he conducted school, chiefly mathematical; M.D., Edin., 1791; settled in London, and L.C.P., 1791;

physician to Westminster Hospital, 1794–1811 ; author of some learned and useful works ; d. in St. George's Fields.
See MEDICAL SOCIETY.

BRADSHAW, John, Serjeant at Law, 1586–1659; b. in Cheshire ; a cousin of Milton; became Ch. Just. of Chester ; presided with great firmness at the trial of Charles I. ; became Pres. of Council of State, and Commissioner of the Great Seal ; bur. in Westminster Abbey, and brutally exhumed at the Restoration.

"From an origl. Painting."   M. vander Gucht.
Oval, in a broad hat. "President of the Prctd. H. Court of Justice."
In Clarendon's "History."
$6\frac{3}{16} \times 4\frac{1}{2}$. $(6\frac{3}{8} \times 3\frac{3}{4})$.   27129.

BRAHAM, John, 1774–1856, great tenor singer, b. in London, of Jewish parents, in very humble circumstances ;' pupil of Leoni, a celebrated Italian singer ; first appearance, Cov. Gard. Theatre, 1787 ; stud. under Rauzzini, at Bath, 1794 ; engaged for Drury Lane, 1796, and for the Italian Opera, 1797 ; stud. in Italy ; reappeared. Cov. Gard., 1801 ; enjoyed long career of success and triumph ; was orig. "Sir Huon" in "Oberon," 1826 ; composed some songs, &c., which were very popular.

J. G. Wood del.   A. Cardon, stipple
Ha. len. to left, looking to front, coat buttoned over light waistcoat ; printed in colours ; published by J. G. Wood, 1806 ; repubd. 1807 by J. P. Thompson.
$15\frac{7}{8} \times 11\frac{3}{16}$. $(9\frac{15}{16} \times 8\frac{1}{4})$.   22809.

BRAMAH, Joseph, 1749–1814, distinguished engineer, the author of many very ingenious and valuable inventions, among which were his hydraulic press, safety lock, various improvements in the steam-engine, in paper-making, constr. of main pipes, wheel-carriages, beer-machine, &c.
See SCIENCE, in which only the back of his head is seen, there being no portrait of him known to exist.

BRANDE, William Thomas, 1788–1866, b. in London, where his father was an apothecary, educ. at private school., Kensington and Westminster ; apprent., 1802, to his brother, a lie. of the Comp. of Apoths. ; removed to Chiswick, where he made the acquaintance of Charles Hatchett, who encouraged his chemical researches ; went, 1803, to Brunswick and Göttingen ; returned, 1804 ; F.R.S., 1809 ; prof. Chem. &c., to Apoth. Comp. 1812 ; suc. Sir H. Davy, at Royal Inst. ; ch. officer, coin dept., Mint, 1854 ; pub. many valuable treatises.

T. Bridgford, A.R.H.A., lith.
Bust-size to left, looking to front, vignette ; facs. signature below.
Ind. proof.
$(7\frac{1}{4} \times 5\frac{1}{4})$.   27539.

BRAY, William, 1736–1832, educ. at Rugby; began in an attorney's office; soon got a place in the Board of Green Cloth, which he held for nearly 50 years; inher. the family estates of Shere and Gomshall, 1803; F.S.A., 1771, and Treasurer of the Society, 1803; frequent contributor to "Archæologia," completed Manning's Hist. of Surrey, 1804–'14; edited "Memoirs, &c., of John Evelyn," &c.

J. Linnell. John Linnell, mez.

Ha. len to left, seated, looking to front, holding a paper in his right hand; "in his 97th year."

Published, March 1st, 1833.

$19\frac{7}{8} \times 16$. $(14\frac{1}{4} \times 12\frac{3}{4})$. 25135.

BRIDGEMAN, Sir Orlando, 1606(?)–1674, Bart., educ. at Queen's Coll., Cambr.; called to the bar, 1632; Serjeant, and Ch. Baron of Exchequer, 1660; presided at trial of regicides; Bart. and Ch. Justice of Com. Pleas; Lord Keeper of the Great Seal, 1667.

R. White.

"Miles et Baronettus;" sh. ha. len. slightly to left, looking to front; oval in border, the bag and mace, one on each side of the arms, below. Two lines of title, below; and, lower, "Printed for Willm. Battersby at Thavies Inn Gate in Holbourne, & Tho : Bassett at the George in Fleet Street."

$10 \times 6\frac{1}{4}$. $(8\frac{9}{16} \times 6)$. 27116.

BRIDGEWATER, Francis Egerton, 3rd Duke of, 1729–1803, brother of John, 2nd Duke, whom he suc., 1748; became celebrated as "The Father of British inland navigation" by his construction of the great Bridgewater Canal, between Worsley, Manchester, and L'pool; d. unm.

J. M. Craig. C. Picart, stipple.

Ha. len. to left, in profile, seated, looking downwards, with head inclined forwards; vignette.

Open letter proof, July 16, 1812.

$14\frac{7}{8} \times 12\frac{7}{8}$. $(7\frac{3}{4} \times 6\frac{1}{2})$. 22022.

BRIDGMAN, Charles, ornamental gardener, practised about 1730; was fashionable in his line, 1735; first used the sunk fence, or "ha-ha;" banished the formal Dutch style, and introduced the more natural and picturesque manner; gardener to the King; member of the St. Luke's Artists' Club.

See ARTISTS, a Society of.

BRIDPORT, Alexander Hood, Lord, 1726–1814, younger brother of Samuel, Visct. Hood (celebr. Admiral); Lieut. in Navy, 1746; Comr. and Post Capn., 1756; Treasr., Greenw. Hosp., 1766; Rear Admiral, 1780; Admiral, 1794; Vice Admiral of Grt. Britain, 1796; distinguished himself on many occasions; second under Howe, June 4, 1794; cr. Baron Bridport; cr. Visct., 1800; Admiral of the Red, 1805.

See COMMEMORATION (1).

BRINDLEY, JAMES, 1716–1772, canal engineer; b. at Wormhill, Derbyshire; appr. to a mill-wright; empl. by the Duke of Bridgewater on his canal from Worsley to Manchester, which he extended to the Mersey; constr. the Grand Trunk Canal in Staffs. and Worcestershire; advised on all similar works throughout the country; used to lie in bed when considering a difficult problem; d. at Turnhurst, Staffs.

F. Parsons.   R. Dunkarton, mez., 1770.
J. C. Smith, 9, 1st state.   24674.

BRISTOL, GEORGE DIGBY, Earl of, 1612–1676, b. at Madrid; cr. M.A., Oxford, 1636; M.P. 1640; one of the Managers of the Impeachment of Strafford, but voted against his attainder; Sec. of State, 1643–'9; Lt.-General, North of Trent; K.G. at Paris, 1652; Sec. of State, P.C., and Lt.-General for England, 1657; incapacitated, as Rom. Cath.

A. van Dyck.   J. Houbraken, 1738.
Oval, with large lace collar; in Birch's " Lives."
A fine early impression, but slightly cut at edges.
(14 × 8¾).   20795.

BRITANNIA BRIDGE. See MENAI STRAITS.

BRITTON, JOHN, 1771–1857, antiquary, topographer, and miscellaneous writer; b. at Kington St. Michael, near Chippenham, Wilts.; where his father was a small shopkeeper, farmer, baker, and maltster; apprent. to a tavern-keeper on Clerkenwell Green, 1787; began compiling song-books, &c., helped in writing a topographical work, " Beauties of Wilts.," 1801, finished in 1825; produced " Architectural Antiquities," " Cathedral Antiquities," &c.

J. Wood, 1845.   C. E. Wagstaff, 1846.
T. Q. len. to left, seated, looking to front, right hand resting on an architectural drawing on table; busts, a model memorial, and bookcase behind; facs. signature below; Jany. 1, 1847, " to accompany the autobiography of the Author."
An impression presented by the personage, with his autograph inscription, to the late Mr. Carpenter, keeper of the prints, &c., Br. Mm.

12½ × 9¾.   (8½ × 6⅞).   23154.

BRITTON, THOMAS, c. 1651–1714, the " Musical Small-Coal Man," b. at Higham Ferrers, apprent. to a coal dealer; afterwards started in business as a dealer in " small-coal;" stud. chemistry, occult sciences, and music, theoretical and practical; established weekly concerts, and a musical club, meeting in a narrow room over his shop, frequented by Handel, Pepusch, and many others, distinguished by talent, learning, and birth; d. of shock from fright, caused by the " practical joke" of a ventriloquist; left a curious collection of musical instruments and books.

J. Woolaston.   J. Simon, mez.
A rare portrait.
J. C. Smith, 27.   27157.

BROCKEDON, WILLIAM, 1787-1854, b. at Totness, son of a watchmaker, whose trade he followed for some years, acquiring great taste for scientific and mechanical pursuits; studied painting in London, 1809-'15; contrib. to Exhibitions of Royal Academy and Br. Institution, 1812-'37; wrote several successful books about the Alpine Passes, &c.; patented various inventions; and helped to form the Geogr. Socy.

C. Turner.   C. Turner, A.R.A., mez.

Sh. T. Q. len. to right, looking to left, sketching, with book in left hand and crayon in right; landscape with Alps behind.

Open letter proof, Jany. 23, 1835.

14 × 10. (10$\frac{11}{16}$ × 8$\frac{3}{10}$).   27204.

BRODIE, SIR BENJAMIN COLLINS, 1783-1862, b. at Winterslow, Wilts.; stud. at Hunterian School and St. George's Hosp., London; Lecturer at St. George's, 1809; Prof. Anatomy and Surgery, Coll. Surg., 1819; Serj.-Surgeon to William IV., 1834; Pres., Coll. Surgeons, 1844; Pres., Royal Socy., 1858; pub. " Psychological Inquiries," and other works; d. at Betchworth, Surrey.

J. J. Halls.   C. Turner, mez., 1821.

Ha. len. to front, seated, holding an open book in left hand, which rests on right; white neckcloth and waistcoat, dark coat, buttoned.

A fine proof before all letters, in the earliest state.

14$\frac{1}{2}$ × 10. (10$\frac{13}{16}$ × 9).   24000.

BROKE, SIR PHILIP BOWES VERE, 1776-1841, entd. R. N. Academy, 1788; appointed, 1792, to Bulldog sloop; present at action off Toulon, 1795; at Cape St. Vincent, 1797; with the channel fleet in victory and capture of French squadron, Oct. 12, 1798, off coast of Ireland; comr., 1799; captain, 1801; in 1813 fought his ship, the Shannon (38 guns), in a memorable engagement against the Chesapeake (49 guns), which he took in a quarter of an hour; Bart., 1813; K.C.B., 1815; rear-admiral, 1830; d. at Broke Hall, Suffolk.

S. Lane.   C. Turner, mez.

Wh. len. with sword drawn; pointing with left hand, to right; a gun in the right background.

Open letter proof; March 25, 1816.

Cut (23$\frac{1}{16}$ × 14$\frac{5}{8}$).   27663.

W. C. Ross, A.R.A.   J. S. Templeton, lith.

Bust, to left, looking to front, wearing a scull-cap; vignette, the shoulders, &c., just indicated; arms and facs. signature below.

Ind proof.

(6$\frac{3}{8}$ × 5$\frac{1}{8}$).   21961.

BROMLEY, HENRY, a pseudonym used by Anthony Wilson, q.v., on the title-page of his " Catalogue of Engraved British Portraits," 4to, London, 1793, founded on Horace Walpole's Collection, with additions.

Barrett.   J. Berry.

Sh. ha. len. to left, with rather long hair, curling at the ends, the bust only slightly sketched ; a copy from a very rare print, in which the portrait, an oval, appears on a scroll, with portraits of Van Dyck, Lely, Faithorne, and Hollar, at the corners, 4to. This copy was pubd. by E. Evans.

$10\frac{7}{16} \times 8\frac{3}{16}$. $(5\frac{5}{16} \times 3\frac{13}{16})$.   26271.

BROMLEY, WILLIAM, 1664–1732, M.P., P.C., Speaker of the House of Commons, 1710–1713 ; Sec. of State, 1713.
M. Dahll, 1712.   J. Smith, mcz.
J. C. Smith, 24.   22810.

BROOKE, MRS. FRANCES, 1724–1789, daughter of Rev. W. Moore ; was mentioned as "a poetic maid" by J. Duncombe, in Feminiad, 1754 ; wrote in a periodical of her own, "The Old Maid ;" pubd. "Virginia," 1756 ; "Lady Julia Mandeville," 1763 ; several other novels, and "Rosina" and "Marian," both set to music as operas by W Shield ; &c.
Catherine Read.   M. Bovi, stipple.
Ha. len. to left, seated, with right hand to head, and elbow on table ; holding an open book on knee with left hand ; oval.
Publish'd May 1790.
$12\frac{16}{16} \times 10\frac{5}{16}$. $(9\frac{3}{8} \times 7\frac{7}{8})$.   27159

BROOKE, GUSTAVUS VAUGHAN, 1818–1866, b. in Dublin ; educ. at Edgeworthstown ; appeared first on stage at T. R. Dublin, 1833, as William Tell ; played in Ireland and Scotland ; appeared at Victoria theatre, London, as Virginius, 1837 ; played in U.S. America, 1851–'3 ; in Australia, New Zealand, 1855–'7 ; drowned in the "London," in Bay of Biscay
A. Wivell, del.   T. Fairland, lith., coloured.
Wh. len. to front, looking to left, in costume, as Othello.
$(22 \times 14\frac{1}{2})$.   26407.

BROOKE, SIR JAMES, 1803–1868, traveller and Rájá of Saráwak ; 2nd son of Thomas Brooke, B.C.S. ; b. at Benares ; educ. at Norwich ; cadet of Infantry in Bengal, at 16 ; served in Burma with a body of native volunteers, formed and drilled by himself, and was wounded at Rangpur ; invalided home ; returned to India, after 4 years ; resigned, 1830 ; sailed for Borneo, 1838 ; suppressed a rebellion in Saráwak, 1840 ; became Rájá, 1841 ; K.C.B., D.C.L., &c.
F. Grant, A.R.A.   G. R. Ward, mez.
T. Q. len., in sailor's jacket, with belt ; water, palms, &c., in distance, on right.
Open letter proof ; April 20, 1849.
$21\frac{1}{2} \times 15\frac{1}{2}$. $(16\frac{1}{4} \times 12\frac{15}{16})$.   22958.

BROOKE, ROBERT GREVILLE, 2nd Baron, 1607–1643, cousin of Fulke, 1st Baron, whom he suc., 1828, educ. at Cambr. ; M.P., Warwick, 1628 ; Recorder of Warwick ; took the side of Parlt. in Civil war ; disting. at Edge Hill, 1642 ; killed by a musket-ball while storming the Cathedral Close, Lichfield, March 2, 1643.

"From the original, in the Collection of the Earl of Warwick," W. Hilton del.   W. T. Fry, stipple.
Full ha. len. to right, looking to front, wearing a cuirass, long hair, sword, &c. ; Feb. 1, 1817.
$14\frac{3}{8} \times 10\frac{5}{8}$. $(7\frac{1}{8} \times 5\frac{1}{2})$.   27151.

BROOKES, Joshua, 1761–1833, anatomist; stud. in London and Paris; taught anatomy, and formed an extensive Museum of Anatomy and Natural History, in which he lectured with great success during 40 years; pub. some valuable professional works on Anatomy, his museum, hygiene, &c., F.R.S., F.L.S.
    T. Phillips, R.A.   J. Fittler.
    Nearly wh. len., to left, seated, holding a pen in right hand which rests on his table, on which an anatomical work lies open ; his left hand rests on his thigh.
    Open letter proof, March 30, 1822.
    $20 \times 15\frac{1}{8}$. $(17\frac{3}{16} \times 13\frac{3}{4})$.   21844.

BROOKS, George, of Twickenham (c. 1815).
    Woodforde.   Heath, stipple.
    Ha. len., slightly to right, seated at table, looking to front, holding a paper in right hand ; papers, pens, &c. on table.
    Open letter proof ; a private plate.
    $17\frac{1}{4} \times 13\frac{1}{2}$. $(11\frac{1}{16} \times 8\frac{8}{16})$.   20932.

BROOMHEAD, Rowland, 1751–1820, Catholic Missionary in Manchester; appointed, 1778, to the ministry, where he by his unremitting and benevolent labours won the affection and respect of all who knew him, through a period of 42 years ; erected St. Augustine's chapel, which became his monument, 21 days after its completion.
    Anon. [Allen ?]   Anon. [Scriven ?], stipple.
    Ha. len. to left, looking to front, holding a book in his right hand, with one finger between the leaves ; a crucifix, &c. on left, in background. Oct. 21, 1820.
    $19\frac{3}{4} \times 14\frac{1}{4}$. $(14\frac{11}{16} \times 11\frac{11}{16})$.   29752. G

BROTHERS, Richard, 1757–1824, religious enthusiast, b. at Placentia, Newfoundland ; midshipman, on board the "Ocean," at 14 ; present at Ushant, and (1781) at the engagement between Rodney and Comte de Grasse; on half-pay, 1783 ; came to London, 1787 ; announced himself as the apostle of a new religion, "Prince of the Hebrews," "Nephew of the Almighty," &c., 1793 ; made many converts, including the distinguished engraver of his portrait ; committed to Bedlam ; released, 1806 ; d. in the house of J. Finlayson, a faithful disciple.
    W. Sharp.   W. Sharp.
    Ha. len. to right, looking to front, white neckcloth, shirt-frill, and waistcoat; dark coat, open ; rays of light from Heaven on his head ; title below, and "Fully believing this to be the man whom God has appointed ;—I engrave his likeness. William Sharp. .   April 16, 1795."
    $8\frac{1}{4} \times 7\frac{3}{16}$. $(5\frac{1}{16} \times 4\frac{1}{2}$, excl. of border)   22491.

BROTHERTON, Joseph, 1783–1857, cotton-manufacturer, politician, M.P. (1832) for Salford, liberal, represented Salford nearly 25 years; free-trader, reformer, generally respected.
Anon.   S. W. Reynolds, mez.
T. Q. len. seated, holding the scroll of a petition; turned to right, looking to left.
Proof before all letters.
14$\frac{7}{16}$ × 10$\frac{1}{8}$. (11$\frac{1}{4}$ × 9).   22811.

BROUGHAM AND VAUX, Henry Peter, Lord, 1778–1868; b. at Edinburgh; a founder of the "Edinb. Review;" M.P. for Camelford, 1810; Attorney-Gen. for Q. Caroline, defended her at trial, 1820; denounced the Holy Alliance, 1823; M.P. for Yorks., 1830; Ld. Chancr. and peer, 1830; resigned, 1834; published "Researches on Light," 1850–'4; &c.
Sir T. Lawrence, P.R.A.   W. Walker, stipple.
T. Q. len. to right, looking to front, hands together on a bundle of papers, pillar and curtain behind.
Private Plate; Ind. proof, Sepr. 1831.
20 × 14$\frac{7}{8}$. (14$\frac{1}{16}$ × 11$\frac{7}{16}$).   22813.

James Lonsdale, 1831.   T. Lupton, mixed mez.
Wh. len. to left, seated, in robes, legs crossed, books on floor, at right; the mace and bag, at left, on table; facs. signature and arms below.
Proof (?) with open letters, Jany. 1, 1832.
                                                    W. Walker, excudit.
22$\frac{5}{8}$ × 16$\frac{3}{16}$. (18$\frac{3}{4}$ × 14$\frac{9}{16}$).   22812.

Anon.   G. Shury, mez.
T. Q. len. to front, looking to right, seated, holding a book in left hand, right hand on arm of chair; bookshelves and curtain behind.
March 12th, 1866.
16$\frac{7}{8}$ × 12$\frac{5}{8}$. (15 × 11$\frac{1}{2}$).   27949.
See also CAROLINE.

BROUGHTON, John Cam Hobhouse, first Baron, 1786–1869; F.R.S., M.P., Dep. Lieut. co. Wilts, politician and littérateur.
J. Lonsdale.   C. Turner, mez.
Ha. len. seated, to front, looking to right.
Open letter proof.
13$\frac{7}{8}$ × 9$\frac{3}{4}$. (10$\frac{3}{4}$ × 8$\frac{3}{4}$).   24119.

BROUNCKER, William Brouncker, 2nd Visct., 1620–1684; cr. M.D., Oxf.; author of many scientific works; first Pres. R.S., 1662, and annually re-elected till he resigned, 1677; Pres. Gresham Coll., &c.
See CHARLES II. (3).

BROWN, Sir George, 1790–1865, joined the 43rd regt. as ensign, 1806; served at Copenhagen, Vimeiro, and Corunna, and in all the actions till June, 1811, when he was promoted

captain, and joined the Staff College; served in Peninsula,
1813 ; major, 1814; severely wounded at Bladensburg; Lt. Col.,
1814; Col. and K. H., 1831 ; Major-Genl. 1841; Adj.-Genl.,
1850; Lt.-Genl., 1851 ; K.C.B.; served in Crimea; G.C.B.;
Genl., 1855 ; Commandr.-in-Chf., Ireland, 1860–'5.
    Hon. H. Graves.   T. L. Atkinson, mez.
T. Q. len. slightly to right, looking to right, in uniform.
Open letter proof, Jany. 1, 1859.
    $20\frac{3}{8} \times 16$.   ($17\frac{1}{2} \times 13\frac{1}{4}$).   27253.

BROWN, LANCELOT, 1715–1773, landscape-gardener ; known as
"Capability Brown ;" b. at Kirkharle, Northumberland; employed by Lord Cobham and other wealthy persons; estab. himself as landscape-gardner and architect ; laid out or altered the
grounds at Kew, Blenheim, Stowe, &c.; made additions to
Burleigh, Prior Park, Corsham, &c.; High Sheriff, Hunts,
1770.
    N. Dance, R.A.   J. K. Sherwin, line and stipple.
    Ha. len., slightly to left, looking to front ; high waistcoat,
buttoned to throat; white neckcloth; coat unbuttoned.
    Open letter proof (?),* artists' names in one line, followed by
title and epitaph in ten (the last eight in two columns) by Rev.
W. Mason, A.M.
    $14 \times 10\frac{1}{4}$.   ($10\frac{1}{4} \times 9\frac{9}{16}$).   21986.
* This is, perhaps, not a proof; the B.M. impression is in the same state.

BROWN, ROBERT, 1773–1858, the most distinguished botanist of
the age ; b. at Montrose ; educ. at Aberdeen and Edinb. ; joined
a fencible regt., 1795, as surgeon and ensign ; attached, 1801,
on the recommendation of Sir Joseph Banks, to H.M.S.
"Investigator " as naturalist, on a survey of the coast of Australia ; Libr. to Linnæan Socy. ; pub. "Prodromus Floræ Novæ
Hollandiæ," 1810–'30, &c. ; F.R.S ; Pres. Lin. Soc., &c.
    H. W. Pickersgill, R.A.   C. Fox, 1837.
    Ha. len. to front, seated, right hand on left leg, which is
crossed over right; glasses in left hand, left elbow on botanical
drawings on table.
    Ind. proof before all letters, except artists' names.
    $14\frac{5}{8} \times 12\frac{1}{4}$.   ($10\frac{3}{4} \times 8\frac{7}{16}$).   27072.
    See also SCIENCE.

BROWN, THOMAS, 1778–1820, metaphysician, b. at the manse
of Kilmabreck, where his father was minister ; educ. at Camberwell, Chiswick, Bromley, Kensington, and Edinburgh ; wrote
criticisms on Darwin's "Zoonomia," 1797 ; pubd., 1798 ; suc.
Stewart in the chair of Moral Philosophy ; wrote some indiffe-
rent poetry.
    G. Watson, P.R.S.A.   H. Cousins, mixed mez.
    T Q. len. to left, seated, looking to front, holding pencil in
right hand, and book in left, on lap.
    Ind. proof with open and scr. letters; May 1st, 1845.
    $20\frac{1}{16} \times 15\frac{1}{16}$.   ($16\frac{1}{8} \times 13\frac{1}{8}$).   24733.
BROWNE, SIR ANTHONY. See MONTAGU.

BROWNE, Isaac Hawkins, the elder, 1705–1760, poet, b. at Burton-on-Trent, where his father was vicar; educ. at Lichfield, Westminster, and Trin. Coll., Cambr., where he grad.; called to the bar; M.P., 1744–'47; wrote several poems, of which the chief was "De Animi Immortalitate," 1754.

Highmore. W. C. Edwards.

Sh. ha. len. to left, looking to front, with long curled wig.

Ind. proof before all letters, except the engraver's name.

$7\frac{13}{16} \times 5\frac{1}{2}$. ($3\frac{13}{16} \times 3$). 28161.

BROWNLOW, Richard, 1553–1638; founder of the Tyrconnel family; ent. at Inner Temple, 1583; ch. prothonotary of Com. Pleas, by which he secured a yearly profit of 600*l*., with which he bought reversion of estates in Linc.; his MSS. pubd. after his death.

Anon. T. Cross.

T. Q. len. to left, seated, looking to front, holding a glove in his left, and a scroll in his right hand; "Ætat. Suæ 86." A frontispiece to his works. His name and title in two lines, below.

Cut, ($6\frac{1}{4} \times 4\frac{5}{8}$). 28046.

BRUCE, James Lewis Knight, 1791–1866, youngest son of John Knight, of Fairlinch, Devon; assumed his mother's name by licence; educ. at Exeter Coll. Oxford; barrister, 1817; K.C., 1829; Vice-Chancr., 1841; Judge of Court of Appeal, 1851.

[G. Richmond ?] [H. Robinson ?], stipple.

Bust, to front, looking to right, vignette.

Ind. Proof before all letters.

$11\frac{7}{8} \times 9$. ($7 \times 6\frac{1}{2}$). 24211.

BRUGGIS, or BRUGIS, Thomas, M.D., author of "Companion for a Chirurgeon," Lond., 1651, 8vo., and "Chirurgical Vade Mecum," with a sup. by E Pratt, M.D., Lond., 1689, 12mo.

Anon. T. Cross.

Bust, to front, oval; above, on left, a surgeon is seen performing an operation on the head of a patient; on the right, a chemist is preparing medicines; below, on left, is a still; on right, a table covered with various instruments.

Cut, 5×3(?). (Oval, $2\frac{1}{4} \times 1\frac{7}{8}$). 29608. K.

BRUNEL, Isambard Kingdom, 1806–1859, engineer; son of Sir M. I. Brunel, whom he assisted in constr. of Thames Tunnel, 1826; engineer of Great Western and other railways, and built Windsor, Chepstow, and Royal Albert bridges; des. the "Great Western," "Great Britain" (screw), and "Great Eastern" steamships.

J. C. Horsley, R.A. H. Cousins, mixed mez.

Full ha. len. to left, facing and looking to front, seated, leaning forward on writing-table, and holding a pencil in right hand.

Open letter proof, March 15, 1858.

$19\frac{7}{8} \times 14\frac{13}{16}$. ($16 \times 12\frac{13}{16}$). 22961.

See also MENAI.

BRUNEL, Sir Marc Isambard, 1769–1849, b. at Hacqueville, Normandy; intended for the Church, but ent. the Navy; made several voyages to West Indies; returned, 1792; emigr. to the U.S.A. during French Revolution, and adopted profession of engineer; came to England; employed at Portsmouth in making ship-blocks by machinery, his own invention; built the Thames Tunnel; Knt.; Vice-pres. R.S., &c.

J. Northcote, R.A.   C. Turner, mez.

T. Q. len. to front, seated, looking to left, with hands on some drawings on table, on which are books, instruments, &c.

A fine proof before all letters.

20 × 14.   (17⅞ × 14).   22212.

See also SCIENCE.

BRUNTON, Miss Anne, 1769–1808, actress, b. in London; appeared on the stage at Bath, 1785, for her father's benefit; soon engaged at Cov. Garden, where she met with great success, in Robert Merry, Della Cruscan poet, 1791, and went with him, 1796, to the U.S. America; he d. there; she afterwards m. Mr. Warren, manager of a theatre.

See HOLMAN

BRYDGES, Sir Samuel Egerton, 1762–1837, b. at Wootton, between Canterbury and Dover, second son of Edward Brydges, preb. of Canterbury and chancellor of Hereford; educ. at Maidstone, Canterbury, and Cambr.; called to the bar. 1787; devoted himself to literary pursuits; claimed the Barony of Chandos for his elder brother, unsuccessfully; cr. Bart., 1814; set up Lee Priory Press, and edited various pieces of early English literature.

[Carloni ?]   [G. B. Nocchi ?], stipple.

Sh. ha. len. to left, looking upwards, left elbow on book on table; collar open; vignette.

Ind. proof before all letters.

8⁷⁄₁₆ × 5¾.   (4 × 4).   27160.

BUCHAN, David Steuart Erskine, 11th Earl of, 1742–1829, 2nd but eldest surv. s. & h. of his father, the 10th Earl, whom he suc., 1767; a patron of literature; pub. "Essays on Fletcher of Saltoun, and Thomson," &c.; inst. an annual commem of Thomson at his birthplace, and erected a tablet to his memory in Richmond Church; a friend of Burns.

S. J. Reynolds.   J. Finlayson, mez.

J. C. Smith, 3, 1st state, as Lord Cardross.   22495.

BUCHANAN, Claudius, 1766–1815, b. near Glasgow, son of a schoolmaster at Inverary; educ. at home and at Glasgow University; went to London, worked in a solicitor's office; resumed intentions of entering the Church; went to Cambr., 1791, and became intimate with Charles Simeon; grad. 1795, and ordained; went to Calcutta, 1796–'7, and became chaplain, and vice-provost, at Fort William; published interesting accounts of tours in India; returned to England, 1808; actively advocated establishment of Indian Episcopacy; D.D., Glasgow, and Cambr.

Slater.　　　　　　　　　　　F. C. Lewis, chalk and dot.

Sh. ha. len. to right, in gown and bands; vignette.
Open letter proof. April 25, 1815.
$16\frac{1}{16} \times 12\frac{3}{8}$. $(8\frac{1}{2} \times 8\frac{1}{4})$. 　　　　　　　22814.

BUCHANAN, George, 1506–1582, historian and scholar, grandson of a poor laird, was born at his father's farm in Stirlingshire; educ. at Killearn and in Paris; served with the French troops brought by Albany to Scotland; stud. at St. Andrews under J. Mair; B.A., 1526; followed Mair to Paris, 1526; B.A., Scotish Coll., 1527; M.A., 1528; Procurator of the Germ. nation, 1529; taught grammar at St. Barbe; wrote against the friars; went to London; to Bordeaux; wrote 4 tragedies, some rather licentious verses; returned to England, 1552; to Paris, 1553; to Scotland, c. 1562; sec. of the Commissn. before Elizabeth, 1568–'9, on the "casket of letters" of Mary Q. of Scots; tutor to the King, 1569; wrote the "Detection," "De Jure Regni," "Historia Scotorum," &c.

From J. J. Boissard's "Icones," 1598.　　　　　　I CH. f.

Bust to left, looking to front, with fur collar, and close cap; "ÆTA SVÆ 76," oval in border, 2 Latin verses below, and sig. Mmm 3.
$4\frac{11}{16} \times 3\frac{9}{16}$. $(4\frac{1}{4} \times 3\frac{1}{4})$.　　　　　　　　E. 1006.–'85.

F. Pourbus.　　　　　　　　　　J. Houbraken, 1741.

Picture "in the collection of Dr. Mead."

Sh. ha. len. to front, oval in border; from Birch's "Lives," 1742.
$14\frac{3}{16} \times 9\frac{1}{4}$. $(14\frac{1}{16} \times 8\frac{3}{4})$.　　　　　　　21812.

　　　　　　　　　　　　　　　R. G[raves?].

Sh. ha. len. to right, looking to front; vignette.
Ind. proof before all letters.
$6\frac{5}{8} \times 4\frac{11}{16}$. $(3\frac{1}{4} \times 3\frac{3}{8})$.　　　　　　　28147. 3.

BUCKHURST, and Lady MARY SACKVILLE. See DORSET.

BUCKINGHAM, George Villiers, Duke of, 1592–1628; the unworthy favourite of James I. and Charles I.; educ. in France; presented at Court, London, where James took a strong fancy to him, and advanced him rapidly; knighted, pensioned, K.G., Visct., Earl, 1617; Marquess, 1619; Duke, 1623; accomp. Charles to Spain, 1623; his intrigues brought on wars with Spain and France; assassinated.

C. Janssens.　　　　　　　　　　Houbraken.

O 62849.　　　　　　　　　　　　　E

From a picture at Somerset House. Oval.

A fine proof, before additional work on the face, on the border, &c.

($13\frac{13}{16} \times 8\frac{5}{8}$). 28157. 2.

C. Janssens. J. Houbraken.

An impression in the ordinary state.

In this there is additional work on the forehead and right cheek, and third sets of cross-hatchings on shadows in the border, &c.; also, the eyes have been made less dark.

$14\frac{1}{4} \times 8\frac{7}{8}$. 20825.

Miereveldt. W. J. Delff, 1626.

Sh. ha. len. to right, looking to front, with strings of pearls, &c. in oval.

Cut ($15\frac{1}{16} \times 11\frac{1}{2}$). 24108.

BUCKINGHAM, GEORGE, 1627–1687, Duke, Marquess and Earle of, Earle of Coventry, Viscount Villiers, Baron of Whaddon, Ld. Ross of Hamlak, K.G., &c.

S. Verelst. J Beckett, mez.

J. C. Smith, 10, 2nd state.

Oval, wearing the collar and the George.

$13\frac{7}{16} \times 9\frac{7}{8}$. ($11\frac{1}{2} \times 9\frac{5}{8}$). 25766.

BUCKINGHAM, GEORGE-NUGENT-GRENVILLE-TEMPLE, 1753–1813, Marquess of, suc. 1779, Marquess, 1784; Lord-Lieutenant of Ireland, 1782, and again 1787.

T. Gainsborough, R.A., 1787. J. K. Sherwin.

T. Q. length, turned to front, looking to left, in robes, with collar of the George, &c.

Proof with open letters.

Published March 20, 1788.

$19\frac{1}{2} \times 14\frac{1}{8}$. ($16\frac{7}{8} \times 13\frac{1}{4}$). 23149.

See also ST. PATRICK.

BUCKINGHAM, HENRY STAFFORD, Duke of, 1454–1483; only son and heir of Humphrey Stafford, *styled* Earl of Stafford; K.B., 1465; K.G., 1474; Lord High Constable, 1483; found guilty in that same year of plotting to place the Earl of Richmond on the throne; beheaded at Salisbury (after no legal trial), and attainted.

From a Picture at Magdalen Coll., Camb.

J. Houbraken, 1747.

In Birch's "Lives."

$14\frac{1}{2} \times 9\frac{1}{4}$. 28156. 2.

BUCKINGHAM, JAMES SILK, 1786–1855, author and traveller; b. at Flushing, near Falmouth, and took early to the sea; captured by the French, imprd. for several months at Corunna; turned to literature; establ. at Calcutta, 1818, a newspaper called the "Calcutta Journal;" expelled from India, 1823, and the paper suppressed; started and conducted other journals, &c.; M.P., 1832–'7; travelled in America; a voluminous writer.

Anon., stipple.

Sh. ha. len. to left, looking to front, holding glasses in right hand; facs. signature below; vignette.

Ind. proof before letters, except facs. signature and address of publishers, Fisher, Sons, & Co., London & Paris.

$11\frac{7}{16} \times 8\frac{15}{16}$. $(4\frac{1}{2} \times 4\frac{1}{4})$. 26647.

BUCKINGHAM AND CHANDOS, RICHARD PLANTAGENET-CAMPBELL - TEMPLE - NUGENT-BRYDGES-CHANDOS-GRENVILLE, Duke of, 1823–1889; educ. at Eton and Oxford; M.P., 1846–'57 ; Lord of Treasury, 1852 ; Pres. of Privy Council, 1866–'7 ; Colon. Sec., 1867–'8 ; Gov. of Madras, 1875–'80 ; G.C.S.I. ; Hon. Col of Yeomanry, &c.

See DERBY CABINET.

BUCKINGHAM AND CHANDOS, RICHARD TEMPLE-NUGENT-BRYDGES-CHANDOS-GRENVILLE, Duke of, 1776–1839, educ. at Oxford and Cambridge ; M.P., Bucks, 1797–1813 ; Commr. for India, 1800–'1 ; P.C. 1806 ; D.C.L., LLD.; K.G., 1820; cr. Earl Temple of Stowe, Marquess of Chandos, and Duke of Buckingham and Chandos, 1822.

Saunders, min. R. Cooper.

Sh. ha. len., looking to left, right hand to breast; oval ; 1815.
Ind. proof with skeleton letters.

$14\frac{5}{8} \times 11\frac{3}{4}$. $(5\frac{3}{4} \times 4\frac{1}{2})$. 27110.

BUCKLAND, WILLIAM, 1784–1850, Geologist, Reader in Mineralogy and Geology at Oxford ; Author of " Vindiciæ Geologicæ," " Reliquiæ Antediluvianæ," &c.; twice Pres. of Geological Society ; D.D., Dean of Westminster, 1845.

T. Phillips, R.A. S. Cousins, mixed mez

Full ha. len. to front, standing, looking to left, holding in both hands the head of a prehistoric animal.

$17 \times 13\frac{1}{16}$. $(13\frac{9}{16} \times 11)$. 21943.

BUCKLE, FRANCIS, a celebrated jockey.

A. Cooper, R.A. Anon.

Ha. len. to left, in profile, as if in the saddle; whip under right arm ; holding reins in left hand; from a likeness taken at Newmarket ; vignette.

$6\frac{1}{2} \times 5\frac{1}{16}$. $(3\frac{1}{8} \times 3\frac{1}{8})$. 22815.

BUDD, RICHARD, 1746–1821, b. at Newbury, Berks, where his father was a banker ; educ. at Jesus Coll., Camb. ; M.B., 1770 ; M.D., 1775 ; rem. to London, 1780, and phys. to St. Barth. Hospl., until 1801 ; F.R.C.P., 1777 ; six times censor, Gulst. lecturer, Harv. orator, and treasr. ; practised little in private.

G. Dance, June 21, 1798. W. Daniell, July 1, 1812.

Sh. ha. len. in profile to right, seated ; vignette.

$10\frac{3}{4} \times 8\frac{1}{16}$. $(8\frac{1}{4} \times 6\frac{1}{4})$. 28146. 6.

BULKLEY, MRS., speaking the Epilogue to " She Stoops to Conquer."

From a " Collection . . . of English Prologues," &c., 1779.

28187. 4.

E 2

BULLER, CHARLES, 1806–1848, b. at Calcutta; educ. at Harrow,
Edinb., and Cambr.; M.P., 1830, for West Looe, attds. for
Liskeard, till death; Sec. to the Bd. of Control, 1841–'2; Judge
Adv., 1846; Q.C., P.C., 1849; Chf. Comr. of Poor Laws till
death; wrote many articles in Edinb. Review, &c.
 Anon.   Day and Son, lith.
 Large bust to front, all below collar only sketched; vignette;
facs. signature below.
 Ind. proof.
 (22½ × 16).   26667.

BULLER, SIR FRANCIS, 1745–1800, of Morval, Cornwall; Judge
of Chester circuit and King's Bench; pubd. " Introduction to
the Law of Trials at Nisi Prius," 1767; d. in Bedford Square.
 M. Browne.   D. Orme, stipple.
 T. Q. len. to left, seated, in robes, with wig, &c., looking to
right; left hand on table, right on arm of chair. March 1st,
1794.
 Cut, (16¾ × 13¼).   26673.

BULWER-LYTTON, EDWARD GEORGE EARLE LYTTON. See
 LYTTON, LORD.

BULWER, WILLIAM HENRY LYTTON EARLE, BARON DALLING
 AND BULWER, 1801–1872, diplomat., second of three sons of
 General W. E. Bulwer, of Wood Dalling; educ. at Sunbury,
 Harrow, and Cambr., where he took no degree; went to the
 Morea for the Greek Committee; entd. the 2d Life Guards,
 1825; become a diplomat, 1829; attaché at Berlin, Paris, the
 Hague; M.P., 1830; wrote several works; Ambassador to
 Spain; G.C.B.; Ambassador at Washington; Commisr. to the
 Danubian Provinces, 1856–8; cr. Baron, 1871.
         D'Orsay, lith. Aug. 15, 1845.
 Full ha. len. to left, seated, in profile, right hand in breast;
facs. signature below; vignette.
 Ind. proof.
 (7½ × 6½).   23581.

BUNBURY, HENRY WILLIAM, amateur draftsman and caricaturist, 1750–1811, b. at Mildenhall, Suffolk; educ. at St.
Catherine's Hall, Cambridge; Col. of W. Suffolk Militia;
equerry to the Duke of York; occasional hon. exhibitor at
Academy; made some illustrations of Shakspere, &c.; but was
really famous for his caricatures, which were full of harmless
humour; an accomplished amateur actor.
 Sir T. Lawrence, R.A.   T. Ryder, stipple.
 T. Q. len. to front, seated, looking slightly to the right of
front; holding a pencil in right hand and a long piece of paper,
on which is his " Long Minuet at Bath;" oval.
 Open letter proof, Apr. 24, 1789.
 16¼ × 12⅝. (12⅜ × 10¹⁄₁₆).   25733.

Sir T. Lawrence, R.A.   H. R. Cook, stipple.
Ha. len. inclined to left, looking to front, one button of coat
fastened across a white waistcoat ; oval ; Oct. 31, 1812.
$(3\frac{1}{16} \times 2\frac{9}{16})$.   E. 1960.–'89.

BUNYAN, John, 1628-1688, b. at Elstow, near Bedford ; son
of a tinker ; served for a short time, 1645, in parliamentary
army ; joined Baptists at Bedford, and preached ; persecuted,
with other dissenters, and thrown into Bedford gaol for 12
years, where he preached, made tagged laces for sale, read, and
wrote part of "Pilgrim's Progress ;" liberated, 1672 ; called
"Bishop of the Baptists ;" wrote other works, "Holy War,"
&c.
(From Mr. Phillips's picture.)   W. Sharp.
T. Q. len. to left, looking to front, seated ; left hand resting on
the Bible, fingers of right hand slightly raised ; he wears his
hair long, bands, and a gown.
Proof before all letters.
$(7\frac{11}{16} \times 6\frac{1}{4})$.   29718.   4.

Anon.   J. Sturt.
Sh. ha. len. slightly to right, looking to front, plain dress,
buttoned up to throat, collar narrow ; oval in border ; inscription on tablet below in 4 lines ; *London, Printed for William
Marshall & sold at the Bible in Newgate Street.*
Prefixed to his "Works," fol. 168–   (Bromley).
$11\frac{3}{16} \times 7\frac{5}{8}$. $(10\frac{3}{4} \times 7\frac{1}{4})$.   26672.

                              Anon., roulette, stipple, &c.
Bust to right, looking to front ; oval, medallion, supported by
figures of hope, religion, &c. ; the figures attributed to T.
Stothard ; within an oval, lengthwise.
$(6\frac{1}{8} \times 7\frac{3}{8})$.   29608.   F.

                                        G. W. Willis, woodcut.
Ha. len. to right, looking to front, holding a book under his
left arm ; on either side, a scene from "Pilgrim's Progress ;"
below, a view of Bunyan's Chapel, Zoar St., Southwark ;
below that, Elstow Church, near Bedford, on the left ; and, on
the right, Bunyan's tomb, Bunhill Fields.
$(9\frac{3}{4} \times 5\frac{3}{4})$.   29718.   5.

BURDETT, Sir Francis, Bart., 1770–1844, politician ; sat in
Parliament nearly 50 years ; became known as the promoter of
Parliamentary Reform and Catholic Emancipation ; Conserva-
tive during latter part of his life.
J. R. Smith.   W. Ward, mez.
J. C. Smith, 17, with the words FIRST FIFTY in the
lowest corner on right (not mentioned by J. C. S.).   22114.

J. Northcote, R.A.   W. Sharp.
Ha. len. to left, looking to front, hands resting on a book ;
" Engraved from a Picture painted during his imprisonment in
the Tower, and Published by Wm. Sharp, ...
Feb. 14, 1811 ; " proof with open letters.
18¾ × 13⅞.   (16⅛ × 13½).   22816.

R. Cosway, R.A.   A. Cardon.
In a classical dress.
Oval. Published   .   by Wm. Richardson, Octr. 15, 1804.
8¾ × 6¼. (4⅓ × 3¾).   E. 1466–'85.

BURGHERSH. *See* **WESTMORLAND.**

BURGHLEY, Sir William Cecil, 1st Baron, 1521–1598, s. &
h. of Richard Cecil of Burghley, near Stamford, co. Northants ;
ed. at Cambr. ; befriended by the Protector Somerset ; *Custos
Brevium* of Com. Pleas., and Sec. of State, 1548 ; Knt., 1551,
and P.C. ; Sec. of State and 40 years leading Minister of the
Crown ; cr. Baron, 1571 ; K.G., 1572 ; Lord Treasurer, &c.
                                   J. Houbraken.
Sh. ha. len. to front, in robes, wearing the collar and George,
and holding staff in left hand ; oval in border ; 1738.
In Birch's " Lives."
14¾ × 9⁵⁄₆. (14 × 8¾).   21980.

   Anon   Modern photo-zincotype from a rare, early portrait,
by an anon. artist.
Bust in oval, slightly to left, looking to front ; ornamented
border with arms in 4 corners.
5⁹⁄₁₆ × 4⁷⁄₁₆. (5¾ × 4⁷⁄₁₆).   29721.   8.
   See also ELIZABETH.

BURGOYNE, Sir John Fox, 1782–1871, Bart., served in
Peninsular War, 1809–14 ; as Inspector-Genl. of Fortifications,
reported to the D. of Wellington on the defenceless condition
of the country, 1845 ; served in Crimea, 1854–5 ; Constable of
the Tower, 1865 ; Field-Marshal, 1868 ; K.C.B., &c.
  G. F. Mulvany, R.H.A.   J. S. Templeton, lith.
Ind. proof, with facs. signature ; vignette.
(14¼ × 11½).   25819.

BURKE, Sir Bernard, 1815–1893, Ulster King-at-Arms, K.C.B.
                              " Spex," lith.
Wh. len., a coloured print, from " Ireland's Eye," May 13,
1875.
(12¾ × 7).   15851.

BURKE, Rt. Hon. Edmund, 1730–1797, statesman, orator, and
writer ; b. in Dublin ; ent. Parlt., 1765 ; opposed Lord North ;
joined Coalition Ministry, 1783 , opposed Pitt ; opened prose-

cution of Warren Hastings, 1786; pubd. "Reflections on the
French Revolution," 1790; separated from his friend, Mr. Fox,
1791; d. at Beaconsfield, Bucks.

G. Romney.   J. Jones, mez.
J. C. Smith, 11, 2nd state.   22111.

BURLINGTON, RICHARD BOYLE, 3rd Earl of, and 4th Earl of
Cork, 1695–1753; disting. for skill in architecture and landsc.-
gardening, and for love of fine arts; built the villa at Chiswick
and the Colonnade of Burlington House, Piccadilly, where the
Royal Academy now stands; friend of Pope, who addressed to
him his "Epistle IV. Of the Use of Riches;" K.G., &c.

Sir G. Kneller.   J. Faber, jun., mez.
J. C. Smith, 208 (Kitcat Club, "Between 15 & 16")
                                                   24057.

BURNET, RT. REV. GILBERT, 1643–1715, b. at Edinburgh;
educ. at home and at Aberdeen; passed his trials, 1661; visited
the English Universities, 1663; F.R.S.; presented to the living
of Saltoun, 1665; prof. Divinity, Glasgow, 1669; defended the
covenanters against Lauderdale; settled in England, 1674;
chaplain to the Rolls Chapel, 1675; pubd. "History of the
Reformation," for which he received the thanks of Parliament,
1679; last vol. pubd., 1714; left England, 1683; returned, 1684,
and dismissed from his chaplaincy, &c.; went to Paris, on
accessn. of James, and to Italy, and the Hague; landed with
William III. at Torbay; Bishop of Salisbury, 1689; &c.

J. Riley.   J. Smith, mez.
J. C. Smith, 29, 2nd state.   21880.

BURNET, JOHN, 1784–1868, engraver and painter, b. near
Edinburgh; apprent. to R. Scott, landscape-engraver, tried
painting, incited by the success of his friend and fellow-student,
Wilkie; came to London, 1806; engraved illustrations, and the
pictures of Wilkie and others; painted also, exhibiting in 1808
and other years; author of several works on Art.

S. P. Denning del.   C. Fox.
Sh. ha. len. to front, looking to left; vignette.
Pubd. Decr. 1, 1827.
$12\frac{1}{8} \times 9\frac{1}{2}$. $(7\frac{3}{4} \times 7\frac{1}{2})$.   24100.

BURNET, REV. THOMAS, c. 1635–1715, educ. at free school,
Northallerton, and Clare Hall, Cambr.; pupil of Tillotson;
fellow of Chr. Coll., 1657; M.A., 1658; proctor, 1661; master
of the Charterhouse, 1685; chaplain and clerk of the closet to
William III., author of some books of considerable eloquence,
and of some absurd theories of the nature and history of the
earth, &c.

G. Kneller.   J. Faber, junr., mez.
J. C. Smith, 51.   21861

BURNETT, SIR WILLIAM, 1779–1861, physician, b. at Montrose,
where he was apprent. to a surgeon; served as surgeon's mate,

and as assist. surgeon in Navy; present at St. Vincent and Cadiz,
at the Nile and Trafalgar; during 5 years, after Trafalgar, in
charge of hospitals for prisoners of war at Portsmouth and
Forton; physician and inspector of hospitals to the Mediterr.
Fleet, 1810; settled at Chichester, 1822; Director Genl. Med.
Dept., R.N., F.R.S., M.D., K.C.H., K.C.B., &c.

Sir M. A. Shee, P.R.A.   H. Cousins, mixed mez.

Wh. len. to front, slightly inclined to left, seated, looking to
front, holding a pen in right hand, which rests on papers on
table; left hand hangs over arm of chair; large folios on floor,
right.

Scr. letter proof (?), 1844
32 × 20¼. (27⅜ × 16¾).   27073.

BURNEY, CHARLES, 1726–1814, b. at Shrewsbury; educ. there
at free school, and at the public school, Chester; stud. music
under Baker, organist at the Cathedral, under his brother James,
organist at Shrewsbury, and under Dr. Arne, in London;
organist at St. Dionis-Backchurch; composed some musical
dramas; organist at Lynn-Regis, 1751; returned to London,
1760; Mus. Bac. and Mus. Doc., 1769; author of "History of
Music," Musical Tours," "Commemoration of Handel," 1784,
&c.; organist, 1789, of Chelsea Coll., where he died.

Sir J. Reynolds.   F. Bartolozzi, stipple.

Ha. len. in Doctor's robes, to front, holding a roll of music
in right hand; April 1, 1784; from collection of Thomas
Thane, 1816, who has noted that "*onely* 20" impressions were
"*taken of the Plate this size.*"
13⅜ × 9. (7₁₆⁵ × 6).   22210.

BURNEY, CHARLES, D.D., 1757–1817, son of Dr. C. Burney,
the historian of music; educ. at Charterhouse and Cambridge,
grad. at Aberdeen, M.A., 1781; LL.D. Aberdeen and Glasgow,
1792; M.A., Cambr., 1808; D.D. by the archbp. of Canterbury,
1812; kept schools, 1782–1813; took orders late in life; rector
of Cliffe, Kent, &c., and Prebend, Lincoln, 1817; pubd. many
critical works.

      W. Sharp.

Ha. len. to front, looking to right, in gown.
Private plate; Ind. proof, Decr 1, 1821.
14₁₆⁷ × 12₁₆⁷. (12⅞ × 10¾).   22818.

BURNEY, FRANCES, 1752–1840, Poet and Novelist; dau. of
Dr. Charles Burney, the historian of music; b. at Lynn Regis;
for some years was Keeper of the Robes and Reader to Q.
Charlotte; m. to M. D'Arblay, a French officer; lived in Paris,
1802–'12; wrote the novels, "Evelina," "Cecilia," the tragedy,
"Edwy and Elgiva," "Memoirs of Dr. Burney," &c.; d. at
Bath.

E. Burney.   C. Turner, mez.

Ha. len. to right, wearing a hat with feathers, hands crossed
on lap; curtain behind her, foliage on right.

Ind. proof before all letters, except artists' names and publication-line, May 16, 1840.

11 × 9. (8 × 7¼¾). 22229.

BURNS, ROBERT, 1759–1796, the national Poet of Scotland; son of a small farmer near Ayr, N.B.; pub. his first vol. of poems 1786; with the proceeds he bought a farm near Dumfries; afterds. received an appointment as Exciseman of his district; d. at Dumfries.

A. Nasmyth. H. S. Sadd, mixed mez.

Sh. ha. len. to front, looking to left, oval in border, facs. signature below.

" Proof," pubd. by A. L. Dick, Brooklyn, N.Y., 1850.

19½ × 15. (15₁²₆ × 12₁⁵₆). 22138.

BURRELL, MISS, of Covent Garden Theatre.

Anon, stipple.

See LA BELLE ASSEMBLÉE. 13867. 3.

BURTON, DECIMUS, 1800–1881, architect, son of James Burton, a successful London builder; designed the Colosseum in Regent's Park, 1822; employed by Govt. in improving Hyde Park, including the erection of the Arch at Hyde Park Corner, 1825; laid out Calverly Park Estate, Tunbridge Wells, 1828; F.R.S.

E. W. Eddis. M. Gauci, lith.

Sh. ha. len. to front, looking to left, the body slightly sketched; heightened with white in places; vignette.

Proof before all letters.

(12⅝ × 11⅜). 27583.

BUSHE, SIR CHARLES KENDAL, 1767–1843; M.P. for Callan; opposed the union; described as " Incorruptible " by Sir Jonah Barrington; Solr.-Gen., and afterwards Ch. Justice, Ireland.

W. Stevenson. D. Lucas, mixed mez.

T. Q. len. to left, seated, holding pencil on paper with right hand; facs. signature below.

Ind. proof before all letters, except artists' names and publication-line, Dublin, Decr. 30, 1841.

20⅛ × 14¼½. (16¼ × 12⅞) 25820.

BUSBY, RICHARD, 1606–1695, b. at Lutton (*alias* Sutton St. Nicholas), Lincolnshire; educ. at Westminster and Oxford; celebrated as Head Master of Westminster School, an office which he held for 58 years; Preb. of Westmr., 1660; canon resid. and treasurer, at Wells; ruled his school with severity, but with extreme care; was " the most pious and benevolent of men; " educated some of the best men and scholars of his time.

Riley J. Watson, mez.

J. C. Smith, 22. 22211.

BUTE, JOHN STUART, 3rd Earl of, 1713–1792, Statesman; repr. peer, 1737–'41, and 1761–'80; K.T.; K.G., after resigning the order of the Thistle; Prime Minister, 1762–'3; when he retired from public life; disting. botanist, and patron of literature and art.

A. Ramsay.   W. Ryland.

Wh. len., in robes.

An engraver's proof, with the arms, but before all letters; signed (autogr.) by the painter, and touched in many places to indicate alterations to be effected.

22½ × 14⁷⁄₁₆.   (20⅝ × 13¼).   24656.

BUTLER, LADY ELEANOR, 1739(?) or 1745(?)–1829, recluse of Llangollen, youngest daughter of Walter Butler, sister of John, who was acknowledged 17th Earl of Ormonde; with Miss S. Ponsonby (q.v.), she lived in a cottage at Plasurwydd, in the Vale of Llangollen, in complete isolation, for about 50 years; eccentric, dressed in almost masculine dress, visited by many curious strangers; celebrated in Miss Anna Seward's " Llangollen Vale," 1796, by Mme. de Genlis, &c.

J. H. Lynch, lith.

Wh. len., with Miss Ponsonby, and a greyhound; a spring falling into a sort of font under an arch in the distance; " The Ladies of Llangollen " are dressed in men's hats, cloth jackets, and skirts.

(8¼ × 7).   25821.

BUTLER, SAMUEL, 1612–1680, poet, son of Samuel Butler, a Worcestershire farmer; his place of education uncertain, after leaving the Cathedral school of Worcester; clerk to Mr. Jefferies, Earl's Croombe; entered service of Elizabeth, Countess of Kent, where he made the acquaintance of Selden; then exchanged into the family of Sir Samuel Luke, Bedfordshire, the original of Hudibras; sec. to Earl of Carbury, and appointed steward of Ludlow Castle; pubd. the poem of Hudibras, 1663–78, and other works.

G. Soest.   G. Vertue.

Sh. ha. len. to left, looking to right, wearing long wig, lace handkerchief, &c.   Oval in border; inscription in Latin, 6 lines, below; ded. to G. Granville, Lord Lansdown.

·14⅝ × 9½.   (13⁷⁄₁₀ × 8¾).   -   21807.

BUTLER, SAMUEL, D.D., 1774–1839; educ. at Rugby and Cambr.; B.A. 1796; master, Shrewsbury School, 1798–1836; Vicar of Kenilworth, 1802; D.D., 1811; Prebend, Lichfield, 1807; bishop, Lichfield, 1836; author of many educational works.

T. Phillips, R.A.   S. Cousins, A.R.A., mez.

T. Q. len. front, seated, in robes, holding a bible on his knee, June 28, 1838.

·19¹³⁄₁₆ × 14⅞.   (16⁵⁄₁₆ × 12¹⁵⁄₁₆).   27220.

BUTLER, WILLIAM, 1535–1618, b. at Ipswich; educ. at Clare Hall, Camb., of which he became a fellow; grad. M.A. and probably incorp. in that degree at Oxf., 1563; Univ. Camb.

granted him license to pract. physic; acquired extraord. reputation, attended Pr. Henry, 1612, in his last illness.

Anon.   Simon Pass.

Sh. ha. len. to front, wearing high embroidered cap, ruff, and gown : left hand resting on book ; oval in frame ; signed *S. P f.* at bottom of oval ; 8 English verses below ; and, at right, *Are to be folde by | Compton Holland.*

$7 \times 4\frac{3}{8}$. $(5\frac{1}{4} \times 4\frac{3}{16})$.   E. 997.–'85.

BUXTON, JEDIDIAH, 1707–1772, an untaught arithmetical genius, b. at Elmton, Derbyshire; his grandfather was the Vicar, and his father the schoolmaster of Elmton, but Jedidiah never learned to write, and continued to be employed all his life long as a farm-labourer; performed extraordinary feats of mental arithmetic, some of which he exhibited to the Royal Society, 1754.

B. Killingbeck.   J. Spilsbury, mez.

J. C. Smith, 7, 2nd state.   22819.

The Christian name, on the print, is spelled Jedediah.

BYNG, GEORGE, c. 1730–1789, Grandson of George, 1st Viscount Torrington; M.P. for Wigan, afterwards for Middlesex, in several parliaments; d. at Bath, Oct. 28.

J. Downman.   J. Grozer, mez.

J. C. Smith, 3, 2nd state.   27644.

BYNG, JOHN, 1704–1757, 4th son of Admiral Visct. Torrington ; ent. Navy at early age, and quickly rose to rank of Admiral of the White ; unsuccessful in an expedition, to drive the French from Minorca, 1756 ; tried by court-martial on his return, and condemned to death, but recom. to mercy; in spite of that recommendation, was shot at Portsmouth, March 14, 1757.

T. Hudson.   R. Houston, mez.

J. C. Smith, 19, 2nd state.   21915.

BYRNE, WILLIAM, 1743–1805, landscape-engraver, b. in London ; educ. at Birmingham, under his uncle, who engraved arms on plate; gained a Socy. of Arts Medal, 1765, for an engraving of Wilson's " Villa Madama"; stud. at Paris under Aliamet and Wille ; Member of Incorpd. Socy. of Artists; engraved " The Antiquities of Great Britain," after Hearne; "Views of the Lakes," after Farrington ; " Scenery of Italy," after Smith ; put in his skies by hand ; was buried at Old St. Pancras.

E. E[dwards], 1804, etched.

Bust, to right, the bust in outline; vignette.

$6\frac{1}{8} \times 4\frac{1}{8}$. $(5 \times 3\frac{1}{2})$.   26272.

BYRON, ANNE ISABELLA, Lady Noel, Baroness Wentworth, 1792–1860, daughter of Sir Ralph Milbanke Noel, Bt., of Kirkby Mallory, Leicestershire; m. to George Gordon, Lord Byron, the poet, 1815 ; separated by mutual consent; widow, 1824 ; distinguished for her works of charity ; d. in St. George's terrace, Regent's Park.

Sir W. J. Newton.   W. H. Mote, stipple.

Ha. len. to front, looking to left, right hand cross her breast;
vignette.
Ind. proof before all letters.
$9\frac{3}{16} \times 6\frac{1}{16}$. ($4\frac{1}{2} \times 3\frac{3}{4}$).   22955.

BYRON, GEORGE GORDON, Lord, 1788–1824, suc. 1798; educ.
at Harrow and Trin. Coll., Camb.; wrote "Hours of Idleness,"
1807, savagely reviewed (by Henry (Lord) Brougham) in the
Edinb. Rev.; Byron replied in "English Bards and Scotch
Reviewers;" pubd. "Childe Harold," 1812–'18; "Prisoner of
Chillon," "Manfred," "Lament of Tasso," "Beppo," "Don
Juan," "Vision of Judgment," "Heaven and Earth," "Werner,"
&c.; took part in the attempt to liberate Greece, 1823; d. at
Missolonghi.
       G. H. Harlow.   H. Meyer, stipple.
   Bust-size, to left, profile, looking downwards; vignette;
Jany. 30, 1816; in Cadell's "Contemporary Portraits."
       $14\frac{3}{4} \times 12\frac{7}{8}$. ($6\frac{1}{2} \times 6$).   E. 1463.–'85.

———

   (Westall?)   (C. Turner?), mez.
   Ha. len. to left, seated, leaning head on right hand, elbow on
a rock; face in profile.
       ($11\frac{1}{8} \times 8\frac{3}{4}$).   E. 23654.   5.

———, at the Villa Diodati near Geneva, 1816.
                          Lith. de Spengler et Cie. à Lausanne.
   Wh. len. to left, in profile, seated on broad balcony, right hand
holding a pen raised; inkstand and books before him on table,
a paper under his left hand; the lake is below, and mountains
beyond; a coloured impression; four verses below, in two
Columns, from Childe Harold, LXXXV, Canto III, "Clear, placid
Leman! . . . . . . a purer spring."
       ($10\frac{1}{4} \times 13\frac{1}{16}$).   23578.

———

   T. Phillips, R.A.   S. W. Reynolds, mixed mez.
   Ha. len. to right, looking to left, with loose collar and cloak,
right hand resting on a table before him.
   Open letter proof; Feby., 1822.
       $9 \times 6\frac{1}{2}$. ($3\frac{7}{8} \times 3\frac{1}{8}$).   E. 1462.–'85.

———

   T. Phillips, R.A.   I. S. Agar, stipple.
   From the same picture, but rather shorter, the hand and table
not appearing.
   Cut. ($4\frac{5}{8} \times 3\frac{1}{2}$).   23555.

———

   T. Holmes.   H. T. Ryall.
   Sh. ha. len. slightly to left, looking to left, with open collar and
cloak; facs. letter below, referring to the portrait (miniature)
by Holmes, dated May 19, 1823.
   Proof; Sepr. 1, 1835; vignette.
       12×9. ($4\frac{1}{8} \times 3\frac{7}{8}$)   E. 1464.–'85.

" From a bust (by Bertolini ?) in the possession of the Hon
Douglas Kinnaird. London.   I. Draper, lith.
Published by J. Watson, 7, Vere Street, Oxford Street ; —
March 1825."
   ($8\frac{1}{16} \times 6\frac{1}{2}$).   E. 1465.–'85.

———

  B. West, R.A.   C. Turner, mez.
Sh. ha. len. to left, looking to front, collar very open, right
hand resting in fold of coat.
  Proof before all letters, except publication-line, Novr. 8th,
1826 (P. Colnaghi and Son) ; in engraved border.
  Cut. (Incl. border, $13\frac{3}{8} \times 11\frac{7}{8}$; excl. border, $10\frac{3}{4} \times 8\frac{1}{2}$).
          28031.

———, at the age of 19.
  G. Sanders.   W. Finden.
  Wh. len. to front, standing, leaning with right hand on a
rock ; by him is a young sailor, holding a boat ready ; a yacht,
sea, and mountains in background ; Novr. 6, 1830.
  $16 \times 13\frac{1}{4}$.   ($9\frac{3}{8} \times 7\frac{1}{4}$).   22494.

BYRON, John, 1st Baron, 1599–1652, Lt. of Tower, 1641–'2 ;
  served the Royal Cause during the Rebellion ; cr. Baron, 1643 ;
  Field-Marshal Genl., Govr. Chester, where he endured a long
  siege, till Feb. 1646 ; Govr. to James, D. of York ; died in Paris.
   P. Paul.   S. de Wilde, etching.
  Sh. ha. len. to left, looking to front, wearing breastplate.
  Proof before all letters.
  $9\frac{7}{16} \times 6\frac{3}{4}$.   ($6\frac{3}{8} \times 5\frac{3}{4}$).   22820.

CABINET.   See ABERDEEN and DERBY.

CADELL, Thomas, the elder, 1742–1802, bookseller and publisher, b. at Bristol ; apprent., 1758, to A. Millar, great bookseller and publisher, in the Strand ; partner with him, 1765 ;
  took the business over, 1767 ; published works of Robertson,
  Gibbon, and Blackstone ; intimate with Dr. Johnson ; liberal to
  authors and assistants ; retired, 1793 ; alderman, 1798 ; sheriff,
  1800–'1.
   Sir W. Beechey. (W. Evans delin.).   H. Meyer, stipple.
  Ha. len. to left, seated, looking to left ; wearing light coat
  with broad lapels.
  Proof before all letters, except the artists' names.
  Cut.   ($8\frac{3}{4} \times 7\frac{3}{16}$).   24657

CADOGAN, William, M.D., 1711–1797, b. in London ; educ.
  at Oriel Coll., Oxf. ; author of " Essay on Children," " On the
  Gout," Harveiian Orations, &c. ; d. in Hanover Square.
   R. E. Pine, 1769.   W. Dickinson, mez.
   J. C. Smith, 12.   22601.

CAIUS, John, 1510–1573, Physician, Anatomist, and Naturalist ;
  b. at Norwich ; educ. there and at Gonville Hall, Cambr. ;

M.D., and Prof. of Greek at Padua, where he stud. anatomy under Vesalius; returned to England; physician to Edward VI., and aftds. to Q. Mary; nine times Pres. of Coll. of Physicians; for many years delivered lectures on anatomy in London; Gonville Hall refounded as Gonville and Caius Coll., 1557, Dr. Caius being declared a co-founder, having endowed and enlarged it; Pres. of the Coll., 1559–1573; d. in London.

J. Faber, senr., mez.

J. C. Smith, 34 (Founders, Camb. XVI.); interm. state, between 2nd and 3rd, with address of Tim: Jordan. 24658.

CALDWELL, Sir Benjamin, c. 1737–1820, Admiral; b. at Liverpool; ent. R. Academy, Portsmouth, 1754; app. to "Isis," 50-gun ship, 1756; served under Boscawen; posted into "Milford" frigate, 1765; served under Rodney and Howe, and took part in action of June 1, 1794; Vice-Adm. of the Blue, 1794; Admiral, 1799; G.C.B., 1820.

See COMMEMORATION (1).

CALLCOTT, Sir Augustus Wall, 1779–1844, younger brother of the musician; landscape-painter, stud. at the R. Academy, and under Hoppner; exhibited his first portrait at the Academy, 1799; exhibited a landscape view of Oxford and two portraits, 1801; soon gained reputation; A.R.A., 1806; R.A., 1810; painted English country scenes, and some of the Dutch coast; began Italian landscapes, 1830; "Raphael and Fornarina," 1837; Knt., same year, surveyor of the Royal Pictures.

J. Linnell. J. Linnell, 1832, mez.

Ha. len. to left, looking to front, wearing a cloak, seals on watch-ribbon, &c.

First proof; pubd. March 1st, 1832, by J. Linnell, who presented this impression to the late Mr. Sheepshanks.

16 × 11. (13⅛ × 9¹³⁄₁₆). 18918.

The same portrait; second proof, with many alterations, the seals being suppressed, work added on face, &c., and some lines very plainly etched on back of chair.

21940.

CALLCOTT, John Wall, 1766–1821, son of a bricklayer and builder, and elder brother of the painter; b. at Kensington, showed early love of music; befriended by Dr. Arnold, Dr. Cooke, and "old Sale;" deputy organist, under Reinhold, till 1785; introduced by Dr. Cooke to the orchestra of the Academy of Ancient Music; composed many fine Glees; Mus. B., 1785; helped Dr. Arnold in founding the Glee Club, 1787, where he gained many prizes; stud. orchestral writing under Haydn; Mus. Doc., 1800.

A. W. Callcott, R.A. F. C. Lewis, stipple.

Ha. len. slightly to right, looking to right, wearing spectacles; vignette.

13⅛ × 9½ (5½ × 6½). 21854.

CAMBRIDGE, ADOLPHUS FREDERICK, Duke of, 1774–1850, fifth son of George III.; educ. at Göttingen; served under the Duke of York in Flanders; Col. in Chf. of the King's German Legion, 1803; Field-Marshal, 1813; Viceroy of Hanover, 1815–1837; m. Princess Wilhelmina Louisa of Hesse Cassel, 1818.

Sir W. Beechey. W. Skelton.
Ha. len. to left, looking to front, wearing star.
Cut. ($18\frac{1}{4} \times 13\frac{13}{16}$).
In Genealogical Chart, 553, 1. 25046. 8.

—

J. Lucas. H. Cousins, mixed mez.
Wh. len. to left, standing, looking to front, in uniform, right hand on hilt of sword, hat with plumes in left; pillar on right; landscape in distance, left; May 20, 1840.
$29\frac{1}{2} \times 19$. ($24\frac{1}{4} \times 16$). 22965.

CAMBRIDGE, AUGUSTA WILHELMINA LOUISA, of Hesse Cassel, 1797–1889, Duchess of; m. 1818.

Anon.

Ha. len. wearing a large hat with a feather.
Proof before letters.
Cut. ($6 \times 3\frac{3}{4}$). 25446. B.
In Genealogical Chart, 553. 1.

—

Partridge del. J. Alais, stipple.
See LA BELLE ASSEMBLÉE, 1818. 13867. 22.

CAMBRIDGE, RICHARD OWEN, poet, 1717–1802, b. in London; educ. at Eton and Oxford; took no degree; entered at Linc. Inn, but did not study; married, 1741, and retired to Whitminster, his family seat, in Gloucestershire; having inherited a fortune in 1748, removed to London, thence to Twickenham, where he enjoyed the intimacy of Gray, Lyttelton, Jenyns, Pitt, Fox, and many other intellectual friends; wrote "Scribleriad," 1751, &c.

O. Humphry, R.A. C Bestland, stipple.
Sh. ha. len. to left, looking to front, oval in border; "Æt. SV. LXI." Arms below in centre. June 1, 1803.
$11\frac{1}{2}$(?) $\times 8\frac{5}{8}$. ($5\frac{3}{8} \times 4\frac{3}{8}$). 28260.

CAMDEN, CHARLES PRATT, 1st Earl, 1713–1794, Lawyer and Statesman; Att.-Gen., 1757; Ld. Chf. Just., 1761; Ld. Chan., 1766; decided against the legality of General Warrants, and opposed the American War; cr. Earl, 1786.

Sir J. Reynolds. S. F. Ravenet
Wh. len. to front, in robes, as Chf. Justice, standing, holding with left hand a large volume which rests on a table, on which are an inkstand, papers, &c.; inscription in a cartouche below, in Latin, 10 lines; "J. Boydell exct. 1766," scratched; and at foot, *publish'd Aug. 12th,* 1766, *by J. Boydell,* &c.
$20\frac{1}{2} \times 15\frac{1}{16}$. ($18\frac{1}{4} \times 13\frac{5}{8}$). 22224.

CAMDEN, John Jeffreys, Marquess, 1759–1840; suc. as 2nd
Earl, 1794; Lord Lieut. of Ireland, 1795–'8; cr. Marquess
Camden and Earl of Brecknock, 1812; held various offices.
  J. Hoppner, R.A.   W. Ward, mez.
  J. C. Smith, 21, 2nd state.   22964.
  Also, a duplicate, in a later state than any described by
J. C. Smith; published by Colnaghi, Son & Co., 1835.
                                               E. 1570.–'88.

CAMDEN, William, 1551–1623, antiquary, b. in London;
  educ. at Chr. Hosp., St. Paul's school, Magd Coll. and Broad-
  gate's Hall (now Pembr. Coll.), Oxf.; B.A., 1573; second
  master of Westminster School, 1575, and head master, 1593;
  Clarencieux King-at-Arms, 1597; publd. his "Britannia,"
  1586, many times reprinted and translated; his Gr. Grammar,
  1597; and other works.
  M. Gherardis (or Geerarts, or Gheeraerts, &c.). (Loder
del)   J. Basire, 1789.
  Sh. ha. len. to front, with ruff; arms above, on left; inscription in Latin below, in 6 lines, followed by the names of the
dedicator and painter, and a chronogram, "hISTORIæ eCCe
. . . . . . eXIIt." March 25, 1789.
  Frontispiece to R. Gough's edn., 3 vols., fol., of that date.
The picture is in the National Portrait Gallery.
    13 7/16 × 8 3/4.   (11 5/16 × 7 4/9).   24067.

CAMERON, Jenny,   –1773, well known for her chivalrous
  attachment to the Royal House of Stuart, lived in Kilbride,
  Lanarkshire, for several years; d. there, and was buried amid
  a clump of trees, near the solitary house of Blacklaw, near
  Kilbride.*
  Anon.   Anon.
  Full ha. len. to right, looking to front, wearing a military
hat, and holding a drawn sword in her right hand; oval in
border; "Sold by P. Griffin, Map and Printseller next ye
Globe Tavern, Fleet Street."
    6 3/8 × 4 5/9.   (Oval, 4 × 3 1/16).   27718.
  * See T. H. Dawson, Abr. Stat. Hist. of Scotland, p. 654, 1853.

CAMPBELL, Colin. See CLYDE, Lord.

CAMPBELL, John, 1st Lord, 1781–1861, disting. lawyer; son
  of a clergyman; b. at Springfield, Cupar, 1781; educ. at St.
  Andrews; called to the bar; M.P. for Stafford, &c.; Sol.-
  Gen., Att.-Gen., and (1841) Ld. Chan. of Ireland and cr. Baron;
  Ld. Chf. Just., 1850; Ld. Chan., 1853; author of "Lives of
  the Chancellors," &c.; d. at Kensington.
  F Grant, R.A.   T. L. Atkinson, mixed mez.
  T. Q. len. to right, seated, in robes, as Lord Chf. Justice; on
table, right, an inkstand and volume lettered "Lives of the
Chancellors;" Aug. 10, 1852.
    20 3/4 × 16.   (17 × 13 1/4).   22967.

CAMPBELL, THOMAS, 1777–1844, b. at Glasgow, and educ. there, at the Univ., where he distinguished himself in classics; pubd. "The Pleasures of Hope," 1799, which ran through four edns. in a year; travelled abroad, and witnessed the battle of Hohenlinden, Decr. 3, 1800, which he commemorated in his poem of that name; wrote many other poems, "Lochiel's Warning," "Gertrude of Wyoming," &c.; Lord Rector of Glasgow University, 1827; pubd. "Letters from the South," "Life and Times of Petrarch," &c.

Sir T. Lawrence.   S. and H. Cousins, mixed mez.
Full ha. len. to front, seated, looking to right, with left hand open, resting on a paper on table.
Proof before all letters, except the artists' names and publication-line, March 1, 1834.
16×12. $(12\frac{1}{4} \times 9\frac{1}{2})$.   21750.

Sir T. Lawrence.   S. and H. Cousins, mixed mez.
The same plate as the one just described; proof before all letters.
       22139.

See also SCOTT, SIR WALTER.

CANNING, RT. HON. GEORGE, 1770–1827, Statesman; b. in London; ent. Parlt. as a supporter of Pitt, 1793; Under-Sec. for For. Affairs, 1796; Sec. for For. Affairs, 1807–'9; again, 1822–'7; suc. Lord Liverpool as Prime Minister, 1827, but d. in same year, at Chiswick.

Sir T. Lawrence, P.R.A.   C. Turner, mez.
Full ha. len. to front, seated; left hand to head, right not seen; white neckcloth and shirt-frill, dark coat, buttoned.
Open letter proof, July 20, 1827.
$15\frac{1}{8} \times 11\frac{1}{16}$. $(11\frac{1}{16} \times 9\frac{1}{8})$.   22140.

CANTERBURY, CHARLES MANNERS-SUTTON, 1st Viscount, 1780–1845, son of the Archbishop of Canterbury; Judge Adv. General, 1809; Speaker of the House of Commons, 1817–'34; Visct. Canterbury, 1835; G. C. B., &c.

H. W. Pickersgill, R.A.   S. Cousins, mixed mez.
T. Q. len. to front, seated in the Speaker's chair, looking to left, hat in left hand, eye-glass in right, which rests on arm of chair.
Open letter proof, April 13, 1835.
$19\frac{11}{16} \times 14\frac{7}{8}$. $(16\frac{3}{4} \times 13\frac{1}{16})$.   21941.

CANUTE II., "THE GREAT," 1017–1036; suc. 1015.
             G. Vertue.
Bust-size, profile to left, wearing a fillet of pearls (?) on his head; from a silver coin.
$11\frac{5}{8} \times 7\frac{11}{16}$. $(11\frac{1}{16} \times 7\frac{3}{16})$.   24648.

     NOTE.—No other portrait of this king is known.

O   82849.   F

CAPON, WILLIAM, 1757–1827, scene-painter and architect, b. at Norwich, son of an artist of some ability, under whom he began painting portraits; preferring architecture, stud. under Novozielski, architect and scene-painter, whom he helped in erection of Opera House and buildings and scenery at Ranelagh; painted scenes for Komble; draftsman and architl. painter to D. of York; exhibited at R.A.; called "Pompous Billy" by Sheridan.

W. Bone, min.   W. Bond.
Ha. len. slightly to right, looking to front, holding compasses in left hand; an architectural drawing behind him; vignette; facs. signature below.
Proof; March 1, 1828.
9 × 6.   (5¼ × 4½).   26245.

CARDIGAN, JAMES THOMAS BRUDENELL. 7th Earl of, 1797–1868; distinguished Cavalry Officer; M.P., 1818–1837; joined 8th Hussars, 1824; Lt.-Col. 11th Hussars, 1836–'54; Col. in Army, 1846; Maj.-Genl., 1854; Lt.-Genl., 1861; Col. 5th Dragoon Gds., 1859–'60, and of his old Regt., the 11th, 1860–'8. In 1854 he led the charge of the Light Brigade at Balaklava; K.C.B., &c.

H. W. Phillips.   G. Zobel, mez.
Sh. ha. len. to left, looking to front, in uniform; oval in border.
Ind. proof, with facs. signature below.
16 × 13.   (11½ × 9²⁄₁₆).   24205.

CARDROSS, LORD.   See BUCHAN.

CAREW, MISS.
Hayter.   Anon., stipple.
See LA BELLE ASSEMBLÉE.   13867   4.

CAREW, BAMPFYLDE MOORE, 1693–1759, "King of the Beggars," son of Rev. Theodore Carew, of Bickley, near Tiverton, co. Devon; his godfathers were the Hon. Hugh Bampfylde and Major the Hon. —— Moore; attracted by the charms of a wild life, he joined the gipsies, with whom he became very popular, and who elected him their King.

R. Phelps.   J. Faber, junr., mez.
J. C. Smith, 56, 1st state.   27158.

CAREY, HENRY, EARL OF MONMOUTH.   See MONMOUTH.

CARLETON, SIR DUDLEY.   See DORCHESTER.

CARLETON, HENRY BOYLE, Lord, c. 1670–1725; M.A., 1693, Cambr.; M.P., 1698–1702, and again later; Chancellor of

Exch., 1701–'8; Princ. Sec. of State, 1708–'10; cr. Baron
Carleton, 1714; Lord Pres., 1721 till death.
Kneller.   J. Houbraken, 1740.
Oval. In Birch's " Lives."
This is the only known portrait of Lord Carleton.
$14\frac{1}{2} \times 9$ (?). $(14\frac{1}{8} \times 8\frac{4}{5})$.   20809.

CARLINI, AGOSTINO (with BARTOLOZZI and CIPRIANI),
    –1790, sculptor and painter, b. at Geneva, came early to
England; original member of the R.A.; succeeded Moser as
keeper, 1783; executed the model of Equestrian Statue of
George III., 1769, port. in oils of a nobleman, 1776, the marble
statue of Dr. Ward, in the hall of Socy of Arts, and figures at
Somerset House; d. in Soho.
G. F. Rigaud.   J. R. Smith, mez.
    J. C. Smith, 30; an intermediate state, between Mr. Smith's
1st and 2nd, the inscription being scratched in full, but before
Boydell's name and address; pubd. by J. R. Smith, No. 10,
Bateman's Buildings, &c. and Wm. Humphrey, No. 70, St.
Martin's Lane, &c., and with the names of the personages,
Cipriani being spelt Cippriani.   2752.

CARLISLE, FREDERICK HOWARD, Fifth Earl of, and GEORGE
SELWYN, Esqre. This Earl, 1748-1825, suc. 1758; was
Lord Lieut. of Ireland, 1780–'2; K.G., 1793; art collector and
poet, satirised by Byron.
    George Augustus Selwyn, 1719–1791, was surveyor to the
Mint; M.P., registrar in Chancery in Barbados; d. in Cleveland Row.
Sir J. Reynolds.   R. B. Parkes, mez.
    Seated at a table, Selwyn caressing a dog, Carlisle holding a
book.
$9\frac{7}{8} \times 10\frac{7}{16}$. $(7 \times 8\frac{1}{2})$.   27254.

CARLISLE, GEORGE WILLIAM FREDERICK HOWARD, 7th Earl
of, 1802–1864, statesman; Chf. Sec., Ireland, 1833–'41; suc. to
the peerage, 1848; Lord Lieut., Ireland, 1855–'63; K.G., &c.
J. Carrick.   S. Bellin, mez.
    T. Q. len. to front, looking to left, as Lord Morpeth; facs.
signature below.
Ind. proof before letters, 1844.
$17\frac{1}{4} \times 13\frac{1}{4}$. $(12\frac{3}{4} \times 10\frac{3}{16})$.   27954.

G. Richmond.   F. Holl, stipple.
Bust, to front, facing and looking to right, vignette.
Proof with skeleton letters; June 6, 1855.
$21\frac{1}{4} \times 17$. $(9\frac{1}{2} \times 7\frac{1}{4})$.   21959.

CARLISLE, LUCY, Countess of, c. 1600–1660, daughter of Henry
Percy, Earl of Northumberland; m (second wife) to James
Hay, Earl of Carlisle, K.G. (c. 1580–1636); d. at Little
Cashiobury House; buried at Petworth.
A. van Dyck.   P. Lombart.

F 2

T. Q. len. to left, looking to front; holding her right hand in water falling from an urn, held by a figure of Cupid, into a basin on left; in a scrolled border.

Cut. (12⅔ × 10¹⁄₁₆, incl. border, ⁹⁄₁₆).　　　　E. 625.–'90.

CARLISLE, MARGARET, Countess of,　　–1676, 3rd daughter of Francis (Russell), 4th Earl of Bedford; m., 1631, to James (Hay), Earl of Carlisle; m. again (his 5th wife) to Edward (Montagu), 2nd Earl of Manchester.

　A. van Dyck.　　　　　　　　　　　　　P. Lombart.

T. Q. len. slightly turned to left, looking to front, a child standing at her knee, on left; in a rect. border ornamented with fruits, &c.

Cut. (12⁷⁄₁₆ × 9¾, incl. border, c. ½).　　　E. 624.–'90.

CARLYLE, THOMAS, 1795–1881, essayist, biographer, and historian; b. at Ecclefechan, Dumfries; educ. at Edinburgh; taught mathematics for some time, but then devoted himself to literature; contr. to "Edinb. Encyclopædia," and "New Edinb. Review;" transl. Goethe's "Wilhelm Meister"; pubd. "Life of Schiller," "Sartor Resartus," "French Revolution," "Chartism," "Essays," "Life of John Stirling," of "Frederick the Great," &c.; refused a G.C.B., 1875; d. at Chelsea.

　　　　　　　　　　　　　　　　　Le Gros, etched.

Ha. len. to right, looking to front, wearing a broad-brimmed hat and cloak.

2nd state (the fourth impression, as per MS. inscription), on thick Ind. paper.

18¼ × 13¾. (17½ × 13⁷⁄₁₆).　　　　　　　27733. 5.

CARNARVON, ANNA SOPHIA,　　–　　eldest daughter of Philip Herbert, 4th Earl of Pembroke, by his first wife; m. (1625) to Robert Dormer, 1st Earl of Carnarvon (c. 1610–1643).

　A. van Dyck.　　　　　　　　　　　　　P. Lombart.

Ha. len., slightly to right, looking to front, hair in curls, wearing pearls, and holding flowers in both hands; in a rect. border of oak leaves and laurel.

Cut. (12 × 9¹⁄₁₆, incl. border, ⅝).　　　　E. 626.–'90.

CAROLINE, QUEEN OF GEORGE II., 1683–1737; Wilhelmina Caroline, dau. of Margrave of Brandenburg-Anspach; m., 1705, to George II. (then Prince of Wales), over whom she exercised a strong influence; d. at St. James's Palace; bur. in Henry VII.'s Chapel, Westminster Abbey.

　J. Vanderbanck, 1736.　　　　　J. Faber, junr., mez.
　J. C. Smith, 63, 1st state.　　　　　　　26675.

CAROLINE, PRINCESS, Third Daughter of George II., 1712–1757.

　H. Hysing.　　　　　　　　　　　J. Faber, mez.
　J. C Smith, 65, 2nd state.　　　　　　　27161.

CAROLINE, MATILDA, 1751–1775, daughter of Frederick, Prince of Wales; m., 1766, to Christian VII, King of Denmark.

Cotes. R. Purcell, mez.

Not described by J. C. Smith.

Sh. ha. len. (like the print by J. Watson, p. 1498), looking to left.

Cut. ($12\frac{5}{8} \times 9\frac{7}{8}$).

In Genealogical Chart, 553. 1.

CAROLINE OF BRUNSWICK, 1768–1821, Queen of George IV., m. 1795; separated, 1796.

Tulkau (?) Schiavonetti.

As Princess of Wales, ha. len. to right, looking to front, wearing hat and feather; oval in border. Published, June, 1795, by Colnaghi & Co.

Cut. ($8\frac{1}{8} \times 7\frac{3}{4}$). 25047.

In Genealogical Chart, 553. 1.

——

Wm. Derby delt. R. Cooper.

Ha. len., wearing a hat with feathers. Published Aug. 1, 1820, by R. Cooper; vignette.

$13\frac{5}{8} \times 11\frac{3}{16}$. ($7 \times 5\frac{3}{8}$). 23593.

——, View of the Interior of the House of Lords, during the trial of the Queen, 1820.

Sir G. Hayter. J. Bromley and J. Porter, mixed mez.

A composition of many figures; the Queen is seated, near the middle of the print; Brougham on her left; Lord Grey standing on the right, checking the interpreter's prolixity; Majocchi, giving evidence, on the left of the interpreter, &c. There is a "Descriptive Catalogue" of the picture in the Art Library, S. K., containing a key to the portraits (189) contained in it, 1823, 4to. (132 F.).

The print is a skeleton-letter proof, March 1, 1832.

($22\frac{5}{8} \times 34\frac{3}{8}$). 23049.

CARPENTER, LADY ALMERIA, 1752–1809, daughter of George, 3rd Lord Carpenter, who was cr. Earl of Tyrconnel, 1761; d. unmarried.

Anon. Page.

Bust, to left, t. q. face; hair dressed high; oval in border; below, "COURT BEAUTIES, N. 4" (from an illustrd. Magazine).

$6\frac{7}{8} \times 4\frac{3}{8}$. ($6\frac{1}{4} \times 3\frac{11}{16}$). 26196.

CARPENTER, MRS. MARGARET SARAH, 1793–1872, b. at Salisbury, daughter of a Captain Geddes, of an Edinb. family; pupil of a drawing-master, and stud. in the picture-gallery of Longford Castle; received the gold medal of the Society of Arts for one of her copies; painted portraits in London, 1814–1866; m. to Mr.

W. H. Carpenter, keeper of the prints, Br. Museum; exhibited
many portraits at the R.A.; d. in London.
W. Carpenter.   W Carpenter, etched.
Bust, to left, in profile; vignette.
9 × 6. (4 × 3).   E. 162.–'91.

CARPENTER, WILLIAM HOOKHAM, 1792–1866, son of a bookseller, pursued the same trade, 1817–'45, when he was appointed
keeper of prints and drawings in the Br. Museum, where he
remained till his death; trustee of Nat. Port. Gallery, 1856 till
death; F.S.A., 1853; author of a monograph on Van Dyck's
etchings, 1844, and a " Guide to the drawings and prints
exhibited to the public in the King's Library," 1858; d. at Br.
Museum.
                                       W. Carpenter, 1847, etched.
Sh. ha. len. to right; vignette.
9 × 6. (6 × 4⅞).   E. 161.–'91.

CARPUE, JOSEPH CONSTANTINE, 1764–1846, Surgeon and
Anatomist; b. in London; educ. at Douai, and at St. George's
Hospital,' where he became surgeon; eminent as a lecturer on
Anatomy and Surgery; was the first to perform the Taliacotian
operation in this country; d. in Upper Charlotte St., Fitzroy
Square; bur. at Chiswick.
C. Turner.   C. Turner, mez.
T. Q. len. to right, seated, left hand and arm on table, on which
are a watch, inkstand, books, papers, &c.; landscape in back-
ground, out of window, on right.
Proof with skeleton letters, May 20, 1822.
20 × 13¾. (16¾ × 12½).   22821.

CARTER, ELIZABETH, 1717–1806, eldest daughter of Nicholas
Carter, D.D., perp. curate, Deal; precocious in desire for
knowledge; wrote a vol. of poems before she was 20, pubd.,
1738; after other essays, translated the works of Epictetus,
1758; made the friendship (for 50 years) of Dr. Johnson, to
whose "Rambler" she contributed two papers; she was
familiar with Hebrew, Greek, Latin, Italian, Spanish, and
German.
T. Lawrence, 1788.   Caroline Watson, stipple.
Sh. ha. len. to left, looking downwards, wearing a cap; oval.
April 4, 1808
The picture is in the National Portrait Gallery.
13¼ × 10½. (9½ × 7₁₆).   22968.

CARY. See FALKLAND.

CARTWRIGHT, Rev. EDMUND, 1743–1823, pub. a poem,
"Armine and Elvira," 1770; is chiefly known for his valuable
invention of the power loom, introduced, 1785, which, though
for some time violently opposed by ignorant and prejudiced
men, was at length generally adopted; received a grant of
10,000l. from Parliament, 1809, as a reward for his services.
See SCIENCE

CASTLEMAINE, Lady. *See* CLEVELAND.

CATESBY, Robert, 1573–1605, second and only surviving son of Sir William Catesby, of Lapworth, Warwickshire, by Anne, daughter of Sir Robert Throckmorton, of Coughton, in same co.; b. at Lapworth; educ. at Douai(?) and Gloucester Hall (now Worcester Coll., Oxf.); imprisoned at Ely, 1588, and later than 1593, for recusancy; adherent of Robert, Earl of Essex, 1601; imprisoned and heavily fined; again in prison, 1603; joined the plot hatched by Thomas Winter; slain at Holbeach, Staff., Novr. 7, 1605.
See CONCILIUM.

CATHARINE OF ARRAGON, 1485–1536; Queen Consort of Henry VIII., 1509; separated, 1531.
Holbein. "In the collection of the Honble. Horace Walpole." J. Houbraken, 1743."
Sh. ha. len., elderly, wearing a close-fitting dark hood.
In Birch's "Lives."
$14\frac{1}{16} \times 9\frac{3}{8}$. $(14\frac{1}{8} \times 8\frac{7}{8})$. 21809.

---

*A. vander Werff. Vermeulen.
(Really after Holbein.)
Sh. ha. len., in a peaked and jewelled headdress.
Cut. $(11\frac{3}{8} \times 6\frac{3}{4})$. 14170.
* Not the original designer.

CATHARINE HOWARD, 1521 (or '2)–1542; Queen of Henry VIII., 1540.
Holbein. "In the Collection of Mr. Richardson." J. Houbraken.
Sh. ha. len., holding a kerchief in her right hand.
In Birch's "Lives."
$14\frac{1}{4} \times 9$. $(13\frac{7}{8} \times 8\frac{1}{2})$. 26676.

CATHARINE PARR, 1509–1548; Queen of Henry VIII., 1543.
*A. vander Werff. Vermeulen.
With her name and 4 verses below.
In Larrey's "History."
$12\frac{3}{8} \times 7\frac{1}{4}$. $(11\frac{7}{16} \times 6\frac{13}{16})$. 27102.
* Not the original designer.

Holbein. H. T. Ryall.
From the original, in the Collection of (the late) Dawson Turner, Esq.
Ha. len., with hands clasped across her breast.
$9\frac{3}{4}$ (?) $\times 7\frac{7}{16}$. $(4\frac{7}{8} \times 3\frac{7}{8})$. 14163.

CATHARINE OF PORTUGAL, Queen Consort of Charles II.,
1638-1705; m. 1662.

Serenissima Catharina Mag: Brit: Fran: & Hiber | Regina.
&c.

Iohn Baptist Caspers.   Ed. Davis.
" Sold by Moses Pitt at the | Angel in St. Pauls Church-
yard."

Wh. len.

Cut. $(17\frac{3}{16} \times 10\frac{9}{16})$.   E. 1290.-'88

After the print by Faithorne.   Dunkarton, mez.
Represented in the dress in which she arrived in England.
Proof before letters.

$12\frac{7}{8} \times 8\frac{5}{16}$. $(11\frac{1}{4} \times 8\frac{5}{16})$.   22497.

J. Huysmans.   Anon., mez.
J. C. Smith, p. 1651, 14, 3rd state.
This would seem almost certainly to be the work of R. Wil-
liams.   22227.

CATHCART, WILLIAM SCHAW, 10th Baron, 1st Viscount, 1st
Earl, 1755-1843, studied for the law, admitted as an advocate
at Edinburgh, 1776; entd. army, 1777; served in America;
Lt. Col. Coldstr. Gds., 1781, exchd. to 29th, of which he became
Col. 1802; Col. in army, 1790; Genl., 1802; took Copenhagen,
1807; K. T.; cr Viscount, 1807; Earl, 1814; Ambassador in
Russia, 1812-'21.

J. Hoppner, R.A.   H. Meyer, mez.
Ha. len. to left, in uniform, with star of the Thistle.
Open letter proof, Novr. 2, 1807.

$13\frac{7}{8} \times 9\frac{13}{16}$. $(12\frac{1}{4} \times 9\frac{13}{16})$.   24206.

Sir J. Reynolds.   W. Sharp, Jany., 1791
Ha. len. to right, looking to left, in the uniform of the 98th
foot, in which he was major, 1774.
Proof before all letters, except the engraver's name and date.

$10\frac{7}{8} \times 8\frac{9}{16}$. $(8\frac{7}{8} \times 7\frac{5}{16})$.   E. 2166.-'89.

CATLEY, ANNE, 1745-1789, apprent. to Joah Bates, musician;
sang in Ireland, 1763, with great success, and in London, on
her return, 1770, down to her last appearance, 1784; d. near
Brentford, at the house of General Lascelles, to whom she is
said to have been married.

W. Lawrenson.   R. Dunkarton, mez.
J. C. Smith, 13, 2d state.   25770.

CAVENDISH, ELIZABETH, Lady.   See SHREWSBURY.

CAVENDISH, HON. HENRY, 1731-1810, b. at Nice, son of Lord
Charles Cavendish; was one of the most eminent natural philo-
sophers of modern times; educ. at Cambridge; devoted himself
to study of chemistry; laid the foundations of pneumatic che-

mistry by his discoveries; wrote little, but with marvellous finish
and accuracy; was "the richest among the learned, and the
" most learned among the rich;" F.R.S.; left 1,200,000*l.* to
his relations.
See SCIENCE.

CAVENDISH. *See* NEWCASTLE, Margaret, Duchess of.

CAWDOR, Caroline, Lady, 1771–1848, eldest daughter of Frederick, 5th Earl of Carlisle; m., 1789, to John Campbell, who
was cr. Baron Cawdor, 1796; d. at Twickenham.
  H. Edridge, 1804.   L. Schiavonetti, 1806, stipple.
  Wh. len. to left, with short, rough hair, looking to front;
wearing a cloak trimmed with fur, resting right hand on a stone
parapet, holding glove in left; trees in distance; private plate.
  Cut.   (13⅛ × 9½, excl. of ruled border, c. 1).   17920.

CECIL. *See* BURGHLEY.

CHALMERS, Alexander, 1759–1834, b. at Aberdeen, where
his father was a printer; educ. there in classics and medicine;
left Aberdeen, c. 1777, and went as far as Portsmouth, to join
a ship, as surgeon; returned, however, to London, devoted himself to journalism and periodical literature; M.A., F.S.A., 1805;
edited "British Essayists," Lives of Burns and Beattie, Fielding's Works, Warton, Gibbon, and many others.
                                  R. J. Lane, lith.
  Sh. ha. len. to right, coat buttoned with one button; facs. signature below; vignette.
  (5½ × 4⅝).   22496.

CHALMERS, George, 1742–1825, b. at Fochabers, Scotland;
· educ. at King's Coll., Old Aberdeen; stud. the law for a time;
· emigr. to Maryland, where he practised 10 years in the courts;
after the declaration of Independence, returned to England,
and was rewarded for his loyalty with a clerkship in Board of
Trade; publd. a number of political, historical, biographical, and
miscellaneous works, "Caledonia," &c.
  H. Edridge.   R. Cooper, stipple.
  Sh. ha. len. to left, looking to front; vignette.
  Open letter proof; March 8, 1813.
  15⅛ × 12¾. (6¼ × 6).   27586.

CHALMERS, Thomas, 1780–1847, Theologian, preacher, and
philanthropist; b. at Anstruther, in Fife; educ. at Univ. of
St. Andrews; minister at Kilmany and Glasgow, 1803–'23;
Prof. of Moral Philosophy at St. Andrews, 1824; Prof. of
Theology, Edinb., 1828; joined Free Kirk, and Principal of
New Coll., 1843; disting. as an eloquent preacher.
  A. Geddes.   W. Ward, mez.
  T. Q. len. to front, seated, right arm resting on table, on which
are papers and an inkstand; Decr. 1822.
  19⅞ × 14. (17¾ × 13⅛).   21909.

CHAMBERS, Sir William, 1729–1796, architect, of Scotch family, b. at Stockholm; educ. at Ripon; supercargo, at 16, with the Swedish E. I. Company; visited Italy and France, stud. at Paris under Clérisseau; on his return, 1755, employed at Kew and taught the Pr. of Wales drawing; gained reputation, and published several works; foundation member and Treasr., R.A.; architect of Somerset House; F.R.S.; &c.

Sir J. Reynolds, P.R.A.　　　　　　S. W. Reynolds, mez.
Ha. len. to left, looking upwards; dark dress, curly hair, white neckcloth; in rectangular border; Feb. 1, 1796.
　　Cut.　(11$\frac{14}{15}$×10).　　　　　　　　　E. 1268.–'86.

Sir J. Reynolds, P.R.A.　　　　　　V. Green, mez.
J. C. Smith, 21, 2nd state.　　　　　　22221.

P. Falconet delt.　　　　　　D. P. Pariset, stipple.
Sh. ha. len. to left, in profile; hair tied at back, curled at side.
　　7$\frac{1}{4}$×5$\frac{3}{4}$.　(4$\frac{3}{4}$×3$\frac{5}{8}$).　　　　　　28300.　17.

Anon.　　　　　　W. Bromley, 1792.
Sh. ha. len. to right, looking to front; oval; for the "European Magazine," April 1, 1796.
　　6$\frac{7}{8}$×4$\frac{7}{16}$.　(3$\frac{7}{8}$×3).　　　　　　15219.　1.

CHAMIER, Anthony, 1725–1780, M.P. for Tamworth, an original member of the Literary Club, and friend of Reynolds, Johnson, Burke, and Goldsmith.
　　Sir J. Reynolds.　　　　　　W. Ward, A.R.A., mez.
　　J. C. Smith, 26, 3rd state.　　　　　　22822.

CHANTREY, Francis Legott, 1781–1842, sculptor, b. at Norton, near Sheffield; son of a carpenter; apprent. to a curver; encouraged by J R. Smith, mezzotintist, and by a statuary of the town of Sheffield; came to London; stud. at Academy; A.R.A., 1816; R.A., 1818; visited France and Italy; made many important statues, busts, and monumental figures; Knt., 1835; left reversion of his property to the Royal Academy.
　　Raeburn.　　　　　　J. Thomson, stipple.
　　Ha. len. to front, facing and looking towards left; Oct. 2, 1820.
　　7$\frac{1}{8}$×5(?).　(4$\frac{5}{16}$×3$\frac{1}{2}$).　　　　　　E. 1264.–'89.

"From an original Painting."　　　　　　J. Thomson, stipple.
Ha. len. to left, looking upwards to front; for the "European Magazine," Feb. 1, 1822.
　　8$\frac{1}{4}$×5$\frac{1}{4}$.　(4$\frac{1}{8}$×3$\frac{3}{8}$).　　　　　　28300.　18.

Sir H. Raeburn.   C. Turner, mez.
Sh. ha len. to front, facing and looking to left; white neck-cloth and frill, dark coat and waistcoat.
Ind. proof before all letters, except artists' names, facs. signature, and publication-line, Feb. 2, 1843.
15 × 11¼.   (10 × 8¼).   22226.

                                 Anon.
Obv., Head on a medal, CHANTREY SCULPTOR ET ARTIUM FAUTOR, round the upper part.
Rev., the statue of Watt, FRANCISCI CHANTREY OPUS, below; engraved in the manner invented by Collas, with waved lines; THE CHANTREY MEDAL, above.
(2¼ diamr.).   28300.   19.

CHAPMAN, WILLIAM, 1749–1832, engineer, friend of Watt and Boulton; engineer of Kildare Canal, &c.; with Rennie, engineer of the London Docks, and of the South Dock and Basin at Hull; took out several patents for inventions, and wrote several essays and reports.
See SCIENCE.

CHARLEMONT, James Caulfield, 4th Visct. and 1st Earl, 1728 –1799; Gov. of Armagh and P.C., 1754; commanded levies for defence of Belfast against the French, 1760; cr. Earl, 1763; Comm.-in-Chf. of the Irish Volunteers, 1780; K.P.; P.R.H.A., F.R.S., F.S.A., &c.
R. Livesay.   J. Dean, mez.
J. C. Smith, 5; but before any inscription below the portrait; an early state, undescribed by J. C. S.   22116.

CHARLES I., 1600–1649, son of James I.; b. at Dunfermline; suc., 1625; m. Henrietta Maria, dau. of Henri IV. of France, 1625; tried in Westminster Hall, Jany., 1649; executed at Whitehall, Jany. 30.
(Delaram).   C. Turner, mez.
Wh. len. as Prince of Wales, on horseback, directed towards right, wearing a hat with plumes, a baton in right hand; land-scape with Richmond Palace in distance; copied from a unique print by Delaram.
15 × 10⁷⁄₁₆.   (12 × 9½).   22499.

Sir A. van Dyck.   L. Vorsterman.
Bust, in armour, to front; marked with the engraver's mono-gram.
(4¼ × 3½).   25403.

Sir A. Van Dyck.   P. Lombart.
Wh. len on horseback, directed towards right, looking to front, holding in his right hand a baton, which rests on his

saddle; on right, a page carrying his helmet; surrounded with
an ornamental border; arms in centre, below; and, underneath,
the title in two lines.
$(20\frac{9}{16} \times 13\frac{5}{8})$.   E. 2.–'88.
NOTE.—The page was M. de St. Antoine. The head of the king was
aftds. erased and replaced with that of Cromwell.

Sir A. van Dyck.   J. Boydell, mez.
J. C. Smith, 1.   23122.

Sir A. van Dyck.   R. Strange, 1770.
Wh. len. in his robes, the crown and orb lying by his right
hand (which should have been his left, as it rests on the hilt of
his sword; probably it is so in the picture).
$21\frac{3}{8} \times 14\frac{1}{8}$. $(19\frac{1}{16} \times 13\frac{5}{8})$.   22225.

—— in three positions.
Sir A. van Dyck.   W. Sharp.
Sh. ha. len. to front, between a profile on the right and a t. q.
face on the left.
Impression on Ind. paper, pubd. Feb. 1, 1815, but dated
above, under centre of subject, Aug. 12, 1817 (100).
$18\frac{9}{16} \times 14\frac{1}{2}$. $(8\frac{1}{2} \times 9\frac{7}{8})$.   26648.

—— with his Queen Consort.
Sir A. van Dyck, 1634.   G. Vertue, 1742.
Sh. t. q. len.; the King, on the left, receives a garland from
the Queen.
$16\frac{1}{4} \times 22\frac{1}{2}$. $(16\frac{1}{16} \times 21\frac{7}{8})$.   23564.

—— with his Queen, Charles, Pr. of Wales, and James, D. of
York.
Sir A. Van Dyck.   B. Baron, 1741.
K. and Q. wh. len., seated, the P. stands by his father on
right; the D. is an infant in the Q.'s arms, on left.
Cut. $(20\frac{3}{16} \times 15\frac{3}{8})$.   25033.
In Genealogical Chart, 553, 1.

—— with his Queen, Charles, Pr. of Wales, and James, D. of
York.
Sir A. van Dyck.   J. Massard, 1784.
This is a reverse of the print by Baron.   23123.

Sir A. van Dyck.   Anon.
Ha. len., in hat and cloak, with the star; in an oval.
This is a copy of Hollar's print, Parthey, 1432.
$5\frac{3}{4} \times 3\frac{7}{8}$.   (Oval, $4\frac{15}{16} \times 3\frac{3}{4}$).   E. 1390.–'85.

E. Lutterell.   M. vander Gucht.
Sh. ha. len. to left, in an oval wreath; crown over arms
below, and inscription, KING CHARLES THE 1ST; a square
border of oak-leaves round the whole.
$11\frac{5}{8} \times 7\frac{1}{4}$ $(11\frac{1}{4} \times 7\frac{3}{8})$.   27992.

—— AND HENRIETTA MARIA ; the King on the left, in an oval, in a title-page to " An History of the Civill Warres of England," Englished by Henry (Carey), Earl of Monmouth (q.v.), 1641–'6, 2 vols., fol., from the Italian of G. F. Biondi, 1637 ; the Queen, in another similar oval, on the right ; Fame blowing two trumpets, between; below is the figure of Henry VII. on the right, and Richard II. on the left ; and the title, in a cartouche, 1641, between ; a battle below.

Anon.   R. E(lstracke).
(7⅝ × 5) ; oval, 1½ × 1¼.   29604.   4.

———

[W. Faithorne?]   W. Faithorne.
In the title-page to "The Reign of King Charles," &c., 1656, folio.
    L. Fagan, p. 75.   29604.   5.

———

Anon.   A. Hertochs.
    Bust, to right, in an oval wreath, supported by two cupids, on a pedestal, on which is an inscription in 10 lines.
    " ÆTERNITATI SACRUM . . . .   *Tacit. Hist. Lib. i.* ; " title to his works, London, 1662, fol., 2 vols.
    Cut.   (12¼ × 7²⁄₁₆).   29604.   3.

———

Anon.   Anon.
    Wh. len. standing on two beasts, "Usurpation and Rebellion ; " six ovals, three on each side, contain portraits of Cromwell and Bradshaw, Ireton and Fairfax, Devereux and Pembroke ; below are figures, on each side, trampling on an armed man at left, and on incendiaries, at right ; under the former is engraved " For ye King ; " under the other, " For ye Kg. & Country."
    Cut.   (6¹¹⁄₁₆ × 3⅝).   29608.   E.

———

W. Marshall del.   R. Vaughan.
    Wh. len. kneeling towards right, holding a crown of thorns, within which appears the word " Gratia"; a beam of light comes to him from a celestial crown, and on the beam are the words " Cœli Specto."
    Cut.   (5¹⁄₆ × 3½).   29608.   D.

———

Anon.   R. White.
    Wh. len. kneeling towards right, holding a crown of thorns; a ship in a storm on the left ; inscription below, in 2 lines, from Tacitus ; letterpress on back.
    6⅝ × 3¹⁴⁄₁₆.   (6 × 3⅞).   29608.   C.

———

Sir A. van Dyck.   G. Vertue.
    Ha. len. in armour, to front, holding a baton in right hand, the crown and sceptre before him, pillars on each side, and a

long inscription below, in 41 lines, quoted from Clarendon, Vol.
III., pag. 197, followed by publication-line, 1757.
13¾ × 9¾. (Port., 4½ × 3¼). 29717. 12.

—— with his QUEEN CONSORT, and the two EARLS of PEM-
BROKE and MONTGOMERY, WILLIAM and PHILIP
HERBERT ; all in a print representing part of the Royal
Palace of THEOBALD'S (interior), perhaps the only existing view
of that palace.
Interior painted by Steenwyck, the figures by Poelemburg,
on Van Balen (picture in possession of Ld. Poulett, at Hinton
St. George). S. Sparrow, jun.
Published, March 20, 1800, by Ed. Harding.
Cut. (10⅜ × 13⅝). 25805.

CHARLES [II., as], PRINCE OF WALES, JAMES, DUKE OF
YORK, PRINCESS MARY, PRINCESS ELIZABETH, and
PRINCESS ANNE, Children of King Charles the First.
Sir A. van Dyck. R. Cooper.
Wh. len., a group ; the Prince of Wales resting his right
hand on the head of a large dog.
18⅝ × 20¾. (15⁹⁄₁₆ × 19⁷⁄₁₆). 25738.

CHARLES II., 1630–1685 ; eldest son of Charles I.; b. at St.
James's ; restored, 1660 ; m. Catherine, Infanta of Portugal,
1662.
Anon. Anon, etched.
On horseback, Miss Lane sitting behind him, and preceded
by her brother, Col. Lane, also on horseback : 4 verses below.
3¾ × 4¾. (3 × 4⅜). E. 355.–'90.
See CHARLES, PRINCE OF WALES, &c., and LANE.

———
Anon. Pieter Stevensz.
On horseback, riding towards the left.
Published by N. Visscher.
9⁷⁄₁₆ × 6¼. (8⁷⁄₁₆ × 6). 25623.

—— as the first Patron of the Royal Society.
J. Evelyn. W. Hollar, 1667.
A bust, on a pedestal, supported by portraits of William,
Visct. Brouncker, the first Pres. R.S., 1661, and Francis Bacon,
Visct. St. Albans, as the representative of Experimental Philo-
sophy ; prefixed to Sprat's Hist. of the R.S.
Parthey, 459. 26660.

———
Anon. P Vanderbanck.
Sh. ha. len. to right, in armour, looking to front, wearing
long wig, lace cravat, the George, &c. ; oval in frame ; "Lon-
" don Printed for Austin Oldisworth at the Golden Bull in
" Cannon Street."
(20¾ × 17). 24101.

Sir G. Kneller.   R. Williams, mez.
J. C. Smith, 11, 3rd state, retouched.   21882.

—— "receiving the first Pine-apple cultivated in England
" from Rose the Gardener, at Dawney Court, Buckingham-
" shire, the seat of the Duchess of Cleveland."
From the original picture at Strawberry Hill ; S. Harding
delin.   R. Graves.
The King, wh. len., on the right, stands, looking to front,
while the gardener kneels, offering him the pine-apple ; fine
garden and house in background.
Ind. proof with open letters.
$13\frac{3}{8} \times 15\frac{5}{8}$. $(10 \times 12\frac{1}{8})$.   **22013.**

Anon.   C. Turner, mez.
Wh. len. to left, looking to front, seated, wearing robes ;
Windsor in the distance, crown and sceptre on table.
Proof before all letters.
$14\frac{1}{2} \times 10\frac{7}{16}$. $(11\frac{3}{4} \times 8\frac{2}{3})$.   **20951.**

Anon.   Anon.
From the Equestrian Statue " at the Entrance of Cornhill."
" Statue Equestre | de | Charles II. | à l'entrée de Cornhill."
Cut. $(8\frac{3}{4} \times 5\frac{7}{8})$.   25603.   2.

CHARLES JAMES EDWARD, Prince, 1720–1788, the " Young
Pretender," eldest son of the old Pretender, grandson of James
II.; b. at Rome ; headed the Rebellion of 1745 ; won the battle
of Preston Pans, and marched as far as Derby ; finally defeated
at Culloden, 1746 ; after various adventures, escaped abroad
from the Isle of Uist ; d. at Rome ; bur. at Frascati.
Tocqué, 1748.   J. G. Wille.
Ha. len., in armour ; oval ; "Carolus Walliæ Princeps ;"· Le
Blanc, 148, 2nd state.
$18\frac{3}{8} \times 13\frac{1}{8}$. $(17\frac{5}{8} \times 12\frac{11}{16})$.   **24250.**

Anon.   J. Daullé, 1744
T Q. len., in armour.
Undescribed proof before all letters, except the engraver's
name ; le Blanc, 149.
$16\frac{3}{4} \times 11\frac{3}{4}$. $(15\frac{13}{16} \times 11)$.   **24684.**

From an original painting (anon.), in the possession of Mr
G. A. Williams, Librarian, Cheltenham.   E. Scriven, stipple.
Wh. len. in a tartan dress, as a boy, facing and looking to
front ; pubd. Oct. 1, 1830, by Charles Tilt, Fleet Street,
London.
$15 \times 10\frac{7}{16}$. $(6\frac{13}{16} \times 4\frac{13}{16})$.   **22173.**

—-- disguised in woman's dress.
Anon.   J. Williams, mez.
J. C. Smith, pp. 1593–'4.   22944.

CHARLOTTE, of MECKLENBURG-STRELITZ, 1744–1818, Queen
Consort of George III., m. 1761.
  F. Coates, R.A.   W. W. Ryland.
  Wh. len. seated, with the Princess Royal, an infant, lying in
her lap.
  Published . . . July 31, 1770.
  $23\frac{5}{8}$(?) × 15. $(21\frac{1}{4} × 13\frac{4}{16})$.   22223.

  J. Zauffely.   R. Houston, mez., 1772.
  J. C. Smith, 25, 2nd state.   22115.

  H. Edridge, 1814.   S. W. Reynolds, 1819,
            mixed etching and mez.
  T. Q. len. seated, to right, looking to front, with hands
folded in lap.
  Open letter proof.
  15 × $10\frac{7}{8}$. $(11 × 8\frac{13}{16})$.   5046. A.
  In Genealogical Chart, 553. 1.

  Sir W. Beechey (?).   B. Smith (?), dotted style.
  Wh. len. holding a little dog in her arms, two other dogs by
her side.
  Proof before letters.
  $23\frac{1}{4} × 16\frac{3}{4}$. $(20\frac{5}{8} × 14\frac{3}{4})$.   22017.
  See also GEORGE III.

CHARLOTTE AUGUSTA, PRINCESS OF WALES, 1796–181$\overset{7}{}$,
daughter of George, Prince of Wales, aftds. George IV.; m.
in 1816 to Prince Leopold of Coburg, aftds. King of the
Belgians.
  Sir T. Lawrence.   M. A. Bourlier.
  As a child, t. q. len. to right, looking to left, holding a bird in
her right hand.
  Published by E. Harding, 19 May, 1806.
  $10\frac{3}{4} × 8\frac{1}{4}$. $(7\frac{3}{4} × 6\frac{1}{2})$.   25049.
  In Genealogical Chart, 553. 1.

  Charlotte Jones.   J. S. Agar, stipple.
  Wh. len., to front, looking to left.
  Ind. proof, inscription scratched.
  Published, March 31, 1814, by Colnaghi and Co.
  $18\frac{7}{8} × 15\frac{3}{8}$. $(11\frac{7}{8} × 8\frac{11}{14})$.   28151.

Sir T. Lawrence. R. Golding.
T. Q. len. to right, looking front.
Dedication to George IV. on a separate plate below.
Proof with etched letters. Published Jany. 1, 1822, by
Messrs. Colnaghi & Co. 22152.
Also an impression with the letters strengthened with a
second line to each.
$22\frac{1}{8} \times 15\frac{1}{4}$. $(18\frac{7}{16} \times 12\frac{11}{16})$. 23551.

[G. Dawe.] Anon., mez.
Wh. len., seated.
Proof before all letters.
$26\frac{1}{2} \times 16\frac{3}{4}$. $(24\frac{15}{16} \times 16\frac{5}{8})$. 23152.

G. Dawe, R.A. H. Dawe and T. Hodgetts, mez.
T. Q. len. seated.
Proof, with inscription scratched.
Cut. $(7\frac{5}{16} \times 13\frac{3}{4})$. 27945.
—— with LEOPOLD, Prince (1790–1865, m. 1816, King of the
Belgians, 1831).
Anon. Anon., chalk and dotted style.
Ha. len., in Opera box; the Princess, on the left, leaning on
her right elbow.
Cut. (16 × 14). 25048.
In Genealogical Chart, 553. 1.

Anon. Anon., etched and stippled.
Ha. len. to left, looking upwards, holding a baby in her arms;
a medallion, supported by a mourning female figure; a broken
tree and weeping willow behind.
Proof before letters, except the date, Nov. 6, 1817, below the
medallion.
Cut. $(9\frac{1}{2} \times 7\frac{1}{2})$. 29717. 17

CHARLOTTE AUGUSTA MATILDA, PRINCESS ROYAL,
eldest daughter of George III., 1766–1828; m. 1797 to the
Hered. Pr. of Würtemberg.
R. H. Ramberg. P. W. Tomkins, stipple.
T. Q. len., seated, with a book; oval.
Cut. $(11 \times 8\frac{3}{4})$. 26725. 1.
Also a duplicate, in Genealogical Chart, 553. 1.
$13\frac{11}{16} \times 10\frac{1}{4}$. 25067. 1.

Sir W. Beechey. Cheesman, stipple.
Ha. len. to right, in oval.
Published 19 May, 1806.
Cut. $(7\frac{1}{4} \times 6\frac{3}{4})$. 25056.
In Genealogical Chart, 553. 1.
CHATHAM, JOHN PITT, 2nd Earl of, K.G., 1756–1835;
eldest son of the great Earl of Chatham, and brother of
O 82849. G

William Pitt; suc. 1778; served in the American War; General
Officer; First Lord of the Admiralty, 1788-'94; commanded
the expedition to Walcheren, 1809.

   J. Hoppner, R.A.   C. Turner, mez.
   Proof before title, &c.
   Published Aug. 31, 1809, by Messrs. Colnaghi & Co.
   13⅜×9¼. (11⅜×9½).   22823.

CHATHAM, WILLIAM PITT, 1st Earl of, 1708-1778, Statesman
and Orator; "the Great Commoner;" Sec. of State, and 1st
Minister with the Duke of Newcastle, 1757, resigned, 1761;
cr. Earl of Chatham, 1766; Ld. Privy Seal and 1st Minister,
1766-'8; seized with sudden illness, while speaking on the
American question, in the House of Lords, April 7, and d.
May 11, at Hayes, Kent.

   W. Hoare.   R. Houston, mez.
   J. C Smith, 94.   22050.

   R. Brompton and J. Wilton, R.A.   J. K. Sherwin.
   T. Q. len. to right, left hand extended; wearing robes and
wig; August 1778.
   15×11⅜. (14×10⅛).   22972.

   [J. K. Sherwin?]   J. K. Sherwin.
   In ordinary dress; figures of Britannia and a Genius holding
a Caduceus below; oval.
   Published   March 25, 1790.
   7⅞×4⅜ (?). (7×4⅜).   29962. B.

—— fainting during his last speech in the House of Lords.
   J. S. Copley, R.A.   F. Bartolozzi, R.A.
   A composition of many figures; that of Chatham is on the
right, supported by several lords, one of whom, wearing the
garter, holds him by the left arm.
   The picture is in the National Gallery, with a key to the
names of the persons represented.
   Proof before all letters, except the artists' names.
   (22⁷⁄₁₆×30½).   22000.

CHAUCER, GEOFFREY, 1328-1400, the "Father of English
Poetry;" b. in London; gained the favour of Edward III.,
who sent him on embassies to France and Italy; author of the
"Canterbury Tales," "Troilus and Creseide," &c.; had a pen-
sion from the Crown; known as a friend of Wycliffe; bur. in
Westminster Abbey.

   Anon.   J. Houbraken, 1741.
   Sh. ha. len. to right, wearing hood, gown, and inkhorn
hanging from button; oval in frame, a lyre, myrtle, &c., below,
in Birch's "Lives."
   14¹³⁄₁₆×9⅞. (14¼×8¾).   21813.

CHELMSFORD, Rt. Hon. Sir Frederick Thesiger, Baron, 1794–1878 ; ent. Navy at an early age ; called to the Bar, 1813 ; K.C., 1834 ; Solicitor-Genl. and Knt., 1844 ; Attorn.-Genl., 1845, and '52 ; Lord Chancellor, and er. Baron, 1858 ; resigned, 1859 ; resumed, 1866–'68.
    See DERBY CABINET.

CHESELDEN, William, 1688–1752, surgeon, b. in Leicestershire ; stud. surgery under Cowper, and rose to the head of his profession ; surgeon to Q. Caroline, St. Thomas's and Chelsea Hospitals ; eminent operator and ophthalmic surgeon ; author of works on Anatomy, Osteology, and Lithotomy ; friend of Pope ; d. of apoplexy, at Bath.
    J. Richardson.   J. Faber, jun., mez.
    J. C. Smith, 70, 1st state.   21742.

CHESTER, Miss, of Covent Garden Theatre.
    J. Jackson, R.A.   S. W. Reynolds, mez.
    Full ha. len. slightly to right, looking to left, wearing a hat with broad leaf and feathers, a scarf, &c.
    Proof with scratched letters ; March 20, 1826.
    14 × 10.   (9¾ × 6¼).   26649.

CHESTERFIELD, Philip Dormer Stanhope, 4th Earl of, 1694–1773 ; suc. his father, 1726 ; educ. at Cambr. ; M.P. for St. Germans and Lostwithiel ; ambas. to Holland, Lord Steward, Lord Lt. of Ireland, Sec. of State, K.G. ; famous chiefly for his wit, his " Letters to his son," and his treatment of Johnson ; friend of Pope, who speaks of his " Attic Wit ; " d. at Chesterfield House, South Audley St. ; bur. at Shelford, Notts.
    T. Gainsborough.   Anon, mez.
    Ha. len. to left, looking to front, wearing the star and ribbon of the Garter, and holding a volume, labelled " Cicero | de | Senect." | in his right hand ; oval at corners, in border.
    Open letter proof ; Jany. 1, 1826.
    13⅛ × 10.   (11⅝ × 10).   24068.

CHEYNE, George, 1671–1743, Physician ; b. in Scotland ; stud. medicine under Pitcairn ; wrote several works on diet, health, and long life ; practised at Bath, where he died.
    I. van Diest.   J. Faber, junr., mez.
    J. C. Smith, 80, 1st state ; " only three known " (besides this ?), according to J. C. S.   27647.

CHICHELE, or CHICHELEY, or CHYCHELE, Henry, c. 1362–1443, educ. at Winchester and Oxf. ; B.C.L., 1389–'90 ; LL.D., 1396 ; rector of St. Stephen's, Walbrook ; ordd., and appointed to archdeaconry, Dorset, 1397, and prebend. at Salisbury, &c. ; sent on mission to Rome, 1405 ; to France, and 1407, to Siena, to Gregory XII. ; bishop of St. David's, 1408 ; Archbishop, Canterbury, 1414 ; founded All Souls', Oxf., 1437, completed, 1443.
    From a window at All Souls'.   F. Bartolozzi, 1772.

Wh. len. to right, crozier in left hand, the right raised as if in the act of benediction.
Cut. $(17\frac{1}{2} \times 9\frac{3}{4})$. 25822.

CHICHESTER, Thomas, 2nd Earl of, and Baron Pelham, 1756–1826; Sec. of State, Postmaster-General, &c.
Hoppner, R.A. S. W. Reynolds, mez.
Ha. len. slightly to left, looking to front.
Open letter proof (?). Published July 4, 1798.
Cut. $(11\frac{5}{16} \times 9\frac{1}{4})$. 27667.

CHIFNEY, Samuel, the younger, 1786–1854; disting. jockey; younger son of S. Chifney (1753?–1807), trainer and jockey; he first rode for the Prince of Wales at Stockbridge, 1802; won the Oaks five times, the Derby twice; kept training-stables; trained for Mr. Thornhill and Lord Darlington; had, with his brother (William), some racehorses, with which they were not successful; d. at Hove, Brighton.
(C. Turner?) C. Turner, mez.
Wh. len. to right, looking to front, about to weigh; saddle, &c., on left arm; horse behind him; scales on right.
Open letter proof (?), Oct. 1807, the year in which Sam Chifney junr. won the Oaks, and his father died.
$18\frac{3}{8} \times 12\frac{7}{8}$. $(16\frac{1}{2} \times 12\frac{7}{8})$. **24102.**

——

B. Marshall del. R. Woodman, stipple.
Ha. len. to left, as if in the saddle, looking to front; left arm slightly extended, as if holding the reins; in jockey's dress; vignette.
Ind. proof, March, 1828.
This appeared in the "Sporting Magazine" (1828), where it accompanied and illustrated a notice of this jockey, then at the height of his reputation; it is there stated that B. Marshall's drawing was executed in 1818.
$7\frac{1}{2} \times 5\frac{7}{16}$. $(5\frac{3}{8} \times 4\frac{1}{2})$. 22824.

CHILD, Francis. *See* ALDERMEN.

CHRISTIAN (Prince), H.R.H. Frederick Christian Charles Augustus, of Schleswig-Holstein, b. 1831, m. 1866, Princess Helena; K.G., &c.
F. Winterhalter. J. A. Vinter, lith., 1866.
T. Q. len. to right. Oval.
$(18\frac{7}{8} \times 15\frac{1}{2})$. 22199.

CHRISTIAN, Helena Augusta Victoria, Princess, 1846– , m. to Prince Christian of Schleswig-Holstein, 1866.
F. Winterhalter. T. Fairland, lith., 1849.
As a child; in a circle.
$(11\frac{7}{8}$ diamr.) 22192.

F. Winterhalter. Léon Noel, lith., 1861.
Before her marriage, as Princess Helena.
(21×15¼). 22187.

CHURCHILL, CHARLES, 1731-1764, satirist; son of a clergyman; b. in Westm.; educ. at Westm.; ordained by Dr. Sherlock; left his profession; m. early, but became dissipated; displayed much ability in his poems and prose writings; the "Rosciad," a severe satire on the Theatres, 1761, "Prophecy of Famine," in favour of Wilkes's party, &c.; satirized Hogarth, who replied with a caricature which has become famous; d., "a spendthrift alike of money and of wit," at Boulogne, while visiting Wilkes.
J. S. C. Schaak. T. Burford, mez.
J. C. Smith, 2. 25769.

CIBBER, MRS. SUSANNAH MARIA, c. 1716-1766, daughter of the elder Arne, "the political upholsterer," of King St., Cov. Garden, and sister of Dr. Arne, the composer; m. to Theophilus, the son of Colley Cibber, from whom she was separated for many years; sang in Handel's operas; acted tragedy, in which she excelled, until her death; buried in Westminster Abbey.
P. van Bleeck. P. van Bleeck, mez.
J. C. Smith, 1, 4th state. 26421.
See also GARRICK, 6.

CIPRIANI, GIOVANNI BATTISTA, 1727-1785, b. at Florence, pupil of Heckford, an English painter; stud. at Rome; came to England, 1755; acquired reputation rapidly; foundation member of R.A.; his compositions popularised by the engravings of his friend, Bartolozzi; exhibited till 1779; his pictures were weak; his best art in his drawings, full of beauty of outline; designed the R.A. diploma; buried at Chelsea.
Rigaud. R. Earlom, stipple.
Ha. len. to right, looking to front, holding palette and brushes in left hand; picture on easel behind, on right; oval.
Open letter proof; Septr. 29, 1789.
8⅝×6⅜. (5⅛×4 7⁄16). 27205.
See also CARLINI.

CLARE, JOHN FITZGIBBON, 1st Earl of. See FITZGIBBON.

CLARENDON, EDWARD HYDE, first Earl of, 1608-1674; Chancellor of Exchequer to Charles I.; Lord Chancellor, 1657; cr. earl and Ld. Chancr., 1661; lost favour and exiled, 1667; wrote "History of the Rebellion," 1670; d. at Rouen.
D. Loggan, ad vivum sculp.
Sh. ha. len. to right, looking to front, in robes, with long hair; the bag is seen behind, on right; 4 lines of inscription, below.
Cut. (11 1⁄16×7 7⁄16). 21969.

CLARENDON, George William Frederick Villiers, 4th
Earl of, 1800–1870; educ. at Cambr.; attaché, 1820–'23;
envoy extr. to Madrid, 1833–'39; G.C.B.; suc., 1838; P.C.;
Ld. Lieut., Ireland, 1847–'52; Gr. Master, order of St. Patrick,
1852; K.G., 1849; Sec. for Foreign Affairs, 1853–'8, 1865–'6,
1868 to death; Amb. Extr. to Paris, 1856; &c.
    J. Catterson Smith.   G. Sanders, mixed mez.
    T. Q. len. in official dipl. uniform, wearing star; books on
table by him, on right.
    Ind. proof before all letters, except artists' names.
    22¾ × 18.   (18 × 14¼).   24208.

    Anon.   Anon.
    Bust, vignette.
    Ind. proof before all letters.
    12 × 9.   (6 × 5½).   24209.
    See also ABERDEEN Cabinet.

CLARK, Edwin,   —   , Chief Assistant Engineer, Britannia
Bridge.
    See MENAI Straits.

CLARK, Sir James, 1788–1870, educ. at Fordyce Gram. Sch.
and King's Coll., Aberdeen; M.R.C.S. Edin., 1809; assist.-
surgeon, R.N., 1809–'16, when placed on half-pay; M.D. Edin.,
1817; phys. at Rome, 1819–'26; in London, 1826–'60; L.R.C.P.,
1826; F.R.S., 1832; first phys. in ord. to the Queen, 1837;
cr. bart., 1837; M. Senate, Univ. Lond., 1838–'65; K.C.B.,
1866; pubd. some medical works and memoirs.
    H. W. Pickersgill, R.A.   G. Zobel, mixed mez.
    T. Q. len. to front, slightly to right, looking to left, seated,
with hands loosely clasped; inkstand and papers on table at left.
    Ind. proof before all letters.
    21¾ × 16¾.   (17⅞ × 14₁₆).   24212.

CLARK, Latimer,   —   , Assistant Engineer at the Conference
about the floating of one of the tubes of the Britannia Bridge.
    See MENAI Straits.

CLARKE, Adam, c. 1762–1832, LL.D., b. at Moybeg, Co.
Londonderry; educ., through the influence of John Wesley, at
the Kingswood School, near Bristol; became proficient in
Oriental literature; itinerant preacher, 1781–1807; settled in
London, 1805, and devoted himself to his Commentary on the
Bible; retired, 1815, to an estate at Millbrook, Lancashire,
bought for him by friends; returned to London, 1823, but went
afterwards to Ruslip, Middlesex, where he died of cholera;
wrote, besides his Commentary, several other works of research.
    T. Mosses.   Robinson.
    Wh. len. seated, at right, turned towards two Buddhist
priests, at left, to whom he is speaking.
    Ind. proof before all letters.
    16¼ × 12¼.   (6₁₆ × 8).   23137.

CLARKE, Sir Alured, c. 1745-1832, ensign in 50th, 1759; captain, 5th foot, 1767; major, 1771; Lt.-col., 1775; exchd. to command of 7th fusiliers, 1777; Govr. Jamaica, 1789; Maj.-Gen.; to India, 1795; Commandr.-in-Chf. Bengal, 1797-8, and Comr.-in-chf. India, 1798; Col. 7th fusiliers; Field-marshal; K.B.; &c.

Sir W. Beechey, R.A., 1794.   J. Bromley, mez.

Ha. len. to front, looking to right, hands resting on sword-hilt.

Open letter proof, Aug. 1, 1833.

21½ × 15½. (16½ × 13,³⁄.).   27541.

CLARKE, Sir Charles Mansfield, 1782-1857, b. in London; educ. at St. Paul's school and St. George's hospital; M.R.C.S., 1802; surgeon to Q. Charlotte's Lying-in-hospital; M.R.C.P.; F.R.C.P.; F.R.S., 1825; M.D. (Lambeth), 1827; phys. to Q. Adelaide, 1830; cr. bart., 1831; author of a work on Diseases of Women.

S. Lane.   T. Hodgetts, mez.

T. Q. len. to front, seated, with right hand to face, right elbow on table, left hand holding a paper.

Open letter proof, Sepr. 1, 1833.

19½ × 13¾. (16¾ × 13¼).   22825.

CLARKE, Edward Daniel, 1769-1822, traveller, antiquary, and mineralogist; b. at Willingdon, Sussex; educ. at Cambridge; travelled extensively in Europe and Asia, 1799-1802; Prof. of Mineralogy, Cambr., 1808; a donor to the public library, Cambr., of antiquities, &c.; author of "Travels;" LL.D.; d. in London.

J. Opie, R.A.   E. Scriven, line and stipple.

Ha. len. to left, facing and looking to front, wearing gown and hood; July 18, 1825.

Ind. proof.

16 × 12¾. (10,⁷⁄₁₆ × 8,⁷⁄₁₆, excl. of ruled border). 22970.

CLARKE, Mary Anne, 1776-1852, b. in London, daughter of a man named Thompson; received a fair education; married to Clarke, a man whose station in society has not been ascertained, 1794; became the mistress of the Duke of York, 1803; very extravagant; sold patronage; accused, but acquitted; occasioned great scandals; imprisoned for libel; retired to Paris, 1815; d. at Boulogne.

Anon.   W. Hopwood, stipple.

T. Q. len. to front, seated, holding a letter in right hand, raising the corner of her veil with her left.

Printed in colours, July 4, 1809.

11½ × 8⅘. (9⅛ × 5¾, excl. of ruled border, ⅔). E. 1063-'88.

CLARKE, Samuel, 1675-1729, b. at Norwich; educ. there and at Cambridge; B.A., 1695; one of the earliest supporters of Newton's principles at that University; ent. the Church; chaplain to Bishop Moore; obtained some preferments, and was appointed rector of St. James's, Westminster, 1709; wrote

many excellent and celebrated works, in philosophy and divinity,
and was offered the mastership of the mint at Newton's
death.

    T. Gibson.   J. Simon, mez.
    J. C. Smith, 40, 2nd state.   22455.

CLARKSON, THOMAS, 1760–1846, the first advocate of the
abolition of Slavery; b. at Wisbech; began his agitation, 1786;
contin. to work in the cause during all the remainder of his
life; he and Wilberforce were vice-presdts. of Anti-Slavery
Society, 1823, when the Emancipation Bill was passed; operated
on for cataract, 1836; d. at Playford Hall, nr. Ipswich.

    A. E. Chalon, R.A.   C. Turner, mez.
    Wh. len. to left, seated, looking to front, left hand on arm of
chair, a pen in right; maps, inkstand, &c., on table, at left.
Proof before all letters.
    22¼ × 17⅝. (17¼ × 13⅞).   22117.

CLAVERHOUSE. *See* DUNDEE.

CLAXTON, CHRISTOPHER, – , ent. Navy, 1804, present at
several engagements, 1806; Lieut., 1810; did useful service in
the Tagus, in co-operation with the troops at Torres Vedras, and
in command of the gun-boats; Commander, 1842; Harbour-
master, Bristol; superintendent of the Nautical arrangements
for floating one of the tubes of the Britannia Bridge.
    See MENAI STRAITS.

CLEAVER, WILLIAM, 1742–1815, eldest son of Rev. W. Cleaver;
educ. at Oxf.; B.A., 1761, fellow of Brasenose; M.A., 1764;
vicar of Northop; preb. Westminster, 1784; Master, Brasenose,
1785; bishop of Chester, 1787; of Bangor, 1800; of St. Asaph,
1806; chiefly remembered for an anecdote connecting his name
with that of De Quincy, who afterwards praised him warmly in
"Confessions of an English opium-eater."

    J. Hoppner, R.A.   J. Ward, mez.
    J. C. Smith, 11, second state.   27997.

CLEMENTINA SOBIESKI, MARIA, 1702–1735, Consort of
"The Old Pretender," 1719.
    Davids.   P. I. Drevet.
    In a rich dress, with large pearls.
    Didot, 487.
    17⅝ × 12⁷⁄₁₆. (17½ × 12¼).   E. 2163–'89.

CLEVELAND, BARBARA VILLIERS, Duchess of, c. 1641–1709,
d. of Sir William Villiers, 2nd Lord Grandison (a gallant
cavalier, killed at siege of Bristol, æt. 30); m. to Roger
Palmer, and went with him to Holland, 1659; made the
acquaintance there of Charles II., whose mistress she became,
and remained for more than 10 years, and over whom she
exercised the most pernicious influence; cr. Countess of Castlemaine (and her husband, Earl), 1660; Duchess of Cleveland,

1670; m. 2ndly, to Beau Fielding, whom she pros. for bigamy ; barbarously ill-treated by him ; d. of dropsy, at Chiswick.

    Sir P. Lely.   T Watson, mez.

    J. C. Smith, 5 (Beauties of Windsor, VI), 2nd state. 22070.

CLIFFORD, GEORGE. *See* CUMBERLAND.

CLIFFORD, THOMAS, First Lord, of Chudleigh, 1630–1673 , Statesman ; educ. at Oxf. ; travelled ; M.P., 1661 ; mentioned by Pepys as of small means ; app. Commissioner for the relief of sick and wounded and prisoners of war, 1664 ; joined the fleet ; present at the great battle, June 3, 1665 ; Knt. ; took part in expedition to Bergen ; present at battle off Harwich ; active at Court, and in Parlt. ; one of the famous Cabal ; cr. Baron, 1672 ; Lord High Treasurer, Treasurer of the Exchequer, &c. ; ruined by the Test Act, 1673 ; resigned office, and retired.

    Sir P. Lely.   H. Crease and W. Holl, stipple.

    Published, Feby. 1, 1817, by Lackington, Allen and Co.

    Proof.

    $14\frac{3}{16} \times 10\frac{5}{16}$. $(7 \times 5\frac{9}{16})$.   27162.

CLIFT, WILLIAM, 1775–1849, b. at Burcombe ; educ. at Bodmin, came to London, 1792 ; apprent. to John Hunter, the great surgeon ; became custodian of Hunter's Museum ; F.R.S. ; contrib. to the " Transactions " of the Royal and Geological Societies ; d. in Hampstead Road.

    Claudet, daguer.   W. Bosley, lith.

    Ha. len. to front, seated, looking to left ; left hand on handle of walking-stick, facs. signature below ; July 12, 1849.

    Ind. paper proof.

    $(8\frac{3}{4} \times 8\frac{1}{16})$.   27631.

CLINT, GEORGE, 1770–1854, painter and engraver, b. in London, son of a hairdresser ; apprent. to a fishmonger ; worked in an attorney's office ; tried house - painting ; began painting miniatures with skill and sentiment of beauty ; took up mezzo-tint, chalk manner, and line ; engraved subjects by Stubbs and Lawrence ; scraped Harlow's " Kemble Family," thrice re-engraved ; painted dramatic scenes and groups ; A.R.A., 1821 ; retired in pique, 1835.

    G. Clint.   T. Lupton, mez.

    Ha. len. to left, looking to front ; holding palette, brushes, and mahl-stick in left hand ; " Paul Pry " picture behind him ; facs. subscripn. and signature below.

    Proof, presented by the engraver, who was Clint's pupil, to A. Cooper, R.A.

    $14\frac{1}{2} \times 10\frac{3}{4}$. $(11\frac{13}{16} \times 9\frac{1}{3})$.   24738.

CLOWES, BUTLER, –1782, mezzotintist, scraped about 30 plates of portraits, subjects, and some caricatures after Collett ; he also published several plates by James Watson and others.

    [B. Clowes.]   S. Harding, stipple and etching.

Sh. ha. len. slightly to right, facing and looking slightly to left, wearing a cap; collar open at throat; oval; copied from his own mez. port. of himself; pubd. Oct. 4, 1802.

$7\frac{5}{8} \times 5\frac{3}{4}$. $(5\frac{1}{4} \times 4\frac{3}{4})$. 26273.

CLYDE, Colin Campbell, 1st Baron, 1792–1863, eld. child of John McLiver (of Glasgow) by Agnes Campbell; b. at Glasgow, where he was educ. and at Gosport; ensign, 9th Foot, in name of Campbell; Lt. Col., 98th Foot, 1835–'53; A.D.C. to the Queen, 1842–'54; commanded 3rd Division under Gough in Punjaub, 1848–9; com. Peshawur district, 1851–'2; Com. Highl. Brig., Crimea, 1854; Col., 67th Foot, 1854–'58; Com. 1st Divn., 1854–'5; Com.-in-Chf., India, 1857; Stormed Lucknow; returned to England, 1858; General, Col. Coldstr. Guards, &c.; cr. Baron, 1858; G.C.B.; K.C.S.I., &c.

Anon.   Anon., mixed mez.

Wh. len. to front, in undress uniform, hat with puggree in left hand.

Ind. proof before all letters.

$30\frac{3}{4} \times 19\frac{1}{2}$. $(25 \times 14\frac{1}{2})$. 24204.

COBBETT, William, 1762–1835, Essayist, Politician, and Agriculturist; edited "The Porcupine's Gazette," and "Weekly Register;" an opponent of Government, 1806–'32; M.P. for Oldham, 1832; was the leading journalist in the movement for Parliamentary Reform; did not live long enough to serve it much in Parliament.

J. R. Smith.   W. Ward, mez.

J. C. Smith, 28. 22222.

COBDEN, Richard, 1804–1865, son of a farmer; b. at Dunford, Midhurst; partner in a Manchester cotton-factory; a leader in the Anti-Corn Law League; M.P. for Stockport, West Riding, and Rochdale; foremost among promoters of Free Trade, Reform, &c.; negotiated the Commercial Treaty with France, 1864; d. in London.

L. Dickinson.   J. H. Baker, stipple.

Bust, to left, looking to front; dark neckcloth; vignette; Newcastle-upon-Tyne, May 1, 1863.

Open letter proof.

$(9\frac{1}{4} \times 8)$. 22906.

COBHAM, Sir Richard Temple, Bart., of Stowe, co. Buckingham, aftds. Viscount, c. 1669–1749; ensign in Pr. George of Denmark's Foot, 1685; suc. his father, 1697; M.P. 1697; disting. in Flemish wars and Siege of Lille, 1708; Maj. Genl., 1709; Lieut. Genl., 1710; envoy to Vienna, cr. Baron Cobham, 1714; P.C.; Visct., 1718; Pope dedicated to him his first "Epistle."

Sir G. Kneller.   J. Faber, junr., mez.

J. C. Smith, 208 (Kitcat, 22). 22826.

COCHRANE, Thomas, Lord. See DUNDONALD.

COCKER, Edward, 1631–1675. Schoolmaster and Penman;
pub. copybooks, "England's Penman," "Cocker's Morals," and
a treatise on Arithmetic, which was very successful and passed
through many editions; hence came the phrase, "According to
Cocker."
 Anon.   R. Gaywood, etched.
 Ha. len., to right, looking to front, holding a pen in right
hand; oval; two pens above, crossed through a laurel wreath;
a winged boy on each side, one reading (on left), the other
writing; four verses below; prefixed to his "Penmanship,"
1664.
 5½×6½. (5¾×6¾).   27647.

COETLOGON, Charles Edward de, c. 1746–1820, Calvinistic
divine, son of the Chevalier Denis de Coetlogon, M.D.; educ.
at Chr. Hospital, and Pembr. Hall, Cambr.; B.A., 1770; M.A.,
1773; assist. chapl. to M. Madan at Lock Hospl., chapl. to
Ld. Mayor Pickett, 1789; Vicar of Godstone, Surrey; gained
much reputation as a preacher; pubd. many sermons and other
works.
 See MADAN, M.

COKE, or COOKE, Sir Edward, c. 1549–1634; Q. Elizabeth's
Atty., 1593; Ch. Justice of King's Bench, 1613; disgraced for
defending the rights of Parliament against James I., 1615;
discharged from the Justiceship, 1616; imprisoned 1621–'2;
published his "Institutes," part 1, 1628.
 [D. Loggan?]   D. Loggan.
 Sh, ha. len. slightly to right, looking to front, in robes, with
chain, ruff, and flat cap; arms below, and inscription in three
lines.
 From "Origines Juridicales."
 11½×7¾(?). (9¼×7½).   26677.

COKE, Thomas William, M.P. See LEICESTER.

COLBORNE, N, William Ridley, 1779–1854, M.P. 1807–
 J. Jackson, R.A.   David Lucas, mez.
 T. Q. len. seated, turned to left, looking to front.
Open letter proof.
 Cut. 13⁷⁄₁₆×9¾(?). (11¾×9½(?)).   27208.

COLCHESTER, Charles Abbot, 1st Lord, 1757–1829, statesman, b. at Abingdon; educ. at Oxford; M.P., 1795; Sec. for
Ireland, 1801; Speaker of the House of Commons, 1802–17;
cr. Baron, 1817.
 J. Northcote, R.A.   C. Picart, stipple.
 T. Q. len. to left, seated, in robes, with mace on right of
print; both hands on arms of chair; coat of arms below, in
middle.
 Cut. (17¾×14¾).   22445.

COLE, Sir Galbraith, Lowry, 1772–1842, second son of
William Willoughby Cole, first Earl of Enniskillen; entd.

army, 1787; major, 1793; present at Guadeloupe, 1784, Lt.
Col.; served in Ireland, 1797; Col., 1801; M.P., 1803; at battle
of Maida, 1806, Maj.-Genl., 1808; in Peninsula, 1809; saved
the day at Albuera; at Salamanca, 1812, and wounded;
Lt.-Genl., 1813; Govr., Mauritius, 1823–'8; Cape of Good
Hope, 1828–'33; Genl., 1830.
> Sir T. Lawrence.   Anon. Mez.
> Ha. len. to front, in uniform, with stars and clasps.
> Proof before all letters.
> $14\frac{7}{16} \times 11$. $(10\frac{1}{8} \times 9)$.   25737.

COLERAINE, HENRY HARE, Lord, 3rd Baron, 1708–1749;
matr. at Oxford, 1712; great collector of prints and drawings,
which he gave partly to his college (Corpus), and partly to the
Socy. of Antiquaries; M.P., Boston, 1730; d. s. p. at
Tottenham, when the peerage became extinct.
> W. Faithorne.   G. Vertue.
> T. Q. len. to right, looking to front, in robes, a coronet in his
right hand, left hand on table. Arms below.
> This plate was begun by Faithorne, and left much unfinished.
An impression (in that state) is in the Br. Mm. It was finished
by Vertue.
> $14\frac{5}{16} \times 9$. $(11\frac{1}{8} \times 8\frac{1}{2})$.   23569.

COLERIDGE, SIR JOHN TAYLOR, 1790–1876, judge; published his edition of Blackstone's "Commentaries," 1825; a
Justice of King's Bench, 1835; retired, 1858.
> Mrs. Carpenter.   S. Cousins, A.R.A., mixed mez.
> T. Q. len. to right, seated, with chin resting on left hand,
the other hand on an open book on his knee; in robes.
> A presented Proof before all letters, except the artists' names,
from Mrs. Carpenter to John Sheepshanks, Esqr. (Sheepshanks
gift). A companion print to the portrait of Sir John Patteson.
> $19\frac{1}{8} \times 15$. $(16\frac{11}{16} \times 12\frac{1}{8})$.   18879.

COLERIDGE, SAMUEL TAYLOR, 1772–1834, poet and philosopher, b. at Ottery St. Mary, son of John Coleridge, Vicar
of the town and master of the Gram. School; educ. at Chr.
Hospital, and Jesus Coll., Cambr.; fled to London, 1793;
enlisted, 15th Dragoons, but discharged, 1794; held liberal
opinions in politics and theology; pub. vol. of poems, Bristol,
1795; occasionally preached, 1796; wrote "Christabel,"
"Kubla Khan," "Lyrical Ballads," which included the
"Ancient Mariner;" "Zapoyla," "Sibylline Leaves," &c.
> J. Northcote, R.A.   W. Say, mez.
> Ha. len. slightly to right, looking to left; high white necker-
chief, dark hair. Pub. by the Engraver, April 20th, 1805.
> Cut. $(12\frac{1}{8} \times 9\frac{1}{16})$.   24659.

> Washington Allston.   S. Cousins, A.R.A., mixed mez.
> T. Q. len. to left, seated, right hand in bosom, left holding a
book; a Gothic arch and window behind, on left. The picture
is in the National Portrait Gallery.

Ind. proof before all letters, except the artists' names and
the words, "Subscribers Proof."
21⅔ × 16. (16⁷⁄₈ × 12⅝).   23761.

COLERIDGE, SARA, 1802–1852, daughter of Samuel Taylor
Coleridge, b. at Greta Hall, near Keswick; brought up under the
care of Southey, and in the frequent society of Wordsworth;
published, at the age of 20, a translation of Dobrizhoffer's Latin
"Account of the Abipones," and wrote and edited many other
works, including her father's writings, after the death of her
husband and cousin, Henry Nelson Coleridge, to whom she was
m. in 1829; with Dora Wordsworth and Edith Southey,
celebrated in Wordsworth's "Trias;" "Phantasmion" was
her chief work.
    S. Lawrence.   R. J. Lane, lith.
    Ha. len. slightly to left, looking to front, wearing a widow's
cap; vignette, in oval: facs. subscription and signature below.
    (11 × 10⅜).   23596.

COLET, JOHN, c. 1467–1519, dean of St. Paul's and founder of
St. Paul's School; son of Sir Henry Colet, twice lord mayor of
London; educ. at Oxf.; M.A. after 7 years of hard study;
held several benefices; great classical and mathematical scholar;
travelled abroad; ordd., 1497; priest, 1498; lectured gratuitously at Oxf., 1497–'8, Erasmus being among his audience, and
afterwards a fast friend; Dean, 1504; founded the school,
1510.
                                        J. Faber, senr., mez.
    J. C. Smith, 58, among the Reformers; the retouched state,
with R. Houston's name substituted for Faber's, &c.
                                                      27669.

COLLARD, WILLIAM FREDERICK, 1776–1866, son of W. Collard
of Wiveliscombe, Somerset, and younger brother of Frederick
William Collard; b. at Wiveliscombe; became, and remained, a
member of the firm of Muzio Clementi & Co., pianoforte-makers,
26, Cheapside, till 1831; partner with his brother, 1831–'42;
inventor of many improvements in the manufacture; d. at
Folkestone.
    J. Lonsdale.   T. Lupton, mez.
    T. Q. len. to front, seated, reading a large book with clasps,
which lies on another book on a table, on which his left arm rests.
    Ind. paper, open letter proof; a private plate.
    20¼ (?) × 15½ (?). (16 × 13).   27075.

COLLINGWOOD, CUTHBERT, 1st Baron, 1750–1810, Admiral,
served constantly under Nelson; under Howe, off Ushant, June
1, 1794; at Trafalgar, 1805, where, by Nelson's death, he suc.
to command; cr. Baron, 1805, with pensions; d. on board his
flagship, "Ville de Paris," while cruising off Minorca.
    Anon.   C. Turner, mez.
    T. Q. len. to right, standing, looking to front, left hand on
hilt of sword; battle at sea in distance on right.

Open letter proof, July 1, 1811.
20 × 13¼¼. (17⅞ × 13½½).   22219.
See also COMMEMORATION (1).

COLLINS, WILLIAM, 1788–1847, subject painter, b. in London, son of a native of Wicklow, picture-cleaner and dealer; stud. 1807 at Academy; gained medal in life-school, 1809, and exhibited his first work; painted portraits occasionally, generally rustic scenes and groups; A.R.A. 1814; R.A. 1820; exhibited constantly; visited Italy; attempted sacred subjects; returned to coast scenes, of which he etched and mezzotinted some; m. 1822, Miss Geddes, sister of Mrs. Carpenter; made many water-colour drawings.
    J. Linnell.   H. Robinson, stipple.
    Ha. len. to front, looking to left; dark clothes and neckcloth; 1808. Prefixed to his "Life" by his son, W. Wilkie Collins.   28300. 17.

COLLYER, REV. DR. WILLIAM BENGO, 1782–1854; b. at Deptford; educ. at school of Leathersellers' Company; at Lewisham, and old college at Homerton; minister to a congregation at Peckham, for which the Hanover Chapel was built, 1816; D.D., Edinb. 1808; preached also at Salters' Hall Chapel; pubd. "Hymns," "Services," &c.
    C. C. Coventry.   J. Young, mez.
    J. C. Smith, 13.
    Open letter proof, undescribed by J. C. Smith.
                                        28772.

COLMAN, GEORGE, 1733–1794, Dramatist, son of Thomas Colman, British envoy at Florence; orig. stud. for the law; wrote the plays of the "Jealous Wife," "Clandestine Marriage," &c.; translated Terence; suc. Foote as manager of the Haymarket Theatre; had a stroke of palsy, 1790; d. at Paddington.
    Sir J. Reynolds.   G. Marchi, mez.
    J. C. Smith, 4, 2nd state.   21935.

COLMAN, GEORGE, the Younger, 1762–1836, educ. at Westminster, Ch. Ch. Coll., Oxf., and King's Coll., Aberdeen; ent. at Linc. Inn; began to write plays, 1784, "Two to One;" "Inkle and Yarico," 1787, followed by "The Mountaineers," "Iron Chest," and many more theatrical and literary pieces; licenser and examiner of plays; celebrated also as a wit.
    J. Jackson, R.A.   T. Lupton, mez.
    Sh. ha. len. to front; oval in border.
    Scratched letter-proof.
    13 × 9¼¼. (10⅞ × 9).   22827.

COLPOYS, SIR JOHN, c. 1742–1821, admiral; entd. navy, c. 1756; lieut., 1770, went to W. Indies; captn. 1773; and commd. various ships till 1793; rear-adml. 1794; vice-adml. 1795; present at the action off L'Orient, 1795, and during the mutiny at Spithead, 1797, and at St. Helen's; Admiral, 1801; Commr.-in-chf., Plymouth, 1803; lord of Admiralty, 1804; Govr. Greenwich Hospital; K.B.; &c.

 Anon.   J. Young, mez.

 J. C. Smith, 13 a. (Appendix); 1st state, not described by Mr. Smith; with open letters, lightly scratched.

                24214.

COLSTON, **Edward**, 1636–1721, Philanthropist; b. at Bristol; made a large **fortune as** a merchant; created and endowed various charitable institutions in his native city, and augmented sixty small livings; d. at Mortlake; bur. at All Saints Church, Bristol, with much pomp.

 J. Richardson.   W. Pether, mez.

 J. C. Smith, 5, but a later state than J. C. S. describes; with [after " Philanthropist," 1817 after "Sculp.," and below,

Sold by Norton and Sons, (🔵) *Corn Street, Bristol. Price 12 Shgs."*

 O. D. H. 16. W. 13.   21855.

 Note.—The impression in the B. M. has the date, but not the address of *Norton & Sons.*

COLVILLE, the Hon. Sir **Charles**, 1770–1843, general, second son of John, ninth Lord Colville of Culross; entd. army, 1781; but did not join till 1787; went to W. Indies, 1791; saw much service there, and in Ireland, 1788, Ferrol and Egypt, 1800–1; Bermuda, 1808; Maj.-Genl., 1810, and took over command of a brigade, under Picton; wounded at Badajoz, and again at Vittoria; G.C.B.; Lt.-Genl.; Genl. &c.

 Sir H. Raeburn, R.A.   G. T. Payne, mez.

 Sh. ha. len. to left, looking to front, in uniform, with stars. Open letter proof; Octr. 15, 1844.

 $15\frac{1}{16} \times 12\frac{1}{4}$. $(11\frac{1}{4} \times 9\frac{3}{4})$.   24109.

COMBE, **Charles**, 1743–1817, physician and numismatist, b. in Southampton Street, Bloomsbury; educ. at Harrow; stud. medicine in London; M.D., Glasgow, 1783; L.C.P., 1784; physician to Br. Lying-in-Hosp., 1789, &c.

 See MEDICAL SOCIETY.

COMBE, **Harvey Christian**, sheriff of London, 1791; Lord Mayor, 1799.

 J. Opie.   C. Turner, mez.

 T. Q. len., seated, in robes. Proof before all letters.

 $19\frac{3}{4} \times 13\frac{3}{4}$. $(17\frac{1}{4} \times 13\frac{1}{4})$.   22828.

 B. Burnell.   W. Evans, stipple.

 Oval. Published, July 1, 1802.

 $11\frac{1}{4} \times 8\frac{7}{16}$ (?) $(6\frac{7}{16} \times 5\frac{5}{16})$.   E. 1467.–'85.

COMBERMERE, STAPLETON COTTON, 1st Visct., 1773–1865, General; b. in Denbighshire; served in Flanders and in Mahratta War, 1798; commanded the allied cavalry in Penins. war; cr. Baron, 1814, and Viscount, 1826; Com.-in-Chf. in India, 1822–'5; Field Marshal, 1855; d. at Clifton.

T. Heaphy. C. Turner, mez.

Wh. len. to right, on horseback, looking back and beckoning to hussars who follow him.

Open letter proof, March 1, 1823.

30 × —. (25$\frac{11}{16}$ × 23$\frac{1}{4}$). 22120.

COMMEMORATION | OF THE VICTORY OF JUNE 1ST, | MDCCXCIV (off Ushant). A collection of medallion portraits of Lord HOWE and the other Naval Officers who took part in this battle; those of HOWE, GRAVES, CALDWELL, GARDINER, BOWYER, BRIDPORT, and PAISLEY, are in the upper part of the plate, among the foliage of an oak; below, the figure of Peace holds a crown over the head of Britannia, who is seated, with the lion, at the foot of the tree, by the sea; below again are the heads, in medallions, of MONTAGUE, PIGOTT, MACKENZIE, PRINGLE, CURTIS, H. HARVEY, PARKER; J. HARVEY, MOLLOY, BAZELEY, GAMBIER, H. SEYMOUR, COTTON, PAKENHAM; COLLINGWOOD, DOUGLASS, DUCKWORTH, PAYNE, BERKELEY, BERTIE, DOMETT; HUTT, NICOLS, WESTCOTT, SCHOMBERG, ELPHINSTONE, and HOPE, arranged in four rows.

R. Smirke, R.A. Landscape and Water by Landseer. Portraits of the Admirals, by Ryder : of the Captains, by Stow. 1803.

Cut. (27 × 16$\frac{3}{4}$). 15594. B.

COMMEMORATION | OF THE | XIVTH FEBRUARY MDCCXCVII. (off Cape St. Vincent). A collection of medallion portraits of Lord ST. VINCENT, and the other Admirals and Captains who took part in that defeat of the Spanish fleet. A figure of Victory stands on a pedestal in the upper part of the print. On the pedestal is the portrait of ST. VINCENT; below are those of SIR C. THOMPSON, BT., L. RADSTOCK, and SIR W. PARKER, BT.; below again, in two rows, above and below the inscription on a wide tablet, are those of FREDERICK, KNOWLES, COLLINGWOOD, WHITSHED, LD. NELSON (a little higher), CALDER, DACRES, SAUMAREZ, MURRAY; SUTTON, TROUBRIDGE, MARTIN, FOLEY, GREY, TOWRY, MILLER, and IRWIN.

R. Smirke, R.A. I. Parker.

Portraits engd. by Worthington. 1803.

26$\frac{1}{2}$ × 19. (23$\frac{3}{4}$ × 16$\frac{13}{16}$). 15594. D.

COMMEMORATION | OF THE | XITH OCTOBER MDCCXCVII. (Camperdown). A collection of medallion portraits of Lord DUNCAN, Sir Richard ONSLOW, and the other naval officers who took part in this battle. DUNCAN and ONSLOW appear just below the car of Britannia, which is drawn over the waves by sea-horses; below again, surrounding the inscription on a wide tablet, are those of SIR HENRY TROLLOPE,

INGLIS, KNIGHT, SIR W. FAIRFAX, SIR THO. BYARD, DRURY; ESSINGTON, WELLS; O'BRYEN, BURGESS; MITCHELL, GREGORY, BLIGH, HOTHAM, WALKER, and PHILLIPS.

R. Smirke, R.A.   J PARKER.

The portraits by Geo. Noble from miniatures by John Smart, 1803.

Cut. $(26\frac{1}{4} \times 16\frac{3}{4})$.   15594.   C.

COMMONS, THE HOUSE OF, "in Sir Robert Walpole's Administration" (1721-1742).

W. Hogarth and Sir J. Thornhill.   A. Fogg, stipple.

A composition of many figures, among which are Sir Robert Walpole, on the left, t. q. len., by the chair, in which Mr. Speaker Onslow is seated; others are Sydney Godolphin, "father of the House," Col. Onslow, Sir Joseph Jekyll, Sir James Thornhill, E. Stables, Clerk of the House, and Mr. Aiskew, Clerk Assistant; with many others unnamed.

$(17\frac{1}{8} \times 14\frac{1}{2})$.   22004.

COMMONS, THE HOUSE OF, in 1860.

J. Phillip, R.A.   T. O. Barlow, mixed mez.

A composition of many figures; Lord Palmerston, Prime Minister, on the left, is addressing the House on the Treaty of Commerce between England and France; on the Treasury Bench are seated Sir George Cornwall Lewis (a note-book in hand), Lord John (aftds. Earl) Russell; Mr. Gladstone, and other members of the Ministry: on the Front Opposition Bench are Mr. Disraeli (aftds. Earl of Beaconsfield), Lord Stanley (aftds. Earl of Derby), Sir E. Bulwer-Lytton (aftd. Lord Lytton), and other prominent members of the Conservative party; the Speaker, Mr. John Evelyn Denison (aftds. Visct. Ossington) in the Chair.

$26\frac{1}{8} \times 32\frac{3}{4}$. $(23 \times 29\frac{1}{4})$.   24196.

COMPTON, HENRY, 1632-1713, sixth and youngest son of Spencer, second Earl of Northampton; b. at Compton; educ. at Oxford, and travelled abroad, after the Restoration, accepted a command in the regiment of the King's Guard; went to Cambr., and was ordd.; rapidly advanced in Church; bishop of Oxford, 1674; of London, 1675; suspended by James for a short time; instrumental in bringing William and Mary to the throne; called the "Protestant Bishop;" d. at Fulham.

I. Rily.   S. Beckett, mez.

J. C. Smith, 26, 3rd state.   24063.

COMYNS, SIR JOHN, c. 1667-1740; son of a barrister; educated at Cambridge; called to the Bar, 1690; M.P. for Maldon; Baron of Exchequer, 1726; Justice of Com. Pleas, 1736; Chief Baron of Exchequer, 1738-'40; Author of "Digest of the Laws of England," and "Reports."

Anon.   J. Houbraken, 1745.

Sh. ha. len., slightly to right, looking to front, in robes, with chain and wig; oval in border.

Proof before all letters, except the engraver's name and the date.

$11\frac{5}{8} \times 7\frac{3}{8}$. $(11\frac{1}{4} \times 6\frac{7}{8})$.   22943.

CONCILIVM Septem Nobilivm Anglorvm conjvrantivm
in Necem iacobi 'i' | magnæ Britanniæ Regis Totivsq.
Anglici convocati Parlementi.
  (Copied from print by Simon Passe.)   Anon.
  Ha. len.; the conspirators in the Gunpowder Plot, Thomas
Percy in the centre; on his left is "Guido Fawkes," then come
Robert Catesby, and Thomas Winter; on Percy's right are
John Wright, Christopher Wright, Robert Winter, and Bates,
Catesby's servant; above is the title, as quoted; beneath are
inscriptions in Latin (12 lines) and French (13 lines) in parallel
columns, and below again another, in German (4 lines), ex-
tending across the plate, which seems to have been used
in an Italian book, some of the letter-press of which is on the
back (1614).
  Apparently, hitherto undescribed.
  $7\frac{1}{2} \times 8\frac{7}{16}$. $(4\frac{1}{4} \times 8\frac{1}{4})$.   26687.

CONFERENCE. *See* MENAI STRAITS.

CONGREVE, WILLIAM, 1672–1728, Dramatist and Wit; b. at
Bardsey Grange, Yorks.; entd. Mid. Temple; estab. his repu-
tation by his comedy, "The Old Bachelor," 1693; wrote also
"Love for Love," "The Double Dealer," "Mourning Bride,"
&c.; was patronised by the Earl of Halifax, and obtained several
Govt. sinecures.
  Sir G. Kneller.   J. Smith, mez.
  J. C. Smith, 540, 2nd state.   22121

CONGREVE, SIR WILLIAM, 1772–1828, son of a lieut.-General;
joined the Army, in which he became a lieut.-Colonel; had
much inventive talent; the rocket which bears his name,
first used in the attack on Boulogne, 1806, was considered for
some time a great instrument in warlike operations; F.R.S.;
M.P., Plymouth.
  J. Lonsdale.   G. Clint, mixed mez.
  Wh. len. to left, raising his hat to shade his eyes, while
"directing the discharge of the Fire Rockets, invented by him,
"into the Town of Copenhagen during the Bombardment . . in
"1807."
  $27\frac{1}{8} \times 20$. $(25\frac{5}{8} \times 19\frac{1}{2})$.   26679.
  See also SCIENCE

CONNAUGHT, ARTHUR WILLIAM PATRICK ALBERT, Prince,
Duke of, 1850–
  F. Winterhalter.   R. J. Lane, lith., 1854.
  As a child, with sword and cross-belt
  $(8\frac{7}{16} \times 6\frac{1}{16})$.   22197
  See also FIRST OF MAY.

  F. Winterhalter.   J. A. Vinter, lith., 1859.
In a circle; with broad collar and loose tie.
Ind. proof with open letters.
  $(12\frac{1}{8}$ diamr.)   22194.

Anon.

With his wife, the Duchess, née Princess Louise of Prussia; married, March 13, 1879.

A coloured print, from the supplement to the "Graphic," March 20, 1879.

$(18\frac{1}{4} \times 14\frac{6}{8})$. 15525.

CONNOLLY, John, 1794–1866, b. at Market Rasen; stud. at Edinb. Univ., 1817–'21; M.D., 1821; physician at Chichester, 1822–'23, at Stratford-on-Avon, 1823–'27; profr. of pract. of medicine, Univ. Coll., London, 1828–'30; pract. at Warwick, 1830–'8; resid. phys. to Middlesex County Asylum, Hanwell, 1839–'44, where he entirely abolished restraint; kept priv. asylum, near Hanwell, 1852 till his death; pubd. some works on the treatment of the insane, &c.

Sir W. Gordon. W. Walker, mez.

T. Q. len. to left, looking to front, seated, with right hand on table, on which are books.

Proof before all letters.

$20\frac{7}{8} \times 16$. $(17\frac{1}{10} \times 13\frac{5}{16})$ 22829.

CONSTABLE, Archibald, 1775–1827, enterprising Scottish bookseller and publisher, commenced business for himself, 1795; started the "Edinburgh Review," pubd. "The Lay of the Last Minstrel," &c.; failed, 1826.

See SCOTT, Sir Walter.

CONSTABLE, John, 1776–1837, landscape-painter, b. at East Bergholt, Suffolk; son of a miller; intended for the church, but preferred art; sketched in his native county; came to London, 1795; stud. in Academy School, 1799; painted portraits; exhibited "A Landscape," 1802; "View on the River Stour," 1819, and elected A.R.A.; R.A., 1829; first appreciated in Paris; esteemed in England after his death; painted in water-colours also; six of his works are in Sheepshanks Gallery.

C. R. Leslie, R.A. D. Lucas, mez.

Ha. len. to left, wearing black coat and neckcloth.

Proof before all letters (1843).

$(6\frac{3}{8} \times 5\frac{1}{16})$. 28298. 2.

CONWAY, Rt. Hon. Henry Seymour, 1720–1795; second son of Francis Seymour, Lord Conway; entd. army, in which he was rapidly promoted; M.P., 1774–'84; Genl., 1772; field-marshal, 1793. Intimate friend of Horace Walpole, his first cousin, who bequeathed to Conway's only child, the Hon. Anne Damer, his most valued possession, Strawberry Hill.

Gainsborough. G. Dupont, mez.

J. C. Smith, 3, 2nd state. 24069.

COOK, James, 1728–1779, Navigator, son of a day-labourer; b. at Marton, Yorks.; apprent. to a grocer at Snaith; released from his indentures, ent. merch. service, and aftds. the Royal Navy; Lieut., 1760; Capt., 1768; made 3 voyages round the globe, 1768–'79; disc. Sandwich Islands, 1776; killed, at Owhyhee, by the natives, Feb. 14.

N. Dance J. K. Sherwin.

H 2

T. Q. len. to left, seated, looking to right, holding a chart, spread before him; his hat lies on a book, on table, to left; April 20, 1779.

11¾ × 10₁₆⁷. (10½ × 8⅓, excl of narrow, ruled border).

22498.

—— The Death of, Feb. 14, 1779.
J. Webber. The figures by F. Bartolozzi, R.A.
The landscape by W. Byrne.
A composition of many figures; Cook is seen, rather to the right of the middle; one of the natives, of whom there is a great crowd, is about to stab him in the back.
Cut. (16¾ × 22⅛). 25843.

COOKE, GEORGE FREDERICK, 1756–1812, eminent actor; apprent. to a printer; tried the navy; took to the stage; after the usual probation in travelling companies, became a star at York, Manchester, Liverpool, Dublin, &c.; appeared, Cov. Garden, 1800, as Richard III., with success; popular also as Macbeth, Iago, Sir Pertinax MacSycophant, Shylock, &c.; played with equal success in U.S. America.
De Wilde del. R. Woodman, stipple.
Wh. len., as Sir Pertinax MacSycophant, facing to front, looking to left; April 10, 1808.
18¾ × 12¼. (16⅜ × 11, including border, 1) 22830.

COOKE, THOMAS POTTER, 1786–1864, b. in London; served in navy, 1796–1802; present at the battle off Cape St. Vincent, 1797; first acted at Royalty theatre, 1804; stage-manager, Surrey theatre, 1809–'16; played at Lyceum, 1820–'2; acted Le Monstre (Frankenstein) 80 nights, Paris, 1825–'6; played William in "Black-eyed Susan," and other sailor parts with unequalled success; last appearance, Princess's theatre, May 2, 1861
[Baugniet ?] C. Baugniet, lith., 1843.
T. Q. len. to right, looking to front, eyeglass in left hand; right hand in coat-pocket; a ship, cliffs, &c., in distance; with autograph presentation from T. P. Cooke to Col. Durrant; the signature in facs.
(12¼ × 11). 25771.

COOKE, THOMAS SIMPSON, familiarly known as Tom Cooke, 1782–1848, singer and composer, b. at Dublin, played a violin solo in public at the age of 7; pupil of Giordani; led a theatre band, at 15; sang the part of "The Seraskier" in Dublin, and soon after at the Lyceum, London, 1813; remained as principal tenor at Drury Lane for 20 years; sometimes led the band, and also that of the Philh. Socy., and Antient Concerts; composed many dramatic pieces, and some delightful glees, &c.
G. Clint, A.R.A. T. Lupton, mez. on steel.
Ha. len. to left, looking to front; coat buttoned; July 4, 1826; with autogr. signature, "T. Cooke 1829."
13⅞ × 10. (11 × 9₁₆⁷) 24110.

COOPER, Sir Astley Paston, 1768–1841, disting. surgeon; 4th son of Rev. S. Cooper, D.D.; b. at Brooke Hall, 7 miles from Norwich; stud. under his uncle, William Cooper, at Guy's Hospital, and under Henry Cline, at St. Thomas's; attained reputation as lecturer on Anatomy, and as operator, at St. Thomas's Hospital; surgeon to the King, and Bart., 1827.

Sir T. Lawrence, P.R.A.   S. Cousins, mez.

Full ha. len. to front, standing, looking to left, right hand resting on table, left in pocket; pillar and curtain behind; Jany. 1, 1830.

$21\frac{1}{4} \times 16\frac{5}{8}$. $(17\frac{3}{8} \times 13\frac{1}{4})$.   22141

COOPER, Bransby Blake, 1792–1853, eldest son of Rev. S. L. Cooper, and nephew of Sir Astley P. Cooper; b. at Great Yarmouth; midshipman, afterwards assist. surg. R.A., 1811–'16; M.R.C.S., 1823; hon. fellow, 1843; memb. of council, 1848; surg. Guy's Hosp. till death; F.R.S., 1829; wrote life of his uncle, 1843, "Lectures," 1851.

E. U. Eddis.   W. H. Simmons, mixed mez.

Sh. t. q. len. to right, leaning on a stone pedestal, right hand to hip.

$22\frac{1}{8} \times 15\frac{3}{4}$. $(18\frac{5}{16} \times 14\frac{1}{8})$.   27074.

COOPER, Richard, –1764, b. in London; stud. under John Pine; practised in Edinb., from 1730 till death; engraved in line and mez., chiefly portraits; was the master of Sir Robert Strange, who was apprent. to him, 1735–'41; bur. in Canongate Churchyard.

G. Schroider.   Anon., mez.

Perhaps, scraped by Cooper himself.

J. C. Smith, 23, p. 1684.   E. 1269.–'86.

COOPER, Samuel, 1780–1848, educ. at Greenwich by Dr. Burney; entd. St. Barthol. Hospl., 1800; M.R.C.S., 1803; entd. the army as surgeon, after the death of his wife, 1813; served at Waterloo; member of Council, Coll. of Surgeons, 1827; Surgeon to Univ. Coll. Hospl. and professor of Surgery, 1831–'48; president, Coll. of Surgeons, 1845; F.R.S., 1846; wrote several excellent surgical works.

A. Morton.   H. Cousins, mixed mez.

T. Q. len. to left, looking to front, seated; on the left is a table, on which are a book, a preparation in spirit, &c.

Open letter proof; March 10, 1840.

$19\frac{13}{16} \times 15$. $(16\frac{9}{16} \times 13\frac{1}{4})$.   27163.

COOTE, Sir Eyre, 1726–1783, b. in Ireland; entd. army and went to India; present at bombardment of Calcutta, 1754; served at Plassey; routed Lally while attempting to besiege Trinchinopoly; returned to England, 1762; received thanks of Parliament, K.B., 1771; Lt.-Genl.; Com. in Chf., Bengal, 1780, defeated Hyder Ali at Porto Novo; but, worn out in health and temper, died at Madras; monument in Westminster Abbey.

W. Lawrenson.   J. Walker, mez.

J. C. Smith, 3, 2nd state.

         24111.

COOTE, Sir Eyre, 1762–1824(?), Lt.-Genl., K.C., M.P., nephew of Sir E. Coote, K.B., Indian Genl.; educ. at Eton; commissioned at 14, and carried the colours at battle of Brooklyn, 1776; served through that campaign, at siege of Charleston, 1780, prisoner at Yorktown; released, returned to England; major, 1783; Lt.-Col., 1788; served in West Indies; Col., 1794; Maj.-Genl., 1798; wounded in Netherlands, served in Mediterranean, took Marabout; Lt. Genl., 1805; Govr. Jamaica; Walcheren, 1809; tried for eccentric conduct, and dismissed, 1815.

E. Shepperson.   T. & R. W. Wallis.
Sh. ha. len. to left, looking to front, in uniform, with star.
Novr., 1815.
Cut. (6⅝ × 4¾).   15242.

COPELAND, Miss F. E., of the Surrey Theatre.
R. E. Drummond.   Alais, stipple.
See LA BELLE ASSEMBLEE, 1820.   13867. 5.

COPLESTON, Edward, 1776–1849, b. at Offwell, Devon, where his father was rector; educ. at home, and at Corp. Xti. Coll., Oxf.; B.A., and fellow, 1795; M.A., 1797, and tutor, –1810; distinguished for scholarship, and for bodily strength and activity; vicar of S. Mary's, Oxf., 1800; profr. of Poetry, 1802; provost of Oriel, 1814; Dean of Chester, 1826; Dean of St. Paul's, and Bishop of Llandaff, 1828; tory politician, and high churchman
T. Phillips, R.A.   S. W. Reynolds & S. Cousin, mez.
T Q. len. to left, seated, in gown, with cap in left hand, looking to right. Oct. 1822.
19¾ × 13⅛. (17⁵⁄₁₆ × 13¹¹⁄₁₆).   25823.

CORAM, Thomas, 1667, or 1668(?)–1751, philanthropist, b. at Lyme Regis, Dorsets.; his father is supposed to have been the captain of a ship; settled at Taunton, Mass., 1694; gave ground, 1703, for a school there; stranded in a ship off Cuxhaven, 1719, and settled in London; one of the trustees for Georgia, 1732; agitated for a Foundling Hospital, which, after 17 years, was established; bur. in the Chapel of that Hospital.
W. Hogarth.   W. Nutter, stipple.
Wh. len. slightly to left, seated, looking to front, holding in right hand the seal of the Royal Charter, gloves in left; sea with ships, on left, in distance; a terrestrial globe on right, in foreground.
Decr. 1, 1796.
22⅝ × 16⁷⁄₁₆. (20 × 13½).   21846.

CORNWALLIS, Charles Cornwallis, 2nd Earl, 1st Marquess, 1738–1805, educ. at Eton and Turin; ensign, 1st Regt. of Foot Guards, 1756; A.D.C. to John, Marquess of Granby, 1758–'9; M.P., Eye, 1760, 1761–'2; Lt.-Col., 1761; suc. as 2nd Earl, 1762; A.D.C. to King George III., and Colonel, 1765; served in Seven Years' War, and in America, capit. at Yorktown, 1781; Gov.-General, India, 1786; fought successfully against

Tippoo Sahib, 1791; cr. Marquess, 1792; General, 1793; again Gov.-General, India, 1804; K.G.; d. at Ghazepore.
Sir W. Beechey, R.A.   J. Ward, mez.
J. C. Smith, 13, 2nd state.   22122.

[J. Bacon, junr.]   G. Dawe, mez.
Colossal statue, in honour of the General, by J. Bacon, junr., 1803.
Open letter proof; a plate not mentioned by J. C. Smith.
$26\frac{1}{4} \times 20\frac{3}{4}$ (?). $(25\frac{7}{8} \times 20\frac{1}{4})$.   29006. A.

CORRY, Rt. Hon. Henry Thomas Lowry, 1803–1873, younger son of the 2nd Earl of Belmore; educ. at Ch. Ch., Oxf.; grad. 1824, with honours; M.P., 1826; Lord of Admiralty, 1841–'5; Sec. to Admir., 1845–'6, and 1858–'9; Vice-Pres., Council of Education, 1866; First Lord of Admiralty, 1867.
See DERBY CABINET.

CORT, Henry, 1740–1800, metallurgist,, b. at Lancaster, navy agent in Surrey St., Strand; set up with a forge and mill, 1775, at Fontley, near Fareham; patented, 1783–'4, a puddling furnace and rolling-mill; ruined by his partner's dishonesty; d. poor, his children receiving insignificant pensions from the State.
Anon.   Anon., mez.
Sh. ha. len. to left, in profile, looking upwards; hair brushed back; coat with high collar.
Ind. proof, with open letters.
$10\frac{9}{16} \times 8\frac{7}{16}$. $(8\frac{3}{4} \times 7\frac{4}{16})$.   22973.

COSWAY, Maria Cecilia Louisa, Mrs., c. 1820, daughter of an innkeeper, named Hadfield, at Leghorn; m. to Richard Cosway (q.v.), the miniature-painter; became known herself as a miniature-painter and fashionable belle in London and Paris; exhibited in R.A. 1781, in which year she was m. to Cosway; left her husband, and sought shelter in the cloister at Lyons; returned, 1804; lived in North Italy for three years; d. 1821, or 1833, at Lodi, where she had established a college for young ladies.
Maria Cosway.   V. Green, mez.
J. C. Smith, 29, 1st state, undescribed by J. C. S.; the inscription in scratched letters, and the margin not entirely cleared of ground; only one known.   22069.

COSWAY, Richard, 1740–1821, miniature-painter, b. at Tiverton, son of the public schoolmaster; pupil of Hudson; stud. in Shipley's School and Royal Academy; A.R.A., 1770; R.A., 1771; his miniatures became the fashion; intimate with the Pr of Wales; painted occasionally in oils; lived in great style, with much vanity and ostentation; believed in Swedenborg and animal magnetism; professed to raise the dead.
R. Cosway, delt.   M. Bovi.

Wh. len., seated on a step, inclined to right, looking to front,
wearing a cloak, hat, and feather; the face, hand, and feather,
tinted red; the background green; March 20, 1786.
$10\frac{1}{2} \times 6\frac{3}{4}$. $(8\frac{1}{2} \times 5\frac{1}{4})$.   25680.

G. Dance del.   W. Daniell, chalk and stipple.
Ha. len. inclined and looking, in profile, to right; vignette.
$11\frac{11}{16} \times 7\frac{3}{4}$. $(8 \times 6\frac{1}{2})$.   E. 28255.   1.

COTES, FRANCIS, 1726–1770, b. in London; son of an apothecary,
formerly Mayor of Galway; stud. under G. Knapton; became
eminent and fashionable as a portait-painter in oils and crayons;
painted " Queen Charlotte with the Princess Royal in her lap,"
1767; drew well, sketched freely, coloured agreeably; foundation member of R.A.
     P. Falconet del. 1768.   D P. Pariset, stipple.
     Sh. ha. len. to right, in profile; circle in border; title on a
tablet below, followed by artists' names and publication-line
     $(6\frac{3}{4} \times 5$; circle, $3\frac{7}{16}$ diamr.$)$.   E. 1963.–'89.

COTMAN, JOHN SELL, 1782–1842, landscape and marine
painter, b. at Norwich, son of a silk-mercer; educ. at City Free
School; intended for his father's business, but preferred art;
stud., and exhibited, London, 1800–'6, chiefly Welsh views at
the R.A.; frequented artists' meetings at Dr. Monro's house;
at Norwich again, 1807, painting portraits; at Yarmouth, later,
pubd. (1811) " Architectural Etchings," &c.; visited Normandy,
1818–'19; painted in water-colours as well as in oil.
     J. P. Davis del., 1818.   [Mrs. Dawson Turner, etch.]
     Ha. len. to right, seated, holding a paper in right hand;
vignette. Private plate.
     $11\frac{7}{8} \times 8\frac{7}{8}$. $(8\frac{1}{2} \times 8\frac{3}{4})$.   27523.

COTTENHAM, SIR CHARLES CHRISTOPHER PEPYS, 1st Earl
of, 1781–1851; lawyer, son of Sir William Weller Pepys,
Bart.; educ. at Harrow and Cambr.; barrister, 1804; K.C.,
1826; M.P., 1831–'6; Sol.-General, 1834, and P.C.; Lord
Chancellor, 1836–'41; cr. Baron, 1836; suc. as 3rd Bart., 1845;
Lord Chancellor, 1846–'50; cr Visct., and Earl, 1850.
     C. R. Leslie, R.A.   H. T. Ryall, mixed style.
     Wh. len to left, in Chancellor's robes, looking to front; mace
and bag on table, on left.
     Open letter proof, March 25, 1842.
     Cut. $(22\frac{1}{8} \times 16\frac{3}{4})$.   22831.

COTTON, CHARLES, 1630–1687, poet, friend of Izaak Walton, b.
at Beresford, Staffordshire; the place of his education doubtful;
acquired considerable knowledge of classics, and of French and
Italian literature; devoted himself to literary pursuits; wrote
poems, not pubd. before his death; " Scarronides, or the First
Book of Virgil Travestie," 1664; translated Corneille's
" Horace," Montaigne, and other works; added a treatise on

fly-fishing to Walton's "Complete Angler," wrote the "Compleat Gamester," 1674, &c.

Sir P. Lely.   W. Humphreys.

Sh. ha. len. to right, looking to front, with breastplate, scarf, long wig, &c. ; facs. 4 lines of verse and signature below. Oct. 1, 1836. The verses quoted are from Cotton's poem, "Contentation."

 12⅛ × 10⅝. (4¾ × 3⅜).   22454.

COTTON, SIR CHARLES, 1753–1812, fifth Bart. ; educ. at Westminster; ent. Navy, 1772; went to N. America; lieut. 1777 ; commander and captain, 1779; served in W. Indies, 1781 ; in Channel fleet, 1793; commanded a ship, June 1, 1794, in Howe's victory off Ushant, and under Cornwallis, 1797, off Penmarcks; Vice-Adm., 1802; Com.-in-Chf. in Tagus, 1807; Com. in Mediter., 1810; in Channel, 1811 ; d. suddenly at Plymouth.

 See COMMEMORATION (1).

COTTON, REV. GEORGE EDWARD LYNCH, 1813–1866, educ. at Westminster and Trin. Coll., Cambr., took a first class in classical tripos, 1836 ; a master at Rugby for 15 years, under Dr. Arnold; head-master of Marlborough College, of which he created the reputation and success; Bishop of Calcutta, 1858 ; drowned accidentally in the Ganges.

E. U. Eddis.   F. Holl, mixed style.

As head-master of Marlborough ; t. q. len. to left, seated, in gown, looking to front, and holding a book in right hand, with a finger between the leaves.

Open letter proof.

 17⅞ × 14⅛. (12 × 9⁷⁄₁₆).   27207.

COTTON, SIR ROBERT BRUCE, 1571–1631, antiquary, eldest son of Thomas Cotton, of Connington, Huntingdonshire; b. at Denton, near Connington; educ. at Westminster, under W. Camden, and at Jesus Coll., Cambr.; B.A., 1585; settled in Westminster, and became a great collector of MSS., coins, and other antiquities; read papers before the Antiquarian Socy.; Camden, Bacon, B. Jonson, Selden, Speed, and others used his library, most part of which is now in the Br. Museum ; knighted 1603; Bart. 1611.

P. van Somer.   G. Vertue, 1744.

Ha. len. to right, looking to front, with ruff; right hand to breast, left hand on an open book ; long Latin inscription below, in 23 lines ; title at top. Engraved for the Society of Antiquaries, Vol. I. P. LXVI.

 14½ × 9½. (14¾ × 8¹³⁄₁₆).   22832.

COUNCIL. *See* ARCTIC.

COVENTRY, MARIA, Countess of, 1733–1760, eldest daughter of John Gunning of Castle Coote, co. Roscommon ; famed, with her sister Elizabeth, for beauty ; very poor ; thought of going on the stage; m. to George William, 6th Earl of Coventry,

1752 ; wanting in sense, manners, and breeding; d. of consumption, or from the use of cosmetics.

J. St. Liotard.   R. Houston, mez.

J. C. Smith, 31, 1st state.   22969.

COVENTRY, THOMAS COVENTRY, Baron, of Aylesborough, 1578–1640, learned judge; son of Sir Thomas Coventry, Knt. ; educ. at Oxford; barrister, 1603 ; Recorder of London, 1616 ; Solr.-General, 1617–'21 ; Knt., 1617 ; M.P., 1620 ; Attorney-General, 1621 ; Lord Keeper, 1625 ; P.C. ; cr. Baron, 1628 ; supported Charles I. in his views of prerogative ; d. at Durham House, Strand.

C. Janssens.   J. Houbraken, 1741.

Sh. ha len. to right, looking to front, in robes ; oval, in border, mace and bag below ; in Birch's "Lives."

$13\frac{13}{16} \times 9\frac{3}{4}$. $(14\frac{1}{2} \times 8\frac{1}{4})$.   22228.

COUTTS, THOMAS, 1735–1822, founder, with his brother James, of the banking-house, Coutts & Co., in the Strand ; 4th son of Lord-provost John Coutts, Edinburgh ; educ. there, at High School ; sole head of the firm, after the death of his brother, 1778 ; banker for George III., and many of the aristocracy ; accomplished gentleman, and very charitable ; amassed a fortune of 900,000l. ; m. twice ; 1st, Susan Starkie ; 2nd, Harriet Mellon, an actress, who, after his death, married the 9th Duke of St. Albans, and d., 1837.

Sir W. Beechey.   R. W. Sievier, stipple.

Ha. len. to left, looking to front ; coat buttoned loosely, white neckcloth ; vignette.

Ind. proof before all letters ; pubd by W. J. White, 1822.

$13\frac{5}{8} \times 11\frac{5}{16}(?)$. $(5\frac{1}{2} \times 5\frac{3}{4})$.   23129.

COWLEY, ABRAHAM, 1618–1667, poet, the son of Thomas Cowley, a stationer ; b. in London ; educ. at Westminster ; pub. "Poetical Blossoms," 1633, repub., 1636, 1637 ; scholar, Trin. Coll. Cambr., 1637 ; pub. "Love's Riddle," and "Naufragium Joculare," 1638 ; B.A., 1639 ; M.A., 1642 ; ejected, 1644, and retired to Oxford ; pub. "The Mistress," 1647 ; collected works, 1656, 4to. ; now little read.

From an Original Drawing in the Possession of Richard Clark, Esqr., Chamberlain of London.   J. Basire, 1813.

Sh. ha len. to left, looking to front, with long hair, dress fastened with three square brooches.

Ind. proof. The crayon drawing is now at Trin. Coll., Cambr., having been presented, 1824, by R. Clark.

$15\frac{5}{8} \times 11\frac{1}{16}$. $(11\frac{1}{4} \times 8\frac{1}{4})$.   28030.

COWPER, WILLIAM, Lord, c. 1670–1723 ; suc. as 3rd Bart. ; went to the Bar ; cr. Baron, 1706 ; Lord Chancr., 1707–'10, 1714–'18 ; cr. Earl, 1718.

Sir G. Kneller.   J. Smith, mez.

J. C. Smith, 65, 2nd state.   22089.

COWPER, WILLIAM, 1731–1800, poet, b. at his father's rectory, Great Berkhampstead ; educ. at Market Street, Herts., and at

Westminster; art. to a solr.; entd. at Mid. Temple, 1748; bar. 1754; suffered from depression and religious melancholia; settled in Temple, 1759; comr. of bankrupts; suffered again from depression and mania, 1763; in 1780–'1, wrote, " Progress of Error," " Truth," " Table-talk," &c.; " Poems" appeared, 1782; the " Task," 1788, and " John Gilpin; " " Tirocinium," translation of Homer, 1785; &c.

Sir T. Lawrence, 1793.   F. Bartolozzi, stipple.
Sh. ha. len. to left, wearing a cap; four verses below.
May 1, 1805.
11×8. (8¼×7).   24215.

COX, MISS ELIZABETH.
    H. D. Hamilton.   R. Laurie, mez.
    J. C. Smith, 15, 2d state.   26423.

COXE, REV. WILLIAM, 1747–1828, educ. at Marylebone grammar school, Eton, and King's Coll., Cambr.; fellow, 1768; deacon, 1771, curate of Denham, Uxbridge; tutor to D. of Marlborough's eldest son, and then to the E. of Pembroke's son, and others; received various preferments; archdeacon, Wilts., 1804; preb., Salisbury, 1791; pubd. " History of the House of Austria," 1807; " Kings of Spain," 1813; " Memoirs of Duke of Marlborough," 1817–'19.

Sir W. Beechey.   R. Dunkarton, mez.
J. C. Smith, 15, but an earlier state than described by him, being an open letter proof.   24213.

CRABBE, GEORGE, 1754–1832, poet, b. at Aldeburgh, went to school at Bungay, aftds. at Stowmarket; chiefly self-educated; contributed verses to Wheble's Magazine, 1772; came to London, 1780; pub. "The Candidate," 1780, "The Library," " The Village; " ordained, 1781; pres. to living of Frome, 1783, and LL.B.; rector of Muston and Allington, 1789; wrote the " Parish Register," " Eustace Grey," " Tales in Verse," 1812, and other poems.

T. Phillips, R.A.   E. Finden.
Full ha. len. to front, seated, with hands clasped together; a church and trees in distance.
Ind. Proof before all letters (pubd. by John Murray, 1834, as frontispiece to Crabbe's " Life and Poems," 8vo.).
9³⁄₁₆×6⅟₈. (3½×3).   26680.
See also SCOTT, SIR WALTER.

CRAGGS, JAMES, senr., 1657–1721, postmaster-general; b. at Wyserley, co. Durham; came to London, 1680; steward to the Duke of Norfolk, 1684, and aftds. to Duke of Marlborough; became an army clothier, 1695; committed to Tower; M.P. for Grampound, 1702–'13; involved in South Sea Scheme; left a million and a half of money.

Sir G. Kneller, 1709.   G. Vertue, 1728.
T. Q. len. to right, facing to front.
15⅜×10⅞ (?). (12¾×10½).   24065.

CRAGGS, James, junr., 1686–1771, War Sec., involved in
the "South Sea Bubble;" d. during the investigation; bur.
in Westm. Abbey, in the same vault with his friend, Addison;
his monument, in the baptistery, is inscribed with an epitaph
by Pope, who was also his friend, and celebrated him in verse.
 Sir G. Kneller.   J. Simon, mez.
J. Smith, 47, 1st state; "only 4 known" (besides this (?)).
                24064.

> Note.—There is an indication, in lower margin, of something,
> perhaps an address, 3⅜ long, having been stopped out, in the middle,
> between the names of painter and engraver; on the impression in the
> B.M. there are strong indications of an address having been beaten
> out, in that part of the margin.

CRANBROOK, Sir Gathorne Gathorne-Hardy, Earl and
Viscount, 1814– , educ. at Shrewsbury and Oxford; B.A.,
1837; barrister, 1840; M.P., 1856–'65, for Leominster, aftds.
for Oxford; Under Sec. for Home Dept., 1858; Pres., Poor
Law Board, 1866; Home Sec., 1867–'8; Sec. for War, 1874–'8;
Sec. for India, 1878–'80; Lord Pres., Council, 1885, 1886;
cr. Visct., 1878; cr. Earl, 1892; P.C., G.C.S.I., &c.
 See DERBY CABINET.

CRANMER, Thomas, 1489–1556, b. at Aslacton, Notts; educ.
there and at Cambr.; B.A., 1512; M.A., 1515; prof. Theol.,
1524; obtained the favour of Henry VIII., 1529; Archbishop
of Canterbury, 1553; pronounced Henry's marriage with
Catherine void; promoted translation of bible, &c.; contributed
largely to establishment of the Ch. of England; pubd. liturgy,
homilies, &c., 1547–'52; condemned for heresy by Mary, 1554;
burnt at Oxford, March 21, 1556.
 H. Holbein.   G. Vertue.
 Sh. ha. len. slightly to right, looking to front, in robes, with
cap, and holding an open book in both hands; oval in border;
two lines of Latin title below, and "Printed for John Wyat at
the Rose in St. Paul's Church Yard."
 10⅜ × 6⅛. (9¼ × 5⅓).   22835.

——— See also "MARTYRS, Protestant," 25736;
and "REFORMERS," 29719. 2.

CRANWORTH, Robert Monsey Rolfe, 1st Baron, 1790–
1868, educ. at Bury, Winchester, and Camb.; M.A., 1815;
barrister, 1816; bencher, 1832; recorder of Bury St. Edmund's,
c. 1830; K.C., M.P.; Sol.-Genl., 1834, and 1835–'9; Baron of
Exch., 1839–'50; one of comrs. of Great Seal, 1850, and Vice-
Chanc.; P.C.; cr. Baron Cranworth of Cranworth, 1850; one
of the two Lord Justices of Appeal in Chancery, 1851; Lord
Chancellor, 1852–'8, and 1865–'7.
 G. Richmond.   F. Holl.
 Bust to left, vignette.
 Open letter proof, 1853.
 22 × 17¼. (8½ × 6).   22962.

 See also ABERDEEN CABINET.

CREW, Nathaniel, 1633-1722, 3rd Baron Crew of Stene, 5th son of John Crew of Stene; entd. at Linc. Coll., Oxf., 1652; B.A., 1656, and soon afterwards a fellow; proctor, 1663; Rector of Linc. Coll. 1668; ordd., 1664; Dean of Chichester, 1669; Clerk of the Closet to Charles II.; Bishop of Oxford, 1671; married the D. of York to Maria d'Este; P.C., 1676; became the subservient instrument of James II.; Dean of Ch. Royal; appd. to the Eccl. Commission; Bishop of Durham; deserted James's cause when lost; excepted from general pardon, 1690; forgiven, on Tillotson's intercession; suc. as 3rd Baron, 1697.

Sir G. Kneller.   D. Loggan.

Sh. ha. len. to right, in robes, looking to front, wearing cap; oval in border; three lines of Latin inscription below.

Cut. $(12\frac{1}{4} \times 9\frac{1}{4})$.   24112.

CROKE, or CROOK, Sir George, 1559-1641, judge and writer; b. at Chilton, Bucks.; of Univ. Coll., Oxford, and Inner Temple; sided with Hampden on the ship-money question; Justice of Com. Pleas and King's Bench; d. at Waterstoke, Oxford.

Anon.   R. Vaughan.

Sh. ha. len. to right, looking to front, in robes, with close cap and ruff, holding a scroll in right hand; oval in border.

Frontispiece to his " Reports."

Cut. $(8 \times 5\frac{3}{16})$.   28043.

CROKER, Rt. Hon. John Wilson, 1780-1857, politician and essayist, b. in Galway, the descendant of an old Devonshire stock; educ. in school kept by the father of Sheridan Knowles, at Cork, and at another kept by French refugees, and at Portarlington, and Trin. Coll., Dublin; B.A., 1800, entd. at Linc. Inn; began to write in the *Times*, and elsewhere; practised as barrister in Ireland; M.P., 1807-'32; helped to start the *Quarterly*; wrote " Talavera," and many other works; Under-Sec. to the Admiralty for 22 years; P.C., &c.

Sir T. Lawrence, P.R.A.   S. Cousins, mez.

Ha. len. to front, seated, wearing white neckcloth, and chain and seals across waistcoat.

Proof before all letters, except artists' names and publication-line, June 1829.

$14\frac{1}{2} \times 10\frac{7}{8}$. (11×9).   22124.

CROME, John (" Old Crome "), 1768-1821, b. at Norwich; son of a poor weaver; began life as a doctor's boy; apprent. to a house-painter; sketched from nature; taught drawing; stud. in a neighbouring collection of pictures, among which were many by Hobbema and other Dutch masters; became known and successful; founded the Norwich Society of Artists, 1805; visited Paris, 1814; painted many delightful landscapes; left some etchings of rural scenes.

D. R. Murphy.   R. W. Sievier, stipple.

Ha. len. to front, looking to left; vignette; Oct. 1821.
Ind. proof.
Prefixed to the 31 etchings of "Norfolk Picturesque Scenery,"
1834.
$13\frac{7}{8} \times 10\frac{7}{8}$. $(5\frac{1}{2} \times 6\frac{3}{4})$. 24066.

[D. R. Murphy.] Anon.
Bust, unfinished, reversed copy from the picture from which
Sievier engraved his print; vignette.
$(4\frac{1}{2} \times 2\frac{3}{4})$. E. 1965.-'89.

"From a Sketch Portrait by one of His Pupils." Woodcut;
engraver's name illegible.
Sh. ha. len. to right, painting at a picture.
$(6 \times 4\frac{2}{5})$. E. 1966.-'89.

CROMPTON, SAMUEL, 1753-1827, inventor of the "mule"
spinning-machine; b. near Bolton, Lancashire; completed his
first mule, after five years' toil, 1779; kept it secret at first, but
gave it to the public, on the strength of promises which were
not kept; refused a partnership in the firm of Peel; received a
trifling grant from Government for an invention which had
revolutionised the trade; d. poor.
Allingham. S. W. Reynolds, mez.
Ha. len. to right, seated, leaning head on right hand, right
elbow on arm of chair; dark coat and waistcoat; March 1828.
14×10. $(12\frac{1}{4} \times 9\frac{3}{4})$. 25824.
See also SCIENCE.

CROMWELL, HENRY, 1628-1675, 4th son of Oliver; Commander-in-Chief, Lord Lieutenant of Ireland, 1655; resigned
1659.
From an original in the possession of Oliver Cromwell, Esqr.,
at Cheshunt, Herts. Dunkarton, mez.
A book-plate to illustrate Clarendon's History.
$10\frac{5}{8} \times 7\frac{7}{8}$. $(8 \times 6\frac{9}{16})$. 26681.

"Drawn and engraved by W. Bond from a half-length portrait,
[Painted by T. Christian, Dà (sic) Sart, in the possession of
Oliver Cromwell, Esqr."]
Vignette. Pubd. Jan. 1, 1820.
Ind. Paper Proof.
$10\frac{1}{8} \times 8\frac{3}{4}$. $(4\frac{1}{8} \times 3\frac{3}{4})$. 28315. E.

CROMWELL, OLIVER, 1599-1658, Lord Protector, Son of
Robert Cromwell, brewer, and M.P. for Huntingdon; b. at
Huntingdon, educ. at the Gr. School there, and at Camb.; M.P.,
1629; leader of the Parl. Army in England, Ireland, Scotland,
1642-'51; dissolved Long Parliament, and became Lord Protector of the Commonwealth, 1653; d. at Whitehall.
[Walker.] P. Lombart.

T. Q. len., a page tying his **sash**; a late impression, with the address of Tho. Hinde.
Cut. $(14\frac{3}{8} \times 10\frac{7}{16})$.   E. 1445.–'89.

(Monogr.) H(ugo) Allardt excudit.
Sh. ha. len. to right, looking to front, in armour; "Olivier Cromwel, Protector," etc., in 3 lines of inscription.
Oval, within an oval border of trophies, engraved upon a separate plate.
Cut. $17\frac{1}{8} \times 14\frac{9}{16}$. (Inner oval, $12\frac{1}{16} \times 9\frac{3}{8}$).   23482.

Vander Werff.   P. Drevet.
Sh. ha. len. to right, looking to front, in armour. "Olivier Cromwel, Protecteur."
Oval, in frame.
$12\frac{5}{16} \times 7\frac{5}{16}$. $(11\frac{11}{16} \times 6\frac{7}{8})$.   E. 1446.–'89.

[R. Walker.]   F. Bartolozzi, R.A., stipple.
Ha. len. in armour, to right, looking rather to left of front, holding truncheon in right hand.
Proof before all letters, except artist's name and publication-line, Oct. 11, 1802.
$(14\frac{7}{8} \times 13)$.   26682.

W. Faithorne.   C. Turner, mez.
Wh. len. to front, standing between two pillars, surrounded with emblematical figures; from the rare print by Faithorne.
Proof before all letters.
$15\frac{1}{2} \times 10\frac{7}{16}$. $(13\frac{3}{8} \times 9\frac{11}{16})$.   22500.

From the Pictures by Lely, Walker, & Cooper.
J. Burnet, mez.
Bust, looking to left, in armour; oval in frame.
Pubd. June, 1850, by E. Gambart & Co.
$21\frac{11}{16} \times 19\frac{1}{2}$. $(17\frac{15}{16} \times 16\frac{7}{8})$.   29752. E.

Anon.   Anon., stipple.
Wh. len. in armour, looking to front; with soldiers and tents in background; in outline.
Proof before letters.
$13\frac{7}{8} \times 8\frac{7}{8}$. $(11\frac{1}{2} \times 6\frac{11}{16})$.   26561.

"From the painting by Cowper (sic) in Sidney Coll. Camb."
J. Bretherton, etched.
Bust, to front, looking to left.
$5\frac{7}{8} \times 5\frac{1}{4}$. $(5\frac{5}{16} \times 4\frac{3}{4})$.   28315. A.

"From an Original by P Lely, 1653."   [J. Thane.]
Bust, to front, looking to left; in armour. Seal, &c., below.
Oval, with facs. signature.
$7\frac{1}{4} \times 4\frac{3}{8}$. (Oval, $3\frac{15}{16} \times 3\frac{3}{16}$).   28315. B.

J. Houbraken.   R. H. Cromek.
Sh. ha. len. profile to left, in armour.
Oval, with a memoir printed below.
Published by Harrison & Co., Decr. 1, 1794.
$2\frac{3}{4} \times 2\frac{3}{8}$. (Oval, $1\frac{7}{8} \times 1\frac{7}{16}$).   28315. C.

Anon.   Peeter Huybrechts.
Ha. len. to right, looking to front, in Oval.
$5\frac{3}{4} \times 4$. (Oval, $5 \times 3\frac{3}{4}$).   E. 1448.–'89.

Anon.   Anon.
Ha. len. to right, looking to front, in armour, holding a baton.
4 verses below, "Cromwellus ducitur Unco. . . . Inv. sat."
(*i.e.*, Juv. Sat.).
$5\frac{3}{4} \times 3\frac{3}{4}$. ($4\frac{3}{4} \times 3\frac{3}{8}$).   E. 1447.–'89.

Anon.   . A Paris chez L. Boissevin.
"Olivier Cromwel."
Sh. ha. len. turned to left, looking to front.
Oval, with arms and 10 lines of inscription below.
Cut. (Oval, $5\frac{9}{16} \times 4\frac{5}{8}$).   E. 1450.–'89.

"Oliverius Cromwel."
Anon.   Anon.
Sh. ha. len. to left, looking to front; in a border.
Oval, 3 lines below. (From a book; fol. 567).
Cut. ($5\frac{1}{4} \times 3\frac{3}{16}$).   E. 1452.–'89.

Anon.   Anon.
"Olivier Cromwel."
Sh. ha. len. to left, looking to front.
Oval, 3 lines of inscription (in Dutch) below.
Cut. (Oval, $4\frac{1}{4} \times 3\frac{3}{16}$).   E. 1453.–'89.

Bullfinch delt.   R. Cooper, stipple.
"From the original in the Collection of Earl Spencer."
In armour, ha. len., coat of arms below.
$9\frac{9}{16} \times 6\frac{1}{8}$. ($6\frac{1}{4} \times 4\frac{1}{4}$).   E. 1454.–'89.
Also, a proof before letters.   E. 1455.–'89.

Sir P. Lely.   Anon., stipple.
Bust, looking to right.
$5\frac{1}{8} \times 3\frac{9}{16}$. ($2\frac{9}{16} \times 2\frac{1}{2}$).   E. 1458.–'89.

Sir P. Lely.   Harding, stipple.
Bust, looking to right.
Pubd..... April 1st, 1794.
$4\frac{11}{16} \times 3\frac{5}{16}$. $(2\frac{5}{8} \times 2\frac{1}{2})$.   E. 1456.–'89.

Anon.   Anon.
A head, looking to the right; vignette, slightly etched.
Cut. $(3 \times 2\frac{5}{8})$.   E. 1459.–'89.

"from a Beautiful Medal by Tho. Simon." Charles Townley,
1801; slightly etched.
A Profile, to the right; in oval; "The Lord of Hosts"
above; below, 9 lines of inscription.
$6\frac{1}{8} \times 4\frac{3}{4}$. $(3\frac{1}{8} \times 2\frac{3}{4})$.   E. 1451.–'89.

P. Delaroche.   Hargrave.
Wh. len., coloured (In the Court Magazine); vignette.
Cut. $(7\frac{1}{4} \times 5)$.   28315. D.

J. Leech.   Anon.
"Take away that bauble." Coloured caricature print (from
"Comic History of England").
Cut. $(4\frac{5}{8} \times 6\frac{1}{2})$.   28315. G.

CROMWELL, RICHARD, 3rd Son of Oliver, 1626–1712; Lord
Protector, 1658; resigned, 1659.
Anon.   John Thane.
Oval, with facs. autograph below.
$7\frac{9}{16} \times 4\frac{3}{8}$. $(3\frac{5}{8} \times 3\frac{1}{2})$.   28315. K.

CROSBY, BRASS, 1725–1793, Attorney; Alderman; M.P. for
Honiton, 1765; Lord Mayor, 1771; imprisoned for a short
time in the Tower, owing to his resisting the Parliament's inter-
diction of printing their debates, and consequent punishment of
printers; returned in triumph to Mansion House after release;
since then Parliament has never again attempted to restrain
printers in that respect.
R. E. Pine.   W. Dickinson, mez.
J. C. Smith, 15.   22836.

CROSSE, ANDREW, 1784–1855, Electrician; made some experiments on the subject of spontaneous generation of insects in
metallic solutions by means or in connection with, a voltaic
current; also on that of the extraction of metals from their
ores, purification of sea-water, &c.
F. Lake.   Weld Taylor, lith.
Bust, to front, light neck-cloth, dark coat and waistcoat;
vignette.
Ind. proof, with facs. signature; July, 1838.
$(6\frac{1}{4} \times 5\frac{1}{4})$.   22837.

O 82849.   I

CROTCH, William, 1775–1847, b. at Norwich, son of a master carpenter, and amateur of music; extremely precocious, played the organ in public, at the age of 5; went to Cambridge, 1786; assistant to Dr. Randall; composed an Oratorio, "The Captivity of Judah," 1789, performed at Trin. Hall; went to Oxford, 1788; org. at Ch. Ch. Coll., 1790; Mus. B., 1794; Mus. Doc., 1799; produced "Palestine," oratorio, 1812, followed by other works; Principal of the R.A.M., 1822.

 Anon.   J. Fittler.

 As a child, ha. len. to front, wearing a broad-brimmed hat placed on the side of his head; music lying on his right arm; an organ behind. May 12, 1779.

 (12⅜ × 9).   26650.

CROWLE. Charles. *See* DILETTANTI SOCIETY.

CROWQUILL, Alfred, pseudonym under which Alfred Henry FORRESTER worked; 1805–1872; humorous draughtsman and author; b. in London; intended for Stock Exchange; preferred literature, writing in the "New Monthly Magazine," to which he became a permanent contributor, 1828; retired from Stock Exchange, 1839; illustrated his own writings; exhibited at R. A., 1845–'46; constant contributor to Illustr. Lond. News; pubd. "Sketch-book," and other works.

 (C. Baugniet?)   C. Baugniet, lith.

 T. Q. len. to right, looking to front, holding a book and pencil, and leaning left arm on a high table; oval.

 (16 × 14).   25825.

CRUDEN, Alexander, 1701–1770, second son of William Cruden, a merchant of Aberdeen, where Alexander was b. and educ.; came to London; employed as a private tutor; bookseller, and corrector for the press, 1732; compiled a "Concordance of the Bible;" subject to derangement of mind; found dead, on his knees, at Islington.

 T. Fry.   T. Trotter.

 Sh. ha. len. to right, looking to front, white neckcloth, high waistcoat, coat without collar, and open; oval; arms below, in oval, in rectang. border.

 Open letter proof.

 9¼ × 7¼. (8¼ × 6⅝)   22971.

CRUIKSHANK, George, 1792–1878, designer and etcher, b. in London, son of Isaac Cruikshank, caricaturist; illustrated books, including P. Egan's "Life in London," in which the literary part was the accompaniment to the plates, "Sketches by Boz," "Oliver Twist," "Nicholas Nickleby," Grimm's "German Popular Stories," 1823–'26, &c.; painted the "Worship of Bacchus," in the Nat. Gallery, and executed the etchings of "The Bottle," &c., in aid of the total abstinence movement.

 S. Thomas.   R. Taylor (?), woodcut.

 Bust, to right, looking to front; vignette; from an illustrated paper.

 (5¼ × 4¼).   E. 1968.–'89.

Anon., woodcut.

Bust, to left, oval; facs. signature below.
$(3 \times 2\frac{7}{16})$.

E. 1969.–'89.

CRUIKSHANK, WILLIAM, 1745–1800, eminent surgeon, b. at
Edinb.; successively a pupil, assistant, and partner of John
Hunter; the publn. of his "Anatomy of the Absorbent Vessels,"
1786, secured him immediate reputation; pubd. other similar
works.

G. Stuart.   W. Say, mez.
Sh. ha. len. to left, looking to front, with turned-down collars,
high coat collar, frill to shirt.
Open letter proof; June 14, 1801; pubd. by W. Say.
$15\frac{3}{16} \times 11\frac{1}{16}$. $(13\frac{11}{16} \times 11\frac{1}{16})$.

27633.

CUBITT, MISS.
R. E. Drummond.   J. Thomson, stipple.
See LA BELLE ASSEMBLÉE, 1818.   13867.   7

CUBITT, SIR WILLIAM, 1785–1861, civil engineer, son of Joseph
Cubitt of Bacton Wood, near Dilham, Norfolk, miller; appr. to
James Lyon, Cabinet-maker, at Stalham; establ. himself as a
mill-wright, 1807; worked aftds. with Messrs. Ransome, of Ipswich; settled in London as civil engineer, 1826; engaged extensively in gasworks, docks, harbours, and canals; constr. the
S. Eastern Railway; knt., 1851.
(Maguire?)   T. H. Maguire, lith., 1850.
T. Q. len. to front, looking to front, seated, hands clasped, left
leg crossed over right, coat buttoned; vignette, with corners
cut off.
Ind. proof; facs. signature below.
$(10 \times 9\frac{1}{4})$.   22201.

CULLEN, WILLIAM, 1712–1790, Physician and Medical writer;
M.D.; Lecturer on Chemistry, Univ. of Glasgow; Prof. of
Medicine, Univ. Edinb.; author of "Lectures on the Materia
Medica."
D. Martin, P W.P.   J. Beugo.
Full ha. len. to left, looking to front, in gown, lecturing;
left hand on book on table, right slightly raised; inkstand,
books, and papers, on table; dedication in three lines, signed by
Peter Hill.
$15 \times 11\frac{1}{4}$. $(12\frac{3}{8} \times 10\frac{9}{16})$.   22220.

CUMBERLAND, ERNEST AUGUSTUS, Duke of, 1771–1799, 5th
son of George III, and King of Hanover.
W. Owen, R.A.   W. Skelton.
Ha. len. in uniform.
Published, June 5, 1815, by W. Skelton.
$19\frac{3}{8} \times 15\frac{7}{16}$. $(17\frac{3}{4} \times 13\frac{3}{4})$.   27244.
Also the Engraver's (?) drawing from the picture, wh. len.
$25 \times 15\frac{3}{8}$.   15593.

W Owen.   W. Skelton.
Another impression of the above-described plate, with the word "Proof" in the lowest corner, on the left.
 Cut.   25046. 6.
In Genealogical Chart, 553. 1.

CUMBERLAND, GEORGE, Author of "Anecdotes of the Life of Julio Bonasoni," 1793; "Lewina," 1793; "Hafod," &c., 1796; "Orig. Tales," 1810; Contrib. to Nicholson's Jour., 1807, '10, '11.
 Branwhite, min.   T. Woolnoth, stipple.
Ha. len. to right, looking to front, seated, holding a note-book and pencil on table before him; vignette.
$7\frac{1}{2} \times 6\frac{1}{4}$. $(3\frac{3}{4} \times 3\frac{7}{8})$.   E. 1967.–'89.

CUMBERLAND, GEORGE CLIFFORD, 3rd Earl of, 1558–1605; M.A. Cambr., 1576; mathematician and navigator; made nine voyages, as commander or Captain; councillor of the North, 1582; on the commission, 1587, for execution of Mary Q. of Scots; K.G., 1592; admiral of a fleet, 1598; Lieut.-Genl., 1599 and 1601; P.C.; died in debt, having greatly wasted the family estate.
 Anon.   R. White; P. Tempest excudit.
Wh. len. to front, dressed for a tournament, seven lines of inscription below; from the Tunno Collection.
 Cut. $(9\frac{1}{8} \times 6\frac{1}{2})$.   27649.

CUMBERLAND, RICHARD, 1732–1811, son of Denison Cumberland, Bishop of Kilmore; educ. at Westminster and Trin. Coll., Cambr.; Sec. to Lord Halifax, empl. on secret mission to Spain and Portugal, which resulted in loss of credit and money; retired to Tunbridge Wells, where he devoted himself to literature; wrote "The West Indian," and other plays, novels, theological tracts, poems, &c.; styled by Goldsmith,
 "The Terence of England, the mender of hearts."
 J. Clover. (J. Jackson del.) E. Scriven, stipple.
Sh. ha. len., to right, seated; vignette.
Pubd., April 12, 1814.
 $15 \times 12\frac{3}{8}$. $(7\frac{1}{4} \times 7\frac{1}{2})$.   27998. 1

 G. Romney.   V. Green, mez., 1771
 J. C. Smith, 32, 1st state.   22118.

CUMBERLAND, WILLIAM AUGUSTUS, Duke of, 1721–'65; youngest son of George II.; Field-Marshal and Comm.-in-Chf.; suppressed the Rebellion in Scotland, 1746, and was called the "Butcher," on account of his inhuman barbarity; concluded Convention of Kloster-Seven in the Seven Years' War, 1757; d. in London.
 Sir J. Reynolds.   C. Spooner, mez.
 J. C. Smith, 10.   21934.

——, on horseback.
 D. Morier.   L. L'Empereur.
 Wh. len., towards right, followed by officer on horseback; a
sentry presenting arms in foreground, on left.
 $21\frac{3}{8} \times 14\frac{1}{2}$.   ($18\frac{3}{4} \times 14\frac{1}{4}$).   23127.

——, on horseback.
 "Done from the Original at Leicester House, Painted by
Mr. John Wootton and Mr. Thomas Hudson;"
                          J. Faber, junr., mez.
 J. C. Smith, 102.   27076.

(Hudson and Wootton).   Engraver not ascertained.
 Wh. len. on horseback, similar to the print by Faber; pro-
bably, a late state of a plate by Brooks.
 J. C. Smith, 29, p. 1685.   25044.
 In Genealogical Chart, 553. 1.

——

[Sherwin.]   I. K. Sherwin.
 Bust, slightly turned to left, looking to front, in uniform,
wearing cocked hat and star; oval, figures of Britannia on
right, and Hercules on left, destroying the Hydra, below;
March 25, 1790.
 Cut. ($6\frac{3}{4} \times 4\frac{1}{2}$).   29717.   16.

CUNNINGHAM, ALLAN, 1785–1842, b. at Blackwood, Dal-
swinton, Dumfriesshire; came to London, 1810, and began
writing for the newspapers; clerk and overseer of Chantrey's
establishment, 1814–'41; wrote poems, Traditionary Tales,
A Romance ("The Maid of Elwar"), "Lives of British
Painters, &c.," ballads, &c.
 [F. W. Wilkin (?).]   Anon., lith.
 Bust, to front, looking rather towards right; vignette.
 Ind. proof before all letters; *FWW* in shield, stamped in
corner, at bottom, on right.
 ($19\frac{1}{2} \times 15\frac{1}{2}$).   24627.

CURRAN, JOHN PHILPOT, 1750–1817, lawyer and politician;
b. at Newmarket, co. Cork; educ. at Trin. Coll., Dublin; went
to the bar, and become a most eloquent and disting. advocate;
M.P. for Kilbeggan, 1783; Master of the Rolls, Ireland, 1806;
resigned, 1814, and aftds. lived chiefly in London, where he
died.
 Sir T. Lawrence.   J. R. Smith, mez.
 J. C. Smith, 50, 2nd state.   20559.

CURTIS, SIR ROGER, 1746–1816, entd. navy, 1762; lieut.,
1771; posted by Lord Howe, 1777, to commd. of flag-ship;
went to Minorca, 1780; assisted materially in defence of Gibraltar, 1782; special envoy, 1789, to Baltic powers; present at
battle of June 1, 1794; rear-admiral; cr. Bart., July 4;

Vice-adml., 1799, Commd.-in-chf., Cape of Good Hope admiral,
1803; G.C.B., &c.
> W. Hamilton.   J. Caldwall.
  Ha. len to left, resting right hand on hilt of sword; ships
engaged in the distance on left.
  Open letter proof, July 7th, 1783.
  16×12. (14- ×11¼).   **22838.**
  See also COMMEMORATION (1).

CURTIS, Sir William, 1752–1829, Lord Mayor, 1795; cr.
Bart. 1802; M.P. for the City, 35 years.
  Sir T. Lawrence.   W. Say, 1830, mez.
  Proof before inscription, except artists' names.
  15½×12½. (12⅞×10).   **22963.**

CURZON. *See* DE LA ZOUCHE.

CUST, Sir John, 1718–1770, third Bart.; suc. 1734, and to
the estates of his maternal uncle, John, Viscount Tyrconnel,
1746; M.P. for Grantham; Speaker in Parliaments of 1761
and 1768. His eldest son was cr. Lord Brownlow, 1776.
  Sir J. Reynolds.   J. Watson, mez.
  J. C. Smith, 42; but an earlier state than any described
by J. C. S.; before the scratched letters of the artists' names,
date, and address. It is an engraver's proof.
  From the Gulston Collection, with these words on the back,
in the handwriting of that great connoisseur, "N 16216. I had
this of Watson . . . . £1. 1. 0."
       24632.

CUTTS, John, Lord; 1661–1707; educ. at Cath. Hall, Cambr.;
cr. LL.D., 1690; distinguished at Buda, 1686, under the Duke
of Lorraine, and, 1688, Lt.-Col. in Holland; came to England
with William III. as Lt.-Col.; distinguised at battle of Boyne,
wounded at Limerick, and cr. Baron Cutts of Gowran, 1690;
wounded at Steinkirk; in Brest expedition, 1694; Col.
Coldstr. Gds.; third in command at Blenheim, 1704; M.P.
1689–1706; Comr.-in-Chf., Ireland, 1705. Very brave, witty,
but vain.
  Sir G. Kneller.   J. Simon, mez.
  J. C. Smith, 51.   **27648.**

DAHL, Michael, 1656–1743, portrait-painter, b. at Stockholm,
where he stud. art; came to England, 1678; travelled in
France and Italy; returned to London, 1688; settled, and
gained high reputation; left many good portraits in royal and
other collections.
  See "ARTISTS," A Society of.

DAILLON, James. *See* LUDE.

DALHOUSIE, George Ramsay, 9th Earl of, 1770–1838, ent.
Army, 1788; Lt.-Col., 1794, serving in W. Indies, 1795; in
Ireland, during the Rebellion, 1798; in Holland, 1799; in

Egypt, 1801; at Walcheren, as Maj. General, 1809; present at Waterloo; General, 1830; cr. Baron, 1815; K.B., G.C.B.; Lt.-Gov. of Nova Scotia, 1816; Gov. of Canada, 1819–'28; Com.-in-Chf., E. Indies, 1829–'32; Capt.-Gen. of Royal Company of Archers in Scotland.

Sir J. W. Gordon, S.A. T. Lupton, mixed mez.

Wh. len. to front, in uniform, left hand resting on staff, plumed hat in right, challenge cups on left.

Open letter proof; inscription on supplementary plate below

25 × 18; (24 × 16½); suppl. plate, 2⅛ × 18. 22142.

DALHOUSIE, James Andrew Ramsay, 10th Earl and 1st Marquess of, 1812–1860, educ. at Oxf.; B.A., 1833; M.P., 1837–'8; suc. as 2nd Baron, 10th Earl, M.A., 1838; Vice-pres., Board of Trade, 1843; P.C.; Pres. Bd. of Trade, 1845–'6; Gov.-Genl. of India, 1847–'56; K.T.; cr. Marquess, 1849; Maj.-Genl., Royal Body Guard of Scottish Archers.

Sir J. W. Gordon, R.A., P.R.S.A. A. Scott, mixed mez.

Wh. len. slightly to right, looking to front, in archer's dress, as Lieut. General of the Royal Company of Archers; Edinb. Castle in the distance, on right.

Ind. proof with open letters.

28¼ × 17⅞. (23⅞ × 14⅞) 27516.

DALHOUSIE. *See* PANMURE.

DALTON, John, 1766–1844, mathematician and natural philosopher; b. near Cockermouth; he taught in a school, while yet a boy; Prof. Math. and nat. philos. at Manchester, 1793; pub. "Meteorological Observations," 1793, and other treatises; invented an "Atomic Theory," by which he will be always remembered.

J. Allen. W. H. Worthington.

T. Q. len. to front, seated, with right hand to head, right elbow on table, on which are some diagrams and apparatus; left hand on arm of chair, left leg crossed over right.

Proof before all letters, except the artists' names, scratched.

18½ × 13. (14½ × 10$\frac{15}{16}$). 21748.

See also SCIENCE.

DALYELL, or DALZIELL, Thomas, c. 1599–1685, of Binns; General; served under Maj. Monro, 1640; in Ireland, 1642; at Worcester; prisoner in Tower, escaped; Lt.-Gen., Russian service, 1655; Comdr.-in-Chf., Scotland, 1666; dispersed Pentland rising; P.C.; &c.

D. Patton. P. Vanderbanck.

Sh. ha. len. to left, looking to front, in armour, with long hair and beard; oval in border; in a medallion below, a naked man, with a sword and a pistol crossed, in a window, behind; below, 12 lines of inscription.

"Fine and extra rare" (Evans).

12¼ × 9$\frac{3}{16}$. (12⅜ × 8¾). 27650.

DAMER, The Hon. Mrs. Anne Seymour, 1748–1828, amateur
sculptor, only child of F. M., Rt. Hon. Henry Seymour Conway; m. the Hon. John Damer, 1767; left a widow by his
suicide, 1776; stud. under Ceracchi, the elder Bacon, and in
France, Italy, and Spain; frequent hon. exhibitor at the R.A.,
1785–1818; modelled her own designs, and even worked on the
marble, but is supposed to have had skilled help with the chisel;
left a statue of George III., one of herself, colossal heads at
Henley Bridge, &c.; linguist, good amateur actress, &c.
    Sir J. Reynolds.   J. R. Smith, mez.
    J C. Smith, 51, 4th state.   22091.

    Walker del.   Mackenzie, stipple.
    Ha. len. to front, leaning her left arm on a pedestal, on
which stands a bust; oval; pubd. Oct. 1, 1801.
    $(3\frac{1}{4} \times 2\frac{1}{2})$.   E. 2008.–'89.

    A. S. Damer. (H. Corbould del.)   J. Thomson, stipple.
    Bust, to front; from a marble bust by herself.
    Open letter proof; Oct. 15, 1827.
    $8\frac{7}{8} \times 5\frac{1}{2}$. $(4\frac{5}{8} \times 3\frac{3}{4})$.   E. 2007.–'89.

DAMPIER, William, 1652–1715, buccaneer, pirate, circum-
navigator, captain in the navy, and hydrographer; went early to
sea; sailed to Bantam, returning 1672; present, as A.B., 1673,
in Sir E. Sprage's flagship, at actions of May 28 and June 4;
went to plantation in Jamaica; joined log-wood cutters,
1675–'8, and pirates, or buccaneers; again, 1679–'91; pubd.
"Voyage round the world," 1697; appointed, 1698, to commd.
an expedition; 1702, found guilty of cruelty to his lieut., and
fined; 1703, kissed the Queen's hand, on starting on another
expedn., this time, privateering; failed, and returned, 1707;
went again, 1708, as pilot to a privateer; returned, 1711.
    T. Murray   C. Sherwin.
    Ha. len. to left, looking to front, holding book of " Voyages "
in right hand.
    $12\frac{1}{2} \times 10\frac{1}{2}$. $(11 \times 9\frac{1}{2})$.   22839.

DANBY, Henry Danvers, Earl of, 1573–1644; 2nd son of Sir
John Danvers; served under Maurice of Nassau and Henri
IV.; then under the Earl of Essex and Lord Mountjoy in Ireland. Cr. Baron and Lord President of Munster by James I.,
and by Charles I., Earl of Danby, 1626; P.C., and K.G.
    Sir A. van Dyck.   V. Green, mez.
    J. C. Smith, 34, 3rd state.   24634.

DANBY, Thomas Osborne. See LEEDS.

DANCE, George, 1740–1825, architect, son of an architect,
brought up in his father's office; travelled in France and Italy,
stud. some time in Rome; member of Incorp. Socy., and sent to
their exhibition his design for Blackfriars' Bridge, 1761; suc.

his father as a city architect, by purchase, 1768; rebuilt Newgate; built Giltspur St. Prison, St. Luke's Hospital, &c.; foundation member of R.A.; professor of architecture, 1798–1805, but never lectured; exhibited some chalk portraits; made many profile portraits.

J. Jackson, R.A.   S. W. Reynolds, mez.

Ha. len. to right, looking to front, holding a crayon in his right hand, and resting both hands on the back of a large thin volume.

Open letter proof; June 30, 1820.

14 × 10.   (9⅘ × 8).   13888.

DANCE, Sir Nathaniel, 1748–1827, commander in the E.I.C. service, ent. that service, 1759; obtained command of a ship, 1787; Commodore of homeward-bound fleet, 1804, engaged the French squadron, under Linois, and put them to flight, for which he was knighted, besides receiving a handsome sum (5,000l.) from the Bombay Insurance Compy., and a pension (500l.) from the E.I.C.; retired; d. at Enfield.

R. Westall, R.A.   C. Turner, mez.

Ha. len. to front, looking to left; in laced coat, one button fastened across chest; July 24, 1805.

13⅞ × 9⅜.   (11⅞ × 9¾).   27524.

DANIEL, Rev. William Barker, c. 1753–1833, educ. at Chr. Coll., Cambr.; B.A., 1787; M.A., 1790; never beneficed; devoted to sport; compiled and wrote "British Rural Sports," 1801, and another book of "Plain Thoughts . . . . upon the Lord's Prayer," 1822, a poor performance; lived for 20 years, and died, in King's Bench.

G. Englehart.   P. W. Tomkins, stipple.

Sh. ha. len. to right, in profile; vignette.

Ind. proof before all letters, except the artists' names and publication-line, Oct. 10, 1811.

10⁷⁄₁₆ × 8¼.   (4½ × 3⅝).   27165.

D'ARBLAY, Madame. See BURNEY, Frances.

DARGAN, William, 1799–1867, Projector of Irish railways, and chief promoter of the Dublin Exhibition of 1853.

G. F. Mulvaney, R.H.A.   W. J. Edwards, line and stipple.

Ha. len. to front, inclined to right, seated; dark neckcloth; dark coat fastened by 2 buttons across chest; vignette; facs. signature below; oval.

Ind. proof.

(9½ × 9).   25826.

DARNLEY, Henry Stuart, Lord, 1546–1567; son of the Earl of Lennox, grandson of Margaret, Q. of James IV.; Consort of Mary Queen of Scots, 1563; murdered.

L. de Heere.   G. Vertue.

Ha. len. to left.

Cut.   (11¼ × 6⅛).   25017.   2.

In Genealogical Chart, 553. 1.

W. Holl.

From the original in the collection of the . . . Earl of
Seaforth.

T. Q. len. to front, with cap and feather. Pubd. by Harding
and Lepard, April 1, 1827.

$9\frac{5}{8} \times 7\frac{5}{16}$. $(5 \times 3\frac{7}{8})$. 14162.

See also MARY, QUEEN OF SCOTS.

DARWIN, ERASMUS, 1731–1802. Poet and physiologist; b. at
Elston, near Newark, Notts; educ. at Cambr.; M.D., Univ. of
Edinb.; practised at Lichfield, and at Derby aftds.; pub. his
Poems, "Botanic Garden," 1781; "Zoonomia," 1793 and
1797; "Phytologia," 1800; F.R.S.; d. at Derby.

J. Rawlinson. J. Heath, stipple.

Ha. len. slightly inclined, and looking, to left; square-cut coat,
open; light neckcloth and waistcoat; May 14, 1804.

$17\frac{3}{16} \times 14\frac{1}{4}$. $(10\frac{7}{8} \times 9\frac{3}{16})$. 21356.

D'AVENANT, SIR WILLIAM, 1605–1668, b. at Oxford, son of a
vintner; educ. at Linc. Coll., Oxf.; page to the Duchess of
Richmond, and afterwards lived in the household of Sir F.
Greville, Lord Brooke; produced a Tragedy, "Alborine, 1629,"
and other plays; suc. B. Jonson as Poet Laureate, 1637;
became entangled, 1641, in political troubles; knighted; confined in Cowes Castle and the Tower; wrote "Gondibert;"
highly esteemed by Milton and Dryden.

J. Greenhill. W. Faithorne.

L. Fagan, p. 32.

Frontispiece to " The Works of Sr. William D'Avenant Kt.,"
Lond. 1762–'3, fol.

26683.

DAVENPORT, MRS., 1759–1843, celebrated actress. *See*
BLANCHARD.

DAVIDSONE, SIR WILLIAM, "Knight and Baronett," Resident
in Holland for "his Majesties most Ancient Kingdome of
Scotland, and sole Comishioner for Ingland and Ireland in the
Citie of Amsterdam, &c.;" ÆTATIS XLVIII YEARS, Anno
MDCLXIIII., on pillar, behind him, on left, and arms above, with
motto, SAPIENTER SI SINCERE.

C. Hagens, del. C. Hagens.

6 lines of inscription at foot. Fine, and very rare; from the
Graaf Collection.

$12\frac{1}{4} \times 9\frac{5}{8}$. $(9\frac{13}{17} \times 8\frac{7}{8})$. 27651.

DAVY, SIR HUMPHRY, 1678–1829, one of the most eminent of
modern chemists; b. at Penzance; intended for med. profession; gave himself up to study of chemistry; Prof. to the
Board of Agriculture, 1802; cr. Bart., 1818; Pres. Royal Socy.,
1820; inventor of the miner's safety-lamp, of the metallic bases
of alkalies and earths, principles of electro-chemistry, &c.

J. Lonsdale.   W. H. Worthington.

T. Q. len. to front, seated; right hand on thigh, left to head; as Pres., Roy. Socy., the mace below, on right; March, 1827.

$17\frac{1}{8} \times 13$. $(14\frac{5}{8} \times 11)$.   22841.

See also SCIENCE, and SCOTT, SIR WALTER.

DAWKINS, JAMES, of Over Norton, 1722–1757, M.P for Hindon, co. Wilts; a great traveller in Asia Minor; discovered the ruins of Baalbec and Palmyra, and pub. an account of the Antiquities of those two famous cities; d. unmarried.

G. Hamilton, 1758.   J. Hall, 1773.

Wh. len. with Robert Wood (q.v.), " First discovering Sight of Palmyra;" they are nearly in the middle of the print, attended by several natives on horse and foot, advancing towards the left.

$19\frac{5}{8}$ (?) $\times 22$. $(17\frac{7}{8} \times 20\frac{1}{4})$.   22012.

DAY, WILLIAM, 1796–1845, lithographer, founder of the business of Day and Son, Lithographers to the Queen and Prince of Wales.

J. T. Smith.   L. Haghe, lith.

Ha. len. to right, looking at a lithographic print, which he holds in both hands.

$(8\frac{3}{8} \times 7)$.   E. 2226.–'89.

——— another impression, printed in lighter ink on a yellowish paper.

                                 E. 1270.–'86.

DAYES, EDWARD, 1763–1804, water-colour painter; pupil of W. Pether, exhibited at R. Academy, 1786; drew topographical subjects, in Indian ink, and tinted, with figures; painted miniatures, and scraped mezzotints; d. by his own hand.

E. Dayes.   W. Holl, stipple.

Sh. ha. len. to right, looking to front; published for his widow; below, " Mr. Edward Dayes, late Draughtsman to H.R.H. the DUKE of YORK."

$8\frac{1}{2} \times 5\frac{11}{16}$. $(3\frac{7}{16} \times 2\frac{1}{2})$.   26247.

DECAMP, MISS MARIA THERESA, 1774–1838, actress, m. to Charles Kemble; successful as " Urania," " Foible," " Catherine," &c.

P. Jean del.   J. Vendramini, stipple.

T. Q. len. to front, looking upwards to left, pointing to heaven with her right hand, a glory round her head; as " Urania;" Octr. 6th, 1802.

$11\frac{1}{2} \times 8\frac{3}{8}$. $(8\frac{1}{2} \times 5\frac{9}{16}$, excl. of border).   26651.

DEFOE, DANIEL, c. 1661–1731, Political and Miscellaneous writer; b. in London; took an active part in politics, as a Whig and Dissenter; pilloried and imprisoned for writing pamphlets; devoted his talents, in latter years, to works of fiction, of which the most celebrated was " Robinson Crusoe," 1719; d. in London; bur. in Bunhill Fields.

Anon. M. Vander Gucht.
Sh. ha. len. to right, looking almost to front, wearing long
wig, gown; oval in ornamented border; below, ———
Laudatur et Alget. | *Juven. Sat. 1.;* prefixed to his "Jure
Divino," 1706, fol.
$10\frac{3}{4} \times 7\frac{1}{8}$ (?). ($10\frac{1}{2} \times 6\frac{1}{8}$). 21827.

DE GREY, Thomas Philip de Grey, Earl, 1781–1859, educ.
at Camb.; M.A., 1801; D.L., North Riding, Yorks., 1803;
Ld. Lt., co. Beds., 1818; Col. Yorks. Hussars, 1819; Yeomanry
A.D.C. to the King, and Col., 1831; suc. as Earl De Grey,
1833; First Ld. of the Admiralty, 1834–'5; P.C.; Yeomanry,
A.D.C. to the Queen, 1837; Ld. Lt., Ireland, 1841–'4; Gr.
Master, Order of St. Patrick, 1841–'4; K.G.
F. Grant, A.R.A. S. W Reynolds, mixed mez.
Wh. len. to front, looking to right; as Col. of the Yorks.
Hussars, landscape in distance, on right.
Open letter proof, Oct. 2, 1850.
$32\frac{1}{4} \times 20\frac{5}{8}$. ($27\frac{1}{8} \times 16\frac{1}{4}$). 27264.

DE LA BECHE, Sir Henry Thomas, 1796–1855, Geologist;
originally in the army; the Geological Survey, and the Museum
of Practical Geology and School of Mines, were established
chiefly upon his recommendation, and of this united Institution
he was Director General; Pres. of the Geol. Socy.; author of
many papers on Geology, "Geological Manual," &c.; Kt., 1848;
C.B.
H. P. Bone. W Walker, mixed mez.
Ha. len. to right, looking to left, wearing spectacles, left arm
resting on a hammer, on rock, left; mountains in background.
Proof before all letters.
$14\frac{7}{8} \times 12$. ($11\frac{15}{16} \times 9$). 22957.

———

J. H. Maguire, lith., 1851.
Ha. len. to front, seated, wearing spectacles, striped waistcoat, &c., left hand to head, left elbow on arm of chair.
Ind. proof, corners cut off; facs. signature below.
($10 \times 9\frac{1}{2}$). 22502.

DE LA ZOUCHE, Robert Curzon, Lord, 1810–1873; Diplo-
mat, etc.
Anon. Anon.
Vignette, head, to front; looking to left; facs. signature below.
Ind. proof before all letters.
$12 \times 9\frac{1}{16}$. ($5\frac{1}{2} \times 4\frac{1}{2}$). 27209.

DELVAUX, Laurent, 1695–1778, sculptor, b. at Ghent; came
to England and was assistant to Bird, temp. George II.; went
to Italy with Scheemakers, 1728; returned here after four
or five years, and found much employment; made some monuments in Westminster Abbey, the bronze lion on Northumberland House, the *Hercules* at the foot of the grand staircase in

the Archducal Palace at Brussels, the *David,* and the thrones in
the Cathedral at Ghent, and at Nivelle, where he died.
Anon. W. Hibbart.
Ha. len. to right, looking to front; left hand resting on a cast
of a bust.
$6\frac{11}{16} \times 5\frac{1}{4}$. $(5\frac{5}{8} \times 4\frac{7}{8})$. E. 1971.–'89.

DENHAM, LADY (Court of Charles II.).
See LA BELLE ASSEMBLÉE, 1820. 13867. 31.

DENHAM, DIXON, 1786–1828, African traveller, b. in London;
Lt.-Col.; assoc. with Dr. Oudney and Captain Clapperton in a
mission from Tripoli to Timbuctoo, in which he endured great
privations and perils, 1822–'4; pubd. "Narrative of Travels
"and Discoveries in Northern and Central Africa," 1826;
F.R.S.; Governor of Sierra Leone, where he died.
T. Phillips, R.A. J. Bromley, mez.
Ha. len. to left, face in profile; right hand just seen above
cloak.
Proof with skeleton letters; March 15, 1831.
$14\frac{3}{8} \times 11\frac{1}{8}$. $(8\frac{5}{16} \times 6\frac{7}{8})$. 24216.

DENISON, SIR WILLIAM THOMAS, 1804–1871; b. in London;
educ. at Eton and R.M.A., Woolwich; 2nd Lieut. R.E., 1826;
Lt.-Governor of Tasmania, 1847–'55; Gov. of N. S. Wales,
1855–1861; Col. R.E., 1860–'68; Gov. of Madras, 1861–'66;
Act. Gov.-Genl., India, 1863–'4; Knt., 1846; K.C.B., 1856;
F.R.A.S., 1834; author of "Varieties of Viceregal Life," 1870,
and many other works.
W. M. Tweedie. J. J. Chant, mixed mez.
Wh. len. to right, in uniform, bareheaded, holding a roll of
paper in right hand, left resting on hilt of sword; hat lying in
chair, on left.
Open letter proof, May 21, 1863.
$29 \times 18\frac{1}{2}$. $(23\frac{7}{16} \times 14\frac{1}{4})$. 27256.

DENMAN, THOMAS DENMAN, Lord, 1779–1854; great lawyer,
earnest opponent of slavery, and promoter of education and
legal reform; Solr.-Gen. to Q. Caroline, 1820; Com. Serjt.,
1822; Ch. Justice of King's Bench, 1832; cr. Baron, 1834;
retired, 1850.
E. A. Eddis. W. Walker, mixed mez.
T. Q. len. to front, seated, looking to right; his right hand
resting on his right knee, his left on arm of chair.
"Second Private Plate."
Proof before letters, except the engraver's address and date,
1st Jany. 1852, in open letters.
$19\frac{1}{4} \times 15$. $(17 \times 12\frac{3}{4})$. 22842.

DENMARK, GEORGE, Prince of, 1653–1708; Consort of
Queen Anne, m. 1683.
P. a Gunst del. (M. Marrebeeck exc.) P. a Gunst.
Sh. ha. len. to right, looking to front, in armour.
$22\frac{1}{2} \times 16\frac{3}{8}$. $(22\frac{1}{8} \times 16\frac{1}{4})$. 23162.

[P. Vanderbanck?]   P. Vanderbanck.
    Sh. ha. len. to right, looking to front, in armour.
    " Sold by P. Vanderbanck over agt. the Hercules Pillers in
    Greek Street near Soho Sold by Christopher Brown at the
    Globe the West end of S. Pauls Church London."
        Cut. (22⅛ × 16⅟₁₆).   E. 359–'90.

─────

    Sir G. Kneller.   J. Smith, mez.
    J. C. Smith, 97, 1st state.   25035.
    In Genealogical Chart, 553. 1.

DENNY, SIR ANTHONY, 1501–1550; favourite of Henry VIII.,
    appointed one of the Council of Edward VI., and one of the
    executors of Henry VIII's Will.
    W. Hollar.   W. Hollar.
    Anno 1541, Ætatis 29. A Circle, cut out of the print, and
    laid down; Parthey, 1387.
    Diamr. 4³⁄₁₆.   E. 45–'89.

DERBY, CHARLES STANLEY, 8th Earl of, 1628–1672, son of
    James, 7th Earl; styled Lord Strange till 1651; joined in
    Booth's rising, Aug. 1659, on behalf of the King; bore the
    third sword at the Coronation. 1661.
    Anon.   A. Blooteling, mez.
    J. C. Smith, K., 1st state.
    Wessely, No. 13.   22067.

DERBY, CHARLOTTE DE LA TREMOUILLE, Countess of, 1601–
    1663; daughter of Claude de la Tremouille, Duc de Thouars,
    wife of James, 7th Earl of Derby; celebrated for her gallant
    defence of Lathom House (a family seat), Lancashire, when
    besieged by the Parliam. forces, 1644 and '45; compelled, 1651,
    to surrender the Isle of Man (then held by the Earls of Derby),
    where she had retired with some of her children; said to have
    been the last person who submitted to the Parliament; d. at
    Knowsley.
    Sir A. van Dyck. (W. Derby del.)   T. A. Dean, stipple.
    Ha. len. to right, looking to front, a collar of pearls round
    throat, and pearls round top of dress; Decr. 1, 1824.
    14⅞ × 10¾. (7½ × 5⅝).   27174.

DERBY, EDWARD GEOFFREY STANLEY, 14th Earl of, 1799–
    1869; b. at Knowsley, Lanc.; educ. at Eton and Ch. Ch., Oxf.;
    M.P. 1821; Under Sec. for Colon., 1827–'8; Chf. Sec., Ireland,
    1830–'3; Sec. for Col., 1833–'4, and 1841–'5; sum. to House of
    Lords as Baron Stanley, 1844; suc. his father, 1851; Prime
    Minister, 1852, 1858–'9, 1866–'8; Chancellor of Oxf., 1852;
    K.G., 1859; transl. Homer's Iliad, 1864.
    H. P. Briggs, R.A.   H. Cousins, mixed mez.
    T. Q. len. to front, looking to left, resting right hand on a
    table.   (10¼ × 8½)   10¼ × 8½

Proof with skeleton letters.
$19\frac{7}{8} \times 15$. $(15\frac{5}{8} \times 12\frac{5}{8})$. 29752. H.

F. Grant. Anon. mez.
Wh. len. to front, looking to left, standing, in robes, as Chancellor of Oxford; part of Ch. Ch. in background, on right;
1860.
$30\frac{1}{4} \times 20$. $(27\frac{1}{2} \times 18)$. 24217.

DERBY CABINET, The (of Edward G. Stanley, 14th Earl)
H. Gales and J. Gilbert. J. Scott, mixed mez.
A composition of 15 portraits, viz. the Earl of Derby, standing, on right, at end of table; behind him are Lord John
Manners and Rt. Hon. H. T. L. Corry; the others, in order,
going towards left, are Rt. Hon. Spencer H. Walpole, Lord
Chelmsford, Earl of Malmesbury, Rt. Hon. Sir Stafford H.
Northcote (see IDDESLEIGH), Duke of Marlborough, Duke of
Buckingham, Duke of Richmond, Rt. Hon. Benjn. Disraeli
(see BEACONSFIELD), Rt. Hon. Sir John S. Pakington (see
HAMPTON), Rt. Hon. Gathorne Hardy (see CRANBROOK), Lord
Stanley (see DERBY), and Earl of Mayo; the Cabinet is represented as "deciding upon the Expedition to Abyssinia."
22×30. $(17\frac{5}{8} \times 26\frac{1}{4})$. 27241.

DERBY, EDWARD HENRY STANLEY, 15th Earl of, 1826–
1893; educ. at Rugby and Cambr.; M.P.; Under Sec. for
Foreign Affairs, 1852; Colon. Sec., 1858; Pres. Board of
Control, 1858; Sec. for India, 1858–'9; For. Sec. 1866–'8,
1874–'8; Colon. Sec., 1882–'5; P.C., K.G., D.C.L., LL.D.,
F.R.S., Chanc., Univ. London, &c.
See DERBY CABINET (as LORD STANLEY), and
COMMONS (2).

DERBY, JAMES STANLEY, 7th Earl of, eminent loyalist; K.G.;
1596–1651; beheaded, after battle of Worcester.
[Loggan?] D. Loggan.
Bust, to right, looking towards front; in cloak, with medal
and star; long hair; 6 lines of inscription below.
"Rare" (Evans).
Cut. $(7\frac{5}{16} \times 5\frac{2}{3})$. 27652.

DERWENTWATER, JAMES RADCLIFFE, 3rd Earl of, 1689–
1716, son of Edward, 2nd Earl; b. in London; shared, with
his parents, the exile of the Stuarts in France; brought up with
the Pretender at St. Germains; suc. to title, 1705; joined the
Pretender in the rising of 1715; taken prisoner at Preston;
tried for treason, and beheaded on Tower Hill.
Sir G. Kneller. G. Vertue, 1714.
T. Q. len. slightly to right, standing, looking to front, coronet
in left hand, right on hip, wearing robes; arms below, and title,
with address of Tho. Bowles.
$(12\frac{5}{8} \times 10\frac{1}{4}$, incl. border, $\frac{1}{4})$. 22231.

DESBOROUGH, DESBOROW. or DISBROWE, John, 1608-
1680, Maj. Genl., bred an Attorney, married Jane, sister of Oliver
Cromwell, 1636 ; 1642-3, captain in his brother-in-law's regiment of horse ; major, at Langport, 1645 ; and at storming of
Bristol, where he commanded the horse ; negotiated surrender of
Woodstock ; Col., 1648, commanded at Yarmouth ; Maj.-Genl.,
fought at Worcester ; a man of violent temper ; arrested, tried,
acquitted, 1666-'7.

 From a picture at Stowe.   Anon., stipple.

 T. Q. len. seated, to right, looking to front, holding gloves in
right hand.

 Proof before all letters ; from the collection of John Young.
 10$\frac{3}{16}$ × 7$\frac{7}{8}$. (7$\frac{7}{8}$ × 6$\frac{5}{16}$).   27653.

DE VEIL, Sir Thomas, Kt., 1684-1746 ; son of Rev. Hans De
Veil, who came to England from Lorraine, and was librarian at
Lambeth ; the son entered the army, as a private ; employed,
partly on account of his knowledge of French and other languages, by Lord Galway, on the Portugal Expedition, as secretary ; when his regiment was reduced, he opened an office in
Scotland Yard, and gained reputation ; began career as Justice
1729, and showed great ability ; seized with apoplexy, while
examining a prisoner, Sep. 6; 1746. He is said, on insufficient
grounds, to have been libelled by Hogarth, in his *Night*, as the
drunken freemason.

 De la Cour.   T. Ryley, mez.

 J. C. Smith, 7.   28003.

DEVONSHIRE, Georgiana, Duchess of, 1757-1806 ; eldest
daughter of 1st Earl Spencer ; m., 1774, to William, 5th Duke
of Devonshire ; charming, a poet, and energetic canvasser.

 T. Gainsborough, R.A.   R. Graves, A.R.A.

 Wh. len. to right, looking to front, wearing a broad-brimmed
hat with feathers ; in a wooded landscape.

 21$\frac{1}{8}$ × 14$\frac{1}{2}$. (16$\frac{1}{4}$ × 10$\frac{1}{2}$).   27257.

DEVONSHIRE, William, Duke of. *See* LORDS JUSTICES.

DEVOTO (DE VOUW ?), Johannes, historical and scene-
painter ; 1738.

 V. Damini.   J. Faber, junr., mez.

 J. C. Smith, 115.   E. 876.-'88.

DIBDIN, Charles, 1745-1814, nautical song writer, b. at Southampton, son of a silversmith ; educ. at Winchester, sang in the
choir, pupil of Kent ; chiefly self-taught in music ; wrote and
composed " The Shepherd's Artifice," 1762, and many other
pieces, including the " Padlock," " Waterman," " Quaker,"
" Liberty Hall," &c. ; wrote 26 entertainments, and hundreds
of sea songs, which did much to inspirit our sailors, and procured for him the name of " Tyrtæus of the British Navy."

 S. Drummond.   W. Ridley, stipple.

 Sh. ha. len. to right, looking to front, wearing shirt with frill.

 (3$\frac{3}{8}$ × 2$\frac{4}{8}$).   E. 248.-'90.

T. Philips. J. Young, mez.
J. C. Smith, 17, 1st state; but erroneously described there
as the portrait of Charles Dibdin the younger. 21930.

DIBDIN, THOMAS, 1771–1841, dramatic and lyric author; eldest
son of Charles Dibdin, the elder; godson of Garrick; apprent.
to an upholsterer; soon quitted trade for the theatre, where he
played, till 1795, in every department of the drama, and wrote
more than 1,000 songs; wrote for Cov. Garden operas, farces,
&c. during half a century.
W. Owen, R.A. J. Young, mez.
J. C. Smith, 18. E. 252.–'90.

DIBDIN, THOMAS FROGNALL, 1776–1847, bibliographer, son of
Thomas, elder brother of Charles Dibdin; b. in India, 1776;
educ. at Reading, at Stockwell, at a school near Brentford, and
at St. John's Coll., Oxf.; B.A. 1801; M.A., B.D., and D.D.,
1825; having at first stud. for the bar, took orders as deacon,
1804, priest, 1805; pubd. poems, 1797; "Introduction to the
Classics," 1802; "Bibliomania," 1809; "Bibliotheca Spence-
riana," &c.
G. Richmond. L. Dickinson, lith.
Sh. ha. len. seated, to left, looking to front, holding in right
hand an open book; vignette.
Ind. proof, with open letters; 1st May, 1840.
(9 × 8½). 22843.

DICKENS, CHARLES, 1812–1870, b. at Landport, Portsea; educ.
at Chatham to a very slight extent; employed in Lamert's
Blacking Warehouse; sent to school in Hampstead Road, then
to another in Henrietta St., Brunswick Square; soon became
an attorney's clerk; stud. shorthand, and reported for "Morning
Chronicle," 1835; began to write in periodicals; "Sketches
by Boz" appeared, 1836, followed by "Pickwick," "Oliver
Twist," "Nicholas Nickleby," and all his other famous novels,
stories, and Christmas books.
W. P. Frith, R.A. T. O. Barlow, mixed mez.
T. Q. len. to right, seated, looking to left, with left hand in
pocket; a desk with books and papers, &c., on the right.
Ind. proof before all letters; signed by the engraver.
24195.
Another, with open letters; August 1st, 1862; much
darkened.
25¼ × 19. (20¾ × 15⅞). 24218.

D. Maclise, A.R.A. Finden.
Full ha. len. to right, seated, looking to left, right hand
raised; oval; facs. subscription and signature below.
Ind. proof; Oct. 1, 1839.
9⅞ × 6¹³⁄₁₆. (5 × 3⅞). 23576.
O 82849. K

—— as "Captain Bobadil" in Ben Jonson's "Every man in his humour."

C. R. Leslie, R.A.   T. H. Maguire, lith.

Wh. len. seated on a bench, turned to right, with left hand raised, in act of speaking to "Tib" (name of the actress not known), who stands in the door-way, on right.

Ind. proof before letters.

Note.—Dickens played this character in 1845,-'47, and '50.

(13 × 16$\frac{9}{16}$).   24621.

————

[Baugniet ?]   Baugniet, 1858, lith.

Sh. ha. len. to left, looking to front; oval, vignette; facs. signature below.

Ind. proof.

(8$\frac{1}{4}$ × 7$\frac{1}{4}$).   23965.

————

Mason & Co. phot., 1868.   J. H. Baker, stipple, 1870.

Bust, to left, profile, vignette; facs. signature and date below.

Ind. proof.

10 × 6$\frac{9}{16}$. (3$\frac{1}{4}$ × 3).   24749.

DICKSON, Sir Alexander, 1777–1840, Maj.-Genl., Royal Artillery; commissioned, 1794; Lt.-Col., 1825; Colonel, 1836; served at capture of Minorca, 1798, and at blockade of Malta, 1800; in Portugal, 1809, at Busaco, Olivenza, Albuera, Badajoz, Ciudad Rodrigo, Salamanca, Burgos, and Madrid, where he commanded the reserve artillery; Inspector of Artillery, 1822; Director General, 1827; G.C.B., &c.

W. Salter.   C. E. Wagstaff.

Standing, t. q. len. to left, plumed hat in right hand, resting left on table; arms of R.A. below.

Open letter proof; Aug. 1, 1841.

20$\frac{11}{16}$ × 14$\frac{7}{16}$. (15$\frac{1}{4}$ × 11$\frac{1}{16}$).   24623.

DIGBY, Sir Kenelm, 1603–1665, only son of Sir Everard Digby; ent. at Glouc. Hall, Oxford, but went abroad early; knt. on his return, 1623; obliged to go to France during Civil War; returned at Restorn.; original member of council, R. S.; wrote some philosophical treatises; a man of varied accomplishments and extraordinary personal strength; d. at his house in Cov. Garden.

Sir A. van Dyck.   R. van Voorst.

Wibiral, 71, 1st state, extremely rare, with full margin.

10$\frac{3}{4}$ × 7$\frac{9}{16}$. 8$\frac{1}{4}$ × 7$\frac{1}{3}$).   26684.

See also BODLEY.

DIGHTON, Robert, 1752–1814, actor, dramatic writer, singer, humorist, portrait-painter, and drawing-master; exhibited with the Free Society of Artists, 1769–'73, small chalk-portraits; published, 1799, satirical portraits of leading counsel, under title of "A Book of Heads," followed by many more caricature portraits; d. at Spring Gardens.

Anon.   Anon.
Ha. len. to left, in profile, holding a crayon in right hand, and
under left arm a portfolio, with inscription, "A Book of Heads,"
&c., to which this was evidently prefixed; "Published by
Bowles and Carver, No. 69 St. Paul's Churchyard, London"
[1799].
    (5¾ × 4⁷⁄₈).   28443.   2.

DILETTANTI SOCIETY, MEMBERS OF THE; established,
    1734, by some noblemen and gentlemen who were desirous of
    advancing the Fine Arts in Great Britain; it consists of 50
    members, and by its aid and encouragement Art Expeditions
    have been sent to the East, and important works published;
    the members formerly dined together periodically at the Thatched
    House Tavern, St. James's Street; they did so in later years at
    Willis's Rooms, King Street, St. James's.
    Sir J. Reynolds (c. 1778).   W. Say, mez.
    A group of seven; Sir W. W. Wynn, on the left; Sir J
    Taylor, Mr. Payne Gallwey, Sir William Hamilton, Mr.
    Richard Thompson, Mr. Stanhope, and Mr. Smith of Heath, on
    the right.
    Proof on Ind. paper.
    23 × 16⁷⁄₈.   (19⁵⁄₈ × 14½).   24256.

    Sir J. Reynolds (c. 1773).   C. Turner, mez.
    A group of seven portraits, viz.:—Lord Mulgrave, holding
    a glass, on the left; next in order, towards the right, Lord
    Dundas, Lord Seaforth, Hon. C. Greville, Charles Crowle,
    Duke of Leeds, and Sir Joseph Banks, on the right.
    Ind. proof.
    22⅞ × 16⅔.   (18¼ × 14½).   24256.   2.

DILLON, CHARLES, 1819–1881, actor, b at Diss; wrote maga-
    zine articles and melodramas, 1836–'38; acted Hamlet at City
    of London Theatre, 1840; stage manager, leading actor, and
    dramatic author, at Marylebone Theatre, 1842; starred in
    every city and important town in Great Britain and Ireland;
    leased and managed Lyceum, 1856–'7, and '8; played at Drury
    Lane, in Australia, U.S. America, &c.
    (From a Daguerreotype).   Anon., on steel.
    Wh. len. to front, as Hamlet, holding a sword in right hand;
    plate arched at top.
    (7¾ × 5¾).   23599.

DISRAELI, BENJAMIN. See BEACONSFIELD, and COM-
    MONS (2).

DOBSON, WILLIAM, 1610–1646, b. in Holborn; succeeded Van
    Dyck as serjeant-painter to Charles I.; was prodigal in his
    habits; imprisoned for debt; d. soon after his release; his
    works were praised by Sir J. Reynolds.
    W. Dobson.   G. White, mez.
    J. C. Smith, 16, 2nd state.   21929.

J. Girtin, etched.
Bust, to left, looking to front, with long hair; printed on orange-coloured paper.
(5⅛ × 3¾). 15217. 1.

DODD, REV WILLIAM, 1729–1777, son of a Lincolnshire clergyman; b. at Bourne, Linc.; sizar at Clare Hall, Camb.; Chaplain to George II.; dismissed, 1774, for endeavouring to procure a place by bribing the Lord Chancellor's wife; pub. "Reflections on Death," "Beauties of Shakspeare," &c.; always extravagant and in difficulties; forged a bond for 4,000l. on Lord Chesterfield, his former pupil; tried, convicted, and hanged, though he had refunded the money.
Anon. Anon., mez.
J. C. Smith, 53, p. 1726. It is almost certainly by, though not signed by, J. R. Smith. 21921.

DODDRIDGE, PHILIP, 1702–1751, nonconformist divine, b. in London; educ. at home, at Kingston, at St. Alban's, and studied under J. Jennings, at Kibworth; minister at Kibworth, 1723; at Market Harborough, where he established an Academy, 1725; at Northampton, 1729; D.D. Aberdeen, 1736; published hymns, sermons, and other works.
Soldi. G. Vertue, 1751.
Sh. ha. len. to right, looking to front, in gown and bands; oval in border.
12¹³⁄₁₆ × 8¼. (12⁵⁄₁₆ × 7½). 22844.

DOHERTY, RT. HON. JOHN, 1783–1850; Solr.-Gen., Ireland, 1827; M.P.; Ch. Justice Com. Pleas, Ireland, 1830; P.C., &c.
J. Catterson Smith. Anon., lith.
Bust, to left, looking to front; vignette.
Proof before all letters; the names of the personage and painter written in pencil. 27211.

DOLLOND, PETER, –1820, son of John Dollond, the eminent optician; made many valuable improvements in optical instruments, and enjoyed a well-deserved reputation.
See SCIENCE

DOMETT, SIR WILLIAM, 1754–1828; ent. Navy, 1769; served under Lord Ducie, Capt. Elphinstone, Capt. Hood, and others; lieut., 1777; present, in the "Robust," off Ushant, July 27, 1778, and off Cape Henry, March 16, 1781; served with Sir S. Hood at St. Kitts, off Dominica, &c.; posted, 1782; flag-captain, 1790–'93; present, June 1, 1794, in Howe's Victory off Ushant; rose to flag rank, 1804; d. at Hawkshurst, Dorset; G.C.B.
See COMMEMORATION (1).

DONKIN, BRYAN, 1768–1855, civil engineer and inventor, b. at Sandoe, Northumberland; his talent for mechanics soon showed

itself in constructing various instruments while yet a child;
made the first machine for paper-making, 1802; finished his
191st in 1851; made improvements in printing-machines, in
stamp-printing, in preserving meat and vegetables, in dividing
and screw-cutting engines, &c.
See SCIENCE.

DONNE, JOHN, 1573–1631, poet and divine, b. in London;
cutd. at Hart Hall, Oxf., 1584; travelled abroad; admitted at
Linc. Inn, 1592; joined the Cadiz voyage in 1596; sec. to Sir
T. Egerton, on his return; wrote his poems, satires, &c., about
this time; degree of M.A. bestowed on him by Univ. of Oxf.
1610; ordd., 1615; Chaplain to James I.; D.D., Cambr.;
Rector of Keyston, and then of Sevenoaks, 1616; Reader to
Lincoln's Inn; Dean of St. Paul's, 1621, with other preferments
afterwards; published many works, sermons, &c.
   [Merian ?]   M. Merian Iun.
   Sh. ha. len. to right, looking to front; oval, in border, in the
title to his "LXXX. Sermons;" Ætat. 42.
   $12\frac{1}{4} \times 7\frac{7}{16}$. $(11\frac{3}{16} \times 7\frac{1}{16})$.   25775.

DORCHESTER, DUDLEY CARLETON, Viscount, 1573–1632;
educ. at Westminster and Oxford; B.A., 1595; travelled
abroad; M.A., 1600; M.P., 1604; suspected, but innocent, of
complicity in Gunpowder Plot; acquitted; Ambassador at
Venice, 1610; at the Hague, 1616; P.C.; cr. Lord Carleton
of Imbercourt, 1626; Visct., and Chf. Sec. of State, 1628 till
death.
   M. Mierevelt.   W. Delff.
   As Sir Dudley Carleton, in oval; lace collar, two chains
round his neck; 4 lines of inscription below.
   $7\frac{1}{4} \times 5\frac{5}{16}$ (?). $(6\frac{5}{16} \times 4\frac{15}{16})$.   27560.

DORSET, CHARLES SACKVILLE, 6th Earl of, 1637–1706; son of
Richard, 5th Earl; served under the Duke of York against the
Dutch, 1665; cr. Earl of Middlesex, 1675; suc. his father as
6th Earl of Dorset, 1677; Lord Chamberlain, K.G., 1691;
patron of literary men; author of "To all you ladies now on
land," and other songs, &c.; d. at Bath.
   Sir G. Kneller.   J. Faber, Junr., mez.
   J. C. Smith, 208 (13).   22065.
   See also LORDS JUSTICES.

DORSET, EDWARD SACKVILLE, fourth Earl of, 1590–1652,
matr. at Oxford, 1605; M.P., 1614, and 1621–'2; K.B., 1616;
suc. 1624; K.G., 1625; High Steward, Chamberlain, &c.;
d. at Dorset House.
   A. van Dyck.   G. Vertue, 1741.
   In Birch's "Lives."
   $14\frac{1}{2} \times 8\frac{1}{2}$ (?). $(13\frac{3}{4} \times 8\frac{3}{4})$.   20889.

DORSET, LIONEL CRANFIELD SACKVILLE, 7th Earl of, 1688–
1765; suc. 1706; held several state offices; cr. Duke, 1720;
Lord Lieut. of Ireland, 1731–'6, 1751–'4.

Sir G. Kneller. I. Smith, mez.
With LADY MARY SACKVILLE, his sister (1688–1705).
J, C. Smith, 27. E. 2122.–'89.

Sir G. Kneller. G. Vertue, 1744.
T. Q. len. to left, looking to front, in robes, wearing the
collar and George, and holding a staff.
17⅛ × 11¹¹⁄₁₆. (16⅝ × 11). 22501.

DORSET, THOMAS SACKVILLE, 1st Earl of, 1536–1608, only
son of Sir Richard Sackville ; educ. at Oxf. and Cambr. ; M.P.,
1557–'67 ; Knt., 1567 ; cr. Baron Buckhurst of Buckhurst, 1567 ;
Ambassador Extr., 1568, 1571, to Paris ; to Holland, 1587 ;
K.G ; Lord High Treasurer, 1598 ; cr. Earl of Dorset, 1604 ;
part author of "Ferrex and Porrex," the first regular English
tragedy ; poet also ; author of "Gorboduc," &c.
"From an Original at Knowle." G. Vertue.
Sh. ha. len. to left, looking to front, wearing the George, and
holding a staff in left hand ; right hand not seen.
14⁵⁄₁₆ × 9⅛. (13⁵⁄₁₀ × 8⅝). 21972.

DOUGLAS, ARCHIBALD, 1748–1827, son of Sir John Stewart,
suc. to estates of Duke of Douglas, 1769, assumed the name and
arms of Douglas ; M.P., 1782 ; cr. Baron, 1790.
G. Willison. V. Green, mez.
J. C. Smith, 39, 2nd state.

DOUGLAS, CAPTAIN (Hon. George ?), – , commanded a
ship, June 1, 1794, in Howe's victory off Ushant.
See COMMEMORATION (1).

DOVER, GEORGE AGAR ELLIS, Lord. See ELLIS.

DOYLE, SIR JOHN, c. 1750–1834, General, 4th son of Charles
Doyle, of Bramblestown, co. Kilkenny ; ensign in 48th Regt.,
1771 ; lieut., 1773, and wounded ; served in America and
Flanders, with distinction ; M.P. (Ireland), 1783 ; Sec. of War
(Ireland), 1796–'9 ; Brig.-General, at Gibraltar, 1799 ; served
in Egypt, under Abercomby ; thanked by Parlt. ; Maj.-Genl.,
1802 ; priv. sec. to Pr. of Wales, 1802–'4 ; Lt.-Gov., Guernsey ;
Bart., 1805 ; General, 1819 ; G.C.B., K.C., &c.
J. Ramsay. W. Say, mez.
T. Q. len. to front, standing, in uniform, looking and facing
to left, pointing with right hand to a paper held in left ; a
horse's head on left, with Indian attendant ; Novr. 1, 1817.
22 × 16. (17⁹⁄₁₆ × 13⅝). 22066.

D'OYLY, GEORGE, 1778–1846, 4th son of the Ven. Matthias
D'Oyly, archdeacon of Lewes and rector of Buxted, Sussex ;
educ. at schools at Dorking, Putney, and Kensington, and, after
that, at Cambr. ; B.A., 1800, second wrangler and second
Smith's prizeman ; fellow, 1801 ; ordd., 1802 ; priest, 1803 ;

curate of Wrotham, 1804; moderator and select preacher,
1809, '10, '11; Rector of Buxted, 1820; of Lambeth and
Sundridge; theologian, controversialist, &c
St. George. Artlett, mixed mez.
T. Q. len. to right, looking to left, seated, in gown; facs.
signature below; the subject arched at top.
Ind proof, 1846.
$12\frac{3}{16} \times 10$. $(9\frac{1}{8} \times 7\frac{3}{16})$.   25827.

DRAKE, SIR FRANCIS, 1540(?)–1596, Admiral and Navigator,
b. at Tavistock; served with distinction in the West Indies and
in the South Seas; circumnavigated the globe, 1577–'80; Knt.
on his return; had a principal share in defeating and destroying
the Spanish Armada; d. off Porto Bello; bur. at sea.
[R. Elstracke ?]
Ha. len. to left, resting right hand on helmet, holding
truncheon in left; window on left, in which hangs a globe; a
landscape beyond; arms and crest, on right, high; inscription
below, in 4 Latin lines, addressed to the reader; above,
FRANCISCVS DRAECK NOBILISSIMVS EQVES ANGLIÆ ANᵒ.
ÆT SVÆ 43.
Out. $(15\frac{1}{2} \times 12)$.   21803.

___

Anon. J. Houbraken.
Sh. ha. len. slightly to left, looking to front, wearing gorget
of steel; oval in border; a naval battle in a cartouche below;
in Birch's "Lives."
$14\frac{5}{8} \times 9\frac{1}{2}$. $(13\frac{1}{2} \times 8\frac{3}{8})$.   E. 356. B. '92.

DRUMMOND, THOMAS, 1797–1840, b. at Edinb.; educ. at the
R.M.A., Woolwich; commissioned to the Royal Engineers;
assist. to Col. Colby, in Trigon. Survey of Great Britain and
Ireland, 1819; invented and first used the "Drummond Light"
(lime-light) during the survey of Ireland, 1825; aftds. priv. sec.
to Earl Spencer and Under-Sec. for Ireland.
H. W. Pickersgill. H. Cousins, mixed mez.
T. Q. len. to front, standing, looking to right; right hand on
hip, left hand resting on papers which lie on a table.
Open letter proof, June 20, 1841.
$19\frac{7}{8} \times 15$. $(17 \times 13\frac{3}{8})$.   24219.

DRUMMOND, WILLIAM, 1585–1649, Poet, b. at Hawthornden,
near Edinb.; educ. at Edinb.; stud. Law at Bourges, but
devoted himself aftds. to Literature; author of a History of
Scotland, Poems, Sonnets, &c.; his Sonnets are the most
admired of his poetry.
C. Janssens. J. Finlayson, mez.
J. C. Smith, 5, 2nd state. 22230.

DRURY, MRS. ELIZABETH, 1596-1610, second daughter of Sir
Robert Drury (1577–1615), of Hardwick House, Suffolk;
celebrated by Dr. Donne, who had determined to celebrate the
anniversary of her death yearly.

Anon. (G. K. Ralph, delin. 1782). J. Basire, 1784.
Wh. len. reclining, her head resting on her left hand, left elbow on pillow; "from the original Painting, in the possession of Sr. J. Cullum, Bart.," an illustration to his "History and Antiquities of Hawsted," &c. 1813; the original portrait is life-size and highly-finished.
Cut. $(5\frac{3}{16} \times 8\frac{7}{8})$ 26195.

DRYANDER, JONAS, 1748–1810, botanist, b. in Sweden; educ. at Gottenburg, and Lund.; grad., 1776; went to Upsala; came to England, 1782; became librarian to Sir J. Banks, and aftds. to the Royal Socy.; original fellow, librarian, and vice-president of the Linnæan Socy., 1788; wrote several valuable works on botany, &c.
G. Dance, June 9, 1795. W. Daniell, stipple.
Sh. ha, len. to right, in profile, seated, with arms folded. Vignette. Pubd. June 1, 1811.
$10\frac{3}{4} \times 7\frac{1}{4}$. $(7\frac{3}{4} \times 6\frac{3}{8})$. 27999. 2.

DRYDEN, JOHN, 1631–1700, poet, b. at Aldwinkle All Saints, Northamptonshire; son of Erasmus, 3d son of Sir Erasmus Dryden, Bart., of Canons Ashby, Northamptonshire; educ. at Tichmarsh, as scholar at Westminster, and again at Trin. Coll., Cambridge, 1650; B.A., 1654; wrote "Heroic Stanzas" on Cromwell's death, "Astræa Redux," on the Restoration, and a "Panegyric," on the Coronation; wrote the "Wild Gallant," 1662–'3, followed by many plays, satires, "Discourse on Satire," translation of Virgil, "Alexander's Feast," &c., &c.
Sir G. Kneller. G. Vertue, 1730.
Ha. len. to right, looking to front, holding wreath in left hand; arms below, name and inscription, with dedication to Edward, Earl of Oxford.
$14\frac{1}{2} \times 9\frac{3}{4}$. $(12\frac{5}{16} \times 8\frac{1}{4})$. 27865. 5.

———
Sir G. Kneller. G. Edelinck.
R. D. 187, 2nd state.

25814.

DUCKWORTH, SIR JOHN THOMAS, 1748–1817, b. at Leatherhead; commanded a ship, June 1, 1794, in Howe's victory off Ushant; Admiral of the White; Commander-in-chf., at Plymouth; M.P., New Romney; res. at Wear, near Exeter.
See COMMEMORATION (1).

DUDLEY, JOHN WILLIAM WARD, Earl of, 1781–1833, Visct. Dudley and Ward, &c.; educ. at Chr. Ch. Coll., Oxf.; B.A., 1802; M.P., 1802–'23; M.A., 1813; Sec. Foreign Affairs, 1827–'8; P.C., cr. Earl, 1827; F.R.S.; &c.
J. Slater del. F. C. Lewis, stipple.
Bust, to front, looking to right; vignette; facs. signature below.
Ind. proof before all letters, except the artists' names.
11×9 $(5\frac{1}{4} \times 5\frac{1}{2})$. 27210.

DUFF, ALEXANDER, 1806–1878, b. at Auchnahyle, Moulin,
Perthshire; educ. at S. Andrews; ordd., 1829; went to India,
reaching Calcutta in May, 1830, after two shipwrecks and the
loss of his books, &c.; successful missionary; returned to
England, in ill-health, 1834; back in India, 1840; in 1843, by
the disruption of the Scotch Church, he lost all his buildings,
books, and apparatus; started afresh, and was again successful;
returned to England, and appointed to the chair of the Free
Church General Assembly, 1851; visited the U.S. America,
1854; D.D., Aberdeen; LL.D., New York; in India again,
1856; home again, 1864; pubd. various works.
  Jn. Faed, R.S.A.   Jas. Faed, mixed mez
  T. Q. len. seated, to front, looking left; facs. signature below
  21⅜ × 16₁⁷₆. (17 × 13¾).   27950.

DUGDALE, STEPHEN, c. 1640–1683, informer, "discoverer of
the" so-called "Popish Plot," had been converted to Romanism
by one Knight, a priest, in 1657 or '8; ingratiated himself
with various priests, and offered information against them;
gave evidence against various persons, including the "five
popish lords," 1678; lost credit, 1681; took to drink, and
died miserably.
  R. White delin.   R. White.
  Sh. ha. len. slightly to right, looking to front; long wig;
  oval in border; "Printed for DORMAN NEWMAN at the Kings
  Armes in ye Poultrey."
  9₁₁₆ × (?). (9¼ × 5½)   27654.

DUGDALE, SIR WILLIAM, 1605–1686, Garter King-at-Arms;
b. at Shustoke, near Coleshill, Warwickshire; educ. at
Coventry; went to London, became a pursuivant extraord.,
1638; Rouge Croix, 1639; Chester Herald, 1644; wrote the
"Monasticon," pubd. 1655–'73, "Antiquities of Warwickshire,"
1656," "History of St. Paul's," 1658," &c.
  W. Hollar delin.   W. Hollar.
  Parthey, 1892.
  10¼ × 6¾. (8½ × 6¾).   25740.
  From the collection of John Young.

DUNCAN, ADAM, 1731–1804, Viscount; son of Alexander
Duncan, Provost of Dundee; b. at Dundee; ent. the Navy,
1746; disting. at Cape St. Vincent; comm. the fleet in North
Sea, and gained, at Camperdown, off the coast of Holland, a
victory over the Dutch under De Winter, Oct. 11, 1797; cr.
Viscount, 1797; d. suddenly at Cornhill, a village on the
border.
  J. Hoppner, R.A.   J. Ward, mez.
  J. C. Smith, 15, 2nd state.   24070.

—— "when victorious off Camperdown."
  H. P. Danloux.   J. R. Smith, mez.
  J. C. Smith, 57.   22086.

—— receiving the sword of the Dutch Admiral (De Winter) on
board the " Venerable," after the battle of Camperdown.
    J. S. Copley, R.A.   J. Ward, mez.
    J. C. Smith, 16, 1st state, a touched proof.   22054.

DUNCAN, Miss,   , afterwards Mrs. Davison; actress;
played Juliana, in the " Honeymoon ; " *see* picture of her, by
M. W. Sharp (-1840), in the Dyce and Forster Collection,
S. K.
    G. H. Harlow.   C. Turner, mixed mez.
    Ha. len. to front, seated ; low dress, high waist, part of an
arch of masonry on right, behind her ; Feb. 11, 1809.
    $16\frac{3}{4} \times 12\frac{1}{2}$.   ($10\frac{1}{2} \times 9$, excl. of tinted border).   27590.

DUNCAN, Thomas, 1807–1845, historical and portrait-painter,
b. at Kinclaven, Perthshire ; painted scenery while yet at
school ; intended for a lawyer, but stud., as soon as free, in
Edinburgh ; R.S.A., 1830 ; exhibited at Academy in London,
1840, '41, '42 ; A.R.A., 1843 ; showed considerable ability in
drawing, composition, and colour ; d. young.
    T. Duncan.   J. Smyth, from a calotype.
    Ha. len. to right, looking to front, with book held by right
hand, and resting on knee ; vignette ; facs. signature below
    Ind. proof.
    $8\frac{5}{8} \times 4\frac{7}{8}$.   ($4\frac{1}{2} \times 4$).   27589.

DUNCOMBE, Thomas Slingsby, 1796–1861, liberal M.P. for
Finsbury, 1834–'61.
    S. W. Reynolds, junr.   S. W. Reynolds, mez.
    Published, May, 1831.
    T. Q. len. with right hand resting on the " Hertford Petition,"
&c.
    $17\frac{13}{16} \times 12\frac{15}{16}$ (?).   ($13\frac{5}{16} \times 10\frac{9}{16}$).   27951.

DUNDAS, Sir David, 1736–1820, Scottish General; pubd.
" Principles of Military Movements," 1788 ; Commander-in-
Chf., 1809–'11 ; G.C.B. ; &c.
    W. Owen, R.A.   S. W. Reynolds, mez.
    Ha. len. to front, looking to left, in uniform, with star, &c. ;
oval in border.
    $14 \times 9\frac{1}{6}$.   ($11\frac{1}{2} \times 9\frac{3}{4}$).   24220.

DUNDAS, Rt. Hon. Robert, 1713–1787, Lawyer ; b. in Edinburgh ; stud. law at Utrecht and Paris ; called to the bar, 1738 ;
Attorney-General, 1742 ; M.P. for Midlothian ; Lord Advocate,
1754 ; Lord Pres. of the Court of Session, 1760.
    H. Raeburn.   W. Sharp.
    T. Q. len. to right, in robes, seated, right hand on arm of
chair, left on table ; curtain and pillar in background.
    Open letter proof, May 1, 1790.
    $19\frac{1}{4} \times 15$.   ($14\frac{3}{4} \times 12$, excl. of border).   22456.

DUNDAS of ASKE, Sir Thomas, 1741–1820 ; 2nd Bart. ;
suc., 1781 ; cr. Baron Dundas of Aske, 1794 ; councillor of

State to the Pr. of Wales, Lord Lieut. and Vice-Admiral of Orkney and Shetland.

See DILETTANTI SOCIETY.

DUNDEE, John Graham, of Claverhouse, Viscount, c. 1649–1689; educ. at St. Andrews, served in French army, and in the Dutch ; distinguished at battle of Seneff ; captn. of troop of Horse against the Noncomformists, where he earned the name of *Bloody Clavers* ; Sheriff of Wigton, 1682 ; P.C., Maj.-Genl. ; Viscount, 1688 ; defeated Genl. Mackay, 1689, at Killiecrankie, where he was mortally wounded.

Sir P. Lely.   J. S. Agar, stipple.

T. Q. len. to left, looking to front.

In Lodge's "Portraits."   Ind. proof.

15 × 10¾.   (7₁₀¹ × 5¾).   27242.

DUNDONALD, Thomas, 10th Earl of, 1775–1863, styled (and well known as) Lord Cochrane, 1775–1831 ; Capt., 106th Foot, 1794 ; ent. Navy ; Capt., 1800, in brig "Speedy ;" in "Impérieuse," 1808, made great havoc among French ; famous for his defeat of the French at Basque Roads, 1809 ; K.B. ; M.P. ; for alleged complicity in frauds on Stock Exch., expelled House of Commons, struck off Navy List, and from the order of the Bath, fined 1,000*l.*, impris. 12 months ; ent. service of Brazil, and aftds. Greece ; suc. his father, 1831 ; reinstated ; Rear-Admiral, G.C.B. ; Com.-in-Chf., W. Indian and N. American Station ; &c.

J. Ramsay.   H. Meyer, mez.

Wh. len. to front, standing, looking to left, holding telescope ; a burning ship in distance. April 1, 1812.

(24⅞ × 16₁₆⁷).   22123.

DUNFERMLINE.   *See* ABERCROMBY.

DUNS, Johannes, Scotus, c. 1265–c.1308, schoolman, known as the "Doctor Subtilis ;" his history very uncertain ; wrote "Opus Oxoniense," and other learned philosophical and logical works, "De Rerum Principio," &c. ; on his monument, erected 1513, at Cologne, is the inscription, "Scotia me genuit, Anglia me suscepit, Gallia me docuit, Colonia me tenet."

Anon.   J. Faber, senr., mez.

J. C. Smith, 30, 3rd state.   27564.

                            F. Chauveau.

Bust, to right, in profile, in a garland of roses, a censer on each side ; MRA, under a crown, in a glory, above ; title on a drapery below.

9₁₆¹¹ × 7⅜.   (9½ × 7₁₆³).   29608.   4.

DUNSTALL,   –1778, comedian, in the print with Shuter and Beard.

See SHUTER.

DURHAM, JOHN GEORGE LAMBTON, first Earl of, 1792–1840,
Lord Privy Seal, Governor of Canada, &c.
　　Sir T. Lawrence.　　　　　　　C. Turner, A.R.A., mez.
　　Open letter proof.　Published April 28th, 1831, by Colnaghi
and Co.
　　15 7/16 × 12.　(10 5/8 × 8 3/8).　　　　　　　　　　　22845.

DURHAM, SIR PHILIP CHARLES HENDERSON CALDERWOOD,
1763–1845, Admiral; 3rd son of James Durham, of Largo,
Fife; entd. Navy, 1777; afloat almost continuously, 1780–1815,
at the defeat of Langara, and the relief of Gibraltar, and elsewhere; with Kempenfelt, on board the " Royal George," when
she foundered, 1782; commanded the " Defence " at Trafalgar,
1805; Comm.-in-Chf. at Portsmouth, 1836–'9 ; G.C.B.
　　F. Grant.　　　　　　　　　　　W. Ward, mez.
　　Full ha. len. slightly to left, looking to front, pointing with
right hand, supporting his sword with left hand and arm,
in uniform; a burning ship in distance, on left.
　　Open letter proof (?), Jany. 1, 1837.
　　17 1/2 × 14.　(15 × 12).　　　　　　　　　　　　　22846.

DWARKANAUTH TAGORE, BABOO, 1794–1846, b. at Calcutta, an eminent Bengali religious reformer; founder of the
Hindu sects known as the Brahmoo Somaj and Vedo Somaj;
the pioneer also of European medicine in India ; travelled and
became well known in France, Italy, and England, visiting the
last country twice, in 1842 and '44; d. in London ; bur. at
Kensal Green.
　　F. R. Say.　　　　　　　　　　　G. R. Ward, mixed mez.
　　Wh. len. to front, in Eastern dress, looking to left, his right
hand resting on an open book, by which are an inkstand and
hookah ; in the distance, at right, a statue; facs. signature.
　　Ind. proof, March 16, 1846.
　　29 3/4 × 18 3/4.　(27 × 16 3/4).　　　　　　　　　　E. 615.-'88.

DYCE, ALEXANDER, 1798–1869, son of Lt.-Gen. Alexander Dyce,
E.I.C.S., b. at Edinburgh; educ. at Edinb. High School and
Exeter Coll., Oxf.; B.A., 1819; ordained, and served curacies,
1822–1825, at Llanteglos, near Fowey, and Nayland, Suffolk ;
settled in London, 1825, and devoted himself to literature ;
edited Shakspere, Middleton, Peele, Webster, Greene, Marlowe,
Ford, Pope, Beattie, and others; bequeathed his valuable library,
pictures, prints, & MSS. to S. K. Museum.
　　From a photograph.　　　　　　C. H. Jeens.
　　Ha. len. to right, seated, looking to front, with coat loosely
buttoned; holding a book in right hand ; facs. subsn. and signature below.
　　Ind. proof.
　　9 15/16 × 6 7/8.　(4 5/8 × 3 1/2).　　　　　　　　　27568.

DYSON, JEREMIAH, 1722–1776, civil servant and politician, clerk
to the House of Commons, 1748-'62 ; M.P. ; held several offices,

P.C.; in the Rockingham Cabinet, but a "King's friend," and opponent of its policy.
Anon.   J. Cochran, mixed stipple.
Ha. len. seated, with thumb in armhole of waistcoat, and holding a paper in the left hand.
A private plate.
$9\frac{1}{8} \times 7\frac{5}{16}$. $(4\frac{5}{8} \times 3\frac{13}{16})$.   20933.

EADGIFU, or EDGIVA, c. 900–953; third Consort of Edward the Elder, King of England.
Anon.   Anon.
T. Q. len., to front, crowned; the sea in the distance.
Below is an inscription in 8 lines, beginning "Edyve the "good queene and noble mother, | to Ethelstane, Edmund, and "Eldred," | . . . . etc., J. P. f.
Cut. $(11 \times 6\frac{3}{4})$.   23159.

EARDLEY-EARDLEY, SIR CULLING, Bart., 1805–1863; politician and publicist.
W. Roeting.   G. S. Sanders, mez. & stipple.
T. Q. len. to front, resting the fingers of his left hand on a table.
Open letter proof. Novr. 15th, 1864.
$20\frac{3}{4} \times 15\frac{1}{4}$. $(17\frac{1}{8} \times 12\frac{1}{4})$.   27258.

EARLE, HENRY, 1789–1838, surgeon, 3rd son of Sir James Earle, b. in Hanover Square, London; apprent. to his father at age of 16; M.C.S., and house-surgeon, St. Bartholomew's, 1808; began practice, 1811; attained some reputation by inventing a bed for cases of fracture of legs; assist. surgeon, St. Bartholomew's, 1815, surgeon, 1827; Professor of Anatomy, R.C.S., 1833; Presidt. R.M. & C.S., 1835–'7; &c.
Behnes. (H. Corbould, del.)   S. Cousins, mez.
Bust, slightly to left, looking to left; the name on pedestal.
A private plate; proof before letters.
$15 \times 11\frac{1}{2}$. (12×9).   27212.

EARLE, SIR JAMES, 1755–1817, surgeon, educ. at St. Barth. Hospl.; assist.-surg. to the Hospl., 1770; surg., 1784 till his death; surg. extraord. to King George III.; wrote several surgical works; F.R.S.; &c.
Sir W. Beechey, R.A.   Dunkarton, mez.
J. C. Smith, 16.
Open letter proof, touched about the face, by the artist for correction. Mr. Smith does not describe this state.   22692.

EARNSHAW, THOMAS, 1749–1829, watch-maker, b. at Ashton-under-Lyne, Lancashire; apprent. to a watch-maker at age of 14; for many years kept a shop at 119, High Holborn; greatly improved and simplified Graham's transit clock at Greenwich Observatory, and first made chronometers within the means of private individuals; invented the cylindrical balance-spring,

&c., unsuccessful in competition for the Longitude reward, but
received a grant of 3,000*l.* for improvements in chronometers.

Sir M. A. Shee, R.A.   S. Bellin, mixed mez.
   Ha. len. to left, light neckcloth and waistcoat, dark coat
unbuttoned, a chronometer on table, left; oval; facs. signature below.
     13×10.   (Oval, $9 \times 7\frac{5}{16}$).   24685.

EAST, SIR EDWARD HYDE, Bart., 1764–1847; b. in Jamaica;
Ch. Justice, Calcutta; M.P., Great Bedwin and Winchester;
d. at Battersea.
   From a statue by F. Chantrey, 1830.   (H. Corbould del.)
                                     F. C. Lewis, stipple.
   Wh. len. seated, to right, right hand raised to his face. The
statue was erected in the Court-House at Calcutta, 1831.
   Open letter proof.
     $17\frac{1}{4} \times 13$.   ($11\frac{1}{2} \times 8\frac{3}{4}$).   E. 281.–'87.

EASTLAKE, SIR CHARLES LOCKE, 1793–1865, b. at Plymouth,
son of a lawyer; educ. at Charterhouse; stud. in Academy
Schools, 1809, and at Paris; painted portraits at Plymouth;
visited Italy and Greece, Malta, and Sicily; lived at Rome for
12 years; exhibited at Academy, 1823–'41; A.R.A., 1827;
R.A., 1830; Sec. to R. Comm. for decoration of Houses of Parliament, 1841; librarian of R. Academy, 1842; Keeper of
National Gallery, 1843; P.R.A., 1850, and knt.; d. at Pisa.
   T. Bridgeford del.   J. Smyth, etched.
   T. Q. len. to left, looking to front, resting left hand on table;
vignette, facs. signature below.
     ($5\frac{3}{8} \times 3\frac{3}{4}$).   28300.   20.

EDGCUMBE, HON. RICHARD. *See* SELWYN, GEORGE.

EDGIVA. *See* EADGIFU.

EDINBURGH, ALFRED ERNEST ALBERT, Prince, Duke of,
1844–   ; second son of H.M. Queen Victoria; Duke of Saxe
Coburg Gotha, 1893.
   F. Winterhalter.   T. Fairland, lith., 1852.
   As a boy; in an oval.
     ($13\frac{1}{2} \times 12\frac{1}{4}$).   22191.

   F. Winterhalter.   J. A. Vinter, lith., 1865.
   Ha. len., in naval uniform, with facs. autogr. signature
below; in an oval.
     ($18\frac{3}{8} \times 15\frac{1}{4}$).   22184.

EDWARD I., "Longshanks," 1239–1307, suc. 1272.
   "Over the gate of Carnarvon Castle, the remains of an
Antient Statue of K. Edward I.   G. Vertue In. & Sculpsit."
   Ha. len. to right, looking to left, with sword in right hand.
     $11\frac{5}{16} \times 7\frac{3}{4}$.   ($10\frac{3}{8} \times 7\frac{1}{4}$).   27095.
     NOTE.—No other portrait of this King is known.

EDWARD III., 1312–1377, suc. 1327.
Wh. len., in armour; from Joshua Barnes's "History."
Six verses below, in two columns.
An inscription in the left corner at top; and, in the right
corner at top, a coat of arms. The Royal arms, England
quartered with France, below, in the middle.
Cut. (11¾ × 7¼).   27542. 1.

"From an antient painting in Windsor Castle." Geo. Vertue,
Delin. et Sculp."
Bust, to right, with sword in right hand, in an oval. On
the sword are two crowns.
11 7/16 × 7 9/16. (11 × 7½).   27178. 11.

EDWARD, PRINCE OF WALES, commonly called the Black Prince,
1330–1376.   [R. White, sc.]
From Joshua Barnes's "History of Edward III."
Wh. len. in armour. 4 verses below, in two columns. An
inscription at top, in the left corner, and "pag. 707" at top,
in the right corner. Above, a coat of arms.
Cut. (11 5/16 × 7¼).   27542. 2.

EDWARD IV., 1441–1483; suc. 1461.
"From an antient Painting in the Royal Collection now at
Kingsington Palace."
Geo. Vertue del.   G. Vertue.
Ha. len. to right, holding a ring.
11½ × 7⅝. (11 1/16 × 7 1/16).   27100.

EDWARD V., 1470–1483; suc. 1483; deposed, 1483.
"From a Limning in a Manuscript-book now in the Library
at Lambeth."
G. Vertue, del.   G. Vertue.
Ha. len. to left, looking to front, wearing an ermine collar
on his cloak.
Cut. (11 1/16 × 7⅛).   27126.

Anon.   Jas. Smith, Sculp.
T. Q. len. holding a flower in his right hand; a crown over
his head; in an oval.
(From a History of England; lettered at top, in right corner,
"Vol. 1," and, in left corner, "Faceing this Reign.") Below
is a representation of the murder of the Princes in the Tower.
14¼ × 9¼. (13⅞ × 8¼).   27990.

EDWARD VI., 1537–1553, only son of Henry VIII. and Jane
Seymour; b. at Hampton Court; suc., 1547.
Anon. (From an original in Kensington Palace.) G. Vertue.
Sh. ha. len., wearing a cap and feather, and collar and George;
from Rapin's "History."
Cut. (11 7/16 × 7 1/16).   27127.

—— Presenting the Charter of Bridewell and Bethlehem Hospitals to the Lord Mayor and Aldermen of London; with Lord Chancellor Goodrick, and others.
   H. Holbein.   G. Vertue, 1750.
   A composition of eleven figures; the young king, seated in the middle, gives the charter to the Lord Mayor, Sir George Barnes, Kt., who kneels, on the left; behind him are the Lord Chancellor and Bishop of Ely, standing; on the other side are the Master of the Rolls, Sir Robert Bowes, and William, Earl of Pembroke, K.G.; on the extreme right, Holbein's own head is seen; 5 lines of inscription below.
   (17⅜ × 20¹¹⁄₁₆).   21971.

EDWARDES, Sir HERBERT BENJAMIN, 1819–1868, entd. Indian Military Service, 1840; present at battle of Moodkee, 1845; of Sobraon, 1846; defeated Moolraj, 1848; K.C.B.; pubd. "A year on the Punjaub Frontier, 1848–'9," 1851.
   H. Moseley.   J. H. Lynch, lith.
   T. Q. len. to left, looking to front, in Indian dress, left hand resting on hilt of sabre; vignette; facs. signature below.
   Ind. proof.   April 17, 1850.
   (14½ × 12¼).   22977.

EDWARDS, EDWARD, 1738–1806, portrait and subject-painter; b. in London, stud. in Duke of Richmond's Gallery and St. Martin's Lane Academy; member of Incorp. Socy. of Artists; taught drawing to support himself, his mother, brother, and sister; A.R.A., 1773; visited Italy, 1775; teacher of Perspective in R.A., 1788; had some knowledge of Architecture, was a tolerable musician, and violinist; pubd. "Treatise on Perspective," and "Anecdotes of Painters;" made some etchings.
   E. Edwards.   A. Cardon, stipple.
   Sh. hn. len. to right, looking to front, holding up a book in his left hand; April 20, 1808.

EDWARDS, W. CAMDEN, 1777–1855, engraver, b. in Monmouthshire; went early in this century to Bungay; engraved in the line manner illustrations for the Bible, "Pilgrim's Progress," and portraits, &c., practising in Norfolk and Suffolk; seems to have been on friendly terms with Mr. and Mrs. Dawson Turner, the Norwich banker and collector, and his wife.; d. and bur. at Bungay.
   Etched by Mrs. Dawson Turner, 1817, finished by W. C. E[dwards].
   Bust to left, looking to right; vignette; below, W. C. Edwards, Engraver, 1815.
   9⅜ × 7⁷⁄₁₆.   (4½ × 4¼).   26275.

EDWIN, JOHN, 1749–1790, disting. comedian, b. in London, son of a watchmaker; appeared at Manchester on the stage, 1765; aftds. at Dublin and Bath; at the Haymarket, 1776, and subsequently at Cov. Garden; particularly successful in parts of old men; besides his comic powers, possessed great ability; as shown by his published " Eccentricities;" d. in Bedford-street ; bur. at St. Paul's, Cov. Garden.

J. Downman delt.   H. Downman, stipple.

T. Q. len. on right, inclined and looking to left, as "Lingo," in Foote's 'Agreeable Surprise'; with Mrs. Wells (q. v.), on left, who is turned towards him, in profile, holding a bowl in her two hands, as " Cowslip ;" printed in colours ; oval.

$18\frac{7}{8} \times 13\frac{1}{8}$.   (Oval, $16 \times 12\frac{3}{16}$).   22504.

EGAN, PIERCE, c. 1772-1849, sporting writer, b. in London, lived in the suburbs ; had established a reputation as " reporter of sporting events," 1812 ; his impromptu epigrams, witticisms, and songs enjoyed a wide circulation; author of " Boxiana," "Life in London," " Finish to the Adventures of Tom, Jerry, and Logic," &c. ; supplied the slang phrases to the re-issue of Grose's "Dictionary of the Vulgar Tongue," as "Lexicon Balatronicum," 1811 ; started the paper which became afterwards " Bell's Life ;" &c.

G. Sharples delin.   "Engraved on steel by C. Turner," mixed mez.

T. Q. len. to right, seated, looking to front, head on left hand, and elbow on table; papers in right hand. Dated June 1st, 1832 ; but mentions, in inscription, the production of "Life in Dublin," at Dublin, Feb. 18. 1834.

(Query: pubd. " at Pierce Egan's tiny crib, in Chancery Lane," 1824 ?—See D. N. B.)

$14\frac{1}{4} \times 10$. $(10\frac{7}{16} \times 8\frac{1}{4})$.   22847.

EGBERT,   —839, King of the West Saxons ; suc. (Wessex) 800, (England) 829.

From a silver coin.   G. Vertue.

Bust, profile to left, crowned; published in Rapin's " History."

Cut. $(11 \times 7\frac{3}{16})$.   27178.   1.

NOTE.—This is the only portrait known of this King.

EGERTON, MRS.

R. E. Drummond.   J. Thomson, stipple.

See LA BELLE ASSEMBLÉE.   13867.   8.

EGG, AUGUSTUS LEOPOLD, 1816-1863, son of the gun-maker in Piccadilly ; b. in Piccadilly ; stud. at R. A., exhibited at R. A. and B. I., at Suffolk St. gallery, 1837-'60 ; A.R.A., 1848 ; R.A., 1860 ; d. at Algiers.

J. Phillip, R.A.   T. O. Barlow, mixed style.

T. Q. len. to right, seated, with a long-haired terrier in his lap ; facs. signature below.

Proof before letters, signed by the painter and engraver; publn. line at top, March 11, 1865.

$15\frac{5}{8} \times 12\frac{7}{16}$. $(11\frac{1}{2} \times 9\frac{3}{8})$.   22976.

O   R2849.   L

EGG, Augustus Leopold—*continued.*
    W. P. Frith, A.R.A.   J. Smyth.
    Ha. len. to front, leaning with right arm on back of chair;
left hand in pocket; vignette; facs. signature below.
    Ind. proof.
    (4½ × 3¾)   28300. 27.

EGMONT, John, second Earl of, 1711–1770; suc. 1748;
first Lord of the Admiralty, 1763; and cr. an English peer;
P.C.; &c.
    T. Hudson.   J Mc. Ardell, mez.
    J. C. Smith, 61.   27130.

EGREMONT, George O'Brien Wyndham, 3rd Earl of, 1751–
1837; eldest son of Charles, 2nd Earl; Lord Lieut., Custos
Rotulorum, and Vice-Admiral of the County of Sussex; F.R.S.,
F.S.A., disting. as a liberal patron of Art; d. unmarried.
    T. Phillips, R.A.   S. W. Reynolds, mixed mez.
    T. Q. len. to right, seated, with right hand to cheek, white
neckcloth, dark coat fastened by one button, right elbow on
table, head of spaniel resting against his hip and looking up
to his face; Jany. 1, 1826.
    15 × 10¾. (13¼ × 10¾).   22090.

ELDON, John Scott, Earl of, 1751–1838; educated at Oxford,
1766; ran away with Miss Surtees, 1772; barrister, 1776;
M.P., 1783; Solr.-Gen., 1788; Atty.-Gen., 1793–'9; Ch. Justice
Com. Pleas, and Baron Eldon, 1799; Ld. Chancr., 1801–'6;
again, 1807; resigned, 1827; cr. Earl, 1821.
    Sir T. Lawrence, P.R.A.   G. T. Doo, 1826.
    Ha. len. seated, to front, arms resting on arms of chair.
    Ind. proof with open letters; May, 1828.
    14¼ × 11. (11 × 8¹³⁄₁₆).   27246.

ELGIN, James Bruce, 8th Earl of, 1811–1863, Statesman and
Diplomatist; Governor of Jamaica, 1842–'46; Gov. General of
Canada, 1846–'54; Ambassador to China, 1857 and 1860; concluded treaties of Tien-tsin and Pekin; Viceroy of India, 1862;
K.T., G.C.B., &c.; d. in the Punjaub.
    Sir F. Grant.   J. Faed, mixed mez.
    Wh. len. to front, inclined and looking to left, standing, in
uniform, resting right hand on a folded paper, which lies on a
table, with despatch-box, seal in case, &c.; left hand on sword-
hilt.
    Open letter proof, June 7, 1864.
    (26¼ × 16).   21951.

ELIOTT, General. *See* HEATHFIELD.

ELIZABETH of York, 1466–1503, Queen of Henry VII., 1486.
Anon.   Anon.
    Ha. len. in oval, in border. In Birch's " Lives."
    Cut. (14½ × 8¾ full).   25018. 1.
    In Genealogical Chart, 553. 1.
    Note.—This is not by Houbraken, as Bromley describes it.

ELIZABETH OF YORK—*continued.*

H. Crease del. W. I. Fry, stipple.
From the original in the collection of the . . . Earl of Essex.
Ha. len., holding a white rose in her right hand.
Published, Decr. 1, 1815.
Cut. $(7\frac{1}{2} \times 5\frac{1}{2})$. 25020.
In Genealogical Chart, 553. 1.

Anon. T. A. Dean.
From the original, in the Collection of the . . . Earl of Essex.
Ha. len., holding a white rose in her right hand.
Published, Feb. 1826, by Harding and Lepard.
$9\frac{11}{16} \times 7\frac{3}{8}$. $(4\frac{5}{8} \times 3\frac{1}{2})$. 14161.

ELIZABETH, QUEEN, 1533–1603, daughter of Henry VIII. by his second wife, Queen Anne Boleyn; b. at Greenwich; suc., 1558, on death of her half-sister, Queen Mary; d. at Richmond; bur. in Westminster Abbey.

From the Original by N. Hilliard.
G. P. Harding del. W. Greatbach.
Published by R. Bentley, 1851.
F. M. O'D., 31.
Cut. $(5\frac{1}{8} \times 4)$. 26193.

Anon. Van Sichem.
Wh. len. to left, orb in right hand, sceptre in left.
Unknown to Bromley.
F. M. O'D., 41.
Cut. $(7\frac{9}{16} \times 4\frac{3}{4})$. 26213.

W. Faithorne.
Wh. len., Enthroned between Lord Burghley, on the left, and Sir Fr. Walsingham, on the right. She holds the sceptre in her right and the orb in her left hand. Below, in a cartouche, is the title of the book, "The Compleat Ambassador," by Sir Dudley Digges, for which this print was the frontispiece.
From the Collection of the late John Young, Esq.
F. M. O'D., 51.—L. Fagan, p. 4.
Cut. $(10\frac{15}{16} \times 6\frac{1}{4})$. 24113.

Jodocus Houdius fecit, Anno 1590.
Sh. ha. len. in ruff, in an oval, at top of a map of England, Ireland, and part of Scotland; figures in the corners.
F. M. O'D., 79.
Map, &c., $6\frac{1}{8} \times 8\frac{5}{8}$. (Oval, $2 \times 1\frac{13}{16}$). 24921.

E. Lutterell delin. P. Vanderbanck.
Bust, with ruff, in an oval, within a border of oak-leaves, &c.
F. M. O'D., 115. Marked at foot, on right, 24.
$11\frac{7}{16} \times 7\frac{15}{16}$. $(11\frac{1}{8} \times 7\frac{11}{16})$. 27991.

ELIZABETH, Queen—*continued.*

T. I. Woodman and H. Mutlow.
Copied from the print engraved by Vanderbanck.
In Harrison's Edition of Rapin's " History of England."
F. M. O'D., 116.
Cut. (7⅝ × 6½). 26192.

Anon.
Sh. ha. len. to front, looking to front, wearing a high ruff,
collar of pearls, and rich dress ; oval in frame ; the defeat of the
Armada below, in a cartouche.
F. M. O'D., 117.
Cut. (14⁷⁄₈ × 8¹¹⁄₆). 29717. 11.

(Ascribed to F. Hillyard.) J. Simon, mez.
Ha. len. with ruff and jewelled dress, in an oval.
Printed and sold by Geo. Bickham.
F. M. O'D., 141. J. C. Smith, 54, 3rd state.
A late impression. 28820.

H. Holbein. A. W. Warren.
Ha. len. to front, face turned slightly to right, looking to
front, wearing crown, high ruff, &c., in rect. frame with corners
cut of, between two pillars ; July 3, 1802. This is a copy of
the print by Vertue, 145.
F. M. O'D., 147.
8⅜ × 5¾. (6¼ × 5½). 29717. 9.

I. Oliver del. C. Turner, mez.
Wh. len., crowned ; from a rare print by Crispin de Passe.
Proof before all letters.
F. M. O'D., 162. 22503.

Crisp : van Queboren, Aᵒ. 1625.
Sh. ha. len., with a great ruff, and a rich dress.
F. M. O'D., 169.
Cut. 6¹⁄₁₀ × 3⅝ (?). (4¹¹⁄₆ × 3¾). 29294.

I. Oliver del. G. Vertue.
Ha. len. slightly turned to left, looking towards left, in superb
dress, wearing crown, high ruff, pearl collars, and holding
sceptre in left hand ; a phœnix above, the bible and sword of
justice below.
F. M. O'D., 188.
11⁷⁄₁₆ × 7⅜ (11 × 7). 29717. 10.

ELIZABETH, QUEEN—*continued.*
Anon. Anon.
Sh. ha. len. to left, in an oval, between pillars. Below,
"Elisabeth Königin von Engellandt." A German print.
Printed in a passe-partout.
$11\frac{7}{16} \times 6\frac{11}{16}$. (The inner plate, $6\frac{3}{4} \times 4\frac{1}{4}$).
Not mentioned by F. M. O'D. E. 103.–'91.

ELIZABETH, OF BOHEMIA, 1596–1662; daughter of James I.,
wife of Frederick V. of Simmerin, 1613.
C. Boel.
T. Q. len. in a rich dress, with great jewels, and with a book
in her left hand.
Below, 8 verses in Latin and 8 in English, by Io. Davies.
"Are to be solde in Lombard Street by John Boswell."
($14\frac{7}{8} \times 10$, excl. of lower part, on which the inscription is
engraved, $2\frac{11}{14} \times 10\frac{5}{16}$ (?)). E. 430.–'85.

Miereveldt. W. J. Delff. 1630.
Sh. ha. len. to left, looking to front, with three rows of pearls
in her hair, and a pendent jewel.
Cut. ($14\frac{1}{4} \times 11\frac{1}{4}$). 25429.
In Genealogical Chart, 553. 1.

G. Honthorst. R. à Voerst. 1631.
Sh. ha. len. to left, looking to front, wearing three rows of
pearls and a pearl pendent, &c.
Oval, in border.
$16\frac{1}{2} \times 12$. ($14\frac{11}{16} \times 11\frac{3}{4}$). 27245.

[Honthorst.] *A. vander Werff. P. à Gunst.
Sh. ha. len. to right, with pearls, &c.; oval in border.
Cut. ($11\frac{3}{4} \times 6\frac{7}{8}$). 25031.
In Genealogical Chart, 553. 1.
* NOTE.—Not the original painter of the portrait.

Honthorst. C. Sherwin, stipple.
Bust, to right, looking to front, in oval.
Published... 4th April, 1787, by J Stockdale.
Cut. ($3\frac{1}{8} \times 2\frac{3}{4}$). 25028.
In Genealogical Chart, 553. 1.

ELIZABETH, PRINCESS, 1635–1650, 2nd daughter of Charles I.
See CHARLES, PRINCE OF WALES, &c.

ELIZABETH, PRINCESS, daughter of George III., 1770–1840,
m. 1818 to Fred. L. Joseph, Landgr. of Hesse Homburg.
H. Ramberg. W. Ward, stipple.
Oval; twining a wreath.
Cut. ($11 \times 8\frac{7}{8}$). 26725. 3.
Also, a duplicate, in Genealogical Chart, 553. 1.
($13 \times 9\frac{1}{8}$). 25067. 2.

ELIZABETH, Princess—continued.

C. Hlatz.   D. Weiss, stipple.

Ha. len. to right, looking to front, with collar of pearls; oval.
11¼ × 8.   (4½ × 3⅜).   25057.   2.

In Genealogical Chart, 553.   1.

ELLA, John, 1802–1888, violinist, a member of the orchestra of
the King's Theatre, 1822, and subs. of the Concerts of Ancient
Music, Philharmonic, &c., retiring in 1848; pupil of Attwood
and Fétis; established, 1845, the "Musical Union," which he
directed until 1880; wrote "Musical Sketches abroad and at
home," a "Personal Memoir of Meyerbeer," and other contributions to newspapers.

  See MUSICAL UNION

ELLENBOROUGH, Edward Law, 1st Lord, 1748–1818,
lawyer and statesman; son of Edmund Law, Bishop of Carlisle; famous for his successful defence of Warren Hastings;
Attorney-General, 1801; Lord Chf. Justice of King's Bench,
1802.

  Sir T. Lawrence, R.A.   C. Turner, mez.

  T Q. len. slightly to right, seated, facing and looking to left,
wearing Chf. Justice's robes and collar, right hand on arm of
chair, left on papers which lie on his desk.

  Open letter proof, Jany. 2, 1809.
  20 × 18⅞.   (17¼ × 13⅛).   22087.

ELLESMERE, Rt. Hon. Francis Egerton, Earl of, 1800–
1857; author, statesman, Ch. Sec. Ireland, &c.

  G. Richmond.   Fr. Holl, stipple.

  Sh. ha. len. to front, looking to right; vignette.

  Ind. proof with open letters.   Jan. 20, 1855.
  21¾ × 16¼   (9¾ × 8).   24221.

ELLESMERE, Thomas Egerton, Baron of, c. 1540–1617,
Viscount Brackley; Atty.-Gen., 1594; Lord Keeper, 1596;
Lord Chancr., 1603–'17; negotiated for a union with Scotland,
1604.

  "From the original at Wootton Court, in Kent."   Trotter.

  Sh. ha. len. to front, in robes, wearing a broad-brimmed hat.
Jany 1, 1794.   Oval; arms below.

  Cut.   (5⅜ × 4⅞).   28000.

ELLICE, Edward, 1781–1863, statesman, b. at Montreal,
Canada; educ. at Winchester and Aberdeen; ent. mercantile
life, 1800; m. a sister of Lord Grey; M.P., Coventry, 1818,
with one short interval, till his death; Sec. to Treasury,
1831–'2; Sec. for War, 1833–'4; one of the chief founders of
the Reform Club, of which he was first chairman; d. at Ardochy,
Glengarry.

  F. Grant, R.A.   J. Scott, mixed mez.

  Wh. len. to front, seated, with left leg crossed over right, a
paper in left hand, books of reports on floor by his chair.

Proof before all letters, except artists' names and publication-line, July 4, 1857.
28 × 18½. (23¹¹⁄₁₆ × 14⅝). 27259.

ELLICOTT, JOHN, c. 1706–1772, clockmaker and man of science, son of John Ellicott, clockmaker; followed his trade at 17, Sweeting's Alley, Royal Exch.; gained great reputation for the beauty and excellence of his workmanship; clockmaker to George III.; submitted an improved pyrometer to the Roy. Socy., 1736; F.R.S., 1738; pubd. several scientific papers; invented a compensating pendulum, 1752; delineated line of moon's motion, 1762; observed transit of Venus, &c.
N. Dance. R. Dunkarton, mez.
J. C Smith, 17, 2nd state. 22233.

ELLIS, GEORGE AGAR, 1797–1833, eldest son of Henry Welbore, 2d. Visct. Clifden; educ. at Oxford; an enlightened patron of art, suggested the purchase of the Angerstein pictures, the foundation of the National Gallery; edited the Ellis, and Walpole and Mann, correspondences; cr. Baron Dover, 1831; d. at Dover House, Whitehall.
J. Jackson. W. Ward, mez.
J. C. Smith, 36; A1 state, undescribed by Mr. J. C. S.; proof before all letters.
24736.

ELLISTON, ROBERT WILLIAM, 1774–1831, eminent actor, b. in London; educ. at St. Paul's School; intended for the church; joined the Bath company at 16; appeared at the Haymarket, 1796, at Cov. Garden, and Drury Lane, 1804–'9; took the Circus (Surrey), but did not succeed; returned to Drury Lane, which he leased, 1819; bankrupt, 1826; went to Olympic; and again to the Surrey, till his death.
G. H. Harlow. C. Turner, mez.
Ha. len. to left, looking rather to right of front, wearing a furred and frogged coat; a pillar behind, on right.
(10½ × 8¹³⁄₁₆). 24071.

ELMORE, ALFRED, 1815–1881, historical painter, b. at Clonakilty, co. Cork; exhibited at R. Acad., Br. Instit., and Suffolk St. Gallery, 1834–'80; " Origin of the Guelph and Ghibelline quarrel " sold for 300l., 1845; A.R.A., 1845; R.A., 1857.
[C. Baugniet.] C. Baugniet, lith., 1857.
Sh. ha. len. slightly to left, looking to front; high waistcoat, dark hair, rather long; vignette; facs. signature below.
(7 × 6). 23617.

ELPHINSTONE, CAPTAIN JOHN, –1801, commanded a ship, June 1, 1794, in Howe's victory off Ushant; d. at Malta.
See COMMEMORATION (1).

ELPHINSTONE, MOUNTSTUART, 1779–1859, 4th son of John, 11th Baron Elphinstone; educ. at Edinb. high school, 1791–'2, and at Kensington; entered Bengal civil service,

landed at Calcutta, 1796; studied diligently; rose rapidly;
present at Assaye and Argaum; resident at Nagpur; ambassador to Cábul; resident at Poona, 1810; Governor of Bombay,
1819–'27; travelled, 1827–'29, in Greece and Italy; wrote
" History of India," &c.
H. W. Pickersgill, R.A. C. E. Wagstaff, mixed mez.
Wh. len. to front, seated, looking to left: on the left is a table
with " History of Caubul," and other books; on the right, a
portfolio leaning against his chair.
Arms below, in centre; facs. signature towards right.
Ind. proof.
$23\frac{1}{8} \times 15\frac{3}{8}$. $(19\frac{5}{16} \times 13\frac{1}{16})$.   23138.

ELPHINSTONE, MOUNTSTUART—*continued.*
 T. Lawrence and Simpson. C. Turner, A.R.A., mez.
Wh. len. seated, to right, looking to front, holding a paper
lifted in his left hand.
Open letter proof, 1833.
$28\frac{7}{8} \times 18\frac{3}{8}$. $(24\frac{1}{2} \times 16\frac{1}{8})$.   29752. F.

EMERSON, WILLIAM, 1701–1782, Mathematician and mechanician; son of a country schoolmaster; b. at Hurworth, Darlington; author of " Doctrine of Fluxions," " Principles of Mechanics," " Method of Increments," &c.; d. at Hurworth.
 Sykes.   C. Turner, mez.
Ha. len. slightly inclined to right, looking to front, light neckcloth, coat buttoned at top by two buttons, open in middle,
buttoned again below; oval in border.
Proof before all letters.
14×10. $(12 \times 9\frac{7}{8})$.   22848.

EMERY, SAMUEL ANDERSON, 1817–1881, actor, son of an actor;
b. in London; first appeared at Fitzroy theatre, 1834; played
at Lyceum, 1843 and 1844–'47; stage manager at Surrey
Theatre, 1848–'9; played at Drury Lane, 1850; at Olympic,
1853; visited America, Australia; a very capable actor; played
at all principal theatres till the year of his death.
 De Wilde.   C. Turner, mez.
Wh. len. to front, inclined to right, looking to left, holding
hat in left hand, right hand raised; as Tyke in the " School of
Reform;" June 14, 1808.
$21\frac{7}{8} \times 15\frac{3}{4}$. $(19\frac{5}{8} \times 15\frac{3}{4})$.   25776.

ENGLAND, KINGS AND QUEENS OF, from William I. to
George II.
Ovals, in four rows (of 8 in each), from left to right; in the
" Chronological Tables " published by Wm. Allen, No. 32,
Dame Street, Dublin.
$16\frac{5}{8} \times 20\frac{3}{4}$. $(15\frac{5}{8} \times 20\frac{1}{2})$.   26206.

ENGLEFIELD, SIR HENRY CHARLES, 1752–1822, eldest of
the five children of Sir Henry Englefield, bart.; suc. to the
baronetcy, 1780; F.S.A., 1779; Vice-pres. and prest. S.A.;

contributed to Archæological works; F.R.S., 1778; F.L.S.;
author of " Description of . . . the Isle of Wight," &c.
  H. Edridge delin.   C. Picart, stipple.
  Sh. ha. len. to left, looking to front, holding papers rolled in
his right hand ; vignette. June 26, 1812.
  Cut. (8¾ × 8¼).   E. 1855.—'89.

ENGLEFIELD, Sir Henry Charles—continued.
  T. Phillips, R.A.   C. Turner, mixed mez.
  Full ha. len. to left, seated ; vases, and an arched window,
with coat of arms, behind, on left.
  Proof before all letters.
  15¼ × 11¼. (12⅝ × 9¾).   22849.

ERNEST, Duke of Saxe-Coburg-Gotha. See ALBERT,
Prince.

ERSKINE, Thomas, Lord, 1750-1823, son of the Earl of
Buchan ; lawyer, orator, and wit ; served in the army, 1768 ;
successfully defended Captain Baillie, 1778, and Ld. G. Gordon,
1781 ; K.C. & M.P., 1783 ; defended Hardy and Horne Tooke,
1794 ; published " View of the Causes and Consequences of the
present war with France," 1797 ; Ld. Chancr. 1806-'7.
  A. Aglio.   Anon., lith.
  Bust, to front, vignette.
  Ind. proof, Novr. 28, 1823.
  (8⅞ × 7⅞)   E. 247.—'90.

  Sir J. Reynolds.   J. Jones, mez.
  J. C. Smith, 25, a late state, retouched, lettering altered, cut
at foot.   21889.

  Sir T. Lawrence.   G. Clint, mez.
  Ha. len. to front, seated, with left arm over the back of a
chair.
  Proof with scratched letters ; May, 1803.
  14 × 10⁵⁄₁₆. (12½ × 10⁵⁄₁₆).   22974.

ESDAILE, William, 1758-1837, banker and print-collector,
4th son of Sir James Esdaile ; received a commercial education, and became a clerk in the bank of Ladbrooke & Co. ; aftds.
in that of the newly-estab. firm of Esdaile, Hammet & Co.,
c. 1780 ; growing rich, began collecting prints, coins, china, books,
&c. ; collection sold after his death, sale lasting 16 days. His
grandson, William Jeffries Esdaile, married, Sep. 27, 1837,
Ianthe Eliza, daughter of P. B. Shelley and Harriet West-
brook.
  G. Sharples delin.   R. Graves. 1826.
  T. Q. len. to left, seated, looking to front, with coat buttoned
up ; holding in right hand an etching by Rembrandt, called
" The Three Trees."

Private plate; Ind. proof before all letters, except the
artists' names, and facs. of the monogram, with which Esdaile
used to mark his prints, &c.
16¼×13½. (9¼×8). 25703.

ESSEX, ARTHUR CAPEL, Earl of, 1632–1683; cr. 1661; Viceroy, Ireland, 1672–'7; connected with the Rye-house Plot;
committed to the Tower, where he was found with his throat
cut.
    P. Lely. E. Luttrell, mez.
    J. C. Smith, 7, 3rd state.
    "Very rare" (Evans). 27525.

ESSEX, THOMAS CROMWELL, Earl of, 1485–1540; minister to
Henry VIII., Chancellor of Exchr.; Constable of Carisbrooke
Castle; cr., 1540; att. and executed, July of same year
    Holbein. (Filian, or P. à Gunst?).
    Sh. ha. len. to left; oval in border.
    Proof before all letters.
    Cut. (11¼×6¼). 23563.

    Holbein. J. Houbraken. 1739.
    Sh. ha. len. to right; oval in border. In Birch's "Lives."
    14¾×9⁷⁄₁₅. (14¹⁄₁₆×8¼×) 21976.

ESSEX, ROBERT DEVEREUX, Earl of, 1567–1601, favourite of
Elizabeth, sent to assist Henri IV.; took Cadiz; Lord Deputy,
Ireland; executed for treason.
    J Oliver. J. Houbraken. 1738.
    Sh. ha. len. to right, looking to front; oval in border. In
Birch's "Lives."
    Cut. (14⅛×8⅝). 24660.

ESSEX, WALTER DEVEREUX, 1st Earl of, 1541–1576, Viscount Hereford, and Lord Ferrers of Chartley; K.G.; cr. Earl,
1572; &c.
    (S. Pass.) (S. Pass.)
    Ha. len in armour, to right, looking to front, in oval; two
Latin verses below.
    From the "Heroologia;" a proof before the letterpress at the
back.
    6⁹⁄₁₆×4¹⁄₁₆. (5⅝×4¹⁄₁₆). 27103.

ETTY, WILLIAM, 1787–1849, historical painter, b. at York, son
of a miller; apprent. to a printer at Hull, 1799; came to London,
1805; stud. in Academy Schools, 1807, and pupil of Lawrence,
1808; sold his first picture, 1811; exhibited at R. A. and B. I.
from that time; travelled abroad; A.R.A., 1824; R.A., 1828;
successful and admired; retired, 1848, having had 130 of his
pictures collected and exhibited that year; d. at York.

Anon.   Anon.
Wh. len. to left, standing with folded arms ; palette, brushes,
&c., behind him ; facs. signature below ; from Arnold's " Magazine of the Fine Arts," 1834.
(8 × 5).   E. 1972.–'89.

ETTY, WILLIAM—*continued.*
W. Etty, R.A.   C. W. Wass, mixed mez.
Sh. ha. len. to left, wearing a cloak with hook and chain
fastening ; oval.
Ind. proof ; January 1st, 1849.
(16½ × 12⅝).   E. 1271.–'86.

From a daguerreotype taken at York, 1849.   W. C. Wass,
                                                            stipple.
Sh. ha. len. to front, looking to right, oval ; facs. subscription
and signature below.
(4⁹⁄₁₆ × 3⁹⁄₁₆).   26249.

                                                       Anon., Lith.
Bust to front, looking to left, dark neckcloth, coat buttoned ;
vignette.
Ind. proof before all letters, except facs. signature below.
(8 × 6¼).   22232.

Anon.   Anon. Woodcut.
Bust to right, in profile ; vignette, in oval ; palette, brushes,
and mahl-stick at bottom of oval, and facs. signature below ;
from an illustrated paper.
(3½ × 2⅛).   E. 1973.–'89.

EVANS, SIR DE LACY, 1787–1870, General, served in India,
Peninsula, America, and France, 1807–'15 ; M.P. for Westminster, 1833–'41, 1846–'65 ; commanded the Spanish legion
in Spain, 1835 ; served in the Crimea, 1854–'5 ; G.C.B.,
1855.
R. Buckner.   G. Zobel, mez.
T. Q. len. to front, looking to right, in uniform.
Ind. proof, with open letters ; Novr. 12, 1856.
20¾ × 15¾.   (16¹⁵⁄₁₆ × 13).   24222.

EVELYN, JOHN, 1620–1706, 4th child and 2nd son of
Richard Evelyn, of Wotton, Surrey ; educ. at Southover Free
School, Lewes, and Ball. Coll., Oxf. ; Hon. D.C.L., 1669 ;
travelled abroad ; returned, 1647 ; went again to France, 1649 ;
returned finally, 1652 ; F.R.S., 1662 ; an active patron of music
and other arts, befriended Gibbons and Hollar ; wrote "Sylva,"
"Diaries," "Sculptura, or the History and Art of Chalco-
graphy," 1662, &c.
R. Nanteuil delin.   R. Nanteuil.

R. Dumesnil, 93, where the later states are erroneously described, and the Greek motto wrongly given. This is a late impression, with Evelyn's monogram on the book on the left, and the triangles on the book on the right; the motto runs, correctly copied, Βούλου τὰς Εικόνας; τῆς ἀρετῆς ὑπόμνημα | μᾶλλον ἢ τοῦ σώματος, καταλιπεῖν.

$9\frac{1}{2} \times 6\frac{13}{16}$. ($9\frac{5}{16} \times 6\frac{11}{16}$). 22204.

EVELYN, Mary, c. 1635–1709, daughter of Sir Richard Browne, the King's ambassador at Paris; m. to John Evelyn, June 27, 1647; joined him in June, 1652, at Sayes Court, Deptford, her father's place, which they left for Wotton in May, 1694, where she died, three years after her husband's death, and was buried beside him.

Anon. Anon., stipple.

Sh. ha. len. to left, looking to front, wearing curls, earrings, and a collar of pearls.

Proof before all letters.

$10\frac{7}{8} \times 8\frac{13}{16}$ (?). ($5\frac{1}{8} \times 4\frac{13}{16}$). 23568.

EVESHAM. *See* SOMERS.

EWART, William, c. 1800, a Liverpool merchant.

Anon. W. Holl, stipple.

Ha. len. to right, looking to front, holding an eyeglass in right hand.

Ind. open letter proof.

$15\frac{3}{8} \times 11\frac{7}{8}$. ($10\frac{1}{8} \times 8\frac{1}{8}$). 20931.

EWART, William, 1798–1869; merchant, liberal politician, M.P. for Liverpool, and afterwards for Dumfries; promoted permissive use of metric system, &c.

E. V. Rippingille. S. W. Reynolds, mez.

Ha. len. seated, to right, with arms folded, books and papers on table; facs. signature below.

Open letter proof (?). Feb. 1838.

$14\frac{3}{8} \times 11$. ($11\frac{3}{8} \times 8\frac{15}{16}$). 22850.

EXMOUTH, Edward Pellew, 1st Viscount, 1757–1833, Admiral; b. at Dover; ent. Navy, 1770; served on Lake Champlain, during American War; knt. for his capture of the French frigate "Cléopâtre," 1793; Com.-in-Chf. on Indian Station, 1803–'9; in Mediterranean, 1809–'13; cr. Visct. Exmouth, 1815; on an expedition to Algiers, enforced abolition of Christian slavery in Barbary States, 1816.

Sir T. Lawrence, R.A. C. Turner, mez.

Ha. len. to front, looking to right; white neckcloth, uniform laced coat, buttoned.

Proof with skeleton letters; Oct. 12, 1815.

14×10. ($11\frac{7}{8} \times 9\frac{7}{8}$). 22085.

EYRE, Sir James, c. 1734–1799, Recorder of London, 1762; resisting the party of Wilkes, became unpopular with the

Council ; Baron of Exchequer, 1772 ; Ch. Baron, 1787 ; Ch.
Justice of Com. Pleas, 1793 ; d. at Ruscombe, Berks.
L. F. Abbott. V. Green, mez.
J. C. Smith, 42, 2nd state. 27260.

FACIUS, JOHANN GOTTLIEB, c. 1750–c. 1802, engraver, b. at
Regensburg ; stud. at Brussels ; came to London ; worked for
Boydell, for whom he and his brother, Georg Sigmund, executed
a number of plates, chiefly etched, and printed in black, brown,
or colours ; their last dated plate is of 1802.
Anon. Anon.
Ha. len. to left, looking to front, seated ; a picture on an easel
is at his right ; his hands are folded before him on a sheet of
paper.
Proof before all letters.
11¼ × 8⅞. (8¼ × 6¾). 27591.

FAIRBAIRN, SIR WILLIAM, 1789–1874, engineer ; b. at Kelso,
Roxb. ; apprent. to an enginewright at Percy Main Colliery ;
came to London, where he worked 2 years as journeyman
mechanic ; settled at Manchester, 1817, and became a great
machine-maker ; originated many improvements in millwork ;
acted with Robert Stephenson in planning and executing the
Britannia and Conway Tubular Bridges ; advocated strongly
the use of iron in shipbuilding ; pubd. " Useful Information for
Engineers," &c., and contrib. largely to "Philsoph. Transactions," &c. ; corresp. member of French Instit. ; Bart., 1869.
P. Westcott. (Picture exhibited, 1849).
T. O. Barlow, mixed mez.
T. Q. len. to front, eyeglass in left hand, right resting on
papers on table.
Ind. proof before all letters ; signed by the engraver (1851).
19⅝ × 15. (15¼ × 11½). 27200.

FAIRFAX, THOMAS, 3rd Lord, 1611–1671, better known as
General, or Sir Thomas, Fairfax ; b. at Denton, Yorks. ; educ.
at Cambr. ; took part against the King, in Civil War ; disting.
at Marston Moor, suc. Earl of Essex as Genl.-in-Chf. of Parl.
Army, and routed that of the King at Naseby, 1645 ; victorious
in West of England ; received Charles from the Scots, in Notts,
1647 ; suc. his father, 1647 ; took no part in trial of the King ;
one of the Commissioners for promoting Restoration ; d. at
Nun Appleton.
R. Walker. W. Faithorne.
L. Fagan, p. 35 (first plate), 3rd state. 24114.

FAITHORNE, WILLIAM, 1616–1691, draftsman and engraver,
b. in London ; brought up under Robert Peake, engraver ;
served with him in the royal army, in the Civil War ; became a
prisoner ; allowed to go abroad ; visited Paris ; returned to
England, c. 1650, and set up a print-shop ; much employed by
the booksellers ; engraved a large number of portraits, many of

which are very fine; published "Art of Graving," 1662; d. in
Printing House Square.
   W. Faithorne.   A. Bannerman.
   Sh. ha. len. to left, looking to front; wearing long hair, cloak,
&c. ; from Walpole's "Catalogue of Engravers," 1763.
   $(6\frac{3}{4} \times 4\frac{1}{2})$.   25461. 6.

FALKLAND, HENRY CARY, Viscount, 1576–1633, Lord Deputy,
Ireland; author, &c.
   Van Somer. (G. P. Harding del.)   J. Brown.
   Wh. len. to front, wearing a hat and feather, and resting
right hand on table.
   Open letter proof, Jany. 1st, 1847.
   $13\frac{1}{8} \times 9\frac{3}{8}$. $(9 \times 5\frac{1}{4})$.   24642.

FALKLAND, LUCIUS CARY, 2nd Viscount, c. 1600–1643, son of
Henry, 1st Viscount; b. at Burford, Oxfordshire; educ. at
Dublin and Cambr.; M.P. for Newport, 1640; opposed the
Court; but, when civil war broke out, sided with the King;
fought at Edge Hill; fell at Newbury, fighting in front rank of
Lord Byron's regiment; beloved friend of Lord Clarendon.
   Sir A. van. Dyck. (W. Hilton, R.A., del.)
                               E. Scriven, stipple.
   T. Q. len. to front, seated, wearing collar with tassels, ruffles,
dark coat and cloak; Feb. 2, 1818.
   $(7\frac{3}{16} \times 5\frac{2}{16})$.   27261.

FARADAY, MICHAEL, 1791–1867, Natural philosopher; son of
a whitesmith; b. at Newington Butts; apprent. to a bookseller
and bookbinder; assist. to Sir H. Davy, at Roy. Instn., 1813;
Prof. of Chemistry there, 1833 ; discov. chlorides of carbon,
condensation of gases, magneto-electricity, &c.; author of many
scientific works and papers; eminent lecturer; d. at Hampton
Court Green; bur. in Highgate Cemetery
   H. W. Pickersgill, R.A.   S. Cousins, mez.
   Ha. len. to right, looking to left, bent slightly forward;
wearing white neck-cloth, dark coat with velvet collar, &c.
   Proof before all letters, except artists' names and publication-
line, Feby. 1, 1830.
   $14\frac{3}{4} \times 11$. $(10\frac{3}{4} \times 9)$.   22143.

   C. Turner, A.R.A., del.   C. Turner, A.R.A., mixed mez.
   Full ha. len. to front, looking to left, with right hand raised,
as in the act of lecturing, left hand resting on a Leyden jar.
   Ind. proof before the title, Oct. 20, 1838.
   $19 \times 12\frac{1}{16}$. $(14\frac{11}{16} \times 11\frac{3}{8})$.   22851.

FARINGTON, JOSEPH, 1747–1821, landscape-painter, b. at
Leigh, Lancashire; pupil of Richard Wilson; gained several
premiums from the Socy. of Arts; member, at 21, of the Incorp.
Socy. of Arts; A.R.A., 1783; R.A., 1785; his colour was
strong and brilliant, but his landscapes lacked poetry and

grandeur; he made numerous topographical drawings; many
of his views of the English lakes and Thames were engraved;
d. of a fall from his horse.

T. Lawrence, R.A.   H. Meyer, stipple.

Ha. len. to left, seated, holding a paper; a landscape roughly
indicated in distance.

Open letter proof; Decr. 22, 1814.

$14\frac{7}{8} \times 11\frac{7}{8}$(?).   ($9\frac{1}{2} \times 7\frac{1}{16}$).   27213.

FARISH, WILLIAM, 1759–1837, son of a clergyman at Carlisle;
educ. at Carlisle Gram. School, and Magdalene Coll., Cambr.;
Senior Wrangler, and first Smith's prizeman, 1778; fellow
and tutor; Prof. of chemistry, 1794–1813; Jacksonian Prof. of
Nat. Philosophy, 1813–'37; in his lectures on Chemistry
"was the first to introduce the application of that science to
the arts and manufactures;" collated to Church of St. Giles,
Cambr., 1800; B.D., 1820; rector of Little Stonham, Suffolk,
1836, where he died.

J. Slater del. 1813.   I. W. Slater, lith

Ha. len. slightly turned, and looking, to left, wearing white
neckcloth, double-breasted waistcoat, and gown; vignette.

Ind. proof with open letters, March 1, 1831.

($7\frac{1}{2} \times 9\frac{3}{8}$).   23167

FARNBOROUGH. *See* LONG.

FARREN, ELIZABETH, c. 1759–1829, distinguished actress,
daughter of George Farren, surgeon and apothecary at Cork,
who became an actor; she began early, playing juvenile parts
at Bath and elsewhere; with her mother and sisters at Wakefield, 1774, under Whitely; at the Haymarket, 1777; suc. Mrs.
Abington in her principal characters; left the stage, and married
Edward, 12th Earl of Derby, as his second wife, 1797.

Sir T. Lawrence.   F. Bartolozzi, stipple.

Wh. len. to left, looking to front, carrying a large muff in
left hand; landscape in background.

Proof with skeleton letters, Feb. 25, 1791.

($19\frac{9}{16} \times 18\frac{7}{16}$).   22979.

—— as Lady Teazle, with T. King, as Sir Peter.

J. Downman.   J. Jones, 1787, stipple.

Wh. len. on left, turned towards King, looking to front; her
left hand on King's shoulder; King, with hands clasped, looking
to right.

Proof, with dotted letters; before names, &c., except those
of the artists, and the publication-line, May 1, 1787.

$22\frac{1}{4} \times 15\frac{7}{8}$.   ($20\frac{3}{8} \times 14\frac{1}{4}$, excl. of border).   21890.

FARREN, WILLIAM, 1786–1861, actor, son of W. Farren of
Cov. Garden theatre; made his first appearance at Plymouth,
c. 1806; played in Ireland; appeared at Cov. Garden, as Sir
P. Teazle, 1818; continued to play there till 1828, at Haymarket in summer seasons; at Drury Lane, 1828–'37, and at

other theatres till 1855, when he retired; famous for his old
men characters.

Anon. Anon., stipple and line.
Ha. len. to left, looking to front, an eye-glass hangs by a
ribbon round his neck; oval in ruled border.
$17\frac{7}{8} \times 14\frac{1}{2}$. (Oval, $8\frac{1}{2} \times 7$). 25777.

FARREN, WILLIAM—*continued.*
J. W Gear del. J. W. Gear, stipple, coloured.
Wh. len. to front, looking to right, as if surprised; as
Ignatius Polyglot in the "Scape-goat;" vignette.
$(8 \times 6\frac{3}{4})$. 26410.

FAUCIT, MRS., of Covent Garden Theatre.
R. E. Drummond. J. Thomson, stipple.
See LA BELLE ASSEMBLÉE, 1817. 13867. 9.

FAUCIT, HELEN, 1819– , daughter of Mrs. Faucit, an
actress of some repute, made her *début* at Cov. Garden, 1836,
as Julia in "The Hunchback;" achieved success, which she
continued in most of Shakspere's heroines, as well as those of
other dramatists; m. Mr. (now Sir) Theodore Martin, 1851;
reappeared at rare intervals; wrote a book "on Some of the
Female Characters of Shakespeare."
Sir W. Allan. L. Dickinson, lith.
T Q. len. to front, looking upwards to right; as Antigone.
$(20\frac{1}{8} \times 17\frac{9}{16})$. 26406.

FAWCETT, JOHN, 1768–1837, actor, and son of an actor;
appeared at Cov. Garden, 1791; gained much reputation as
"Dr. Pangloss," "Caleb Quotem," "Job Thornbury;" joined
the English Opera, 1813; Manager of Cov. Garden until 1836.
G. H. Harlow. W. Say, mez.
Full ha. len. to right, white neckcloth, dark coat buttoned
loosely; hat and stick in right hand, over which left is crossed,
holding glove.
Proof with skeleton letters.
$(18\frac{1}{4} \times 13\frac{7}{8})$. 21903.

FAWKES, GUY, 1570–1606, Gunpowder Plot conspirator, only
son and second child of Edward Fawkes of York, by his wife
Edith, both protestants, the father a notary, or proctor;
Guy was educ. at Free School, York, brought up a protestant; became a catholic after his mother's second marriage; left England for Flanders, 1593, and joined Spanish
Army as a soldier of fortune; present at capture of Calais,
1595; drawn into the Plot by T. Winter, or Catesby, 1604;
tried and tortured, Novr., 1605; executed, Jany. 31, 1606, with
Winter, Rookwood, and Keyes.
See CONCILIUM.

FERGUSON, ADAM, 1723–1816, b. at Logierait, Perthshire;
educ. at home, at Perth gram. school, and at St. Andrews;
M.A., 1742; went to Edinb. to study divinity; priv. sec. to

Lord Milton, 1742; deputy-chaplain to the Black Watch (then
the 43rd. Regt.); soon afterwards chaplain; present at Fontenoy,
1745; gave up clerical profession, 1754; Advocates' Librarian,
1757; Prof. Moral Philos., Glasgow, 1758; of Natural Philos.,
Edinb., 1759; of Pneumatics and Moral Philos., 1764; LL.D.;
wrote "Essay on Civil Society," "History of the Progress and
Termination of the Roman Republic," &c.

W. Evans delin.   J. B. Lane, stipple.
Ha. len. to left, seated; vignette; March 17, 1815.
$14\frac{7}{8} \times 12\frac{1}{2}$. $(8\frac{5}{8} \times 8\frac{3}{4})$.   28001.

FERGUSON, SIR ADAM, 1771–1855, Keeper of the Regalia in
Scotland, eldest son of Prof. Adam Ferguson (q. v.); companion of Sir Walter Scott at Edinb. Univ.; one of the 19
original members of the society, "called by way of excellence
the Club;" ent. the army, 1800, and served in the Peninsular
War, under Wellington; taken prisoner, 1812; released, 1814;
retired, 1816; knt., 1822.
   See SCOTT, Sir WALTER.

FERGUSON, JAMES, 1710–1776, Astronomer and Mechanician;
   b. in Banffshire; son of a labourer; kept sheep in his youth;
   overcame great difficulties in pursuit of knowledge; practised
   as a clockmaker and portrait painter; came to London, 1743;
   devoted himself to philosophical experiments and lecturing;
   F.R.S., without fees; pensioned by George III., 1760; author
   of "Astronomy on Newton's Principles," &c.
   J. Townsend.   R. Stewart, mez.
   J. C. Smith, 5.   22081.

FERRAR, or FARRAR, ROBERT.
   See "MARTYRS, PROTESTANT," a group.   25736.

FEVERSHAM, LOUIS DE DURAS, second Earl of, 1641–1709,
   Visct. Sondes of Lees Court, Baron Duras of Holdenby, &c.;
   also Marquis de Blanquefort in France; naturalised, 1665,
   Captn. of the Duke of York's Horse Guards, of which he
   became Colonel, 1667; cr. Baron Duras, 1673; suc. 1677; Lt.-
   Genl., 1678, and 1685; Master of the Horse, Ld. Chambn.,
   Lord Keeper; commanded at Sedgmoor.
   I. Riley.   I. Beckett, mez.
   J. C. Smith, 33, 2nd state.
   From the collection of John Young.   23144.

FIELDING, HENRY, 1707–1754, b. at Sharpham Park, Glaston-
   bury, Somersets; son of Edmund Fielding, aftds. a general;
   second cousin of Lady Mary W. Montagu; educ. at Motcombe,
   under Mr. Oliver, at Eton, and Leyden; began writing plays,
   1728, original and adapted from Molière; author of "Tom
   Thumb," 1730; "Pasquin," 1736; barrister, 1740; wrote
   "Joseph Andrews," 1742, "Miscellanies," 1743; made a J.P.,

Westminster, 1748, aftds. for Middlesex; wrote "Tom Jones," 1749; d. at Lisbon.

W. Hogarth delin. J. Basire.

Sh. ha. len. to left, in profile, wearing long wig; oval, in border, with books, masks, laurels, scales, paper signed by him, and sword of Justice, below.

$(7\frac{1}{3} \times 4\frac{1}{5})$. 26685.

FIELDING, Sir John, -1780, half-brother of Henry Fielding, the novelist; blind; magistrate at Bow Street, 1761-'80.

Hone. J. McArdell, mez.

J. C. Smith, 65, 1st state, which is only mentioned by J. C. S. on the strength of Sir M. M. Sykes' Sale Catalogue. This is not the Sykes print.

The only book lettered is the "Holy Bible;" the "Plan" is not lettered, and there is no inscription below.

The size is as given by J. C. S. 22079.

———

W. Peters, R.A. W. Dickinson, mez.

"As Chairman of the Quarter Sessions for the City of "Westminster."

J. C. Smith, 20; "Republished from the Original Plate in "the possession of Henry Pownall, Esq., by Barclay, Gerard "Street." This late state was unknown to J. C. S. It is quite modern. 23108.

FIRST OF MAY, 1851.

The Duke of Wellington presenting a casket to his Godson, Prince Arthur, afterwards Duke of Connaught, on his first birthday, May 1, 1851.

F. Winterhalter. S. Cousins, mez.

The Duke is on the left; the Queen holds the infant Prince in her arms; the Prince Consort stands behind her.

Proof before all letters, except the publication-line at top.

$21\frac{3}{4} \times 22\frac{7}{8}$. $(16\frac{1}{2} \times 19\frac{1}{2})$. 23759.

FIRST READING of a New Work, The.

[C. Baugniet.] C. Baugniet, lith., 1852.

A composition of 8 figures, viz. (beginning on the left), J. B. Cramer, W. Sterndale Bennett, Ed. Schultz, Lindsay Sloper, Me. Belleville-Oury, Mrs. Anderson, Jules Benedict, and G. A. Osborne; Mrs. Anderson is seated near the right side of the print, the others are standing; W. S. Bennett, at the pianoforte, places a piece of music on the desk; Osborne, with hat in left hand, is on the extreme right. India proof.

$(15 \times 23\frac{1}{4})$. 23780.

FISHER, John, 1459-1535, Bishop; b. at Beverley; educ. at Camb.; Confessor and Chaplain to Margaret, Countess of Richmond; Bishop of Rochester, 1504; refused to recognise the supremacy of Henry VIII. as head of the Church ; imprisoned, and executed on Tower Hill.

H. Holbein.   J. Houbraken.

Sh. ha. len. slightly to right, looking to right, in robes, with furred scarf and low cap ; oval in border, a cupid below, bearing a bishop's hat ; axe and head lower down ; from a picture "In the Collection of Mr. Richardson."

$14\frac{5}{8} \times 8\frac{15}{16}$.   ($13\frac{7}{8} \times 8\frac{1}{2}$).   21811

FITTLER, JAMES, 1758–1835, engraver, b. in London ; stud. in Academy Schools, 1788 ; attained high distinction ; engraved portraits, landscapes, sea-pieces, and topography ; Marine engraver to George III. ; illustrated Bell's "Theatre," Dibdin's "Ædes Althorpianæ," "Illustrated Bible," "Scotia Depicta," &c. ; A. E., 1800 ; worked in line manner ; d. at Turnham Green.

E. F. Burney, delin.   Anon.

Head, as medallion, to left in profile ; name and date, 1797, in oval ; below, a group of four female figures ; one holding an open "Cabinet Bible ;" another, a palette and brushes ; a third a mallet and cross ; the fourth, a plan and compasses ; inscribed beneath,—" to lead the Fine Arts into the service of Religion. "Vide Proposals for Publishing the Cabinet Bible."

$8\frac{16}{10} \times 5\frac{7}{10}$.   ($5\frac{5}{8} \times 3\frac{1}{16}$).   E. 1981–89.

FITZGIBBON, JOHN, 1ST EARL OF CLARE, 1749–1802, Lawyer and Statesman ; son of John Fitzgibbon, M.P. ; educ. at Dublin Univ. ; Attorney-General for Ireland, 1784 ; Lord Chancellor of Ireland and Baron Fitzgibbon, 1789 ; Viscount, 1793 ; Earl of Clare, 1795 ; Baron Fitzgibbon in British Peerage, 1799 ; played a chief part in carrying Act of Union ; but, on entering House of Peers, did not distinguish himself as might have been expected ; d. in Ely Place, Dublin ; bur. at St. Peter's Church.

C. G. Stuart.   C. H. Hodges, mez.

J. C. Smith, 14, 2nd state.   22083.

FITZHERBERT, MARIA ANNE, 1756–1837, youngest daughter of Walter Smythe, of Brambridge, Hampshire ; m., 1775, to Edward Weld, of Lulworth Castle, Dorset, who died same year ; m. to Thomas Fitzherbert, of Swynnerton in Staffordshire, 1778, widow again, 1781 ; m. to the Prince of Wales, afterwards George IV., Decr. 21, 1785, in her own drawing-room ; appeared as his wife, and was so treated everywhere, until 1803 ; retired from Court on an annuity of 6000l.

J. Russell, R.A.   J. Collyer, stipple.

T. Q. len. to right, seated, leaning her chin on left hand ; a curtain behind her, trees in distance, on right ; 24 Decr, 1792.

$13\frac{7}{8} \times 10\frac{6}{16}$.   ($11\frac{4}{16} \times 8\frac{1}{4}$, incl. ruled border, $1\frac{1}{4}$ at top, 1 at sides, $1\frac{1}{8}$ below).   22011.

FITZHERBERT, MARIA ANNE—*continued.*
Anon. Anon., etched.
Sh. ha. len. to right in profile, wearing a hat with feathers;
caricature, printed in brown ink; oval.
Cut. (4½ × 3¾). 29874. 1.

FITZJAMES, CAPTAIN JAMES, –1848, ent. Navy, 1825,
served in the Mediterranean and in Euphrates expedition;
Lieut., 1838; served in Egypt and China; Commander, 1842;
Post Captain, 1845; Commanded "Erebus," under Sir F.
Franklin, in Northern explorations, in which he perished, with
his leader and companions.
See ARCTIC COUNCIL.

FITZJAMES, JAMES, *See* BERWICK, DUKE OF.

FITZWILLIAM, RICHARD FITZWILLIAM, 7th Viscount, of
Meryon, 1745–1816, eldest son of Richard, 6th Viscount; suc.,
1776; d. unmarried; left his South Sea stock, books, pictures,
prints, &c. to the Univ. of Cambr.; founder of the Fitzwilliam
Museum.
H. Howard, R.A. C. Turner, mez.
T. Q. len. to right, seated, facing and looking to front, wearing
furred gown; right hand on arm of chair, left on open book on
table; coat of arms below.
18 × 12¼. (15¼ × 12½). 22082.

FITZ-WYGRAM, SIR ROBERT, 1773–1843, Bart., M.P., Dep.
Lieut., Essex, &c.
T. Phillips, R.A. J. Brown.
Ha. len. seated, to left, looking to right, holding a paper in left
hand.
Ind. proof with scratched letters. 1837.
13⅝ × 10⅚. (9 × 7½). 20644

FLAMSTEED, REV. JOHN, 1646–1719, First Astronomer Royal;
b. at Denby, near Derby; only son of Stephen Flamsteed, a
maltster; educ. at Derby Free School, which he was obliged by
bad health to leave, 1662; educ. himself; turned attention to
astronomy; explained the equation of time, 1667; pub. the
rules in a tract, 1673; came to London, 1670; M.A., Cambr.,
per literas regias, 1674; "Astronomer Observator," 1675;
ordained, 1675; worked in the Observatory at Greenwich until
his death; pubd. "Historia Cœlestis Britannica."
T. Gibson, 1712. G. Vertue, 1721.
Sh. ha. len. to left, looking to front, wearing wig, bands, and
gown; left hand to breast; oval in border; title in Latin
below.
12¾ × 8¾. (11¼ × 8¼). 22236.

FLAXMAN, JOHN, 1755–1826, sculptor, son of J. Flaxman, a
modeller; b. at York; stud. from classical models in his father's
shop; exhibited, 1767, at Free Socy. of Artists; stud. at R. A.;

exhibited wax portraits, 1770, and in following years; also clay models, and groups, 1786, and '87; employed by Wedgwoods; visited Rome; A.R.A., 1797; R.A., 1800; Prof. of Sculpture, 1810; wrote on Art.

J. Flaxman. A. R. Freebairn.

Bust, to left, in profile, in a circle; from the original model by Flaxman; engraved, in the manner invented by A. Collas, with waved lines; facs. signature below; prefixed to the series of the "Shield of Achilles."

Cut. ($6\frac{3}{4}$ diamr.). E. 1976.–'89.

FLAXMAN, John—*continued.*

J. Flaxman. Anon., woodcut.

Bust, to left, in profile, copied from the print engraved after the medallion; in an oval.

Oval, $4\frac{3}{4} \times 3\frac{15}{16}$. ($3\frac{1}{16} \times 2\frac{1}{4}$). E. 1975.–'89.

—

J. Jackson, R.A. C. Turner, mez.

Ha. len. to left, looking to front; white collar, waistcoat dark and high, black coat with high full collar.

Ind. proof, with open letters; May 1, 1827.

14×10. ($10 \times 8\frac{3}{16}$). 22506.

—

J. Jackson. Pannier.

Ha. len. to left, looking to front, oval.

$12\frac{3}{4} \times 9\frac{1}{2}$. ($5\frac{15}{16} \times 4\frac{3}{4}$). 21938.

—

J. Jackson. R. Woodman, stipple.

Ha. len. to left, looking to front; from the "Portrait Gallery "of distinguished Poets," &c., Vol. III., 1853.

Cut. ($4\frac{7}{8} \times 4\frac{1}{8}$). 23589.

—

J. Jackson, R.A. W. C. Edwards.

Ha. len. to left, looking to front; facs. signatures of Flaxman and Jackson below.

Cut. ($3\frac{3}{16} \times 2\frac{5}{8}$). E. 1974.–'89.

—

W. Derby. J. Thomson, stipple.

Ha. len. slightly to left, looking to front; vignette; facs. signature below.

Cut. ($3\frac{7}{8} \times 4$). 28300. 24.

FLEETWOOD, Charles, c. 1620–1692, Parliamentary General; son of Sir Thomas Fleetwood; m. Mrs. Ireton (Bridget Cromwell); Lord Deputy of Ireland; favoured return of Charles II.; was excepted from the Act of Pardon at the Restoration, but ultimately included; m. again twice; d. in obscurity; bur. in Bunhill Fields Cemetery.

R. Walker. J. Houbraken, 1740.

Sh. ha. len. to left, looking to front, in armour, with white collar, long hair; oval in border, vignette with lion and fasces below; in Birch's " Lives."

$14\frac{3}{4} \times 9\frac{1}{4}$. $(14\frac{1}{8} \times 8\frac{3}{4})$.   21819.

FLETCHER, JOHN, 1579–1625, younger son of Dr. Richard Fletcher, aftds. Bishop of London; admitted (?) a pensioner of Bene't (Corp.) Coll., Cambr., Oct. 15, 1591; intimate friend (1584–1616) of Francis Beaumont, with whom he wrote many plays of exceptional merit; about 15 were by his own pen alone, 1618–'25; probably Shakspere had a hand in the " Two Noble Kinsmen," 1634, and Fletcher in "Henry VIII.;" buried at St. Saviour's, Southwark.

Anon.   "Ad Archetypum " (?).   G. Vertue. 1729.
Sh. ha. len. to left, looking to front; oval in border; LUSIT AMABILITER, with comic and tragic masks, above; arms below, with inscription in five lines.

$14\frac{5}{8} \times 9\frac{1}{4}$. $(13\frac{1}{4} \times 8\frac{3}{4})$.   27865. 6.

FLOOD, RT. HON. HENRY, 1732–1791; M.P., Vice-Treasurer of Ireland, &c.

From a miniature.   Anon.
Bust, face in profile, to left; oval.

$10\frac{5}{8} \times 8\frac{5}{8}$. $(4\frac{1}{4} \times 3\frac{1}{2})$.   22852.

FOLEY, JOHN HENRY, 1818–1874, b. at Dublin; stud. at R.A., 1835; A.R.A., 1849; R.A., 1858; made statues of Hampden and Selden for St. Stephen's Hall, Westminster; group of Asia and figure of Pr. Consort for Albert Memorial; and many other works.

T. S[cott], monogram.   Anon., woodcut.
Sh. ha. len. slightly inclined to right, looking to left; vignette in oval; from the "Illustrated London News," Sepr. 12, 1874.

$(6\frac{1}{2} \times 6\frac{3}{8})$.   E. 1985.–'89.

Anon.   Anon., woodcut.
Sh. ha. len. to right, looking to front; vignette, in oval, with sculptor's tools below, followed by facs. signature; from an illustrated paper.

$(3\frac{3}{4} \times 2\frac{3}{4})$.   E. 1983.–'89.

Anon.   Anon., woodcut.
Bust to right, wearing a cap with tassel; vignette, from an illustrated paper.

(6×5).   E. 1984.–'89.

FOLKES, MARTIN, 1690–1754, b. in Queen St., Linc. Inn Fields; educ. at Clare Hall, Cambr.; M.A., Cambr., 1717; D.C.L., Oxf., 1746; F.R.S., 1714, at age of 23; Vice-Pres., 1722–'3; Pres., 1741–1753; F.S.A., 1720; Vice-Pres., and Pres., 1749–54, when he d.; pub. " Tables " of Coins; helped

Theobald in notes on Shakspere ; sale of his collections of books, prints, drawings, pictures, gems, coins, &c., lasted 56 days, 1756, and brought 3,090*l.* 5*s.*

W. Hogarth, 1741.   J. Faber, Junr., 1742, mez.
J. C. Smith, 132, but a later state than described by Mr. Smith, having the address at foot, "London. *Printed for* R. Wilkinson, *No. 58 Cornhill.*"   E. 1652.-'89.

FOLKES, MARTIN—*continued.*
     T. Hudson.   J. McArdell, mez.
     J. C. Smith, 68.   22234.

FOLLETT, SIR WILLIAM WEBB, 1798-1845, M.P., Chester ; Solr.-Gen., 1834-'5, 1841-'3 ; Atty.-Gen., 1844.
     F. R. Say.   G. R. Ward, mez.
     As Solr.-Gen., t. q. len. seated, to left, looking to front, with head resting on left hand, right holding a book on his right knee.
     Open letter proof ; August 1st, 1842.
     $20\frac{1}{4} \times 15\frac{1}{4}$. $(16\frac{5}{8} \times 13\frac{9}{16})$ 22978.

     A. E. Chalon, R.A.   H. T. Ryall.
     Ha. len. seated, to left, looking to right.
     Ind. proof, with scratched letters ; 1836.
     $13 \times 10\frac{3}{16}$. $(8\frac{7}{8} \times 7\frac{1}{16})$.   20629.

FOOTE, MISS.
     R. E. Drummond.   R. Cooper, stipple.
     See LA BELLE ASSEMBLÉE.   13867.   10.

FOOTE, SAMUEL, 1721-1777, b. at Truro ; educ. at Oxford, but preferred the stage, and opened the Haymarket, 1747 ; became famous as a wit, writer, and mimic ; broke his leg, 1766, and suffered amputation ; scandalously libelled, 1766 ; acquitted of all guilt, but broken down by the slander ; d. at Dover.
     Sir J. Reynolds.   T. Blackmore, mez.
     J. C. Smith, 2, 3rd state.   26433.

     Zauffely.   J. Finlayson, mez.
     With Thomas Weston (q. v.), in the "Devil on Two Sticks."
     J. C. Smith, 6, 2nd state.   26420.

—— as "Major Sturgeon" in the "Mayor of Garratt."
     J. Zauffely.   J. G. Haid, mez.
     J. C. Smith, 2, 1st state.   29136.

—— in the character of Doctor Squintum. Epilogue to the Minor.
     From a "Collection . . . . of English Prologues," &c., 1779.   28187.   5.

FORBES, EDWARD, 1815-1854, Natural Philosopher ; son of a banker in the Isle of Man ; attended Jameson's lectures at Edinb. Univ. ; trav. on Continent ; attached to Govt. scient.

expedition in Asia Minor, 1841; Prof. of Botany, King's Coll.,
London; Prof. of Nat. History in Univ., Edinb.; Pres. Geol.
Socy.; author of many works on Nat. Hist. subjects; F.R.S.
  [Maguire.]   T. H. Maguire, lith., 1850.
  Full ha. len. to front, seated, looking to left, holding a book
in right hand with forefinger between leaves; vignette, corners
cut off; facs. signature below.
  (9¾ × 9¼).   22507.

FORD, EDWARD, 1746–1809, surgeon; educ. under Dr. John
  Ford, Bristol; surgeon to the Westminster Dispensary, 1780–
  1801, to which he was a benefactor; d. at Sherborne.
  See MEDICAL SOCIETY.

FORDYCE, GEORGE, 1736–1802; b. at Aberdeen; settled as a
  physician in London, 1759, and attained considerable eminence;
  Senior physician, St. Thomas's Hospl.; M.D.; F.R.S.; &c.
    T. Phillips.   G. Keating, mez.
    J. C. Smith, 4.   22457.

FORRESTER, ALFRED HENRY. *See* CROWQUILL, ALFRED.

FORSTER, FRANK,   –   , Resident Engineer to the Bangor
  District, c. 1850.
  See MENAI STRAITS.

FORTESCUE, JOHN FORTESCUE ALAND, Baron, of Credan, in
  the Kingdom of Ireland, 1670–1746; Baron of Exchequer,
  1717–'8; a justice of King's Bench, 1718–'29; of Com. Pleas,
  1729–'46; cr. Baron, 1746.
    Sir G. Kneller.   J. Faber, jun., mez.
    J. C. Smith, 2.   27655.

FOWLER, ROBERT, c. 1726–1801, third son of G. Fowler, of
  Skendleby Thorpe, Lincolnshire; King's scholar at West-
  minster, 1744; B.A., at Trin. Coll., Cambr., 1747; M.A., 1751;
  D.D., 1764; chaplain to George II., 1756; preb. Westminster,
  1765; bishop of Killaloe, 1771; Archbishop of Dublin, 1779;
  Irish P.C.; &c.
    G. Dance, Novr. 23, 1795.   W. Daniell.
    Ha. len. to right, in profile; seated.
    Pubd. April 1, 1809. Vignette.
    10⅝ × 7½.   (7¼ × 5⅛).   28146. 7.

FOX, RT. HON. CHARLES JAMES, 1749–1806, statesman; second
  son of the 1st Lord Holland; M.P., 1768; famous as an orator,
  and the great Parliamentary opponent and rival of Pitt; Foreign
  Sec., 1782 and 1806; moved the "Representation," 1784, which
  was carried in the House of Commons by a majority of one.
    Sir J. Reynolds.   J. Jones, mez.
    J. C. Smith, 28, 3rd state, undescribed, without address of
  Austin, and with date, 1789.   21888.

FOX, RT. HON. CHARLES JAMES—*continued.*
   J. R. Smith.   S. W. Reynolds, mez.
   Wh. len. slightly to right, seated, looking to front, left hand holding spectacles, and resting on papers on table ; landscape out of window.
   Open letter proof, Oct. 13, 1806.
   $26\frac{1}{8} \times 18\frac{1}{2}$. $(24\frac{1}{4} \times 17\frac{3}{4})$.   22084.

FOX, HENRY RICHARD VASSALL, 3rd Lord Holland, and ELIZABETH VASSALL, Lady Holland.
   See HOLLAND.

FOX, SIR STEPHEN, 1627–1716, "Domestick servant to King Charles ye 2d during his exile ; " built hospitals and a church ; clerk of the Green Cloth ; projector of Chelsea hospital, to which he contributed 13,000*l.* ; Lord of the Treasury ; M.P.
   J. Baker.   J Simon, mez.
   J. C. Smith, 60.   22505.

FOXE, JOHN, 1516–1587, martyrologist, b. at Boston, Lincoln-shire ; a pupil of John Hawarden, of Brasenose Coll., Oxf. ; prob. fellow of Magdalen, 1538 ; fellow, 1539 ; B.A., 1537 ; M.A., 1543 ; resigned fellowship, 1545 ; tutor to the orphan children of Henry Howard, Earl of Surrey ; pubd. theological tracts, advocated advanced reforming views, 1548 and onward ; ordd. deacon, 1550 ; fled to Strasburg, 1554 ; began writing his "Actes and Monuments ; " went to Frankfort, and Basel ; returned to England ; priest, 1560 ; "Actes," &c., published by Day, 1563 ; d. in Grub Street.
   Anon.   G. Glover.
   Sh. ha. len. in hat, to front ; "ANNO DO. 1587 . . ÆTAT. 70."
4 Latin verses below.
   $9\frac{1}{2} \times 6\frac{3}{4}$. $(7\frac{7}{8} \times 6\frac{3}{8})$.   26659.

FRANCIS, SIR PHILIP, 1740–1818, Politician, son of Rev. Philip Francis ; b. at Dublin ; empl. by Fox and aftds. by Pitt ; member of Council, Bengal, 1774–'80 ; ent. Parliament as an adherent of the Whigs, 1784 ; aided prosecution of Warren Hastings ; believed by many to have been the author of the "Letters of Junius ;" G.C.B., &c.
   J. Lonsdale.   T Lupton, mez.
   Ha. len. to front, facing and looking to right, wearing light neckcloth and waistcoat, ribbon and star, coat fastened across chest by one button.
   Lettered "proof," but with inscription in three lines, June 4, 1817.
   $14\frac{1}{2} \times 11$. $(11\frac{1}{4} \times 9\frac{1}{2})$.   22080.

FRANKLIN, SIR JOHN, 1786–1847 ; Rear Admiral and Arctic explorer ; b. at Spilsby, Lincolns. ; midshipman, 1800 ; present at battle of Copenhagen, 1801 ; accomp. Flinders, on Australian Expedition ; disting. at Trafalgar, 1805, and New Orleans, 1814 ; explored Arctic coast of N. America, 1818–'19, and 1825 ; Knt., Governor of Van Diemen's Land, seven years ;

F.R.S. ; sailed on Arctic Expedition, with " Erebus " and
"Terror," 1845 ; d. on board his ship off Point Felix, Arct.
Ocean, June 11, 1847.
    G. R. Lewis.   F. C. Lewis, stipple.
    T. Q. len. to front, seated, holding in right hand a prismatic
compass ; Fort Enterprise in the background.
    Ind. proof, Jany. 1, 1824.
    $13\frac{1}{8} \times 11$. $(8 \times 6\frac{3}{4})$.   27247.

FRANKLIN, Sir John—continued.
    T. H. Maguire.   Negelen, lith.
    T. Q. len. to front, looking to left ; resting left hand on sword-
hilt.
    Ind. proof ; facs. signature below ; vignette.
    $(14\frac{1}{8} \times 10)$.   27248.
    See also ARCTIC COUNCIL.

FREDERICK LOUIS, 1707–1751, Prince of Wales, K.G.,
eldest son of George II. ; b. at Hanover ; m. Princess Augusta
of Saxe-Gotha, 1736 ; pre-deceased his father.
    Anon.   Anon., mez.
    J. C. Smith 47, p. 1690.   24646.

    Vanloo.   B. Baron, 1753.
    Wh. len. in robes, with the star, collar, and George.
    Cut. $(20\frac{3}{8} \times 14\frac{1}{4})$.   25042.
    In Genealogical Chart, 553. 1.

—— The Six Children of.
    Du Pan.   J. Faber, mez.
    J. C. Smith, 147, 3rd state.   27146.

FREELING, Sir Francis, 1764–1836, Bart., Sec. to Genl. Post
Office ; F.S.A., &c.
    G. Jones, R.A.   C. Turner, A.R.A., mez.
    Wh. len. seated, to left, looking to front, at a table on which he
rests his right hand ; an open despatch-box on floor, at his left.
    Proof before all letters.
    $25\frac{3}{4} \times 18\frac{1}{2}$. $(22\frac{5}{16} \times 16\frac{9}{16})$.   22853.

FREIND, John, M.D., 1675–1728, physician and politician, b.
at Croton, near Brackley, Northamptonshire ; educ. at Westminster and Ch. Ch., Oxf., where he attracted the notice of
Dean Aldrich, and gained the friendship of Atterbury ; B.A.,
1698 ; M.A., 1701 ; M.B., 1703 ; M.D., by dipl. 1707 ;
lectured on Chemistry ; accomp. Lord Peterborough, 1705, in
his brilliant campaign in Spain ; visited Italy ; returned to
England, 1707 ; F.R.S., 1712 ; went with Duke of Ormonde,
as his physician, to Flanders ; F.C.P., 1716 ; M.P., 1722 ; com.
to Tower, 1723 ; released 3 months later ; Physician to Q.
Caroline.
    M. Dahl.   G. Vertue, 1730.

Full ha. len. to right, looking to front, seated at table on which
are an inkstand, paper, and books. Bust of Hippocrates behind;
inscription below.
 Cut. Last line of Sapphic stanza missing. (9⅝ × 7₁⅛).
              24661.

FRERE, JOHN HOOKHAM, 1769–1846, Diplomatist and author,
son of John Frere, of Roydon, Norfolk; b. in London; educ.
at Eton and Cambridge; friend of Canning; Under Sec. for
Foreign Affairs; Envoy to Lisbon, and aftds. to Madrid, and
Berlin; wrote in " Microcosm," and " Anti-Jacobin; " author
of humorous poem, " The Monks and the Giants," translations
from classics, &c.; d. at Malta.
 J. Hoppner, R.A.   W. W. Barney, mez.
 J. C. Smith, 7.   22980.

FRITH, WILLIAM POWELL, 1819– , b. at Studley, near Ripon;
stud. in Sass's Art Academy; exhibited, 1839, at B.I.; and at
R.A., 1840; A.R.A., 1845; R.A., 1852; painted " The Derby
Day " and " Railway Station," and many other popular pieces;
pubd. " Autobiography," 1887, and " Further Reminiscences,"
1888; retired, 1890.
 A. Egg.   J. Smyth, etched.
 T. Q. len. to left, seated, looking to front; left arm on back of
chair; vignette; facs. signature below.
 Cut. (4⅝ × 3¾).   28300. 25.

FRODSHAM, WILLIAM J. See SCIENCE.

FROST, W. E., 1810–1877, b. at Wandsworth; student at
R.A., 1829; painted portraits and allegorical pictures; A.R.A.,
1846; R.A., 1870; resigned, 1876; exhibited many pictures at
R.A. and B.I.
              Anon., woodcut.
 Sh. ha. len. to left, looking to front; vignette; from an illustrated paper.
 (4¼ × 3¾).   E. 1982.–'89.

FRY, MRS. ELIZABETH, 1780–1845, b. at Earlham, Norfolk;
eldest child of John Gurney, banker in Norwich, of an old
Quaker family; m. at 20 to Joseph Fry; became recognised as
a minister; interested herself in prison reform, in which she
was very successful, owing to wonderful personal influence;
started " nightly shelter for the homeless," District Visiting
Society, Royal Manor Hall Asylum, and other benevolent schemes.
 Drawn, Etchd. and Pubd. by Richd. Dighton, 1820.
 Wh. len. to right, in profile, seated, in prison, holding before
her an open book on a table.
 Cut. (10¼ × 9⅝).   23594.

FRY, Mrs. ELIZABETH—*continued.*
R. Dighton, 1820. W. T. Fry, 1821.
Ha. len. to right, in profile, copied from Dighton's print;
allegorical objects on border; group at top, representing charity,
a boy giving alms to a boy beggar.
Ind. proof, Aug. 1, 1821.
$9\frac{14}{16} \times 5\frac{15}{16}$. ($2\frac{1}{16} \times 1\frac{1}{2}$, excl. of border). 23595.

G. Richmond. S. Cousins, mixed mez.
Wh. len. to front, standing, wearing light shawl and cap,
dark dress.
Open letter proof, March 1, 1850.
$31\frac{3}{4} \times 20\frac{3}{4}$. ($26\frac{3}{8} \times 16\frac{1}{2}$) 21946.

FRYE, THOMAS, 1710–1762, b. in or near Dublin; came to
London with Stoppelaer, and soon painted and engraved portraits
of the Prince (Frederick) of Wales and others; managed china
factory at Bow; scraped portraits of George III. and his Queen,
and life-size heads, chiefly from imagination; his pictures
were correctly coloured and well finished; he was also a good
miniaturist.
T. Frye. T. Frye, mez.
J. C. Smith, 6, but a proof before the inscription; undescribed
state.
Cut. $18\frac{3}{4} \times 12\frac{1}{8}$. ($17\frac{3}{8} \times 12\frac{1}{8}$). 29453. B.
Also an impression in the ordinary state. E. 3.–'85.

Frye. Frye, mez.
J. C. Smith, 7, 2nd state. E. 1978.–'89.

Frye. Anon., etched.
Bust to left; copy, reversed, of the small portrait by himself
(J. C. Smith, 7, 1st state).
5×4. ($4\frac{1}{16} \times 4$). E. 1977.–'89.

FULLER, ISAAC, 1606–1672, historical and portrait-painter;
stud. in France, under Perrier; practised in England, painting
"wall-pieces," thus decorating several London taverns, and
portraits; he executed a picture in Wadham Coll. Chapel, and
another at Magdalen; his own portrait of himself is at Queen's
Coll.; he left a few etchings.
I. Fuller. T. Chambars.
Sh. ha. len. to right, looking to front; oval; from Walpole's
"Anecdotes."
Cut. ($5\frac{7}{16} \times 3\frac{11}{16}$). E. 1980.–'89.

FULLER, JOHN, –1833; of Rose Hill, Sussex; M.P., 1801,
1802, 1806; "Honest Jack;" was reprimanded for swearing
at the Speaker.
Anon. C. Turner, mez.

T. Q. len. seated, to left, looking to front; on a table at his left
is a paper addressed to him, "*J. Fuller Esqr. M.P.* | Rose Hill
| Sussex | June 10 | 1806."
Engraver's Proof before letters.
$19\frac{1}{4} \times 13\frac{3}{4}$. $(17\frac{5}{16} \times 13\frac{3}{4})$.   24734.

FULLER, Thomas, 1608-1661, b. at Aldwinckle, Northants;
ent. Queen's Coll., Cambr., at the age of 12; B.A., 1624; M.A.,
1628; Fellow of Sidney Coll., and Preb. of Salisbury, 1631;
Rector of Broad Windsor, Dorsets, 1634; Minister at the Savoy,
1641; chaplain to the royalist army; returning to London, 1646,
received various preferments, recovered his stall and preachership
at the Savoy, of which he had been deprived; eloquent preacher;
author of "Holy and Profane State," "Pisgah-Sight of
Palestine," "Worthies of England;" &c.
[Loggan.]   D. Loggan.
Ha. len. to front, in gown, with broad white collar, and long
hair; oval in border; " METHODUS MATER MEMORIÆ," on scroll
above; four verses below.
$11\frac{9}{16} \times 7\frac{1}{16}$. $(11\frac{3}{16} \times 7)$.   22235.

FUSELI, Henry, 1741-1825, b. at Zurich, educ. for the church;
stud. in Rome; exhibited in Spring Gardens, 1775; came to
London, 1779; A.R.A., 1788; R.A., 1790; exhibited a "Milton
Gallery" of 47 pictures; Keeper and Lecturer on painting at the
Academy; his lectures were published; an accomplished linguist;
as a painter, executed huge and bold pictures, deficient in beauty,
as in colour and drawing.
J. Opie, R.A.   [W.] Ridley, stipple.
Sh. ha. len. to right, looking to front; oval; pubd. by Vernor
& Hood (the father of Tom Hood), Jan. 31, 1801.
$6\frac{6}{8} \times 4\frac{6}{8}$. $(3\frac{6}{8} \times 2\frac{1}{16})$.   26276.

___

H. G. Harlow.   E. Scriven, line and stipple.
T. Q. len. to front, seated, looking to left; left elbow on arm of
chair, hand to head; facs. signature below; for the " Library of
the Fine Arts, 1831."
Cut. $(4 \times 3\frac{6}{8})$.   28300. 26.

___

M. Haughton, min.   [W.] Evans, stipple.
Ha. len. to front, seated, looking up to right, his right elbow
on the arm of his chair, hand to head.
Open letter proof (?).
$11\frac{6}{8} \times 8\frac{1}{8}$. $(7 \times 5\frac{6}{8})$.   27214.

___

T. Lawrence, R.A., del.   T. Holloway.
Sh. ha. len. to right, with flowing hair, white neckcloth, dress
slightly sketched; vignette; "Αει ϐαλεοντι εοικος, *Homer*,"
below; Octr. 28, 1796; numbered, 168.
$10\frac{7}{8} \times 9\frac{7}{16}$. $(7\frac{1}{8} \times 7\frac{7}{8})$.   28297. 1

FUSELI, HENRY—*continued.*
 Sir T. Lawrence, P.R.A.   W. C. Edwards.
 Sh. ha. len. to right; copy of the print by T. Holloway;
vignette; facs. signature below.
  Cut. (2$\frac{11}{16}$×2$\frac{1}{4}$).   15219. 3.

———

 Baily sculp.; H. Corbould del. T. Thomson, stipple.
 Bust to front, looking to left; from a bust by Baily; vignette;
a line of Greek below, ινερίδων α νυ ειναι φαμεν, followed by a
facs. signature.
 Ind. proof, March 1, 1825; for the " European Magazine."
 8$\frac{3}{4}$×5$\frac{1}{2}$. (4×4).   E. 1979.-'89.

FUST. *See* JENNER, SIR HERBERT.

FYERS, WILLIAM, –1829, Royal Engineers; Lt.-General,
 Aug. 12, 1819; d. Oct., 1829. His portrait is in the Garrison
 Library, Gibraltar.
  J. Hoppner, R.A.   H. Meyer, mez.
 Ha. len. to left, in uniform, looking to front; The Rock in the
distance.
 Proof before all letters.
 13$\frac{14}{16}$×10. (12×10).   F. 2167.-'89.

GAINSBOROUGH, THOMAS, 1727–1788, b. at Sudbury, son of a
 clothier, came to London, 1742; had lessons from Gravelot; stud.
 at St. Martin's Lane Academy; pupil of F. Hayman; after 4
 years, returned to his native place, and painted portraits and
 landscapes; married at 19; went to Ipswich; then to Bath;
 foundation member of the R. A.; acquired great reputation;
 quarrelled with the Academy; excellent amateur of music; one
 of the greatest of British painters.
  T. Gainsborough.   H. Meyer, chalk and dot.
 Ha. len. to right, looking towards left of front; white neckcloth; coat open down to the third button; vignette.
 Proof before all letters.
  Cut. (6$\frac{7}{8}$×5$\frac{3}{8}$).   27526.
 Subsequently pubd. by Cadell & Davies, 1810.

GALLWEY, STEPHEN PAYNE, c. 1745– , of Tofts Hall,
 Norfolk; assumed name and arms of Gallwey.
 See DILETTANTI SOCIETY.

GALT, JOHN, 1779–1839, novelist, b. at Irvine, Ayrshire; son
 of the commander of a West Indiaman; educ. in a desultory
 way at various schools, at Irvine and Greenock; clerk in Custom House, Greenock; went to London, 1803; wrote poetry,
 and went into a business, which had a brief life; entd. at Linc.
 Inn; went abroad on a commercial mission; travelled with
 Byron from Gibraltar to Malta; took a house at Mycone; returned to London; went once more abroad, 1814; again at
 home soon after; author of "Voyages," "Life of Wolsey,"

"Tragedies," "The Majolo," "Ayrshire Legatees," "Annals of the Parish," "Lawrie Todd," "Autobiography," &c.

I. Irvine.   R. Graves.

Full ha. len. to left, seated, with hands loosely clasped; vignette; face. signature below.

Ind. proof, 1833.

$8\frac{3}{16} \times 5\frac{1}{8}$. ($4\frac{1}{4} \times 3\frac{1}{2}$).   22854.

GAMBIER, James, Lord, 1756–1833, b. at Bahama Islands; ent. Navy; post-cap., 1788; comm. a ship in Howe's Victory off Ushant, 1794; co-operated with Lord Cathcart in capture of Danish Navy, 1807; cr. Lord Gambier, and Comm.-in-Chf. of Channel Fleet, 1808; many years Lord of Admiralty; Admiral of the Fleet, 1830.

Sir W. Beechey.   G. Clint, mez.

Ha. len. to front, looking to right, in uniform; wearing a medal over coat fastened by two or three buttons.

Proof with skeleton letters; Septr. 2, 1808.

$13\frac{3}{4} \times 9\frac{3}{4}$. ($11\frac{3}{4} \times 9\frac{3}{4}$).   22078.

See also COMMEMORATION (1).

GANDON, James, 1742–1823, architect, b. in London, well educated in classics and mathematics; showed early talent for drawing; stud. at St. Martin's Lane Academy; gained a premium from the Socy. of Arts, 1757; articled pupil to Sir W. Chambers; began practice on his own account, c. 1765; stud. at R. A., and contributed to Academy exhibitions, 1774–'80; built New Custom House and Docks in Dublin, 1781, and other works; retired, 1808; etched several plates after Wilson.

H. Hone, R.A.   H. Meyer, stipple.

Ha. len. to right, looking to front, in coat with furred collar; right hand raised to level of breast; a view of the Custom House, Dublin, in distance.

Ind. proof before all letters, except the artists' names.

$9\frac{1}{8} \times 7\frac{1}{4}$. ($5 \times 4\frac{1}{8}$, excl. of ruled border, $\frac{5}{8}$).   21853.

GARDINER, Stephen, 1483–1555, b. at Bury, Suffolk; Archdeacon of Norfolk and Leicester; Vice-chancellor, Cambr. Univ.; bishop of Winchester; committed to the Fleet, and to the Tower; d. at Whitehall.

From a picture at Trin. Hall, Cambr.

S. Harding del.   W. N. Gardiner, stipple.

Ha. len. to front, holding a book in right hand. May 1, 1795.

$7\frac{7}{16} \times 5\frac{3}{8}$. ($5\frac{1}{4} \times 4\frac{3}{8}$).   27262.

GARDNER, Alan, Lord, 1742–1808, b. at Uttoxeter, ent. the Navy, 1755; Post-Capt., 1766; Com. and Commander-in-Chf., Jamaica, 1785; Lord of Admiralty, 1790; Rear-Adm., 1793; present, June 1, 1794, at the victory off Ushant; Vice-

Admiral, and Bart., 1794; Admiral, 1799; Peer of Ireland, 1800.
See COMMEMORATION (1).

GARRICK, DAVID, 1716–1779, pupil of Dr. Johnson, with whom he came to London, 1736; intended for the law, went into the wine trade; went on the stage at Ipswich, 1741; so successful that he tried Richard III. at Goodman's Fields, with immediate and decisive triumph; became the most celebrated and accomplished of English actors, in Tragedy and Comedy; wrote or adapted nearly forty plays; acted Shakspere, and reformed the style of the stage.

   T. Hudson.   J. Dixon, mez.
   J. C. Smith, 6, 1 A state, not described, "David Garrick, Esqr.," in scratched letters.   22855.

Sir J. Reynolds.   T. Watson, mez.
   J. C. Smith, 16, intermed. state between 1 and 11; with "Prologue," artists' names, and publication-line, as described, but before "David Garrick . . . . . servant Thos. Watson."
                                 28480.

   T. Gainsborough.   V. Green, mez.
   J. C. Smith, 46, 2nd state.   24072.

   Zauffely.   L. Dickinson, lith.
   Sh. ha. len. to front, looking to right, collar open at throat; oval; facs. signature below; marked, "PROOF."
   (12$\frac{15}{16}$ × 10$\frac{1}{2}$).   26408.
—— as Richard the Third.
   N. Dance, R.A.   J. Dixon, mez.
   J. C. Smith, 15, 2nd state.   21918.
—— as Richard III.
   W. Hogarth.   W. Hogarth and C. Grignion.
   Wh. len. to front, on couch, in tent; right hand raised with separated fingers, sword grasped in left; bivouack and tents in distance, on left; 1746.
   16$\frac{1}{4}$ × 20$\frac{1}{4}$(?).   (15$\frac{5}{16}$ × 20).   21845.

   Zauffely.   J. Dixon, mez.
   As Abel Drugger, in the "Alchymist."
   J. C. Smith, 18, 2nd state.   E. 269.–'89.
—— in the Character of a Countryman. Prologue to Barbarossa. From a "Collection . . . of English Prologues," &c., 1779.
                           28187. 6.

   Zauffely.   J. MacArdell, mez.
   With Mrs. Cibber, as Jaffier and Belvidera, in "Venice Preserved."
   J. C. Smith, 80, 2nd state.   25741.

GARRICK, DAVID—*continued.*
 Zauffely.   J. Finlayson, mez.
 As Sir John Brute, with **Parsons** and other actors.
  J. C. Smith, 8.   26413.

 G. Carter.   J. Caldwall and S. Smith.
 "Immortality of Garrick;" a composition of many figures;
 on the left, above an empty tomb, the body of Garrick is carried,
 recumbent, by two angels; the right foreground is occupied by
 a crowd of actors and actresses, doing respectful homage;
 while above is the figure of Shakspere, accompanied by two
 Muses, ready to welcome the great actor to Parnassus, on whose
 summit Apollo strikes his lyre, surrounded by the rest of the
 Muses. The figures are by Caldwall, the landscape by S. Smith;
 January 20, 1783.
  19⅛ × 24½. (17½ × 23⁵⁄₁₆).   29751

GARRICK, Mrs.
 R. E. Drummond.   J. Thomson, stipple.
 See LA BELLE ASSEMBLÉE, 1818.   13867. 11.

GARTH, SIR SAMUEL, 1661–1719, Physician and poet, eldest
 son of William Garth of Bowland Forest, West Riding, Yorks;
 educ. at Cambr.; M.D., 1691; F.R.C.P., 1693; rose to first rank
 in his profession; Knt., 1714; Phys. to the King, Phys.-Genl.
 to the Army; pub. the "Dispensary," and other poems; bur. at
 Harrow.
 Sir G. Kneller.   J. Simon, mez.
 J. C. Smith, 68, 1st state.   22239.

GAUNT, JOHN OF, Duke of Lancaster. *See* LANCASTER.

GAY, JOHN, 1688–1732, Poet and dramatist; b. near Barnstaple;
 appr. to a mercer in London; became known by his "Rural
 Sports," 1711; wrote the "Beggar's Opera," and other
 comedies and farces; also "Fables;" spent latter years of his
 life in the house of the Duke of Queensberry; bur. in Westminster Abbey.
 Zincke.   W. Smith, mez.
 J. C. Smith, 1, 2nd state.   22074.

GEORGE I., 1660–1727; GEORGE AUGUSTUS, son of Ernest,
 Elector of Hanover, and Sophia, granddaughter of James I.;
 m. Sophia Dorothea of Zell, 1682; Elector, 1698; King of
 England, on death of Queen Anne, 1714; d. at Osnaburg.
 Sir G. Kneller.   J. Faber, junr., mez.
 J. C. Smith, 153.   21863.

GEORGE II., 1683–1760, GEORGE AUGUSTUS, only son of
 George I. and his Queen, Sophia Dorothea of Zell; b. at
 Hanover; m., in 1705, Princess Caroline of Brandenburg-
 Auspach, who d., 1737; disting. himself at Oudenarde, and

 O 82849.   N

(when King) at Dettingen ; suc., 1760 ; bur. in Henry VII.'s
Chapel, Westminster Abbey.

    R. E. Pine.   W. Dickinson, mez.
    J. C. Smith, 26, 3rd state.   25779.

GEORGE II.—continued.

    P. à Gunst del.   P. à Gunst.
                                M. Marrebeeck excudit.
    Ha. len. in armour; oval in border decorated with branches
of laurel ; title on scroll, below.
    $23\frac{7}{10} \times 19\frac{1}{4}$. $(22\frac{3}{4} \times 18\frac{1}{2})$.   24683.

GEORGE III., 1738–1820, eldest son of Frederick, Prince of
Wales; b. at Norfolk House, St. James's Square ; cr. Pr. of
Wales, on his father's death, 1751 ; suc. his grandfather,
George II., 1760 ; m. Princess Charlotte of Mecklenburg-
Strelitz, 1761 ; d. at Windsor Castle.

    D. Luders, 1751.   J. McArdell, mez.
    J. C. Smith, 84.   27164.
    As Prince of Wales ; oval.

    A. Ramsay.   W. W. Ryland.
    Wh. len. in robes, with left hand on a table.
    Published April 11th, 1762.
    $23\frac{1}{2} \times 15$. $(20\frac{3}{4} \times 13\frac{1}{2})$.   21990.

—— with Queen Charlotte and family.
    J. Zauffely.   R. Earlom, mez., 1770.
    J. C. Smith, 2nd state.   27113.

    J. Zauffely.   R. Houston, mez., 1772.
    T. Q. len. seated.
    J. C. Smith, 43, 2nd state.   22073.

    Frye.   W. Pether, mez.
    Ha. len. looking to right, wearing collar of the Garter.
    J. C. Smith, 17, 2nd state.   25045.
    In Genealogical Chart, 553.   1.

    Sir J. Reynolds.   Dickinson and Watson, mez.
    J. C. Smith, 27, 1st state (?).
    Cut at foot.   E. 341.–90.

    S. Myers.   J. McArdell, mez.
    Sh. ha. len. in profile to the left.
    J. C. Smith, 85, 1st state.   24115.

—— on his favourite charger, Adonis.
    Sir W. Beechey, R.A.   J Ward, mez.
    J. C. Smith, 20.   23128.

GEORGE III.—*continued.*
—— at Review.
    Sir W. Beechey, R.A.   J. Ward, mez.
    J. C. Smith, 22.   25829.

    Anon.   W. Skelton.
    Sh. ha. len. to front, looking to left, in Admiral's uniform, and
wearing a cocked hat.
    Published Oct. 25th, 1810.
    $19\frac{7}{8} \times 15\frac{3}{16}$ (?). $(18 \times 14\frac{7}{16})$.   25046.
    In Genealogical Chart, 553.   1.

                   [D. Orme (?)], chalk and dotted style.
    Wh. len. seated, receiving the Persian ambassador who bows
low, on the right; the King, on the left, is surrounded by his
ministers, attendants, &c.
    Proof before all letters.
    At foot, in middle, scratched; "July 22, 1796, Orme 14 Old
Bond Street."
    $19\frac{1}{2} \times 24\frac{1}{2}$. $(17\frac{1}{16} \times 23\frac{1}{4})$.   25743.

    E. Dayes.   J. Neagle.
    In the "Royal Procession in St. Paul's on St. George's Day
1789, the day appointed for a General Thanksgiving for the
King's happy Recovery."
    $18\frac{5}{8} \times 27\frac{7}{16}$. $(16\frac{1}{2} \times 26\frac{9}{16})$ 25844.   1.

    E. Dayes.   R. Pollard, etched and aquatinted.
    In the "View of the Choir of St. Paul's, on the Day of
"Solemn Thanksgiving for the Recovery of His Majesty, April
"23, 1789."
    $18\frac{1}{3} \times 27\frac{1}{16}$. $(15\frac{5}{8} \times 25\frac{3}{4})$.   25844.   2.

    Anon. [Dighton].   Anon. [Dighton].
    "Our Sovereign Lord the King | as he appeared the Moment
previous to the Dreadful mischief intended him | by the Horrid
Assassin James Hadfield," etc., 6 lines of inscription. A coloured
print.
    "Pubd. May 19th, 1800, by Dighton, Charing Cross."
    Cut. $(8\frac{1}{4} \times 7\frac{1}{2})$.   29046.

    T. Stothard.   P. Roberts, stipple.
    "The Royal Family of England in the year 1787, a group
including the King, the Queen, and the rest of the Royal
Family; numerals below, to correspond with those on a key.
    Cut. $(6\frac{15}{16} \times 9\frac{1}{2})$.   26729.

    Anon.   Anon.
    "His Late Most Excellent Majesty King George III."
    Ha. len. seated, wearing a cap, and a dressing gown, decorated

with a star. "From an original drawing taken at the age of 82 in the 60th year of his Reign." Vignette. Published, March, 1820 . . . and sold by . . . R. Cooper, No. 1, Edward Street, Hampstead Road.

$15\frac{5}{8} \times 12\frac{7}{8}$. ($9\frac{1}{2} \times 8\frac{3}{4}$). E. 358.-'90.

GEORGE IV., 1762–1830; m. Princess Caroline Amelia Elizabeth, dau. of the Duke of Brunswick, 1795; separated, 1796; Regent, 1811; suc. 1821.

[J. Cruikshank.] [G. Maile], stipple.

Wh. len. to right; the Pavilion at Brighton in distance.

Proof before all letters.

$11\frac{3}{4} \times 8\frac{7}{8}$. ($8\frac{3}{4} \times 6\frac{1}{4}$). 28411.

—— as Prince Regent.

G. H. Harlow. W. Ward, mez.

On horseback, in Hussar uniform, turned to the right, with sword raised.

Published Feby. 6th, 1811, by J. P. Thompson.

J. C. Smith, 40, 2nd state. 15589.

——

T. Phillips, R.A. W Ward, A.R.A., mez.

On horseback, in Hussar uniform, facing to front.

A Progress Proof (before all letters), on which the artist has marked alterations (to be made) with a pencil. This state is not described by J. C. Smith (41). 15590.

——

T. Phillips, R.A. W. Skelton.

Sh. ha. len. to front, looking to left; in uniform, with the Golden Fleece.

Published, March 4th, 1819.

$20 \times 15\frac{7}{16}$. (18×14). 25046. 2.

In Genealogical Chart, 553. 1.

——

J. Holmes. J. Holmes.

Ha. len. to front, wearing the Golden Fleece, and Star of the Garter; pillar and curtain behind on right.

Published, Jany. 1, 1829, by Colnaghi, Son & Co.

$20\frac{1}{2} \times 15$. ($17 \times 14\frac{1}{2}$). 27943.

——

Sir T. Lawrence, P.R.A. T. Hodgetts, mez.

Wh. len. in robes.

Proof before the title.

Published June, 1829, by M. Colnaghi.

Cut. ($24\frac{3}{4} \times 16\frac{7}{8}$). 24073.

——

Sir T. Lawrence, P.R.A. W. Finden.

Wh. len. with left arm over the back of the sofa on which he is seated, looking to front.

$27\frac{5}{16} \times 18\frac{3}{8}$. ($23\frac{1}{16} \times 16$). 21847.

GEORGE IV.—*continued.*
—— when Prince of Wales.

J. S. Copley, R.A.   C. Turner, mez.

Wh. len. on horseback, at a review; directed to the left, attended by Lord Heathfield, General Turner, Col. Bloomfield and Baron Eben; Col. Quintin in the distance. The picture was exhibited at the Royal Academy, in 1810.
Proof with skeleton letters, mostly cut off.
(26¼ × 22⅛).   15591

GEORGE V., PRINCE, of Cumberland, afterwards King of Hanover, 1819–1878; suc. 1851.

F. Krüger.   Luderitz, lith., 1825.

Ha. len. slightly to left, looking to front, in uniform.
Cut. (9¾ × 7⅔).   25061.
In Genealogical Chart, 553. 1.

GERBIER, SIR BALTHAZAR, c. 1591–1667, miniature-painter, b. at Antwerp; resided long in Italy, where he was highly esteemed; knighted by Charles I., who appointed him Master of the Ceremonies at the Court; had been patronised by the Duke of Buckingham; more a courtier than a painter; led an eventful life, described by Walpole in his "Anecdotes."

A. van Dyck.   J. Meyssens.

Ha. len. to left, looking to front, holding a folded paper in his right hand; wearing a broad collar, long hair, and a cloak, &c.
6 9⁄16 × 4⅜. (5 9⁄16 × 4½).   E. 1298.–'88.

GERBIER FAMILY.

A. Van Dyck.   W. Walker.

Wh. len., Gerbier himself, on left, leans on the back of his wife's chair; she is seated, holding an infant on her lap, and directed to the right; before her are three children; two more approach from the right, and other three are on the right; landscape in distance. Feb. 1, 1766.

NOTE.—In the print by McArdell, mez., the picture is attributed to Rubens, to whom some parts of it are probably due. It was most likely a joint production of the two painters.
Cut. (15½ × 22 1⁄10).   24628.

GERMAINE, LORD GEORGE. *See* SACKVILLE.

GETHING (or GETHINGE), RICHARD, 1585(?)–1652(?), calligrapher, of Hereford, a pupil of John Davies, the famous writing-master; considered superior to his master; started business in Fetter Lane, London, at the "Hand and Pen;" published a copybook, 1616; "Chirographia," 1645, engraved by Goddart; "Caligraphotechnia," 1652.

Anon.   (J. Chantry ?)

Ha. len. slightly to right, looking to front, wearing a ruff; oval; two pens above, crossed, in a wreath; about the oval, RICHARDUS GETHINGE HEREFORDIENSIS. Æt: 32; below, 6 English verses, signed W. B.; outside, on right, an arm and hand, holding a pen; above VIVE LA, and below, PLVME, in flourished writing. Prefixed to " Caligraphotechnia.". *Rare*, from the Burleigh James collection.

Cut. (7$\frac{2}{16}$×10$\frac{5}{8}$; oval, 3$\frac{3}{4}$×3). 27977.

GIBBON, EDWARD, 1737–1794, historian, b. at Putney; educ. at Westminster, and Magdalen Coll., Oxf.; became a Rom. Catholic, 1753; was sent to Lausanne, 1754, and recanted; learned French, stud. Latin, travelled through Switzerland; returned to England, 1758; wrote " Essai sur l'Étude de la Littérature, 1758–'61; went to Rome, 1764; M.P., 1774; wrote " Decline and Fall of the Roman Empire," 1776–'88.

Sir J. Reynolds. Anon.
Sh. ha. len. to front, looking to left; the name and date of birth above; oval in border, Romulus and Remus with the she-wolf on one side, and the Roman eagle on the other side, of a figure leaning on a column and gazing on the ruins of the Colosseum, below.

Cut. (6$\frac{1}{8}$×4$\frac{1}{2}$). 27527.

GIBBONS, GRINLING, 1648–1720, wood-carver and sculptor, of Dutch origin, b. at Rotterdam; lived in Belle Sauvage Court, Ludgate Hill, aftds. in Bow St.; worked at Windsor, and executed much of the carving for the choir of St. Paul's, the wooden throne at Canterbury, the statues of Charles II. at Chelsea and James II. at Whitehall, carvings at Chatsworth, Petworth, Blenheim, Wimpole, Cassiobury, &c.; he had many pupils, who assisted him in his carving and statuary work; according to Evelyn, he was " likewise musical, and very civil, sober, and discreete in his discourse."

Sir G. Kneller. J. Smith, mez.
J. C. Smith, 105, 1st state. 21867

——, with Mrs. Gibbons, his wife.
Mrs. Gibbons had 9 or 10 children, all baptised at St. Paul's, Cov. Garden, including 5 daughters; she d. 1719, and was buried in that church.

J. Closterman. J. Smith, mez.
J. C. Smith, 106, 2nd state. 21868.

GIBBONS. *See* ARTISTS, A SOCIETY OF.
Nothing seems to be known of this artist's life.

GIBBS, JAMES, 1674–1754, architect, A.M., F.R.S.; b. near Aberdeen; stud. in Holland and Italy; came to England, c. 1710; built several London churches, the Radcliffe Library at Oxford, &c.; pubd. some works on Architecture; d. in London.

J. Williams. J. McArdell, mez.
J. C. Smith, 88, 1st state. 25742.

GIBBS, SIR VICARY, 1752–1820, justice of Com. Pleas, 1812; Ld. Ch. Baron, 1813; Ch.-justice of Com. Pleas, 1814; resigned, 1818.

W. Owen, R.A. S. W. Reynolds & T. Lupton, mez.

T. Q. len. to right, seated, looking to left, in robes, resting right elbow on one, and left hand on the other, arm of his chair. Open letter proof. April 6th, 1815.
19½ × 14.   (16⅝ × 14).   22985.

GIBSON, EDMUND, 1669–1748, learned divine, b. at Bampton, Westmoreland; educ. at Queen's Coll., Oxf.; precentor, Chichester; rector, Lambeth; bishop of Lincoln, 1716; and of London, 1720; edited Camden, &c.
I. Ellys.   G. Vertue, 1727.
T. Q. len. to left, seated, in robes, looking to front, and holding a book on his right knee; 4 lines of inscription below.
Cut.   (12⅔ × 10₁⁄₁₆).   27601.

GIBSON, JOHN, R.A., 1790–1866, sculptor; b. at Conway, Wales; went to Rome, and stud. under Canova and Thorwaldsen, 1817; exec. statues of the Queen, Mr. Huskisson, Sir Robert Peel, &c.; exhib. his "Tinted Venus," 1862; d. at Rome.
P. Williams.   C. Wagstaff, mixed mez.
Full ha. len. to right, looking to front, wearing cap and loose coat; sculptor's tools in left hand, right hand clasping left wrist; figure of "Cupid tormenting the soul" on the right, in background.
Ind. proof, with skeleton letters; August, 1845.
15⅞ × 12.   (12 × 8⅛).   21957.

GIBSON, RICHARD, 1615–1690, painter, commonly called "The Dwarf," being only 3 ft. 10 in. in height; b. in Cumberland (probably); page to a lady at Mortlake; pupil of Franz Cleyn; married to Anne Shepherd, also a dwarf, in presence of Charles I. and his Queen; rose into repute, and was sent to Holland to teach the Princess Mary; instructed Q. Anne also; painted portrait of Cromwell several times.
Anon.   A. Walker.
Sh. ha. len. to left, looking to front, with long hair; oval; his wife, in another oval, below, on the right.
In Walpole's "Anecdotes," Vol. III., 1763.
Cut.   (6½ × 4½).   E. 1988.–'89.

GILBERT, DAVIES GIDDY, 1767–1840, b. at St. Erth, Cornwall; his family name was Giddy, but he assumed the name and arms of Gilbert, 1817, having married the daughter of a wealthy Sussex gentleman of that name; used his wealth to advance science, and to assist talented explorers, whom poverty might have kept in obscurity; helped Sir Humphry Davy in this way; author of several papers, &c.; Pres. Royal Socy., 1829; M.P., Bodmin, 1806–'32.
H. Howard, R.A.   S. Cousins, mez.
Ha. len. to front, seated; white neckcloth, dark coat, fastened by two buttons.
Proof before all letters.
13⅞ × 10½.   (10¾ × 9).   21741.
See also SCIENCE.

GILBERT, Sir John, 1817–   ; exhibited first in 1836; has
painted many pictures in oil as well as in water-colours; worked
for many years on the "Illustrated London News," and on
book-illustrations, excelling in spirited "Charges of Cavalry,"
and such pictures as "The Field of the Cloth of Gold," 1874,
"Tewkesbury Abbey," "Crusaders," &c.; associate, 1852;
member, 1853; and President of R. S. of Painters in Water-
colours; A.R.A., 1872; R.A., 1876.
 [J. Gilbert (?)]   J. Knight, woodcut.
 Bust, to front, looking to left, wearing a cap; with palette,
brushes, bottles, &c., below; arched at top.
 15 × 11. (14¾ × 11).   E. 1987.–'89.

 A. Gilbert.   Smeeton & Tilly, woodcut.
 Bust to right; oval; for an illustrated paper. Inscription in
French, printed below.
 $(7\frac{3}{16} \times 6\frac{9}{16})$.   E. 1986.–'89.

GILL, Thomas, c. 1694, son of **Thomas Gill**, M.D., of Edmonton,
a celebrated physician, who d. there, 1714.
 T. Murray.   J. Smith, mez.
 J. C. Smith, 108.   E. 2124.–'89.

GILLIES, John, 1747–1836, historian and scholar, b. at Brechin,
in Forfarshire, eldest son of a merchant; educ. at Brechin, and
Glasgow Univ.; came to London, went abroad as tutor to the
sons of the 2d Earl of Hopetoun; returned to England, 1784;
LL.D.; F.R.S.; F.S.A.; Historiographer for Scotland, 1793;
author of a "History of Greece," &c.
 J. Opie, R.A. (W. Evans delin.) C. Picart, stipple.
 Sh. ha. len. to right, looking rather to left, with coat buttoned,
and high collar; vignette; Feb. 1, 1813.
 14¾ × 11⅓. (7⅞ × 7¼).   27998. 2

GILLRAY, James, c. 1757–1815, caricaturist; apprent. to a
heraldic engraver; joined some strolling players; returned, dis-
gusted; stud. at R. A.; designed illustrations for the "Deserted
Village," and engraved them himself, 1784; continued to
execute serious engravings, while he became the most eminent
of English caricaturists, producing over 1,200 political and
miscellaneous caricatures; the last is dated, 1811; intemperate
in habits, he then fell into imbecility and delirium, in which he
died.
 J. Gillray, min.   C. Turner, mez.
 Ha. len. to left, looking to front, wearing a high-collared coat,
buttoned loosely, a frill, and a light striped waistcoat; oval in
ruled border; April 19, 1819.
 15½ × 12. (Oval, 9¾ × 7¹⁵⁄₁₆).   24074.

 Anon.   Anon., etched.
 Sh. ha. len. to right, looking to front; caricatures on wall
behind him; vignette; "James Gillray. | The Caricaturist," in
facs. (?), below.
 6⅞ × 5. (5¾ × 4½).   26251.

GILPIN, SAWREY, 1733–1807, animal painter, b. at Carlisle;
intended for commerce, but turned to art; became pupil of
Samuel Scott, marine-painter, whom he left, 1758, to devote
himself to painting animals; patronised by the Duke of Cumberland; president of the Incorp. Society, where he exhibited
1763, 1764, 1770; A.R.A., 1795; R.A., 1797; drew horses
well; etched a small book of them, and some plates of oxen, &c.
 G. Dance, 1798.   W. Daniell, stipple.
 Sh. ha. len. to right, in profile; vignette; March 15, 1810.
 10¾ × 8. (7¼ × 5½).   27216.

GIRTIN, THOMAS, 1775–1802, water-colour painter, b. in Southwark; pupil of Dayes; painted views in London, then in
Scotland, and visited York, Durham, Cumberland, Westmoreland, and other places; exhibited at the R. A., 1794–'98;
an admirable artist, bold, vigorous, and skilful; etched some
views in Paris, to which effects were added in aquatint from his
drawings.
 J. Opie, R.A.   S. W. Reynolds, mez.
 Ha. len. to front, looking to left; white neckcloth, coat
buttoned; holding a crayon in right hand.
 Pubd. May 16, 1817, by J. Girtin, engraver, &c., brother of
the artist represented.
 14⅞ × 10½. (12⅛ × 10⅜).   21901.

 G. Dance, 1798.   W. Daniell, stipple.
 Sh. ha. len. seated, to right, in profile; vignette; April 2, 1814.
 10¾ × 8. (7⅝ × 6).   28255. 2.

GLADSTONE, SIR JOHN, 1764–1851, merchant, son of Thomas
Gladstone, and father of Rt. Hon. W. E. Gladstone; b. at
Leith; eminent W. Ind. merchant at Liverpool for nearly 60
years; M.P. for Woodstock; cr. Bart., 1846.
 Anon.   Anon.
 Wh. len. standing, to front, looking to left, holding eyeglass
in right hand; left resting on books on table; ships at sea, in
distance.
 Ind. proof before all letters.
 (24 × 15³⁄₁₆).   22856.

GLADSTONE, RT. HON. WILLIAM EWART, 1809– ; Statesman and Author; Colonial Sec.; Master of the Mint; Chancellor of the Exchequer; four times Prime Minister.
 Anon.   Anon., lith.
 Bust, slightly to right.
 (6½ × 4).   29627. 96.
 See also ABERDEEN CABINET, and COMMONS (2).

GLENELG, CHARLES GRANT, Lord, 1778–1866; Chief Sec.
Ireland, 1819–'22; Presidt. Board of Trade, 1827–'28; cr.
Baron, 1835; Colonial Sec., 1834–'39.
 T. C. Thompson.   C. Turner, mez.

T. Q. len. to left, looking to front, left hand on hip, right on book, lettered "Ireland," and "5."
Open letter proof; March 14, 1820.
$19\frac{7}{8} \times 13\frac{1}{16}$. ($16\frac{7}{16} \times 12\frac{1}{16}$). 22860.

GLOUCESTER, HENRY STUART, Duke of, 1639–1660, youngest son of K. Charles I.; suc., 1659.
S. Luttichuys. C. van Dalen, junior.
Sh. ha. len. to front, in armour, with long hair.; oval in border.
$15 \times 11\frac{3}{16}$. ($14\frac{5}{8} \times 10\frac{3}{4}$). 24626.

GLOUCESTER, WILLIAM, Duke of, 1689–1700.
Sir G. Kneller. I. Smith, mez. [1691].

As a child, with a "shock-dog."
J. C. Smith, 111, 1st state. 24116.

GLOUCESTER, WILLIAM FREDERICK, Duke of, 1776–1834, son of William, Duke of Gloucester.
Sir J. Reynolds. Caroline Watson, stipple.
As a boy, wh. len. in a Van Dyck dress.
Proof before the title.
Published, Augt. 14th, 1784, by John Boydell, &c. (Scratched below.)
$12\frac{7}{16} \times 8\frac{3}{8}$. ($11\frac{1}{4} \times 8$). 22857.

———

Sir W. Beechey. W. Say, mez.
T. Q. len. to left, seated, in uniform with star.
Published March 22, 1819. Proof with scratched letters.
$22\frac{1}{8} \times 16\frac{1}{8}$. ($18\frac{1}{4} \times 13\frac{5}{8}$). 25058. I.
In Genealogical Chart, 558. 1.

———

Sir W. Beechey, R.A. W. Say, mez.
T. Q. len. to right, in robes, with the collar and George.
Published Jany. 2nd, 1826.
$21\frac{7}{8} \times 15\frac{1}{16}$. ($17\frac{7}{8} \times 13\frac{1}{8}$). 21906.

GLOUCESTER, MARIA, Duchess of, 1739–1807. See WALDEGRAVE

GLOUCESTER. See MARY, DUCHESS OF GLOUCESTER.

GLOVER, JOHN, 1767–1849, water-colour painter, son of a small farmer, b. at Houghton-on-the-Hill; self-taught; stud. water-colour drawing and music at Appleby, where he was master of the Free School; practised later in oils, and made many etchings; induced to visit London, was one of the promoters and first members of the Water-colour Society, of which he was President, 1815; one of the founders of Socy. of Br. Artists; went to Australia, 1831; d. in Tasmania.
Skinner Prout. C. K. Childs (?), woodcut.

Ha. len. to left, sleeping, in travelling dress; vignette; facs.
signature below.
($3\frac{1}{2} \times 3$). E. 2006.-'89.

GLOVER, Miss P., — , actress; daughter of Mrs. Glover;
appeared first as "Juliet" to Kean's "Romeo," her mother
playing the Nurse, April 29, 1822; and again, with Liston, in
"Paul Pry;" in the print with LISTON (q. v.).

GLYNN, JOHN, 1722–1779, politician and lawyer, second son of
William Glynn, of Glynn, in Cardinham, Cornwall; educ. at
Oxford; barrister, 1748; serj.-at-law, 1763; recorder of Exeter,
1764; supported Wilkes, for whom he acted, 1763, in appl. for
writ of hab. corp., and in actions following; for John Almon,
1765; and for Wilkes, against his outlawry, 1768; M.P. 1768,
1774, for Middlesex; Recorder of the City, 1772; &c.
R. Houston. R. Houston, mez.
With J. Wilkes and Rev. J. Horne (q. v.).
J. C. Smith, 48. 22093.

GODFREY, SIR EDMUNDBURY, –1678, magistrate before
whom Titus Oates had sworn his information; found murdered
near Primrose Hill.
Anon. Vander Banck.
Sh. ha. len. to right, looking to front; oval, in border.
Cut. ($13\frac{3}{8} \times 10$). 24662.

GODOLPHIN, SIDNEY GODOLPHIN, Earl of, 1645–1712, Lord
High Treasurer to Q. Anne, 1702–'10; dismissed with a
pension, 4,000l. a year; K.G., 1704; cr. Earl, 1706.
Sir G. Kneller. J. Houbraken.
Sh. ha. len. to left, looking to front, holding a staff of office;
oval in border. In Birch's "Lives."
$14\frac{3}{8} \times 9\frac{1}{4}$. ($14 \times 8\frac{3}{8}$). 20806.

Sir G. Kneller. J. Smith, mez.
J. C. Smith, 116. 22077.
See also LORDS JUSTICES.

GODOLPHIN, SYDNEY, M.P., "Father of the House," during Sir
Robert Walpole's Administration.
See COMMONS.

GODWIN, GEORGE, 1815–1888, F.R.S., F.S.A., architect, son of
an architect, b. at Brompton; gained a medal from the
R.I.B.A., 1835, for an essay on Concrete; pubd. a work, 1838,
on "Churches of London;" one of the founders, 1839, and
Hon. Sec., of the London Art Union; built several London
Churches, and restored that of S. Mary Redcliffe, Bristol;
editor of "The Builder" for nearly 40 years; published
"History in Ruins," and other works.
Anon. Anon., woodcut.
Bust, to front, looking to left; for an illustrated paper;
circular.
($3\frac{1}{4}$ diamr.). E. 1989.-'89.

GODWIN, MARY WOLLSTONECRAFT, 1759–1797, set up a
school at Islington, 1782, adopted revolutionary ideas, and

wrote an answer to Burke's " Essay ; " became violently attached
to Fuseli, the painter; afterwards to a Mr. Imlay; advocated
" the Rights of Woman," free love, &c.; married William
Godwin, the writer; gave birth to a daughter, Mary, afterwards
the second wife of Shelley, the poet.
J. Opie, R.A.   W. T. Annis, mez.
J. C. Smith, 5.   24075.

GODWIN, WILLIAM, 1756–1836, Political and Miscell. writer;
b. at Wisbeach, son of a dissenting minister; began preaching
at Stowmarket; turned to literature, 1783; pubd. "Political
Justice," 1793, in favour of French Revolutionary Principles;
"Caleb Williams," 1794, excited much attention; connected
himself with Mary Wollstonecraft, whom he married, 1797;
spent some time in Ireland, 1800; m. again, 1801; opened a
book-shop, under name of Edward Baldwin, in Skinner Street;
visited Edinburgh, 1816; app. Yeoman usher of Exch. by
Earl Grey; d. at his residence, New Palace Yard, Westminster.
J. Northcote, R.A.   G. Dawe, mez.
J. C. Smith, 4, 1st state.   22237.

GOFFRIE,   –   , viola-player; in England, 1853;
still living (1894), in U.S. America.
See MUSICAL UNION

GOLDSMITH, OLIVER, 1728–1774, b. at Pallas, near Bally-
mahon, Longford; educ. at Elphin, Athlone, Edgeworthstown,
and, as a sizar, at Trin. Coll., Dublin, 1744; B.A., 1749;
intended for the church, a profession for which "he had no
liking;" helped by a kind but injudicious uncle, Contarine;
went to Edinb., 1752; to Leyden, 1753; to Louvain, Paris,
Strasburg, Germany, Switzerland, Italy, 1755–'6; returned,
destitute, to London; after many adventures and struggles,
became an author; wrote "Vicar of Wakefield," "Chinese
Letters," "Animated Nature," "The Traveller," "Good-
natured Man," "She stoops to conquer," "Deserted Village,"
"Haunch of Venison," &c.
Sir J Reynolds.   Jos. Marchi, mez.
J. C. Smith, 7, 3rd state,   27294.

GOOCH, ROBERT, 1784–1830, physician, b. at Yarmouth, Norf.,
son of Robert Gooch, a sea-Captain; educ. at a private day-
school, and apprent. at 15 to G. Borrett, surg.-apoth.; went to
Edinb. Univ., 1804; M.D., 1807; worked in London, under
Astley Cooper; began general pract., 1808; L.C.P., 1812; in
ill-health, 1826, obtained post of librarian to the King; wrote
on the "Most Important Diseases of Women," and other similar
subjects.
J. Linnell.   J. Linnell.
Ha. len. to right, looking to front, seated by a table on which
are books; holding a paper in right hand.
Ind. proof with open letters, May 1st, 1831.
15⅛ × 11. (11⅝ × 9 7/16).   22858.

GOODALL, JOSEPH, 1760–1840, educ. at Eton and King's Coll., Cambr.; Canon of Windsor; rector of West Holey; D.D.; provost of Eton, where he died.
Jackson. C. Turner, mez.
T. Q. len. to left, looking to front, seated, holding a closed book in left hand; wearing gown and bands.
Proof before all letters.
$19\frac{7}{8} \times 13\frac{1}{8}$. ($15\frac{4}{16} \times 11\frac{1}{2}$). 27952.

GORDON, LORD GEORGE, 1751–1793, younger son of Cosmo George, 3rd Duke of Gordon, b. in London; received a commission as ensign, "when in petticoats;" became afterwards a midshipman, served on American station, rose to be a lieutenant, 1772, and resigned; M.P., 1774; President of the Protestant Association; tried for High Treason, 1781, in connection with the famous riots, and acquitted; convicted of libel; d. in Newgate.
R. Bran. Anon. [R. Bran?].
Wh. len. to front, carrying his hat in left hand, and in right his stick, with which he points to the roll of the Protestant Petition; his right foot rests on a volume, entitled POPERY; in the distance the various divisions of the Protestant Association are drawn up.
$13\frac{7}{8} \times 9\frac{7}{8}$. ($12\frac{3}{8} \times 9$). 25778.

GORDON, GEORGE, 5th Duke of, 1770–1836, educ. at Eton and Cambridge; ent. army, 1790; General, 1819; served in Ireland, during the Rebellion, 1798; in Holland, 1799; at Walcheren, 1809; M.P., 1806–7; G.C.B.; suc. 1827.
J. McKenzie. C. Turner, A.R.A., mez.
T. Q. len. seated, to left, looking to front, holding watch in his left hand.
Proof before letters. Septr. 1st, 1830.
$15\frac{1}{2} \times 12\frac{3}{8}$. ($12\frac{1}{2} \times 10\frac{9}{16}$). 22859.

G. Sanders. J. Lucas, mez.
T. Q. len. in Highland dress, to right, looking to left.
Open letter proof. Sepr. 1st, 1836.
$21\frac{3}{4} \times 16\frac{5}{16}$. ($17\frac{5}{16} \times 12\frac{3}{8}$). 22984.

GORDON, SIR JOHN WATSON, 1790–1864, b. at Edinburgh, son of Capt. Watson, R.N.; intended for the Artillery; stud. at Edinburgh, where he painted many portraits, and succeeded Raeburn, on the death of that artist, in the chief practice; R.S.A., 1826; exhibited also in London, 1827; A.R.A., 1841; R.A., 1850, P.R.S.A., and knighted; his portraits are vigorous and full of character and expression; obtained a medal at Paris, 1855.
J. W. Gordon. W. Walker, mixed mez.
Ha. len. to right, looking to front, coat buttoned at neck.
Proof before all letters.
$16 \times 12\frac{3}{8}$. ($12\frac{7}{8} \times 10\frac{1}{4}$). 22461.

GOUGH, HUGH, 1st Viscount, 1779–1868; b. at Woodstown, co.
Limerick; disting. in Penins. War; Com.-in-Chf. in China;
cr. Bart., 1842; Com.-in-Chf. in India; defeated Mahrattas at
Maharajpore, 1843; victorious at Moodkee, Sobraon, Goojerat,
&c., in the Sikh wars; cr. Baron, 1846; Viscount, 1849;
G.C.B., &c.; d. at St. Helen's, near Dublin.
    F. Grant, R.A.   G. Saunders, mixed mez.
  Wh. len. to front, facing, looking, and pointing to left, with
right hand extended; left hand, on sword hilt, holding white
helmet; a gun in background.
  Open letter proof. Jany. 1, 1856.
  $31 \times 19\frac{1}{2}$. $(26\frac{1}{4} \times 16\frac{1}{4})$.   22982.

GOULBURN, RT. HON. HENRY, 1784–1856; Ch. Sec. Ireland,
1821–'7; Chancellor of the Exchequer; Home Sec.; &c.
  G. Richmond.   R. A. Artlett, stipple.
  Ha. len. seated, to right, looking to front, with arms folded.
  Open letter proof.
  Cut. $(16 \times 12\frac{1}{2})$.   22988.

GOW, NATHANIEL, or NEIL, 1727–1807; b. at Strathband,
Perthshire, of humble parents; showed precocious talent for
music, and at 9 began to play the violin; received some lessons
from John Cameron; became famous as a player of Scotch
tunes, strathspeys and reels; is said to have had an uncom-
monly powerful bow hand, "particularly in the up-stroke;"
published several collections of tunes, including many of his
own composition; d. at Inver, near Dunkeld.
  H. Raeburn, R.A.   W. Say, mez.
  T. Q. len. to front, seated, wearing plaid breeches and stockings, and playing the violin.
  $21\frac{7}{8} \times 15\frac{7}{8}$. $(17\frac{7}{8} \times 13\frac{13}{16})$.   22997.

GOWER, JOHN, c. 1325–1408, poet, of good birth, probably of
the family of Sir Robert Gower, a large landowner in Suffolk
and Kent; wrote of the Kentish insurrection (1381) with apparent
personal knowledge; travelled abroad and read widely; wrote
"Confessio Amantis" at request of Richard II., to whom it was
first dedicated; lived in the priory of St. Mary Overies, where
he married, 1397, Agnes Groundolf; became blind, 1400;
author of "Speculum Meditantis," and "Vox Clamantis;"
buried in St. Mary Overies (now St. Saviour's) Church.
  "Ex Monumento."   G. Vertue, 1727.
  Sh. ha. len. to right, in profile; wearing collar of SS and
swan medal, the badge of Henry IV., to whom the poet had
transferred the dedication of his "Confessio."
  $14\frac{1}{4} \times 9\frac{8}{16}$. $(13\frac{1}{8} \times 8\frac{11}{16})$.   27865. 1.

GOWER, JOHN, 2nd Baron; c. 1690–1754; suc., 1709; cr.
Earl, 1746; P.C.; one of the Lords of the Regency, 1743.
  Vanloo.   J. Faber, junr., mez.
  J. C. Smith, 163, 2nd state, retouched.   27543.

GRAFTON, CHARLES FITZ-ROY, 2nd Duke of, 1683–1757; suc., 1690; Lord Lieut., Ireland, 1721–'3; suc. as Earl of Arlington, 1722.

   Vanloo, 1739.   J. Faber, junr., 1749, mez.
   J. C. Smith, 165.   .27656.

GRAHAM, GEORGE, 1675–1751, mechanician, b. at Horsgills, Kirklinton, Cumberland; apprent. to a watchmaker, London, 1688; attracted the notice of the celebrated Tompion, who treated him with great kindness, and to whose business he ultimately succeeded; invented the compensating pendulum; made the most complete planetarium, and in cabinet form, for Lord Orrery; for Halley he made the great mural quadrant, and the fine transit instrt. and zenith-sector, used by Bradley, and some apparatus for the French Govt.; F.R.S.; bur. in Westminster Abbey.

   T. Hudson.   J. Faber, junr., mez.
   J. C. Smith, 166.   22072.

   [Hudson].   T. Ryley, mez.
   J. C. Smith, 10.   E. 1587.–'85.

GRAHAM, SIR JAMES ROBERT GEORGE, 1792–1861, 2nd Bart., educ. at Westminster and Ch. Ch., Oxf.; M.P., 1818, 1820–'1, 1826–'9, 1829–1861, First Lord of Admiralty, 1830–'4, and 1852–'5; Home Sec., 1841–'6; K.C.B., F.R.S.; author of "Corn and Currency," &c.

   See ABERDEEN CABINET.

GRAHAM, JOHN. *See* DUNDEE.

GRAHAM, THOMAS. *See* LYNEDOCH.

GRAHAM, THOMAS, 1805–1869, Chemist, b. at Glasgow; educ. at the Univ. Glasg.; stud. Chemistry under Dr. T. Thomson, and at Edinb.; Prof. Chem. at Andersonian Inst., Glasg., 1830–'7; Prof. Chem., Univ. Coll., London, 1837; Master of Mint, 1855; made investigations as to the laws of diffusion of gases, the nature of arseniates and phosphates, &c.; one of the first Presidents, Chem. Socy.; served on com. for ventilating Houses of Parliament, and in investigating Water-Supply of London.

   Claudet, daguer.   W. Bosley, lith.
   Ha. len. to front, seated, looking to left; left arm resting on table; coat buttoned loosely, striped neckcloth; Aug. 21, 1849.
   $(8\frac{3}{4} \times 8\frac{1}{4})$.   27634.

GRAMMONT, ELIZABETH, Comtesse de ("Lady Grammont"), eldest daughter of Sir George Hamilton, 4th son of the 1st Earl of Abercorn; "la belle Hamilton," one of the best and loveliest of the Court beauties, under Charles II.; m. to Philibert, Comte de Grammont, wit, and favourite of that King, 1668; accomp.

him to France, 1669, where he suc. to great wealth and position
by his elder brother's death; she survived that of her husband,
1709, but a short time.

Sir P. Lely. J. MacArdell, mez.
J. C. Smith, 91, 3rd state. 22240.

GRANBY, JOHN MANNERS, Marquis of, 1721-1770, eldest
son of the 3rd Duke of Rutland, served in Germany; chiefly
helped to gain the victory of Minden, 1759; Commander-in-
Chf., 1766.

Sir J. Reynolds. R. Houston, mez.
J. C. Smith, 50. 26703.

GRANT, RT. HON. CHARLES. See GLENELG.

GRANT, SIR FRANCIS, 1803-1878; exhibited at the Academy,
1834; A.R.A., 1842; R.A., 1851; successful portrait-painter;
succeeded Sir Charles Eastlake as P.R.A., 1866, and was
knighted soon afterwards.

From a photograph. Anon., woodcut.
Ha. len. seated, to left, reading a paper
For the "Graphic," Oct. 19, 1878.
($6\frac{7}{16} \times 6\frac{5}{8}$). E. 1990.-'89.

GRANT, ULYSSES SIMPSON, 1822-1885, 18th President of the
U.S. America; b. at Point Pleasant, Ohio; educ. at West
Point, 1839-'43; 2nd lieut., 1845; served in Mexico; Capt.,
1853; resigned, 1854; served in Civil War, 1861; Brig.
General, '61; captured Vicksburg, 1863; took the entire
command; Lieut.-Genl., 1864; received Lee's surrender, 1865;
General, 1866; President, 1868, and again, 1872.

Engraved and Printed at the Bureau of Engraving and
Printing, U.S. Treasury Department. Geo. B. McCartel, Chief,
Geo. W. Casilear, Supt. Eng.

Bust to right, in profile; vignette; facs. signature below.
Ind. proof.
$4\frac{7}{8} \times 4$. ($2\frac{3}{4} \times 2\frac{2}{3}$). 27847.

GRANT, SIR WILLIAM, 1754-1832, b. at Moray; Atty.-Gen. at
Quebec; Ch.-Justice of Chester; Solr.-Gen.; M.P.; Master of
the Rolls, 1801-'18; d. at Dawlish.

Sir T. Lawrence. R. Golding.
Wh. len. seated, to left, looking to front, in robes, holding a
paper in right hand; left resting on arm of his chair.
Proof with open letters; the inscription being on a supple-
mentary plate at foot.
Cut. ($22\frac{9}{16} \times 14\frac{1}{16}$). 22981.

GRANVILLE, GRANVILLE GEORGE LEVESON-GOWER, 2nd Earl,
1815-1891, statesman; Lord Pres. of Council, 1852-'8, and
1859-'66; Colon. Sec., 1868; For. Sec., 1870-'74, and 1880-
'85; Col. Sec., 1886; K.G., P.C., Chanc. Univ. Lond., &c.
See ABERDEEN CABINET.

GRANVILLE, JOHN CARTERET, Earl, 1690–1763, Statesman; son of George, 1st Baron Carteret, and Grace Granville, daughter of John, 1st Earl of Bath, cr. Countess Granville; Lord Lieut. of Ireland, 1724, 1729; Sec. of State, 1721, 1742, 1746; suc. as Earl Granville, 1744; K.G., 1749; Lord Pres. of Council, 1751; D.C.L., &c.
Vander Smissen. T. Major.
Sh. ha. len. slightly to left, looking to front, in robes of the Garter; oval in border; vignette below; Sept. 12, 1757.
$15\frac{1}{8} \times 9\frac{1}{2}$. $(14\frac{1}{8} \times 8\frac{5}{8})$. 22452.

GRANVILLE, SOPHIA, Countess, –1745, Lady Sophia Fermor, eldest daughter of Thomas, Earl of Pomfret; m. (second wife), 1744, to John Carteret, 2nd Earl Granville.
F. Zincke. T. Major.
Sh. ha. len. to front, wearing large ear-drops, a low dress, and pearls; oval in border ornamented with flowers; 1755.
$12\frac{3}{4} \times 8\frac{7}{8}$. $(12\frac{1}{16} \times 8\frac{1}{4})$. 27544.

GRATTAN, RT. HON. HENRY, 1750–1820, entered Irish Parlt. 1775, advocated Free Trade, Equality for Roman Catholics, and opposed the Union; M.P (Engl. Parlt.), 1805; buried in Westminster Abbey.
J. Ramsay. C. Turner, mez.
T. Q. len. seated, to right; left hand on papers lying on table.
Open letter proof; Oct. 25, 1806.
$19\frac{1}{2} \times 13\frac{5}{8}$. $(17\frac{3}{4} \times 13\frac{7}{8})$. 20472.

——
A. Pope. E. Scriven, line and stipple.
Wh. len. to front, looking to right, leaning with left hand on a table, and holding a roll of paper in his right hand.
Ind. proof, with open letters.
$18\frac{3}{4} \times 13\frac{7}{8}$. $(14\frac{5}{8} \times 10\frac{1}{4})$. 22986.

GRAVES, ROBERT, 1798–1873, engraver, b. in St. Pancras, London, a member of the family of print-dealers; pupil of John Romney, the engraver, and stud. in life-school, Ship Yard; practised in line manner; illustrated Waverley novels; elected A.E., 1836; executed many prints, after Wilkie, Landseer, Webster, Copley, Eastlake, as well as Reynolds and Gainsborough; d. at Highgate Road; buried in Highgate Cemetery.
J. Miller. F. Fairland, lith.
T. Q. len. to front, seated, looking to left, holding etching-needle in right hand; vignette.
Ind. proof before all letters, presented to R. Graves by the lithographer, with an autograph inscription, 1847.
$(13 \times 11\frac{1}{4})$. 27215.

GRAVES, THOMAS, Lord, 1725–1802, 2nd son of Rear Admiral Thomas Graves, of Thanckes, co. Cornwall; b. at Thanckes; entd. navy very young; M.P. for East Looe, 1775; commanded in American war, 1781; second, under Howe, in French war,

1793; Admiral, 1794; disting. and badly wounded in Victory of 1st June, 1794, over the French fleet; cr. Lord Graves, Baron of Gravesend, co. Londonderry, 1794, with pension, 1,000*l.* a year.

   J. Northcote, R.A.   F. Bartolozzi.

T. Q. len. to front, looking to left, left hand on sword-hilt, right in sling; ships engaged, in distance; private plate.

   Proof before all letters.

   20¼ × 15½.   (17⅝ × 13,⁹,).   22016.

   See also COMMEMORATION (1).

GRAY, JOHN EDWARD, 1800–1875, Zoologist; b. at Walsall, of a family of naturalists; ent. the Br. Museum at an early age; keeper of the Zoological Collection, 1840; superint. arrangement of the collection, and wrote catalogues of many sections; author of many papers, treatises, &c., joint Editor of the zoological part of "Voyages of Erebus and Terror," 1839–'43; d. at the B. Museum.

   Maguire.   T. H. Maguire, lith., 1851.

Ha. len. to front, looking to left, wearing spectacles, coat buttoned across chest; vignette, corners cut off; facs. signature below.

   (10½ × 9¾).   27670.

GRAY, THOMAS, 1716–1771, poet, son of Philip Gray, "money scrivener;" b. in Cornhill, London; educ. at Eton, in "quadruple alliance" with Hor. Walpole, Rd. West, and Thos. Ashton, and at Peterhouse, Cambr., where he wrote some poetry, but left without taking a degree, 1738; went abroad with Walpole, 1739; quarrelled, 1741, and returned alone; went back to Peterhouse, 1742; LL.B., 1743; author of the "Eton Ode," "Ode to Spring," "On the death of a favourite Cat," "Elegy in a Country Churchyard," "Pindaric Odes," "The Bard," &c. Declined the Laureateship, 1757; Prof. of Mod. Hist., Cambr., 1768.

   [J. G. Eckhardt.]   J. S. Müller.

Full ba. len. to right, leaning with left elbow on a table, holding a paper in his right hand, which rests upon his left wrist. In the original picture, exhibited at S. K., May, 1867, the paper in the poet's hand was described as the MS. of the "Eton Ode."

   Proof before the title, &c. (?).

   12 × 9⅞.   (11¾ × 9).   26662.

GREEN, CHARLES, 1785–1870, b. in Goswell Road; son of a fruiterer; made a balloon ascent, 1821; another, on the back of a pony, 1828; made the great Nassau balloon, 1836, in which year he went in it from London to Weilburg, with T. Monck Mason and Robert Holland, the latter paying the expenses; made his last of 527 ascents, 1852.

   J. Hollins.   G. T. Payne, mixed mez.

T. Q. len. to left, seated, holding a barometer in his right hand, and resting his left hand and forearm on a map, on table.
Published, June 5, 1838.
$22\frac{9}{16} \times 16\frac{8}{16}$. ($15\frac{5}{8} \times 12\frac{1}{4}$). 27077.

GREEN, CHARLES—*continued*; in "*A Consultation previous to an Aerial Voyage from London to Weilburg in Nassau, | on the 7th day of November, 1836;*" in centre, seated at table is Robert HOLLOND, M.P. (*q. v.*); to his left, Thomas Monck MASON (*q. v.*); and at the end of table, on right of subject, Charles GREEN, wearing a fur cap; on the left are portraits of three of Mr. Hollond's friends, W. Prideaux, J. Hollins (the painter), and W. M. James, behind Mr. Hollond.
J. Hollins, A.R.A. J. H. Robinson.
The picture was exhibited, 1888.
Proof before all letters, except the artists' names.
$12\frac{5}{16} \times 14\frac{5}{8}$. ($8 \times 11\frac{1}{4}$). 18887
Also, an Ind. proof, with skeleton letters, Novr. 7, 1843.
27078.

GREEN, VALENTINE, 1739–1813, mezzotintist, b. in Worcestershire, son of a dancing-master; pupil of Robert Hancock; came to London; exhibited at Spring Gardens, 1766; member of Incorp. Society of Artists, 1767; A.E., 1775, and mezzotinto engraver to the King; obtained the exclusive privilege of engraving the pictures at Düsseldorf, and completed 20 plates; keeper of the Br. Instn., 1805 till death; he was an admirable engraver.
L. F. Abbott. V. Green, mez.
J. C. Smith, 57, 2nd state. 24224.

GREGORY, JAMES, 1753–1821, b. at Aberdeen; educ. there and at Edinburgh; and, for a short time, at Ch. Ch. Oxf.; gained considerable classical taste and knowledge; studied, 1773–'4, at St. George's Hospl.; M.D., 1774; professor of institutes of medicine, Edinb., 1776; of pract. of medicine, 1790; pubd. "Conspectus," and other works.
Sir G. Chalmers. R. Earlom, mez.
J. C. Smith, 17. 27132.

GREGORY, JOHN, 1745–1813, Treasurer of the Whig Club, instituted, 1774; Commissr. of Taxes, J.P., etc.
"From the Original Picture." J. R. Smith, mez.
J. C. Smith, 69, an intermediate state, between the first and second, as described; and before the words, "To be had of Mr. Jenkins," &c.; with open letters. 24714.

GRENVILL, or GREENVILL, SIR BEVILL, 1596–1643; loyalist; educ. at Exeter Coll., Oxon.; knighted for services in Scotland; killed at Lansdown.
Anon. R. Cooper, stipple.
Sh. ha. len. slightly to right, in armour, broad lace collar, baldrick, &c.
$15\frac{11}{16} \times 12\frac{3}{4}$. ($8\frac{1}{4} \times 6\frac{1}{8}$). 22861.

GRENVILLE, Rt. Hon. George, 1712-1720, Statesman; son
of Richard Grenville, Esq.; M.P., 1741; Lord of Admiralty,
1744; Treasurer of Navy, 1754, 1756, 1761; First Lord of
Admiralty, 1763; Prime Min. and Chanc. of Excheq., 1763-'5;
contest with Wilkes began during his administration, and the
American Stamp Act introduced; P.C., &c.

 W. Hoare, R.A.   R. Houston, mez.
  J. C. Smith, 53, 2nd state.   22071.

GRENVILLE, Rt. Hon. Thomas, 1755–1846, statesman and
book collector, 2nd son of George Grenville; educ. at Ch.
Ch., Oxf.; ensign, Coldstr. Guards, 1778; lieut. in regt. of
foot, aftds. known as 80th; left the army, and M.P., 1780;
entrusted with task of arranging terms of treaty with U.S.
America, 1782; lost seat, 1784; M.P. again, 1790; P.C. 1798;
ambassador to Berlin, 1799, but shipwrecked; Ch. Just. in. Eyre,
South of Trent, 1800–'17; First Lord of Adm.; retired, 1818,
devoted his energy and time to collecting books; left his
library to the Br. Museum.

 J. Hoppner, R.A.   C. Turner, mez.
  Ha. len. to left, seated, Novr. 1, 1808.
  $14 \times 9\frac{1}{2}$. $(11\frac{11}{16} \times 9\frac{1}{8})$.   27529.

GRENVILLE, William-Wyndham, Lord, 1759–1834, statesman; 3rd son of George Grenville; M.P., 1782; filled some
high offices; cr. Baron, 1790; Sec. for Foreign Affairs, 1791–
1801; Prime Minister, 1806–'7; favoured Catholic Emancipation; Chancellor of Oxford University; Gov. of Charter-house;
P.C., &c.

 J. Hoppner, R.A.   S. W. Reynolds, mez.
  T. Q. len. to left, seated, looking to front, holding in left hand
a book which rests on his thigh, right hand on right thigh; dark
coat, fastened by one button.
  Open letter proof, Aug. 1, 1800.
  20×14. $(16\frac{1}{8} \times 13\frac{1}{4})$.   21900.

 T. Phillips, R.A.   J. Fittler, A.R.A.
  T. Q. len. to left, in his Chancellor's robes, right hand resting
on a book on table; Ch. Ch. Coll., Oxford, in distance; March,
1812.
  $21 \times 15\frac{1}{4}$. $(16\frac{7}{8} \times 13\frac{1}{4})$.   22983.

GRESHAM, Sir Thomas, 1519–1579, youngest son of Sir
Richard Gresham, "King's Merchant;" educ. at Caius Coll.,
Cambr.; apprent. to his uncle, Sir John Gresham, merchant;
employed abroad in public financial business, under Edward VI.,
Mary and Elizabeth; Knt. by Queen Elizabeth, who frequently
visited him, in Bishopsgate, at the house which he left as a
College; built, chiefly at his own charge, the Royal Exchange;
founded the "Gresham Lectures."

 Sir A. More.   R. Thew, stipple.

T. Q. len. to right, seated, looking to front, wearing a flat cap,
gloves in right hand, ring on first finger of left.
Open letter proof, Jan?. 1, 1792.
15⅞ × 11¾. (13 × 10½). 23121.

GREVILLE, THE HON. CHARLES FRANCIS, 1749–1809, son of
Francis, 8th Baron Brooke of Beauchamp's Court, 1st Earl of
Warwick; connoisseur, dilettante, F.R.S.; d.s.p.
See DILLETANTI SOCIETY, and TOWNELEY.

GREY, CHARLES GREY, 1st Earl, 1729–1807, General; wounded
at Minden, when A.D.C. to Prince Ferdinand of Brunswick,
1759; fought in American War, 1777–'82; in West Indies,
1794; cr. Baron, 1801; Earl, 1806.
   T. Lawrence, R.A.   J. Collyer, A.R.A., stipple.
   As Sir Charles Grey, K.B., T. Q. len. to front, looking to left,
in uniform; castle in the distance, and masts of ships, &c.
   Proof with scratched letters; May 29, 1797.
   18 × 14. (14¾ × 11⅜). 24225.

GREY, CHARLES, 2nd Earl, 1764–1845, statesman; son of the
1st Earl; educ. at Eton and King's Coll., Cambr.; M.P., 1786,
'90, '96, 1802, 1806–'7, for Co. Northumberland; one of the
managers of the trial of Warren Hastings, for the Ho. of Commons,
1787; First Lord of the Admiralty, P.C., 1806; M.P., Tavistock,
1807; suc. as 2nd Earl, 1807; First Lord of Treasury, 1830–
'34; K.G., 1831; carried first Reform Bill.
   Sir T. Lawrence.   S. Cousins, mez.
   Full ha. len. to front, right hand in breast of buttoned coat,
left arm resting on a high pedestal; white cravat and waistcoat,
light coloured trousers; landscape in distance, on left.
   Proof with skeleton letters, July 1830.
   16 × 11. (13½ × 9). 21942.
   See also REFORM BANQUET and CAROLINE.

GREY, SIR GEORGE, 2nd Bart., 1799–1882, educ. at Oxf.; M.A.,
1824; barrister, 1826; M.P., 1832; Judge Adv. Genl., 1839–
'41; home sec., 1846–'52, 1855–'8, and 1861–'6; Colon. Sec.,
1854–'5; Chanc., Duchy of Lancaster, 1841, and 1859–'61;
P.C. &c.
   See ABERDEEN CABINET.

GREY, LADY JANE, 1537–1554, daughter of Henry Grey,
Marquess of Dorset, and niece of Henry VIII.; famous for
beauty and accomplishments; m. to Lord Guildford, and
proclaimed Queen, 1553; arrested by Queen Mary, and
executed in the Tower.
   "From an original" (anon.). G. Vertue, 1748.
   Sh. ha. len. to front, wearing low, dark cap, small ruff, two
pearl collars, pearl brooch, and two strings of pearls falling from
it; oval in border; arms and insignia below, and a female
figure weeping. The plate is "Inscrib'd to   Algernon

Seymour Duke of Somerset," the owner of the picture from which it was engraved.
$18\frac{1}{2} \times 22\frac{1}{2}$. ($17\frac{3}{8} \times 21\frac{13}{16}$). 21973.

GREY, Lady Jane.
Anon. T. A. Dean.
T. Q. len. to front, holding a book in her left, which rests upon her right hand. From the Original in the Collection of the Earl of Stamford and Warrington.
Pubd. by Harding, Triphook, and Lepard, Septr. 1, 1825.
$9\frac{7}{8} \times 7\frac{1}{8}$. ($5 \times 3\frac{3}{4}$). 14353.

GRINDAL, Edmund, c. 1519–1583, son of William Grindal, a well-to-do farmer, at Hensingham, St. Bees, Cumberland; educ. at Magdalen Coll., Chr. Coll., and Pembr. Hall, Cambr.; B.A., 1538, and fellow; M.A., 1541; ordd., 1544; proctor, 1548–'9; chaplain to Ridley, bishop of London; precentor, St. Paul's, 1541; preb. Westminster, 1552; on Mary's accession went to Strasburg, &c.; returned to England, 1559; Master, Pembr. Hall, and bishop of London; Archbp., York, 1570; Canterbury, 1575; suspended, 1577; restored, 1582.
Lens. M. vander Gucht.
Ha. len. to front, holding an open book with both hands before him. Oval, in border; three lines of inscription below.
$10\frac{1}{8} \times 6\frac{1}{8}$. ($9\frac{7}{8} \times 5\frac{7}{8}$). 27166.

GROSE, Francis, c. 1731–1791, antiquary, b. at Greenford, eldest son of Francis Grose, or Grosse, a native of Berne in Switzerland, and a prosperous jeweller at Richmond, in Surrey; the son received a classical education, and stud. art in Shipley's school; exhib. drawings at R. A., 1769, and following years; Richmond Herald, 1755–'63; Adj., and paymaster, Hants. Militia; Cap., Surrey Militia, 1778; pub. "Antiquities of England," &c., 1773; "Class. Dictionary of the Vulgar Tongue," and other works; F.S.A., &c.
N. Dance delin. F. Bartolozzi.
Wh. len. to front, standing, looking to left, leaning on stick with right hand, left in waistcoat pocket; vignette.
$10\frac{7}{8} \times 7\frac{15}{16}$. ($8 \times 6\frac{1}{2}$). 24103.

GUILFORD, Rt. Hon Francis North, Baron, 1637–1685; second son of Dudley, 4th Lord North; barrister, 1661; K.C., 1668; Solr.-Gen., and Kt., 1671; M.P., 1672–'5; Atty.-Gen., 1673; Ld. Ch.-Justice of Com. Pleas, 1675–'82; P.C., 1679; Ld. Keeper, 1682; cr. Baron, 1683.
D. Loggan. D. Loggan.
Sh. ha. len. to right, looking to front, wearing robes; oval in border.
$14\frac{11}{16} \times 10\frac{11}{16}$. ($13\frac{1}{2} \times 10\frac{1}{2}$). 26686.
See NORTH.

GUNNING. *See* ARGYLL and COVENTRY.

GUNPOWDER PLOT Conspirators. *See* Concilium.

GURNEY, Maria, Lady,   –   daughter of William Hawes,
M.D., m. to Sir John Gurney (1768–1845), Baron of Exchequer
and Knt. (1832); mother of Russell and John Hampden
Gurney.
Anon.   Anon., stipple.
Ha. len. to front, slightly inclined to left, seated, wearing a lace
cap and broad collar; vignette.
Proof before all letters.
10 × 7½. (5½ × 5).   20934.

GUTHRIE, George James,1785–1856, b. in London; M.R.C.S.,
1801; member of council, 1824; president, 1833, '41, '54;
assist. surg., 29th Regt., 1801; served in Canada, 1803–'8;
Peninsula, 1808–'14; at Waterloo, 1815; surg. on half-pay
1814; lect. in London, 1816–'45; first who used lithotrite, 1816;
founded infirmary for diseases of the eye; assist. surg., Westmr.
Hospl., 1823; surg., 1827–'43; Professor of anatomy and
surgery, 1828–'31; F.R.S., 1827; author of several valuable
surgical works.
H. Room.   W Walker, mez.
Ha. len. to right, looking to front, seated, holding a paper in
right hand.
Proof before all letters, except the publication-line and
the words, "Private Plate."
16⁵⁄₁₆ × 12⁵⁄₁₆. (14 × 10¾).   22862.

GUY, Thomas, 1644–1724, Philanthropist; traded as a book-
seller, and speculated successfully in South Sea Stock; founded
Guy's Hospital, 1721, and spent 200,000l. on it; erected also
Almshouses at Tamworth, and left money to Christ's Hospital.
J. Bacon, R.A. (J. T. Viner pinx.)   A. M. Huffam, mez.
From the statue at Guy's Hospital; wh. len. to front;
looking to right, assisting a sick man to rise, and inviting him
to enter the hospital.
Proof with skeleton letters.
27½(?) × 18½. (24 × 15¾).   22075.

GWYN, Eleanor, 1650–1687, actress, and mistress to Charles II.,
b. at Hereford; sold oranges in the Theatre Royal, as a girl,
in London; owed her theatrical training to Hart, the actor;
acted many parts in Howard's, Dryden's, Otway's, and other
plays; much satirised when taken up by the King; but kind,
gentle, witty, pretty, "wild, and of an agreeable humour;" and
mother of the 1st Duke of St. Alban's.
Sir P. Lely.   G. Valck.
T. Q. len. to front, seated on a bank, holding a lamb; landscape
in the distance; two English verses below, "The Sculpters
part . . . . . shew her Will;" and the privilege
beneath; 2nd state.
(12⁹⁄₁₆ × 9½).   27263.

GWYN, ELLEN—*continued*; speaking the Epilogue to "Sir Patient Fancy."

Dod del. Cook.

From a "Collection . . . of English Prologues," &c. 1779. 28187. 7.

GYLES, HENRY, c. 1640–1700, glass-painter, practised chiefly at York, where he lived and was probably born; painted the east window at University Coll., Oxon, 1687, and some more windows in Oxford; painted historical subjects also and landscapes; established a school of glass-painting at York, which maintained its reputation for nearly a century.

Anon. (Gyles?). F. Place, mez.

Sh. ha. len. to right, looking to front, wearing long curled hair, a shirt open at the collar, loose gown; oval in border; below, "*Glasspainting for windows, as Armes, Sundyals, History, Landskipt, &c. Done by Henry Gyles of the City of York.*;" evidently a trade-card. It is very rare.

$4\frac{9}{16} \times 3\frac{1}{4}$. ($4\frac{1}{8} \times 3\frac{1}{4}$; oval, $3\frac{3}{4} \times 3\frac{1}{16}$). 17082

With this are two cuttings, and a copy of the print, a little larger; cut. ($5\frac{1}{16} \times 3\frac{5}{8}$). 17083.

HACKER, FRANCIS, Colonel; "Regicide;" executed at Tyburn, 1660.

Anon. Anon.

Sh. ha. len. to right, looking to front; long hair, wide collar, breastplate, &c.

$11\frac{1}{4} \times 8\frac{1}{8}$. ($6\frac{3}{16} \times 5\frac{9}{16}$). 22863.

HACKET, JOHN, 1592–1670, son of Andrew Hacket, a prosperous tailor, of Scottish extraction, educ. at Westminster, and Trin. Coll., Cambr.; ord. 1618; chaplain to Lord Keeper Williams; received several preferments; chaplain to King James; preb. of Aylesbury, Linc. Cath., 1623; Archdeacon of Bedford, 1631; member of committee for religion, 1641; canon of St. Paul's; bishop (1661) of Lichfield and Coventry, where he restored the Cathedral, 1669; benefactor to Trin. Coll., Cambr

Anon. W. Faithorne.

L. Fagan, p. 39, 2nd state, with 4 verses below.

Prefixed to "A Century of Sermons," 1675. 27565.

HADDOCK, NICHOLAS, 1686–1746, Admiral, youngest son of Sir Richard Haddock, entd. navy as a volunteer, 1699; midshipman, 1702; at Cadiz and Vigo; Lieut., 1704; captain, 1707; contributed largely to the victory at Cape Passaro; Rear-Admiral, 1734; Vice-admiral, 1741; retired, 1742; but promoted Admiral, 1744.

Rumsey. Johnson, mez.

J. C. Smith; under name of Faber, junr., 67, 3rd state, altered from the portrait of George, Lord Carpenter.

This impression was in the Gulston Collection. 27546.

HADEN, Francis Seymour, 1818–   ; surgeon and amateur
artist; educ. at Univ. Coll., London, and the Sorbonne, Paris;
F.R.C.S., 1857; author of letters on "Earth to Earth" burial,
and of a monograph on Rembrandt's Etched work; he has
published some remarkable etchings; is Pres. of the Society of
Painter-Etchers, and Vice-Pres. of the Obstetrical Society of
London.
  [Lacretelle.]   J. E. Lacretelle, 1878, etch.
  T. Q. len. slightly to right, looking to front, legs crossed, a
drawing board on knee, and a pencil in right hand; vignette;
below, "I think this a very good portrait. F. S. H."[aden], in
pencil.
  12 × 7¼. (10 × 6⅝).   E. 2267.–'89.

HAIGHTON, John, c. 1755–1823, physician and physiologist,
b. in Lancashire; pupil of Else; surgeon to the Guards;
demonstrator of anatomy, at St. Thomas's, under H. Cline;
resigned, 1789, succeeding Dr. Skeete as lecturer on physiology,
and lecturing also on midwifery; called "the Merciless Doctor;"
M.D., F.R.S.; wrote several medical works.
  H. Ashby.   J. Kennerly, stipple.
  Full ha. len. seated, to right, looking to left, with right hand
to face; right elbow on table, on which are a book, a skull, &c.
  Cut. (17¹⁵⁄₁₆ × 13¹³⁄₁₆).   22693.
  See also MEDICAL SOCIETY.

HALE, Sir Matthew, 1609–1676, Lawyer and Author; b. at
Alderley, Gloucestershire; stud. at Oxf. and Linc. Inn; de-
fended Strafford, Laud, Hamilton, and Charles I.; Justice of
Com. Bench, under Cromwell; Chief Baron of Exch. and Ld.
Chf.-Justice, after Restoration; wrote on Law, Morals,
Mathematics, &c.
  J. M. Wright.   G. Vertue, 1735.
  T. Q. len. slightly turned to right, looking to front, holding a roll
of papers in left hand, right hand to girdle, wearing his robes
as Chf.-Justice; C . . . . R, embroidered on the hangings behind
him; arms below, and title in 4 lines.
  12⅓ × 7¾(?). (9⅘ × 7½).   22508.

HALE, William Hale, 1795–1870, son of John Hale, a surgeon,
of Lynn, Norfolk; educ. at Charterhouse, and Oriel Coll., Oxf.;
B.A., 1817; ordd., 1818; M.A., 1820; chaplain to the Bishop
of Chester, 1824; preacher to the Charterhouse, 1823–'42,
where he was appointed Master; Archdeacon of St. Albans,
1839; of Middlesex, 1840; of London, 1842; Vicar of St.
Giles, Cripplegate, 1847–'57; Tory, opponent of reforms, antiquary; pubd. various works.
  T. A. Woolnoth.   W. Walker, mez.
  Ha. len. slightly to right, looking to front.
  Open letter proof, April 1st, 1850.
  15½ × 11⅞. (12¹⁄₁₆ × 9⅝).   25828.

HALFORD, Sir HENRY, 1766–1844, physician, 2nd son of
Dr. James Vaughan, a successful physician at Leicester; educ.
at Ch. Ch., Oxf.; B.A., 1788; M.D., 1791; studied some time
at Edinb.; settled in London; soon made his way; physician
to Middlesex Hosp., and Physician Extr. to the King, 1793;
F.R.C.S., 1794; inherited a large property on the death of
Lady Denbigh, widow of his mother's cousin, Sir Charles
Halford, 7th Bart.; took the name of Halford; cr. a Bart.,
1809; G. C. H.

Sir T. Lawrence.   C. Turner, A.R.A., mez.
T. Q. len to right, seated, looking to front, wearing the star of
the Order of Hanover; left hand on papers on table.
Proof before all letters, except the artists' names; June 24,
1830.
20 × 14.   (15$\frac{14}{16}$ × 12$\frac{1}{2}$).   22864.

HALIBURTON, THOMAS CHANDLER, 1796–1865, son of the
Hon. William Otis Haliburton, Just. of Com. Pleas (Nova
Scotia); b. at Windsor, Nova Scotia; educ. at Gram. Sch. and
King's Coll. there; barrister, 1820; Ch.-Just. Com. Pleas, 1828
–'40; transferred to Supreme Court, 1842; resigned, 1856, and
settled in England; began authorship, 1825; wrote articles in
" Nova Scotia " newspaper, 1835 (signed " Sam Slick, a Yankee
Pedlar "), " The Attaché," " The Bubbles of Canada," "The
Clockmaker," " Letter-bag of the Gt. Western," "Old Judge."
E. U. Eddis delt.   M Ganci, lith.
Sh. ha. len. to left, looking to right.
Ind. proof; Jany. 7th, 1839.
(12$\frac{1}{4}$ × 12$\frac{3}{4}$).   24686.

HALIFAX, CHARLES MONTAGU, 1st Earl of, 1661–1715, Grand-
son of the 1st Earl of Manchester; educ. at Westminster, and
Trin. Coll., Cambr.; M.P. for Durham, and Malden; Chanc.
of Exchequer; First Comm. of Treasury; cr. Baron Halifax,
1700, and Earl, and K.G., 1714; disting. for love of literature
and ability in Parlt.; wrote some poetry, and (with Prior),
"The City and the Country Mouse," a burl. of Dryden's
"Hind and Panther;" bur. in Westmr. Abbey; Pope, in
" Epilogue to the Satires," says,
          " Thus Somers once, and Halifax, were mine."
Sir G. Kneller.   G. Vertue, 1716.
Ha. len. to front, in robes of the Garter, wearing the George
and Star; oval in border; arms below; title in 4 lines, and
artists' names.
Cut.   (15$\frac{1}{4}$ × 11$\frac{1}{4}$).   26688.

HALIFAX, CHARLES WOOD, 1st Viscount, 1800–1885, states-
man, educ. at Eton and Oriel Coll., Oxf.; B.A., 1821; M.A.,
1824; M.P., 1826; Chanc. of Exch., 1846–'52; P.C.; Pres.
Board of Control, 1852–'5; First Lord of Admiralty, 1855–'8;
G.C.B.; Sec. of State for India, and Pres. of Council, 1859–'66;
Lord Privy Seal, 1870–'4; cr. Visct., 1866.
See ABERDEEN CABINET.

HALIFAX, George Savile, Marquess of, 1630-1695, Statesman; contributed to the Restoration of Charles II.; Pres. of Council, under James II.; Speaker of the House of Lords in the Convention Parliament; Lord Privy Seal, under William III.; author of "Character of a Trimmer."

Anon.   J. Houbraken, 1740.

Sh. ha. len. slightly turned to right, looking to front, wearing lace collar, long wig, gown, &c.; oval in border; vignette below, in which he is shown offering the crown to William and Mary.

In Birch's "Lives."

14¾ × 9¼.   (14⅛ × 8¾).   21977.

HALL, Robert, 1764-1831, celebrated Baptist minister, b. at Arnsby, Leicestershire; educ. at Bristol and King's Coll., Aberdeen; minister at Bristol and Cambridge; eloquent pulpit orator; twice insane, but recovered; pubd. sermons, &c.

Anon. [Bramwhite?].   Anon. [Finden?].

Ha. len. to front, leaning with his left arm and elbow on an open book, in the pulpit; vignette.

Ind. proof before all letters.

14⅞ × 12⅜.   (7½ × 8½).   23158.

HALLAM, Henry, 1777-1859, historian, b. at Windsor; settled in London; devoted himself entirely to literary labour; gained wide reputation by his "History of Europe during the Middle Ages," "Constitutional History of England," "Introduction to the Literature of Europe," &c.; F.R.A.S., &c.

T. Phillips, R.A.   H. Cousins, mez.

Ha. len. to front, looking to left; dark neckcloth, coat, and background

Open letter proof; Feb. 26, 1841.

15¾ × 12.   (11¾ × 9½).   21947.

HALLEY, Edmund, 1656-1742, Astronomer, son of a tradesman in Winchester St.; b. at Haggerston, near London; educ. at St. Paul's school, and Queen's Coll., Oxford; early stud. astronomy; went to St. Helena, 1676, and collected materials for his Chart of Magnetic Variation, pubd. 1701; Savil. Prof., 1703; Sec. R.S., 1713; Astr. Royal, 1719; author of many remarkable works and papers, on astronomy, magnetism, mechanics, &c; induced Newton to publish his "Principia," paying the expense of the work, which he presented to James II.; d. at Greenwich.

T. Murray, 1712.   J. Faber, junr., mez., 1722.

J. C. Smith, 173, 3rd state.   24076.

HAMILTON, Elizabeth, Duchess of, and aftds. of Argyll, See ARGYLL.

HAMILTON, Emma Hart, afterwards Lady, c. 1761-1815, b. in humble circumstances; nursemaid at Hawardine, near Chester, came to London, 1777; exhibited by Dr. Graham, a noted quack, as the goddess Hygeia; her beauty and grace made her a much-sought model for artists, of whom Romney was one especially devoted; m. to Sir William Hamilton, 1791; obtained great influence at the Neapolitan Court; the object of Nelson's passionate attachment; d. in poverty, near Calais.

A. Kauffmann.   R. Morghen.

As the comic Muse; T. Q. len. inclined slightly to right, looking to front; with a mask in her right hand, and pushing back a curtain with her left; 2 Latin verses below, " Quam Veteres . . . ' in Latio:"

17$\frac{3}{16}$ × 12$\frac{1}{2}$.   (13$\frac{1}{4}$ × 10$\frac{9}{16}$).   24117.

HAMILTON, EMMA HART, Lady,—*continued*.

G. Romney.   R. Earlom, stipple.

T. Q. len.to right, right hand to breast, left knee on a pedestal, on which stands a vase, from which springs a " sensitive plant," towards which she extends her left hand; inscribed "SENSI-BILITY."

Open letter proof; March 25, 1789.

14$\frac{7}{8}$ × 11$\frac{3}{8}$.   (12$\frac{5}{16}$ × 9$\frac{9}{16}$).

H. P Horne, 50, 1st state.   24077.

HAMILTON, JAMES, 3rd Marquess, aftds. 1st Duke of, 1606–1649; son of James, 2nd Marquess; intimate friend of Charles I. from boyhood; commd. the fleet, when troubles broke out in Scotland. cr. Duke, 1643; aftds. suspected of betraying the King; marched against Cromwell, but was defeated and taken at Preston ; beheaded.

A. van Dyck.   P. van Lisebetten.

Ha. len. to front, slightly inclined to left, in armour, holding truncheon in right hand, which rests on helmet.

Not mentioned by Weber ; F. Wibiral, 140, 1st state.

11 × 7$\frac{3}{4}$.   (9$\frac{11}{16}$ × 7$\frac{1}{2}$).   21965.

HAMILTON, SIR WILLIAM, 1730–1803, b. in Scotland; diplomatist, antiquary, and virtuoso; ambassador at Naples, 1764–1800; pubd. " Campi Phlegræi;" husband of the famous Lady Hamilton.

See DILETTANTI SOCIETY

HAMILTON, CAPTAIN WILLIAM ALEXANDER BAILLIE, 1803–, b. at Normanby, Yorks; ent. Navy, 1816 ; Lieut., 1823 ; served off Morea, in suppression of piracy ; Post-cap., 1828 ; priv. Sec. to Lord Haddington, First Lord of Admiralty, 1841 ; Second Sec. of Admiralty, 1845.

See ARCTIC COUNCIL.

HAMILTON, WILLIAM GERARD, 1729–1796, statesman, P.C., and Chancellor of the Exchequer (Ireland) ; called "Single Speech Hamilton."

I. R. Smith.   W. Evans, stipple.

Ha. len. seated, to right, with left elbow resting on a table.

8$\frac{15}{16}$ × 5$\frac{1}{16}$.   (4$\frac{5}{8}$ × 3$\frac{1}{2}$).   22865.

HAMILTON, William Richard, 1777–1859, antiquary and
diplomat, b. in London, son of Rev. Anthony Hamilton, D.D.;
educ. at Harrow; priv. sec. to Lord Elgin, at Constantinople,
1799; sent on dipl. mission to Egypt, 1801, when he rescued
the Rosetta stone from the French; helped very much in
collecting and removing the famous Greek Marbles; Und. Sec.
For. Affairs, 1809–22; minister at Naples till 1825; author of
"Ægyptiaca," 1809, &c.; F.R.S., one of the founders of the
R.G.S.; Trustee of the Br. Musm.; Sec., Dilettanti Socy.
[Baugniet.]   Baugniet, lith., 1850.
T. Q. len. to left, seated, looking to front, holding a minia-
ture(?) in a case with both hands; oval; vignette.
(14¼ × 13¼).   27181.

HAMILTON; it is not possible to say of which of the family of
artists, named Hamilton, this is the portrait; there were three
sons of James Hamilton living about 1730; but they all painted
abroad, and not in England.
    See ARTISTS, A SOCIETY OF.

HAMPDEN, JOHN, 1594–1643, eldest son of William Hampden,
of Hampden, Bucks., and Elizabeth Cromwell, aunt of the Lord
Protector; b. in London; educ. at Thame and Oxford; stud. in
Inner Temple; in Parliament, 1636; resisted the imposition of
Ship-money, and became a leading patriot; one of the "Five
Members" whom Charles I. attempted to have arrested, Jany.,
1642; among the first to take up arms against the king; mortally
wounded in a skirmish with Prince Rupert, at Chalgrove Field,
Bucks., June 18, 1643; d. at Thame, June 24.
    Anon.   Audran.
    Sh. ha. len. to right, looking to front, wearing a loose gown,
long hair, white cravat; oval in border; in Peck's "Life of
Milton " (?); of very dubious authenticity. Sir R. Ellys is said
to have bought the picture at a stall, and to have named it.
    13⅞ × 9¾.   (12⅝ × 9⅜).   24664.

HAMPTON, RT. HON. SIR JOHN SOMERSET PAKINGTON, Baron,
1799–1880; M.P., 1837–'74, for Droitwich; P.C. and Colon.
Sec., 1852; First Lord of Admiralty, 1858–'9, and 1866;
Sec. for War, 1867; Bart., 1846; G.C.B., 1859; cr. Baron,
1874; First Civil Service Commissioner.
    See DERBY CABINET.

HANDEL, GEORGE FREDERICK, 1685–1759, the great composer;
b. at Halle, son of a surgeon, in spite of whom he devoted
himself to music; pupil of Zachau; sent to Berlin; at the death
of his father, went to Hamburg, where he soon conducted the
orchestra; visited Italy, 1706; returned to Germany, 1709;
came to England, 1710, composed 39 Italian Operas, 19 English
Oratorios, and many other works, vocal and instrumental;
naturalised British subject, 1726; d. in Brook St., Grosvenor
Square.
    [From Roubilliac's Statue] B. Rebecca del.   F. Bartolozzi,
                                                          stipple.

Wh. len. seated, wearing a loose cap and robe, holding a lyre on which he seems to play; a cupid at his feet; Jany. 1, 1789; commonly prefixed to Dr. Arnold's Edition of Handel's works.
$14\frac{1}{2} \times 10\frac{7}{8}$. ($11\frac{1}{8} \times 8\frac{13}{16}$). E. 250.–'90.

HANDEL, George Frederick—*continued*.
G. B. Cipriani del. F. Bartolozzi.
Bust, in a medallion, to right, looking to front, supported by a figure (Fame) on right and a cupid on left; another cupid behind, on right; inscription below, in three lines.
Ind. proof; 2nd state; the plate and border reduced in height.
Cut. ($12\frac{3}{4} \times 10\frac{3}{8}$). 29604. 8.

T Hudson. W. Bromley.
T. Q. len. to front, looking to right, holding a large sheet of paper in left hand.
Proof before all letters, except the artists' names, scratched.
Cut. ($11\frac{3}{4} \times 9\frac{1}{8}$). 22019.

C. Jäger. J. Bankel.
Sh. ha. len. to left, looking to right, wearing full wig, lace cravat, embroidered coat.
$11\frac{3}{8} \times 9\frac{1}{8}$. ($7\frac{1}{8} \times 5\frac{1}{16}$). 26550.

HANKINSON, Thomas Edwards, 1805–1843, poet and divine, educ. at Corp. Chr. Coll., Cambr., B.A., 1828; M.A., 1831; curate at King's Lynn, and aftds. incumbent, St. Matthew's Chapel, Denmark Hill; pub. sermons and lectures; won the Seatonian prize at Cambr. for English Verse, nine times, 1831–'38.
Anon. Anon., lith.
Sh. ha. len. to front, wearing gown.
Ind. proof before all letters.
($8\frac{3}{4} \times 7\frac{1}{8}$). 23587.

HANSARD, Luke, 1752–1828, printer, b. at Norwich, son of Thomas Hansard, a manufacturer; educ. at Boston gram. school; apprent. to Stephen White, printer, Norwich; entered as compositor in the printing-office of John Hughs, printer to the House of Commons, and became manager and partner, 1774; printed the "Journals," 1774–1828; introduced technical improvements.
S. Lane. F. C. Lewis, stipple.
Sh. ha. len. to left, looking to front, holding a paper in left hand; facs. subscription and signature below; vignette.
$10\frac{15}{16} \times 8\frac{1}{2}$ (?). ($7\frac{1}{8} \times 6$). 27293.

HANWAY, Jonas, 1712–1786, b. at Portsmouth; took to trade; travelled in Russia and Persia; returned to England; pubd. his travels, 1753; became distinguished as a philanthropist, founding or improving the Marine Society, Foundling and Magdalen Hospitals, &c.; spent his wealth on benevolent objects; was the first man who carried an umbrella in London.
E. Edwards. R. Dunkarton, mez.
J. C. Smith, 23, 2nd state. 24226.

HARDINGE, Henry Hardinge, Viscount, 1785–1856; served
in Peninsula, 1809–'14; Sec. War, 1828–'30, 1841–'4; Govr.-
Genl. India, 1844–'8; defeated the Sikhs at Moodkee and
Ferozeshaw, 1845; made peace, 1846; cr. Viscount, 1846;
Master Genl. of Ordnance, 1852; Commander-in-Chf., 1852;
Field-Marshal, 1855.
    Eddis.   Fr. Holl, 1836.
    Sh. ha. len. to front, as Maj. Gen., Sir Henry, K.C.B., &c.;
in uniform.
    Proof with scratched letters.
    Cut. (8$\frac{1}{16}$ × 7$\frac{1}{8}$).   29431.   B.
    Another impression, with letters strengthened, and "Printed
by Wilkinson & Dawe."   20630.

    F. Grant, R.A.   J. Faed, mez.
T. Q. len. rather inclined to left, looking and facing to front;
in uniform, as "Vicount" (sic), G.C.B., P.C., &c.
    Open letter Ind. proof; November 1, 1851.
    16$\frac{1}{4}$ × 12$\frac{1}{4}$. (11$\frac{1}{2}$ × 8$\frac{3}{8}$).   21950.

    F. Grant, A.R.A.   S. W. Reynolds, mixed mez.
    Wh. len. on horseback, directed towards left, with his staff,
on the field of Ferozeshah; a composition of many figures;
dead and wounded soldiers, tents, guns, &c., in distance on left.
    Ind. proof with skeleton letters, Decr. 10, 1849.
    25 × 33$\frac{3}{8}$. (20$\frac{7}{8}$ × 31$\frac{1}{4}$).   25744.
    See also WATERLOO BANQUET.

HARDWICK, Thomas, 1752–1829, architect, b. at New Brentford, son of a builder; stud. under Sir W. Chambers, and in the
R.A. schools; exhibited at the R.A., 1772–'76; travelled abroad
for three years; exhibited continually; rebuilt and built several
churches, including that of St. Marylebone, 1813–'17, which he
designed; Clerk of the Works at Hampton Court Palace; buried
at Brentford.
    G. Dance, 1795.   W. Daniell, chalk and dot.
    Sh. ha. len. to right, in profile, seated; hair tied behind;
vignette. April 2, 1814.
    10$\frac{1}{4}$ × 8. (7$\frac{1}{2}$ × 6).   E. 1999.–'89.

HARDWICKE, Philip Yorke, 1st Earl of, 1690–1764, Lawyer
and Statesman; son of Philip Yorke, attorney, at Dover; ent.
Parliament, 1719; Att.-General, 1724; Ld. Chf.-Justice and
Baron Hardwicke, 1733; Lord Chancellor, 1737; cr. Earl, 1754.
    A. Ramsay.   B. Baron.
    Wh. len. slightly turned to left, in Chancellor's robes; left
hand extended, as in the act of speaking; right hand resting
on the bag containing the great seal, by which lies the mace on a
table; 1749.
    (18$\frac{1}{4}$ × 12$\frac{1}{4}$).   22001.

HARDY, Sir Charles, c. 1713–1780; grandson of Sir Thomas
Hardy; son of an admiral; commanded the Ryc, 40 guns, 1741;
knighted, 1755, and Govr. New York; Rear-Admiral of White;
under Boscawen at Louisberg, 1758; under Hawke at Belleisle,
1764; M.P., 1771; Admiral of White, commanding grand
fleet, 1779.

G. Romney.   W. Dickinson, mez.
J. C. Smith, 36.
The publication-line has been cut off at foot.   24663.

HARDY, Sir Thomas, 1769–1839, midshipman, 1781; lieut.,
1793, in Nelson's squadron; app. by Nelson to command of a
brig, La Mutine, 1797; flag-captain to Nelson, on board the
Victory, July, 1803; devoted friend of Nelson, whose last breath
he received, Oct. 21, 1805; Bart., Vice-Admiral, Gov. of
Greenwich Hospital, &c.
See NELSON, Death of.

HARE, Julius Charles, 1795–1855, 3rd son of Francis Hare-
Naylor; educ. at Tonbridge School, abroad, at the Charterhouse, and Trin. Coll., Cambr., 1812–'18; went to the Temple;
returned to Cambr., as classical lecturer, 1822; translated
Niebuhr with Thirlwall; ordd., 1826; presented to family
living, Hurstmonceaux, 1832; select preacher, Cambr., 1839;
Archdeacon, Lewes, 1840; pubd. many works, sermons,
pamphlets, letters, &c.

G. Richmond.   H. Robinson, stipple.
Bust to front, looking to right; vignette; facs. signature
below.
Ind. proof, Jany. 1, 1852.
22¾ × 16⅞.   (8¼ × 7½).   25830.

HARGRAVE, Francis, 1741–1821, barrister, and disting. as a
legal writer; Recorder of L'pool, 1806; Author of "State
Trials," and "Juridical Arguments and collections;" broke down,
1813, from overwork and anxiety; his mind showed symptoms
of failure; his library purchased for 8,000l. by House of
Commons, to relieve him from embarrassment.

Sir J. Reynolds.   J. Jones, mez.
J. C. Smith, 33, 1st state.   22458.

HARGREAVES, John, 1783–1873, of Larkhill House, Blackburn, admitted as Attorney, 1806; Coroner of Blackburn, 1810
–'65; Clerk to the Police Comnrs.; Town Clerk, 1851–'4, &c.

T. H. Illidge.   C. Turner, A.R.A., mez.
Nearly wh. len. to left, seated, looking to front, fingers of
right hand in waistcoat; papers, inkstand, and books, on table,
at left.
Scr. letter proof, July 2nd, 1836, London and Blackburn.
21¾(?) × 15¹⁵⁄₁₆.   (18¹³⁄₁₆ × 14).   23166.

J. Lonsdale.   S. W. Reynolds, mixed mez.
Full ha. len. to front, seated, looking to right, holding gloves
in left hand, which rests on back of chair.

Proof before all letters, the names of the personage and artists being written under in pencil.
$13\frac{7}{8} \times 10$. $(11\frac{5}{8} \times 9\frac{7}{8})$. 22866.

HARLEY, John Pritt, 1786–1858, eminent actor, b. in London; apprent. to a linen-draper, 1801; acted in Kent and Sussex, 1807–'13; appeared in London at English Opera House, 1815; played chief parts at Drury Lane, 1815–'35, 1838, 1841–'8; at St. James', 1835; at Cov. Garden 1838–'40; at Princess's, 1850 till death; especially great in Shaksperean clowns.
T. C. Wageman del. T. Woolnoth, stipple.
Ha. len. to front, looking to right.
Open letter proof; July 1st, 1822.
$12 \times 9\frac{3}{8}$. $(5\frac{11}{16} \times 4\frac{1}{2}$, excl. of ruled border.) 21852.

HARRINGTON, James, 1611–1677, political writer, b. in Northants.; travelled abroad; placed by Parliament about the person of Charles I.; published his political ideas, in "The Commonwealth of Oceana;" after Restoration, impris. in Tower, and at St. Nicholas's Island, Plymouth; released on bail afterwards; d. deranged.
Marchi, mez.
J. C. Smith, 8, 2nd state. 22026.

HARRIS, George Harris, Baron, 1746–1829; General, command. at the capture of Seringapatam; cr., 1815; G.C.B.
A. W. Devis. S. W. Reynolds, mez.
Ha. len. to left, looking to front; in uniform.
Open letter proof; July 1st, 1824.
$13\frac{3}{8} \times 9\frac{7}{8}$. $(11\frac{7}{8} \times 9\frac{7}{8})$. 25745.

HARRIS, Moses, 1731–c. 1785, entomologist and amateur artist, member of the Aurelian Society; drew from the life, engraved, and coloured, moths and butterflies, during 20 years, pubd. under title of "The Aurelian," 1766; the engraving was his first attempt, and well done; the colouring, very brilliant; pubd. other works; exhibited a frame of insects at the R.A., 1785, after which we hear no more of him living.
M. Harris. M. Harris, 1780.
Ha. len. to right, face in profile; oval, in border; round the upper half of the oval is the name and "*Æta.* 49."; the outer border is ornamented with a butterfly-net, palette, books, flowers, and insects.
$(8 \times 6$, border; oval, $4\frac{3}{4} \times 3\frac{7}{8})$. E. 1994.–'89.

HARRISON, John, 1693–1776, b. at Foulby, near Pontefract; brought up as a carpenter, under his father, who also repaired clocks and watches; made improvements in clocks; invented a machine for determining longitude at sea; came to London, 1735; sent on a voyage to Lisbon, to try the new machine; invented the compensation-curb, and several timekeepers for ascertaining the longitude at sea; received tardy acknowledgment of his inventions, and 24,000*l.* reward; had a musical ear,

and invented a curious monochord; d. in Red Lion Square;
bur. in Hampstead Churchyard; an eight-day clock by him is in
S. K. Museum.

    J. Wright.   J. R. Smith, mez.
    J. C. Smith, 74, cut, but a touched proof; the touches on
many parts of the face; " *Harrison, Author of the Timekeeper,*"
written below, on the mount, probably by the engraver.
    $(13_{16}^{1} \times 10_{16}^{7})$.   27133.

HARRISON, John;—*continued.*
    T. King.   P. L. Tassaert, mez.
    J. C. Smith, 1, 2nd state.   E. 1585.–'85.

HARROWBY, Dudley Ryder, Earl of, 1762–1847; Chan-
cellor, Duchy of Lancaster; Sec. of State; Ambassador to
Berlin, etc.
    Madame Meunier.   H. B. Hall.
    Ha. len. seated, to right, looking to front, with folded arms.
Ind. proof, with scratched lettering. 1837.
    $13_{16}^{4} \times 10_{4}^{1}$. $(8_{4}^{3} \times 7_{16}^{1})$.   20631

HARTLEY, Elizabeth, Mrs.,   –1824, celebrated actress,
first appeared at Bath, c. 1771; became very popular in tragedy,
quite as much, perhaps, on account of her beauty as of her
talent; retired, 1780; d. at Woolwich.
    Sir J. Reynolds.   W. Nutter, stipple.
    Ha. len. to front, as " A Bacchante," looking to left,
holding a naked boy in her arms; April 14, 1801.
    $(19_{3}^{1} \times 15_{16}^{5})$.   21992.

HARVEY, Captain H.,   – , commanded a ship, June 1,
1794, in Howe's victory off Ushant.
    See COMMEMORATION (1).

HARVEY, Captain John, 1740–1794, lived at Sandwich,
where he was Mayor, 1774; ent. Navy, 1755, and rendered
eminent services; highly regarded by Hood, Rodney, and
Howe; his arm was shattered by a ball, when commanding the
Brunswick, June 1, 1794, and he died at Portsmouth from the
effects of the wound.
    See COMMEMORATION (1).

HARVEY, William, M.D., 1578–1657; physician; famous for
his discovery of the circulation of the blood; b. at Folkestone;
educ. at Camb.; M.D., at Padua; Physician to St. Barth. Hosp.,
and to James I. and Charles I.; pub. his great discovery, 1628,
in " Exercitatio Anatomica de Motu Cordis," &c.; left his
library and property to the Coll. of Physicians.
    Bemmel.   J. Houbraken, 1739.
    Sh. ha. len. to right, looking to front; broad collar and black
gown; grey hair; oval in border; title at top; below, an
anatomical chart of the heart, arteries, and veins, with herbs,
and the sceptre of Esculapius.
    $14_{8}^{5} \times 9_{16}^{3}$. $(14_{16}^{1} \times 8_{4}^{3})$.   21818.

HARVEY, WILLIAM, 1796–1866, wood-engraver and designer, b.
at Newcastle, apprent. to Thomas Bewick, whom he assisted
in illustrations of Æsop's "Fables;" came to London, 1817;
stud. under B. R. Haydon, whose "Dentatus" he cut; designed
for wood and copper, and illustrated many works; d. at
Richmond.
   Monogram, T. S[cott].
              Monogram, M[ason] J[ackson], woodcut.
   Bust, in profile, to left; circular; from an illustrated paper.
(5$\frac{1}{16}$ diamr.)   E. 1993.–89.

HASE, HENRY, 1763–1829, Chief Cashier of the Bank of England.
   F. W. Wilkin.   C. Wilkin, stipple.
   Bust, to front, looking to right; vignette.
   Ind. proof; Jany. 10, 1821.
   15$\frac{1}{16}$ × 12$\frac{1}{2}$. (7$\frac{3}{4}$ × 6$\frac{3}{8}$).   27592.

HASTINGS, FRANCIS RAWDON-HASTINGS, Marquess of, 1754–
1826; ent. Army 1771; Lt. Col., 1778; A.D.C. to George III.,
and Colonel, 1782; cr. Baron Rawdon of Rawdon, 1783; F.R.S.;
suc. as Earl of Moira (Ireland), 1793; General, 1803; P.C.;
Master General of the Ordnance, 1806–'7; Gov.-Genl. of Bengal, 1812–'23; K.G.; Com.-in-Chf. in India, 1823; cr. Visct.
Loudoun, Earl of Rawdon, Marq. of Hastings, 1816; G.C.B.,
G.C.H.; Gov. of Malta; &c.
   Sir M. A. Shee, R.A.   G. Clint, mez.
   Wh. len. to front, facing and looking to left, right hand
extended, holding a roll of paper; sword in left hand.
   Pubd. by Colnaghi, Son, & Co.
   28 × 18. (27$\frac{1}{4}$ × 18).   21937.

HASTINGS, WARREN, 1732–1818, statesman; Clerk in the
E. I. Company, 1750; member of Council, Calcutta, 1761;
Gov. of Bengal, 1772; Gov. General of India, 1772–'85;
impeached, 1788; after a trial of more than seven years,
acquitted, 1795; D.C.L.; d. at Daylesford, Worcestershire.
   Sir T. Lawrence.   W. Say, mez.
   T. Q. len. to front, seated, with hands clasped, legs crossed;
coat buttoned.
   (13$\frac{5}{8}$ × 10$\frac{1}{2}$.)   22025.

   E. Dayes.   R. Pollard, aquat. and etched.
   In the scene of his trial, a composition of many figures.
   (15$\frac{3}{4}$ × 25$\frac{3}{4}$.)   27112.

HATCHETT, CHARLES, 1765 (?)–1847, chemist, son of a coach-
builder in Long Acre; F.R.S., 1797; member of Literary Club,
1809; author of treatises and papers in Nicholson's Journal
and Philos. Transactions, &c.
   See SCIENCE.

HATTON, SIR CHRISTOPHER, 1540–1591, Lord Chancellor under
Elizabeth; Chancellor of Univ. Oxford, &c.

Ketel pinx.   W. Hilton, R.A., del.   E. Scriven, stipple.
Hn. len. to right, looking to front, wearing a triple chain and
jewel pendant.
    14⅝×10¾.   (7½×5¾).   26167.

HAVELOCK, Sir Henry, 1795–1857, b. at Ford Hall, Bishop
    Wearmouth; educ. at Charterhouse; stud. at Mid. Temple,
    1813–'14; ent. army, 1815; D.A.A.G., in Burmese War,
    1824–'6; present at capture of Cabul, 1839; at siege of
    Jallalabad, 1841; C.B., 1842; K.C.B., 1857; at Ferozeshah
    and Sobraon; com. a column in Ind. Mutiny, defeated Nana
    Sahib, 1857, recapt. Cawnpore; Bart., '57.
        [Baugniet.]   C. Baugniet, lith., 1857.
        Sh. ha. len. to right, looking to left, in undress uniform;
    vignette; facs. signature below.
        (9×7).   23612.
        In the wrapper, in which this portrait was published, with
    those of Genl. Williams, D. Maclise, Col. Lake, Lt. Teesdale,
    and A. Elmore (q. v.).

        W. Crabbe.   J. Sinclair, mixed mez.
        T. Q. len. to front, looking and facing to left, resting both
    hands on hilt of sword; tents and buildings in distance; facs.
    signature below, on right.
        Ind. proof before all other letters.
        22×17¼.   (16⅜×13₁₆³).   21955.

HAWKE, Edward, Lord, 1705–1781; entd. navy, 1720; won a
    victory over the French off Finisterre, 1747, being then Rear-
    Admiral of White; K.B. 1749; M.P.; defeated French fleet off
    Belleisle; Vice-Admiral, 1765; Admiral and Comr.-in-Chf.,
    1768; First Lord, 1766–1771; cr. Baron, 1776.
        G. Knapton.   J. McArdell, mez.
        J. C. Smith, 103, 1st state.   E. 401.–'86.

        F. Cotes, R.A.   J. Hall.
        Full ha. len. to front, facing and looking to left, right hand
    on hilt of sword; sea and ships in distance, on left; rocks
    behind him, on right; title, &c., in six lines, on tablet, below.
        Pubd., Decr. 1, 1793.
        15×11½.   (14¼×10⅞).   22241.
        See also TRIUMPH OF BRITANNIA.

HAWKESBURY, Charles Jenkinson, Lord, 1727–1808; son
    of Col. Jenkinson; educ. at Oxf.; Lord of the Treasury, 1767–
    '73; Sec. of War, 1778–'82; Presidt. Board of Trade, 1784–
    1801; cr. Lord Hawkesbury, 1786; and Earl of Liverpool, 1796.
        G. Romney.   J. Murphy, mez.
        J. C. Smith, 6, early 1st state with skeleton letters, not
    described by J. C. S.; the publication-line cut off.
                                              E. 2255.–'86.
        Also, an impression in the 2nd state.   22511.

HAWKESWORTH, John, 1715–1773, a great contributor to the "Gentleman's Magazine;" author of part of the "Adventurer," and other works; edited Swift, and undertook (1772) the writing of "Cook's Voyages," for which he received 6,000*l*.; but the adverse criticisms and excitement which followed that publication affected his health, and he died at the house of his friend, Dr. Grant, Novr. 17, 1773.

Sir J. Reynolds.   Jas. Watson, mez.

J. C. Smith, 73, 2nd state.   26689.

HAWKWOOD, Sir John (Giovanni della Guglia),   – 1393; English soldier of fortune, b. at Sible Hedingham, Essex; d. at Florence, where his monument is.

For the Socy. Antiquaries.   T. Patch, 1771

Ha. len. on horseback, in profile to right; arms below and five lines of inscription, beginning "IOANNES · ACVTVS · EQVES &c. . . . PAVLI · VCCELLI · OPVS | 1436," &c.

$13\frac{1}{8} \times 9$. $(10\frac{1}{4} \times 8)$.   22867.

HAYDON, Benjamin Robert, 1786–1846, historical painter, b. at Plymouth; educ. there and at Plympton; stud. at R. A., 1804; painted ambitious pictures, some of which, being refused at the R. A., led him to quarrel with the Academy, 1812; received prizes from Br. Instn.; painted several successful pictures while suffering great privations; founded a school, taught some pupils who rose to eminence; imprisoned for debt; released by friends; disappointed, lost his reason, and committed suicide.

D. Wilkie, R.A., 1815.   Mrs. Dawson Turner, etched.

Sh. ha. len. to left, in profile; the body slightly indicated with a few lines; vignette.

$9\frac{1}{4} \times 7(?)$. $(5\frac{1}{4} \times 4\frac{1}{2})$.   27530

Anon.   W. Harvey.

Bust, to left, looking to front; curling hair; wide open collar.

Ind. proof; Aug. 1, 1820.

Cut. $(3\frac{9}{16} \times 2\frac{1}{4})$.   E. 1991.–'89.

HAYES, Sir John McNamara, c. 1750–1809, physician, b. at Limerick; army surgeon in N. America and W. Indies; physn. to the forces; M.D. Reims, 1784; L.C.P., 1786; physician Extr. to the Pr. of Wales, 1791; to Westminster Hosp., 1792–'4; cr. Bart., 1797; Insp. Genl., Milit. Dept., Woolwich; &c.

See MEDICAL SOCIETY.

HAYLEY, William, 1745–1800, poet, b. at Chichester; educ. at Eton and Trin. Hall, Cambr.; stud. Spanish and wrote several poems, while at Cambr., but took no degree; entered at Mid. Temple, but never practised law; author of "Essay on Painting," "Triumphs of Music," and "Triumphs of Temper" (both ridiculed by Byron), "Essay on Old Maids," "Life of Cowper," "Life of Romney," &c.; d. at Felpham, Chichester.

G. Romney.   J. Jacobe, 1779, mez.

J. C. Smith, 4. The portrait, which is very scarce, has no lettering except the artists' names; and, though Mr. Smith does not call it a proof, in this state, it was so described by the late Edward Evans and Domenic Colnaghi.

                                                 22024.

HAYMAN, FRANCIS, 1708–1776, history-painter, b. at Exeter; pupil of Robert Brown, a portrait-painter; painted scenes at Drury Lane, and illustrated Shakspere, 1744, Milton, 1749, Pope, and Cervantes; painted historical designs for Vauxhall Gardens, which gained him great reputation; member of St. Martin's Lane Academy, Incorp. Socy. of Artists, of which he was for a short time president; foundation member of R. A.; friend of Hogarth.

    P. Falconet del., 1769.   D. P. Pariset, stipple.

Bust, to right, in profile; circular in border; the name on a tablet, and P. Falconet's address, &c., below.

    $8\frac{1}{2} \times 5\frac{1}{4}$. $(6\frac{7}{8} \times 4\frac{1}{8}$; $3\frac{7}{16}$ diamr., circle).   28300.   30.

HAYTER, SIR GEORGE, Knt. 1792–1871, painter of history and portraits; b. in London, son of Charles Hayter, portrait-painter; stud. at R. Academy; went to sea as a midshipman, 1808; but returned to study painting; awarded a premium, 1815, of 200 guineas; practised miniature; painter of miniatures to Princess Charlotte and Prince of Saxe-Coburg; stud. at Rome, 3 years; exhibited portraits, 1820; went to Italy again, 1826–'31; Portrait and History-Painter to Queen Victoria, 1837; d. in Marylebone.

    G. Hayter, 1822.   G. Hayter "Aquâ forte Fecit, 1824 (?), Woburn Abbey."

Ind. proof.

    $6\frac{1}{4} \times 4\frac{1}{4}$.   27239.

HEARD, SIR ISAAC, 1730–1822, Garter King of Arms.

    A. W. Devis.   C. Turner, mez.

Hd. len. to right, looking to front. Ætat. 87.

Open letter proof. Published, Oct. 28, 1817, by Boydell & Co.

    $19\frac{7}{8} \times 14$. $(11\frac{3}{8} \times 9\frac{1}{2})$.   22868.

HEARDSON, EDWARD, Cook to the Ad Libitum Society, c. 1790.

    J. Barry, min.   J. R. Smith, mez.

    J. C. Smith, 78, 2nd state.   E. 2126.–'89.

HEARNE, THOMAS, 1678–1735, historical antiquary, son of George Hearne, parish clerk at White Waltham, Berks; educ. at Bray and at Edm. Hall, Oxford; B.A., 1699; M.A., 1703; worked for many years in the Bodl. Library; second keeper 1721; archi-typographus and esquire bedell in Civ. Law, 1715, but resigned;

excluded from the library, because a non-juror; 1716; author of a diary, 1705–'35, now being published in full, "Reliquiæ Bodleianæ," and editor or author of many learned works on antiquarian subjects.

P. Tillemans d. G. Vertue, 1723.

Ha. len. to left, wearing long hair and gown, holding an open book in his right hand, the left resting on his hip; a bookcase in background.

$7\frac{7}{8} \times 5\frac{1}{4}$. ($6\frac{1}{2} \times 4\frac{13}{16}$). 25781.

This is the first of the two (1723) plates engraved by Vertue in 4to, having "ROB. *of* GLOU | CESTER" on the open book.

HEARNE, THOMAS,—*continued.*

[Tillemans and Vertue.] Parr.

Copied from Vertue's plate. On each side, beginning at the top, is one of the following verses printed, outside the plate-mark:—

> *Hearnius* behold! in Closet close-y-pent,
> Of sober Face, with learned Dust besprent;
> To *future* Ages will his *Dulness* last,
> Who hath preserv'd the *Dulness* of the *past*.

On the open book are the words "OATH of ALLEG.," in allusion to Hearne's non-juring principles.

This print appears on the title-page of the "Impartial "Memorials of the Life and Writings of Thomas Hearne, M.A., "by several hands," Lond. MDCCXXXVI.

$2\frac{5}{8} \times 2\frac{5}{16}$. ($2\frac{1}{2} \times 2\frac{1}{8}$). E. 1704.–'88.

HEATH, JAMES, 1757–1834, engraver, b. in London; articled to Collyer; illustrated Lord Orford's works, Bell's "Poets," "Novelist's Magazine," &c., gaining great reputation; engraved larger plates also, "Death of Major Pierson," after Copley; "The Riots of 1780," after Wheatley, &c.; A.E., 1791; Engraver to the King, 1794; lost much property, and nearly his life, by fire, 1789; retired to Great Coram Street, where he died.

T. Kearsley. S. W. Reynolds, mez.

Ha. len. to left, looking to front; in a rectangular border; landscape in the distance, on the left. "London, Published . . . . . . 1795;" some more address has been removed.

$13\frac{7}{8} \times 10\frac{1}{4}$. ($12\frac{1}{16} \times 10\frac{1}{16}$). 29730.

———

L. F. Abbott. J. R. Smith, mez.

J. C. Smith, 79, a touched proof before all letters, undescribed; the touching is on either side of the face, the nose, &c.

22462.

———

"From an Original Painting." Anon., stipple.

Sh. ha. len. to left, looking to front; white neckcloth; coat buttoned across; oval; published in "Monthly Mirror," June 1, 1796.

$6\frac{3}{4} \times 4\frac{3}{8}$. ($3\frac{5}{8} \times 2\frac{13}{16}$). 28300. 31.

HEATHFIELD, GEORGE ELIOTT, Baron, 1717–1790, entered
army, 1735; Commander at Gibraltar, 1775; defended it
against the French and Spanish Fleets, 1779–'82, and repulsed
the great attack, 1782; cr. Baron, 1787.

    Sir J. Reynolds.   R. Earlom, stipple.
Hn. len. to front, looking to left, holding key and chain; in
background, a gun on left, and a mortar on right.

    Proof before all letters, except the artists' names and publi-
cation-line, Novr. 1st, 1788.
    $19\frac{1}{8} \times 13\frac{3}{4}$(?). $(16\frac{3}{4} \times 13\frac{5}{8})$.   21858.

    Sir J. Reynolds.   G. T. Doo, 1836.
Full, ha. len. to front, looking to left, holding key and chain;
guns in background.
    Pubd., July, 1836.
    $20\frac{1}{2} \times 14\frac{1}{2}$. $(9\frac{5}{16} \times 7\frac{1}{4})$.   18843.

    As "General ELIOTT, on the King's Bastion, Gibraltar,
Septr. 13, 1782."
    G. F. Kochler.   T. Malton, etch. and aqunt.
Wh. len. to left, pointing with right hand; in a composition
of many figures.
    (Cut?) $19\frac{1}{16} \times 24\frac{1}{4}$. $(16\frac{9}{16} \times 23)$.   22975.

    J. S. Copley, R.A.   W. Sharp.
In "THE SIEGE AND RELIEF OF GIBRALTAR;"
wh. len. on horseback, at the head of his staff, on right,
directed towards left, with outstretched right hand, pointing to
the fighting ships on the left; pubd. by J. S. Copley, March 27,
1810; a composition of many figures.
    $25\frac{3}{4}$(?)$\times 33\frac{7}{8}$. $(22\frac{7}{8} \times 32\frac{1}{4})$.   21995.

    J. Trumbull.   W. Sharp.
In "The SORTIE made by the GARRISON of GIBRAL-
TAR in the Morning of the 27 of Novr. 1781," a composition
of many figures; wh. len. on right, with his staff, Eliott extends
his right hand over a figure of a dying officer, who lies on the
ground, raising his left hand.
    Skeleton-letter proof, Jany. 1, 1799.
    $23\frac{5}{8}$(?)$\times 31\frac{1}{4}$. $(19\frac{7}{8} \times 30\frac{1}{4})$.   21996.

HEAVISIDE, JOHN, 1748–1828, Surgeon Extraordinary to the
King, F.R.S., F.A.S., &c.; resided at Geddons, Herts; d. at
Hampstead.
    J. Zauffely, R.A.   R. Earlom, mez.
    J. C. Smith, 22, 2nd state.
    Cut: the inscription after "&c.," is all gone.
                                      22694.

    Sir W. Beechey, R.A.   W. Say, mez.
Ha. len. to left, in plain coat, buttoned, looking to front.
Pubd. July 16, 1803.
    $14\frac{13}{16}$(?)$\times 10\frac{7}{8}$ $(12\frac{1}{4} \times 10\frac{13}{16})$.   21905.

HEBER, REGINALD, 1783–1826, b. at Malpas, Cheshire; educ. at Whitchurch, then under Dr. Bristowe, at Neasden, and Oxf.; won prizes, and elected fellow, 1805, ord. 1807; incumb. Hodnet; preb. St. Asaph, 1812; Bampton lecturer, 1815; preacher at Linc. Inn, 1822; Bishop, Calcutta, 1822–'6; pubd. poems, Bampton lectures, &c.

T. Phillips R.A.   S. W. Reynolds, mez.

Ha. len. to left, looking to front, in robes, holding cap in right hand.

Open letter proof; Augt., 1824.

19⅞ × 13¼⅜. (17¼ × 13 7/11).   22993.

HEBERDEN, WILLIAM, 1710–1801, educ. at Cambridge, and began to practise there as a physician; came to London, 1748, and soon acquired great reputation; F.R.S., 1769; author of several medical works; d. at his house in Pall Mall.

Sir W. Beechey, R.A.   J. Ward, mez.

J. C. Smith, 24; a lettered impression, not described by J. C. S.   27217.

HEEMSKERK, EGBERT VAN, 1645–1704, subject-painter, b. at Haerlem, where he stud.; came early to England, where he was patronized by Lord Rochester; painted Dutch humorous scenes, fairs, drunken brawls, &c.; d. in London.

See RILEY.

HEIDEGGER, JOHN JAMES, c. 1659–1749, b. at Zurich (?); came to England, and began managing the Opera, 1713; partner in management with Handel, 1720; instituted masquerades, and ridotti, or balls; gave up the Haymarket Theatre, 1734; resumed it, 1737; was very ugly; commonly known as the "Swiss Count" (Tatler); very charitable; wrote or translated several libretti; d. in Maid of Honour Row, Richmond.

Vanloo.   J. Faber, junr., mez.

J. C. Smith, 184, 2nd state.   27545.

HELENA, PRINCESS.

See CHRISTIAN, PRINCESS.

HEMMINGWAY, – Contractor for the Masonry of the Britannia Bridge.

See MENAI STRAITS.

HENDERSON, JOHN, 1747–1785, disting. actor; b. in London; acquired great reputation at Drury Lane and Cov. Garden Theatres in "Falstaff," "Richard III.," "Macbeth," and other Shaksperian characters.

G. Romney.   J. Jones, mez.

In the character of "Macbeth."

J. C. Smith, 37, 2nd state.   24891.

HENLEY, ROBERT HENLEY, LORD. See NORTHINGTON.

HENNING, JOHN, Senr., of Paisley, carpenter; father of John Henning, the sculptor (1771–1851)

Anon. Anon., woodcut.
Bust, to left, in profile, in an oval ; facs. signature below.
Ind proof.
Oval, $4\frac{3}{4} \times 3\frac{5}{8}$; bust, $2\frac{1}{8}\frac{3}{8} \times 2$). E. 1992.-'88.

HENRIETTA MARIA, Queen of Charles I., 1609–
1669 ; dau. of Henri IV. of France ; b. at Paris ; m. to
Charles I., 1625 ; withdrew to France 1644 ; d. at the Convent
of Chaillot.
A. van Dyck. R. Strange, 1784.
Wh. len. seated, with her two sons, Charles, Prince of Wales,
and James, Duke of York, as children.
$42\frac{11}{16} \times 18\frac{4}{16}$. ($22\frac{13}{16} \times 18$). 22242.

———

Vander Werff. C. Simonneau.
Sh. ha. len. to right, looking to front ; oval in border ; arms
and title below.
$12\frac{4}{16} \times 7\frac{5}{16}$. ($11\frac{5}{8} \times 7\frac{1}{16}$). 29710. 8.

HENRIETTA, Duchess of Orleans, 1644–1670, youngest
daughter of Charles I., m. 1661.
(Sir P. Lely ?) J. Brown.
T. Q. len. to left, looking to front, with child and basket of
flowers.
Ind. proof, with etched letters.
$16\frac{3}{4} \times 13$. ($9\frac{7}{8} \times 7\frac{5}{8}$). 26664.

HENRY I., Beauclerk, 1070–1135, suc., 1100.
Anon. G. Vertue.
Bust, profile to left, crowned ; from a silver coin and a seal
in wax.
$11\frac{1}{2} \times 7\frac{1}{2}$. ($11 \times 7\frac{7}{16}$). 27178. 5.
Note.—No other portrait of this King is known.

HENRY II., Plantagenet, "Shortmantle," 1133–1189, suc.,
1154.
From the print in Montfaucon's "Antiquities," taken "from
the Effigie on his monument at Font-evraud in Anjou," where
he was buried.
Anon. G. Vertue.
Ha. len. to right, crowned, holding sceptre in right hand
27096.
Note.—No other portrait of this King is known.

HENRY III., of Winchester, 1207–1272 ; suc., 1216.
Anon. G. Vertue.
From his monument at Westminster.
Ha. len. to right, crowned.
Cut. (11 (nearly) $\times 7\frac{1}{2}$). 27178. 8.

HENRY IV., 1366–1413 ; suc., 1399.
Anon. G. Vertue.

Ha. len. holding in his right hand a rose, and the sceptre in his left. " Taken from a Picture at Hampton Court, Herefordshire."
11$\frac{5}{16}$ × 7$\frac{1}{2}$ (nearly).   (11$\frac{3}{16}$ × 7$\frac{1}{2}$).   27097.

HENRY V., 1388–1422, suc., 1413.
Anon.   G. Vertue.
From an Antient Picture now in the Palace at Kensington.
Ha. len. to left, in profile.
Cut. (10$\frac{7}{8}$ × 6$\frac{7}{8}$).   27098.

HENRY VI., 1421–1472 ; suc. 1422 ; deposed, 1461.
"Painted on Bord, in the Palace of Kensington." G. Vertue.
Ha. len. to left, hands folded together, wearing a rich collar and cross pendent.
11$\frac{3}{16}$ × 7$\frac{5}{16}$. (11 × 7$\frac{1}{16}$).   27099.

"Engraved after a drawing taken from the original painting on glass in the magnificent Chapel " of King's Coll., Camb.
Mr. Orde del.   J. Bretherton, stipple.
25$\frac{3}{16}$ × 13$\frac{3}{16}$. (23$\frac{7}{8}$ × 12$\frac{1}{4}$).   26690.

HENRY VII., 1455–1509, suc., 1485.
"From an antient Limning in the Royal Collection."
                                                        G. Vertue.
Ha. len. to right, looking to front, holding sceptre in his right and orb in his left hand. On the right, below, is the portrait of his Queen, Elizabeth of York, in small.
Cut. (10$\frac{1}{2}$ × 7).   27178. 10.
Also, a copy, reversed, in Genealogical Chart, 553. 1.
Cut. (10$\frac{3}{4}$ × 6$\frac{7}{8}$).   25017.

—— with his Queen ; together with Henry VIII., as Prince of Wales, and Jane Seymour.
R. Van Leemput, after Holbein.   G. Vertue.
Wh. len. all standing ; from the famous tapestry.
Cut. 19 × 22$\frac{3}{4}$. (18 × 21$\frac{1}{2}$).   27642.

HENRY VIII., 1491–1547, suc. 1509, married six times.
Anon.   Woodcut, early German.
Wh. len. on horseback.
Cut. (14$\frac{7}{8}$ × 11$\frac{1}{4}$).   E. 469.–'87.

Holbein.   J. Houbraken, Amst., 1750.
Wearing a collar of rubies.
14$\frac{1}{2}$ × 8$\frac{15}{16}$. (14$\frac{1}{8}$ × 8$\frac{1}{2}$).   E. 186.–'85.

—— presenting the Charter to the Barber-Surgeons' Company.
Holbein.   B. Barron, 1736.
The king, looking to front, seated, rather to the right of the centre of the composition, holds in his left hand the sword of justice, and with his right gives the charter to the barber-surgeons, eight of whom kneel on the left and three on the right of the print.
(17$\frac{9}{16}$ × 29$\frac{7}{10}$)   24682.

HENRY FREDERICK, Prince of Wales, 1594–1612.
"From an extreme rare Print by S. Pass." (1612).

Dunkarton, mez.

Wh. len. with a pike. Coat of arms below, with the three feathers.
Proof before letters.
$13\frac{3}{4} \times 10\frac{2}{3}$.   ($10\frac{2}{3} \times 8\frac{1}{4}$).   22243.

HENRY, Rev. Robert, 1718–1790, Historian; son of a farmer; b. at St. Ninian's, Stirlingshire, 1718; educ. at Edinb. Univ.; Moderator of General Assembly, 1774; D.D.; Author of a "History of Great Britain."
D. Martin.   J. Caldwall.

Sh. ha. len. to front, in gown, facing and looking to left; oval in ruled border.
Proof before all letters.
($9\frac{7}{8} \times 7\frac{9}{16}$; oval, $6\frac{9}{16} \times 5\frac{1}{16}$).   22509.

HENRY, William, 1774–1836, Chemist, b. at Manchester, son of Thomas Henry, F.R.S.; educ. at Manchester Academy; went to Edin. Univ., 1795; M.D., 1807; author of many scientific works on chemistry and medicine, "Elements of Exp. Chemistry," "Cursory Remarks on Music," &c.; F.G.S.; F.R.S. *See* SCIENCE.

HENSLOW, Rev. John Stevens, 1796–1861, botanist; b. at Rochester; educ. at Cambr.; Prof. of Mineralogy, 1822; Prof. of Botany, 1825; retired, 1837, on being appointed Rector of Hitcham, Suff.; Author of a "Catalogue of British Plants," "Principles of Botany," &c.; d. at Hitcham.
[Maguire.]   T. H. Maguire, lith., 1851.

Ha. len. to front, seated, holding eye-glasses in right hand, right arm resting on books on table; vignette; rectilin., but corners cut off; facs. signature below.
($10 \times 9\frac{7}{16}$).   22512.

HERBERT of Chirbury, Edward, Lord, 1581–1648, Philosopher, educ. at Oxford, K.B., 1603; served in Netherlands, 1610–'14; twice Ambassador to France; cr. Irish peer, 1624; English Baron, 1629; neutral in the Civil War; author of "Tractatus de Veritate," "Memoirs," &c.
J. Oliver.   A. Walker.

Wh. len. to left, lying by a spring, resting on his right elbow.
$8\frac{1}{4} \times 9\frac{3}{4}$.   ($7\frac{1}{4} \times 8\frac{1}{16}$).   25780.

HERBERT, George, 1593–1632, younger brother of Edward, Lord Herbert of Chirbury, b. at Montgomery Castle; educ. at Westminster and Trin. Coll., Cambr.; fellow and Univ. Orator, 1619; ord. and made prebend. of Layton Ecclesia, Linc.; presented, 1630, to living of Bemerton; author of "The Temple," 1631, and other works in prose and verse.

Copied from the scarce print by R. White prefixed to the "Temple," eleventh edition, 1678–'9.

G. Clint, A.R.A., delin.   E. Smith.

Sh. ha. len. to right, looking to front, wearing a cap, broad collar, and long hair.

Ind. proof; Nov. 1, 1822.

8 × 5¼. (3¹³⁄₁₆ × 3).   27265.

HERBERT, Rt. Hon. Sidney, aftds. Lord, of Lea, 1810–1861, Statesman, son of the Earl of Pembroke; Sec. of State for War, under Sir Robert Peel, Lord Aberdeen, and Lord Palmerston; cr. Lord Herbert of Lea, 1861; d. from effects of overwork.

F. Grant, A.R.A.   G. R. Ward, mez.

T. Q. len. to front, looking and facing to left, leaning with right hand on walking-stick; landscape with water in background.

Ind. proof; Novr. 29, 1847.

20⁷⁄₁₆ × 15³⁄₁₆ (16¼ × 13¹⁄₁₆).   21956.

See also ABERDEEN CABINET.

HERKOMER, Hubert, 1849– ; b. at Waal, in Bavaria; stud. at Southampton, in the Art School, at Munich, 1865, under Prof. Echter, and at South Kensington; member of Inst. of Painters in Water-colours; exhibited at R. A.; gained a grand medal at Paris Exhibn., 1878; practised etching; A.R.A., 1879; founded a school of Art at Bushey, Herts.; officer of Legion of Honour, 1889; R.A., 1890.

Pilotel, etched.

Bust, to front, looking to right; vignette.

6¼ × 4¾. (4⅞ × 4½).   E. 1998.–'89.

HEROES. See NAVAL.

HEROES of the Peninsular.

J. P. Knight, A.R.A.

A group of 31 figures, including the Duke of Wellington.

Key-Plate to the above-mentioned print (which is not in the S. K. Collection), giving the names of the personages represented.

(9 × 16¼).   13569. 6.

HERRICK, Robert, 1591–1674, divine and poet, son of Nicholas Herrick, goldsmith in Cheapside; educ. (probably) at Westminster and St. John's Coll., and Trin. Hall, Cambr.; B.A., 1616–'17; M.A., 1620; admitted to living of Dean Prior, Ashburton, Devon, 1629; ejected, 1647; restored, 1662; author of "Hesperides," 1648, &c.

Copy from the frontispiece of the "Hesperides," 1648, by W. Marshall.   Schiavonetti.

Bust, to right, in profile; oval; seal and fncs. signature below.

6¹³⁄₁₆ × 4¹¹⁄₁₆. (4¹¹⁄₁₆ × 3½).   29639. 157.

HERRIES, Rt. Hon. John Charles, 1778–1855; Statesman; Master of the Mint; Presdt. of Board of Trade; Chancellor of Exchequer, 1827; Sec. at War, 1834.

W. A. Boxall.   W. Walker, mez.
Ha. len. seated, to front, holding a book.
A Private Plate. Published, March 1, 1853.
$16 \times 12\frac{1}{4}$. $(12\frac{5}{8} \times 10\frac{1}{16})$.   22994.

HERRING, JOHN FREDERICK, 1795–1865, b. in Surrey, son of
American parents, began on signboards and coach panels; went
to Doncaster, worked in a stable, drove a coach, and painted
horses; soon noticed, and befriended by A. Cooper, R.A.,
established himself as a successful animal painter; produced
many good pictures of that kind, some of which were engraved
and very popular; member of Society of Br. Artists; d. at
Tunbridge Wells.
    W. Betham.   J. B. Hunt, stipple on steel.
Sh. ha. len. to front; vignette; facs. signature below.
Cut. $(4\frac{3}{4} \times 4\frac{1}{4})$.   27289.

HERRING, THOMAS, 1693–1757, son of a clergyman; b. at
Walsoken, Norfolk; educ. at Camb.; fellow of Corp. Chr.
Coll.; Dean of Rochester, 1731; Bishop of Bangor, 1737;
Archb. of York, 1743; zealously supported reigning dynasty
during the Rebellion, 1745; Archb. of Canterbury, 1747; d.
at Croydon.
    T. Hudson.   J. Faber, jun., mez.
    J. C. Smith, 186   21864.

HERSCHEL, SIR JOHN FREDERICK WILLIAM, 1792–1871, son
of Sir William Herschel; b. at Slough; educ. at St. John's
Coll., Cambr.; Senior Wrangler and first Smith's Prizeman,
1813; with Sir. J South, made observations, 1821–'3;
re-examined the stars discovered by his father, and observed
many other new stars, 1824–'32; made astr. observ. at Cape,
1834–'8; Knt. of Guelphic Order, 1836; Bart., 1838; P.R.A.S.,
1848; Master of Mint, 1850–'5; pub. many discoveries in
Astronomy, Optics, Chemistry, Photography, &c.; d. at
Collingwood, Hawkhurst.
    H. W. Pickersgill, R.A.   W. Ward, mez.
    Ha. len. to front, in gown, looking rather upwards; a globe,
on right; 1835.
    $15\frac{1}{2} \times 11\frac{2}{16}$. $(11\frac{1}{4} \times 8\frac{1}{4})$.   25782.

HERSCHEL, SIR WILLIAM, 1738–1822, Astronomer; son of a
musician at Hanover; early showed talent for music; came to
England; organist at Halifax, aftds. at Bath; turned to study
of astronomy and mathematics; constr. a large telescope; discovered a new planet, "Georgium Sidus" (now known as
"Herschel"), and became famous; astronomer to George III.;
removed to Slough; Knt.; D.C.L., Oxford; contrib. 69 papers
to "Philosophical Transactions," 1780–1815; besides his astr.
discoveries, made researches in optics, heat, &c.; F.R.S.
    F Reyberg, 1814.   J. Godby, stipple.

Sh. ha. len. to right; tops of trees and stars in distance;
Novr. 1, 1814.
$12\frac{1}{2}\times9$. ($9\frac{3}{8}\times7\frac{1}{2}$).   24118.
See also SCIENCE.

HERVEY, Hon. Augustus, 1724–1779; entd. navy, 1744,
married privately to the notorious Miss Chudleigh; M.P. for St.
Edmondsbury; Capt. R.N., Col. of Marines, Com.-in-Chf.
in Mediterranean, 1763; suc. his brother as 3rd Earl of Bristol,
1775.
Sir J. Reynolds.   E. Fisher, mez.
J. C. Smith, 28, 2nd state.   27593.

HERVEY, Rev. James, 1714–1758, devotional writer; b. near
Northampton; educ. at Oxf.; suc. his father as Rector of
Weston Favell; wrote " Meditations and Contemplations," and
" Theron and Aspasia," once very popular.
I. Williams.   I. Dixon, mez.
J. C. Smith, 20, 2nd state.   22459.

HERVEY, John, Lord, 1696–1743, eldest son of the 1st Earl of
Bristol; educ. at Westminster and Clare Hall, Cambridge;
disting. as an orator in both Houses of Parliament; Lord Privy
Seal; cr. Baron, 1733; suffered from epilepsy, and used to paint
his face; ridiculed by Pope as " Sporus " and " Lord Fanny; "
Princess Caroline said to have been in love with him; he
m. the beautiful Mary Lepell; wrote " Memoirs of the Reign of
George II.; " bur. in Ickworth Church, Suffolk.
Vanloo.   J. Faber, junr., mez.
J. C. Smith, 188, 1st state.   25746.

HESSE-HOMBURG, Frederick Louis Joseph, 1769–1829,
Landgrave of, m. Elizabeth, daughter of George III., 1818.
C. Hlotz.   D. Weiss, stipple.
Ha. len. slightly to left, looking to front, in uniform; oval.
$11\frac{1}{8}\times8\frac{1}{16}$. ($4\frac{1}{2}\times3\frac{3}{8}$).   25057. 1.
In Genealogical Chart, 553. 1.

HILL, Aaron, 1685–1750; educ. at Westminster; wrote poems,
plays, &c.; manager of King's Theatre, Haymarket; a friend
of Pope, who quarrelled with him aftds.; bur. in West Cloister,
Westminster Abbey; a " Collection of Letters never before
" printed : written by Alexander Pope, and other ingenious
" gentlemen, to Aaron Hill," was pub. in 1751.
Anon.   H. Hulsbergh.
Sh. ha. len. to front, wearing long wig, lace-collar open at
throat, left hand partly seen; oval in border, title at top, " Ætatis
suæ 24 A°. Domī 1709 " below, and arms at bottom.
$10\frac{3}{4}\times6\frac{1}{2}$. ($10\frac{7}{16}\times6\frac{1}{4}$; oval, $7\frac{1}{4}\times5\frac{3}{4}$).   24665.

HILL, Sir John, 1716–1775, b. at Peterborough; apothecary in
Westminster; practised as a physician; wrote many books,
novels, farces, &c., and invented quack medicines; pub. " System
of Botany," 17 vols., folio, which procured him the order of

Vasa from the King of Sweden; often involved in quarrels with
wits of the day; d. of gout.
    F. Cotes, R.A.   R. Houston, mez.
    J. C. Smith, 64, 2nd state.   22510.

HILL, Rev. Rowland, 1744–1833, preacher, 6th son of Sir
    Rowland Hill, 1st Bart.; educ. at Shrewsbury, Eton, and
    Cambr.; B.A. with honours, 1769; ord., 1773, and curate of
    Kingston, Somersets.; was refused priest's orders, on account
    of his irregularities; preached everywhere he could; then at
    Wotton, Gloucestershire, and (1783) at Surrey Chapel, built
    for him; pubd. his "Village Dialogues," 1810; first Chairman
    of Rel. Tract Socy., &c.
        M. R. S. del.   J. Linnell.
        Ha. len. to left, seated, holding a book in right hand; vignette.
        Ind., open letter proof, March, 1827.
        14 × 10⅛.   (8¾ × 7½).   22991.

HILL, Rowland, Viscount, 1772–1842, entered the army, 1790;
    Lt.-Col., 1794; Col., 1800; Maj.-Genl., 1805; Lt.-Genl.,
    1812; General, 1825; distinguished at Aboukir, 1801; com-
    manded second division of Brit. army in Peninsular war,
    distinguished at storming of Almarez, 1812; G.C.B., 1815;
    M.P., 1812–'4; cr. Baron, 1814; G.C.H., 1818; Visct., 1842.
        H. W. Pickersgill, R.A.   C. Turner, A.R.A., mez.
        Wh. len. to front, looking to left, charger held by a trooper on
    right. The General holds a cocked hat in his right hand.
        Open letter proof; May 14, 1834.
        28½ × 19½.   (25 × 17).   24740.
        See also WATERLOO BANQUET.

HILL, Sir Rowland, 1795–1879, K.C.B., advocate and initiator
    of postal reform, 1837; Secretary to the Postmaster General,
    1846; Chief Sec., 1854.
        A. Wivell, junr.   W. O. Geller, mixed mez.
        T. Q. len. seated, to right; holding a paper in left hand.
        Ind. proof, with open letters. Published, May 1st, 1848.
        19 × 14.   (14⅛ × 11).   E. 1656.–'89.

————

        [W. Taylor.]   W. Taylor, lith.
        Head, to right; vignette; facs. signature below.
        Proof on India paper.
        (7 × 5).   E. 1657.–'89.

HILLS, Robert, 1769–1844, painter and etcher of animals; b. at
    Islington; one of the first members of the Water-colour Society,
    and for many years its secretary; the Br. Museum has a large
    number of his etchings of animals; d. in Golden Square.
        J. Jackson, R.A.   W. T. Fry, chalk and dot.
        Ha. len. slightly directed to right, looking to front, seated,
    with crayon in right hand, as in the act of drawing on a sheet
    of paper; a figure of a stag behind, on right; vignette.

Open letter proof; March, 1823.
$17\frac{1}{16} \times 14\frac{1}{4}$. $(9\frac{1}{2} \times 8\frac{3}{8})$. 21739.

HINDERWELL, Thomas, 1744–1825, historian, b. at Scarborough, son of a master-mariner and shipowner; educ. at Scarborough and at Coxwold gram. school; mayor of Scarborough, 1781, '84, '90, 1800; presid. of Amicable Society, &c.; best known as author of "History of Scarborough."

J. Jackson, R.A., del. J. Posselwhite, chalk and dot.

A head, to left, in profile, at age of 79; vignette; a private plate.

$9\frac{3}{16} \times 6\frac{1}{2}$. $(3\frac{7}{8} \times 2\frac{3}{4})$. 18109.

HOARE, Prince, 1755–1834, painter of history and portraits, son of W. Hoare, R.A., b. at Bath; pupil of his father; gained a Society of Arts' premium, 1772, and came to London; entd. the Academy schools; stud. at Rome, 1776, under Mengs; returned, 1780; unsuccessful, tried literature, writing comic operas, &c., some of which held the stage; foreign secretary to the R.A., 1799; wrote some works on Art.

Sir T. Lawrence. C. Turner, A.R.A., mez.

Head only, to right; white neckcloth; vignette; facs. signature below; July 25, 1831

14×10. $(5 \times 5\frac{1}{4})$. 23130.

HOARE, Sir Richard Colt, 1758–1838, historian of Wiltshire, only son of Richard Hoare (cr. Bart., 1786); educ. at priv. schools, and introduced early into the family bank; travelled abroad, 1785–'7; suc. to the Baronetcy, 1787; travelled again, 1788–'91, and through Wales and Ireland, 1792–1807; author of "Ancient History of North and South Wiltshire," 1812–'21; F.R.S., F.S.A., &c.; wrote many other works.

H. Edridge, A.R.A. H. Meyer, stipple.

T. Q. len. to left, seated, looking to front, holding an open folio book and pen; books and antiquities in background. This appeared in the "Pedigrees of the Families of Hoare," and in Vol. 1 of "History of Modern Wiltshire."

$12\frac{3}{8} \times 9\frac{6}{16}$. $(9\frac{3}{8} \times 7\frac{3}{8})$. 22869.

HOARE, William, 1706–1792, portrait and history-painter, b. at Eye, Suffolk; pupil of Grisoni; went to Rome; returned, after nine years, and settled at Bath, where he painted portraits in oil and crayons with the greatest success; foundation member of the R. A., where he exhibited for the last time, 1779; some etchings by him are known; d. at Bath.

P. Hoare. S. W. Reynolds, mez.

Sh. ha. len. to left; white neckcloth; hair curled at ends; dark coat, not buttoned; oval in border; Feb. 1, 1796.

Cut. $(12 \times 9\frac{5}{8})$. 28298. 3.

[P. Hoare.] Page, stipple.

Sh. ha. len. to left; small copy of the print by S. W. Reynolds. Letter-press below and on back.

$(1\frac{15}{16} \times 1\frac{9}{16})$. 15219. 4.

HOADLY, Benjamin, 1676–1761, b. at Westerham, Kent; educ. at home, and at Cath. Hall, Cambr.; B.A., 1696; fellow, 1697; M.A., 1699; coll. tutor, 1699–1701; ord., 1701; lecturer at St. Mildred's, Poultry; Rector of St. Peter-le-poor, Broad St., 1704; led the "Low Church" party; Rector of Streatham, 1710; D.D., 1715, and Bishop of Bangor; of Hereford, 1721; of Salisbury, 1723; of Winchester, 1734; a cripple, obliged to preach kneeling; pubd. many controversial works, sermons, &c.

W. Hogarth.   B. Baron.

 T. Q. len. to right, seated in robes, as Prelate of the Order of the Garter, looking to front, wearing the George, &c.

 $16\frac{7}{8} \times 11\frac{3}{4}$. $(14 \times 11\frac{1}{8})$ 20920.

HOBBES, Thomas, of Malmesbury, 1588–1679, philosopher; b. at Malmesbury; educ. at Magdalen Hall, Oxf.; tutor in Duke of Devonshire's family; mathem. tutor to Pr. of Wales, 1647; his "Leviathan" and other works appeared at Amsterdam, 1668, and were equally praised and blamed by his contemporaries; d. at Chatsworth; epitaph suggested for his tomb, "This is the Philosopher's Stone."

 [Faithorne?]   W. Faithorne.

 L. Fagan, p. 41, 2nd state.   26692

HOBHOUSE, Sir John Cam. *See* BROUGHTON.

HOBSON, Thomas, 1544–1630, carrier of Cambridge, who by prudence, common sense, and economy amassed a fortune, out of which he was able to endow Cambridge with a handsome stone conduit, supplied by an aqueduct, whereby his memory is better preserved than in Milton's quibbling epitaphs; d. at the time of the plague.

 [Payne.]   J. Payne.

 Ha. len. to front, wearing broad-brimmed hat and cloak; carrying before him a bag, in which his right hand is partly hidden; 8 English verses below, "Laugh not to see . . . . . a thrifty Father."

 "*Cum priuileg: Are to be sould by P. Stent.*"

 $8\frac{11}{16} \times 6\frac{5}{16}$. $(6\frac{3}{4} \times 5\frac{7}{8})$.   26693.

HODGES, William, 1744–1797, landscape-painter, b. in London, son of a blacksmith; stud. in Shipley's drawing school, noticed by R. Wilson, who took him as assistant and pupil; scene-painter at Derby; exhibited at Spring Gardens, 1770–72; draftsman to Cap. Cook's second expedition; exhibited at R. A., 1776; went to India, where he acquired some money; returned, 1784; A.R.A., 1786; R.A., 1787; his best works were Indian views and one of Windsor.

 R. Westall.   J. Thornthwait.

 Sh. ha. len. to right, looking to front; loose white neckcloth, coat buttoned; oval; June 1, 1792.

 Cut. $(3\frac{11}{16} \times 3\frac{1}{16})$.   28300.   32.

HODGSON, Rev. Francis, 1781–1852, b. at Croydon; educ. at Eton and King's Coll., Cambr.; B.A., 1804; M.A., 1807;

B.D., 1840; a fellow at King's, 1802; a master, 1806, at Eton for a year; wrote for magazines, &c.; tutor at Kings, 1807; a friend of Byron; curate of Bradden, and Bakewell, 1816; archdeacon of Derby, 1836; provost of Eton, 1840, and rector of Cottesford; pubd. poems, &c.

F. Grant.   W. Walker, mez.
Ha. len. to front, in gown, with bands.
Open letter proof; April 1st, 1850. A private plate.
15⅝ × 11⅞. (12⁷⁄₁₆ × 9¼).   23157.

HOGARTH, WILLIAM, 1697–1764, subject-painter and engraver, b. in London; apprent. to a silversmith; student in St. Martin's Lane Academy; set up as engraver of plate, 1720; began illustrating books, 1723; painting portraits, soon after; ran away with and married Sir J. Thornhill's daughter; painted and engraved many satirical subjects, "Harlot's Progress," "Rake's Progress," "Marriage à la Mode," "Southwark Fair," "Enraged Musician," "Industry and Idleness," &c.

Hogarth.   Anon.
Wh. len. to right, seated; painting the Comic Muse; March 29, 1758; 4th state (see A. Dobson).
Cut. (14⅜ × 13⅜).   27249.

___

Hogarth.   S. Ireland, etched.
Sh. ha. len. to right, looking to front; long curled wig; holding a palette.
Cut. (7⅞ × 7).   E. 2000.–'89.

___

Weltdon and Hogarth.   C. Townley, mez.
J. C. Smith, 10.   E. 1562.–'85.

___

       L. C. Wyon.
Bust to right, in profile, on a medal; reverse shows three figures, with motto, "He through the eye corrects the heart," surrounding the upper part of the medal; below, "Art Union of London, 1848." Above, "The Hogarth Medal." Both engraved on one plate.
5¼ × 8⅜(?). (2½ diamr.).   15219, 5.

HOGG, JAMES, 1782–1835, "The Ettrick Shepherd," native of Scotland, a shepherd; began rhyming at 18; noticed by Sir Walter Scott; produced an "Essay on Sheep," which won for him a premium; a vol. of ballads, called "The Mountain Bard," the "Forest Minstrel," and "Queen's Wake," 1813; contributed to "Blackwood," &c.; firm friend and companion of Sir Walter Scott; d. at Altrive Lake, on the Yarrow, leaving a widow and five children totally destitute.
See SCOTT, SIR WALTER.

HOLCROFT, THOMAS, 1745–1809, dramatist, novelist, and translator, b. in Orange Court, Leicester Fields, London, son of

Q 2

a man who kept a shoemaker's shop and let horses for hire, but
aftds. left London in poverty and became a pedlar; the son
became a stable-boy at Newmarket for three years; returned to
London, worked as a cobbler, for his father; went to Liverpool,
1764, and taught reading to children; returned to London,
worked as a shoemaker again; wrote occasionally in newspapers; engaged as prompter at a Dublin theatre, 1770–'1;
returned to London; wrote "The Crisis," 1778, followed by
"Duplicity," a translation of the "Mariage de Figaro," "The
Road to Ruin," and many other pieces.
Opie (picture exhibited, 1804; aftds. (1878) in the possession
of Mr. C. L. Kenney).   Anon. [T. Hodgetts?], mez.
Ha. len. to front, with coat buttoned across chest, holding
pair of spectacles.
Proof before all letters; later impressions have "Longmans
exc. 1816."
$11\frac{7}{8} \times 8\frac{11}{16}$. $(8\frac{3}{4} \times 7\frac{3}{16})$.   24666.

HOLL, FRANCIS MONTAGUE, known as Frank, 1845–1888,
portrait and subject-painter, eldest son of F. Holl, the engraver;
b. in Kentish Town; educ. at University Coll., London;
entered the R. A. schools, 1861; gained a gold medal, 1863,
and the travelling studentship, 1868; exhibited, 1864 and
following years; A.R.A., 1878.
                                            Anon., woodcut.
Sh. ha. len. to left. Vignette, from the "Graphic," May 3,
1879.
$(5\frac{1}{2} \times 4\frac{1}{4})$.   E. 1997.–'89.

HOLLAND, HENRY RICH, Earl of, 1590–1649, loyalist, K.G.,
Ambassador to France; General of Horse against the Scots,
1639; executed as a traitor to Parliament.
A van Dyck.   P. Clouet.
Ha. len. in armour, to left, looking to front.
Wibiral, 102, 2nd state.
$10\frac{3}{8} \times 7\frac{1}{2}$. $(9\frac{1}{4} \times 7\frac{1}{4})$.   E. 271.–'89

HOLLAND, HENRY RICHARD VASSALL FOX, 3rd Lord, 1773–
1840, statesman; nephew of Charles James Fox; known as
a leader of the Whig Party; Chancellor of the Duchy of
Lancaster, 1830 and 1834.
J. R. Smith.   S. W. Reynolds, mez.
Wh. len. to right, seated, looking to front, hands folded
together, right arm resting on arm of chair, left leg crossed over
right; paper, book, and pen and inkstand, on table, right; a
bust of C. J. Fox, above, on right; a dog on left; Oct. 13,
1806; published by the engraver.
26×18. $(24 \times 17\frac{7}{8})$.   22030.

——, with Elizabeth Vassall, LADY HOLLAND, 1770–1845,
m. 1st to Sir Godfrey Webster, Bart., 2nd to Lord Holland;
and JOHN ALLEN, M.D., 1770–1843, librarian.
C. R. Leslie, R.A.   S. W. Reynolds, mixed mez.
Wh. len. figures in the library at Holland House; Lord

Holland at table on left, Lady Holland on right, both seated;
Dr. Allen, behind table, standing; a servant on extreme right,
holding a portfolio. The picture was exhibited (350) on loan
at S. K. M., 1868.

Ind. proof; June 10, 1847.

(?) × 31¼. (22¾ × 29).   22146.

HOLLINS, JOHN, 1799–1855, b. at Birmingham; exhibited
portraits, 1818; came to London, 1822; travelled in Italy,
1825–'7; contributed largely to exhibitions at the R. A.;
A.R.A., 1842; d. unmarried, in Berners St.

See GREEN (2).

HOLLIS, THOMAS, 1720–1774, b. in London, educ. at home, and
at Amsterdam, and under Dr. Ward, the Gresham professor;
travelled abroad, collecting books and curiosities; contributed
generously to Harvard Coll., U.S.A., the public library at Berne,
and other foreign institutions; F.R.S., F.S.A., made valuable
presents to the Br. Museum; great friend to democratic
government; gentle and agreeable in manners.

[Cipriani.]   J. B. Cipriani, 1767.
A head, to front, on a pyramid, the top of which is not seen;
title on pedestal; inscription (from Plutarch) in 7 lines at foot;
in right lower corner, a profile of the personage, to right,
smiling.

11 × 8⁴⁄₅. (10¾ × 8¹⁄₁₆).   29718. 11.

HOLLIS, SIR TRETSWELL. *See* NAVAL HEROES (2).

HOLLOND, ROBERT, 1808–1877, educ. at C. C. Coll., Camb.,
B.A., 1828; M.A., 1831; barrister, 1834; M.P., 1837–'52;
made, at his own expense, in company with T. Monck Mason
and Charles Green, a voyage in the Nassau balloon from
London to Weilburg, 1836.

See GREEN (2).

HOLMAN, JAMES, 1791–1857, blind traveller, entd. navy as
first-class volunteer, 1791, rose to lieutenant's rank, constantly
afloat till 1810; invalided, lost his sight from illness, appointed
naval knight of Windsor; travelled through Europe, 1819–'21,
Russia, &c., 1822–'24; taken for a spy in Russia, and conducted to the frontier; published "Voyage round the World,"
and other books of travel.

J. P. Knight, R.A.   J. R. Jackson, mez.
Full ha. len. slightly to right, seated, head turned towards
left; white beard and hair; left hand raised, right on chair-arm.
Proof before the name; May 23, 1849.

15⅞ × 12¼. (12¹⁄₁₆ × 9¼).   22989.

HOLMAN, JOSEPH GEORGE, c. 1760–1817, actor, educ. at
Oxford, and intended for the Church; preferred the stage;
appeared at Cov. Garden, 1784, as Romeo, and obtained such
success that he became a rival of Kemble; bought a share in
the Dublin theatre, c. 1801; afterwards went to the U.S.

America, and took a theatre in Charlestown; wrote several
successful plays; d. at Long Island.
 M. Brown.   T. Park, mez.
 J. C. Smith, 4, 2nd state.
 With Miss Brunton (q. v.).   26424.

HOLROYD, Sir George Sowley, 1757–1831, of Gray's Inn;
puisne judge of King's Bench, 1816.
 S. W. Reynolds, junr.   S. W. Reynolds, mixed mez.
 T. Q. len. to front, seated, in wig and robes, right hand
slightly forward, open; left resting on a paper; 1834.
 19$\frac{1}{16}$ × 14. (17$\frac{1}{4}$ × 13$\frac{1}{2}$).   24622

HOLT, Sir John, 1642–1709; judge; opposed the tyranny of
James II., 1685–'8; Ch. Justice of King's Bench, 1689; pub-
lished "Reports of Pleas of the Crown," 1708; P.C.; &c.
 Sir G. Kneller.   R. White.
 Sh. ha. len. to right, looking to front, in wig and robes, with
chain; oval in border. Three lines of inscription below, and
"Printed and sold by John King at the Globe against the
Church in the Poultry."
 "Scarce" (Evans). Cut. (18$\frac{3}{4}$ × 10$\frac{1}{2}$).   24078.

HOLT, T., 1752– , of Petworth, Sussex; farmer, insurance-
agent, and teetotaller, accustomed to walk to London once or
twice every year, a distance of 50 miles, in 13 hours, and back
again on the day after the morrow, a feat which he performed
in his 85th year (1836).
 H. W. Phillips del.   R. J. Lane, A.R.A., lith.
 Wh. len. to left, carrying an umbrella; a milestone is seen
on the right.
 (6$\frac{3}{4}$ × 6)   24730.

HOME, Sir Everard, Bart., 1756–1832, surgeon; pupil of John
Hunter; Sergeant-surgeon to George III.; Pres. R.C.S.;
Vice-Pres. R.S.; Author of "Lectures on Comparative
Anatomy," &c.
 Sir W. Beechey, R.A.   W. Sharp
 T. Q. len. to front, seated, holding a paper in left hand on
knee, resting right hand on papers on table; coat buttoned up.
A private plate.
 20$\frac{1}{2}$ × 15$\frac{1}{4}$. (16$\frac{11}{16}$ × 13$\frac{1}{2}$).   21838.

HOME, Rev. John, 1722–1808, b. at Leith, son of the town-
clerk; educ. at the gram. school and at Edinb. University;
licensed as a probationer, 1745; enlisted in Coll. volunteers;
went to Dunbar, Prestonpans, and Falkirk; prisoner, conf.
in Doune Castle, but escaped; minister at Athelstaneford,
E. Lothian; wrote "Agis," and "Douglas," both refused by
Garrick; "Douglas" produced at Edinb., 1756, with great
success, and by Rich, at Cov. Garden, 1757; he resigned his
charge at Athelstaneford, became private sec. to Lord Bute,
and tutor to the Pr. of Wales; "Agis" accepted by Garrick,

1758, and "Siege of Aquileia," 1760; and other works followed.

H. Raeburn. Andrew Birrell, May 9, 1799.
Full ha. len. to left, seated; trees and sky seen through an opening on the left.
17$\frac{1}{16}$ × 12. (13$\frac{1}{4}$ × 10$\frac{1}{2}$). **24120.**

HONE, NATHANIEL, 1718–1784, portrait painter, b. in Dublin; came to England, settled in London; member of the Incorp. Socy. of Artists and a Foundation R. A.; painted in oils, miniature, and enamel; quarrelled with Reynolds and the Academy; made an exhibition of his own works, 1775; executed some etchings and mezzotints; d. in Rathbone Place; buried at Hendon.

Hone. E. Fisher, mez.
J. C. Smith, 30, 2nd state; cut. E. 1272.-'86.

HOOD, ALEXANDER. See BRIDPORT AND COMMEMORA-TION (1).

HOOD, SAMUEL, 1st Viscount, 1724–1816, Admiral; b. at But-leigh, Somersets.; son of Rev. Samuel Hood, and elder brother of Lord Bridport; ent. Navy.; disting. in Seven Years' War against the French; Bart., 1778; raised to Irish Peerage, 1782, for his services against De Grasse in W. Indies; Com.-in-chf. in Mediterranean, took Toulon and reduced Corsica, 1793–'4; cr. Visct. Hood in English Peerage, 1796; Gov. of Greenwich Hospital; d. at Bath.

L. F. Abbott. V. Green, mez.
J. C. Smith, 66, 2nd state, undescribed, before last 20 words of inscription, and with "P" over arms, and "Published by "L. F. Abbott Caroline Street; Bedford Square Decemr. 1st; "1795" at foot. **22028.**

HOOD, SIR SAMUEL, 1762–1814, ent. Navy, at 14; present at Rodney's action, April 12, 1782; in the Mediterranean, in "Juno," and disting. at Toulon and Corsica, 1793–'4; comm. "Zealous" at the Nile, 1798; reduced Tobago and Guiana, 1803; lost an arm, off Rochefort, where he took French frigates, &c., 1806; M.P., Westminster, 1806; served at Copenhagen, 1807; K.B.; Bart., 1809; Vice-Admiral, 1811; Com.-in-chf., E. Indies, d. at Madras.

J. Hoppner, R.A. G. Clint, mez.
Wh. len. to front, looking to left, leaning left hand on the fluke of an anchor; ships at sea, fighting, in distance, on left.
Open letter proof; May 2, 1808.
27 × 16. (25$\frac{3}{4}$ × 15$\frac{3}{8}$). **25783.**

HOOK, THEODORE EDWARD, 1788–1841, novelist and miscel-laneous writer, son of James Hook, composer, was b. in Charlotte Stt., Bedford Square; partially educ. at private schools and at Harrow (for a short time); began to write words for his father's songs at 16; produced a number of farces and

melodramas; practical joker and hoaxer; appointed account-
general and treasurer, Mauritius, 1813; condemned by the
Treasury to refund defalcations, imprisoned, 1823–'5, though
morally guiltless, and his property confiscated; editor of "John
Bull," author of novels, "Sayings and Doings," &c.

  E. N. Eddis delt.   **M. Gauci**, lith.
  Bust, to left, looking to front; coloured vignette.
  (11½ × 11½).   E. 195.–'93.

HOOKER, SIR JOSEPH DALTON, M.D., R.N., K.C.S.I., C.B.,
P.R.S., F.L.S., &c., 1817– ; second and only surviving son
of the late Sir William Jackson Hooker; b. at Halesworth,
Suffolk; educ. at Glasgow; M.D., 1839; accompanied Sir J.
C. Ross in his expedition; went to India, 1847; Assist.-Director,
Kew, 1855; suc. his father as Director, 1865; resigned, 1885;
has written valuable works on botanical subjects.

  F. Stone, A.R.A. (exhibited, 1852).   W. Walker, mez.
  Wh. len. seated, "surrounded by his native (Lepcha)
" collectors, in the Rhododendron region of the Himalayas,
" examining the plants gathered during the day's march." It
was adapted from a water-colour drawing made at Darjeeling
by the late Mr. Tayler, B.C.S.
  Proof before all letters; the later state was " Publish'd, Aug. 1,
1856, by the Engraver."
  Cut.   (22⅜ × 18⅜).   27148.

HOOKER, RICHARD, c. 1554–1600, b. at Heavitree, Exeter; educ.
at Exeter Grammar School, and by the kindness of Bishop
at Exeat Corpus Xti. Coll., Oxf.; B.A., 1574; M.A., 1577,
and a fellow; ordd., c. 1581, and preached at Paul's Cross;
presented to Drayton-Beauchamp, Bucks, 1584; Master of the
Temple, 1585; had a controversy with Travers; Rector of
Boscombe, Wilts, and preb., Salisbury, 1591; presd. to Bishops-
bourne, Kent, 1595, where he died; pubd. " Laws of Ecclesiast.
Polity," &c.

  [Faithorne.]   W. Faithorne.
  Fagan, p. 42.   26658.

HOOKER, SIR WILLIAM JACKSON, 1785–1858, Botanist; b. at
Norwich; made extensive travels, collecting plants, 1806–'14;
Reg. Prof. of Botany, Glasgow, 1820; Knt., 1836; Director of
Kew Gardens, 1841; ed. " Botanical Miscellany," and " Journal
of Botany;" pub. " Tour in Iceland," " Flora Scotica," &c.; d.
at Kew.

  [Maguire.]   T. H. Maguire, lith., 1851.
  Ha. len. to right, seated, with left elbow and arm resting on
a table; coat fastened by 3 buttons; rectil., with angles cut off,
vignette; facs. signature below.
  (10 × 9½).   22513.

HOOPER, JOHN, 1495–1555, Bishop of Gloucester. See " MAR-
TYRS, PROTESTANT," and " REFORMERS."

HOOPER, Robert, 1773–1835, medical writer; educ. at Pembr. Coll., Oxf.; B.A., 1803; M.A., and M.B., 1804; M.D., St. Andrews, 1805; L.R.C.P., 1805; lectured on medicine for many years; wrote a number of valuable works.
See MEDICAL SOCIETY.

HOPE, The Hon. Sir Alexander, 1769–1837, son of the second Earl of Hopetoun; General; Gov. of Tynemouth, Clifford's fort, Edinburgh Castle, and Chelsea Hospital; M.P., Dumfries, &c.; G.C.B.; D.C.L. Oxon.; d. at Chelsea.
Sir T. Lawrence, 1810.   W. Walker, stipple, 1825.
Ha. len. to right, looking to front; in uniform.
Open letter proof.
15 × 11½.   (8¼ × 6⅛).   27531.

HOPE, Henry, 1736–1811, merchant, b. at Boston; joined his uncles, great merchants in Amsterdam, 1760; became head of the firm, on death of Adrian Hope, 1780; settled in Harley Stt., London, 1794; d. there, leaving a fine collection of pictures, and bequeathing more than a million sterling, chiefly to his niece's husband, his successor in business, John Williams Hope.
Sir J. Reynolds.   C. H. Hodges, mez.
J. C. Smith, 17, 2nd state.   28256.

HOPE, Sir William Johnstone, 1766–1831, b. at Finchley; ent. Navy, 1777; lieut., 1782; with Nelson, on board the "Boreas," 1787; commanded "Bellerophon," June 1, 1794, in Howe's victory off Ushant; Commander-in-chf. at Leith; Rear-Admiral; K.C.B.; Vice-Admiral; Lord of Admiralty; treasurer of Greenwich Hosp.; M.P., Dumfries.
See COMMEMORATION (1).

HOPPNER, John, 1758–1810; portrait-painter, b. at White-chapel, of German parents; began as a chorister in the Chapel Royal; admitted as a student in R. A., 1775; gained gold medal, 1782; attained high rank in his profession; A.R.A., 1793; R.A., 1795; became most successful and celebrated; fell into chronic ill-health and irritability; published "Oriental Tales translated into English Verse," 1810.
J. Hoppner, R.A.   C. Turner, mez.
Sh. ha. len. to right, looking to front, coat buttoned across chest.
Open letter proof.
The picture is in the Council Room of the Royal Academy.
13¼(?) × 9⅞.   (11¾ × 9⅝).   21892.

J. Hoppner. (J. Wright delt.)   H. Meyer, stipple.
Sh. ha. len. to right, looking to front, coat buttoned across chest; vignette; June 4, 1812.
14¾ × 12¾.   (7 × 6¼).   E. 2001.–'89.

Sir J Reynolds.   J. Posselwhite, stipple.

Sh. ha. len. to left, looking to front, hair curling at ends; high-collared coat; vignette.

Ind. proof, with artists' names only.

$6\frac{9}{16} \times 5\frac{1}{4}$. $(4\frac{1}{2} \times 2\frac{1}{4})$.   E. 2002.–'89.

HORNER, FRANCIS, 1778–1817, b. at Edinburgh; educ. there, at High School and University; Barrister, littérateur, became eminent political leader; settled in London, 1803; friend of Brougham, Mackintosh, Romilly; M.P.; Chairman of Bullion Committee, 1810; visited Italy, 1814; d. at Pisa.

H. Raeburn, R.A.   S. W. Reynolds, mez., 1818.

T. Q. len. seated, to left, looking to front, right hand resting on an open book on a table.

$15\frac{7}{8} \times 11\frac{13}{16}$. $(14\frac{1}{4} \times 11\frac{1}{4})$.   22029.

HORSLEY, SAMUEL, 1733–1806, mathematician and eloquent preacher; sec. to the Royal Society, 1773; edit. the works of Sir I. Newton; Bishop of St. David's, 1788; of Rochester, 1793; of St. Asaph, 1802.

J. Green.   H. Meyer, mez.

T. Q. len. to left, seated, looking to front, wearing wig and robes, holding book in right hand; the star of the Bath is on his gown.

Open letter proof; July 24, 1813.

$19\frac{3}{4} \times 13\frac{7}{8}$. $(16\frac{3}{4} \times 13\frac{3}{4})$.   22027.

HOWARD OF EFFINGHAM, CHARLES, Lord, 1536–1624, grandson of Thomas, 2nd Duke of Norfolk; ent. army early; disting. in suppression of the rebellion headed by Earls of Northumberland and Westmorland, 1568; Lord High Admiral, 1585; rend. great services in preparation against, and defeating, the Spanish Armada, 1588; took Cadiz, 1596, and destr. Spanish fleet; Lt.-General of England, 1599; suppressed Essex's revolt, and captured him; present at death of Q. Elizabeth; Ambas. to Spain, 1604; retired, 1618; through long career, with unsullied honour, enjoyed the esteem and confidence of his countrymen.

See NAVAL HEROES (I).

HOWARD, EDWARD C.,   –   chemist, contributed papers on "New Fulminating Mercury," 1800, and "Stony and Metalline substances," 1802, to Nicholson's Journal and Philosophical Transactions.

See SCIENCE.

HOWARD, JOHN, 1726–1790, celebrated philanthropist; b. at Hackney; apprent. to a grocer, but gave up trade, owing to weak health; went abroad; returned, he married a widow, who d. three years later; embarked for Lisbon, 1756, after the earthquake; captured and imprisoned by the French; released, retired to New Forest; m. again, 1758; sheriff, 1773; visited gaols in England and abroad; received thanks of

Parliament; visited lazarettos, and pubd. an account of them, 1789; d. of a fever.

[Gillray.] J. Gillray, 1788.
Wh. len., in a prison, bestowing charity on the family of a wounded soldier; a composition of seven figures, of which one is that of the gaoler at the door; one of the children kneels, kissing his left hand; the wife supports the prisoner, on the left; an inscription below in two columns on either side of the title, "The Triumph of Benevolence," and a quotation of three lines of poetry.

(18¼ × 23½). 24229.

HOWARD, ANNABELLA, Lady, 1675–1728, the 4th wife of Sir Robert Howard, the poet and dramatist; her maiden name was Dives; she was a maid of honour; m. after her husband's death (1698) to Dr. Edmund Martin, Canon of Windsor.

Sir G. Kneller. J. Smith, mez. (1697).
J. C. Smith, 136, 2nd state (?). E. 2120.–'89.

HOWDEN, JOHN FRANCIS CRADOCK, Baron, 1759–1839, only son of John Cradock, Archbp. Dublin; entered the army 1777, becoming finally General, 1814; distinguished, and wounded, 1793, at the capture of Martinique; Quarter-Master-Genl., Ireland, 1797; M.P.; G.C.B.; superseded in Portugal by Sir A. Wellesley; Govr. of Cape of Good Hope; cr. Baron, 1819.

Sir T. Lawrence. W. Say, 1805, mez.
T. Q. len. to right, looking to front, left hand on hilt of sword. Lettering cut off at bottom.

(17¾ × 14). 25773.

HOWE, RICHARD, 1726–1799, 4th Visct., 1st Earl; second surviving son of Emanuel, 2nd Visct.; educ. at Eton; ent. Navy at 14; Post Captain, 1745, for his defeat of two French ships bearing assistance to the Young Pretender; suc. his brother, the 3rd Visct., 1758; defeated French squadron and took two ships, 1759; com. the Fleet, and was Commissioner for pacification of America, 1776; successfully engaged French Fleet under D'Estaing off Rhode Island, 1778; relieved Gibraltar, 1782; cr. Earl, 1788; in comd. of Chan. Fleet, gained the victory of 1st June, 1794, over the French; sup. Mutiny of Nore, 1797; K.G.; called "Black Dick" by sailors.

J. S. Copley, R.A. R. Dunkarton, mez.
J. C. Smith, 26. 27218.

See also TRIUMPH OF BRITANNIA, and COMMEMORATION (1).

HOWLEY, WILLIAM, 1766–1848, b. at Ropley, Hants; educ. at Winchester, and New Coll., Oxf.; B.A., 1787; M.A., 1791; B.D. and D.D., 1805; tutor to the Pr. of Orange, afterwards William II. (of Holland), at Oxford; fellow, Winchester Coll., and Canon of Ch. Ch., 1804; Reg. Prof.; vicar

of Bishop's Sutton, 1796; Andover, 1802; Rector, Bradford
Peverell, 1811; P.C., 1813, and Bishop of London; Archbp.
Canterbury, 1828; supported the bill of pains, &c. against
Q. Caroline; opposed Cath. Emancipation, Reform and Educa-
tion Bills, &c.

Sir T. Lawrence, R.A.   C. Turner, mez.

As Bishop of London; t. q. len. seated, slightly turned to
right, looking to left, in robes.

Open letter proof.

Cut. $(18 \times 14\frac{1}{16})$.   22990.

See also VICTORIA, Coronation, Sacrament, and Marriage
of Queen; and VICTORIA, PRINCESS ROYAL, Christening of.

HUDDART, CAPTAIN JOSEPH, 1741–1816, hydrographer and
manufacturer; b. at Allonby, Cumb.; son of a shoemaker and
farmer; educ. at Allonby in the parish school; showed aptitude
for mathematics and mechanics; went to sea; stud. navigation
and survey of ports; app. to command E. I. C. ship "Royal
Admiral," 1778; made 4 voyages to the East; retired, 1788;
elder brother of Trin. House, and F.R.S., 1791; manufactured
cordage, by which he made a fortune.

See SCIENCE.

HUDSON, GEORGE, the "Railway King," c. 1800–1871, b. at
York, of which city he was thrice elected Lord Mayor; made
a large fortune by successful R'way speculations, particularly
during the R'way mania, 1845–'6; M.P., Sunderland, as a
Conservative, 1845–'59, but rejected at the latter date, his
great fortune and reputation as a R'way oracle having melted
away.

F. Grant, A.R.A.   G. R. Ward, mez.

Wh. len. to front, holding a roll of paper in right hand; left
hand on hip; a chair behind him, on left; on right a table
with books and papers, and two pillars in background; July 25,
1848.

Ind. proof (or "First Class Print").

$29\frac{1}{2} \times 18\frac{3}{4}$. (25×16).   27079.

HUDSON, JEFFREY, 1619–1682, celebrated dwarf, b. at Oke-
ham, Rutlandshire; taken into the service of the Duchess of
Buckingham, at Burleigh, between the ages of 7 and 8; served
up in a cold pie, at an entertainment given to Charles I. and
his Queen; sent to France, 1630, and taken prisoner by a
Flemish pirate; Capt. of Horse in Civil Wars; fought a duel
on horseback with Mr. Crofts, whom he killed; made captive
again at sea by a Turkish rover, and carried into slavery;
redeemed, and settled in his native place for a time; committed
to Gatehouse, 1682, as a Papist; d. there.

Anon. Published by W. Richardson.

Wh. len. to front, slightly inclined to right, looking to front;
a table on the right, balustrade behind, &c.; in a broad, heavy
border.

$7\frac{1}{4} \times 5\frac{5}{8}$. $(1\frac{11}{16} \times 1\frac{1}{4}$, excl. border, $1\frac{7}{16})$.   E. 357.–90.

HUDSON, Jeffrey,—*continued.*
   D. Mytens. (G. P. Harding del.)   J. Stow.
   Wh. len. to right, looking to front; with his dog; a landscape with river, &c. in distance; printed in colours; Decr. 1,
1810.
   10⅝ × 7⅞. (7¼ × 5½).   E. 1202.–'87.

HUGHES, Mrs.
   Sir P. Lely.   Cooper, stipple.
   See LA BELLE ASSEMBLÉE, 1819.   13867. 27.

HULLMANDEL, Charles Joseph, 1789–1850, lithographer,
son of a German musician; b. in London, devoted to art;
travelled abroad, tried lithography, 1818, very successfully;
his instruction was sought by artists and amateurs; made
several inventions in improving the process, including litho-tint
and stump-work on the stone; died in London.
                               G. B. Black, lith
   Ha. len. to front, black neckcloth, white waistcoat; vignette;
facs. subscription and signature below.
   Ind. proof.
   (6¾ × 7).   E. 1995.–'89.

HULME, Nathaniel, 1732–1807, physician, b. at Hulme Thorp,
near Halifax; stud. at Guy's; M.D., Edinb., 1765; physician
to the City of London Lying-in Hosp., before 1772; to the
Charterhouse, 1774; M.R.C.P.; F.R.S., 1794; &c.
   See MEDICAL SOCIETY.

HUME, Joseph, 1777–1855, Politician and Financial Reformer;
b. at Montrose; M.D., Edinb., 1796; Surgeon, Interpreter,
Paymaster, and Postmaster, in India, 1799–1808; M.P. for
Weymouth, Middlesex, and Montrose, 1812–1855; prom.
promoter of Financial and Parliamentary Reform, and of
National Education.
   G. P. A. Healy.   F. Bacon, mixed mez.
   T. Q. len. to front, seated, with left hand on thigh, right
hand hanging over edge of table on which right arm rests; coat
fastened by two buttons; Sepr. 10, 1845.
   20⅞ × 16. (16¾ × 13¼).   22129.

HUMPHRY, Ozias, 1742–1810, miniature-painter, b. at
Honiton; practised at Bath; came, 1764, to London, where he
had unexampled success; went with Romney to Rome, 1773–'7;
to India, 1785–'8; R.A., 1790; failing sight obliged him first
to adopt crayons, with which he soon excelled, and, finally,
c. 1797, to give up practice.
   G. Romney.   V. Green, mez.
   J. C. Smith, 70, undescribed, intermediate state between the
1st and 2nd described by Mr. Smith; with "*Publish'd May
18th 1772, by V. Green,* | *Salisbury Street, Strand,*" scratched
in the middle; but before the addresses of the second state.
                                 24080.

HUMPHRY, Ozias—*continued*.
  G. Romney, 1772.   Caroline Watson, 1784, stipple.
  Ha. len. to left, in profile, holding a book to breast with right hand, a finger between the leaves; wearing a loose gown. From the picture at Knole.
  $7\frac{3}{4} \times 6\frac{1}{2}$. $(5\frac{1}{4} \times 4\frac{6}{16})$.   13881.

  [Moeglich ?]   A. L. Moeglich, stipple.
  Sh. ha. len. to left, in profile, in circular border, the name on a tablet below.
  $8\frac{1}{16} \times 5\frac{1}{4}$. ($3\frac{5}{8}$ diamr.)   25671.   7.

HUNT, Henry, 1773–1835, b. near Upavon, Wilts; educ. at various schools; intended for the Church, preferred farming; friend of Horne Tooke; violent reformer; thrown several times into prison; presided at meeting which led to Peterloo massacre; confined in Ilchester Gaol, 1820, and wrote there his egotistical and wordy memoirs; liberated, 1822; M.P., 1831; lost influence; retired, 1833; devoted himself to manufacture of blacking.
  Hutchisson.   Cooper, stipple.
  As "The Champion of the Radicals;" sh. ha. len. to right, looking to front; vignette.
  $14 \times 11\frac{1}{16}$. $(7\frac{1}{2} \times 7\frac{1}{2})$.   22870.

HUNTER, John, 1728–1793, Comparative Anatomist and distinguished **Surgeon**; youngest son of a farmer, near Glasgow; worked as a cabinet-maker for 3 years; came to London, 1748, as assistant to his brother, Dr. William Hunter; attended Cheselden, at Chelsea Hospital, and Pott, at St. Bartholomew's; House Surgeon at St. George's, 1756; abroad, as Surgeon on the Staff till 1763; devoted himself to anatomy and philosophy of Natural History; formed the collection illustr. of Comp. Anatomy, Coll. Surg.; contributed often to "Philosophical Transactions."
  Sir J. Reynolds.   W. Sharp.
  T. Q. len. to right, looking upwards, seated at table, on which rests left elbow, hand to chin; right hand, over arm of chair, holds a pen; Jany. 1, 1788.
  20×15. $(16\frac{3}{4} \times 13\frac{1}{2})$.   26694.

HUNTINGTON, Rev. William, 1774–1813, "S. S." (Sinner Saved), b. in Kent, Calvinist dissenting preacher; author of "Arminian Skeleton," "Bank of Faith," &c.; minister at Thames Ditton and in London.
  D. Pellegrini, 1803.   J. Godby, stipple.
  T. Q. len. to right, seated at table, looking to front, holding a pen in his right hand; left hand resting on a paper.
  Ind. open letter proof, "Pubd. Novr. 1, 1813, by E. Hunt-"ington, 55 High Street, Bloomsbury."
  Cut. $(18\frac{1}{16} \times 15\frac{1}{16})$.   22992.

HURDIS, Rev. James, D.D., 1763–1801, poet, b. at Bishopstone, Sussex; educ. at Chichester and Oxford; B.A., 1785; curate of Burwash, 6 years; published "Village Curate," 1788, "Adriano," &c.; pres. to living of Bishopstone, 1791; Prof. Poetry, Oxford, 1793; friend of Cowper and Hayley; wrote some poor criticisms on Shakspere and Gibbon.

    Sharples del. 1784.   J. H. Hurdis, etched, &c., 1842.

    Sh. ha. len. to left, in profile, oval in heavy, ornamented border, a shell at top, fruits and foliage at sides.

    Ind. proof.

    15 × 12.   (14½ × 11; oval, 8½ × 6¼).   29718. 13.

HUSKISSON, Rt. Hon. William, 1770–1830, Statesman; b. at Birt's Moreton Court, Warwicks.; ent. Parliament as a supporter of Pitt, 1792; Und. Sec. for War, 1795–1801; Sec. to the Treasury, 1804; Pres. Board of Trade, 1822; Colon. Minister, 1827; d. from injuries received at opening of L'pool and Manchester R'way.

    J. Graham (Gilbert, R.S.A.).   W. Ward, mixed mez.

    T. Q. len. to front, looking to left, resting right hand on paper on table, holding a folded paper in left; pillar and curtain behind.

    Scr. letter proof, Aug. 1831.

    (17½½ × 14 $\frac{7}{8}$).   22126.

HUTCHINSON, John, 1615–1664, son of Sir Thomas Hutchinson, Knt.; b. at Owthorpe, Notts.; educ. at Cambr.; M.P. for that town; member of the Court which tried Charles I.; arrested, 1663; d. during imprisonment in Sandown Castle, 1664; his "Memoirs" were written by his widow, Lucy Hutchinson, dau. of Sir Allen Apsley, Lieut. of the Tower.

    Anon.   I. Neagle.

    T. Q. len. to right, pointing to right with right hand, looking to front, in armour; a page, on left, carries his helmet; arms below; Sepr. 1, 1806.

    12¼ × 9½. (8½ × 6½).   22871.

HUTCHINSON, Rt. Hon. John Hely, 1715–1794, son of Francis Hely; went to the Bar; M.P.; m. (1751) Christiana Nickson, niece and heiress of R. Hutchinson, whose name he assumed; Prime Serjt., 1762; Provost, 1774; Sec. 1777; d. in Dublin.

    Sir J. Reynolds.   J. Watson, mez.

    J. C. Smith, 79, 2nd state.   24629.

HUTT, Captain John, 1746–1794, lieut., R.N., 1780; served in W. Indies; made prisoner, and exchanged; app. to command of several ships; commanded the "Queen," June 1, 1794, in Howe's victory off Ushant, when he received the wound from the effects of which he died.

    See COMMEMORATION (1).

IBBETSON, Julius Cæsar, 1759–1817, landscape and figure-painter; b. at Scarborough; educ. at first by the Moravians, aftds. at a Quaker school at Leeds; apprent. to a ship-painter; came to London, 1777, without money or friends; exhibited at the R.A., 1785; befriended by Capt. Baillie; went to China with Col. Cathcart, 1788, but returned immediately; boon companion of Morland; in difficulties, went to Liverpool; returned to London, 1800; retired to Masham, Yorks., where he died; pubd. "An Accidence or Gamut of Painting," 1803.

 J. R. Smith.   R. Cooper.
 Sh. ha. len. to right, seated, looking to front; right hand hanging over chair-back, holding a crayon.
 $9\frac{7}{8} \times 7\frac{3}{8}$. $(4\frac{1}{10} \times 3\frac{1}{4})$.   27219.

IDDESLEIGH, Rt. Hon. Sir Stafford Henry Northcote, 1st Earl of, 1818–1887; M.P.; Pres., Board of Trade, 1866–'7; Sec. for India, 1867–'8; Chanc. of Exchequer, 1874–'80; First Lord of Treasury, 1885; suc. as 8th Bart., 1851; cr. Earl, 1885; Foreign Sec., 1886; G.C.B., P.C., &c.
 See DERBY CABINET.

INGLIS, Sir Robert Harry, 1786–1855, educ. at Winchester, and Ch. Ch., Oxf.; M.P. for Dundalk, 1820–'6, aftds. for Ripon, and Oxford, where he ousted Sir R. Peel; opposed all the Liberal Reforms; F.R.S., etc.

                 Anon., mez.
 Wh. len. in gown, to left, with right hand raised, as if speaking.
 Ind. proof before all letters.
 $25\frac{7}{8} \times 18\frac{1}{4}$. $(23\frac{7}{8} \times 15\frac{1}{2})$.   24741.

INSTALLATION of Knights of the Order of Saint Patrick.
 See ST. PATRICK.

IRETON, Henry, 1610–1651, General and Statesman of the Commonwealth; b. at Attenborough, Notts.; educ. at Oxf. and the Middle Temple; joined the Parl. Army at the outbreak of the Civil War; mar. Bridget Cromwell, dau. of the Protector; sat as one of the judges on the trial of Charles I.; Lord Deputy of Ireland, 1650; d. of the plague, before Limerick.

 Cooper.   J. Houbraken, 1741.
 Sh. ha. len. to left, looking to front, in armour; oval in border; in Birch's "Lives."
 $14\frac{3}{4} \times 9\frac{5}{16}$. $(14 \times 8\frac{3}{4})$.   21814.

IRVING, Edward, 1792–1834, b. at Annan; graduated at Edinb., 1809; master of the "Mathematical School" at Haddington, 1810; of the academy at Kirkcaldy, 1812; obtained license to preach, 1812; went to Edinb., 1818; came to London, 1822; preached in Hatton Garden; became famous at once; preached in Regent Square; the "unknown tongues" heard, 1830; founded the "Holy Catholic Apostolic Church;" deprived, 1833.

 A. Robertson.   H. Meyer, stipple.
 Ha. len. to front, looking to right, in the pulpit.
 Ind. proof, with open letters; August 27, 1823.
 $13\frac{1}{2} \times 11\frac{5}{8}$. $(11\frac{9}{16} \times 8\frac{13}{16})$.   22995.

IRVING, Washington, 1783–1859, son of a Scotch father and English mother, b. at New York; a very distinguished author; wrote the famous "History of New York, by D. Knickerbocker," 1809; "Sketch-book," 1819; "Bracebridge Hall," "Tales of a Traveller," "Life of Columbus," "Conquest of Granada," &c.

W. A. (Washington Allston?), etched.

Wh. len. to left, seated on a bank, wearing a white hat with a black band; his left leg crossed over his right knee; a dog is sitting by him, on the right; vignette.

Facs. signature below

(4¼ × 3½).   25226.

JACKSON, Cyril, 1746–1819, educ. at Halifax, Manchester, Westminster, and Ch. Ch., Oxf.; B.A., 1768; M.A., 1771; B.D., 1777; D.D., 1781; sub-preceptor to the two eldest sons of George III.; ordd., preacher at Linc. Inn, 1779–'83; canon of Ch. Ch., Oxf., and Dean, 1783; rector of Kirkby in Cleveland, and preb., Southwell, 1786.

From the statue by Chantrey.   Freebairn.

Wh. len. seated, towards right, on a high pedestal; the statue is in the north transept, Ch. Ch. Cath., Oxf.

Ind. proof.

21⅞ × 16.   (17 × 7).   E. 282.–'87.

JACKSON, John, 1744–1821, village tailor at Lastingham, in the North Riding of Yorks.; father of John Jackson, R.A., whom he most reluctantly permitted to desert his trade for **Art.**

J. Jackson, R.A.   J. Posselwhite, stipple.

Bust, to front, looking to right; the shoulders and chest, &c., sketched only in line; "ÆT. 78, 1821;" vignette; a private plate.

Ind. proof with open letters.

9¼ × 6¼.   (4⅜ × 5⅜).   18108.

JACKSON, John, 1769–1845, pugilist, known as "Gentleman Jackson," son of a London builder; b. in London; appeared only thrice in the prize-ring, June 9, 1788, against Fewterel of Birmingham, whom he defeated; March 12, 1789, against George (Ingleston), by whom he was defeated, owing to an accident; April 15, 1795, against Mendoza, whom he beat in 10½ minutes; establ. a school of boxing; landlord of the "Sun and Punch Bowl," Holborn, and of the "Cock" at Sutton; Byron was one of his pupils, had a great regard for him, and twice alludes to him in his notes to his poems, as well as in "Hints from Horace;" bur. in Brompton Cemetery.

B. Marshall.   C. Turner, mez.

Wh. len. to front, holding in right hand his hat which he places on pedestal of the statue of "The Boxer;" a picture of two men fighting in background; May 19, 1810.

25½ × 17¾.   (22⅞ × 17¼).   22031.

JACKSON, John, 1778–1831, portrait-painter, son of the village tailor at Lastingham, Yorks.; apprent. to his father; showed

early talent for drawing; released by the kindness of friends,
and assisted by Sir George Beaumont to study at the R. A.;
A.R.A., 1815; travelled and stud. abroad; R.A., 1817; visited
North Italy, 1818; member of Acad. of S. Luke; exhibited at
the R. Academy, chiefly portraits, till 1830; married twice;
died poor, in St. John's Wood, leaving no provision for his
family.

    J. Jackson.   C. Thompson, stipple.

    Ha. len. to left, looking to front, holding palette and brushes;
facs. signature below; vignette.

    Cut. $(5\frac{1}{4} \times 4\frac{1}{8})$.   28300.   33.

JACKSON, JOHN—*continued*.

    J. Jackson, R.A.   W. Ward, mez.

    Ha. len. to left, looking to front, holding palette and brushes
in left hand.

    Open letter proof, May 21, 1832.

    $13\frac{1}{2} \times 10$. (10×8).   22996.

JACKSON, JOSEPH DEVONSHER, 1783–1857, of Trin. Coll.
Camb.; M.P., Bandon, and Dublin Univy.; King's Sergeant,
and Solr. and Atty.-Gen. in Ireland; one of the Justices of Com.
Pleas, Ireland.

    G. Richmond.   J. Brown, stipple.

    Ha. len. to front, slightly inclined to left, seated, looking
to right; left hand, gloved, resting on papers.

    Ind. proof with skeleton letters; 1837.

    $13\frac{7}{8} \times 10\frac{1}{4}$. $(8\frac{3}{4} \times 7)$.   20632.

JACKSON, WILLIAM, "of Exeter," 1730–1803, son of a grocer
in that city, pupil of John Silvester, organist of Exeter Cathedral,
and (1748) of John Travers, in London; pubd. songs, 1755,
which became popular immediately, "Sonatas," "Elegies," and
many other works, now forgotten, except his service in F.;
painted landscapes in the style of his friend, Gainsborough,
with much skill; d. of dropsy.

    Anon.   Anon., mez.

    J. C. Smith, 94, p. 1735.   27594.

JACOB, JOHN, 1813–1858, Indian General; b. at Woolavington,
Somerset; educ. at home, and at Addiscombe; ent. E. I. C.
Service, 1828; organised Sind Cavalry; won great fame at
Meanee, Dubba, &c.; tardily promoted; C.B., 1843; com. in
Upper Sind; Lt.-Col., 1855; A.D.C. to the Queen, 1857, and
Col.; d. at Jacobabad.

    Anon.   Anon., mez.

    Ha. len. standing, to left, in undress uniform, right arm
resting on high piece of furniture.

    Ind. proof before all letters.

    $20\frac{3}{4} \times 16\frac{1}{4}$. $(16\frac{3}{16} \times 12\frac{1}{2})$.   27268.

JAMES IV. (of Scotland), 1473–1513, suc. 1488.

    Anon.   Anon.

259

Ha. len. to left, in oval, holding a thistle.
Cut. (6 × 4¾). 25020.
In Genealogical Chart, 553. 1.

JAMES V. (of Scotland), 1512–1542, suc. 1513.
Anon. Anon.
Ha. len. to right, with fingers of right hand to the jewel which
hangs from his collar of the Order of the Thistle; in oval.
6⁹⁄₁₆ × 5½. (6 × 4¾). 25022.
In Genealogical Chart, 553. 1.

JAMES VI. OF SCOTLAND (I. of England), 1566–1625, only son
of Henry Stuart, Earl of Darnley, and Mary Queen of Scots;
b. in Edinb. Castle; crowned, when a child, as James VI. of
Scotland; suc. to English throne, 1603.
Licinio Veneziano. G. Vertue.
As a child; with Matthew, Earl of Lennox (1526, ob.
1571); Margaret Douglas, Countess of Lennox, wife of Matthew
(ob. 1578); and Charles Stuart, Earl of Lennox (a boy), 1555–
1576, all kneeling before the cenotaph of Henry Stuart, Lord
Darnley.
Cut. (16⅝ × 21₇⁄₁₆). 23140.

Anon. Vaughan.
Ha. len. with crown, sceptre, and orb.
Above, "BEATI PACIFICI." 4 English verses below.
6₁₀⁄₁₆ × 4⅜. (5⅞ × 4). 26517.

Anon. Anon.
Ha. len. in oval, to front. Under, "Jacobus VI. Scotorum."
Cut. (6 × 4¾). 25023.
In Genealogical Chart, 553. 1.

Anon. Anon.
In an oval, within a rectangular border. Below, "Jacobus I.
König van Engelland." A German print. Printed in a passe-
partout.
10¾ × 6⅝. (The inner plate, 6₁₁⁄₁₆ × 4₉⁄₁₆). E. 102.–'91.

—— with his Queen and Prince Henry.
[S. de Pass.] [S. de Pass.]
A small oval, from a silver plate.
Cut. (2₆⁄₁₆ × 1¾). E. 1453 A.–'85.
With this is an impression of the reverse, bearing the Coats
of the King and Queen and the Prince's Feathers.
Cut. (2₇⁄₁₆ × 1₁₆⁄₁₆). E. 1453 B.–'85.

Van Dyck. J. Smith, mez., 1721.
J. C. Smith, 139, 2nd state. 22244.

R 2

JAMES I.—*continued.*

[F. Delaram.]   C. Turner, mez.
On horseback, to left; a view of London in background;
from an extremely rare print by Delaram.
Proof before all letters.
$13\frac{3}{8} \times 10\frac{1}{2}$. $(11\frac{1}{4} \times 8\frac{7}{8})$.   22515.

—— with his family and Frederick, King of Bohemia, also with
his family.
[W. de Pass.]   C. Turner.
The king is sitting on the throne, in the centre, surrounded
by the other personages represented, of whom two (princesses,
deceased) sit on the steps of the throne, having skulls in their
laps, palm branches in their hands, and crowns on their heads;
from a rare print by William de Pass.
Proof before all letters, except Woodburn's publication-line,
Aug. 4, 1813.
$13\frac{3}{8} \times 17\frac{1}{4}$ $(10\frac{3}{8} \times 14\frac{7}{8})$.   22514.

JAMES II., second son of Charles I.; 1633–1701; commanded
English Fleet in the war with the Dutch; suc. his brother,
Charles II., 1685; endeavoured to restore the Rom. Cath
religion; compelled to abdicate, 1688; fled to France; assisted
by Louis XIV., made unsuccessful attempt to recover Ireland,
1689–'90; d. at St. Germans.
Anon. [Giffart ?].   P. Giffart.
Sh. ha. len in armour, with long wig, turned slightly to left,
facing towards right, looking to front, wearing the George,
oval in border.
$26\frac{1}{8} \times 19\frac{1}{4}$. $(25\frac{3}{4} \times 19$; oval, $19\frac{3}{8} \times 16\frac{5}{8})$.   23784.

———

Sir G. Kneller.   R. White, 1685.
"Sold by R. White in Bloomsbury Market | Neare the
Golden Heart, 1685."
Oval; in armour, with long wig.
Cut. $(18\frac{5}{16} \times 13\frac{7}{8})$.   24681.
See also CHARLES, PRINCE OF WALES, &c.

JAMES FRANCIS EDWARD, Prince, 1688–1766, eldest son of
James II.; known as the "Chevalier St. George," or "The
Old Pretender;" father of "The Young Pretender."
A. S. Belle.   F. Chéreau, Senior.
In an oval; wearing a wig, armour, and scarf.
$15\frac{7}{8} \times 10\frac{11}{16}$. $(14\frac{7}{16} \times 10\frac{5}{16})$.   26695.

———

De Troy.   Edelinck.
Ha. len. in an oval, in armour, to left, looking to right.
R. D. 211, 2nd state.
Cut. $(19\frac{1}{4} \times 17\frac{1}{2}$ (?)).   25785.

—— with his Sister, Loui-a Maria.
N. de Largillière.   J. Smith, mez.
J. C. Smith, 247, 3rd state, retouched.   22282.

JAMES, W. M. *See* GREEN (2).

JAMESON, ANNA BROWNELL, 1794–1860, authoress, b. at
Dublin, eldest daughter of D. Brownell Murphy, a miniature-
painter of talent; came to England, 1798, and became go-
verness in the family of the Marquis of Winchester for 4 years,
and elsewhere; wrote "A Lady's Diary," published as "The
Diary of an Ennuyée, 1826; married Robert Jameson, a barrister, 1825; wrote "Loves of the Poets," "Celebrated Female
Sovereigns," the accompanying memoirs to "The Beauties of
the Court of Charles II.," "Sacred and Legendary Art,"
"Legends of the Saints," "Legends of the Madonna," &c.

    H. P. Briggs, R.A.   R. J. Lane, A.R.A., lith.

    Ha. len. seated, turned and looking to right, holding a
handkerchief in her raised right hand, the right elbow resting
on the arm of her chair; vignette.

    Ind. proof.

    (9¼ × 10).   E. 1280.–'86.

JAMESON, GEORGE, 1586–1644, portrait-painter, "the Scotch
Van Dyck;" b. at Aberdeen, son of an architect and member
of the guild; stud., with Van Dyck, under Rubens; returned to
Aberdeen, 1620; married there, 1624; lived in Edinburgh,
c. 1630–'44; painted portraits, some historical subjects and
landscapes, also some miniatures; painted Charles I., 1633, at
Edinburgh.

    G. Jameson, 1623.   A. Jameson, 1728, etched.

    Ha. len. to right, looking to front, standing on the left, behind
his wife; his young son is on the right; the painter holds a
palette and brushes.

    The picture is at Cullen-house (Lord Finlater's).

    The etcher of this plate was Alexander, the great-grandson
of the painter.

    8½ × 6⅗.   (7¾ × 6¹⁄₁₆).   24081.

JANE SEYMOUR, 1509(?)–1537; Queen of Henry VIII.,
1536.

    [Holbein.]   Anon.

    Sh. ha. len. to left, with two necklaces and a jewel.

    In Birch's "Lives;" ascribed by Bromley to Houbraken, by
whom it was certainly not engraved.

    14½ (nearly) × 8⅝.   (14 × 8½).   27280.

———

    Holbein.   R. Cooper.

    Ha. len. to left, her left hand lying in her right.

    The picture is in the Collection of . . the Duke of Bedford.

    Published Jan. 1, 1823, by Harding, Mavor, and Lepard.

    Cut.   (4⅛ × 3¼).   14164.

JARDINE, SIR WILLIAM, Bart., 1800–1874, Naturalist; b. in
North Hanover Street, Edinb.; educ. at Edinb. Univ.; became
a good botanist and geologist; particularly disting. for his
knowledge of animals, especially birds; made his museum, at

Jardine Hall, one of the finest private collections in the
country; suc. his father in title, 1821 ; pubd. "Contributions to
Ornithology," &c.; ed. "Naturalist's Library."

Maguire. T. H. Maguire, lith., 1849.
Full ha. len. to front, looking to left, wearing a plaid waistcoat; left hand on hip; rectilin. with corners cut off; facs.
signature below.
(10¼ × 9¼). 27168.

JARRETT, −1886, horn-player. *See* MUSICAL UNION.

JAY, WILLIAM, 1769–1853, dissenting minister, son of a stone-
cutter and mason; b. at Tisbury, Wiltshire; educ. at Marlborough, under Cornelius Winter; began preaching at the age
of 16; preached at Surrey Chapel, 1788; ministered at various
places until 1791, when he was ordd. pastor at Bath; styled by
Sheridan the most natural orator he ever heard.

T. Langdon. T. Overton.
Sh. ha. len. to left, looking to front, in gown; vignette.
Ind. proof; April 1, 1817.
14 × 11½. (6¼ × 7½). 23155.

JEFFREY, FRANCIS, Lord, 1773–1850, Lawyer and writer; b.
at Edinburgh; educ. at High School and Glasgow Univ.;
called to Scotch bar, 1794; took part in founding "Edinburgh
Review," of which he was editor, 1802–'29; Lord Advocate,
1830; M.P., Edinburgh, 1832; raised to Scotch Bench, 1834.

Sir G. Hayter. E. Coombes, aquatint and mez.
Ha. len. to right, in profile, seated; the body in outline, with
aquatint ground, over which the engraver has worked on the
face, collar of coat, and other parts, in mezzotint, accentuated
with a few touches of the needle, here and there.

Proof, with facs. signature.
11½ × 9¼. (8⅝ × 7⁷⁄₁₆). 22128.
See also SCOTT, SIR WALTER.

JEFFREYS, GEORGE JEFFREYS, Lord, c. 1640–1689; judge; as
Ch. Justice of King's Bench, held the "bloody assize" after
the defeat of Monmouth's rebellion, 1685; Lord Chanc. and
cr. a peer, 1685; sent to the Tower, 1688, where he died.

Sir G. Kneller. R. White.
Sh. ha. len. to right, looking to front, in robes; oval, in
border, the mace and bag below.
Cut. (14¹⁄₁₀ × 10⅜). 27538.

JEKYLL, SIR JOSEPH, 1664–1738, lawyer; Master of the Rolls,
1717–'38; published "Judicial Authority of the Master of the
Rolls;" M.P., one of the managers of Sacheverell's trial.

M. Dahl. G. Vertue.
Sh. ha. len. to right, looking to front, in robes; arms below;
oval, in border.
Cut. (13¾ × 10). 24718.
See also COMMONS.

JEKYLL, Joseph, 1753–1837; celebrated wit, politician, and lawyer, one of the Masters of the High Court of Chancery; F.R.S., F.S.A.; M.P. for Calne, 1787–1816.

  Sir T. Lawrence, R.A.   W. Say, mez.

  Ha. len. to left, looking to front; a drapery behind. Jany. 1, 1818.

  $13\frac{3}{4} \times 9\frac{7}{8}$. $(12\frac{1}{4} \times 9\frac{13}{10})$.   22023.

JENNER, Edward, 1749–1823, b. at Berkeley, Gloucestershire; stud. in London under John Hunter; settled at Berkeley as a Med. Practitioner; investigated the relation of cow-pox and small-pox, until 1796; gained great honours and rewards for his discovery of vaccination, one of the most valuable blessings ever conferred on humanity; M.D.; F.R.S.; &c.

  J. Northcote.   W. Say, mez.

  T. Q. len. to right, seated, looking to left, turning the leaves of an open book on table with right hand; right leg crossed over left; Aug. 20, 1804.

  17×12. $(15\frac{1}{2} \times 12)$.   27267.

  See also MEDICAL SOCIETY, and SCIENCE.

JENNER, Sir Herbert, 1777–1852, judge; made Dean of the Arches, and judge of the Prerogative Court of Canterbury, 1834; took the additional name of FUST, 1842.

  F. Y. Hurlstone.   W. Walker, mez.

  T. Q. len. seated, to front, looking slightly to right. Private plate, April, 1835.

  $16\frac{3}{16} \times 12\frac{1}{4}$. $(11\frac{3}{4} \times 9\frac{7}{16})$.   24620.

JENYNS, Soame, 1704–1787, miscellaneous writer, son of Sir Roger Jenyns, Kt. of Bottisham Hall, Cambridge; b. in London; educ. at St. John's Coll., Cambr.; left, without degree, 1725; pubd. "Art of Dancing," poem, 1727, and "Poems," 1752, collected; M.P., 1742–1780; wrote "Free Inquiry into the Nature and Origin of Evil," 1757; "View of the Internal Evidence of the Christian Religion," 1776; tenth edn., 1798; "Disquisitions," 1782; &c.

  Sir J. Reynolds.   W. Dickinson, 1776, mez.

  J. C. Smith, 40.

  Walpole (Cor. VI., p. 477) calls the picture, from which this print is copied, a "proof of Sir Joshua's art, who could "give a strong resemblance of so uncouth a countenance without "leaving it disagreeable."   27266.

JERROLD, Douglas, 1803–1857, Humorist and Dramatist; became known by his "Black-eyed Susan," "Rent Day," and other popular plays; contrib. humorous tales to "Blackwood" and "Punch;" founded "Jerrold's Shilling Magazine" and "Lloyd's Weekly Newspaper."

  K. Meadows delt.   H. Robinson, stipple, 1815.

  Ha. len. to left, seated, looking to front, eye-glasses hanging by ribbon; vignette, June 8, 1846.

  $20\frac{1}{2} \times 15\frac{1}{2}$. $(9\frac{1}{2} \times 9\frac{1}{4})$.   21962.

JERVIS, John. *See* COMMEMORATION (2) and SAINT-VINCENT

JERVIS, Sir John, 1802–1856, lawyer; Atty.-gen., 1846-'50;
Ch. Justice of Common Pleas, 1850.
    H. Weigall.   S. Shury, mixed mez.
    T. Q. len. to left, seated, looking to front, in robes, his right
holding a paper and resting on a table.
    Open letter proof, Feb. 4, 1857.
    21×16. $(16\frac{1}{8} \times 13\frac{1}{4})$.   22997

JESSOP, William, author of "Letters on an improvement in
process of blasting rocks with gunpowder" (Nic. Journal, ix.,
1804, and Gilbert's Annal. xxii., 1806), and of "Blasting of
Rocks" (Quarterly Journal Sci. xxl., 1826).
    See SCIENCE.

JOHN, "Lackland," King of England, 1160–1216, suc. 1199.
    From his monument at Worcester.   G. Vertue.
    Ha. len. to right, looking to front, crowned.
    $11\frac{3}{8} \times 7\frac{6}{10}$. $(11\frac{1}{10} \times 7\frac{3}{10})$.   27178.   9.

JOHNSON, James, 1777–1845, physician, b. at Ballinderry;
educ. in his native parish, and apprent. (1792) to a surg.-
apothecary at Port Glenone, Antrim, for 2 years; 2 more at
Belfast; then to London, without money or friends, but passed
very well at Surgeons' Hall, 1798; served in navy; went in
expedition to Egypt; returned invalided; served in North Sea,
and in the East, till 1806; at Walcheren, 1809; surg.-in-
ordinary to the Duke of Clarence, and physician extraordinary
to him when King, 1830; published several works on medical
subjects, &c.
    J. Wood.   G. H. Phillips, mixed mez.
    T. Q. len. to front, seated, with pencil in right, and left hand
holding an open book on table.
    Open letter proof, July, 1835.
    Cut. $(16\frac{7}{8} \times 13\frac{3}{4})$.   22695.

JOHNSON. Samuel, 1709–1784, lexicographer, son of Michael
Johnson, bookseller at Lichfield; educ. at Lichfield and Stour-
bridge; precocious, indolent at games, immoderately fond of
old romances; sent to Pembr. Coll., Oxf., 1728-'9, and resided
occasionally till 1731; endured hard struggles with poverty;
married Mrs. Porter, 1735; tried school-keeping; came to
London, 1737, with Garrick; wrote "Irene;" contributed to the
"Gentleman's Magazine;" wrote "Parliamentary Debates,"
1741-'4; "London," 1738; "Life of Savage," 1744, "Dictionary," 1747-'55; "Vanity of Human Wishes," "Rambler,"
&c.; LL.D. of Dublin and Oxford.
    Sir J. Reynolds.   J. Watson, mez.
    J. C. Smith, 82, 2nd state; the address cut off; modern.
                                  E. 1648.-'89.

    J. Barry, R.A.   A. Smith, A.R.A.
    Bust to right, looking to front; vignette.
    Open letter proof, March 1, 1808.
    $13 \times 10\frac{7}{10}$. (7×6).   22872.

JOHNSTONE, John Henry, 1751–1829, comedian; b. at
Tipperary, enlisted; but advised by his Colonel, who heard him
sing, to go upon the stage, where he met with great success;
appeared in London, 1783; on his voice beginning to fail,
became an admirable performer of Irish characters; d. in
Tavistock-row, Cov. Garden, leaving considerable property to
the children of his daughter, Mrs. Wallack.

De Wilde.   Anon., stipple.
  Wh. len. to front, looking to left, " in the character of Tully
" in O'Keef's comedy of The London Hermit, or Rambles in
" Dorsetshire "; Oct. 21, 1816.
  $17\frac{1}{2} \times 13\frac{1}{4}$. $(15\frac{8}{16} \times 11\frac{11}{16})$.   22873.

JONES, Inigo, c. 1572–1651, b. in London, apprenticed to a
joiner, early distinguished for skill in landscape and designs; stud.
at Rome and Venice; employed at Copenhagen by K. Christian
IV.; returned to England, c. 1606; surveyor-general in reversion, and architect to the Queen and Prince Henry; made
scenery and machinery for Court Masques; returned to Italy
for some years; built the Banqueting House in Whitehall,
1619; built many additions to St. Paul's, and other works at
Oxford, in London, and elsewhere; made a handsome fortune,
but suffered heavily at the Revolution.

Van Dyck.   R. van Voerst.
  Ha. len. to front, looking to left, holding in left hand a paper.
One of the "Icones Principum," &c., published by Gillis Hen-
driex; Wibiral, 72, 5th state.
  $(9\frac{3}{8} \times 6\frac{1}{4}.)$ 27134.

Van Dyck.   V. Green, mez.
J. C. Smith, 77   E. 2003.–'89.

Van Dyck.   E. Smith.
  Bust, to front, looking to right; wearing cap and broad collar.
March, 1821.
  $7\frac{3}{8} \times 4\frac{3}{8}$. $(2\frac{5}{8} \times 1\frac{7}{8})$.   15214. 1.

JONES, John, c. 1800–1882, b. in Middlesex; apprent. to a tailor;
estab. himself, c. 1825, as a tailor and army clothier, in Waterloo Place; retired, 1850, but retained a share in the business;
lived in chambers till 1865, when he removed to Piccadilly;
formed a magnificent collection of pictures, enamels, miniatures, porcelain, furniture, ivories, &c., which he bequeathed to
the South Kensington Museum.

R. Deighton delin.   J. Brown.
  Wh. len. to left, in profile, holding glass to eye, wearing hat
and overcoat; facs. signature below; vignette.
  Ind. proof.
  9×6. $(5\frac{7}{8} \times 2\frac{1}{2})$.   29390. A.

JONES, John Paul, 1747–1792, b. at Kircudbright; entered
the service of America; displayed much bravery and skill in

descents on various parts of the British coasts; and in his famous
fight with the Serapis, 1779; entered the service of Russia,
1788; d. at Paris.

Anon.   Anon., mez.
J. C. Smith, 97, p. 1735.   27532.

JONES, OWEN, 1809–1874, architect and ornament-designer, b. in
London; educ. at Charterhouse, and at a private school; pupil
of Vulliamy, and stud. at the R.A.; travelled in Europe and the
East, 1830–1836; produced a work on the Alhambra which
occupied him for several years, and involved him in difficulties;
published various works on design and ornament, on which,
especially Eastern, he became an authority.

T. S[cott], monogram.   Anon., woodcut.
Bust to front, looking to left, vignette; oval; from an illustrated paper.
(7 × 6¼).   E. 2004.–'89.

T. S[cott], monogram.   Anon., woodcut.
Bust, to left, wearing spectacles; vignette; circular; from an
illustrated paper.
(3½ × 3¾).   E. 2005.–'89.

JONSON, BENJAMIN, c. 1573–1637, b. in Westminster (?), of
the family of the Johnstons of Annandale; educ. at Westminster; set to bricklayer's work; escaped to Flanders, where
he killed one of the enemy in single fight; returned, married,
1592, and began to write for the stage, 1595; friend of Drummond of Hawthornden and of W. Shakspere, who acted in
"Every Man in his humour," 1598; wrote many successful
plays, masques, &c.

G. Honthorst.   G. Vertue.
Sh. ha. len. to front, cloak over right shoulder; name and
wreath above; oval in border; four verses below, followed by
dedication, 1730, and artists' names.
14¼ × 9⅝. (13¾ × 9¼).   27865. 2.

"From an original picture."   W. C. Edwards.
Sh. ha. len. to right, looking to front.
Open letter proof.
9 × 6⅟₁₆. (5⅝ × 4⅓).   E. 18.–'94.

JORDAN, DOROTHEA, or DOROTHY, BLAND, commonly known
as Mrs. Jordan (an assumed name), c. 1762–1816, popular and
charming actress; mistress of the Duke of Clarence, afterwards William IV.; b. at Waterford; appeared on the Dublin
stage, 1777, as Phœbe in "As You Like It;" came to England,
1782; appeared, 1785, at Drury Lane; her connection with the
Duke lasted from 1791 to 1811; d. at St. Cloud.

H. Bunbury del.   C. Knight, stipple.
Wh. len., as Viola in "Twelfth Night," in the scene of the
duel with Sir Andrew Aguecheek, a composition of seven

figures; she is on the right, supported by Fabian and Antonio. March 10, 1788.

$16\frac{3}{8} \times 21\frac{3}{8}$. ($13\frac{7}{8} \times 20\frac{1}{4}$). 26432.

JORDAN, Dorothea—*continued.*

G. Romney. J. Ogborne, stipple.

H. P. Horne, 72, 1st state. 21839.

KATER, Capt. Henry, 1777–1835, b. at Bristol, intended for the law; ent. army, 1794, 12th Regt. of foot, in India; engaged on the trigonometr. survey of India; after seven years of this, returned home; devoted himself to science; constr. standards of weights and measures; invented the floating collimator, for astr. observations; &c.

See SCIENCE.

KATHARINE of ARRAGON, KATHARINE of BRAGANZA, or PORTUGAL. *See* CATHARINE.

KAUFFMANN, Angelica, 1740–1807, R.A., history and portrait-painter, b. at Coire, capital of the Grisons, daughter of John Joseph Kauffmann, portrait-painter; showed precocious talent; visited Milan, Florence, Rome, with her father, painting portraits; accomplished linguist and musician; came to England, 1765; original member of the R.A.; married twice, the first time unhappily; retired to Rome, 1782, with her second husband.

Sir J. Reynolds. F. Bartolozzi, stipple.

Ha. len. to right, seated, holding with both hands a print, or drawing, and a crayon in her left hand; a long curl descends on each side of her neck; *John Boydell excudit*, 1780; oval.

($9\frac{7}{16} \times 8$). 25663.

Also, the same portrait, a proof before the title; pub. Sepr. 3, 1780; printed in reddish-brown ink.

$12\frac{1}{2} \times 10\frac{3}{8}$. 21998.

——

A. Kauffmann. T. Burke, stipple.

Wh. len. seated, turned slightly to the right, "in the character of Design, listening to the Inspiration of Poetry;" Jany. 5, 1787; circular.

$17\frac{7}{8} \times 14$. ($12\frac{3}{8}$ diamr.). 26696.

——

Anon., stipple.

Ha. len. slightly to right, looking to left, a feather in her hair; an easel behind her; rectilin., but with the corners cut off; published, Feb. 1, 1800, by Vernor and Hood (the father of Tom Hood), Poultry.

$5\frac{7}{8} \times 3\frac{13}{16}$ (?). ($3\frac{1}{2} \times 2\frac{7}{8}$). E. 2009.–'89.

——

F. Moeglich. J. F. Bause, stipple.

Bust, to left, in profile; from a bas-relief in wax, executed at Rome; oval.

$7\frac{1}{8} \times 4\frac{3}{4}$ ($4\frac{5}{16} \times 3\frac{11}{16}$). 25609. 9.

KAUFFMAN, ANGELICA—*continued.*

A. Kauffman. A. H. Payne.

Sh. ha. len. slightly turned to left, looking to front; as a Bacchante; light drapery, grapes and vine-leaves in her hair; oval, in border. The picture is in the Berlin Gallery.

$9 \times 7\frac{1}{4}$. $(6 \times 4\frac{7}{8})$. E. 2010.–'89.

KAYE, JOHN, 1783–1853, b. at Hammersmith; educ. under Dr. Charles Burney, and at Cambridge; B.A., 1804; senior wrangler and senior Chancellor's medallist; M.A., 1807; B.D., 1814; D.D., 1815; master of his Coll., 1814; Reg. Prof. Div., 1816; bishop of Bristol, 1820; of Lincoln, 1827; F.R.S.; &c.

S. Lane. H. T. Ryall, mixed mez.

T. Q. len. to right, looking to left, seated, in robes; Lincoln Cathedral in background, on right; facs. signature below.

Ind. proof, Apl. 2, 1842.

$21\frac{7}{8} \times 18$. $(17\frac{1}{4} \times 13\frac{1}{16})$. 25832.

KEAN, EDMUND, c. 1787–1833, eminent tragedian, son of a scene-carpenter, his mother being the daughter of G. S. Carey; she deserted him; he went to sea; aftds. engaged under Moses Kean, and (later) J. P. Kemble, whose rival he was afterwards to become; assisted in his first efforts by Miss Tidswell, an actress; acted with success at Edinburgh, when only 16; appeared at Drury Lane, as Shylock, 1814; unequalled as Othello and Sir Giles Overreach; he visited America twice; managed Richmond Theatre after his return.

Wageman del. J. Thomson, stipple.

Ha. len. to right, looking to left; in armour and cloak, as Coriolanus; 1820.

$(4\frac{1}{2} \times 2\frac{13}{16})$. 26221.

J. J. Halls. C. Turner, mez.

Wh. len. to left, looking to front, as Richard III., wearing ermine hat, embroidered and furred cloak, boots and spurs, &c., and holding a baton in his right hand; Novr. 24, 1814.

26×15. $(23\frac{3}{4} \times 15)$. 26697.

KEATE, ROBERT, 1777–1857, Surgeon, 4th son of William Keate, D.D., rector of Laverton, Somerset, nephew of Thomas Keate, and younger brother of John Keate, head master of Eton; educ. at Bath Gram. School till 1792; apprent. to his uncle, Surg.-Genl. to the Army; ent. St. George's Hosp., 1793; "hosp.-mate," Chelsea Hosp., 1794; memb. Surg. Corpn., 1798, and staff-surg. in the army; serg.-surg. to William IV.; and to Q. Victoria, 1841.

J. P. Knight, R.A. J. R. Jackson, mixed mez.

T. Q. len. to left, seated, looking to front; facs. signature below.

Proof before all letters, except the artists' names and facs. signature.

Cut. $(17\frac{3}{4} \times 13\frac{3}{4})$. 22696.

KEBLE, John, 1792–1866, divine and poet, b. at Fairford; educ. by his father; scholar at Corp. Xti. Coll., Oxf., 1806; double first class, 1811; fellow of Oriel; private tutor, 1813–1816; College tutor, 1818, public examiner, 1821–'3; entd. the Church; returned to Fairford; refused preferments on account of his father's bad health; vicar of Hursley, 1836–'66; the primary author of the "Oxford Movement;" wrote the "Christian Year," &c.

G. Richmond. W. Holl, stipple.
Bust, to right; vignette; facs. signature below.
Ind. proof, Decr. 3, 1863.
12 × 9¼. (5½ × 5). 22998.

KEITH, James Francis Edward, 1696–1758, commonly called Marshal Keith, youngest son of William, 9th Earl Marischal; fought for James Stuart at Sherriffmuir; was attainted, and went abroad; first entered Spanish army; next engaged in that of Russia, where he rose to the rank of Genl.; visited England, 1740, and introduced to George II. by Russian Ambassador; entered service of Frederick of Prussia, who made him a Field-Marshal; killed in battle of Hochkirch.

A. Ramsay. A. van Haecken, mez.
J. C. Smith, 10, only mentions one impression, in the Brit. Musm.
This is from the Gulston Colln. 27595.

KELLY, Hugh, 1739–1777, born at Killarney; came to London, 1760; after struggling for years, succeeded as dramatic author with his comedy, "False Delicacy," and other pieces; called to the bar, 1774, but died soon after.

H. Hamilton. J. Boydell, mez.
J. C. Smith, 4, 2nd state. 27269.

KELLY, Michael, c. 1764–1826, b. at Dublin, taught singing by Passerini, Peretti, St. Giorgio, and Rauzzini, by whose advice he was sent to Naples to study, 1779, under Finaroli, and Aprile, with whom he travelled through Italy to Vienna, where he was engaged at the Court Theatre, and enjoyed the intimate friendship of Mozart, returned to England, 1787; appeared at Drury Lane; composed operas; engaged in wine trade; called by Sheridan, "composer of wine and importer of music;" pubd. "Reminiscences," 1826, really written by Th. Hook.

J. Lonsdale. C. Turner, mez.
Ha. len. to front, seated, holding a roll of music.
Open letter proof, June 1, 1825; with autogr. inscription by Kelly "to his friend John Taylor, Esqre., Augt. 28th, 1825."

14 × 10. (10¾ × 8½). 22246.

KEMBLE, Charles, 1775–1854, brother of J. P. Kemble and Mrs. Siddons; educ. at Douai; appeared first at Sheffield as Orlando in "As You Like It," and at Drury Lane, as Malcolm in

"Macbeth," 1794; joined his brother at Cov. Garden, 1803, with Mrs. Siddons; unsuccessful and unpromising at first, became successful by dint of of unremitting study and exertions; went to America, 1832 ; retired, 1836.

G. H. Harlow.   T. Lupton, mez.

Ha. len. to front, looking upwards to right, holding a pen in right hand ; papers lie on a table before him.

Open letter proof, Feb. 1, 1819.   22245.

KEMBLE, CHARLES—*continued.*

Monogram, J. R. C[ruikshank].

Wh. len. as Friar Michael in "Maid Marian," red cross on breast, staff in hand ; looking upwards to right ; etched, with aquatint ground, coloured by hand.

$7\frac{7}{8} \times 4\frac{12}{16}$. $(6\frac{1}{8} \times 3\frac{3}{4})$.   26431.

R. J. Lane, A.R.A., lith.

"Sixteen Portraits of Charles Kemble Esq.," fifteen of which are in character, on one sheet, as Macbeth, Macduff, Leon, Hamlet, Benedick, the Stranger, Othello, Cassio, Falconbridge, Falstaff, Shylock, Mark Antony, Mercutio, Iago ; 1840.

Ind. proof.

$15\frac{1}{8} \times 9\frac{5}{8}$ (the Ind. paper) ; the portraits are of various sizes, one, $1\frac{9}{16} \times 3\frac{6}{16}$; one, $1\frac{7}{16} \times 2\frac{3}{16}$; one, $2\frac{3}{16} \times 1\frac{6}{16}$; nine, $1\frac{7}{16} \times 1\frac{1}{16}$; and one, a circle, $1\frac{3}{16}$ diamr.   26405.

KEMBLE, FRANCES ANNE (called "Fanny"), 1809– , daughter of Charles Kemble ; b. in Newman Street, London ; made her first appearance at Cov. Garden, 1829, as Juliet ; afterwards played Belvidera, the Grecian Daughter, Mrs. Beverley, Portia, and other leading parts ; visited America, performing with great success, 1832 ; m. to Mr. P. Butler ; divorced 1839 ; author of "Poems," "Records of Girlhood," and other works.

Anon.   Anon., lith.

Ha. len. to right, in profile, leaning on the parapet of a balcony, as Juliet ; vignette.

$(6 \times 5\frac{1}{4})$.   26428.

J. Hayter del.   R. J. Lane, A.R.A., lith.

Ha. len. to left, in profile, leaning on the stone parapet of a balcony, looking downwards ; vignette.

Ind. proof.

$(5\frac{1}{2} \times 6\frac{1}{4})$.   23598.

(name illegible), lith.

Wh. len. as Juliet, with the Nurse ; turned towards left, looking back ; the Nurse is on the left, supporting her.

Ind. proof, touched with pencil.

(8×6).   29429.

KEMBLE, JOHN PHILIP, 1757–1823, distinguished actor, eldest
son of Roger Kemble, manager of a provincial company; b. at
Prescot, in Lancashire; educ. at Douai, where he was a fellow-
student of Talma; joined a strolling company; performed with
éclat at Liverpool, Edinburgh, York, &c.; appeared at Drury
Lane, 1783, with complete success, as Hamlet; became first
tragedian of the age; retired, 1817; author of a few pieces;
d. at Lausanne.

Chinnery, min.   J. Heath, stipple.
 Sh. ha. len. to front, wearing a furred cloak; oval; Feb. 1,
1779.
 $9\frac{7}{8} \times 8\frac{7}{16}$. $(4\frac{1}{2} \times 3\frac{11}{16})$.   E. 1468.–'85.

 Sir T. Lawrence, R.A.   W Ward, junr., mez.
 Wh. len. to left, seated, as "Cato," looking to front and
upwards.
 Proof before all letters.
 $34 \times 21\frac{1}{2}$. $(31\frac{1}{4} \times 21\frac{1}{2})$.   22032.

KEMPENFELT, RICHARD, 1720–1782, son of a Swedish officer,
who had entered the English service; Post Captain, 1757;
Captain of the Fleet, under Sir Charles Hardy, 1778; intercepted and destroyed a large portion of the French Fleet on its
way to the West Indies, 1781; Rear-Admiral; went down in
the "Royal George," at Spithead.

Tilly Kettle.   R. Earlom, mez.
J. C. Smith, 25, 1st state.   21857.

KENN, or KEN, THOMAS, 1637–1711, b. at Berkhampstead;
educ. at Winchester, and New Coll., Oxf.; B.A. 1661; M.A.,
1664; rector, Little Easton, Essex, 1663–'5; chapl. to Morley,
bishop of Winchester; rector, Brightstone, I. of Wight, 1667;
preb., Winchester, rector of East Woodhay; chapl. to Q. Mary
at the Hague; bishop of Bath and Wells, 1685; one of the
seven bishops who petitioned against the Second Declaration of
Indulgence; sent to the Tower; acquitted; deprived, 1691, for
refusing to take the oath of allegiance.

Anon.   G. Vertue.
 Sh. ha. len. to front, head to right, looking to front, oval in
border; arms below, and 2 lines of inscription.
 $6\frac{7}{16} \times 4\frac{1}{4}$. $(6\frac{3}{16} \times 3\frac{7}{8})$.   26698.
 See also "BISHOPS, SEVEN."   26668.

KENNETT, WHITE, 1660–1728, educ. at Oxford; whilst
shooting, in 1689, dangerously wounded in the forehead by his
gun bursting, both tables of the skull being broken; successfully
trepanned, and wore a black velvet patch afterwards; ent. the
Church; esteemed by Tenison; wrote many sermons and other
works, including his "Compleat History of England;" bishop
of Peterborough, 1718.

Faber.   Faber, senr., mez.
J. C. Smith, 50, 1st state (?).
 The plate is cut at bottom.   24121.

KENT, EDWARD, Duke of, 1767–1820, son of George III,
and father of H.M. Queen Victoria.
  Sir W. Beechey.   W. Skelton
  Ha. len. to front, looking to right, in uniform, with star.
  In the lowest corner, on the left, is the word " Proof."
  Published, Novr., 1, 1815.
  19¾ × 15½. (18 × 13¼).   27243.
  Also a duplicate, in Genealogical Chart, 553. 1. 25046/5.

KENT, VICTORIA MARIE LOUISE, of Saxe-Coburg-Gotha-
Saalfeld, Duchess of; 1786–1861; m. 1818; mother of H. M.
Queen Victoria.
  S. C. Smith.   R. J. Lane, lith.
  Ha. len. to front, wearing a broad-brimmed hat.
  Ind. proof.
  Cut. (7⅞ × 6¼).   25052.
  In Genealogical Chart, 553. 1.

  W. C. Ross, A.R.A.   F. Bacon.
  Ha. len. seated, wearing a turban.
  Published, May 24, 1841, by Colnaghi and Puckle.
  Ind proof.
  14½ × 10⅞. (7¹⁄₁₆ × 5½).   27946.

-—— with her daughter, PRINCESS VICTORIA.
  Sir W. Beechey, R.A.   " Etched by W. Skelton."
  T. Q. len. seated, to right, looking to front, and with her left
arm round the infant Princess, who stands on the sofa by her.
Proof before letters, except the artists' names.
  13¹⁶ × 11. (11¼ × 9½).   24737.
    NOTE.—This is to a large extent engraved, though the engraver calls
    it only " etched."

—— with her daughter, Princess Victoria.
  G. Hayter.   Anon., lith.
  T. Q. len. the Duchess, seated, to right, with her right arm
round the Princess, who stands by her, looking to front.
  Cut. (18½ × 13⁷⁄₁₆).   25064.
  In Genealogical Chart, 553. 1

  F. Winterhalter, 1843.   Léon Noel, lith., 1846.
  Wh. len. to right, looking to front; in a landscape.
  (24⅞ × 16¼).   22153.

  F. Winterhalter.   J. A Vinter lith., 1861.
  (14⁷⁄₁₆ × 11¾).   22174.

  Ha. len. seated, to right.

  Partridge del.   I. Alais, stipple.
  See LA BELLE ASSEMBLÉE, 1818.   13867. 24.

KENT, WILLIAM, 1685-1748, architect and painter, b. in York-
shire; apprent. to a coach-painter, but ran away to London,
c. 1704; sent to Rome, by kindness of friends; painted the
altar-piece which Hogarth ridiculed; designed monument to
Shakspere in Westminster Abbey; built Devonshire House,
and other mansions, the Horse Guards, &c.; gained great reputation as landscape gardener.
See ARTISTS, A SOCIETY OF.

KENYON, LLOYD, 1st Lord, 1733-1802, b. at Gredington, Flint-
shire; art. to an attorney at Nantwich; called to the bar;
defended Lord George Gordon; Attorney-General, 1782; Master
of the Rolls, and Bart., 1784; Lord Chf.-Justice, and Baron
Kenyon, 1788; d. at Bath.
    G. Romney.   W. Holl, stipple.
   T. Q. to left, seated, in robes, looking to front, holding a pen
in right hand, a paper folded in left.
   Open letter proof, August 1, 1804.
   H. P. Horne, 73, 1st state.
   24 × 17⅛. (17 × 13¼).   22874.

KEPPEL, HON. AUGUSTUS, 1725-1786, second son of 2nd Earl of
Albemarle; entd. navy, and saw service; Admiral of the fleet,
1778, but accused of misconduct by his second in command,
Sir Hugh Palliser; tried by court-martial, 1779, and acquitted;
first lord of Admiralty, 1782; cr. Viscount.
    Sir J. Reynolds.   E. Fisher, mez.
    J. C. Smith, 34, 2nd state.   26699.
   See also TRIUMPH OF BRITANNIA.

KEY, CHARLES ASTON, 1793-1849, surgeon, b. in Southwark,
eldest son of Thomas Key, med. pracr.; educ. at Buntingford
Gram. School; apprent. to his father, 1810; cancelled, 1815;
a pupil at Guy's, and of Astley Cooper; qualified, 1821, and
appointed first assist. surg. at Guy's; and surg., 1824; gained
large practice, and elected F.R.S.; lecturer at Guy's, till 1844;
one of the first elected fellows of R.C.S., member of Council;
Surgeon to Pr. Albert, 1847; contributed to "Guy's Hosp.
Reports" some valuable papers on surgical subjects.
    G. Richmond.   F. Holl, stipple.
   Bust, to front, looking to right; vignette.
   Open letter proof; June 28, 1851.
   20 9⁄16 × 16⅞. (8¼ × 6).   22999.

KEY, SIR JOHN, 1794-1858, Lord Mayor of London, 1830, and
again in 1831; cr. Bart., 1831; chamberlain of the City, 1853.
                        Anon. [C. Turner], mez.
   T. Q. to left, looking to front, wearing the robes and chain.
   Proof before letters.
   19⅞ × 13⅞. (15¼ × 11¾).   27547.

KILLIGREW, ANNE, 1660-1685, amateur artist, daughter of
Dr. H. Killigrew, Master of the Savoy; painted landscapes and
portraits in Lely's manner, and some pieces of still life and

history; maid of honour to the Duchess of York; described by
Anthony à Wood as "a Grace for beauty, and a Muse for wit;"
her genius in poetry and painting celebrated by Dryden; d. of
small-pox; buried in Savoy Chapel.

Anne Killigrew.   T. Chambars.

 Sh. ha. len. to left, looking to front; hair in curls; pearl
earring.

 In Walpole's " Anecdotes," Vol. 3, 1763.

 Cut. (5 7/16 × 4⅝).   25461. 11.

KILLIGREW, ANNE—*continued.*

 A. Killigrew.   J. Beckett, mez.

 J. C. Smith, 56, 2nd state.   25748.

KILWARDEN, ARTHUR WOLFE, 1739–1803, Irish Judge;
educ. at Trin. Coll., Dublin; called to the bar, 1766; Solicitor-
General, 1787; Attorney-General, 1789; succ. Lord Clonmel
as Chf. Justice of King's Bench, Ireland; murdered by mob,
when returning from the country, during an insurrection in
Dublin.

 H. Hamilton, 1795.   F. Bartolozzi, R.A.

 Sh. ha. len. to left, looking to front; loose collar and dark
gown; oval in rectang. frame; arms below; 20th Novr., 1800.
Open letter proof (?).

 14¼ × 11½. (11 × 9).   22463.

KING, JAMES, 1750–1784, Captn. R.N., served under Capn. W.
Norton, Capn. Palliser, and Capn. Jervis in the Mediterranean;
lieut., 1771; accompanied Capn. Cook, in his third voyage, as
a competent astronomer; at the time of Cook's death he was on
shore, and suc. in repulsing the natives' attack; Post Capn.,
1780; LL.D.; F.R.S.; &c.

 J. Webber.   F. Bartolozzi, stipple.

 Ha. len. to left, looking to front, in oval.

 June 4th, 1784.

 11⅜ × 8⅞. (4 7/16 × 3⅝).   27596.

KING, JOHN, c. 1559–1621, b. at Worminghall, Bucks.; educ.
at Westminster, and Ch. Ch., Oxf.; B.A., 1579–'80; M.A.,
1582–3; archdeacon, Notts, 1590; chaplain to lord-keeper, Sir
T. Egerton; rector of St. Andrew's, Holborn, 1597; preb., St.
Paul's, 1599; chapl. to the Queen; D.D., 1601; Dean of Ch.
Ch., 1605; Vice-chancellor of Oxf., 1607–1610; bishop of
London, 1611.

 N. Lockey.   S. Pass.

 Ha. len. in robes, to front, holding an open book in both
hands; 12 verses below, in two columns : " Are to be sould in
" Popes head Ally by I S. & G. Humble."

 7 3/16 × 4¼ (?). (7 × 4 7/16).   E. 998.–'85.

KING, PETER KING, Baron, 1669–1734, nephew of John Locke;
jurist and philosopher; endeavoured to reconcile dissenters to
the Church; cr. a peer, Baron of Ockham, Lord Chancellor,
1725–1733. Author of several works.

 Anon.   G. Vertue, 1725.

Sh. ha. len. to left, looking to front, in robes; oval in border; the mace, &c., below the oval.
$(12\frac{1}{8} \times 10)$. 22464.

KING, PETER, 7th Baron, 1775-1833, economical writer, &c.
E. U. Eddis. M. Gauci, lith.
Sh. ha. len. to front, looking to right, the face slightly tinted.
$(12\frac{1}{2} \times 11)$. 23583.

KING, THOMAS, 1730-1805, comedian, played tragic characters at first, in a provincial company, unsuccessfully; became one of the greatest actors of his day in comedy; excelled as a *raconteur* and mimic; unfortunately addicted to gambling; buried at St. Paul's, Cov. Garden.
J. Zanffely. R. Earlom, mez.
J. C. Smith, 26, 1st state.
He is represented here with Mrs. Baddeley (q. v.). 24255.

——, in the Character of Fame. Prologue to the Maid of the Oaks.
From a "Collection . . . of English Prologues," &c. 1779. 28187. 8.

KINGS AND QUEENS OF ENGLAND. *See* ENGLAND

KINGSDOWN, THOMAS PEMBERTON LEIGH, Lord, 1793-1867, called to the bar, 1816; K.C., 1829; M.P., 1831, Atty.-Gen. to the Prince of Wales, 1841; Chan. and Keeper of Great Seal to H.R.H., P.C., 1843; cr. Baron, 1858.
[G. Richmond ?]. Anon. [H. Robinson ?], stipple.
Bust, to front, looking to right; vignette.
Ind. proof before all letters.
$11\frac{7}{8} \times 8\frac{7}{8}$. $(6 \times 4\frac{3}{4})$. 24210.

KIPPIS, ANDREW, D.D., 1725-1795, nonconformist minister and biographer, b. at Nottingham; son of a silk-hosier; educ. at Sleaford, and at the Academy, Northampton, under Dr. Doddridge; settled at Boston, 1746; went to Dorking, 1750, and to Westminster, 1753; remained there 43 years; F.S.A., 1778; F.R.S., 1779; edited the 2nd edition of the "Biographia Britannica" with Dr. Towers, as far as "Fastolf;" &c.
W. Artaud. F. Bartolozzi.
Sh. ha. len. to front, seated, wearing a wig; coat buttoned.
Open letter proof (?); Octr. 20th, 1792.
$12\frac{5}{8} \times 9\frac{7}{8}$. $(10\frac{7}{8} \times 9\frac{3}{16})$. 22875.

KIRBY, JOSHUA, 1716-1774, b. at Parham, Suffolk; topographical draftsman; began as a coach and house-painter, at Ipswich, c. 1738; induced by early friendship with Gainsborough to try landscape-painting; studied linear perspective, and lectured on that science; clerk of the works at Kew; edited a second edition of Brook Taylor's "Perspective," 1754; pubd. "Perspective of Architecture," 1761; President of Incorp.

Socy. for a year; his views of Kew Palace were engraved by
Woollett, 1763; F.R.S., &c.
Gainsborough.   Dixon, mez.
J. C. Smith, 21.   24082.

KIRBY, Rev. William, M.A., 1759–1850, entomologist, educ. at
Ipswich Grammar School, and Caius Coll. Cambr.; rector of
Barham, Suffolk; canon of Norwich; rural dean of Claydon;
president of Ipswich Museum; published many works on
entomology, and, in collaboration with William Spence, the
famous "Introduction to Entomology;" founded a new order
of insects, *Strepsiptera*; F.R.S., 1818; Hon. Presdt., Entomol.
Socy., 1837.
H. Howard, R.A.   T. Lupton, mez.
Ha. len. to front, looking to right; drapery behind him; his
left hand rests on a folio book, lettered on the side, Insecta.
Proof (?), with inscription in open letters; Aug. 1, 1828.
$13\frac{1}{4} \times 10\frac{1}{8}$ ($10\frac{13}{16} \times 8\frac{7}{8}$).   21907.

[Howard.]   T. H. Maguire, lith., 1850.
Full ha. len. to front, looking to right; from the same
picture as the above print; facs. signature below; rectilin.,
with corners cut off; vignette.
$(9\frac{1}{4} \times 9\frac{1}{4})$.   22516.

[Spence?]   W. B. Spence, lith.
T. Q. len. to left, seated, reading a paper.
Ind. proof, Novr. 23/'48; "in his 90th year, Barham Rectory."
$(9\frac{1}{4} \times 7\frac{1}{16})$.   22200

KIRWAN, Very Rev Walter Blake, c. 1754–1805, Irish
divine and preacher; b. in Galway; educ. at St. Omer and
Louvain; priest in Rom. Cath. Ch.; chaplain, 1778, to the
Neapolitan Embassy, London; conformed to Prot. Ch. in
Ireland, 1787; very popular preacher; Preb., Dublin Cathedral,
1788; Dean of Killala, 1800; d. of fever at Mount Pleasant,
near Dublin.
H. D. Hamilton, R.H.A.   W. Ward, mez.
J. C. Smith, 52, 2nd state.   24227.

KITCHINER, William, M.D., c. 1775–1827, b. in London;
educ. at Eton, and M.D. of Glasgow; devoted himself to
science; wrote gastronomical works, and others on diet, optics,
vocal music, &c., and collected a fine musical library.
C. Turner.   C. Turner, mez.
Wh. len. to left, holding a book in his left hand; behind on
right is a piano, on which are books and music; on the left, a
telescope, and a stuffed tiger, with hat and coat lying on it.
Open letter proof; Sepr. 1, 1827.
$20\frac{3}{16} \times 14\frac{1}{8}$. ($16\frac{3}{4} \times 11\frac{3}{16}$).   22876.

KNELLER, SIR GODFREY, 1648–1723, Bart., portrait-painter, b. at Lübeck, of an ancient family ; pupil of Bol, at Amsterdam, and had some instruction from Rembrandt ; visited Rome and Venice, 1672 ; came to England, 1674 ; painted the King's portrait, and those of all the most eminent persons of the day, 43 in the Kit-Cat Club, ten "Beauties" at Hampton Court, and ten sovereigns ; d. at Kneller Hall, Twickenham.

Kneller.   J. H. Robinson.

Ha. len. to right, looking to front ; long hair ; loose gown ; oval in border.

Ind. proof before all letters, except engraver's name.

Engraved for Walpole's "Anecdotes," Vol. 2, 1849.

$8\frac{5}{16} \times 5\frac{1}{4}$. $(4\frac{1}{2} \times 3\frac{3}{8})$.   26259.

Kneller.   J. Beckett, mez.

J. C. Smith, 59, 1st state.   22877

—— "Portrait Painter."

[Kneller.]   Anon., stipple.

Bust, to right, looking to front ; long wig ; vignette.

$5\frac{7}{8} \times 3\frac{7}{8}$. $(4\frac{1}{4} \times 3\frac{1}{2})$.   26252.

[Kneller.]   Anon.

Bust, to right, looking to front ; long wig.

$(4\frac{1}{8} \times 3\frac{7}{8})$.   23588.

Kneller.   J. Girtin, etched.

Bust, to left, looking to front ; from J. Girtin's "Seventy-five Portraits of Celebrated Painters," 1817 ; printed on tinted paper.

$(5\frac{1}{8} \times 3\frac{3}{4})$.   15217.   2

KNIGHT, EDWARD, 1774–1826, actor, commonly known as "Little Knight," b. at Birmingham ; began as a painter, but took to the stage at Newcastle and Staffordshire, as "Hob" in "Hob in the Well ;" recovering from the stage-fright which drove him at first to quit the boards, he appeared again, and with success, in N. Wales ; acted at Stafford for some years ; joined York Circuit, c. 1803 ; came to Drury Lane and Lyceum ; successful in many characters from "Jerry Blossom" and "Simple" to "Diego" in the "Kiss ;" wrote one musical farce, "The Sailor and Soldier," 1805, without merit.

J. P. Knight.   H. Dawe, mez.

Head and shoulders, to front, chin on hands, resting on the front of a box in theatre ; a playbill under right hand, with "As you like it," and "Hit or Miss," on it ; painted by his son.

Open letter proof (?), Jany. 1, 1825.

$15\frac{1}{2} \times 11\frac{3}{4}$. $(11\frac{3}{4} \times 9\frac{1}{2})$.   22247.

KNIGHT, Richard Payne, 1750–1824, numismatist, eldest son
of Rev. Thomas Knight, of Wormesley Grange, Herefordshire;
of weak health, not sent to school before age of 14; went to
Italy, 1767, for several years, and again, 1777; kept a journal,
translated by Goethe; travelled again, 1785; collected bronzes,
antiques, coins, &c.; inherited the estates, 1764, and built a
mansion, where he entertained Lord Nelson and Lady Hamilton;
M.P., 1780–1806; wrote on antiquarian subjects; bequeathed
his collections, valued at 50,000*l.* to the Br. Musenm.

Sir T. Lawrence. [C. Turner?], mez.

Ha. len. to left, seated, holding a pair of spectacles in his left
hand.

Ind. proof before all letters.

$15\frac{3}{4} \times 12\frac{3}{4}$. $(11 \times 8\frac{7}{8})$. 23000.

KNIGHT, Thomas Andrew, 1758–1838, Vegetable Physiologist;
b. near Hereford; educ. at Balliol Coll., Oxford; laid before
the Royal Society his paper on inheritance of disease among
fruit trees, and propag. of debility by grafting, 1795; author
of accounts of experimental researches into vegetable fecunda-
tion, &c.; separate publications on fruits; F.R.S.; suc. Sir
Joseph Banks as Pres. Hort. Socy.; his " Physiological and
Horticultural papers, with Life," pub., 1841.

S. Cole. S. Cousins, A.R.A., mixed mez.

Ha. len. to front, seated, dark coat and waistcoat, white neckcloth, right hand resting on table before him; pillar on right;
May 1, 1836.

$13\frac{7}{8} \times 10\frac{7}{8}$. $(10\frac{0}{16} \times 9)$. 25747.

KNIGHTON, Sir William, 1776–1836, b. at Beer Ferris,
Devon; educ. at Newton Bushell, at Tavistock, under his uncle,
Dr. Bredall, a surgeon, and at Guy's Hospl.; assist. surgeon at
Royal Naval Hospl., Plymouth; settled at Devonport, 1797;
came to London, 1803; removed to Edinb.; received a degree
from the Archbp. of Cant., and M.D., Aberdeen; attended
Marquis Wellesley to Spain; Physn. to Prince of Wales, 1810;
cr. Bart., 1812; private sec., and keeper of the privy purse to the
King, over whom he acquired a strong and beneficial influence.

Sir T. Lawrence. C. Turner, mez.

Sh. ha. len. to right, looking front.

Proof before all letters, except the artists' names and publication-line, Oct. 20, 1823.

$15\frac{1}{4} \times 12$. $(9\frac{7}{8} \times 8\frac{1}{4})$. 27671.

KNOWLES, James Sheridan, 1784–1840, dramatist, b. at
Cork; son of James Knowles, the lexicographer; educ. at his
father's school in Cork; came with the family to London, 1793;
made early efforts in verse, and in play-writing; left home after
his father's second marriage; served in militia as ensign,
1804–'5; studied medicine; M.D., Aberdeen; wrote small
tragedies; went on the stage; wrote for E. Kean, 1810, "Leo,

or the Gipsy;" pubd. poems; kept a school; wrote. "Caius
Gracchus," "Virginius," "The Hunchback," "Love-Chase," &c.
    S. S. Osgood.   H. S. Sadd, mixed mez.
  Full ha. len. to front, looking to left; hands crossed; left
elbow resting on a stone pedestal; face. signature below;
Oct. 10, 1840.
    $17\frac{1}{4} \times 13\frac{9}{16}$. ($13\frac{1}{8} \times 10\frac{1}{2}$).   24637

KNOX, JOHN, 1505–1572, educ. at Edinb. University, 1524;
ordd. priest, before 1530; professed the reformed doctrines,
1542; charged with complicity in the murder of Beatoun,
condemned to the galleys, 1547; released, went to England;
well received; consulted and employed, 1549; on accession of
Mary, fled to Geneva; welcomed by Calvin, 1554; returned to
Scotland, 1555; joined the lords of congregation, instituted
protestant worship, preached against bishops and clergy, 1556;
returned to Geneva, 1557; began a translation of Bible into
English, &c., 1558; his confession of faith adopted by the
parliament, 1560; preached at coronation of James VI., 1567.
  Anon. (From an original picture in Calder House.)
                                          W. Penny.
  Ha. len. slightly to right, looking to right, holding an open
book.
  Ind. proof, Aug. 1828.
  ($10\frac{3}{8} \times 8\frac{3}{4}$).   25831

LACY, JOHN, c. 1620–1681, comedian and dramatist, b. at Doncaster, bred a dancing-master; entered the army; subsequently
took to the stage; acquired such celebrity there that Charles II.
had his portrait painted in three of his best characters; the
picture is at Windsor Castle; he wrote "The Dumb Lady,"
"Sir Hercules Buffoon," "Old Troop," and "Sawney the Scot,"
comedies.
  Anon.   W. Hopkins, etched.
  Wh. len. in three characters, viz., "Teague" in "The Committee," "Scruple," in "The Cheats;" and "Galliard," in "The
Variety;" pubd. 1825.
  ($12\frac{3}{4} \times 9\frac{13}{16}$).   26411.

LAKE, GERARD, Viscount, 1744–1808, General; commanded,
Ireland, 1797; sent to India; took Agra, defeated Mahrattas,
near Delhi, restored the Mogul, 1803; defeated Holkar, at
Furruckabad, 1804; took Bhurtpore, 1805; with
LAKE, LT.-COLONEL THE HON. FRANCIS GERARD, his son,
1772–1836; suc. 1808; Maj.-Gen., 1811; Lt.-Gen., 1821.
  Place.   R. Cooper, stipple.
  Both wh. len., at the battle of Laswari, the General's horse
having just been shot under him, on left.
  ($19\frac{1}{8} \times 14\frac{7}{8}$).   23007.

LAKE, COL. SIR HENRY ATTWELL, c. 1809–1881, 3rd son of Sir
James S. W. Lake, Bart., joined Madras Engineers, 1826;

Captn., 1841; Lt.-Col., 1855; ent. Turkish service, sacrificing a valuable post in India, went to Kars, where he rendered great services throughout the siege; called by the Russians "The English Todleben;" returned to England, 1856; A.D.C. to the Queen, with rank of Colonel; Chf. Comm. Police, Dublin, 1858–'77; K.C.B., 1875.

   [Baugniet.]   C. Baugniet, lith., 1857
   Ha. len. to front, looking to left; in uniform; vignette; facs. signature below.
   (10 × 8).   23615.

LAKE, JOHN, Bishop of Chichester. *See* "BISHOPS, SEVEN."
                                           26668.

LAMB, CHARLES, 1775–1834, essayist, b. in London; educ. at Christ's Hospital till 1789, when he became a clerk in the India House; retired with a handsome annuity, 1825; publ. poems, written with Coleridge and Lloyd, 1797; "John Woodvil," a tragedy, 1802; "Essays of Elia," "Tales from Shakspeare," &c.

   H. Meyer.   H. Meyer, stipple.
   Ha. len. to front, seated, looking to right; coat loosely buttoned; vignette.
   Ind. proof, Jany. 1, 1828.
   $8\frac{7}{8} \times 5\frac{11}{16}$. $(5\frac{3}{8} \times 4\frac{7}{8})$.   22878.

LAMBARDE, WILLIAM, 1536–1601, historian of Kent, b. in parish of St. Nicholas Acon, London; eldest son of John Lambarde, draper, alderman, and sheriff; ent. at Linc. Inn, April 12, 1556; studied Ang.-Saxon, and history with L. Nowell; author of a paraphrase of the Ang.-Saxon laws, 1568; "Perambulation of Kent," 1576, the first county history; bencher, and J.P., 1579; wrote "Eirenarcha," "Archeion," &c.; master in Chancery, 1592; keeper of the Rolls records, 1597, and of those in the Tower, 1601.

                                         G. Vertue.
   Bust, to front, slightly turned and looking to left; wearing a gauffred collar, a high coat, and a flat cap; oval, in border; DEO PATRIÆ TIBI, above; below, name, arms, and date of death.
   $8\frac{1}{2} \times 6\frac{1}{4}$. $(8\frac{5}{16} \times 5\frac{1}{8})$.   27597.

LAMBERT, AYLMER BOURKE, 1761–1842, b. at Bath; educ. at Hackney School, and St. Mary Hall, Oxf., where he never graduated; orig. Fellow of Lin. Socy., 1788, and Vice-presidt., 1796–1842; contributed to their Transactions, and pubd. other works, especially his "Pinus;" F.R.S.; &c.

   J. Russell, R.A.   [W.] Holl [the elder].
   Sh. ha. len. to front, looking to right; oval, surrounded with branches of plants; name and titles below on a tablet.
   (Oval, $5\frac{1}{16} \times 4\frac{1}{16}$).

Below again is a vignette, with deer browsing and resting in a glade of a wood.

Reinagle, A.R.A. ![John] Landseer.
The whole, $(15\frac{1}{4} \times 9\frac{1}{4})$. 28152

LAMBERT, DANIEL, 1770–1809, famous for his great corpulence, b. at Leicester; when aged 23, weighed 32 stone; began to exhibit himself in London and provinces, 1806; weighed 52 stone, 11 lbs., shortly before his death; d., on a "business tour," at Warrington.

H. Singleton. C. Turner, mixed mez.
Wh. len. to front, seated, slightly inclined to left, looking to front; hat on table, on which his right hand and arm rest.
Open letter proof (?).
$(23\frac{1}{2} \times 17\frac{7}{8})$. 22038.

LAMBERT, GEORGE, 1710–1765, landscape-painter, b. in Kent; imitated Poussin; greatly assisted the theatres at Lincoln's Inn Fields and Covent Garden by his admirable scene-painting; a friend of Hogarth; first president of the Incorp. Socy. of Artists; founder of the Beefsteak Club; assisted in decorating the India House with pictures of the Company's settlements.

J. Vanderbanck. J. Faber, mez
J. C. Smith, 214, 2nd state. 21862.

(Vanderbanck). A. Bannerman.
Ha. len. to right, looking to front, holding in left hand a print of a landscape. For Walpole's "Anecdotes," Vol. 4, 1771.
$(6\frac{1}{4} \times 5\frac{3}{4})$. E. 2185.–'89.

J. Vanderbanck. H. Robinson.
Ha. len. to left, looking to front, holding in his right hand a print, on which a landscape is represented. For Walpole's "Anecdotes," 5th Edn., 1826–'8.
Ind. proof, Oct. 15, 1827.
$8\frac{12}{12} \times 5\frac{5}{8}$. $(4\frac{3}{4} \times 3\frac{11}{16})$. 26253.

LAMBERT, JOHN, 1620–1694, Parliamentary General; disting. at Marston Moor and Naseby; opposed Cromwell's taking the title of King, and compelled Richard Cromwell to abdicate; resisted General Monk at the Restoration; banished, after this, for life to Guernsey, where he died.

R. Walker. J. Houbraken, 1739.
Sh. ha. len. in armour, to left, facing and looking to right; long hair, lace round throat; oval in border; from Birch's "Lives."
$14\frac{7}{8} \times 9\frac{5}{8}$. $(14\frac{1}{6} \times 8\frac{3}{4})$. 21979.

LANCASTER, JOHN OF GAUNT, Duke of, 1340–1399; suc. 1361; Regent of England, 1377.
G. Vertue del. G. Vertue.

Ha. len. slightly to left, wearing a crown, and holding the
sceptre in his left hand.

"Painted on Glass in an Ancient Window in ye Library of
All Souls Coll., Oxon."

(11 × 7⅛). 27178. 12.

LANDER, RICHARD, 1804–1833, African explorer; b. in Cornwall; accomp. Clapperton in his expedition to the Niger, 1825; returned, after Clapperton's death, and in a second expedition, 1830, navigated the Niger from its upper waters to the sea; perished in a third expedition.

W. Brockedon, F.R.S.   C. Turner, A.R.A., mez.

Ha. len. in "African costume," open at throat; slightly turned to right, looking to left; July 13, 1835.

14 × 10. (10¾ × 9¾) 22035.

LANDON, LETITIA ELIZABETH, 1802–1838, b. in London, daughter of an army-agent; at an early age showed poetic talent, contributing to the "Annuals" numerous pieces, signed "L. E. L.;" her principal poems were the "Improvisatrice," "Troubadour," "Golden Violet," "Venetian Bracelet," "Zenana," &c.; wrote several novels; married Mr. G. Maclean, 1838; went to Cape Coast Castle; d. Oct. 15, from the effects of an accidental overdose of prussic acid.

D. Maclise.   E. Finden, stipple.

T. Q. len. to front; left hand slightly extended; high bow of ribbon on head; white dress with broad sash and buckle; facs. subscription and signature below, dated "Cape Coast Castle—October 12."

20 1/16 × 16¼ (?). (13 5/16 × 11 13/16). 22518.

LANDSEER, SIR EDWIN HENRY, 1802–1873, animal-painter, b. in London; precocious, admitted at the age of 14 to the R. A. schools, where he exhibited in the same year, and again constantly; A.R.A., 1826; R.A., 1831; very popular painter; suffered much in health during the last 20 years of his life; Kt., 1850; refused the office of P.R.A., offered to him on the death of Sir C. Eastlake, 1865.

Anon.   Woodcut.

Bust, to front, loose neckcloth; oval.
Ind. proof, from an illustrated paper.

(11 × 8¼). E. 2186.–'89

R.M. (monogram), woodcut.

Head, to front; from an illustrated paper; vignette, in oval.

(5¼ × 4). E. 2187.–'89.

LANE, COLONEL, and LANE, MISS. See CHARLES II.

E. 355.–'90.

LANE, "MRS." JANE, —1689, of Bentley Hall, Stafford, co. Warwick; assisted in concealment and escape of Charles II.; fled to France, where she was received by Charles with honour;

ent. service of Princess of Orange; received pension, 1,000*l.*
per annum, and presents, at Restoration; pension confirmed by
James II. and William III.; m. to Sir Clement Fisher, after
Restoration.
Anon.   Anon.
Sh. ha. len. with broad lace collar; oval in border; name on
tablet below, within the border; for Clarendon's "Rebellion."
6$\frac{7}{16}$ × 4$\frac{7}{16}$ (?). (Oval, 3$\frac{5}{8}$ × 2$\frac{3}{4}$).   27135.
See also CHARLES II.

LANGDALE, HENRY BICKERSTETH, Lord, 1783–1851; lawyer;
Master of the Rolls and Baron, 1836.
   G. Richmond.   H. Robinson, stipple.
   Bust to right; vignette.
   Ind. proof before all letters, except the artists' names.
   23$\frac{1}{4}$ × 17$\frac{3}{16}$. (8 × 9).   23005.

LANKESTER, EDWIN, 1814–1874, b. at Melton, Suffolk; educ.
at Woodbridge; stud. Medicine at Univ. Coll. London; grad.,
Heidelberg; Lecturer in Materia Medica, and Botany at St.
George's Sch. of Med., 1843; Superint., Food Collections,
S.K.M., 1858; Prof. Nat. Hist., New Coll., London; Coroner,
Centr. Middlesex, 1862; prolific writer on Scientific and Sani-
tary subjects; transl. Schleiden's "Principles of Scientific
Botany;" ed. "The Natural Hist. of Deeside," by command
of the Queen; d. at Margate.
   [Maguire.]   T. H. Maguire, lith., 1852.
   Full ha. len. to front, slightly inclined, facing, and looking to
right; right hand raised; facs. signature below; corners cut
off; Ipswich.
   (10 × 9).   27169.

LANSDOWNE, HENRY PETTY-FITZMAURICE, 3rd Marquess
of, 1780–1863; statesman; M.P., 1801; Chanc. of the Exchequer, 1806; Home Sec., 1828; Ld. Presid. and Leader of
the House of Lords, 1831–'41; influential liberal to the end of
his life; K.G., &c.
   Sir F Grant, P.R.A.   J. R. Jackson, mez.
   Ha. len. slightly inclined, and looking, towards left; seated;
left hand on arm of chair; glass hanging by a ribbon.
   Ind. proof before all letters, except publication-line, scratched
at top; Aug. 8, 1857.
   17$\frac{3}{8}$ × 13$\frac{1}{2}$. (12 × 9$\frac{1}{2}$).   21749.

   Sir T. Lawrence.   J. Bromley, mixed mez.
   T. Q. len. to front, looking to left, leaning with left hand on
a pillar; landscape in distance, on right.
   Proof before letters, except artists' names and publication-
line, Aug. 25, 1831.
   16$\frac{1}{5}$ × 11$\frac{1}{4}$. (13$\frac{1}{4}$ × 8$\frac{5}{8}$).   22125.
   See also ABERDEEN CABINET.

LANSDOWNE, William Fitzmaurice Petty, 1st Marquess
of, 1737–1805, Statesman; son of John, Earl of Shelburne;
M.P., 1761; Pres. Board of Trade, 1763; Sec. of State for
Southern Dept., 1766–'8 ; Sec. Foreign Affairs, and Pr. Minister,
1782–'3 ; cr Marquess, 1784; collected one of the finest private
libraries ever formed ; K.G., &c.
 T. Gainsborough, R.A.   F. Bartolozzi, stipple.
 Ha. len. to left, looking to front ; wearing the Star of the
Garter ; oval, 1787.
 Open letter proof.
 H. P. Horne's Catalogue, 44.
 11 × 8⅞. (8³⁄₁₆ × 6¹¹⁄₁₆).   22250.

LARDNER, Dionysius, 1793–1859, b. in Dublin, son of a solicitor ; began in his father's office, but soon left that for Trin.
Coll. ; B.A., 1817 ; remained for 10 years at the University,
publishing various treatises on scientific subjects, the steam-
engine, &c. ; received the gold medal of the R. Dublin Socy. ;
contributed to Encyclopædias; prof. Nat. Phil., London, 1827 ;
went to the U.S. America, 1840, and lectured ; pubd. "Cabinet
Encyclopædia," "Railway Economy," "Museum of Science
and Art," &c.; D.C.L., F.R.S.
 T. Bridgford, A.R.H.A., del.   Anon., lith.
 Sh. ha. len. to left, looking to front ; vignette ; facs. signature
below.
 Ind. proof.
 (7 × 5½).   27550.

LAROON, Marcellus (known as "Captain Laroon"), 1679–
1772, subject-painter ; b. in Bow Street ; showed early talent
for drawing ; travelled abroad with Sir J. Williamson as a page,
and in the suite of Earl of Manchester ; stud. painting and
music ; quarrelled with his father ; went on the stage ; returned
to painting, 1707 ; joined the army in Holland, and in Spain ;
served in England till 1734 ; clever artist, as painter and
musician.
 See ARTISTS, A Society of.

LATHAM, John, 1761–1843, b. at Gawsworth, Cheshire ; educ.
at Oxford ; practised as a physician in Manchester, Oxford,
and London ; attained great eminence in his profession ; M.D.,
F.R.S., Pres. Roy. Coll. of Physicians, 1814.
 J. Jackson, R.A.   R. W. Sievier, stipple.
 T. Q. len. to left, seated, looking to front, in robes, as Pres.
R.C.P.
 Open letter Ind. proof, May 1, 1816
 17⅜ × 13⁷⁄₁₀. (12³⁄₁₀ × 9¹¹⁄₁₆).   27171

LATIMER, Hugh, D.D., c. 1485–1555, educ. at Cambr. ; fellow
of Clare Hall, and B.A., 1510 ; M.A., 1514; D.D., 1524;
preached the reformed doctrines ; patronised by Cromwell ;

Bishop of Worcester, 1535; resigned, 1539; imprisoned till
1547; burnt at Oxford.
                                        J. Faber, senr., mez.
    J. C. Smith, 58, among the Reformers; 2nd state, with
name of Houston as engraver.   24667.
    See also "REFORMERS," a Group.
    See also "MARTYRS, PROTESTANT," a Group. 25736.

LAUD, WILLIAM, 1573–1645, b. at Reading; educ. at Oxford;
    Dean of Gloucester, 1616; Bishop of London, 1628; Arch-
    bishop of Canterbury, 1633; became prominent as a partisan of
    Charles I. in his conflict with Parliament; impeached and con-
    demned by the Long Parliament, 1640; beheaded, 1645.
        A. van Dyck.   J. Watson, mez.
        J. C. Smith, 90, 3rd state.   21744.
        See also BODLEY.

LAUDERDALE, JOHN (MAITLAND), 1st Duke of, 1616–1682,
    statesman; son of John, 1st Earl of Lauderdale; Covenanter
    in early life; joined Royalists, 1647; after Restoration, cr.
    Duke, Lord High Comm. of Scotland; one of the "Cabal"
    Ministry; K.G.; &c.
        J. Riley.   J. Beckett, mez.
        J. C. Smith, 61, 3rd state.   22033.

————
        Sir P. Lely.   J. Houbraken, 1740.
        Sh. ha. len. to front, oval in border.
        In Birch's "Lives."
        $14\frac{3}{4} \times 9\frac{1}{16}$. ($14\frac{1}{2} \times 8\frac{3}{4}$).   20813.

LAURIE, SIR PETER, Lord Mayor of London, 1832–'3, President
    of Bridewell and Bethlehem Hospitals, &c.
        T. Phillips, R.A.   J. Scott, mez.
        T. Q. len. to front, looking to left, in robes.
        Ind. proof with open letters. Publd., July, 1839.
        $21\frac{1}{8} \times 15\frac{7}{8}$. ($16\frac{1}{8} \times 12\frac{3}{8}$).   25751.

LAURIE, SIR ROBERT,   –1804, 5th Bart., of Maxwellton;
    Lt.-General; M.P., Dumfriesshire, Knight Marshal of Scotland;
    Colonel of 8th King's Royal Irish Light Dragoons, &c.
        W. Owen.   J. Ward, mez.
        J. C. Smith, 29, 2nd state.   29731.

LAWRENCE, SIR HENRY MONTGOMERY, 1806–1857; K.C.B.,
    Colonel; served in Cabul campaign, 1843; and the Sutlej,
    1845; Chf. Commissr. for governing Punjaub, 1849; of Oude,
    1856; d. of wounds, defending Lucknow.
        J. R. Dicksee.   A. N. Sanders.
        Ha. len. to left, seated, looking to front, wearing the star, in
    morning dress; holding a paper in right hand.
        Open letter proof, Decr. 3, 1866.
        $18\frac{5}{16} \times 15$. ($13\frac{5}{8} \times 11$).   23006.

LAWRENCE, Sir Thomas, 1769–1830, portrait-painter, b. at
Bristol; showed precocious genius; gained a premium from the
Society of Arts, 1785; admitted a student at R. A., 1785;
began exhibiting immediately; A.R.A., 1791; King's painter
in ordinary, 1792; R.A., 1794; visited Paris, 1814; Kt., 1815;
visited Italy, 1818–'20; P.R.A., 1820; went to Paris, 1825, to
paint portraits of Charles X. and Dauphin; received the Legion
of Honour decoration; d. suddenly; buried in St. Paul's.
[Lane.] R. J. Lane, A.R.A., lith.
Head, in 3 positions, "from a plaster cast, taken at the age
" of thirty-four, in the possession of an attached friend."
Ind. proof, 1830.
$(7\frac{5}{8} \times 9\frac{13}{16}$, incl. border, $\frac{15}{16})$. 13896.

T. Lawrence del. F. C. Lewis, stipple.
Head, to front, "aged 35;" vignette.
Proof with scratched letters.
$10\frac{1}{4} \times 8\frac{1}{8}$. $(2\frac{1}{4} \times 2\frac{1}{4})$. 26261

A. E. Chalon, R.A., 1828 ("sketched from memory").
M. Gauci, lith.
Bust, in profile to right; chain over shoulder; vignette;
facs. signature.
Ind. proof, May, 1830.
$(5\frac{1}{4} \times 5\frac{5}{8})$. E. 2190.–'89.

(Sir T Lawrence ?). C. Turner, mez.
Ha. len. to front, wearing the chain and badge of President
R.A.
Proof before letters, except the publication-line, Feb. 1,
1830.
$20\frac{7}{16} \times 14$. $(12\frac{3}{16} \times 10\frac{3}{4}$, including border, $\frac{5}{8})$. 22879.

Sir T. Lawrence. S. Cousins, mez.
Ha. len. to front; white neckcloth, coat with high collar,
buttoned.
Proof with scratched letters; April 22, 1830.
Cut. $(12\frac{2}{3} \times 9\frac{13}{16})$. E. 2188.–'89.

C. Landseer. J. Thomson, stipple.
Ha. len., inclined to right, looking to front; holding in his
left hand the President's badge; left elbow resting on a table;
facs. signature below.
Ind. proof, 1831.
$9 \times 5\frac{3}{4}$. $(4\frac{1}{2} \times 3\frac{1}{4})$. E. 2189.–'89.

LAWRENCE, Sir William, 1783–1867, Bart., b. at Cirencester; educ. at Gloucester; apprenticed, 1799, to J. Abernethy, assist.-surgeon, St. Barth. Hosp., who apptd. him

demonstrator, 1801; M.C.S., 1805; assist.-surg., St. Barth. Hosp.; F.R.S.; surg. to Lond. Infirmy. for Diseases of the Eye, 1814; Surgeon to Bridewell and Bethlehem Hospls., 1815; to St. Barth., 1824–1865; pubd. several medical works; Surg. Extraord., and (1857) Sergeant-Surg. to the Queen; cr. Bart., 1867.

H. W. Pickersgill, R.A.   E. R. Whitfield.

T. Q. len. to front, standing, looking to right; left hand resting on a book on a table.

Proof before all letters, except the artists' names.

20 × 16. (16¼ × 13¼).   23004.

LAWSON, John Joseph,   – , printer of *The Times*; sentenced by Mr. Justice Littledale, Jany. 30, 1839, to "be " committed to the custody of the Marshal of the Marshalsea " for the space of one calendar month; that he pay to her " majesty a fine of 200*l.*, and that he be further imprisoned till " such fine be paid," for a libel against Sir John Conroy, which appeared some time before in *The Times* newspaper.

J. Sant.   D. Lucas, mez.

T. Q. len. to right, seated, looking to front; left hand in breast, a copy of *The Times* in his right hand; on the left is a grated window; facs. signature, dated "February 1839," below; published, March, 1840.

14 × 10$\frac{9}{10}$. (9½ × 7¼).   27548.

LAZARUS, Henry, 1815–1895, distinguished clarionettist, b. in London; stud. under Blizard, a bandmaster; second clarionet, 1838, at Sacred Harm. Socy.; suc. to Willman's place, at his death, as first clarionet at the Opera, all principal concerts, and festivals; famous for his full and beautiful tone, excellent phrasing, and neat and expressive execution; taught at the R. Acad. Music since 1854, and at the Military School of Music, Kneller Hall, Hounslow, since 1858, until late years.

See MUSICAL UNION.

LEBECK,   , celebrated cook and tavern-keeper in London, in the early part of the 18th century. The picture has been exhibited as the portrait of Christopher Kat, at whose tavern the Kit-cat Club, named after him, used to meet.

Sir G. Kneller.   A. Miller, mez.

J. C. Smith, 29, 2nd state.   28004.

LEE, John, 1783–1866, Astronomer and Antiquary; eldest son of John Fiott, merchant, of an old Burgundian house; assumed maternal name, Lee, 1815, being descended from Ld. Chf. Justice Lee; educ. at Cambr.; 5th Wrangler, 1806; Fellow and Travelling Bachelor of his Coll. (St. John's); travelled on Continent and in East, where he amassed a very valuable collection of antiquities; author of "Antiquarian Researches in the Ionian Islands;" LL.D., Q.C., member of Advocates of Doctors' Commons; Pres. Royal Astr. Society; erected an Observatory at Hartwell, Bucks.

[Maguire.]   T. H. Maguire, lith., 1849.

Full ha. len. to front, seated, looking to right, right hand on
open book; rect. with corners cut off; vignette; facs. signature below.
(10 × 9½).   24638.

LEE, NATHANIEL, c. 1653-1692, said to have been son of
Richard Lee, D.D.; educ. at Westminster, and Trin. Coll.,
Cambr.; B.A., 1667/8; came to London, fell in with Rochester and his set, whose vices he imitated, to the detriment of
his health; attempted acting, 1672, unsuccessfully; wrote
plays, "Nero," "Gloriana," "Sophonisba," "The Rival
Queens," "Œdipus," &c.; confined in Bethlehem Hospital,
1684-'89; found dead in the street, after an orgy.
       Dobson.   J. Watts, mez.
       J. C. Smith, 5.   24643.

LEEDS, FRANCIS GODOLPHIN OSBORNE, 5th Duke of, 1751-
1799, educ. at Westminster and Oxford; M.P., 1774, 1775;
F.R.S.; P.C.; Ambassador Extr. to Paris, 1783; Foreign
Sec., 1783-'91; suc., 1789; K.G.; &c.
   See DILETTANTI SOCIETY (as Marq. of Carmarthen).

LEEDS, THOMAS OSBORNE, Duke of, 1631-1712, Statesman,
Duke, 1694.
       P. Lely Pinxit.   A. Blooteling Fec. et ex.
       As Earl of Danby. In an oval laurel border.
       Very scarce and fine.
       10½ × 6⅞.   (9⅛ × 6¼).   25774.

LEES, SIR HARCOURT, 1776-1852, political pamphleteer, eldest
son of Sir John Lees, Bart.; educ. at Trin. Coll., Cambr.;
B.A., 1799; M.A., 1802; Rector and Vicar, Killaney, Down;
preb. of Fennor, Cashel, 1800, and of Tullycorbet, Clogher,
1801; resigned both, 1808; pubd. several pamphlets in support
of protestant ascendency.
       T. C. Thompson, R.H.A.   H. Meyer, stipple.
       Ha. len. seated, to left; "The Great Protestant Advocate."
       Vignette; Ind. proof; March 20, 1824.
       14 × 11⅜.   (11 × 10¾).   27598.

LEFROY, RT. HON. THOMAS LANGLOIS, 1776-1869; Baron of
the Exchequer (Ireland), 1841; ch. justice of Queen's Bench
(Ireland), 1852-'60; M.P. for Dublin University; P.C.; &c.
       Catterson Smith.   G. Zobel, mixed mez.
       T. Q. len. to right, looking to front, seated, in robes, writing
in note-book on his knee.
       Ind. proof with open letters, July 30, 1855.
       21½ × 16⅞.   (16⅞ × 13).   24230.

LEGGE, HENRY BILSON, RT. HON., 1708-1764, Statesman;
third son of 1st Earl of Dartmouth; ent. navy, but aftds. took
to public life; Lord of the Admiralty, 1746; Lord of Treasury,

1747; Envoy to Berlin, 1748 ; Chanc. of Exchequer, 1754, 1756, 1757-'59; d. at Tunbridge Wells.
W. Hoare. R. Houston, mez.
J. C. Smith, 70, 2nd state. 22034.

LEICESTER, SIR JOHN FLEMING, first Baron de Tabley, 1762-1827; a munificent patron of the fine arts, cr. Baron, 1826.
Sir J. Reynolds and J. Northcote, R.A.
S. W. Reynolds, mez.
Wh. len. to right, looking to left, and pointing with sword to right; his horse on left, the bridle over his right arm; in uniform, as Col. of the Cheshire Provisional Cavalry.
June 13, 1800.
$25\frac{1}{4} \times 15$. $(23\frac{13}{16} \times 15)$. 27533.
NOTE.—This is from the last picture painted by Sir J. Reynolds.

LEICESTER, ROBERT DUDLEY, 1532(?)-1588, favourite of Q. Elizabeth, imprisoned in Tower and sentenced to execution for supporting Lady J. Grey; pardoned; K.G.; Chancellor of Oxford; &c.
C. van Sichem.
Wh. len. in armour, sea and ships behind. Marked "fol. 662" in top right corner.
$(7\frac{1}{4} \times 5\frac{9}{16})$. 25487.

Anon. [C. van Sichem ?]
Wh. len on horseback, to right, looking front.
In a "History of the Netherlands" (Bromley). Marked "10" at foot in right corner.
Cut. $(10 \times 6\frac{1}{8})$. 23449.

(From a picture in the Collection of Sir Rob. Worsley, Bart.)
J. Houbraken, 1738.
Sh. ha. len. to left, looking to front, sword-hilt in left hand; oval in border.
In Birch's "Lives."
$14\frac{1}{2} \times 8\frac{1}{16}$. $(13\frac{3}{4} \times 8\frac{1}{2})$. 27118.

LEICESTER, THOMAS WILLIAM COKE, 1st Earl of Leicester, 1752-1842, son of W. R. Coke, Esqre.; many years M.P. for Norfolk; well known for his excellent management of the Holkham estate, and as one of the most active improvers of English agriculture; cr. Earl of Leicester, 1837.
Sir T. Lawrence, R.A. C. Turner, mez.
Wh. len. to front, looking and facing to left; left hand on hip, right resting on papers on table by his side.
Open letter proof, July 14, 1814.
$27\frac{1}{2} \times 16\frac{3}{4}$. $(24\frac{1}{16} \times 14\frac{1}{2})$. 22119.

LEIGH, ANTHONY, -1692, comedian, b. in Northamptonshire; a member (1672) of the Duke of York's company in Dorset Gardens, and in the highest favour with Charles II.

O 82849. T

and the public; played the Friar in Dryden's "Spanish Friar,"
Feb. 1681–2, and many other original parts of importance;
d. of a fever; Kneller was commissioned by Charles, Earl of
Dorset, to paint this portrait, which was "highly finished and
extremely like him."

Sir G. Kneller.   J. Smith, mez.
J. C Smith, 155, 3rd state.   21877

LEIGHTON, ROBERT, D.D., 1611–1684, sent to Edinb. Univ.,
1627; M.A., 1631; travelled abroad, and acquired languages;
returned to Scotland, licensed, 1641, inducted to parish of
Newbattle; gained great reputation as a preacher; principal of
the Univ., Edinb., 1653, and Profr. of Divinity; Bishop of
Dunblane, 1661; Archbishop of Glasgow, 1669; resigned,
1672; his resignation accepted, 1674; retired to Sussex;
pubd. "Rules and Instructions for a Holy Life," Sermons,
Commentaries, &c.

Anon.   R. Strange.
Sh. ha. len. to left, in gown, looking to front; oval in border;
"Ætat. 42, 1654," in a selection from his works, 1758.

$6\frac{3}{8} \times 4$ (?). $(6 \times 3\frac{1}{4})$.   26700.

LEINSTER, WILLIAM ROBERT FITZGERALD, 2nd Duke of,
1749–1805, Marquis of Kildare, &c., M.P. Dublin.

M. A. Shee, R.A.   C. Turner, mez.
Wh. len. to front, looking to left; resting fingers of right
hand on table; London, Pub. Novr. 24, 1804.

Fine proof before inscription. There are traces of the
artists' names, in right and left lower corners, below which
again they are engraved on a supplementary plate, which is
otherwise blank.

$(26\frac{1}{8} \times 18\frac{1}{4})$.   24742.

LELY, SIR PETER, 1617–1680, celebrated painter, b. at Soest,
in Westphalia; arrived in England just after the death of Van
Dyck, 1641; after painting landscapes and subjects, he became
the fashionable portrait-painter of the time; painted Charles I.,
Cromwell, Charles II., the "Beauties" at Hampton Court, &c.;
knighted, 1680; d. Novr. 30 in same year.

Lely.   A. de Jode
Ha. len. to left, looking to front; long wig, right hand to
breast, landscape behind him.

$13\frac{7}{8} \times 11\frac{1}{10}$ (?). $(12\frac{1}{2} \times 11)$.   E. 223.–'93.

Lely.   I. Beckett, mez.
J. C. Smith, 63, 2nd state,   27136.

[Lely.]   Anon.
Ha. len. to left, looking to front; long wig.
In the "Universal Magazine."

$7\frac{3}{8} \times 4\frac{1}{4}$. $(6\frac{1}{8} \times 3\frac{15}{16})$.   15219. 6.

LELY, Sir Peter—*continued*.

Lely. J. Corner.

Ha. len. to left, looking to front; long wig; right hand to breast. Below, in the border, is a copy of the portrait of Frances, Duchess of Richmond, painted by Lely.

Proof before all letters.

$10\frac{1}{4} \times 7\frac{7}{8}$. ($5\frac{1}{8} \times 3\frac{7}{8}$, including border; $4 \times 3\frac{3}{16}$, excl. border). 26260.

[Lely.] Anon.

Bust to left, looking to front, with long wig; oval.

Cut out from some larger print.

($1\frac{7}{8} \times 1\frac{5}{8}$). 15219. 7.

LENNOX, Margaret Douglas, Countess of, 1515–1577, wife of Mathew Stuart, 4th Earl of Lennox, brother of Lord Darnley; niece of Henry VIII.; b. at Harbottle; imprisoned by Henry VIII. and Elizabeth; buried in Westminster Abbey.

From an original picture, anon., at Hampton Court.

(F. Ross del.) J. Brown, stipple.

Wh. len. to front, in a dark dress, trimmed with fur; a little dog plays at her feet, on right of print; for the Granger Society.

Ind proof, 1841.

$12\frac{1}{16} \times 9$. ($8\frac{15}{16} \times 5\frac{1}{16}$). 24641.

LENS, Bernard, 1680–1740, miniature-painter, b. in London, son of B. Lens, a mezzotintist, and taught by him; became one of the best miniaturists of his time; enameller and miniature-painter to George II.; excelled in water-colour copies from Rubens, Van Dyck, and other great masters; drawing-master to Christ's Hospital, &c.; prepared a drawing-book, published after his death; scraped some plates; d. at Knightsbridge.

B. Lens. Anon., stipple.

Ha. len. to front, looking to right, holding palette and brushes in left hand.

Pubd. Novr. 1, 1824, by E. Evans.

$6\frac{1}{8} \times 4\frac{1}{8}$. ($4\frac{3}{8} \times 3\frac{3}{8}$). 26254.

LENTHALL, William, 1591–1662 (or '63), M.P., Speaker; Master of the Rolls; sat in H. of Lords as Lord Lenthall

S. Cooper, min. (G. P. Harding del.) J. Brown.

Pubd. Decr. 20, 1847

Bust, to right, looking to front, oval in border.

$10\frac{1}{8} \times 7\frac{1}{8}$. ($4 \times 3\frac{1}{8}$). 24720.

LEOPOLD, K. of Belgians. *See* CHARLOTTE, Princess.

LEOPOLD, George Duncan Albert, Prince, 1853–1884.

[Winterhalter?] Anon. [J. A. Vinter?], lith.

As a child; in a circle, cut round.

($12\frac{1}{4}$ diamr.) 22195.

LESLIE, Sir John, 1766–1832, mathematician and natural philosopher, b. at Largo in Fife; educ. at St. Andrews and

Edinb. ; came to London, 1790; went to Etruria, Staffs., as
tutor to the young Wedgwoods, 1790–'92 ; after a few months
in Holland, returned to Largo for ten years, studying and
making experimental research ; mounted several instruments
for use in sciences of heat and meteorology, &c.; gained the
Rumford medal, 1805 ; Prof. Math., Edinb., 1805 ; Prof. Nat.
Ph., 1819; pubd. many scientific works.
See SCIENCE

L'ESTRANGE, Sir Roger, 1616–1704, Political writer and
partisan ; b. in Norfolk ; educ. at Camb. ; sided with the King
in Civil War; prisoner at Lynn, sentenced to be shot, 1644 ;
imprisoned in Newgate 4 years; escaped to Continent;
returned, 1653, and pardoned by Cromwell; licenser of Press,
after Restoration ; wrote in favour of the Court; Knt. by
James II., but afterwards lost all his appointments.
  Sir G. Kneller.   R. White.
  Sh. ha. len. to front; long wig ; oval in border ; motto, Vos
Non Vobis, above ; arms below.
  Cut. ($13\frac{3}{4} \times 10\frac{7}{16}$)   21820.

LETTSOM, John Coakley, 1744–1815, physician, b. at Little
Vandyke, one of the Virgin Islands, W. Indies ; appr. to A.
Sutcliff, surgeon, at Settle, Yorks.; M.D. Leyden, 1769;
L.R.C.P., 1770, and F.S.A.; F.R.S., 1771 ; a rigid Quaker,
most successful in his profession ; LL.D., member of several
Academies and Literary Societies.
See MEDICAL SOCIETY.

LEVETT, Sir Richard,   –1711, Lord Mayor London, 1699.
  R. White.   R. White, 1700.
  Sh. ha. len. to right, looking to front, in oval, surrounded with
civic emblems.
  Cut. ($13\frac{3}{8} \times 10\frac{1}{4}$).   E. 198.–'91.
  See also ALDERMEN.

LEWIS, Sir George Cornewall, 1806–1863, statesman, Bart. ;
educ. at Eton and Oxford ; B.A., 1828 ; Chf. Commr. of Poor
Laws, 1839 ; M.P., Herefordsh., 1847, and Sec. to Board of
Control ; Sec. of Treasury, 1850 ; Home Sec. ; War Sec., 1861 ;
author of several works, particularly the "Inquiry into the
Credibility of Early Roman History," "Influence of Authority
in Matters of Opinion," &c.
  See COMMONS (2).

LEWIS, Lee, actor, speaking a Prologue in the Character of
Harlequin.
  From a "Collection   of English Prologues," &c.,
1779.   28187.   9.

LEWIS, Lady Maria Theresa, 1803–1865, daughter of George
Villiers, 3rd son of the 1st Earl of Clarendon, and sister to
the 4th Earl ; m. 1st, 1830, to Thomas Henry Lister, of Army-
tage Park, Staffordshire, who d. 1842 ; 2nd, 1844, to Sir

George Cornewall Lewis, Bart., M.P., who d. 1863; authoress
of "Clarendon and his Contemporaries," &c. ; d. at Oxford.
  G. S. Newton, R.A.   S. Cousins, mixed mez.
  Ha. len. to front, as Mrs. Lister, wearing a high headdress,
curls, a cross hanging from a ribbon round her neck; leaning
with both arms on the parapet of a balcony.
  Open letter proof, 1st Octr. 1834.
  14⅜ × 10⅚. (10½ × 8¼).   27080.

LEWIS, Sir Thomas Frankland, 1780–1855, Bart., M.P., Sec.
Treasury; Treasurer of Navy, 1830.
  F. Watts.   T. H. Maguire, lith.
  Ha. len. seated, to left, facs. signature below.
  (12½ × 9½).   27170.

LEWIS, William Thomas, 1748–1811, Comedian; b. at Orms-
kirk, Lancashire; brought to Ireland, 1749; educ. at Armagh;
went on the stage when young; appeared at Dublin as "Belcour"
in the "West Indian," 1771, and at Edinb.; at Covent Garden,
1773, where he played parts formerly filled by Barry and Woodward, and became deputy manager; d. at Westbourne Place,
King's Road, Chelsea.
  M. Shee.   J. Jones, mez.
  J. C. Smith, 47, 1st state.   21887.

LIGONIER, Sir John Ligonier, 1st Earl, 1678–1770, of an
ancient French family; served, with great distinction, through
Marlborough's campaigns; Knt. banneret at Dettingen, 1743;
cr. Visct., 1757; Field-Marshal; Col. 1st Foot Guards; cr.
Baron Ligonier of Ripley, 1763; cr. Earl, 1766; K.B., F.R.S.
  Sir J. Reynolds.   E. Fisher, mez.
  J. C. Smith, 38, 2nd state.   22249.

LINDLEY, John, 1799–1865, Botanist; b. near Norwich; assist.
Loudon in his "Encyclopædia of Plants;" Prof. of Botany in
Univ. Coll., London, 1829; advocated Natural System of Botany
in oppos. to Linnæus; pub. "The Vegetable Kingdom," "Flora
Medica," "Fossil Flora of Great Britain," &c.; received Copley
Gold Medal of the Royal Society.
  Maguire.   T. H. Maguire, lith., 1849.
  Full ha. len. to front, arms folded over coat, buttoned up;
vignette; corners cut off.
  (9½ × 9).   22517.

LINDLEY, Robert, 1776–1855, b. at Rotherham, precocious
performer on violin, at 5, and violoncello, at 9 years; pupil
of Cervetto; engaged at the Brighton Theatre; succeeded
Sperati as principal violoncello at the Opera and chief concerts,
1794, and held that position till his retirement, 1851; composed
concertos, &c.; an admirable violoncellist.
  W. Davison.   J. P. Quilley, mez.
  T. Q. len. to front, seated, holding his violoncello with left
hand, a pinch of snuff in his right; his bow, music, and snuff-
box, open, on table by him, on which his right arm rests.
  Ind. paper; marked, "proof," in left lower corner.
  20½ × 13⅙. (17½ × 13⅛).   24122.

LINDSEY, ROBERT BERTIE, 1st Earl of, 1582–1642, son of
Peregrine, Lord Willoughby of Eresby, b. in London; educ. at
Cambr.; suc. as 10th Baron, 1601; served at Amiens, Cadiz,
and in Low Countries; Lord Great Chamberlain, Admiral,
Capt.-General, Governor of a Fleet, and cr. Earl of Lindsey,
1626; P.C., 1628; K.G., 1630; Lord High Admiral, 1635;
Genl.-in-Chf., 1642; wounded at Edge Hill, and d. of
his wounds.

C. Janssens. J. Houbraken, 1742.
Sh. ha. len., slightly inclined to left, looking to front, in
armour; oval in border; in Birch's "Lives."
$14\frac{3}{4} \times 9\frac{5}{16}$. $(14\frac{3}{16} \times 8\frac{3}{4})$. 24668.

LINGARD, JOHN, 1771–1851, b. at Winchester, the son of
humble parents, educ. at Douai, 1782–1793; priest, 1795, at
Crook Hall, Durham; wrote papers on Antiquities, afterwards
expanded into 2 vols., and a "History of England," 1819–1830,
for which he received the degrees of D.D. and LL.D. from Pius
VII., and from Leo XII. the gold medal, which is usually
given only to Cardinals and princes; he wrote many other
works, mainly in defence of the doctrines of the Roman Catholic
Church.

J. Lonsdale. H. Cousins, mixed mez.
T. Q. len. to left, seated, looking to right; a pen in right hand;
books and papers on table on left; a bookcase and drapery
behind.
Open letter proof, with facs. signature below, May 1, 1836.
$20\frac{3}{4} \times 15\frac{5}{16}$. $(17\frac{1}{4} \times 12\frac{9}{16})$. 23003.

LINLEY WILLIAM, c. 1767–1835, youngest son of Thomas
Linley, the composer; educ. at St. Paul's and Harrow; stud.
music under his father and Abel; civil servant in Madras;
returned with a competence, devoted himself to literature and
music; composed many glees, songs, &c., and two comic operas,
two novels, and some poetry.

Sir T. Lawrence. T. Lupton, mez.
Ha. len. to front, slightly inclined, and looking to left; with
long hair; one button of coat fastened; 1840.
$15\frac{3}{4} \times 11$. $(11\frac{13}{16} \times 9\frac{1}{8})$. 24083.

LINWOOD, MISS MARY, 1755–1845, celebrated for her needle-
work, b. at Birmingham, removed early in life to Leicester;
exhibited a collection of her worsted-work, Hanover Sqr.-Rooms,
1798, afterwards in Leicester Square, later in Edinburgh,
Dublin, and other great towns; worked over 100 copies chiefly
from originals of great masters; enjoyed great reputation
and popularity; her collection, after her death, realised only a
trifling sum.

Anon. P. W. Tomkins, chalk and dot.
Wh. len. to left, seated, looking to front, by a stream in a
wood; holding a crayon in right hand, and resting left arm on a
portfolio.
Proof with skeleton letters; April 29, 1806.
$18\frac{5}{8} \times 14\frac{11}{16}$. $(15\frac{5}{8} \times 12\frac{5}{8})$. 22466.

LINWOOD, Miss Mary—*continued.*
    Anon.   J. Hopwood, junr., stipple.
    Sh. ha. len. inclined to right, looking to front; hair in ringlets,
    lace round top of low dress; high waist; oval in border, a
    reversed copy from the preceding print; a basket of flowers,
    harp, and books below. Oct. 1, 1817.
        $7\frac{3}{8} \times 4\frac{1}{2}$(?). ($8 \times 2\frac{3}{8}$, oval).   15219. 8.

LISCOMBE, Thomas, a labourer, murderer of Sarah Ford, the
    wife of a farmer, of North Huish, Devon, Oct. 17, 1812; when
    apprehended, he confessed another murder, on the 20th of pre-
    ceding January; his portrait was taken in Exeter Gaol.
    W. Brockedon.   F. C. Lewis, stipple and aquatint.
    Bust, to front, rough hair, white neckcloth, scowling brows;
    vignette; March 12, 1813.
        $16\frac{11}{16} \times 13\frac{2}{8}$. ($15\frac{1}{4} \times 11$).   28005.

LISLE, Sir George,   −1648; son of a bookseller in London,
    Royalist; shot, after the surrender of Colchester, with Sir
    Charles Lucas.
    Anon.   M. vander Gucht.
    Sh. ha. len to right, looking to front, wearing a gorget and
    baldrick; oval in border; name on a tablet below.
        Cut ($6\frac{9}{16} \times 3\frac{3}{4}$).   27137.
    See also LUCAS.

LISTER, George, celebrated feeder and trainer of fighting
    cocks, c. 1800.
    W. Artaud.   W. Say, mez.
    Ha. len. to front, with short curled wig, striped waistcoat,
    left hand partly seen.
        Scratched letter proof, March 10, 1804.
        $14\frac{7}{8} \times 10\frac{15}{16}$. ($13\frac{3}{16} \times 10\frac{15}{16}$).   27953.

LISTER, Mrs. *See* LEWIS, Lady Maria Theresa.

LISTON, John, 1777–1846, a very popular low comedian; b. in
    St. Anne's, Soho; began as a teacher in a day school; took
    part in amateur theatricals with C. Mathews; was discovered in
    a provincial company by C. Kemble; engaged at Haymarket,
    1805; next, at Cov. Garden; later, at Drury Lane, at 40*l.* a
    week; at Olympic, aftds., under Madame Vestris, with 100*l.*
    weekly salary; d. rich.
    J. Jackson, R.A.   W. Ward, A.R.A., mez.
    Sh. ha. len. to front, looking rather towards right; coat with
    high collar, buttoned up; eye-glass hanging by broad ribbon.
    "Finished" proof before all letters, the word "Finished"
    being written (by the engraver?) in the lower margin, on
    right.
        $13\frac{7}{8} \times 9\frac{7}{8}$. ($11\frac{7}{8} \times 9\frac{1}{4}$).   21922.

LISTON, JOHN—*continued*.
   G. Clint, A.R.A.   T. Lupton, mez.
   Wh. len. as Paul Pry, with Madame Vestris, Miss P. Glover, and Mr. Williams; Liston stands at right, facing to left, and pointing to door which the others defend.
   Open letter proof, July 1, 1828.
   $20\frac{3}{8} \times 16$. $(18\frac{7}{16} \times 14\frac{3}{8})$ 24254.
   See also BLANCHARD

LISTON, ROBERT, 1794–1848; surgeon; eminent as lecturer and operator at Edinburgh; afterwards surgeon to North London Hospital, and Professor of Surgery at Univ. Coll., London; author of " Principles of Surgery," &c.
   C. Turner, A.R.A., del.   C. Turner, mez.
   Full hn. len. to front, looking to left; left hand resting on books on table; curtain behind; facs. signature below.
   Open letter proof, Jany. 16, 1840.
   $19 \times 13\frac{1}{8}$. $(14 \times 10\frac{7}{8})$.   21963.

LITTLETON, SIR THOMAS, c. 1421–1481, jurist, of Inner Temple, K.B. Wrote a work on " Tenures."
   Anon.   Anon. (Vaughan ?)
   Wh. len. to right, kneeling; a motto, "Ung Dieu et Ung Roy, " issuing from his lips. Below, "The true portraiture of " Judge Littleton the Famous English Lawyer."
   Cut. $7\frac{1}{2}(?) \times 5\frac{3}{4}$. $(6\frac{7}{8} \times 5\frac{1}{8})$.   26701

LIVERPOOL, 1ST EARL OF. *See* **HAWKESBURY.**

LIVERPOOL, ROBERT BANKS JENKINSON, 2nd Earl of, 1770–1828, Statesman, son of 1st Earl; educ. at Charterhouse and Oxford; M.P. for Rye, 1790; Foreign Sec., 1801–'4; Home Sec., 1804, 1807; Sec. for War, 1807–'12; suc. 1808; Premier, 1812–'27; K.G.; d. at Combe Wood.
   Sir T. Lawrence.   Anon., mixed mez.
   T. Q. len. slightly turned to right, looking to front, hands folded together; from the picture belonging to the Queen
   Proof before all letters.
   $21\frac{7}{8} \times 15\frac{7}{8}$. $(17\frac{3}{8} \times 13\frac{3}{4})$.   22880.

LIVERSEEGE, HENRY, 1803–1832, subject-painter, b. at Manchester; exhibited at Manchester, 1827, three small pictures of Banditti; came to London; exhibited at Academy, 1828; stud. at British Museum and British Institution; exhibited for a few years at Manchester and in London; dramatic in style, brilliant in colour, but wanting in refinement; had very bad health; d. suddenly, at Manchester.
   W. Bradley.   H. Cousins, mixed mez.
   T. Q. len. inclined to right, looking to front, seated; holding crayon in right hand; left hand resting on paper on table; facs. signature below. July 1, 1835.
   $11\frac{1}{2} \times 9$. $(8\frac{1}{2} \times 6\frac{11}{16})$.   E. 2191.–'89.

LLOYD, William, Bishop of St. Asaph. *See* BISHOPS, the
SEVEN, GROUP (2). 26668.

LOCKE, John, 1632–1704, Philosopher, stud. Chemistry and
Medicine; sec. to Lord Shaftesbury, 1672; fled to Holland, to
escape a Government prosecution, under suspicion of complicity
in Monmouth's rebellion; returned after the Revolution, 1689;
author of the "Essay on the Human Understanding," a
"Treatise on Civil Government," &c.
Sir G. Kneller. J. Smith, mez.
J. C. Smith, 157, 2nd state. 21881

LOCKE, Joseph, 1805–1860, civil engineer; b. at Attercliffe,
near Sheffield; worked under G. Stephenson at Newcastle,
under whom he was empl. in construction of Manch. and
L'pool R'way; constr. r'ways between Warrington and Birmingham, Lancaster and Preston, Sheffield and Manchester, London
and Southampton, and some on the Continent; M.P., Honiton,
1847–'60; Pres. I.C.E.; memb., Legion of Honour; d. at
Moffat.
F. Grant, A.R.A. H. Cousins, mixed mez.
Wh. len. to left, looking to front; left hand in pocket, cane in
right, hat and gloves on a bank beside him, on right; June 1,
1849.
30¾ × 19½. (26¾ × 16⅛). 25749.
See also MENAI.

LOCKHART, John Gibson, LL.D., 1793–1854, critic, novelist,
and biographer; b. in Glasgow; educ. at Balliol Coll., Oxf.;
admitted a Scottish advocate, 1816, but soon left the law for
literature; contributed to "Blackwood," 1817; became a friend,
and married the daughter (Sophia) of Walter Scott; wrote
"Valerius," "Adam Blair," &c., and the life of his father-in-
law.
F. Grant, R.A. J. Faed, mixed mez.
Ha. len. slightly to left, looking rather to right; the hands
together.
Open letter proof (?); Jany. 31st, 1856.
15¾ × 12½. (11⅞ × 9½). 23001.
See also SCOTT, Sir Walter.

LONDONDERRY, Charles William, 3rd Marquess. *See*
STEWART.

LONDONDERRY, Robert Stewart, 2nd Marquess of, 1769–
1822; better known as Visct. Castlereagh; son of 1st Marquess;
b. at Mount Stewart, co. Down; educ. at Cambridge; M.P. in
Irish, aftds. in British, Parliament; Chief Sec. for Ireland; took
prom. part in Union, 1801; Sec. for War and Colonies, 1805,
1807; Foreign Sec., 1812–'22; Plenipo. to Congr. of Vienna,
1814; suc. as 2nd Marquess, 1821; K.G., &c.; com. suicide,
1822, at North Cray Place; bur. in Westmr. Abbey.
Sir T. Lawrence. C. Turner, mez.

Wh. len. to right, looking to left, in robes of the Garter.
Fine proof before border and all letters, but cut.
(25¼ × 16⅛). 24084.
Another proof, with a finely-ruled border, 1½ in. wide, but
before all letters. 22881.

LONG, RIGHT HON. CHARLES, 1761–1838; Politician, educ. at
Camb.; M.P., 1789–1826; friend of Pitt, and consistent Tory;
P.C. 1805; **Paymaster** of the forces; Chief Sec., Ireland; cr.
Baron Farnborough, 1826; a good judge of painting and archi-
tecture; collector of pictures and sculptures; Trustee of Nat.
Gallery, &c.
H. Edridge. C. Picart.
Bust, to front, looking to left. Published Jan. 11, 1810.
14⅞ × (cut). (6¾ × 5½). 27998. 3.

LONSDALE, JAMES, 1777–1839, portrait-painter; b. in Lancashire; came early to London; pupil of Romney; stud. in
Academy schools; on the death of Opie, bought his house in
Berners St., where he lived the rest of his life; painted good
portraits, his subjects being chiefly gentlemen, including many
of the most distinguished of the day; exhibited at the R.A.;
was one of the founders of the Society of British Artists, where
he exhibited, 1824–'37.
[J. Lonsdale ?] C. Turner, mez.
Ha. len. to right, looking to front; coat buttoned up; hair
scanty on top of head.
Proof before all letters.
14 × 9¹⁵⁄₁₆. (9¹⁵⁄₁₆ × 8³⁄₁₆). 27221.

LORDS, View of the Interior of the House of, during the Trial
of Queen Caroline, 1820. *See* CAROLINE.

LORDS JUSTICES, THEIR EXCELLENCIES THE, For the Administration of the Government during the Absence of the King.
[White.] R. White, 1695.
A set of seven ovals on one plate, not mentioned by Bromley,
though he describes another similar set. In the centre is
THOMAS [TENISON], Archbishop of Canterbury, 1636–
1715; Archbp. 1694; above, on left, is SOMERS, JOHN, Lord,
1651–1716, Lord Keeper, P.C., Lord High Chancellor, &c.;
above, on right, PEMBROKE, THOMAS HERBERT, 8th Earl of,
1656–1733, Lord Privy Seal, P.C., K.G., Lord High Admiral,
&c.; on left, middle, DEVONSHIRE, WILLIAM, 4th Earl of,
1641–1707, cr. Duke, 1694, Lord Steward, K.G., &c.; on right,
middle, SHREWSBURY, CHARLES, 12th Earl of, 1660–1718,
cr. Duke, 1694, Principal Sec. of State, P.C., K.G., &c.; on left,
below, DORSET, CHARLES, 6th Earl of, 1637–1706, Lord
Chamberlain, P.C., K.G., F.R.S., &c.; and on right, below,
GODOLPHIN, SIDNEY, Earl of, c. 1644–1712, First Lord of
Treasury, P.C., K.G., &c., cr. Earl, 1706.

"Printed and Sold by John King at the Globe against the Church in the Poultry."

The name of each personage is on a label, below his portrait.

From the Tunno Collection, sold, 1863.

$15\frac{1}{8} \times 11$(?). $(13\frac{15}{16} \times 10\frac{3}{4})$. 27563.

LORNE, Louise Caroline Alberta, Princess, 1848– 4th dau. and 6th child of H.M. Queen Victoria; m. to the Marquess of, 1871.

F. Winterhalter. T. Fairland, lith., 1851.

As a child; in a circle.

$(11\frac{7}{8}$ diamr.). 22193.

A. Graefle. J. A. Vinter, lith., 1864.

As Princess Louise, before her marriage.

T. Q. len. to left, looking to front.

$(20\frac{3}{8} \times 15\frac{5}{8})$. 22188.

LOUDON, John Claudius, 1783–1843, writer on Agriculture, Botany, and Gardening; b. at Cambuslang, Lanarks.; author of the Encyclopædias of Gardening, &c.; contrib. to "Horticultural Transactions," &c.; d. at Bayswater.

J. Linnell (?). Anon., stipple.

Ha. len. to left, seated, looking to front; vignette; facs. signature below.

Ind. proof, 1845.

$9 \times 5\frac{3}{4}$. $(4\frac{1}{4} \times 3\frac{5}{8})$. 27600

LOUGHBOROUGH, Alexander, Baron. *See* ROSSLYN.

LOUISA MARIA, Princess, 1692–1712, 6th child of James II.; d. unmarried. *See* JAMES FRANCIS EDWARD, the "Old Pretender."

LOUISE, Princess. *See* LORNE.

LOUTHERBOURG, Philip James de, 1740–1812, b. at Strassburg, son of a miniature-painter, of noble Polish family; pupil of Vanloo, at Paris; member of the French Academy at the early age of 22; visited Switzerland, Germany, Italy, painting portraits, landscapes, and battles; engaged by Garrick, at 500*l*. a year, to superintend scenery and machinery at Drury Lane, where he showed wonderful talent and ingenuity, for many years; R.A., 1781; was very eccentric.

Anon. (J. Jackson del.) H. Meyer stipple.

Bust to front, looking to left; white neckcloth, coat buttoned across; vignette.

Open letter proof.

$(6 \times 6\frac{1}{4})$. 28298. 4.

Anon. Page, stipple.

Sh. ha. len. to left, looking rather to right; coat fastened by one button; high collar; oval, "from the Original Picture in "the Possession of Mrs. Loutherbourg;" Aug. 1, 1814.

$6\frac{3}{8} \times 4\frac{1}{8}$. $(4\frac{1}{16} \times 3\frac{3}{8})$. 28300. 34.

LOVAT, Simon Fraser, 11th Lord, c. 1667–1747, b. near Inverness; Capt. in Lord Tullibardine's Regt.; went to France, and gained favour with James II. and the Pretender; employed by them on a mission to Scotland, 1702, and betrayed them; ent. Jesuits' Coll., St. Omer; returned to Scotland; opposed rising of 1715; claimed dignity of Lord Lovat, which was allowed; impl. in Rebellion of 1745; beheaded on Tower Hill.

Hogarth del.   Hogarth, etched.
Described in Cat. of Political and Personal Satires, Br. Museum, Vol. III., Part 1, 1877; 2801, 2nd state; p. 609.
$14\frac{7}{16} \times 9\frac{3}{8}$. $(13\frac{1}{4} \times 8\frac{13}{16})$.   22467.

LOVER, Samuel, 1797–1868, b. in Dublin, began as a painter, elected an Academician of the Royal Hibernian Society of Arts, of which he became Secretary; took to literature, wrote "Legends and Tales," "Irish Sketches," "Handy Andy," Songs, Lyrics of Ireland," &c., and gave an entertainment, "Irish Evenings," in which he embodied songs and music of his own composition.

Baugniet.   Baugniet, lith.
Sh. ha. len. to left, looking to front, holding an eye-glass in right hand; vignette; facs. signature.
Ind. proof, 1844.
$(8 \times 8\frac{3}{8})$.   26653.

LOWE, Sir Hudson, 1769–1844, Irish General, served in the French War; Governor of St. Helena, with charge of Napoleon, 1816; sailed for England, 1821; his "Memoirs" pubd., 1854.

Anon.   Anon.
Published for Henry Colburn, March, 1836.
Sha. ha. len. to front, looking to left, in uniform, bareheaded.
Ind. proof, with open letters; vignette.
$7\frac{3}{4} \times 5\frac{1}{16}$. $(3\frac{1}{4} \times 3)$ 22882.

LOWRY, Wilson, 1762–1824, Engraver and Mineralogist, son of a portrait-painter; b. at Whitehaven; began as house-painter at Worcester, where he began engraving also; came to London, 1779, and ent. R.A. schools; engr. most of the machinery for Rees' "Encyclopædia," and several other such works, and illustrated some architectural treatises; invented his ruling-machine, c. 1790; a good mathem. draughtsman, with knowledge of anatomy, geology, mineralogy, precious stones, and surgery; d. in London; F.R.S., M.G S., &c.

J. Linnell del.   J. Linnell & W. Blake.
Bust to right, looking nearly to front; with shirt frill; vignette.
Ind. proof, Jan. 1, 1825.
$10 \times 7\frac{3}{4}$. $(5\frac{1}{2} \times 4\frac{1}{4})$.   27222.

LOWTH, Robert, D.D., 1710–1787, 2nd son of William Lowth, divine; educ. at Winchester, and New Coll., Oxf.; B.A.,

1733; M.A., 1737; wrote poems while at Winchester; vicar of Overton, Hants., 1735; Profr. of Poetry, Oxf., delivered remarkable series of lectures on Hebrew poetry; tutor to Lords George and Fred. Cavendish, 1749; Archdeacon, Winchester, 1750; Rector of Woodhay, Hants, 1753; D.D., 1754; Bishop of St. David's, 1766; then of Oxford, and of London, 1777, and Dean of the Chapel Royal; P.C.; refused Canterbury; pubd. "Prelectiones," Lectures, controversial pamphlets, poems, sermons, &c.

R. E. Pine. J. K. Sherwin.

T. Q. len. to left, seated, in robes, right hand raised; books before him.

$17\frac{5}{8} \times 13\frac{3}{4}$. ($13\frac{3}{8} \times 10\frac{5}{8}$). 21835.

LUCAN, PATRICK SARSFIELD, Earl of, –1693; b. at Lucan, co. Dublin; second son of Patrick Sarsfield of that place; suc. his elder brother in the estate; served in France; Lieut. of Guards; raised a troop of horse, 1688, in Ireland, for the service of James II., and was app. Col., with rank of Brig.-General; commanded Irish horse at the Boyne, 1690; highly distinguished at siege of Limerick, and cr. Baron Rosberry, Visct. of Tully, Earl of Lucan, 1691; Col. of Life Guards; Com.-in-Chf. in Ireland, but superseded; retired to France; fought at Steinkerk; killed at battle of Landen.

Lady Bingham. F. Tilliard.

Bust to right, in armour, looking to front; oval in decorated border; arms below; an Irish motto below and above; title in five lines, on tablet.

$11\frac{3}{16} \times 7\frac{15}{16}$. ($10\frac{7}{16} \times 7\frac{1}{2}$). 21967.

LUCAS, SIR CHARLES, –1648, Royalist Commander, youngest brother of Lord Lucas, and heir to his title and estate; brought up in the Low Countries, under the Prince of Orange; very brave, and reputed the best Commander of Horse in the world; commanded the right wing of the King's Army at Marston Moor, 1644; with SIR GEORGE LISLE, who with Lucas defended Colchester, when besieged by Fairfax; both barbarously shot after surrender, Aug. 28, 1648.

The former, after Dobson; the latter, Anon. G. Vertue.

Both sh. ha. len., Lisle on the left, Lucas on the right; in separate ovals; Lucas wearing a breastplate; 41 lines of inscription, from Clarendon, &c., below; in a border of oak-leaves and acorns.

$12\frac{11}{16} \times 8\frac{3}{4}$. (Ovals, $3 \times 2\frac{5}{8}$). E. 200.–'91.

(*See also* LISLE.)

W. Dobson. Anon. [G. Vertue?].

Ha. len. to left, turned and looking to right, in armour, his right hand resting on his helmet, which is on a table before him, with a pistol; from illustrated "Clarendon."

$6\frac{3}{4} \times 4$. ($6\frac{3}{8} \times 3\frac{3}{4}$). 27138.

LUDE, James Daillon, Count du, 1634–1726, of a noble French family, came to England, and obtained a benefice in Bucks, but was deprived of it on preaching a sermon in favour of James II.; joined the non-jurors in London ; tried "for High Treason for preaching an Orthodox sermon," Aug. 20, 1693 ; author of " Demonology," &c.

J. Fry.   P. Pelham, mez.
J. C. Smith, 25.   20921.

LUDLOW, Edmund, 1620–1693, b. at Maiden Bradley, Wilts. ; educ. at Oxford and Temple; took arms on the Parliamentary side; fought at Edge Hill, 1642; M.P. for Wilts, 1645 ; one of the Judges at trial of Charles I.; sent by Cromwell to Ireland, where he was Lieut.-General of Horse, 1650 ; withdrew to Switzerland at the Restoration, the late King's Judges having been excepted from the Act of Indemnity; returned to London aftwds., but obliged to retire again to Switzerland ; d. at Vevay ; his " Memoirs " published, 1698–'9.

Anon.   S. F. Ravenet.
Bust, in armour, to left, looking to front; oval, in border ; arms below, and title on tablet; prefixed to the " Memoirs," 1771.
$10\frac{1}{4} \times 6\frac{1}{4}$. $(9\frac{1}{16} \times 6\frac{3}{10})$ 25786.

LUSHINGTON, Sir Stephen, 1782–1873 ; ecclesiastical lawyer, Judge of Consistory Court, 1828, of High Court of Admiralty, 1838 ; retired, 1867.

W. I. Newton, min.   W. Walker, mez.
Ha. len. to front, with arms folded, looking to left, seated ; facs. signature below. May, 1834.
$15\frac{1}{8} \times 11\frac{3}{4}$. $(10\frac{7}{8} \times 8\frac{3}{8})$,   26702.

LYNDHURST, John Singleton Copley, Lord, 1772–1863 ; son of J. S. Copley, R.A. ; M.P. for Yarmouth ; Ch. Justice of Chester, Sol.-Gen., Atty.-Gen., Master of the Rolls ; Ld. Chan. and Baron Lyndhurst, 1827 ; Ch. Baron of Exchequer, 1830– '4 ; again Ld. Chan. 1834, and a third time, 1841–'6.

Sir W. C. Ross, R.A.   W. Walker, stipple.
Ha. len. to right, looking to front.
$15\frac{7}{8} \times 12\frac{7}{8}$. $(11\frac{3}{4} \times 9\frac{1}{4})$.   22883.

A. Wivell.   H. Dawe, mez.
T. Q. len. seated, to left, in robes, holding a paper in left hand.
Proof before letters, except artists' names and publisher's address; March, 1837.
$20\frac{7}{8} \times 14\frac{1}{16}$. $(17\frac{5}{16} \times 13\frac{1}{16})$.   22884.

A. F. Chalon.   R. A. Artlett, stipple.
Sh. ha. len. to right, seated, looking to front.
Ind. proof with scratched letters, 1838.
$13\frac{1}{8} \times 10\frac{1}{8}$ $(8\frac{7}{8} \times 7\frac{1}{8})$.   20633.

LYNEDOCH, Thomas Graham, of Balgowan, 1st Lord, 1748–1843, third son and only surviving child of Thomas Græme, laird of Balgowan; educ. at Ch. Ch. Coll., Oxf., 1766–'8; m., 1774; after the early death of his beloved wife, he travelled; lived in Spain and Portugal, 1780–'85; bought Lednoch, or Lynedoch, 1787; served as volunteer, 1793, A.D.C. under Lord Mulgrave; raised the "Perthshire Volunteers," or 90th Foot, of which he was Lt.-Col., 1794; served at Gibraltar, and in the Peninsula, under Sir J. Moore; gained victory of Barossa, 1811; made a daring attempt on Bergen-op-Zoom; cr. Baron Lynedoch, 1814; General, 1821; G.C.B., &c.

J. Hoppner, R.A. S. W Reynolds, mez.

Ha. len. to left, looking to front, in uniform, as Colonel Graham of 90th Regt.

Cut. $11\frac{15}{16} \times 9\frac{7}{8}$. 27864.

Sir T. Lawrence. T. Hodgetts, mez.

Wh. len. to front, in uniform, hands folded together and holding drawn sword across chest; looking to right; a burning town in distance; title, &c., on a suppl. plate, below; Jany. 1, 1829.

$23\frac{13}{16} \times 16$. $(23\frac{3}{16} \times 15\frac{7}{16})$; suppl. plate, $4\frac{1}{8} \times 16$. 22037.

LYONS, Edmund, 1st Baron, 1790–1858, Admiral and Diplomat; son of John Lyons, Esq.; educ. at Hyde Abbey School, Winchester; Midshipman, 1801; Post Captain, 1814; K.C.H.; Knt., 1835; Bart., 1840; served with distinction; Commander of the Fleet in Black Sea, during Crimean War; 1853–'5; G.C.B., 1855; cr. Baron Lyons of Christ Church; Vice-Admiral; &c.

R. Buckner. G Zobel, mixed mez.

T. Q. len. to front, looking to left, in uniform, holding sword in left hand, right hand raised to height of belt; sea and forts in distance; he stands between a gun and the bulwark of the ship on board which he is supposed to be.

Ind. proof, Novr. 12, 1856.

$20\frac{7}{8} \times 16$. $(16\frac{1}{8} \times 13)$. 22130.

LYSONS, Samuel, 1763–1819, Antiquary and topographer, b. at Rodmarton, co. Gloucester; ent. Temple; assisted his brother Daniel in compilation of "Magna Britannia;" wrote on Roman Antiquities in England; Keeper of the Records in the Tower of London; F.R.S., F.S.A.

Sir T. Lawrence, R.A. S. W. Reynolds, mez.

Sh. ha. len. to front, looking to right; white neckcloth, coat buttoned across chest, dark background; oval in grounded border; June 1, 1804; title within the work; artists' names, &c., below.

$12\frac{3}{16} \times 9\frac{7}{8}$. $(11\frac{15}{16} \times 9\frac{7}{8})$. 22036.

LYTTELTON, Rt. Hon George, 1st Lord, 1709–1773, Poet and historian; son of Sir Thomas Lyttelton, 4th Bart.; b. at Hagley, Worcestershire; educ. at Eton and Oxford; ent.

Parlt. 1730; opposed Sir R. Walpole; Lord of the Treasury, 1744; Chancellor of the Exchequer, 1755; suc. his father as 5th Bart., 1751; cr. Baron Lyttelton, 1756; author of "Dialogues of the Dead," "History of Henry II.," Poems, &c.

 B. West, R.A.   R. Dunkarton, mez.
 J. C. Smith, 30, 2nd state.   22248.

LYTTON, EDWARD GEORGE EARLE-LYTTON-BULWER-LYTTON, 1st Baron Lytton, 1806–1873, third and youngest son of General William Earle Bulwer, of Heydon Hall, Norfolk; b. in London; educ. at Cambr., where he gained the Chancellor's medal; M.A., 1835; M.P., 1852, 1857, 1859, 1856–'6; sec. for Colon. Dept., 1858–'9; P.C.; added the name of Lytton to his surname; printed some poems, and many novels, incl. "Falkland," "Pelham," "Eugene Aram," &c.; successful as a Parliamentary orator; at first a Whig; aftds. a Tory; Bart., 1838; D.C.L., Oxf., 1853; LL.D., Cambr., 1864; cr. Baron, 1866.

 R. J. Lane delin.   G. Cook, line and stipple.
 Sh. ha. len. to right, seated, looking to left; right hand to chin; vignette.
 Ind. proof, 1848.
 $9\frac{1}{2} \times 6\frac{1}{2}$. $(3\frac{3}{4} \times 3\frac{1}{2})$.   23579.

 D. Maclise, R.A.   W. J. Edwards, stipple.
 Ha. len. to front, left hand to head, left elbow resting on a pillar; oval; facs. signature below, on right.
 Ind. proof, Jany, 1st, 1853.
 $21\frac{15}{16} \times 16\frac{3}{4}$. $(13\frac{11}{16} \times 11\frac{3}{4})$.   25750.
 See also COMMONS (2).

LYTTON, SIR WILLIAM HENRY, Baron Dalling and Bulwer See BULWER.

McADAM, JOHN LOUDON, 1756–1836; b. at Kirkcudbright, in Scotland; known as the inventor of the system of road-making which bears his name; received a Government reward of 10,000l.; the honour of knighthood, which he declined to accept, was conferred on his son.

 Anon. [C. Turner?].   C. Turner, mez.
 Ha. len. to left, looking to front; hair thin, and descending on forehead; light neckcloth; dark coat, full, and held together in front by one button.
 Open letter proof, Sepr. 20, 1825.
 14×10. $(10\frac{7}{16} \times 8\frac{3}{4})$.   22041

McALPINE, MISS, of Covent Garden Theatre.
 Anon.   Anon., stipple.
 See LA BELLE ASSEMBLÉE, 1817. 13867.   14.

MACARDELL, JAMES, c. 1729–1765, b. in Cow-lane (aftds. called Greek-street), Dublin; a pupil of John Brooks, with whom he came to London, c. 1747; soon aftds. begun on his

own account, and c. 1754 established himself at the Golden
Head, Covent Garden, where he executed and pubd. many
very beautiful engravings in mezzotinto; highly appreciated
by Sir J. Reynolds, who expressed the belief that his own
fame would be preserved by MacArdell's prints; but in Hampstead Churchyard.

J. MacArdell.   R. Earlom, mez.
    J. C. Smith, 28, 2nd state.   21859.

MACARTNEY, GEORGE, Earl, 1737-1806; Envoy to Russia,
1764; Chief Sec. to Lord Lieut. of Ireland, 1769-'72; Govr.,
Grenada and Tobago, 1775; Governor of Madras, 1781;
Ambassador to China, 1792.

    M. Brown.   H. Hudson, mez.
    J. C. Smith, 6, 3rd state.   27082.

MACAULAY, CATHARINE, 1733-1791, sister of John Sawbridge,
q.v.; married first, 1760, Dr. George Macaulay, a physician in
London; pubd. "History of England," 1763-'83; married
secondly, 1778, Mr. Graham; went to America, and visited
Washington, 1785; d. at Binfield, Berks.

    Kath. Read.   J. Spilsbury, mez.
    J. C. Smith, 30.   22259.

MACAULAY, RT. HON. THOMAS BABINGTON, Lord Macaulay,
1800-1859, historian, poet, orator, and politician; educ. at Trin.
Coll., Cambridge, where he obtained the Craven scholarship,
other high honours, and a fellowship, 1822; called to the bar;
bencher, 1849; contributed to Edinb. Rev.; M.P., 1830; fifth
member of Council of India, 1834; returned, 1838; Sec. at
War, 1839; wrote "Lays of Ancient Rome," "History of England," &c.; cr. Baron, 1857.

    F. Grant, R.A.   J. Faed, mixed mez.
    Sh. ha. len. to front, looking to right, seated, left arm over
back of chair.
    Open letter proof (?); May 20th, 1854.
    $15\frac{7}{8} \times 12\frac{7}{8}$. $(11\frac{1}{4} \times 9\frac{1}{2})$.   23008.

MACBRIDE, JOHN,   -1800; Admiral, entd. R.N. as A.B.,
c. 1754; 1761, commd. a cutter; posted to Renown frigate, 1765;
to Jason, 1766; in the Bienfaisant he took part in the action off
Ushant, July 23, 1778; M.P. Plymouth, admiral, 1799.

    J. Northcote, R.A.   J. Fittler.
    As Captain; t.q. len. to left, in uniform, left hand on hip, right
resting on hilt of sword; ship in distance, left. March, 1792.
    $19\frac{7}{16} \times 14\frac{5}{8}$. $(16\frac{1}{2} \times 13\frac{5}{16})$.   23096.

MACCLESFIELD, THOMAS PARKER, Earl of, 1666-1732, Recorder (Derby), M.P., 1705, and 1708-'10; Lord Chief Justice,
1710-1718; P.C., cr. Baron Parker, 1716; Lord Chancellor,
1718-1725; cr. Earl, 1721; impeached for gross frauds,
unanimously condemned, fined, and committed to the Tower,

where he lay 6 weeks, till the heavy fine (30,000*l.*) was paid; passed the rest of his life in retirement.

Sir G. Kneller.   G. Vertue, 1722.

T. Q. len. to left, looking to front, in wig and robes, with right hand on the bag, left on hilt of sword.

15¾ × 10⅘. (12½ × 10₁₀¹).   25787.

MACCLURE, Sir Robert John Le Mesurier, 1807–1873, b. at Wexford; educ. at Winchester and Sandhurst; ent. the Navy, and served in Canada, America, and W. Indies, 1837–'46; in Coast Guard 1846–'8; accomp. Sir John Ross in search of Franklin, 1848; commanded the "Investigator" in an exploring expedition, and discovered the North West Passage, 1850; Knt. for this service, and awarded a grant of 5,000*l.* for the discovery; Rear-Admiral; C.B., 1859; d. at Portsmouth.

S. Pearce.   J. Scott, mixed mez.

T. Q. len. to front, facing and looking to left, right hand in side-pocket, telescope under left arm, gun at his back; an Arctic scene in distance.

Proof on Ind. paper, facs. signature below, on right.

21½ × 16¼. (17 × 13½).   27270.

MACCULLOCH, John, 1773–1835, Physician and Geologist; b. in Guernsey; grad. at 18, as M.A., Edinb.; Chemist to the Ordnance Board, 1803; undertook for Govt. the mineralogical and geological survey of Scotland, and completed it, 1832; pubd. "Geological Classification of Rocks," &c.; M.D., F.R.S.

B. R. Faulkner.   C. E. Wagstaff, mixed stipple and mez.

T. Q. len. to front, seated, looking to right, holding pencil on paper on table to his right; left hand on arm of chair.

Open letter Ind. proof, April, 1837.

18 × 14. (15¾ × 12¾).   22206.

MACDONALD, Flora (or Flory, as spelt by herself), 1722–1790, dau. of Macdonald of South Uist, Hebrides; after the defeat of Charles Edward, the young Pretender, at Culloden, she assisted his escape in disguise, as a maid-servant, at the risk of her own life, 1746; impris. in Tower for a short time, but included in Act of Indemnity, 1747; m. to Allan Macdonald, the younger, of Kingsburgh, Skye, 1750; emigr. with him to N. Carolina; returned to Skye; bur. at Kilmuir in a shroud made from the sheets in which Charles Edward had slept at Kingsburgh.

I. Markluin.   Anon. mez. (style of Burford).

J. C. Smith, p. 1695, 64.   29740.

MACDONELL, Æneas Ronaldson, of Glengarry and Inverie, 1818– ; a boy at Eton at the time of his father's death; aftds. sold the heavily-encumbered estate, and emigr. with his family and clan to Australia, 1840.

A. Robertson.   E. Finden, stipple.

Wh. len. to right, looking back to left, in highland dress; a deer-hound with him, and a dead deer at his feet; he holds a hunting-horn in his right hand, raised; a lake and mountains in the distance; dedicated to the Clan Macdonell by the Editor and Publishers of the Amulet.

Ind. proof.

$9\frac{1}{4} \times 6\frac{1}{16}$. $(3\frac{1}{16} \times 3)$.　　　　　　　　　　　E. 1061.-'88.

MACKAY, ——, actor, c. 1830.
　　W. Allan, A.R.A.　　　　　　　　　　　　J. Horsburgh.
　　Ha. len. to front, looking to left, as if surprised; in the character of Bailie Nicol Jarvie.
　　Ind. proof.
　　$15\frac{7}{16} \times 10\frac{1}{4}$. $(7\frac{3}{4} \times 6\frac{7}{16}.)$　　　　　　　　　　25789.

MACKENZIE, HENRY, 1745-1831, essayist, lawyer, and novelist; son of an eminent physician at Edinb.; Attorney in the Scottish Court of Exchequer, 1764, and Crown Agent; author of "The Man of Feeling," "The Man of the World," &c.; pubd. a series of Essays under the titles of "The Mirror" and "The Lounger," two tragedies, and other works.
　　A. Geddes.　　　　　　　　　　　　　　　R. Rhodes.
　　Wh. len. to left, seated in library, looking to right, arms folded, pen in right hand; wearing dressing-gown and cap.
　　Ind. proof, Feb., 1822, signed autogr. by And". Geddes, below.
　　$18\frac{1}{4} \times 13\frac{1}{4}$. $(16\frac{1}{4} \times 12\frac{1}{4})$.　　　　　　　　　22256.
　　See also SCOTT, SIR WALTER.

MACKENZIE, CAPTAIN THOMAS,　　—　　, commanded a ship, June 1, 1794, in Howe's victory off Ushant; rose to flag rank.
　　See COMMEMORATION (1).

MACKLIN, CHARLES, 1697 (?)-1797, actor, b. in the north of Ireland, son of William McLaughlin; led a wandering life; was an actor, 1725, in a booth, at Southwark, and at Linc. Inn, 1730, at Drury Lane, 1733; soon made a reputation; at Haymarket, 1734, and again at Drury Lane; killed a man in a quarrel; had a fracas with Quin, whom "he pommelled damnably;" gave lessons in acting, when dismissed from Drury Lane, in consequence of the strike; opened the Haymarket; returned to Drury Lane; wrote some plays of high merit; was a great stage-manager; d. in poverty.
　　Dod del.　　　　　　　　　　　　　　　　Walker.
　　Speaking his Farewell Epilogue to the Refusal in 1753.
　　Pubd. by Fielding and Walker, Novr. 20th, 1779, from a "Collection . of English Prologues," &c.　　28187. 10.

MACLAINE, ARCHIBALD, D.D., 1722-1804, b. at Monaghan, Ireland; educ. at Glasgow Univ.; minister of the Engl. Church at the Hague, 1745-'94; returned subsequently to England, and settled at Bath; pubd. a translation of Mosheim's Ecclesiast.

U 2

History, which has been praised by some, but severely handled by other critics; &c.

C. H. Hodges. C. H. Hodges, 1796, mez.
Mentioned, but not described, by J. C. Smith, p. 625.
Sh. ha. len. to right, looking to front, 1796.
$10\frac{5}{8} \times 8\frac{1}{4}$. $(9\frac{7}{16} \times 8\frac{3}{16})$. 28257.

MACLEAY, ALEXANDER, 1767–1848, b. in Co. Ross; educ. for commercial life; left that, and became chief clerk in the Prisoners of War Office, 1795; head of Correspondence Dept. of the Transport Board, 1797; Sec. to the Board, 1806–18, when it was abolished, and he retired on a pension; Colon. Sec., N.S. Wales, 1825; 27 years Sec. of the Linnæan Socy.; F.R.S.; &c.

Sir T. Lawrence. C. Fox.
Sh. ha. len. to right, seated, looking to front; vignette.
Open letter proof. Private plate (?)
$11\frac{3}{4} \times 9\frac{5}{8}$. $(7\frac{3}{4} \times 7)$. 18607.

MACLISE, DANIEL, 1806–1870, subject and history-painter, b. at Cork, son of a soldier in the Elgin Fencibles; began as a clerk in a Bank; soon left this, and entered the Cork School of Art; sketched portraits; came to London; stud. in Acad. School, 1828; gained a prize, 1831; painted portraits, and soon afterwards subjects; R.A., 1840; executed several pictures for the decoration of the palace at Westminster.

E. M. Ward, A.R.A. J. Smyth.
T. Q. len. to front, seated, looking to left; vignette.
$(5\frac{3}{8} \times 4\frac{3}{8})$. 28300. 35.

C. Baugniet, 1857. Baugniet, lith.
Sh. ha. len. to front, looking to right; vignette; oval; facs. signature below. Oct. 15, 1857.
$(9 \times 7\frac{1}{4})$. 24231.

Monogram, T. S[cott]. Monogram, M[ason] J[ackson], woodcut.
Ha. len. to left, looking to front; from the "Illustrated London News."
$(11\frac{7}{8} \times 9\frac{1}{4})$. E. 2192.–'89.

MACMAHON, SIR JOHN, 1754–1817, Bart.; b. in Ireland; M.P. Aldborough; d. at Bath.

Sir T. Lawrence, R.A. C. Turner.
Full ha. len. seated, to front, holding a paper in right hand. Proof before all letters, except the artists' names, and publication-line, Feby. 16, 1815.
20×14. $(14\frac{11}{16} \times 11\frac{7}{16})$. 28258.

MACPHERSON, JAMES, 1738–1796, b. in Inverneesh; schoolmaster at Ruthven; published "Fragments of Ancient Poetry translated from the Gaelic," 1760, "Fingal, an Ancient Epic

Poem, translated from the Gaelic," 1762, which caused much
controversy; inventor of "Ossian;" M.P., Camelford, 1780-'90.
Sir J. Reynolds. W. Bond, stipple.
Ha. len. to front, facing and looking to left; holding in right
hand a roll of paper.
(7½×6). 22255.

MADAN, MARTIN, 1726-1790, and COETLOGON, CHARLES
EDWARD DE, q. v.; Madan was called to the bar, but left law
for the pulpit; chaplain to the Lock Hospl., where his preaching
was much admired; d. at Epsom, and was buried at Ken-
sington; pubd. several sermons and controversial works,
"Thelyphthora," &c; defended polygamy.
George James. J. Watson, mez.
J. C. Smith, 94, 2nd state.
From the Gulston Collection. 25833.

MADDOCK, SIR THOMAS HERBERT, 1792-1870, Knt., President of the Council of India, Deputy Governor of Bengal, &c.
Anon. Anon., lith.
T. Q. len. to left, in profile; left hand resting on a book upon
a table; facs. signature below.
(10×7). 28491.

MAINWARING, SIR PHILIP. See STRAFFORD.

MALCOLM, Sir JOHN, 1769-1833, Scottish General, historian,
orientalist; went to India, 1783; employed by Govr.-Genl.,
Marq. of Wellesley, 1798; envoy to Persia 1799, 1810;
returned to Europe, 1811; pubd. "History of Persia," 1825;
Govr., Bombay, 1827-'30.
From marble statues by Sir F. Chantrey.
H. Corbould del. S. Cousins, mez.
Wh. len. to right, in uniform, with cloak, star, sword, &c.
Open letter proof.
21¼×13⅛. (14¾×7). E. 280.-'87.

G. Hayter, 1815. R. J. Lane, A.R.A. lith., 1832.
Sh. ha. len. slightly to left, looking to right; facs. signature
below.
(8½×8). 27224.

MALMESBURY, JAMES HARRIS, 1st Earl of, 1746-1820,
diplomat; son of James Harris, author of "Hermes;" b. at
Salisbury; educ. at Oxford and Leyden; Sec. of Legation,
Madrid, 1768; Minister, Berlin; St. Petersburg, the Hague;
negotiated the marriage between the Pr. of Wales and Princess
Caroline, 1794; cr. Baron, 1788, and Earl, 1800; d. in
London.
Sir T. Lawrence. W. Ward, mez.
J. C. Smith, 56, 1st state. 22519.

MALMESBURY, James Howard, 3rd Earl of, 1807–1889,
Foreign Sec., 1852, 1858–'9; Privy Seal, 1866–'8, and 1874–'6;
P.C.; G.C.B.; D.C.L., &c.
See DERBY CABINET.

MALTBY, Edward, 1770–1859, b. at Norwich, and educ. there,
and at Pembr. hall, Cambr.; Preb., Lincoln; Vicar of Buckden,
Hunts; Bishop of Chichester, 1831; of Durham, 1836; resigned, 1856; edit. "Morell's Lexicon Græco-Prosodiacum,"
and pubd. Sermons, Psalms, and Hymns, &c.
    Sir W. Beechey, R.A.   T. Lupton, mez.
    T. Q. len. to left, standing, looking to front, in robes, a book
in his left, and his glasses in right hand,
    Open letter proof; Sepr. 3, 1834.
    21×16. $(16\frac{3}{4} \times 13)$.   22885.

MALTHUS, Thomas Robert, 1766–1834, b. near Dorking,
Surrey; educ. at, and fellow of, Jesus Coll., Cambr.; ord.,
and took curacy in Surrey; appointed, 1805, Prof. Mod. Histy.
and Polit. Economy at the E. Ind. Coll., Haileybury, and held
that post till his death; pubd. an "Essay on the Principle of
Population," and other works; F.R.S.
    J. Linnell.   J. Linnell, mixed mez.
    T. Q. len. to right, seated, looking to front, holding a book
with both hands.
    Pubd. Jany. 1, 1834.
    $17\frac{7}{8} \times 13\frac{5}{8}$. $(13\frac{7}{8} \times 11\frac{3}{8})$.   25834.

MALTON, Thomas, 1748–1804, following his father's tastes as a
draughtsman, exhibited drawings in Dublin and London;
published "Elements of Geometry," "Complete treatise on
Perspective," "Picturesque Tour through London and Westminster," "Views of Oxford," "Views in London and Bath."
    Gab. Stuart.   W. Barney, mez.
    J. C. Smith, 10.   23153.

MANGEON, Miss, of Drury Lane Theatre.
    R. E. Drummond.   Anon., stipple.
    See LA BELLE ASSEMBLÉE, 1817.   13867. 12.

MANNERS, Lord John James Robert, 1818– , second son
of John Henry, 5th Duke of Rutland; b. at Belvoir Castle;
educ. at Eton and Cambr.; M.A., 1839; M.P., 1841; opposed
repeal of Corn Laws, Free Trade, &c.; P.C. 1852; in Lord
Derby's Administrations, 1852, 1858, 1866; Postmaster-
General, 1874, G.C.B., &c.; suc. to Dukedom of Rutland,
1887.
    See DERBY CABINET.

MANNERS, Thomas, Lord, son of Lord George Manners-
Sutton; Solicitor-General (England), 1802; Baron of Exche-
quer (England), 1805; cr. Lord Manners, and appointed Lord
Chancellor of Ireland, 1807–'27.
    T. C. Thompson, R.H.A.   S. W. Reynolds, mez.

Wh. len. to front, facing and looking to left, his right hand resting on the handle of a cane; buildings in distance; hat and book on a table which is covered with his robes.

Open letter proof, March 1826.

25 × 15.   (23⅜ × 15).   22039.

MANNERS-SUTTON, CHARLES.   *See* CANTERBURY.

MANNING, WILLIAM, 1763–1835, M.P., Govr. Bank of England 40 years, &c.

J. Lonsdale.   C. Turner, mez.

Wh. len. seated, to right, looking to left, in court suit.

Pubd., Sepr. 18, 1813.

23¾ × 14¾.   (22⅝ × 14¼).   22886.

MANSEL, WILLIAM LORT, D.D., 1751–1820 ; educ. at Trin. Coll., Cambridge ; fellow, and aftds. Master ; Rector of Barwick, Yorks. ; Bishop of Bristol, 1808 ; pubd. one sermon.

T. Kirkby.   W. Say, mez.

T. Q. len. to right, in robes, looking to front, holding his cap in right hand, which hangs by his side, a roll of paper in his left, which rests on a high-backed chair.

Pubd., May 1, 1812.

20 × 13¼.   (18⅛ × 13⅛).   27549.

MANSFIELD, SIR JAMES, 1738–1821, M.P. for Cambridge University, 1776 ; Solicitor-General, 1780 ; 1783–'4 ; Chief Justice of County Court (Chester), 1799, of Common Pleas, and knighted, 1804 ; surrendered, 1814.

L. Vaslet.   J. Jones, mez.

J. C. Smith, 52, 1st state.   27665.

MANSFIELD, WILLIAM MURRAY, Earl of, 1705–1793 ; 4th son of David, 5th Viscount Stormont ; educ. at Westminster and Ch. Ch. Coll., Oxford ; M.A., 1730 ; barrister, 1730 ; Solr.-Genl., 1742 ; M.P., 1742, '47, 1754–'56 ; Attorn.-Genl., 1754 ; Ld. Chf. Justice and Baron, 1756, and P.C. ; his house and property destroyed in Gordon riots, 1780 ; cr. Earl of Mansfield, co. Notts., 1776 ; cr. Earl of Mansfield, co. Middlesex, 1792.

Martin, 1770.   Martin, 1775.

Wh. len. to left, seated, looking to front, wearing wig and robes ; his right hand resting on an open book.

"Published March 1st, 1775, by David Martin, Dean Street, Soho."

Cut.   (22 × 16).   E. 211.–93.

Sir J. Reynolds.   F. Bartolozzi, line & stipple.

T. Q. len. to right, seated, looking to front, wearing robes, collar, wig, &c. ; a paper, addressed " to the Earl of Mansfield," lies on some books on a table at his left ; " Publish'd 24th Augt. 1786."

Proof before all letters, except the artists' names and publication-line, scratched.
20½ × 15¼. (16⅞ × 13⅜). 21831.

MANSFIELD, William Murray, Earl of—*continued.*
Grimaldi. J. Jones, stipple.
T. Q. to right, seated, looking to front; pubd., June 1st, 1797.
11¹⅜ × 9⅝. (6¾ × 5½). E. 1294.–'88.

MANTELL, Gideon Algernon, 1790–1852, Geologist; son of a shoemaker; b. at Lewes; apprent. to a surgeon; pract. at Lewes, and elsewhere, for many years; wrote "The Fossils of the South Downs," "Wonders of Geology," "Medals of Creation," &c.; eminent as a lecturer; his geological collection bought for the Br. Museum; d. in Chester Square; LL.D., F.R.S., &c.
Sentics del., & Mayall phot. W. T. Davey, mez.
Sh. ha. len. slightly to right, looking to front, white neck-cloth, dark coat and waistcoat, cloak fastened across his chest by a cord with tassels; oval.
Open letter proof.
13⅜ × 10¾. (9¹⁵⁄₁₆ × 7⅞). 22887.

MARGARET of Anjou, 1429–1482, daughter of René, Duke of Lorraine; Queen of Henry VI., 1445, Foundress of Queen's Coll., Camb., 1446.
J. Faber, senr., mez.
J. C. Smith (Founders), 34, 2nd state.
A very doubtful portrait. 27172.

MARGARET Tudor, 1489–1539; daughter of Henry VII., Queen of James IV. of Scotland, 1503.
Holbein. T. Cheesman.
From the picture in the Collection of the Marquis of Lothian.
Ha. len. to right, wearing a necklace of pearls, in couples.
Published, July 1, 1819, by Lackington, Hughes, & Co.
Cut. (7¼ × 5¹⁄₁₆). 25019.
In Genealogical Chart, 553. 1.

Holbein. J. Cochran.
Ha. len. to right, wearing a necklace of pearls, in couples.
Published Dec. 1, 1836, by Harding and Lepard.
9⅞ × 7¼. (4⅞ × 3⅞). 14351.

MARKHAM, William, 1720–1807; b. in Ireland; educ. at Westminster and Ch. Ch. Coll., Oxf.; Master of Westminster School; preceptor to the Prince of Wales and the Duke of York; Preb., Durham, Dean of Rochester and Ch. Ch., Oxf.; Bishop of Chester, 1771; Archbishop of York, 1777; published various sermons and charges, 1752–'91; died in South Audley Street, at his house; buried, Westminster Abbey.
Hoppner. J. Heath.

T. Q. len. to left, seated, his hat on his knee, a walking-stick in his left hand; his legs crossed.
Proof before all letters, except the artists' names.
$21\frac{3}{8} \times 15\frac{1}{4}$. ($17\frac{7}{16} \times 13\frac{9}{16}$). 24232.

MARLBOROUGH, CHARLES SPENCER, 2nd Duke of, 1706–1758, 3rd but eldest surviving son of Charles Spencer, 3rd Earl of Sunderland; suc., 1733; commanded the foot guards at Dettingen; Lt.-General, 1747; Lord Steward; K.G.; P.C.; Lord Keeper, and Master-Genl. of Ordnance, 1755; Com.-in-Chf. of Forces agst. France in Germany, and General of Foot, 1758; d. of a fever, at Münster, Westphalia.
Sir J. Reynolds, 1758. R. Houston, mez.
J. C. Smith, 77, 2nd state. 24630.

Sir J. Reynolds. C. Turner, mez.
Wh. len. with his Duchess (b. Hon. Elizabeth Trevor) and family; on the left, his eldest son stands by the Duke, who is seated; the Duchess is in the centre, and the remaining (5) children in front of her, and towards the right of the picture.
Open letter proof, Oct. 24, 1815.
($29\frac{7}{8} \times 26\frac{1}{4}$). 22562.

MARLBOROUGH, JOHN CHURCHILL, 1650–1722; General and Statesman; son of Sir Winston Churchill; fought under Turenne, 1674; helped to defeat Monmouth, 1685; deserted James II, 1688; cr. Earl, 1689; Commr.-in-chf., assisted in defeat of James II., in Ireland, 1690; dismissed on charge of treason, 1692, but released; Ambassador at the Hague; Captain-Genl. of the forces under Anne; drove the French out of Guelderland, and captured Liège; cr. Duke, 1702; won the victories of Blenheim, Ramillies, Oudenarde, Malplaquet, 1704–'9; recalled, charged with peculation, dismissed, 1710; restored, 1714; organised defence against Jacobites.
Sir G. Kneller. J. Smith, mez.
J. C. Smith, 163, 1st state. 21872.

NOTE.—The same engraver scraped a companion portrait of the Duchess, after the picture by the same painter (see below, 21873).

Sir G. Kneller. R. Sheppard.
Ha. len. slightly to left, looking to front, in armour, with long wig, wearing the George; oval in border; arms, and 6 lines of titles, &c., below.
Cut. ($14\frac{3}{8} \times 8\frac{3}{4}$). E. 199.–'01.

A. vander Werff. P. van Gunst.
T. Q. len. to right, looking to front, in armour, wearing a cloak, long wig, &c., and holding a baton in right hand.
Three lines of titles, followed by 12 Latin verses, arranged in two columns, below.
$24\frac{1}{4} \times 15\frac{3}{4}$. ($18\frac{9}{16} \times 15\frac{1}{16}$). 24233.

MARLBOROUGH, John Churchill—*continued.*
    Smirke, R.A.   Rhodes.
    Bust, in medallion, suspended on a pedestal by a winged
figure (Fame ?) on left ; incense rises from a vase, above ;
behind are trees and a hill ; vignette ; July, 1796.
    Cut. (10¼ × 8¼).   29608. N.

MARLBOROUGH, John Winston Spencer-Churchill, 6th
    Duke of, 1822–1883, educ. at Eton, and Oxford ; M.P., Wood-
    stock, 1844–'5, 1847, 1852–'7 ; D.C.L. ; suc., 1857 ; Lord
    Steward of Household, 1866 ; P.C. ; Lord Pres. of Council,
    1867–'8 ; K.G., &c.
    See DERBY CABINET.

MARLBOROUGH, Sarah, Duchess of, 1660–1744, youngest
    dau. of Richard Jennings ; m., 1678, to Colonel John Churchill,
    aftds. 1st Duke of Marlborough ; lady of the bed-chamber,
    1683, to the Princess Ann, over whom she gained great influ-
    ence, which she lost, 1710 ; retired from Court.
    Sir G. Kneller, 1705.   J. Smith, mez.
    J. C. Smith, 165, 1st state.   21873.
    Companion to the portrait of John, Duke of Marlborough, by the same
    engraver after the picture by the same painter (*see* above, 21872).

MARRYAT, Frederick, 1792–1848 ; Captn. R.N., C.B., novelist,
    author of " Peter Simple," " Jacob Faithful," " Midshipman
    Easy," &c., &c. ; inventor of the Code of Signals used in the
    R.N., in the mercantile service, and by foreign nations ; saw
    much service under Lord Cochrane, and gained a high repu-
    tation for bravery ; received the decoration of C.B. for his
    services in the Burmese War, and the cross of the Legion of
    Honour from Louis Philippe for his Code of Signals, when
    translated into French.
    W. Behnes.   C. Cook.
    Ha. len. to left, arms folded ; leaning against a pillar ; vignette.
    Open letter proof, 1851 (R. Bentley).
    9½ × 6⁷⁄₁₀. (5¼ × 3¾).   27672.

MARSTON, H., eminent actor, c. 1850.
    From a Daguerreotype.   Anon.
    Wh. len., as Marc Antony, in an ornamented border.
    (5⅞ × 4⁹⁄₁₆).   23568.

MARTIN, John, 1789–1854, landscape-painter, b. at Haydon
    Bridge, near Hexham ; intended for a heraldic painter, " began
    as a coach-painter," as he says himself, " then as a china-
    painter ;" sent to Newcastle ; came to London, 1806 ; exhi-
    bited, 1812–1853 ; quarrelled with the R. Academy ; his
    " Joshua," " Fall of Babylon," " Belshazzar's Feast," among
    his most famous works, some of which were engraved by him-
    self ; illustrated " Paradise Lost," the Bible, &c.
    W. Derby   J. Thomson, stipple.

Wh. len. to right, seated, looking to front ; left hand in breast
of plaid dressing-gown ; right leg crossed over left ; easel on
right ; vignette ; facs. signature below.
Ind. paper proof.
8¼ × 6¹⁄₁₆. (5½ × 5⅜). E. 2190.–'89.

MARTIN, JOHN—*continued.*
[Derby.] E. Bocourt (?) del. J. Guillaume, woodcut.
Sh. ha. len. to left, looking to front ; from an illustrated paper.
(4¼ × 3¼). E. 2194.–'89.

MARTIN, LADY. *See* FAUCIT, HELEN.

MARTYRS, PROTESTANT (a Group), viz. :—
　Above, on left,
　　NICHOLAS RIDLEY, (q. v.), bishop of London.
　Above, on right,
　　JOHN HOOPER, bishop of Gloucester, 1495–1555, fled
　to Zurich, 1539 ; consecrd., 1550 ; burnt.
　In centre,
　　THOMAS CRANMER, (q. v.), archbishop of Canterbury.
　Below, on left,
　　HUGH LATIMER, (q. v.), bishop of Worcester.
　Below, on right,
　　ROBERT FERRAR or FARRAR, bishop of St. Davids,
　　. . . . –1555, educ. at Oxford ; consecrd., 1548 ; imprisd. in
　Queen's Bench ; depr. 1554 ; burnt at Carmarthen.
[White.] R. White.
Ovals in border ; title at top, " *The Bishops who suffer'd* |
" MARTYRDOM | for the | *Protestant Faith ;* under the
" Persecution of | Q. MARY y⁰ 1st."
15 × 11¼. (14⁷⁄₁₆ × 10¾). 25736.
　See BISHOPS, THE SEVEN, a companion plate.
26668.

MARVELL, ANDREW, 1620–1678, distinguished political writer ;
educ. at Trin. Coll., Cambr. ; travelled abroad for several years ;
Sec. to Br. Legation at Constantinople ; Latin Sec. to Milton,
1657 ; M.P. for Hull, after Restoration, with a salary from his
constituents ; reputed wittiest man of his time ; wrote many
poems, humorous and satirical, and prose tracts ; favourite of
Charles, all whose offers of liberality he steadily refused ;
suffered from malicious attacks in latter years.
J. B. Cipriani, 1760.
" From a portrait painted in the year 1660, in the possession
of Thomas Hollis," &c. ; bust, to right, looking to front ;
vignette, surrounded with a wreath of oak-leaves and bays ;
inscription below, in 11 lines.
10¾ × 6¹⁵⁄₁₆. (7⅞ × 5½). 29718. 6.

MARY OF ENGLAND, 1488–1533 ; daughter of Henry VII. ;
formerly Queen Consort of Louis XII. of France ; with Charles
Brandon, Duke of Suffolk, her second husband, –1545.
G. Vertue, 1748.

Both ha. len. Mary on the left, whose left hand is clasped by her husband with his left. He wears the Collar and George, she holds in her right hand a bulb (?) from which springs a winged Caduceus.

"Inscribed to . . . John Lord Carteret Earl of Granville, "from an Original in his possession." Marked in upper right corner, Pl. III.

Cut. (18¼ × 21¼). 24245.

MARY I., QUEEN OF ENGLAND, 1516–1558, dau. of Henry VIII. by his first wife, Catharine of Arragon ; b. at Greenwich ; suc. her half-brother, Edward VI., 1553 ; m. to Philip II. of Spain, 1554.

Sir A. More. G. Vertue.
"From a picture in possession of the Right Honble. the Earl of Oxford."

Sh. ha. len. to front; oval in border; a papal tiara, over a crown, between a cross and a crosier, above ; arms, &c., below.
11¾ × 7¹¹⁄₁₆. (11½ × 7³⁄₁₆). 29717. 8.

Sir A. More. J. Vazquez, 1793.
T. Q. len. to left, seated, looking to front, wearing a collar and jewel, and a girdle of precious stones ; holding a flower in right hand ; description in 4 (Spanish) lines below.
(13⁴⁄₆ × 10¼). 21825.

T. Geminus. Photozincotype.
Sh. ha. len. to front, with sceptre in left hand; in an ornamented border of figures, scroll-work, &c. ; the original is the title of Vesalius's Anatomy, c. 1545.
(14½ × 10). 29604. 10.

Franz Hogenberg, 1555. Photozincotype.
Sh. ha. len. slightly to left, looking to front, in oval within an ornamented border ; title round the oval ; below " VERITAS × TEMPORIS × FILIA ; " F. H. at top ; the original is a rare print.
(12¼ × 8¾). 29717. 6.

MARY STUART, QUEEN OF SCOTS, 1542–1587, only child of James V. of Scotland ; m. 1st to the Dauphin (1558), aftds. Francis II. of France ; 2nd (1565) to Henry, Lord Darnley ; 3rd (1567) to the Earl of Bothwell ; beheaded, 1587.

F. Zucchero. F. Bartolozzi.
Wh. len., with her son (James), on whose head she lays her right hand ; pubd. Jany. 26, 1779, by J. Boydell.
19¼ × 12¾. (15⁹⁄₆ × 10¾). 25025.
In Genealogical Chart, 553. 1

From " an Ancient Painting " (in St. James's Palace).
G. Vertue, 1735.
Full. ha. len. to front ; oval in decorated border ; arms below.
(11 × 7¼). 29717. 7.

MARY STUART—*continued.*

I. Oliver. J. K. Sherwin, stipple.

Bust, to right, in obl. oval; crown, &c., and long dedication below.

Cut. ($8\frac{1}{2} \times 5\frac{1}{2}$). 25032.

In Genealogical Chart, 553. 1.

Anon. Anon.

A medal, profile to right. Inscription round it, "MARIA STOWAR SCOTI ANGLI."

Cut. ($2\frac{1}{16}$ diamr.) 25027.

In Genealogical Chart, 553. 1.

Anon. J. Thomson.

T. Q. to front, wearing a jewel, which she touches with the fingers of her right hand.

From the original in the Collection of . . . the Earl of Morton. Published, Oct. 1, 1824, by Harding, Triphook, and Lepard.

$9\frac{7}{8} \times 6\frac{3}{4}$. ($4\frac{7}{8} \times 3\frac{7}{8}$). 14354.

——, with her 2nd husband, Henry Stuart, Earl of Darnley.

Elstracke. R. Dunkarton, mez.

Wh. len., Darnley on the left; Mary on the right, in a rich dress; after a drawing from the unique print by Elstracke, in the Collection of Sir M. M. Sykes; arms of France and Scotland below, in centre.

Open letter proof; pubd. by S. Woodburn, who bought the original in the Sykes sale for 81*l*. 18*s*., in 1824.

$14\frac{3}{4} \times 10\frac{7}{16}$. ($11\frac{13}{16} \times 9\frac{3}{16}$). 22521.

MARY, eldest daughter of K. Charles I., 1631–1660; Consort of William Prince of Orange, 1641.

G. Hondthorst Pinxit. P. Soutman Inven. &c.
I. Suyderhoef, Sculp. A°. 1643.

Bust, to right, looking to front; in an oval border, decorated with figures of amorini, &c.

$17\frac{1}{16} \times 14$. ($16\frac{7}{8} \times 13\frac{13}{16}$). 25567.

Ger. van Hondthorst | pinxit. Corn. Vischer | Sculpsit. |
P. Soutman | dirigente | . . . 1649.

Bust, to left, looking to front; in an oval, within a border.

$16\frac{9}{16} \times 12$. ($14\frac{1}{4} \times 11\frac{9}{16}$). 24715.

See also CHARLES, PRINCE OF WALES, &c.

MARY BEATRICE D'ESTE, Queen of England, 1658–1718, dau. of Alfonso IV., Duke of Modena; affianced to James, Duke of York (aftds. James II.), soon after the death of his Duchess, Anne Hyde, 1671; m. to him, 1673; left England, 1688; d. at St. Germains.

N. de Largillière. J. Smith, mez.

J. C. Smith, 171, 1st state. 22520.

MARY II., QUEEN, 1662-1694, dau. of James II.; m. to William
Prince of Orange, aftds. William III., 1677 ; Queen of England,
1689; d. at Kensington Palace.
    Sir G. Kneller.   G. Valck.
    22¼ × 16¼.   (21¹⅜ × 15⅞).   25810. 2.

    NOTE.—This is the companion print to 25810. 1, though Bromley does
       not mention it; but it is evidently by the same engraver. Also, a
       duplicate, in Genealogical Chart, 553. 1,—cut, but more brilliant.
                                                             25634.

    G. Netscher.   J. Houbraken, 1750.
    Sh. ha. len. to left, looking to front, with pearl necklace ; oval
in border.
    Cut. (13⅜ × 8¼).   25018. 3.
    In Genealogical Chart, 553. 1.

    Sir G. Kneller.   J. Smith, mez.
    J. C. Smith, 172, 2nd state.   21876.

MARY, PRINCESS, daughter of George III., 1776-1857, afterwards Duchess of Gloucester.
    H. Ramberg del.   W. Nutter, stipple.
    Oval, with a basket.
    Cut. (10⅜ × 8⅜).   26725. 4.
    Also, a duplicate in Genealogical Chart, 553. 1.
    Open letter proof.
    13⅞ × 10½.   25067. 4.

                                    M. A. Bourlier, stipple.
    T. Q. len. to front, looking to left.
    Published by Harding, May 19, 1806.
    Cut. (7¾ × 6).   25059. 1.
    In Genealogical Chart, 553. 1.

    Beechey.   W. Say, mez.
    Wh. len. to right, seated, looking to front ; a landscape, with
Windsor Castle, in distance, on the right.
    Cut. (17½ × 13¼).   25058. 2.
    In Genealogical Chart, 553. 1.

——, WITH SOPHIA, AND AMELIA, PRINCESSES.
    J. S. Copley, R.A.   F. Bartolozzi, R.A., stipple.
    Wh. len. with three dogs ; the two younger Princesses are in a
little carriage, drawn by the eldest, who raises a tambourine in
her left hand.
    22¼ × 16½.   (19½ × 14⅝).   25062.
    In Genealogical Chart, 553. 1.

MASKELYNE, NEVIL, 1732-1811, Astronomer Royal; b. in
    London, educ. at Westminster and Cambridge ; B.A., 1754;

M.A., 1757; B.D., 1768; D.D., 1777; F.R.S., 1758; ordained,
1755; employed to observe transit of Venus, 1761; Astr.
Royal, 1765; member of Fr. Institute, 1802.
    See SCIENCE.

MASON, THOMAS MONCK,   aëronaut.
    Wrote account of Green's voyage in a balloon from London
to Weiburg, 1836; and " Aeronautica," 1838.
    See GREEN (2).

MASTERS, ROBERT, 1713–1798, b. in London; educ. at Corp.
Chr. Coll., Cambr.; fellow and B.D.; presented, 1756, to Coll.
living of Landbeach, Cambr.; and, later, in addition, to that of
Linton, which he changed for Waterbeach; wrote " History of
Corp. Chr. Coll.," " Memoirs of Thomas Baker," " Catalogue
of the Pictures in the University of Cambridge," &c.; F.S.A.
    T. Kerrich delt.   Facius, stipple.
    Ha. len. to left, looking to front, but slightly to right; wearing
a full-bottomed wig.
    Decr. 1st, 1795.
    $14\frac{1}{6} \times 10\frac{7}{8}$. $(11\frac{11}{16} \times 8\frac{9}{16})$.   E. 1649.–'89.

MATHEW, FATHER THEOBALD, 1790–1856, b. at Thomastown,
near Cashel, Tipperary; educ. at Kilkenny and Maynooth;
ordd., 1814; became the " Apostle of Temperance," Presidt. of
the " Total Abstinence Socy.," 1838; devoted himself and his
resources to the cause; received later a pension of 300l. a year
from the Civil List.
    S. West.   W. O. Geller, mixed mez.
    T. Q. len. to front, standing, looking to left, hands extended in
act of preaching; landscape in background; Feb. 1, 1848.
    $21\frac{1}{2} \times 16$. $(17\frac{1}{4} \times 13\frac{9}{16})$.   23013.

MATHEWS, CHARLES, 1776–1835, distinguished comedian
and " entertainer; " son of a London bookseller, a Wesleyan;
educ. at Merch. Taylors' School, apprenticed to his father's
trade; preferred the stage; rambled with strolling companies;
soon achieved eminence; for 16 years previous to his death
" entertained" crowded audiences with his " Mathews at
Home," in Great Britain, Ireland, and U.S., America; d. at
Liverpool.
    J. Lonsdale.   C. Turner, mez.
    Ha. len. to front, looking to left; right hand in breast of
cont.
    Open letter proof, Novr. 1, 1826.
    $18\frac{7}{8} \times 9\frac{3}{4}$. $(10\frac{1}{2} \times 8\frac{1}{4})$.   21897.

    T. Jones del.   T. Jones, etched.
    Wh. len. in 15 different characters, beside his own; " *The
Matthewsorama for* 1827—*or* | *Cockney Gleanings,—Aint
that a good un now?* "; quotations in 16 columns below;
coloured; March 26, 1827; pubd. by G. Humphrey.
    $11\frac{7}{18}(?) \times 15\frac{1}{4}(?)$. $(8\frac{1}{4} \times 14\frac{1}{4})$.   27026.
    See also BLANCHARD.

MATTHEW Paris, c. 1195–1259, a Benedictine monk of St.
Alban's; mathematician, poet, divine, and historian; wrote
"Historia Angliæ ad ultimum annum Henrici III.," founded on
the "Flores of Roger" of Wendover; wrote also "Vitæ duorum
Offarum, Merciæ Regum," and other works.
Anon. Anon.
Wh. len. to front, looking to left; below, an inscription in 3 lines
"Matthæi Parisiensis historici," &c. "desumpta."
Prefixed to his "Historia," 1684(?).
Cut. (8¼ × 8¾). 26655.

MATTHEWS, Henry, 1789–1828, son of John Matthews of
Belmont, Hereford; educ. at Eton and King's Coll., Cambr.;
puisne Judge of Supreme Court, Ceylon; author of the "Diary
of an Invalid," praised by Byron and others.
Anon., lith.
Bust, to right, looking to front; vignette.
Ind. proof.
(4 × 3). 27173.

MATTOCKS, George, –1804, an admirable singer and a
handsome man; d. at Edinburgh.
With Mrs. Quick (q. v.). Anon., mez.
J. C. Smith, 107, p. 1738. 26422.

MATTOCKS, Mrs., wife of G. Mattocks, speaking the Prologue
to "Know Your Own Mind."
From a "Collection of English Prologues," &c., 1779.
28187. 11.

MAUDSLAY, Henry, 1771–1831, engineer, b. at Woolwich,
entered the Arsenal, where his father, who had served in the
Royal Artillery (1756–'76), was an artificer; became very
expert; worked for Bramah, 1789, but left him, 1798; patented
many inventions, and improved the lathe; made a measuring
machine to divide the inch by 10,000.
See SCIENCE.

MAULE, Fox. See PANMURE.

MAURICE, Frederick Denison, 1805–1872, educ. at Cambridge, and subsequently at Oxford; B.A., 1831; Chapl. and
Reader at Linc. Inn, and Theol. Prof., King's Coll., 1846;
retired from latter post some years after; incumbent, St. Peter's
Chapel, Vere St., Marylebone; worked with Rev. Chas. Kingsley at improved education of working men; pubd. a novel, when
young, "Eustace Conway," and many Lectures, Sermons, and
other Theological books.
S. Lawrence. J. H. Lynch, lith.
Bust, to right; vignette.
Open letter proof; Oct. 14, 1858.
(7¾ × 6½). 25752.

MAVOR, WILLIAM FORDYCE, LL.D., 1758–1837, b. at New Deer, Aberdeenshire; at the age of 17, taught in a school at Burford, Oxfordshire, and afterwards started a school at Woodstock; obtained a title for orders, and got the vicarage of Hurley, Berks.; also rector of Stonesfield, and of Bladon-with-Woodstock, where he died; author of a "Spelling Book," and other educational works, which formerly had a high reputation, now superseded.

Saxon.   C. Turner, A.R.A., mez.

Ha. len. to right, seated, right elbow on arm of chair, right hand to chin.

Ind. proof ; March 1, 1829.

$9 \times 5\frac{3}{8}$. $(5\frac{3}{16} \times 4\frac{1}{4})$.   27602.

MAXWELL, THOMAS, c. 1688, Major-Genl., Commander of the Dragoons in Ireland, &c., said (by Noble) to have been of a good family in Scotland.

J. Closterman.   J. Smith, mez.

J. C. Smith, 180, 2nd state.

           E. 204.–'92.

MAYERNE, SIR THEODORE TURQUET DE, 1573–1655, Physician and Chemist; b. at Geneva; physician to Henry IV. of France, on whose death he came to England; Physn. to James I., and Knt.; by his chemical knowledge assisted Petitot, the enamellist, in preparation of colours for his miniatures; physn. to Charles I. and II.; bur. in vaults of St. Martin-in-the-Fields; bequeathed his library to the College of Physicians.

Anon.   Anon.

Ha. len. to left, seated, looking to front, holding in left hand a skull, to which he points with right hand; Æt. 82; prefixed to his "Works," according to Bromley; title, &c., in 5 (Latin) lines, below.

$(9\frac{1}{4} \times 9\frac{9}{16})$.   26661

MAYHEW, JONATHAN, 1720–1766, "D.D., Pastor of the West
" Church | in Boston, in New England, an assertor of the civil
" | and religious liberties of the Country and Mankind, | who,
" overplied by public energies, died of a nervous fever, | July
" VIIII., MDCCLXVI., aged XXXXV.;" one of the most energetic opponents of England and promoters of the war of Independence; b. at Martha's Vineyard; grad. at Harv., 1744; ordained, 1747; published sermons and controversial tracts.

Cipriani.   J. B. Cipriani, 1767.

Bust, to right, looking to front, two olive branches crossed below; and, lower again, inscription in five lines, as given above.

$9\frac{1}{4} \times 7$. $(9\frac{1}{8} \times 6\frac{7}{8})$.   29118.   12.

MAYO, RICHARD SOUTHWELL BOURKE, 6th Earl of, 1822–1872; M.P., 1847–'66; Sec. for Ireland, 1852, 1858, 1866; Gov.-General, India, and K.P., 1868; assassinated in Andaman Islands; G.M.S.I., M.A., P.C., LL.D., &c.

See DERBY CABINET.

MEAD, RICHARD, 1673-1754, son of Rev. Matthew Mead; b. at
Stepney; stud. at Utrecht under Grævius, and under Herman
and Pitcairn at Leyden; intimate with Boerhave; grad. at
Padua, 1695; began practice in his native parish, 1696; physician, St. Thomas' Hospital, and removed to Crutched Friars,
1703; M.D. Oxf. by dipl., 1707; F.C.P., 1716; Censor, 1716,
'19, '24; Physn. in Ord. to George II., 1727; wrote many
learned works on medical subjects.

   A. Ramsay.   B. Baron, 1749.
   Wh. len. to right, seated, in Doctor's robes, looking to front;
a table with books on it, at right; a statue behind, in niche;
arms in centre below.
   Cut.   (18⅝ × 12⅜).   22258.

MEAUTYS, SIR THOMAS, -1649, M.P., Clerk of the Privy
Council, &c.
   Anon.   Greatbach.
   Wh. len. to right, looking to front, holding a pike, in a
landscape; from a picture in possession of Lord Verulam.
   Ind. proof, with open letters.
   12¾ × 9.   (9₁₆¹ × 5⅝).   24640.

MEDICAL SOCIETY OF LONDON, The Principal Institutors of
the, Founded, 1773, James Sims, M.D., 1740-1820, President.
   S. Medley.   N. Branwhite, stipple.
   A composition of 22 figures, of whom 14 are seated, the others
standing; Novr. 10, 1801; for names, see Key-plate.
   20¾(?) × 24 (18⅝ × 22₁₆⁷.).   22468.

—— Key to the above plate.
                                            Anon.
   Printed by R. & H Causton, 21, Finch Lane, Cornhill.
   The figures are in outline, the names printed below (from
type); viz.:—
James Sims, M.D., President, F.A.S. & R. Ir. Ac., &c. (q. v.).

2. Sir John M. Hayes, Bart.	12. W. Babington, M.D.
3. J. C. Lettsom, M. & LL.D.	13. C. Combe, M.D.
	14. J. Aikin, M.D., F.L.S.
4. W. Saunders, M.D., F.R.S.	15. T. Bradley, M.D.
	16. R. J. Thornton, M.D.
5. N. Hulme, M.D., F.R.S.	17. J. Shadwell, M.D.
6. E. Jenner, M.D., F.R.S.	18. J. Haighton, M.D.
7. W. Woodville, M.D., F.L.S.	19. R. Hooper, M.D., F.L.S.
8. J. Relph, M.D.	20. E. Ford, F.S.A.
9. S. Walker, M.D.	21. Mr. Ware, Surgeon.
10. J. H. Myers, M.D.	22. Mr. Blair, Surgeon.
11. E. Bancroft, M.D., F.R.S.	

   (4⅓ × 8¾).   22468A.

MEDINA, SIR JOHN BAPTIST, 1660-1711, portrait-painter, son
of a Spanish captain; b. at Brussels, where he stud. painting;
m. young, and came to England, 1686; painted portraits for

several years in London; settled at Edinburgh, where he had extensive practice in portraiture; painted history, landscapes, &c., occasionally, but succeeded best with portraits; Knt.; d. at Edinburgh; buried at Greyfriars.

Medina.   T. Chambars.

Sh. ha. len. to left, looking to front; in Walpole's "Anecdotes," Vol. III., 1763.

Cut. $(5\frac{11}{16} \times 4\frac{13}{16})$.   25461.   14.

MEE, Mrs. ANNE,   –1851, miniature-painter, daughter of John Foldsone, a painter, who d. young; having married unfortunately, she had to support her mother and 8 brothers and sisters; exhibited at the R.A., 1815–1836; obtained a good practice and many commissions from George IV; d. at a great age.

A. Mee.   H. Meyer, stipple.

T. Q. len. to right, seated, looking to front, holding a paper, on one side of which is a female portrait; on the other side, which is turned up, is inscribed, "Gallery of Beauties by Anne Mee."

Ind. paper proof with inscription scratched; June 1, 1812.

$13\frac{1}{8} \times 10\frac{7}{8}$. $(9\frac{5}{16} \times 7\frac{5}{8}$, including ruled border, $1\frac{1}{4})$.   22888.

MELBOURNE, WILLIAM LAMB, 2nd Visct., 1779–1848 statesman; educ. at Eton, Cambr., and Glasgow; stud. at Linc. Inn; M.P., Sec. for Ireland, 1827, under Canning; Home Sec. under Earl Grey, 1830; Premier, 1834, and 1835–'41.

Sir G. Hayter.   C. Turner, A.R.A., mixed mez.

T. Q. len. to right, resting finger-tips of right hand on papers on table; coat open, dark neckcloth, coat, vest, &c.; white shirt.

Open letter proof, March 25, 1839.

$21\frac{7}{8} \times 16$. $(16\frac{1}{16} \times 12\frac{1}{4})$.   22131.

MELLON, Miss HARRIET, 1775–1837, actress, dau. of Matthew Mellon, actor; made début at Drury Lane as "Lydia Languish," 1795; m. to Thomas Coutts, the banker, 1814; inher. his property, 1822; m. aftds. to William, 9th Duke of St. Albans, 1827; left her property to Miss Angela Burdett, who took the name of Coutts (cr. Baroness, 1871).

Sir W. Beechey, R.A.   C. Turner, mez.

Ha. len. to front, looking to left, with right hand raised, " in the character of Volante in the Honey Moon;" she is saying "It is the Count," Act. 2, Scene 3.

Scr. letter proof; Jany. 16, 1806.

$17\frac{7}{8} \times 13$. $(10\frac{3}{14} \times 9\frac{1}{16})$.   22257.

—— in the Character of Mrs. Page.

I. J. Masquerier.   W. Say, mixed mez.

Wh. len. to left, facing and looking to front, holding an open letter in left hand; view of Windsor in distance; ded. to Lady Templetown.

Open letter proof; Oct. 24, 1804.

$26\frac{13}{16} \times 16\frac{3}{4}$ $(25\frac{3}{8} \times 16\frac{1}{4})$.   22889.

MELVILLE, HENRY DUNDAS, 1st Viscount, 1740–1811, son of the Lord Pres. of Court of Session; educ. at Edinb.; successively Sol.-General for Scotland, 1773; lord-adv., 1775; ent. Parlt.; Treasr. of Navy; Home Sec., 1791; for War, 1794; ally of Pitt; cr. Visct., 1802; first lord of Admiralty; impeached, 1805, and very unpopular, but acquitted by the Lords; d. at Edinburgh.

   G. Romney   J. Young, mez.
   J. C. Smith, 21, 1st state.   22088.

   Sir T. Lawrence, R.A.   C. Turner, mez.
   T. Q. len. to front, looking to right, holding a roll of paper in right hand, and resting finger-tips of left on paper on table; coat buttoned across chest.
   Ind. proof before all letters, except artists' names and publication-line, Decr. 1, 1810.
   $20 \times 13\frac{7}{8}$. $(17 \times 13\frac{1}{4})$.   22890.

MENAI STRAITS, Conference of Engineers at the, Preparatory to floating one of the tubes of the Britannia Bridge.
   J. Lucas.   J. Scott, mixed mez.
   A composition of 14 figures, seated and standing, of which 12 are portraits, viz., Admiral Moorsom, L. & E. Clark, F. Forster, G. P. Bidder, R. Stephenson, M.P., Mr. Hemmingway, Cap. Claxton, R.N., C. H. Wild, A. Ross, J. Locke, M.P., and J. K. Brunel; R. Stephenson is seated in the centre, Admiral Moorsom stands on the left, Mr. Locke sits on the right, Brunel still further to the right; facs. signature of R. Stephenson in centre, below; Jany., 1858.
   $26\frac{1}{4} \times 32\frac{1}{4}$. $(21\frac{9}{16} \times 28\frac{1}{4})$.   23048. 1.
   See KEY-PLATE.

   Key-plate of the engraving of the, . . . with the names of the persons represented.
   $(7\frac{1}{8} \times 9\frac{7}{16})$.   23048. 2.

MERRY, Miss.
   R. E. Drummond.   R. Cooper, stipple.
   See LA BELLE ASSEMBLÉE.   13867. 13.

MEYER, JEREMIAH, 1735–1789, "miniature-painter in enamel," b. at Würtemberg, came to England, 1749; stud. under Zincke; obtained a premium, 1761, of the Society of Arts for the likeness of George III. (intended for a die), which was engraved by J. McArdell, and frequently copied; appointed miniature-painter to the Queen, and enameller to the King, 1764; d. at Kew.
   J. C. Smith, 24.   24104.

MEYER, JEREMIAH—*continued*.
[Dance.] Anon.
Sh. ha. len. to front, looking to left, long hair curling at the
end, white neckcloth, coat buttoned across with two buttons.
Pubd. April 16, 1793, by W. Richardson.
$7\frac{1}{4} \times 5\frac{3}{4}$. $(5\frac{1}{16} \times 4\frac{7}{16})$. E. 1300.–'88.

MEYRICK, SIR SAMUEL RUSH, 1783–1848, educ. at Oxf.;
practised many years in Eccl. and Adm. Courts; antiquary;
accumulated a great collection of armour at Goodrich Court,
Herefordshire; wrote a "Critical Inquiry into Antient Armour,"
1824, and the descriptive matter to J. Skelton's "Engraved
Illustrations of Ancient Arms," &c.; LL.D., F.S.A., K.H.
His collection, exhibited at S. K. 1869–'72, dispersed gradually
and privately by Mr. Pratt, No. 3, Avery Row, Lower Grosvenor
Street.
H. P. Briggs, R.A. W. Skelton.
T. Q. len. to front, looking to right, resting right arm on a
steel breast-plate, holding a pen in his right hand; left hand on
hip. Novr. 4, 1833.
$8\frac{3}{4} \times 7\frac{1}{3}$. $(5\frac{5}{8} \times 4\frac{1}{4})$. 23012.

MIDDLESEX, RACHEL FANE, Countess of, 1613–1680, daughter
of Francis, Earl of Westmoreland, widow of Henry, Earl of
Bath, and m. to Lionel Cranfield, 3rd Earl of Middlesex, who
d. *s. p.*, 1674, leaving her a second time a widow; buried at
Tavistock, Devon.
A. van Dyck. P. Lombart.
T. Q. to left, looking to front, wearing ringlets, pearl earrings, a brooch with pearl pendants, and other jewels on sleeves
and girdle, and in her hair; holding some flowers on a table by
her, on the left of the print; London; but printed in Paris.
$13\frac{7}{8} \times 9\frac{11}{16}$. $(12\frac{1}{2} \times 9\frac{9}{16})$. E. 990.–'87.

MIDDLETON, MRS.
Anon. Anon.
See LA BELLE ASSEMBLÉE, 1820. 13867. 29.

MIDDLETON, SIR CHARLES, Admiral. *See* BARHAM, LORD.

MIDDLETON, CONYERS, 1683–1750, b. at York, educ. at, and
fellow (1706) of, Trin. Coll., Cambr.; D.D.; Principal Librarian,
c. 1722; late in life, presd. to living of Hascomb, Surrey; distinguished and bitter controversialist; wrote "Life of Cicero," &c.
Echardt, 1746. J. Faber, junr., mez.
J. C. Smith, 241. 26663.

MIDDLETON, SIR HUGH. *See* MYDDELTON.

MIDDLETON, THOMAS FANSHAWE, 1769–1822, b. at Kedleston,
Derbyshire; educ. at Chr. Hospital and Pembroke Hall,
Cambr.; B.A., 1792; curate, Gainsborough, Linc., 1793;
Rector, Tansor, 1795; D.D., 1808; Preb. Linc., 1809; Arch-
deacon, Huntingdon, 1812; Vicar of St. Pancras and Rector

of Rottenham, 1811; first Bishop of Calcutta, 1814; publd. a
great work on the Greek Article, and Sermons, Charges, &c.
    J. Jackson del.   H. Meyer, stipple.
    T. Q. len. to front, seated, in robes, looking to left, right arm
resting on arm of chair; vignette. Sep. 7, 1815.
    $14\frac{3}{4} \times 12\frac{7}{8}$. $(11\frac{1}{2} \times 8\frac{3}{4})$ 28002.

MILL, John Stuart, 1806–1873, son of James Mill, author of
"The History of India;" educ. by his father; clerk in the India
House, 1823; ch. Examiner of India Correspondence, 1856;
co-editor of Westminster Review with Sir William Molesworth,
and Editor, 1835–'40; M.P., 1865; author of "System of
Logic," 1843, Essays, Dissertations, "Principles of Political
Economy," &c.
    G. F. Watts, R.A.   P. A. Rajon, etching.
    Sh. ha. len. slightly to right, looking to front; facs. signature
below.
    $12\frac{3}{8} \times 9\frac{7}{8}$. $(10 \times 7\frac{7}{8})$.   27071.

MILLAIS, Sir John Everett, 1829– , contemporary painter,
b. at Southampton; stud. in Sass's Academy and the Royal
Academy School, where he gained prizes; exhibited first in
1846; joined the founders of the so-called "Pre-Raphaelite
School;" R.A., 1863; one of the most successful of modern
painters; cr. Bart., 1885.
                                              Pilotel, etched.
    Bust to right; vignette; for "The Artist."
    $6\frac{7}{16} \times 4\frac{5}{8}$. $(4\frac{3}{4} \times 4\frac{5}{8})$.   E. 2200.–'89.

MILLER, Edward, 1731–1807, b. at Norwich; stud. under Dr.
Burney; elected organist of Doncaster, 1756, upon the recommendation of Nares; Mus. Doc., Cambr., 1786; composed
elegies, songs, sonatas, flute solos, psalm tunes, &c.; author of
"The Elements of Thorough-bass and Composition," and a
"History of Doncaster," 1804; d. at Doncaster.
    T. Hardy.   T. Hardy, stipple.
    Ha. len. to right, seated, looking to front, coat unbuttoned;
curtain behind.
    $10\frac{9}{16} \times 7\frac{5}{16}$. $(8\frac{1}{8} \times 6\frac{5}{8})$.   27604.

MILLER, Hugh, 1802–1856, Geologist, son of a coasting trader,
b. at Cromarty; self-educated; a stonemason, aftds. clerk in a
bank; Editor of the Free Church Paper, "The Witness;"
author of "The Old Red Sandstone," "Footprints of the
Creator," "Testimony of the Rocks," &c.; driven by overwork
to insanity and suicide.
    W. Bonnar, R.S.A.   W. & T. Bonnar, mixed mez.
    T. Q. len. slightly to left, seated on a bank, facing and looking
to front, a plaid over his knees, a stick (in his right hand)
lightly held also by the fingers of his left hand; facs. subscr.
and signature below, on right.
    Ind. proof before all letters, except artists' names and the
above-mentioned facsimile.
    $17\frac{7}{8} \times 14\frac{7}{16}$. $(15\frac{3}{8} \times 12\frac{1}{4})$.   23009.

MILLER, Patrick, of Dalswinton, 1731–1815, projector of steam navigation; author of "Triple Vessel and Wheels," Edinb., 1787, fol. ; made experiments with paddle-boats, which resulted in the invention of the steam-boat; introduced fiorin grass into Scotland.

    See SCIENCE.

MILLER, Thomas, 1731–1804, b. at Norwich, son of a pavior, and brother of Edward Miller, Mus. Doc., organist at Doncaster ; Thomas became a noted bookseller at Bungay, Suff.

    H. Edridge, min.   E. Scriven, stipple.

    Sh. hn. len. to left, looking to front, right hand in breast of coat ; oval, in border ; a private plate.

    Ind. proof.

    $8\frac{7}{8} \times 6\frac{7}{16}$.   (Oval, $2\frac{11}{16} \times 2\frac{1}{4}$).   E. 1301.–'88.

MILMAN, Henry Hart, 1791–1868, D.D. ; youngest son of Sir Francis Milman, Bart., educ. at Eton and Brazenose Coll., Oxf. ; won the Newdegate Prize, 1812 ; fellow of Braz., 1815 ; ord., 1817 ; Vicar, St. Mary's, Reading ; Prof. of Poetry, Oxf., 1821 ; Rector, St. Margaret's, Westminster, and a Canon ; Dean of St. Paul's, 1849 ; wrote "Fazio, a Tragedy," Poems, Sermons, and other works.

    T. A. Woolnoth.   W. Walker, mez.

    T. Q. len. slightly to right, looking to front, an open book held with both hands on his lap.

    Proof before all letters, except the publication-line, May 1, 1852.

    $16\frac{1}{4} \times 13\frac{7}{16}$.   ($13\frac{1}{4} \times 10\frac{1}{4}$).   22891.

MILTON, John, 1608–1674, b. in Bread St., Cheapside, son of a scrivener, by whom he was first educ. ; then at St. Paul's School, and Chr. Coll., Cambr. ; after graduating, he went to Horton, Bucks, where his father was settled ; there wrote "Comus" and "Lycidas," and probably there also "L' Allegro" and "Il Penseroso ;" travelled abroad, 1638 ; became a schoolmaster in London, and wrote tracts against hierarchy ; Latin Sec. to the Commonwealth ; became blind, 1654 ; wrote "Iconoclastes," "Paradise Lost," 1667, for which he received 5l., "Paradise Regained," 1671, "Samson Agonistes," &c. ; bur. in St. Giles's, Cripplegate.

    C. Janssens (the picture in the possession of Thomas Hollis, F.R.S., &c.).   I. B. Cipriani, 1760.

    Sh. hn. len. slightly to right, looking to front ; a boy of ten years of age ; in a wreath of roses rising to a point at top ; vignette ; name and inscription below in 11 lines ; painted in 1618, the first year of Janssens' visit to England.

    $10\frac{3}{16} \times 7$.   ($7\frac{1}{2} \times 5\frac{3}{8}$).   E. 1292.–'88.

    "From a bust in plaster, modelled from the life, now in the possession of Thomas Hollis, F.R. and A.SS."   I. B. Cipriani, 1760.

Sh. ha. len., to right, looking to front, in a garland of laurels;
vignette; the name and inscription in 17 lines below.
   10¼ × 7¹⁄₁₆;   (7½ × 5¾).   E. 1293.-'88.

MILTON, JOHN—*continued*.
   W. Faithorne del.   W. Faithorne.
   L. Fagan, pp. 48, 49; 2nd state.   24680.

———

G. Vertue, 1725.
   Sh. ha. len. to front, in a cloak; oval, in border; the name
above, with " Ætat. 62. A°. D. 1670;" six lines from Dryden
below,
        " Three Poets in three distant ages born
        . . . . the former Two;"
dedicated to Algernon, Earl of Hertford.
   14⅜ × 9¹⁄₁₆.   (Oval, 8 × 7).   **27865.   4.**

MINGS, CHRISTOPHER. *See* NAVAL HEROES (2).

MINTO, GILBERT ELLIOT MURRAY KYNYNMOND, 2nd Earl of,
   1782-1859, Privy Seal, 1846; resigned, 1852.
   Sir F. Grant.   Anon.
   T. Q. len. to right, seated, holding a paper in his right hand.
   Ind. proof.
   14½ × 11⅞.   (10 × 7⅞).   24123.

MITFORD, MARY RUSSELL, 1787-1855, b. at Alresford, the
   daughter of a physician practising at Reading, a reckless,
   selfish, gambler, who dissipated two fortunes, and afterwards
   lived for thirty years on the earnings of his daughter; she
   had received a good education at Chelsea, and pubd. verses,
   1806, and for the stage " Julian," 1823, " Foscari," 1826,
   " Rienzi," 1828, " Charles the First," also " Our Village," her
   most successful work, " Recollections," &c.
   F. R. Say delin.   Thomson.
   Bust to left, looking to front, wearing a cap and frilled
   collar; vignette; facs. signature below; Oct. 1, 1831.
   8⅛ × 5¹⁄₁₆.   (3¾ × 3¼).   22892.

MITFORD, WILLIAM, 1744-1827, historian, brother of Lord
   Redesdale, b. in London; educ. at Queen's Coll., Oxf.; ent.
   Middle Temple, but never practised law; Lt.-Col., South
   Hants, Militia; M.P., 1785-1818; for a time, Prof. Anc. Hist.,
   R.A.; pubd. " History of Greece," 1784-1818; " Essay upon
   Harmony in Language; " &c.
   H. Edridge delin.   C. Picart, stipple.
   Ha. len. to left, seated, looking to front, holding a paper in
   left hand; a curtain behind him; vignette. Feb. 7, 1811.
   14¹⁵⁄₁₆ × 12¹³⁄₁₆.   (9 × 8¼).   27223.

MOHUN, CHARLES MOHUN, 5th Baron,1675 (?)-1712, duellist;
   eldest son of 4th Baron; accomplice in the murder of W.

Mountfort, and acquitted by the Peers, at the age of 17 ; served
with distinction in Flanders ; was implicated in other disgrace-
ful brawls, duels, and murders ; took part in debates in House
of Lords ; carried copy of Act of succession to Electress
Sophia ; finally was killed in a duel by the Duke of Hamilton.

J. Faber, mez.
In Kit-Cat Club.   J. C. Smith, 208 (23).   22893.

MOIR, David Macbeth, 1798–1851, b. at Musselburgh, co.
Edinburgh ; educ. at Edin. University, and practised as a
surgeon with great success ; contributed to Blackwood, signing
"Δ" ; two vols. of poems, which first appeared there, " The
Legend of Genevieve," and " Domestic Verses," were published
afterwards separately, as also his humorous novel, " The Life of
Mansie Waugh ; " he wrote also "Outlines of the Ancient
History of Medicine."

Sir J. W. Gordon, P.R.S.A., R.A.   G. Faed, mez.
T. Q. len., to right, seated, looking to front, holding a pencil
in right hand and a note-book in the left ; facs. signature below
Ind. proof.
Cut. $(12\frac{9}{16} \times 10)$ 22894.

MOLESWORTH, Sir William, 8th Bart., 1810–1855 ; politician
and author, educ. privately, in Germany, and at Cambr. and
Edinb. ; travelled in Italy, and stud. Arabic ; M.P., 1832 ;
friend of Grote and James Mill ; started the " London Review ; "
M.P., Leeds, 1837 ; for Southwark, 1845 ; first Commissioner
of Works, under Aberdeen, 1853 : Colonial Secretary, &c.
Anon.   Walker, mez.
T. Q. len. to right, left hand in bosom.
Open letter proof ; pubd. March 15, 1856.
$14\frac{7}{8} \times 11\frac{1}{2}$. $(10\frac{7}{8} \times 8\frac{1}{2})$.   24234.
See ABERDEEN CABINET.

MOLLOY, Captain,   –   , commanded a ship, June 1, 1794,
in Howe's victory off Ushant.
See COMMEMORATION (1).

MONAMY, Peter, c. 1670–1749, b. in Jersey ; practised in
London ; apprenticed to a house-and-sign-painter on London
Bridge ; was afterwards " reckon'd the finest painter of ship-
ping in England ; " d. in Westminster.
[P. Stubly.]   J. Bretherton, etched.
Ha. len to left, looking to front, holding in his right hand a
sea-piece, to which he points with his left ; in Walpole's " Anec-
dotes," Vol. IV., 1771.
$6\frac{13}{16} \times 5\frac{1}{8}$. $(5\frac{1}{2} \times 4\frac{13}{16})$.   E. 2196.–'89.

P. Stubly.   S. Freeman.
Ha. len. to right, looking to front, holding in his left hand a
sea-piece, to which he points with his right. In Walpole's
" Anecdotes," Vol. II., 1849.
Proof before all letters, on India paper.
$8\frac{1}{2} \times 5\frac{1}{8}$. $(4\frac{9}{16} \times 3\frac{1}{8})$.   E. 2195.–'89.

MONBODDO, JAMES BURNET, or BURNETT, Lord, 1714-1799, Scotch lawyer, philosopher, and author; Judge of Court of Session; published "Dissertation on the Origin and Progress of Language," 1774-'92, "Ancient Metaphysics," 1779-'99.

J. Brown.   Chas. Sherwin, stipple.
Sh. ha. len. to right, with wig, bands, and gown.
Oval, 12th April, 1787.
$6\frac{1}{4} \times 4\frac{3}{16}$. $(2\frac{5}{8} \times 2\frac{3}{16})$.   26674.

MONCKTON, HON. MARY, 1747-1840, youngest child of John Monckton, 1st Viscount Galway; m., 1786, (2nd wife) to Edmund, 7th Earl of Cork; highly esteemed in London Society; said by Boswell to have been "used to talk together [with "Johnson] with all imaginable ease;" d. in New Burlington Street.

Sir J. Reynolds.   J. Jacobé, mez.
J. C. Smith, 6, 2nd state; from collection of Sir Thomas Lawrence, whose mark is in the left corner, at foot.   22042.

MONCREIFF, JAMES, 1811- ; 2nd son of Sir James W. Moncreiff, 9th Bart., of Tulliebole, Kinross-shire; b. at Edinb.; educ. at the High School and University, Edinb.; adm.-advocate, 1833; Solr.-Genl. (Scotland), 1850-'1, and Lord Advocate till 1852; M.P. Leith, 1852-'9; Edinb., 1859-'68; Univs. of Glasgow and Aberdeen; Lord Adv. again, 1852-'58, 1859-'66; 1868-'69; Lord J. Clerk, and Pres. Court of Session; P.C.; cr. Bart., 1871; Baron Moncreiff of Tulliebole, 1874, &c.

J. W. Gordon.   S. Cousins, mixed mez.
As Dean of Faculty; ha. len. slightly to right, looking to front, wearing a ribbon and jewel.
Open letter proof.   Private plate; May 1, 1829.
$14\frac{7}{16} \times 10\frac{15}{16}$. $(11\frac{3}{4} \times 9\frac{3}{4})$.   28259.

MONK, JAMES HENRY, 1784-1856, D.D.; educ. at, and fellow and tutor of, Trin. Coll., Cambr.; Reg. Prof. Greek, Univ. Cambr.; Dean of Peterborough, 1822; Bishop of Gloucester, 1830, and 1st Bishop of Gloucester and Bristol, on the union of those sees, 1836; publd. some very learned works, Life of Dr. R. Bentley, &c.

W. Gush.   F. Bacon, mixed mez.
T. Q. len. to front, seated, looking to right, a roll of paper in his right hand; arms below, in centre. Oct. 10, 1843.
$21\frac{3}{16} \times 16\frac{3}{8}$. $(16\frac{9}{16} \times 13\frac{3}{16})$.   22895.

MONMOUTH, HENRY (CAREY), 2nd Earl of, 1596-1661, distinguished for his scholarship, and especially in modern languages; translated several works from the French and Italian, the most important being Biondi's History of the Civil Wars of England (see Charles I.), and Paul Paruta's History of Venice, 1658, fol.

                              (W. Marshall.)

Bust, to left, in profile; on pedestal, the following inscription: HENRICUS | *Dom* CARY *Baro*; | *de Loppington* | *Com. de* | MONMOVTH | ; and,at foot, *Prœ·nob: Ord: Baln* EQVES.
Cut. $(5\frac{9}{16} \times 3\frac{7}{16})$. 29717. 14.

MONMOUTH, HENRY (CARRY)—*continued.*
W. Faithorne (?). W. Faithorne.
L. Fagan, p. 49, 2nd state.
Cut. $(8\frac{3}{4} \times 5\frac{7}{8})$. 27585.

MONMOUTH, JAMES, Duke of, 1649–1685, natural son of Charles II. and Lucy Walters; ordered to leave England on account of his intrigues against James, Duke of York; headed the insurrection, 1685 ; defeated at Sedgemoor, and executed on Tower Hill.
Sir P. Lely. A. Blooteling.
T. Q. len. to left, looking to front, in robes of the garter, with long hair, hat with plumes in right hand, left hand resting on hilt of sword ; titles, &c., in 5 lines, at foot.
$(12\frac{9}{16} \times 9\frac{15}{16})$. 21828.

Netcher and Wyke. W. Baillie, mez.
J. C. Smith, 4, 1st state. 24105.

MONTAGU, SIR ANTHONY BROWNE, 1st Viscount, c. 1527–1592; Statesman; great grandson of John Neville (3rd son of Richard, Earl of Salisbury, and Marquess of Montagu) ; Knt., 1547 ; M.P. ; cr. Visct., 1554 ; K.G., 1555 ; Ambas. Extr. to the Pope, 1555 ; a staunch Catholic under Elizabeth, who nevertheless esteemed him highly ; sat on trial of Mary Queen of Scots.
(From the original picture in the possession of Thomas Baylis, Esq.) G. P. Harding del. J. Brown, stipple.
Sh. hn. len. to front, wearing a jewelled cap, a rich dress, the George, &c.; inscription within border, in 14 lines ; title below, July 1, 1845.
$11\frac{9}{16} \times 7\frac{7}{8}$. $(5\frac{1}{8} \times 4\frac{5}{16})$. 22453.

MONTAGU, EDWARD WORTLEY, 1713–1776, son of Edward Wortley Montagu and his wife, Lady Mary, the celebrated writer of the well-known letters ; ran away when a boy, and led a roaming life ; on his return became M.P. ; driven abroad by his embarrassments ; converted in Italy to Catholicism, in Egypt to Mahometanism, and resided in the East ; d. at Padua.
W. Peters. J. R. Smith, mez.
J. C. Smith, 111, 2nd state. 22040.

MONTAGU, ELIZABETH, Mrs., 1720–1800, daughter of Matthew Robinson, Esq., of West Layton, Yorks. ; partly educ. by Dr. Conyers Middleton, her grandmother's second husband, and displayed considerable talent ; m. (1742) to Edward Montagu, Esq., of Denton Hall, who d., 1775, leaving her so wealthy as to become a leader of literary society and founder of the *Blue*

Stocking Club, or coterie ; pub. several works ; friend of Pope, Pulteney, Johnson, Goldsmith, Reynolds, &c.

Sir J. Reynolds.   J. R. Smith, mez.

J. C. Smith, 112, 2nd state.   22254.

MONTAGU, LADY MARY WORTLEY, c. 1690–1762, dau. of Evelyn Pierrepont, 5th Earl of Kingston, aftds. Marquess of Dorchester and Duke of Kingston, of Thoresby Park, Notts. ; m. to Edward Wortley Montagu, whom she accomp. to Constantinople, when he was ambassador there ; while abroad, wrote the " Letters " which made her literary fame ; introduced inoculation for small-pox from Turkey into England ; returned home, 1718, and became Pope's neighbour at Twickenham, living there at Savile House ; later, lived many years in Italy and France ; returned finally, 1761 ; at one time a great friend of Pope, but latterly at bitter enmity, each satirising the other ; celebrated as " Sappho " by Pope in his poems ; d. in George St., Hanover Square ; buried in Grosvenor Chapel, South Audley St.

See PORTLAND, 2ND DUKE OF.

MONTAGU, CAPTAIN JAMES, 1752–1794, 3rd son of Adm. John Montagu ; lieut., and commander, 1773 ; served on N. Amer. Stn., and in North Sea, Channel, and E. Indies ; posted, 1775 ; commanded a ship, the Montagu, June 1st, 1794, in Howe's victory off Ushant ; lost his life in the action.

See COMMEMORATION (1).

MONTEAGLE, THOMAS SPRING RICE, Lord, 1790–1866 ; Colonl. Sec., Chancellor and Comptroller of Exchequer ; cr. Baron, 1839.

J. Linnell.   J. Linnell, mez.

Ha. len. to right, seated, holding a book. March 15, 1836.

$18\frac{1}{4} \times 13\frac{3}{4}$. $(14\frac{11}{16} \times 11\frac{1}{8})$.   23033.

MONTGOMERY, JAMES, 1771–1854, Poet ; son of a Moravian missionary ; b. in Ayrshire ; shopman, for some time, to a London bookseller ; aftds. wrote for the press, conducted the " Sheffield Iris " for many years ; pub. the " Wanderer of Switzerland," " The World before the Flood," Hymns, &c. ; received a Govt. pension.

J. R. Smith.   C. Turner, mixed mez.

Ha. len. to right, seated, holding a book in right hand ; coat buttoned across chest ; inkstand on table, on right ; July 1, 1819.

14×10. $(10\frac{3}{8} \times 8\frac{5}{16})$.   22469.

MONTGOMERY, ROBERT, 1807–1855, b. at Bath, son of Gomery, a famous theatrical clown, who had shortened his name by dropping the first syllable, unless that syllable was added gratuitously by the son, who entd. at Linc. Coll., Oxf., 1830 ; B.A., 1833 ; M.A., 1838 ; ord., 1835 ; curate of Whittington ; at Percy

St. Chapel, 1836–'8, at St. Jude's, Glasgow, till Decr. 1842; again at Percy St., 1843, till his death; author of Poems, severely-reviewed by Macaulay, and other works.

C. Baugniet.   C. Baugniet, lith.
Ha. len. to front, looking to right, with right hand raised, preaching. Facs. signature below. 1845.
(13½ × 11¾).   25836.

MONTROSE, JAMES GRAHAM, 1st Marquess of, 1612–1650, General, son of the 4th Earl; b. in Edinb.; first joined the Covenanters; aftds. took the part of Charles I., who cr. him Marquess; defeated Lord Elcho at Tippermuir, 1644, and the Marquess of Argyll at Inverlochie, 1645; fled from the kingdom after his defeat by Leslie, near Selkirk, 1645; on his return, was captured and executed.

Sir A. van Dyck.   J. Houbraken, 1740.
Sh. ha. len. to left, looking to front, in armour, with long hair; oval in border, a battle below. In Birch's " Lives."
14¾ × 9⁵⁄₁₆. (14½ × 8¾).   21982.

MOODY, JOHN, 1727–1812, comedian; appeared at Drury Lane, 1759; succeeded brilliantly in Irish characters, that of O'Flaherty being a special favourite; behaved with proper spirit towards rioters at Drury Lane, 1763; d. at Shepherd's Bush; buried at Barnes.

B. vander Gucht.   J. Saunders, mez.
J. C. Smith, 9, 5th state, not mentioned by Mr. Smith, with address of Sayer & Bennett, June 1777.
With Packer (q. v.).   26416.

———

T. Hardy.   T. Hardy, mez.
J. C. Smith, 1st state.   22252.
See also PARSONS.

MOON, SIR FRANCIS GRAHAM, Bart., 1796–1871, son of Christopher Moon, printseller and publisher; sheriff, 1843; Alderman, 1844; Lord Mayor, 1854–'5; Bart., and Chev. Leg. of Honour, 1855; F.S.A., magistrate for Middlesex, Commr. of Lieutenancy for London, connoisseur and patron of Art.

G. T. Doo, F.R.S.   G. T. Doo.
Ha. len. inclined to left, looking to front, wearing robes and badge.
Ind. proof before letters, except the artists' names and titles.
17¼ × 13⅛. (11¼ × 9⁷⁄₁₆)   25835.

MOORE, HENRY, 1831–   , contemporary painter; of a York-shire family; has painted landscapes and sea views with success; A.R.A., 1884; R.A., 1893.

Pilotel.   Pilotel, etched.
Bust, to right, wearing beard; vignette, for " The Artist."
6¼ × 4⅗. (5 × 4⁵⁄₁₆).   E. 2199.–'89.

MOORE, Dr. John, 1730–1802, Physician and Miscellaneous Writer; b. at Stirling; educ. as a physician; practised at Glasgow; accomp. the young Duke of Hamilton abroad, 1772–'8; settled in London, where he pub. books of travels, "Medical Sketches," "Zeluco," and other tales; one of his sons was the gallant Sir John Moore, who fell at Corunna; d. at Richmond.

Sir T. Lawrence, R.A.   G. Keating, mez.
J. C. Smith, 6, 1st state.   21939.

MOORE, Sir John, 1761–1809, son of Dr. John Moore; b. at Glasgow; ent. Army, 1776; served with distinction in Corsica, West Indies, Holland, and Egypt, 1795–1802; Commander-in-chf. of the British Army in Portugal, 1808; fell, on his famous retreat from Saldanha, in the Battle of Corunna; Lt.-General; K.B., &c.

Sir T. Lawrence, R.A.   C. Turner, mixed mez.
Ha. len. to front, in uniform, three buttons of coat fastened, wearing the star of the Bath.
Scratched letter proof.
(12½ × 10).   21896.

MOORE, Thomas, 1779–1852, b. in Dublin, son of a grocer and spirit-seller; precocious, he contributed verses to "Anthologia Hibernica," at the age of 13; educ. at Trin. Coll., Dublin; stud. law in London, and pubd. his translation of Anacreon; pubd. the "Poetical Works of the late Thomas Little, Esq.," 1801, of which he was aftds. ashamed; later, "Epistles," "Intercepted Letters," "Irish Melodies," "Lalla Rookh," "Fudge Family," "Loves of the Angels," &c.

M. A. Shee, R.A.   J. Burnet.
Full ha. len. to left, seated, holding an eye-glass in right hand, and resting the left arm on a table, on which are books and papers; in a rectangular border of ruled lines.
Open letter proof; February, 1820.
13⅛ × 9¼. (Excl. of border, 9⅜ × 7⅝).   22003.

———

G. S. Newton.   W. H. Watt.
Sh. ha. len. to front, looking to left; eye-glass hanging by a ribbon, oval in border.
Ind. proof with open letters; June, 1828.
14¹⁄₁₆ × 10¾. (10¼ × 8⁷⁄₁₆).   22896.
See also SCOTT, Sir Walter.

MOORSOM, Admiral Constantine Richard, 1792–1861; ent. Navy, 1809; Lieut., 1812; h. p., 1827; Rear-Adm. 1851; Vice-Adm., 1857; Chairman of the Chester and Holyhead Railway; author of an essay "On the Principles of Naval "Tactics," priv. printed, 1843; pubd., with additions, 1846. See MENAI Straits.

MORE, Hannah, 1744–1833, authoress; dau. of a village schoolmaster in Gloucestershire; wrote "Percy" and other

tragedies; aftds. wrote moral tales and essays; achieved her
greatest success with the " Shepherd of Salisbury Plain,"
and " Cœlebs in search of a Wife ; " d. at Clifton.
    H. W. Pickersgill, A.R.A.   W. H. Worthington.
    T. Q. len. to front, seated, holding in right hand a pair of
spectacles in case; wearing a high cap with frills; a letter
inscribed to *W. Wilberforce Esq.* on table beside her ; March
1, 1824.
    $17\frac{1}{4} \times 13$. $(13\frac{3}{4} \times 11)$.   22005.

MORE, Sir John, 1453(?)–1530, father of Sir Thomas More ;
sergeant, 1503 ; judge of Com. Pleas, 1518 ; judge of K. B.,
1520, or 1523 ; mentioned in terms of deepest respect and
tenderness in his son's Latin epitaph, 1532.
    Holbein.   R. Dalton.
    An etching, tinted by hand; inscription below, written by
hand, " Judge More Sr. Tho: More's Father," &c.
    Bust to right, furred robe, and cap ; vignette.
    $14\frac{1}{2} \times 11\frac{3}{4}$. $(12\frac{1}{4} \times 10\frac{1}{4})$.   23139.

MORE, Sir Thomas, 1480–1535, Statesman ; M.P., 1503 ;
wrote " Utopia," 1518 ; Speaker, 1523 ; Lord Chancellor, 1529 ;
resigned, 1532 ; published " Apologie," 1533 ; imprisoned for
refusing oath of supremacy ; attainted, 1534 ; executed, 1535.
    Holbein.   J. Houbraken, 1740.
    Sh. ha. len. to left, wearing furred robe, with chain ; oval in
border.
    In Birch's " Lives."
    $14\frac{2}{3} \times 9\frac{3}{16}$. $(14 \times 8\frac{11}{16})$.   27119.

———
    Anon.   T. Holloway.
    Bust, to front, wearing fur collar and flat hat.
    From Lavater's " Essays on Physiognomy," Vol. 2, p. 262.
    Cut. $(9\frac{1}{2} \times 7\frac{1}{16})$.   E. 183.–'93.

MORETT, Hubert, a famous jeweller, temp. Henry VIII. ;
executed many of Holbein's designs.
    H. Holbein.   (M. Bacciarelli del,)   J. Folkema.
    Full ha. len. to front, handsomely dressed, with a collar of
fur, a jewel in his hat, and a chain round his neck ; grasping a
dagger in his right hand. The picture, in the Dresden gallery,
was long attributed to L. da Vinci (see " Holbein and his Time,"
by Dr. A Woltman, London, 4to, 1872, p. 404).
    Cut. (11×9).   26360.

MORGAN, Sydney, Lady, c. 1780–1859, b. in Dublin, daughter
of a musician named Owenson ; began publishing verses at the
age of 14, and novels at that of 16 ; " The Wild Irish Girl,"
1801, made her famous ; married to Sir T. C. Morgan, 1811 ;
pubd. " France," " Italy," " Florence Macarthy," &c.
    S. Lover   R. Cooper, stipple.

Full. ha. len. to left, seated ; her left arm resting on two
books. June 14, 1825 ; in a rectangular border of waved
lines.
12$\frac{11}{16}$ × 9$\frac{1}{2}$.   (Excl. of border, 5$\frac{3}{16}$ × 4$\frac{1}{4}$).   22470.

MORIER, JAMES, 1780–1849, traveller and novelist, having
received a good education, became Sec. of the Br. Embassy in
Persia ; published " Journey through Persia in 1808–'9," 1812 ;
"Adventures of Hajji Baba of Ispahan," 1824–'28 ; " Zohrab,
the Hostage," 1832 ; " Ayesha, the Maid of Kars," 1834 ; &c.
  W. Boxall.   S. W. Reynolds, mixed mez.
  Full. ha. len. to left, seated, looking to front, with hands folded
together.   July 1st, 1850.
  14$\frac{7}{8}$ × 10$\frac{7}{8}$.   (10$\frac{1}{8}$ × 8$\frac{3}{16}$).   24235.

MORLAND, GEORGE, 1763–1804, b. in the Haymarket, son of
Henry Morland, the painter ; early showed genius for art,
painted first children and genre ; famous afterwards chiefly for
animal pictures ; ruined and destroyed by dissolute habits ;
married the sister of W. Ward, engraver ; his wife died three
days after him ; both buried at St. James' Chapel, Tottenham
Court Road.
  R. Muller.   W. Ward, mez.
  J. C. Smith, 60.   E. 322.–'89.

———

  J. R. Smith.   I. R. Smith, mez.
  J. C. Smith, 115.   23015.

———

  J. R. Smith, 1792.   (R. W. Satchwell del.)
                                        C. Picart, stipple.
  Bust to left ; looking to front ; vignette.
  (3$\frac{1}{4}$ × 2$\frac{1}{2}$)   E. 2197.–'89.

———

  Bell del.   G. Scott, etched and stippled.
  T. Q. len. to left, looking to front, seated, sketching ; sheep,
a tree, and palings, in the distance ; oval ; pubd., Feb. 26,
1805.
  7$\frac{7}{16}$ × 4$\frac{7}{8}$.   (4$\frac{7}{8}$ × 3$\frac{13}{16}$).   26255.

MORLEY, GEORGE, 1597–1684, b. in London ; educ. at Westminster and Oxford ; attended Charles I. till his death, when
he retired to Holland ; Bishop of Worcester, 1660 ; Principal
Manager of the Savoy Conference, 1661 ; Bishop of Winchester, 1662.
  Sir P. Lely.   G. Vertue, 1740.
  Sh. ha. len. slightly inclined to left, looking to front,
wearing robes and square cap ; oval in border, the garter surrounding the arms of the see of Winchester (incorrect, because
reversed) below.
  11$\frac{1}{4}$ × 9$\frac{5}{16}$.   (13$\frac{11}{16}$ × 9$\frac{13}{16}$).   22471.

MORNINGTON, ANNE HILL, Countess of, 1740–1831, daughter
of Arthur Hill-Trevor, 1st Visct. Dungannon; m. to Garret
Wellesley, 1st Earl of Mornington, amateur musical composer,
1759; became the mother of the Marquess Wellesley, Gov.-
Genl. of India, and the 1st Duke of Wellington.
  Lady Burghersh.   T. Hodgetts, mixed mez.
  Wh. len., slightly turned, and looking to left; seated, holding
in right hand a copy of the LONDON GAZETTE EXTRA-
ORDINARY; a letter from her son, the Duke of Wellington,
dated *Waterloo, June 19, 1815*, on the table by her side; busts,
pictures, &c., around her, and in background; Jany. 1, 1839.
  (20¼ × 15).   23010.

MORPETH.   *See* CARLISLE.

MORRIS, CAPTAIN CHARLES, 1746–1838, served in the 17th
Regt. in the American war; exch. into Dragoons, and subsequently into Life Guards; extremely popular writer of convivial
songs, which he sang with great effect; d. at Dorking; "Lyra
Urbanica," a collection of his songs, pubd. after his death.
  A. J. Oliver, A.R.A.   T. Hodgetts, mez.
  Ha. len. to left, looking to front, short grey hair, white neckcloth, coat buttoned across; June 21, 1808.
  14⅜ × 10⅞.   (11₁₀⁷ × 9¼).   26654.

MORRISON, ROBERT, 1782–1834, D.D.; b. at Morpeth, was
ord. as a missionary of the London Miss. Socy., Jany., 1807;
landed at Canton in Sepr.; lived there remainder of his life,
except during a visit to England, 1824–'26; translated the
Bible into Chinese, pubd. a Dicty. of the Chinese language, &c.
  J. Chinnery.   C. Turner, A.R.A., mez.
  Wh. len. to left, seated, in gown, looking to front; behind, on
left, are two Chinese, assisting him in his translation of the
Bible.
  Open letter proof; March 29, 1830.
  24⅞ × 18₁₆⁹.   (21₁₀¹ × 16₁₀¹⁴).   23014.

MORTIMER, JOHN HAMILTON, 1741–1779, b. at Eastbourne;
pupil of Hudson, afterwards of Pine; gained prizes for
historical pictures from the Society of Arts; A.R.A., 1778;
of dissipated habits, by which his health was shattered; d.
suddenly in Norfolk St., Strand.
  J. H. Mortimer.   V. Green, mez.
  J. C. Smith, 87, 2nd state.   24085.

  R. Wilson.   J. R. Jobbins, lith.
  Wh. len. to left, looking to right, sketching; some blocks of
ruined buildings behind and at his feet; landscape in distance;
printed for J. Britton, 1842, who had the picture then;
published with a pamphlet of 4 pp., in cover, "On the Paintings
and merits of Richard Wilson, R.A.," &c.
  (6⅞ × 5⅝).   28443.   B.

MORTON, JAMES DOUGLAS, 4th Earl of, 1530–1581, Chancellor
to Mary, 1563; took part in the murder of Rizzio, and fled to
England; pardoned, through Bothwell's influence; refused to
share in the plot against Darnley; Regent of Scotland, 1572;
his administration was arbitrary, burdensome, and odious;
charged with complicity in Darnley's murder, tried, condemned,
and beheaded, still calmly protesting his innocence.

From a picture "in the Possession of the . . Earl of
Morton." J. Houbraken, 1740.
Sh. ha. len. to left, looking to right; in oval.
$14\frac{11}{16} \times 9\frac{1}{4}$. $(14\frac{1}{8} \times 8\frac{3}{4})$. 26704.

MORTON, THOMAS, 1764–1838, dramatist; b. in co. Durham;
educ. at school in Soho Square; member of Linc. Inn; produced
"Cure for the Heartache," 1797; "Speed the Plough," 1798;
"School of Reform," 1805.
Sir M. A. Shee, P.R.A. T. W. Hunt, stipple.
Ha. len. to right, seated, looking to front; coat loosely
buttoned.
Ind. proof.
$14\frac{3}{8} \times 10\frac{13}{16}$. $(9\frac{9}{16} \times 8)$. 21746.

MUDGE, THOMAS, 1715–1794, son of a clergyman; b. at Exeter;
appr. to G. Graham, celebrated watchmaker; became eminent
in his business, and noted for his improvements in chronometers,
for which he received a Parliamentary grant of 3,000l.; kept a
shop in Fleet St.; d. at his son's house at Walworth.
N. Dance, R.A. C. Townley, mez., 1772.
J. C. Smith, 16, 2nd state. 22897.

MULGRAVE, HENRY PHIPPS, Earl of, 1755–1831, ent. Army,
1775; Col., 1793; General, 1809; M.P., Totness, 1784–'90,
Scarborough, 1790–'94; suc. 1792; cr. a peer of Gr. Britain,
1794, as Baron Mulgrave; Chancellor of the Duchy of Lancaster, Foreign Sec.; First Lord of the Admiralty; Master-
Gen. of Ordnance, 1810–'18; cr. Viscount Normanby, and Earl
of Mulgrave, 1812.
T. Lawrence, R.A. C. Turner, mez.
Published Aug. 13, 1808.
$13\frac{7}{8} \times 9\frac{7}{8}$. $(11\frac{3}{4} \times 9\frac{3}{4})$. 22898.
See also DILETTANTI SOCIETY.

MULGRAVE, JOHN SHEFFIELD, Earl of, 1649–1720, suc. 1658,
as 3rd Earl; served against the Dutch with Pr. Rupert; sent
to the relief of Tangier, 1680; Lord Chamberlain, 1685; cr.
Marquess of Normanby, 1694; D. of Normanby and D. of
Buckingham, 1703.
Sir G. Kneller. J. Smith, mez.
J. C. Smith, 186, 3rd state. 22112.
See also SHEFFIELD.
See also NORMANBY.

MULREADY, WILLIAM, 1786–1863, b. at Ennis, co. Clare, son
of a breeches-maker; studied in the Academy schools; illustrated many of Newbery's books for children; began exhibiting, 1803; became successful as a subject-painter, R.A., 1817;
led a solitary life; buried at Kensal Green. Some of his best
works came by the Sheepshanks gift to the S.K. Museum.

   J. Linnell.   J. Thomson, stipple.

   Ha. len. to front, looking to right; as President of the Artists'
Annuity Fund; the plate presented by the engraver to the
Committee for the Report, in which it appeared for many
years.

   $5 \times 2\frac{1}{8}$(?). $(3\frac{1}{8} \times 2\frac{1}{4})$.   28300.   36.

   P. Mulready del., 1829.   J. H. Robinson, etched.

   Bust, to right, in profile; as President (1815–'17, 1820–
'22, 1824–'26, 1828–'30), of the Artists' Annuity Fund; vignette.

   $4 \times 3\frac{1}{4}$. $(2\frac{1}{4} \times 2\frac{1}{4})$.   29023.   A.

MUNDEN, JOSEPH SHEPHERD, 1758–1832, distinguished comedian; son of a poulterer; b. in London; suc. Edwin at Cov.
Garden, 1790; engaged at Drury Lane, 1813; noted as "Sir
Francis Gripe," "Jemmy Jumps," "Old Rapid," "Brum-
magem," &c.; celebrated by C. Lamb in the "Essays of Elia;"
retired, 1824.

   J. Opie, R.A.   S. W. Reynolds, mez., 1804.

   Ha. len. to front, looking to left; white neckcloth, one button
of coat fastened; a paper in right hand; in rectang. grounded
border.

   15×11. $(12\frac{1}{4} \times 10\frac{3}{4})$.   22253.

MUNRO, SIR THOMAS, 1760–1827, cadet in India, 1778; disting.
in Mahratta War; present at capture of Seringapatam, 1799;
administrator of territory ceded by the Nizam, 1801; K.C.B.,
1819; Gov. of Madras, 1820; cr. Bart. for services in Burmese
War, 1825; Maj.-General; d. in India.

   Sir M. A. Shee, P.R.A.   S. Cousins, mixed mez.

   Wh. len. to front, looking to left, in uniform, with collar,
star, &c.; left hand resting on a map of India on table, right
hand holding sword at level of belt; despatch-box on floor, at
left.

   Open letter proof (?); title on separate plate at foot.

   $30 \times 20\frac{5}{8}$. $(29 \times 19\frac{7}{8})$; title-plate, $1\frac{7}{8}$(?)$\times 20\frac{1}{4}$.   25790.

MURCHISON, SIR RODERICK IMPEY, 1792–1871, b. at Tarra-
dale, Ross-shire; educ. at Durham, the Military Coll., Gr.
Marlow, and Edinb. Univ.; ent. army, 1807; served in Penins.
campaign; and at Vimiera; ret. as Captain, 1815, and devoted
himself to science, especially Geology; examined borderland of
Wales and England (1830), and found the rocks which he called
"Silurian;" made geol. survey of Russia, 1840; called attention to gold in Australia, 1841–'8; Knt., 1846; twice Pres.

Geol. Socy. ; Pr. Geogr. Socy. ; friend of Livingstone ; F.R.S. ; Director-Genl. of Geol. Survey of Grt. Britain, 1853 ; K.C.B., 1863 ; Bart., 1866 ; Author of "Siluria," &c.
H. W. Pickersgill.   W. Walker, mixed mez.
Ha. len. to front, wearing collar, medal, and star ; looking to right ; hands resting on book before him, lettered SILURIAN SYSTEM. MURCHISON.
Proof before all letters.
$15\frac{3}{4} \times 12$. $(14 \times 11\frac{7}{16})$.   25788.

MURDOCH, WILLIAM, one of Matthew Boulton's workmen, and his most efficient assistant.
See SCIENCE.

MURPHY, ARTHUR, 1727–1805, b. in Co. Roscommon ; stud. at St. Omer's ; settled in London, and became celebrated as a playwright ; friend of Foote and Garrick, and biographer of the latter ; wrote " The Upholsterer," "The Orphan of China " ; pubd. " Gray's Inn Journal," and the " Auditor ;" translated Tacitus ; d. at Brompton-row, Knightsbridge, in his 78th year.
N. Dance, R.A.   W. Ward, A.R.A., mez.
J. C. Smith, 63, 2nd state.   22251

MURRAY, SIR GEORGE, 1772–1846, General and Statesman ; b. in Perthsh. ; educ. at Edinb. ; entd. the army, 1789 ; served in the French wars ; Governor of the Royal Military Coll., 1819 ; Master-Genl. of the Ordnance, 1834–'5, 1841 ; M.P. for Perthshire ; Colon. Sec., 1828–'30 ; G.C.B., &c.
Sir T. Lawrence, P.R.A.   H. Meyer, mez.
Sh. ha. len. to front, looking to left, in undress uniform.
Ind. paper proof, March 1, 1841.
$13\frac{1}{2} \times 9\frac{11}{16}$. $(11\frac{5}{8} \times 9\frac{5}{8})$ 24086.

H. W. Pickersgill, R.A.   C. Fox.
Wh. len. to front, looking to right, in uniform, with cloak ; his hat hangs from his left hand ; right hand on hip ; landscape with hills in distance.
Ind. proof.
$(25\frac{1}{8} \times 15\frac{5}{16})$.   23016.

MURRAY, SIR JOHN ARCHIBALD, by courtesy, Lord, 1788–1868 ; educ. at Edinb. High School and Westminster ; entd. as an advocate at the Scottish bar, 1800 ; on staff of Edinb. Review, from the beginning ; M.P., 1832 ; Lord Advocate, 1834 ; knighted, and raised to the bench, 1839 ; sat 20 years as Lord of Sessions ; d. at age of 80.
Sir H. Raeburn, R.A.   W. Walker, mez.
Sh. ha. len. to left, looking to front ; coat buttoned ; white neckcloth.
Private plate ; proof ; Feb., 1835.
17×13. $(11\frac{1}{2} \times 9\frac{1}{4})$ 23164.

MURRAY, THOMAS, 1666–1724, painter, b. in Scotland; came
early to London; studied under Riley, and painted portraits;
remarkable for good looks and elegant manners; was very
successful, and acquired some fortune.

 T. Murray.   J. Smith, mez.

 J. C. Smith, 188, undescribed 1st state, before any inscription.

                     27666.

MUSGRAVE, THOMAS, 1788–1860, son of a tradesman at Cam-
bridge; entd. at Trin. Coll., 1806; 14th wrangler, 1810;
fellow, and M.A., 1813; Almoner's Prof. of Arabic, 1821;
Sen. Proctor and Bursar, 1831; incumbent of St. Mary's,
Cambr.; D.D., and Bishop of Hereford, 1837; Archbishop of
York, 1847; pubd. 2 charges, 1839, 1849.

 F. R. Say.   J. R. Jackson, mixed mez.

 T. Q. len. slightly to right, looking to left, in robes, standing;
a book in his right hand; Aug. 1, 1851.

 21⁵⁄₁₆ × 15⅛. (17½ × 13¾).   27635.

MUSICAL UNION, THE, an association, managed by a President, Vice-President, Committee of 15 noblemen and gentlemen, and a Director, John Ella; it gave eight afternoon
concerts of classical chamber music every season in London,
1844–1880. It was founded by John Ella (q. v.), at whose
house the first meetings were held; they were afterwards
held at the Hanover Square Rooms, and lastly at St. James's
Hall.

 [Baugniet.]   C. Baugniet, lith., 1853.

 "L'Analyse. Souvenir de l'Union Musicale (9me Saison);"
A group of the 15 principal artists who had at that time
appeared at these concerts, (beginning at left) viz., Bazzini,
H. Blagrove, Goffrie, Blumenthal, Vieuxtemps, Lazarus,
S. Pratten, Jarrett, F. Hiller, Barret, Baumann, Lind-
painter, Spohr, Molique, H. Berlioz, and the director, J. Ella.

 F. Hiller is seated at the Piano-forte, from which he turns
towards Spohr, Berlioz, and the others on his left; Vieuxtemps, holding his violin in his left hand, stands on the other
side; Ella is on the extreme right, holding a pen in his left
hand, raised to his chin.

 The angles rounded off; proof.

 (15¼ × 23¼).   23781.

MYDDELTON, SIR HUGH, 1560 (?)–1631, son of Richard Myddelton, Governor of Denbigh Castle; b. at Denbigh; became
a goldsmith in London; acquired great wealth by working
mines in Wales, and invested his profits in constructing the
"New River," to supply London with fresh water, 1609–1613;
M.P. for Denbigh, 1603; cr. Bart., 1622.

 C. Janssens, 1632.   G. Vertue, 1722.

 T. Q. len., slightly to right, looking to front; wearing broad
ruff, chain, and jewel; his left hand rests on a shell, from

which flows a stream of water; arms above, on the right; title,
&c., below, in 5 lines, Engl. and Latin.
$14\frac{11}{16} \times 10\frac{3}{4}$. ($11\frac{7}{8} \times 9\frac{7}{16}$).   21826.

MYDDELTON, Sir Hugh—*continued*.
　C. Janssens.   [W. Walker ?], stipple.
　From the same picture as the print described above.
　Proof before all letters.
　($7 \times 5\frac{11}{16}$).   E. 1291.-'88.

MYERS, Joseph Hart, c. 1800, M.D., Physician to the Portu-
　guese Hospital, &c.
　　See MEDICAL SOCIETY.

MYLNE, Robert, 1734–1811, architect and engineer, b. at
　Edinburgh, son of an architect; visited Paris, and Rome, where
　he studied five years, gaining the first prize in architecture,
　1758, in the Academy of S. Luke; went to Naples, Sicily,
　Florence, and other cities; returned, built Blackfriars Bridge;
　surveyor of St. Paul's and of New River Compy.'s works; clerk
　of the Works at Greenwich Hospital; built Almack's, &c.
　Anon.   Anon.
　Head, in profile to right; oval in border.
　Proof before all letters.
　$7\frac{1}{4} \times 5\frac{7}{16}$. ($5\frac{9}{16} \times 4\frac{3}{8}$).   E. 2201.-'89.
　　See also SCIENCE.

NANKING Treaty of Peace and Commerce between Great
　Britain and China, The signing and sealing of the ; in the State
　Cabin of H.M.S. " Cornwallis," Aug. 29, 1842 ; with portraits
　of Her Majesty's Plenipotentiary, Sir Henry Pottinger, the
　Naval and Military Commanders-in-Chief, the Chinese Com-
　missioners, and many other officers and officials.
　　Captain J. Platt.   J. Burnet, mixed mez.
　　A composition of many figures ; the Imperial Commissioners
　are seated at a table in the middle; Sir H. Pottinger sits by
　them, on the left; the rest are ranged on each side, seated and
　standing.
　　Proof before all letters.
　　Cut. (?) $\times 33\frac{1}{4}$. ($12\frac{1}{8} \times 31\frac{3}{4}$).   25846.

————

　A key to the names of the (56) personages represented in the
　print, on the back of the prospectus.
　($4\frac{7}{8} \times 12\frac{5}{16}$).   25846. A.

NAPIER, Sir Charles James, 1782–1853; b. in Ireland; entd.
　the army, served in the suppression of the Irish rebellion, 1798,
　and in Spain, 1808–'13; commanded army of Bengal, and
　defeated Ameers, 1843; annexed Scinde and governed it, 1843–
　'7; Commr.-in-Chf. in India against the Sikhs, 1849; resigned,
　1850; G.C.B.; &c.
　From a photograph.   J. Skelton.
　T. Q. len. seated, to front, looking to left ; Novr. 24, 1849.
　($13 \times 9\frac{7}{8}$).   23019.

NAPIER, Sir Charles, 1786–1860, son of Capt. the Hon. Chas. Napier, R.N.; commanded the Portuguese Constitutional fleet, and established Doña Maria on the Portuguese throne, 1833; successfully concluded the Turco-Egyptian war between the Porte and Mohammed Ali, 1840 ; Comr.-in-Chf. of Baltic fleet in the Russian War, 1854; K.C.B.; M.P. for Marylebone and Southwark; advocated naval reform and improvement of condition of seamen; d. at Merchistoun Hall, Hants.

  J. Simpson.   J. Porter, mez.

  Ha. len. to front, looking to right, in uniform, wearing star, &c. Open letter proof; July 26th, 1841.

  14½ × 11. (11 9/16 × 9 9/16).   22899

  From an Original Drawing.   Gauci, lith.

  Wh. len. as Admiral, and C.B., before he was K.C.B.; on deck, with left arm extended, giving orders ; wearing an ordinary tall hat; resting with right hand on a curiously-shaped cutlass.

  Ind. proof, 1834.

  (15 4/5 × 11½)   E. 1304.–'88.

NAPIER, Sir John, of Merchiston, 1550–1617, son of Sir Alexander Napier; b. at Merchiston Castle, Edinburgh, 1550; ent. Univ of St. Andrews, 1562–'3; suc. his father, 1608; pubd. his famous discovery of the method of Logarithms, 1614.

  Brown del.   J. Beugo, stipple.

  Sh. ha. len. to front, slightly inclined to left, looking to front; oval in a wreath of oak and thistle intertwined, an eye in glory above ; arms below, and title, with a quotation, in 4 lines, from Hume's Hist. Vol. VII., p. 35, 8th edit., 1775; engraved from a drawing by Mr. Brown in the possession of the Earl of Buchan, who published a " Life of John Napier," 1787.

  Cut. (Oval, 2 7/16 × 1 6/16).   25753.

NARES, James, 1715–1783, b. at Stanwell, Middlesex, chorister in Chapel Royal, under B. Gates ; pupil of Pepusch; deputy for Pigott, organist at Windsor; went to York as organist, 1734; organist and composer, Chapel Royal, and Mus. Doc., Cambr., 1756 ; master of the children, 1757 ; pubd. Harpsichord Lessons, Services, Anthems, Glees, Catches, &c.

  G. Engleheart. (J Hoppner del.) W. Ward, stipple.

  Sh. ha. len. to left, looking to front, wearing curled wig; Ætat. 65; prefixed to his " Morning and Evening Service," &c., 1788 ; oval, cut out.

  (5½ × 4½).   E. 2015.–'89.

NASH, Richard, 1675–1761, b. at Swansea; Master of the Ceremonies at Bath, 1704, became known as Beau Nash, and celebrated as a leader and dictator of fashion; retained his office more than 50 years; towards the end of his life was

forsaken by society ; d. in comparative indigence ; his life was
written by Goldsmith.

    T. Hudson.   J. Faber, junr., mez.

    J. C. Smith, 253, 1st state.   22014.

NASMYTH, ALEXANDER, 1758–1840, landscape-painter, and
dexterous mechanic, b. at Edinb.; pupil of Allan Ramsay;
visited Italy ; settled at Edinb. ; painted portraits ; more successful in landscapes ; assisted Miller in his early experiments with
paddle-boats, which led to the invention of the steamboat.

    See SCIENCE.

NAVAL HEROES (1), viz., SOUTHWELL, SIR ROBERT,   –
1599 ; HOWARD OF EFFINGHAM, CHARLES, Baron, K.G.,
1536–1624 ; SEYMOUR, OF SUDLEY, THOMAS, Lord High
Admiral,   –1549 ; RUTLAND, HENRY, Earl of, c. 1525–
1563, Admiral ; SHEFFIELD, EDMUND, Lord, aftds. Earl of
Mulgrave, c. 1564–1646 ; NORTHUMBERLAND, ALGERNON
PERCY, Earl of, Lord High Admiral, 1602–1668 ; WARWICK,
ROBERT RICH, Earl of, Lord High Admiral, 1587–1658.

    R. Smirke.   W. Sharp.

    7 ovals, on a rock ; sea-nymphs below ; vignette.

    Proof.

    (10½ × 8¼).   26381. 2.

——— (2), viz., MINGS, CHRISTOPHER, Admiral,   –1666 ;
PENNINGTON, SIR JOHN, Lord High Admiral,   –1646 ;
HOLLIS, SIR FRETSWELL, Admiral,   –1672 ; BERKLEY,
SIR WILLIAM, Vice-Admiral,   –1666 ; ALLEN, CAPTAIN WIL-
LIAM (of the *Bonadventure*),   –1698 ; SPRAGUE, SIR E.,
Admiral,   –1673 ; PENN, WILLIAM, Admiral, 1621–1670 ;
SHEFFIELD, EDMUND, Lord, c. 1564–1646, Admiral.

    G. Noble. 1803.   T. Holloway.

    8 ovals, on the side of a monument ; Neptune below ; vignette.

    (11¼ × 8½).   26381. 1.

NAYLER, SIR GEORGE, 1764(?)–1831, Garter King-of-Arms, &c.

    W. Beechey, R.A.   E. Scriven.

    Ha. len. to right, looking to front, wearing three decorations.

A private plate, according to Evans.

    Ind. proof with open letters.

    16⁷⁄₈ × 12¼. (9¾ × 8¼).   21745.

NELSON, HORATIO, VISCOUNT, 1758–1805 ; 5th son of Rev. E.
Nelson ; educ. at High School, Norwich ; midshipman, 1770 ;
Post Captn., 1779 ; Commodore, 1795 ; Rear-Admiral of Blue,
1797 ; cr. Viscount Nelson of the Nile, 1801 ; Vice-Admiral
of White, 1804 ; captured Elba, 1796 ; won the battles of
Nile and Trafalgar, at the latter of which he was killed.

    Westall, R.A.   Golding.

Wh. len. to left, receiving the sword of the dying commander of the *San Nicolas*, off Cape St. Vincent, Feb. 14, 1797; a composition of many figures.
Ind. proof before all letters, except the artists' names.
Cut. ($8\frac{3}{8} \times 7$). 18928.

—— receiving the swords of the Spanish officers on board the "San Josef," after the surrender of that ship, in the battle of Cape St. Vincent, Feb. 14, 1797.
T. J. Barker. C. G. Lewis, mixed stipple.
Nelson stands just to the left of the centre of the composition, with left hand extended courteously to receive the sword of the Spanish captain; a composition of many figures.
$28\frac{1}{4} \times 47$. ($24\frac{1}{4} \times 44$). 27679.

—— on board the "San **Josef,"** in the battle of Cape St. Vincent.
D. Orme. D. Orme, stipple
Nelson, just to the right of the centre, with right hand extended, is about to receive the sword of the Spanish captain, which is presented by another officer, kneeling on one knee, and pointing with left hand to the captain who is dying, or dead, on the deck; a composition of many figures.
Open letter proof; June 2, 1800.
$20\frac{1}{8} \times 24\frac{1}{4}$. ($17 \times 23$). 22015.

——
J. Hoppner, R.A. H. Meyer, stipple.
Wh. len. to left, looking to front; sea and ships in distance, on left.
Proof before all letters; *inlaid.*
($20\frac{5}{16} \times 12\frac{7}{8}$). 22018.

——, The Death of Lord Viscount, K.B.
B. West, P.R.A. J. Heath.
Nelson, near the middle of the print, directed towards the right, looks upwards, while his left hand is pressed by Hardy, who kneels on one knee by him; a composition of many figures; May 1, 1811.
$19\frac{7}{8} \times 25$. ($17\frac{1}{4} \times 23\frac{7}{8}$). 25837.

——, ——
West. Heath.
Outline key to the Portraits in the print from Mr West's picture of the Death of Lord Nelson.
$16\frac{7}{8} \times 24$. 25837. A.

——, ——
D. Maclise, R.A. C. W. Sharpe.
A composition of many figures; Nelson in the middle; from the picture in the Palace of Westminster; pubd. by the Art Union of London, 1876.
Ind. proof.
$16\frac{5}{8} \times 48\frac{1}{4}$. ($11\frac{7}{8} \times 45\frac{3}{16}$). 27567.

NELSON, Horatio, Viscount—*continued.*

Anon. S. Lines.

From the statue erected by the inhabitants of Birmingham, A.D. MDCCCIX.

$12\frac{3}{4} \times 8\frac{1}{4}$. $(11\frac{5}{8} \times 8\frac{1}{8})$. 26222.

Anon. Anon.

Bust, directed to front, the face turned towards right; in a glory, with laurel and oak-leaves at sides; below, a trophy of arms and flags, on either side of the pedestal; vignette.

Proof before all letters.

Cut. $(7\frac{1}{4} \times 5)$. 29608. O.

From a cast by Thaller. P. W. Tompkins, stipple.

Bust, to front, looking to right, supported by two winged figures, one of whom (Victory?), on the left, places a wreath on his head, while the other (Fame?), on the right, blows two uplifted trumpets; below, eight verses, over a plan of the order of battle of Trafalgar; beneath is a dedication "*To the* Queen," in 6 lines, and a biography in 22 lines; 2 lines giving the history of the portrait, and publication-line, follow at foot, with facs. signature, "left hand."

17 × 13. (Bust, $2\frac{5}{16} \times 1\frac{13}{16}$). 29718. 15.

NEWCASTLE, Henry Pelham, 4th Duke of, 1785–1851, suc., 1795; educ. at Eton; Bearer of the sword "Curtana" at Coron. of George IV.; D.C.L., Oxon; K.G., &c.

H. W. Pickersgill, R.A. W. H. Mote.

Hn. len. to front, seated, looking to left.

Ind. proof, with scratched letters. Published, 1836.

$13\frac{1}{8} \times 10\frac{1}{4}$. $(9\frac{1}{8} \times 7\frac{1}{4})$. 20636.

NEWCASTLE, Henry Pelham Fiennes-Pelham-Clinton, 5th Duke of, 1811–1864, educ. at Ch. Ch. Coll., Oxford; B.A., 1832; M.P. for South Notts., 1832, 1835, 1837, 1841–'6; P.C., 1841; Cab. Minister, 1846; declared for Free Trade; suc., 1851; Sec. for War, 1854–'5, for Colonies, 1859; K.G., D.C.L.

Sir J. W. Gordon, P.R.S.A. G. Zobel, mixed mez.

T. Q. len. to front, facing and looking to left, resting both hands before him on a folded paper, which rests on a table; facs. signature below.

Ind. proof, Oct. 28, 1864.

$20\frac{7}{8} \times 16\frac{7}{16}$. $(16\frac{1}{8} \times 13\frac{1}{4})$. 22132.

See also ABERDEEN CABINET.

NEWCASTLE, Margaret, Duchess of, –1673, daughter of Sir Thomas Lucas; 2nd wife of William, 1st Duke of Newcastle (1592–1676); a voluminous writer, severely criticised by Walpole and others.

Abr à Diepenbeke. P. van Schuppen.

347

Wh. len. in niche, an embl. figure on each side ; twelve verses
below, on a tablet ; *rare.*
11¼ × 6¾. (10½ × 6⁷⁄₁₆).   24124.

Diepenbeke.   Alais, stipple.
See LA BELLE ASSEMBLÉE, 1819.   13867.   30.

NEWCASTLE, THOMAS PELHAM-HOLLES, 1st Duke of, 1694–
1768; suc. as Lord Pelham, 1712; cr. Duke, 1715; had great
political power, from the fall of Walpole to 1762; Prime
Minister, K.G., P.C., &c.
  W. Hoare.   J. MacArdell, mez.
  J. C. Smith, 136, 2nd state.   22043.

NEWCASTLE, WILLIAM CAVENDISH, 1st Duke of, 1592–1676;
son of Sir Charles Cavendish ; cr. Earl of Newcastle, 1628 ;
Governor of the Prince of Wales; disting. for his gallantry in
the Royal Army, during the Civil war ; retired abroad after
Marston Moor, and settled at Antwerp ; cr. Duke, at the
Restoration ; Author of a Treatise on Horsemanship ; P.C.,
K.G., &c.
  A. van Dyck.   G. Vertue.
  Sh. ha. len. slightly turned towards right, looking to front ;
broad lace collar, star, &c. ; oval in border ; 1739.
  In Birch's Lives."
  14³⁄₁₆ × 9⁵⁄₁₆. (13⅞ × 8⅞).   22472.

NEWLAND, ABRAHAM, 1730–1807, Chief Cashier of the Bank
of England from 1778 to his death; left by will 200,000*l.*
  G. Romney.   J. Grozer, mez.
  J. C. Smith, 18, 1st state.   24087.

NEWPORT, SIR JOHN, Bart., 1754–1843 ; M.P., Chancellor and
Comptroller of the Exchequer in Ireland, &c.
  J. Ramsay.   T. Lupton, mez.
  T. Q. len. to left, seated, looking to front, holding in right
hand a roll, inscribed, "Ireland 1806 | Corn Intercourse
Act."
  Open letter proof. Published, May 22, 1828, by Colnaghi,
Son, and Co.
  15⅞ × 12½. (13 × 10⁵⁄₁₆).   27551.

NEWTON, SIR ISAAC, 1642–1726, b. at Woolsthorpe, Linc. ;
educ. at Grantham Gram. Sch., and Trin. Coll., Cambr. ; discov.
method of Fluxions, 1665; suc. Isaac Barrow as Lucasian
Prof. of Mathematics, 1669; published his discoveries in his
lectures, 1669–'71 ; presented the first book of his " Principia "
to the Royal Society, 1686 ; M.P. for Cambr. Univ., 1689–'90 ;
Master of the Mint, 1699 ; P.R.S., 1704 ; Knt., 1705 ; d. at
his house, Kensington ; bur. in Westminster Abbey.
  Sir G. Kneller.   J. Smith, mez., 1712.
  J. C. Smith, 190, 2nd state.   21870.

NEWTON, Sir Isaac—*continued.*
    Sir J. Thornhill.   J. Simon, mez.
    J. C. Smith, 110, 2nd state; address erased.   21926.

    Sir G. Kneller, 1689.   T. O. Barlow, mixed mez.
    Ha. len. to left, looking to right; hair long, and light in
colour; right hand resting on left wrist; loose collar and gown.
Ind. proof, signed by the engraver in pencil.
    $19\frac{3}{4} \times 15\frac{1}{4}$. $(14\frac{5}{16} \times 11\frac{6}{8})$.   24194.

NEWTON, Robert, D.D., 1780–1854, a Wesleyan minister;
son of a farmer; b. at Roxby, N.R., Yorks.; began preaching
when a lad; minist. in London, 1812; in Liverpool, 1820;
in Manchester, Liverpool, Leeds, and Stockport, till his death,
at York; Pres. Wesl. Conf., 1824, '32, '40, '48 : sermons pubd.,
much commended, 1856.
    H. Calvert.   T. O. Barlow, mixed mez.
    T. Q. len. to front, standing; his right hand holds a folded
paper, and rests on a table.
    Open letter proof; March 17, 1852.
    $19\frac{3}{4} \times 14\frac{7}{8}$. $(15\frac{1}{4} \times 11\frac{7}{8})$.   27083.

NEWTON, Thomas, 1704–1782, b. at Lichfield; educ. at
Cambr.; Rector of St. Mary-le-Bow; Dean of St. Paul's;
Bishop of Bristol, 1761; edited Milton's Poems, and pubd.
"Dissertations on the Prophecies," 1754; d. suddenly; bur. at
St. Paul's.
    Sir J. Reynolds.   T Watson, mez.
    J. C. Smith, 27, 2nd state.   22260.

NEWTON, William, 1735–1790, brother to James Newton,
engraver; architect; clerk of the works at Greenwich Hospital,
and designed some of the additional buildings; member of
Incorp. Socy. of Artists, 1766; exhibited at Academy, 1776 and
'80; pubd. the first English translation of the "De Architectura"
of Vitruvius, 1771, and superintended publication of the third
vol. of Stuart's "Antiquities of Athens;" died at Sidford,
Devon.
    R. Smirk del.   I. Newton, stipple.
    Head, in profile to right; oval, in the style of a basso-rilievo.
    $5\frac{1}{16} \times 4\frac{7}{16}$. $(3\frac{5}{8} \times 3\frac{1}{8})$.   15219.   10.

NICHOLAS, Abraham, 1692–1744 (?), writing-master and
private schoolmaster, London, and attds. at Clapham; highly
commended by George Bickham for the mastery of hand in one
of his copy-books, of which he pubd. three; went abroad, about
1722 (to Virginia?), and d. abroad.
    Anon.   Anon.
    Sh. ha. len. slightly inclined towards right, looking to front;
long wig, open collar; oval in border, decorated with formal
garlands of oak-leaves; name on border, in middle, at bottom.
    $(7 \times 10\frac{11}{16}$; oval, $5\frac{5}{8} \times 4\frac{5}{16})$.   29718.   3.

NICHOLAS, Sir Edward, 1593–1669, Secretary of State to Charles I. and II.; attended Charles I. to Oxford; retired to Jersey and Caen, 1646; with the D. of York at Breda and Antwerp, 1651; met the King at Aix, 1654; returned with Charles to England, 1660; retired, 1662, to East Horsley, Surrey, where he died.

Sir P. Lely. Vertue.

T. Q. len. seated at table, to left, looking to front. "Ætat. suæ LXX. 1662."

$14\frac{3}{8} \times$ (?). Cut. $(11\frac{1}{8} \times 8\frac{3}{4})$. 22900.

NICHOLL, Sir John, Knt., 1759–1838; educ. at Cowbridge, Bristol, and St. John's Coll., Oxf.; B.C.L., 1780; D.C.L., 1785; adm. at Doct. Commons, 1785; Commissioner to enquire into state of law in Jersey; K. Adv., Knt., 1798; M.P., 1802–'32; opposed Cath. Emancipation and all Reform Bills; Dean of Arches, P.C. Judge of the Prerogative Court of Canterbury, and Vicar General to the Archbishop.

W. Owen, R.A. H. Meyer, mez.

T. Q. len. seated, to left, looking to front, in judge's robes, right hand resting on table.

Open letter proof; April 7, 1819.

$20 \times 13\frac{7}{8}$. $(17\frac{3}{8} \times 13\frac{1}{8})$. 23020.

NICHOLS, John, 1745–1826, learned printer and author, F.S.A.; b. at Islington; at the age of 12, apprent. to W. Bowyer, who took him into partnership, 1766; on Bowyer's decease, 1777, suc. to the entire business; edited the "Gentleman's Magazine," 1778–1826; pubd. "Select Collection of Misc. Poems," 1780–'2; Bibliotheca Topographica; "History, &c., of Leicester," 1795–1815; &c.

J. Jackson, 1811 H. Meyer, mez.

Sh. ha. len. to front, wearing large spectacles; high waistcoat, buttoned to chin; "Ætat. LXVI.;" books, inkstand, pens, and paper, on table behind, on right.

Open letter proof.

$13 \times 10\frac{1}{2}$. $(8\frac{1}{4} \times 6\frac{3}{4})$. **23018.**

H. Edridge delin. A. Cardon, stipple.

Ha. len. to right, seated, wearing large spectacles, and holding a cross-headed stick with both hands; Nov. 17, 1814; vignette.

$14\frac{1}{8} \times 11\frac{7}{8}$. $(8\frac{1}{4} \times 7\frac{1}{4})$. E. 1302.–'88.

NICHOLSON, Francis, 1753–1844, water-colour painter, b. at Pickering, had some lessons from an artist at Scarborough; after two visits to London, settled at Whitby, painting horses, dogs, &c., and teaching; exhibited at the Academy, 1789; left Whitby, 1792, and, after staying for a time at various places, came to London, where he established himself as an artist; one of the founders of the Water-Colour Society, 1804; painted landscapes, waterfalls, &c., and executed some lithographs.

J. Green. M. Gauci, lith.

Sh.-ha. len. to right, looking to front; furred collar to his
cont.; vignette.
India paper proof, printed by Hullmandel.
(10¼ × 8½). E. 1273.-'86.

NICHOLSON, JOHN, 1821–1857; Brig.-General; born in Dublin; educ. at Dungannon; ensign, 1839; served at Jalalabad,
1840; at Kabul and Gazni, 1841, taken prisoner, but escaped,
after great hardships; adjt., 1843; in Kashmir, 1846; Capt.,
1848; put down rebellion, at Multan; served in 2nd Sikh war,
with great distinction; Br. Lt.-Col., 1854; exercised wonderful
influence in Punjab; commanded Punjab col. during Mutiny;
killed at Delhi.
T. F. Dicksee. A. N. Sanders, mixed mez.
Ha. len. to front, looking to right, both hands resting on hilt
of sword; bareheaded, in uniform.
Open letter proof; June 1st, 1867.
18¼ × 15⅜. (13⅞ × 11). 23021.

NICHOLSON, PETER, 1765–1844, architect, son of a stonemason;
b. at Preston Kirk, East Lothian; apprent. to a cabinet-maker,
came to London; pubd. "The Carpenter's New Guide," 1792,
for which he engraved the plates, "The Student's Instructor,"
and other works; returned to Scotland, 1800; settled at
Glasgow as an architect; afterwards at Carlisle; returned to
London, where he pubd. "Architectural Dictionary," &c.; went
to Morpeth, 1829, to Newcastle, 1832, to Carlisle, 1841; where
he died, poor, and receiving a small pension.
H. Adlard, stipple on steel.
Ha. len. slightly to right, looking to right; coat buttoned;
compasses in right hand, a paper in left; vignette.
Cut. (5¼ × 4⅞). 28414. 2.

T. Heaphy. C. Armstrong.
Ha. len. seated, looking to left; holding a paper in left hand,
compasses in right; within a ruled border.
7½ × 5⁷⁄₁₆ (?). (5⅝ × 4⁵⁄₁₀, including border). 15219. 11.

NICOLS, CAPTAIN , — , commanded a ship, June
1, 1794, in Howe's victory off Ushant.
See COMMEMORATION (1).

NOEL, BAPTIST WRIOTHESLEY, 1799–1873, b. at Leightmont,
Scotland; son of Sir G. N. Noel, Bart., and brother to Lord
Gainsborough; grad. Univ. Cambr., 1826; minister at St.
John's Chapel, Bedford Row, till 1848, when he joined the
Baptists, in John St., where he suc. to the pulpit on the death
of Rev. J. H. Evans; pubd. many sermons, meditations, essays.
G. Richmond. W. J. Edwards, stipple.
Bust, slightly to right, looking to front; vignette.
Open letter proof; June 24, 1851.
22 × 17. (8¼ × 7). 25838.

NOLLEKENS, Joseph, 1737–1823, sculptor, son of "Old Nollekens," the portrait-painter; b. in Soho; studied in Shipley's school, and worked under Scheemakers; gained Society of Arts premiums, 1759 and '60; saved money, and went to Rome; gained another premium and the gold medal of the Roman Academy, 1761; returned, 1770, and soon acquired reputation and employment; executed some groups and many busts; A.R.A., 1771; R.A., 1772; left a fortune, over 200,000*l.*, at his death; buried in Paddington Churchyard.

Anon.   Anon.
Bust, to right; oval in a border; in the European Magazine, July 1, 1788.
6⅞ × 4⅞. (5⅝ × 3³⁄₁₆, including border).   15219. 12.

Sir W. Beechey, R.A.   C. Turner, mez.
Ha. len. slightly to left, looking to front, holding in his right hand a modelling tool, leaning his right elbow on a table, on which is the model of a monumental group.
Proof with open letters; touched on the hair, whisker, collar, background, and elsewhere, to indicate alterations to be made; signed in pencil by the engraver. Publd. Decr. 24, 1814.
14 × 10.   (11⅛ × 9⅞).   22261.

F. Abbot.   (W. Evans del.)   J. Vendramini, chalk and dot.
Ha. len. to front, looking to right; his right hand resting on the bust of Charles James Fox; vignette.
Open letter proof; pubd. Oct. 21, 1816.
15 × 10(?).   (7¼ × 8).   28298.   5.

G. Dance del.   W. Daniell.
Sh. ha. len. to right, in profile, seated; vignette.
Proof, before all letters, except the name of the person represented.
10¾ × 8.   (6 × 5¼).   26265.

J. Jackson, R.A.   W. Bond, stipple.
Sh. ha. len. to front; vignette; Oct., 1828.
Ind. paper proof.
Prefixed to J. T. Smith's "Nollekens and his Times," 1829.
8¹⁵⁄₁₆ × 5⅞.   (6 × 4½).   26264.

NORFOLK, Charles Howard, 11th Duke of, Earl of Surrey and Arundel, 1746–1815; M.P. 1780, and 1784–'6; suc., 1786; F.R.S., P.S.A., &c.
Gainsborough, 1783.   I. K. Sherwin, 1790.
Wh. len. slightly to left, in robes, as Marshal of England, holding a staff.
Published June 20, 1790, though Evans calls it "a private plate."
26½ × 19¾.   (24 × 18).   24079.

NORFOLK, Thomas Howard, 3rd Duke of, 1473–1554, eldest son of Thomas, 2nd Duke; cr. Earl of Surrey, 1514; commanded at Flodden; Lord Deputy, Ireland, 1520-'22; Earl Marshal, 1534; attainted, 1547, on disgrace of his niece, Q. Katharine Howard; impris. in Tower, 1546–'53; rest., D. of Norfolk, 1553; K.G.; Bearer of Crown at Coronation of Q. Mary; Lieut.-General of the Queen's Army.

    H. Holbein.   L. Vorsterman.

    Ha. len. to front, " Æ. 66, Obyt. 1654," above, on right; with staff, as Earl Marshal, wearing the Collar and George; title in two (Latin) lines; artists' names and privilége, &c., in another line, below; " Visitur in Ædibus Arondelianis Londini."

    (9⅝ × 7¾).   21964.

NORFOLK, Thomas Howard, 4th Duke of, 1536–1572, K.G., suc. 1554; Lieutenant in the North; proposed husband of Mary, Queen of Scots, imprisoned in the Tower, 1569; released, but recommitted, 1571; executed.

    Holbein.   Houbraken, 1735.

    Sh. ha. len. slightly to left, looking to front, in oval.

    In Birch's " Lives."

    Cut. (14⅛ × 8¾).   20792.

NORMANBY, Constantine Henry Phipps, Marquess of, 1797 –1863, statesman and novelist; Home Secretary, 1839–'41; Ambassador at Paris, 1846–'52.

    H. P. Briggs, R.A.   C. Turner, A.R.A., mez.

    As Earl of Mulgrave, Lord Lieutenant of Ireland, 1836; T. Q. len. to front, looking to right.

    19¼ × 13⅛. (14⅝ × 11⅜).   23011.

NORTH, Frederick, Lord, aftds. 2nd Earl of Guilford, 1732 –1792, Statesman; son of the 1st Earl of Guilford; ent. Parliament, 1754; Chanc. of Exchequer, 1767; Prime Minister, 1770–'82; opposed the cause and claims of the American Colonists; suc. as 2nd Earl, 1790.

    N. Dance, R.A.   T. Burke, mez.

    J. C. Smith, 6, 1st state.   21919.

NORTH, Roger, c. 1650–1734, youngest son of Dudley, 4th Lord North; stud. at Temple; Steward of the Courts to Archbp. Sheldon; wrote an " Examen " of Kennet's Hist. of England, in defence of the Stuarts; also " Lives " of his three brothers, &c.

    Sir P. Lely, 1680.   G. Vertue, 1740.

    Sh. ha. len. to left, looking to front, wearing long wig and gown; " Ætatis cir. 30," prefixed to his Examen of Kennet's History.

    (8 × 6).   22523.

NORTHAMPTON, Henry Howard, 1st Earl of, 1540–1614, Statesman; page to Bishop Gardiner; educ. at King's Coll.

and Trin. Hall, Cambr.; M.A., Camb., 1566; Oxf., 1568; P.C., 1603; cr. Baron Howard, of Marnhill, and Earl of Northampton, 1604; K.G., 1605; Lord Keeper, 1608; &c.

Zucchero. W. Bond.
Sh. ha. len. to front, wearing a high hat with broad brim, the collar, and George; in Lodge's Portraits, large series.
Cut. (7$\frac{1}{16}$ × 5$\frac{5}{8}$). 28147. 1.

NORTHAMPTON, SPENCER JOSHUA ALWYNE COMPTON, 2nd Marquess of, 1790–1851; educ. at Trin. Coll., Cambr.; M.P., Northampton, 1812; worked with Wilberforce and others for abolition of slavery and reform of crim. law; spent many years in Italy; suc., 1828; full of literary, artistic, and scientific tastes and acquirements; P. Geol. Socy.; twice Pres. of Br. Association; P.R.S., 1838–'49; Pres. Arch. Inst.; d. at Castle Ashby, Northants.

"Commenced by the late Thomas Phillips, R.A.," finished by H. W. Phillipps. Painted for the Royal Society; Exhibited at the R. A., 1847.

W. Walker, mixed mez.
T. Q. len. to left, holding in right hand a book, which rests on table.
Ind. proof before all letters, except the engraver's name, address, and date, Nov. 25, 1848.
22 × 16$\frac{1}{4}$. (18$\frac{1}{4}$ × 14$\frac{1}{2}$). 24631.

NORTHCOTE, JAMES, 1746–1831, historical and portrait-painter, b. at Plymouth, son of a watchmaker, served his time as his father's apprentice; fled, with his elder brother, from his father's house, on foot, to London, 1771, with an introduction to Sir J. Reynolds, who received him into his house for five years; studied at the R. A.; returned to Devonshire, where he made a little money by portrait-painting; went to Italy, 1777–'80; returned, painted portraits and some subjects; rapidly gained reputation; A.R.A., 1786; R.A., 1787; wrote "Life of Sir J. Reynolds," "Fables," illustrated by himself, "Life of Titian;" d. rich, in Argyll St.

J. Opie. W. Ridley, stipple.
Ha. len. to right, looking to front; coat loosely buttoned; high collar; oval.
Pubd., Octr., 30, 1799.
6$\frac{1}{4}$ × 4$\frac{1}{2}$. (3$\frac{1}{2}$ × 2$\frac{2}{3}$). 28300. 40.

Anon. J. Condé, stipple.
Bust, slightly inclined to right, the face in profile to right; oval.
Cut. (4$\frac{5}{16}$ × 3$\frac{2}{3}$). 28300. 58.

G. Dance del., March 2, 1793. W. Daniell, chalk and dot. 1809.
Sh. ha. len. to right, the face in profile; vignette.
10$\frac{3}{8}$ × 7$\frac{1}{8}$. (6$\frac{1}{4}$ × 4$\frac{4}{5}$). E. 1299.–'88.

O 82849. Z

NORTHCOTE, James—*continued*.

G. Dance, 1793. P. Audinet.
Sh. ha. len. to right, the face in profile; vignette; facs.
signature below.
Published in the Gentleman's Magazine, Sepr. 1, 1831.
$7\frac{3}{8} \times 5$. $(3\frac{11}{16} \times 2\frac{1}{2})$. 28300. 39.

Prince Hoare del. Anon., stipple.
Sh. ha. len. to left, the face in profile; oval.
$5\frac{5}{16} \times 4\frac{3}{8}$. $(3\frac{11}{16} \times 2\frac{7}{16})$. 28300. 37.

Prince Hoare del. J. de Claussin, etched.
Head, to right, "from the Original Sketch;" vignette.
$10\frac{1}{8} \times 7\frac{7}{8}$. $(6 \times 5\frac{1}{4})$. E., 2202.-'89.

J. Northcote. H. Meyer, stipple.
Ha. len. to right, looking to front, holding a palette in left,
and a brush in right hand; wearing a dressing-gown.
Published by T. Cadell and W. Davies, Novr. 1, 1815.
Cut. $(7 \times 5\frac{1}{2})$. 28298. 6.

G. H. Harlow. F. C. Lewis, stipple.
T. Q. len. to right, seated, holding spectacles in right hand; a
picture ("Burial of the Princes in the Tower") in the background, on right.
Scratch-letter proof; June 1, 1824.
16×11. (10×8). 21837.

A. Wivell. B. Holl, stipple.
Bust, to left, wearing a cap; vignette; facs. signature below;
for the "Library of the Fine Arts," 1831.
$8\frac{3}{4} \times 5\frac{3}{4}$. $(3\frac{1}{4} \times 2\frac{1}{3})$. 28300. 41.

NORTHCOTE, Samuel, Senior, of Plymouth, 1786; father of
the painter; watchmaker, lived in Market St., Plymouth;
unitarian, of humble origin; steadily opposed his son's wish to
be an artist.
J. Northcote. S. W. Reynolds, mez.
Sh. ha. len. slightly to right, looking to right, white hair,
curling at the ends, white neckerchief; oval in rectang. border.
$13\frac{3}{8} \times 9\frac{1}{16}$. $(9\frac{1}{8} \times 7\frac{3}{4})$. 27978. 2.

NORTHCOTE, Samuel (Junior), of Plymouth, 1785; elder
brother of the painter, whom he accompanied in his flight on
foot to London from their father's house; he himself returned
at once to Plymouth.
J. Northcote. S. W. Reynolds, mez.
Sh. ha. len. to front, looking to right; high collar, white
neckerchief, striped waistcoat; two lower corners of portrait
rounded, in rectang. border.
$13\frac{3}{8} \times 10$. $(9\frac{5}{16} \times 7\frac{13}{16})$. 27978. 1.

NORTHCOTE, Rt. Hon. Sir Stafford H. *See* IDDES-
LEIGH, and DERBY CABINET.

NORTHINGTON, Robert Henley, Earl of, c. 1708-1772,
educated at Westminster and St. John's Coll., Oxford; M.A.,
1733; M.P., Bath, 1747; Recorder of Bath; K.C., 1751;
Attorney-General, 1756; Lord Keeper, and P.C., 1757; cr.
Baron, 1760; Ld. Chancr., 1761-'6; cr. Earl, 1764; Ld. Presi-
dent, 1766-'7; &c.
 T. Hudson.   J. McArdell, mez.
 J. C. Smith, 104.   24228.

NORTHUMBERLAND, Algernon Percy, Earl of. *See*
NAVAL Heroes (1).

NORTON, Hon. Mrs. Caroline Elizabeth Sarah, 1808-1877,
2nd daughter of Thomas, and gr.-daughter of Rt. Hon. R. B.
Sheridan, brought up by her mother at Hampstead; showed
early signs of literary talent, in the " Dandies' Rout," illustrated
by herself; m. to Hon. George C. Norton, from whom she
was separated not long after; prod. "Sorrows of Rosalie,"
1829; the "Coquette" and "Wife and Woman's Reward,"
novels, 1835; followed by poems, ballads, " Martyr," a tragedy,
" Tales and Sketches," &c.
 F. Grant, A.R.A.   T. Fairland, lith.
 Sh. ha. len. to right, looking rather towards left of front, a
broadly-checked shawl over her left shoulder. Decr. 20th, 1847.
 $(11\frac{3}{4} \times 9\frac{3}{16})$ 24732.

NOTT, Sir William, 1782-1845, educ. at Cowbridge; entd.
Indian Army, 1800; commd. the troops in Sind and Lower
Affghanistan, 1839, and captured Khelat; accomplished his
brilliant and successful march from Candahar by Gazni, which
he took and demolished, to Kabul, during the insurrection of
1841-'2; General; G.C.B., &c.; d. at Carmarthen.
 J. D. Francis.   G. T. Payne, mez.
 Ha. len. to front, wearing cloak, star, and medal.
 Open letter proof, May 12, 1845.
 $15\frac{1}{8} \times 11\frac{11}{16}$. $(11\frac{1}{4} \times 9\frac{3}{8})$.   23017.

NOTTINGHAM, Charles Howard, 1st Earl of, 1536-1624,
son of William, Lord Howard of Effingham; Lord High
Admiral of England; commanded the fleet against the Spanish
Armada, 1588; cr. Earl of Nottingham for his capture of Cadiz,
1596; Lieut.-General of England, 1599; defeated and captured
Essex, 1601; Ambassador to Spain, 1604.
 F. Zucchero.   J. Houbraken, 1739.
 Sh. ha. len. to left, wearing embroidered cap and robes, with
the collar and George; oval in border, a naval battle, below.
 In Birch's " Lives."
 $14\frac{13}{16} \times 9\frac{5}{16}$. $(14\frac{1}{8} \times 8\frac{3}{8})$.   21983.

NOTTINGHAM, Daniel Finch, 2nd Earl of, 1647-1730,
Statesman; son of Heneage Finch, 1st Earl; First Commr. of

Admiralty under Charles II.; one of the Commissioners sent by James II. to treat with the Prince of Orange; Principal Sec. of State under William III. and Queen Anne; P.C., &c.

Sir G. Kneller.   J. Houbraken.

Sh. ha. len. to right, looking to front, in robes, with long wig; oval in border, arms below.

$14\frac{3}{8} \times 8\frac{1}{4}$. ($13\frac{5}{8} \times 8\frac{3}{8}$).   21981.

NOTTINGHAM, HENEAGE FINCH, 1st Earl of, 1621–1682, Lawyer and Statesman; son of Sir Heneage Finch, Recorder of London; educ. at Westminster, and Ch. Ch. Coll., Oxf.; called to the Bar, 1645; M.P., Canterbury, 1660; Sol.-Gen., 1660; cr. Bart., 1660; M.P., Univ. Oxf., 1665; Attorney-Gen., 1670; Lord Chanc., 1675; famous as an orator; cr. Earl of Nottingham, 1681; P.C., &c.

Sir G. Kneller.   R. White, 1681.

Sh. ha. len. to left, in robes, looking to front; oval, in border decorated with mace and bag, on either side of arms; title in 3 lines below.

$15\frac{5}{16} \times 11\frac{1}{8}$. ($13\frac{3}{4} \times 10\frac{5}{8}$).   21968.

NUGENT, SIR GEORGE, 1757–1849; cr. Bart., 1806; Lt.-Genl.; Colonel of 6th Regt. of Foot; Govr. of St. Mawes; Comr.-in-chf. in India; Field-Marshal; &c.

J. Downman, A.R.A.   R. Woodman, stipple.

Ha. len. to right, in uniform, bareheaded.

A private plate (?), not mentioned by Evans, Bryan, &c.

$18\frac{3}{8} \times 14$. ($14\frac{1}{2} \times 11\frac{7}{8}$, or, exclusive of border, $12 \times 9\frac{3}{8}$).

27552.

NUNN, WILLIAM, 1787–1840; educ. at St. John's Coll., Cambr.; M.A.; Minister of St. Clement's, Manchester; a "Lancashire worthy."

H. Wyatt delin 1823.   John Ford, lith.

Sh. ha. len. to front, in bands and gown, looking to right; vignette; this seems to have been drawn on stone with a pen.

(5×4).   22700.

OAKELEY, SIR CHARLES, Bart., 1751–1826; b. at Forton, Staffs.; educ. at Shrewsbury; ent. E.I.C. Service, 1766; assist.-sec., and sec., 1767–'80; Pres. of Committee of assigned revenue (of Nabob of Arcot), 1781–'4; Pres. of Board of Revenue, Madras, 1786–'88; Govr. of Madras, 1790–'94.

T. Barber, 1816.   S. W. Reynolds, mez.

Ha. len. to right, looking to front.

Open letter proof.

$13\frac{7}{16} \times 10\frac{1}{16}$. ($11\frac{7}{16} \times 9\frac{3}{8}$).   20927.

OATES, TITUS, 1649–1705, son of a Baptist preacher; educ. at Cambr., and ent. church; joined Ch. of Rome, 1677, and turned informer against persons accused of complicity in a popish plot; brought many noblemen and others to the scaffold; on James's accession was convicted of perjury, pilloried, and flogged;

in William's reign, received a small pension, and rejoined the
Baptists, who expelled him, 1701, as "a disorderly person and
a hypocrite."
    T. Hawker.   R. Tompson excudit, mez.
    J. C. Smith, 32.   24088.

O'CONNELL, DANIEL, 1775–1847, b. at Cahirciveen, Kerry;
called to the Irish Bar, 1798; rose to national influence by his
struggle for Catholic Emancipation, 1809–'28; M.P., 1830;
began his Repeal agitation, 1831; sentenced to fine and imprisonment for this agitation, 1843; judgment reversed, 1844;
d. at Genoa.
    H. Newton, M.S.W.C.   Maclure & Macdonald, lith.
    Wh. len. to right, looking, and pointing with right hand, to
left; holding hat in left hand; coat buttoned up; a staircase
behind him.
    Ind. proof, May 30, 1844.
    (16 × 12).   22155.

OCTAVIUS, PRINCE, 1779–1783, and PRINCE ALFRED, 1780–
1782, sons of George III.
    Anon.   Anon., stipple.
    T. Q. len. seated at table, on which are shells; Octavius, on
the right, holds a cup and ball. A dog's head on the left.
    Proof before all letters.
    Cut. (8½ × 7¾).   25060.
    In Genealogical Chart, 553. 1.

OGILBY, or OGILVY, JOHN, 1600–1676, b. at Edinburgh;
became a dancing master; went to Ireland with Strafford; was
made master of the revels; built a theatre, but lost his property
in the Rebellion; settled at Cambridge, and translated Virgil;
at the age of 54 he learnt Greek, and translated the Iliad (1660)
and Odyssey (1665); pubd. a splendid edn. of the Bible;
restored to his place in Ireland, and again built a theatre;
became King's Printer in London after the Great Fire, and
published many books.
    Sir P. Lely.   W. Faithorne.
    L. Fagan, p. 51. It is the frontispiece to Ogilby's translation
of Virgil, 1654, fol.   25791.

OGLE, SIR CHALONER, 1680–1750, admiral; b. at Kirkby, near
Newcastle-on-Tyne; knighted, 1723, for killing Roberts, the
pirate; Rear-Admiral of the Blue; led the attack, March 9,
1741, and took the forts of Chamba, S. Iago, and S. Philip, at
Carthagena; M.P. for Rochester; bur. at Twickenham.
    C. Zincke.   J. Faber, jun., mez.
    J. C. Smith, 259, 1st state. This plate was subsequently
altered to serve for the portrait of Sir Edward Hawke, and
again for that of Lord Duncan.   27659.

OGLETHORPE, JAMES EDWARD, 1683–1785, son of Sir Theophilus
Oglethorpe; educ. at Oxford; ensign in the Guards, 1706; served

under Prince Eugene against the Turks; M.P. for Haslemere; settled the Colony of Georgia; philanthropist, eulogised by Johnson, Pope, and Thomson; shot snipe where Conduit St. now stands; d. at Cranham Hall, Essex.

S. Ireland delt.   S. Ireland, etched.

Wh. len. to left, in profile, seated, "Sketch'd from Life at " the sale of Dr. Johnson's books, Feby. 18, 1785, where " the Genl. was reading a book he had purchas'd without " spectacles," vignette.

$8\frac{1}{4} \times 6\frac{1}{4}$. $(7\frac{3}{4} \times 5\frac{5}{8})$.   22901.

OLIVER, Isaac, 1556–1617 (some say he died later), miniature-painter, pupil of Hilliard and Zucchero; became eminent, and received very high prices for his portraits; painted Queen Elizabeth, Mary Queen of Scots, Prince Henry, Ben Jonson, Sir Philip Sidney (full length), and many others; not so successful with oils; executed fine pen-drawings; wrote a treatise on Limning; d. at his house in Blackfriars; buried in the church of St. Anne's there.

I. Oliver.   J. Miller.

Ha. len. to right, looking to front, wearing a ruff and slashed doublet; from Walpole's "Anecdotes of Painting."

Cut. $(6\frac{1}{4} \times 4\frac{1}{2})$.   25461.   17

[I. Oliver.]   I. Girtin, etched.

Ha. len. to right, looking to front, as in the print by J. Miller. In Girtin's " Seventy-five Portraits of celebrated Painters," 4to, 1817. Printed on orange-coloured paper.

Cut. $(5\frac{1}{16} \times 3\frac{11}{16})$.   15217.   3.

OLIVER, Peter, 1601–1660, miniature-painter, b. in London, eldest son of Isaac Oliver, whom he excelled; many fine portraits by him are preserved; was distinguished also for miniature water-colour copies of the works of great masters; etched some similar subjects; buried near his father.

Van Dyck.   Anon.

Ha. len. to right, looking and pointing to left with left hand; wearing a cloak.

Proof before all letters, except the painter's name (?).

Cut. $(8\frac{1}{16} \times 6\frac{3}{4})$.   E. 2204.–'89.

Van Dyck.   W. Finden.

Ha. len. to right, looking and pointing to left with left hand; wearing a cloak.

Cut. $(4\frac{1}{2} \times 3\frac{1}{2})$.   E. 2205.–'89.

P. Oliver.   T. Chambars.

Sh. ha. len. slightly to right, looking to front, wearing a hat; in H. Walpole's "Anecdotes of Painting."

Cut. $(5\frac{3}{4} \times 4\frac{3}{4})$.   25461.   8.

OLIVER, RICHARD,   –1784, Alderman and M.P., 1770;
imprisoned for a short time in the Tower, 1771.
"Painted in the Tower by R. Pine, 1772."

W. Dickinson, mez.
   J. C. Smith, 55, 2nd state.   22902.

O'NEILL, ELIZABETH, c. 1791–1872, celebrated Tragic actress,
particularly successful as Belvidera, Juliet, &c.; m. (1819) to
William Wrixon Becher, who was cr. a Bart., 1831.
A. W. Devis.   H. Meyer, mez.
Wh. len. to front, looking to right, in the character of Belvidera; the Bridge of Sighs, Venice, in the distance, on left;
the title, &c., on a supplementary plate, at foot; Jany. 1, 1816.
26¼ × 17½. (25¾ × 16⁵⁄₁₆); suppl. plate, 2 × 17½   27139.

   W. Devis.   Meyer, stipple.
See LA BELLE ASSEMBLÉE.   13867. 15

ONSLOW, ARTHUR, Rt. Hon. 1691–1768, eldest son of Foot
Onslow, M.P. for Guildford, 1719; M.P. for Surrey; treasurer
of Navy, 1734–'42; unanimously elected Speaker of the House
of Commons, 1727, and continued to hold that position until
1761, when he received the unanimous thanks of the house,
and a pension of 3,000l. a year; P.C; bur. at Thames Ditton.
Hysing.   J Faber, mez.
   J. C. Smith, 262, 2nd state.   27657
   See also COMMONS.

ONSLOW, COLONEL RICHARD,   –1760, second son of Foot
Onslow; soldier; rose to be Col. of 39th regt., 1738; of the
8th, 1739; Adj.-Genl., 1742; Brig.-Genl.; served in Germany, pres. at Dettingen; Maj.-Genl.; Col. of Gren. Guards,
1745; Lieut. Genl. and Govr. of Fort William, 1752; Govr. of
Plymouth, 1759; M.P., Guildford, 1727–'60. *See* COMMONS.

OPIE, AMELIA, Mrs., 1769–1853, b. at Norwich; daughter of
Dr. James Alderson; was the second wife, 1798, of John Opie,
the painter; wrote numerous tales, once very popular, "Father
and Daughter," "Murder will out," "The Ruffian Boy," "The
odd-tempered Man," "Illustration of Lying," &c.; joined the
Quakers, 1825, after which she pubd. only "Detraction Displayed" and "Lays for the Dead."
   J. Opie, 1798.   Mrs. Dawson Turner.
Bust, to front, the hair coming down on the forehead;
vignette. A private plate.
9 × 6¾. (5¾ × 4⅔).   22473.

OPIE, JOHN, 1761–1807, historical and portrait-painter, b. near
Truro, of humble origin; taken up by Dr. Wolcot ("Peter
Pindar"), who brought him to London, c. 1780, on a sort of
partnership compact, which soon broke down; A.R.A., 1787;
R.A., 1788; contributed 5 pictures to Boydell's Shakspere
series; painted and exhibited many compositions and portraits;

married twice, his second wife being the clever authoress; he
struggled hard for a competence, and died of overwork and
brain-disease.

J. Opie. W. Ridley, stipple.
Ha. len. to left, looking to front, holding palette in left hand
and brush in right; oval; in "European Magazine," Decr. 1,
1798.
$6\frac{1}{2} \times 4\frac{7}{16}$. $(3\frac{7}{16} \times 2\frac{7}{8})$. 28300. 45.

OPIE, JOHN—*continued.*
J. Opie. W. Ridley, stipple.
Ha. len to right, looking to front; oval.
$6\frac{5}{8} \times 4\frac{5}{8}$. $(3\frac{3}{16} \times 2\frac{11}{16})$. 28300. 43.

J. Opie. S. W. Reynolds, mez.
Ha. len. to left, looking to front; in a narrow square border.
June 1, 1802. Dedicated to Alderman Boydell; published by
John Jeffryes, Clapham Road.
$13\frac{7}{8} \times 10$. $(10\frac{9}{16} \times 8\frac{11}{16})$. 23022.

[Opie.] Hopwood, stipple.
Bust, to right, looking to front; oval; July 1, 1807.
$6\frac{1}{4} \times 4\frac{5}{8}$. $(3\frac{1}{8} \times 2\frac{3}{8})$. 28300. 44.

W. Holl, stipple.
Sh. ha. len. to right, looking to front, seated, holding palette
and brushes in left hand, with right extended, as in the act of
painting.
Proof before letters, except the engraver's name lightly
etched.
$12\frac{5}{8} \times 9\frac{5}{8}$. $(4\frac{1}{8} \times 3\frac{3}{8})$. 28300. 42.

ORFORD, EDWARD RUSSELL, 1st Earl of, 1653–1727, nephew
of William, 1st Duke of Bedford; Commander, R.N., 1672;
Captain, after 1672; groom of the bedchamber to James, D.
of York; resigned his post after execution of his cousin,
Lord William Russell; promoted the Revolution; Admiral,
M.P.; gained the battle of La Hogue, 1692; Comm. in
Mediterranean; cr. Baron Shingey of Cambr., Visct. Barfleur,
and Earl of Orford, 1697; First Lord of Admiralty.
T. Gibson. G. Vertue, 1716.
Full ha. len. to left, looking to front; left hand on hip, right
hand resting on, and pointing to, a folded paper on table; a
pillar behind on right; a curtain on left.
Cut. $(12\frac{1}{4} \times 10)$. 22475.

Sir G. Kneller. J. Houbraken, 1742.
Sh. ha. len. to right, looking to front, in oval.
$14\frac{3}{4} \times 9\frac{4}{16}$. $(14\frac{5}{16} \times 8\frac{7}{8})$. 20807.

——. *See* WALPOLE, HORACE and ROBERT.

ORKNEY, George Hamilton, Earl of, 1665-1737, Brig.-General to William III. in Flanders and Ireland; K.T., Governor of Edinburgh Castle, &c.

Maingaud.   Houbraken.

In Birch's "Lives."

$14\frac{11}{16} \times 9\frac{3}{4}$. $(14\frac{1}{8} \times 8\frac{7}{8})$.   20829.

ORMONDE, James Butler, Duke of, 1665-1745, suc. his father, as Earl of Ossory, 1680, and his grandfather, as 2nd Duke of Ormonde, 1688 ; K.G. ; held high commands under William III. and under Q. Anne ; Lord Lieut. of Ireland, 1703-'6, and 1710-'12 ; impeached, after accession of George I. ; left England, and resided chiefly at Avignon ; d. at Madrid.

M. Dahl.   S. Gribelin.

T. Q. len. to left, looking to front, in armour, with baton, a battle in distance ; oval in border, supported by winged figures ; arms on left ; inscription in 13 lines below, with date, 1713 ; "Sold by Phil Overton," &c.

Cut. $(14\frac{1}{8} \times 9)$.   29608.   9.

Sir G. Kneller.   J. Smith, mez.

J. C. Smith, 194.   22046.

OSBALDESTON, Richard, -1764, educ. at St. John's Coll., and fellow of Peterhouse, Cambr.; Dean of York; Bishop of Carlisle, 1747; transld. to London, 1762; pubd. three separate sermons, 1723, '48, '52.

T. Hudson.   J. McArdell, mez.

J. C. Smith, 141, 2nd state.   23065.

OSBORNE, George Alexander, 1806-1893, b. at Limerick, where his father was lay-vicar and organist ; self-instructed pianist to age of 18, when he went to Belgium, where he was received and patronised by the Prince de Chimay, Cherubini's friend; went to Paris, 1826, and stud. under Pixis, Fétis, and Kalkbrenner ; intimate with Chopin and Berlioz; settled in London, 1843, and became a popular teacher ; composed P.F. and violin duets, with de Bériot, Lafont, Artôt, and Ernst, "La Pluie des Perles," a brilliant P.F. piece, &c.

See FIRST READING.

OSBORNE, Thomas. See LEEDS.

OSSINGTON, Visct. See DENISON, J. E.

OSSORY, Thomas, Lord Butler, Earl of, 1634-1680, son of James, 1st Marquess and Duke of Ormonde ; General of the Horse in Ireland ; distinguished in the war with the Dutch, 1673; P.C. ; K.G. ; &c.

Sir P. Lely.   P. Vanderbanck.

Sh. ha. len. to right, head turned slightly to left, but looking to front, in armour, with long hair, wearing the George.

Oval, in border, with arms below, and 6 lines of titles, &c.

Cut. $(17\frac{1}{8} \times 12\frac{1}{8})$ 27658.

OTTLEY, WILLIAM YOUNG, 1771–1836, son of an officer in the
Guards; educ. at Richmond (Yorks.) and Winchester; pupil
of Cuitt, the elder; studied in the Academy schools; best
known as a writer on Art, and illustrator of his own books;
pubd. "An Inquiry into the Origin and Early History of
Engraving upon Copper and on Wood," 1816; "The Italian
School of Design," 1823, &c.; Keeper of the Prints, Br.
Museum, 1823, till his death.
  W. Riviere.   F. C. Lewis, stipple.
  Bust, to right; vignette; facs. signature below; a private plate.
  $12\frac{1}{4} \times 9\frac{7}{16}$. (6×5).   27225.

OTWAY, THOMAS, 1652–1685, dramatist, b. at Trottin, Sussex;
son of Rev. H. Otway, rector of Woolbeding; educ. at
Winchester, and Ch. Ch. Coll., Oxf.; left without a degree;
tried the stage; failed as an actor; more successful as a writer;
prod. "Alcibiades," 1675; "Don Carlos," 1676; "Titus and
Berenice," "Cheats of Scapin," 1677; "Friendship in Fashion,"
1678; "Caius Marius," "The Orphan," "Venice Preserved,"
&c.; died in poverty.
  M. Beal.   J. Houbraken, 1741.
  Sh. ha. len. to left, leaning head on right hand; oval in
border.
  From Birch's "Lives."
  $14\frac{3}{4} \times 9\frac{3}{8}$. $(14\frac{1}{4} \times 8\frac{1}{4})$ 21817.

OWEN, JOHN, 1616–1683, b. at Stadham, Oxfords.; educ. at
Queen's Coll., Oxf.; chaplain to Sir Richard Dormer, and after-
wards to John, Lord Lovelace; presd. to living of Fordham,
Essex, and removed to Coggeshall; renounced Presbytery for
Independence; preached before the House of Commons, the
day after the execution of Charles I., and again before O.
Cromwell, who became one of his firmest friends; Dean, Chr
Ch., Oxf., 1651; Vice-Chancr., 1652; retired, and afterwards
ministered in Leadenhall St., and resided at Woburn and
Ealing; pubd. many theological works.
  Anon.   Vertue.
  Ha. len. in cap, bands, and gown, to right, looking to left;
bookcase on right.
  Oval in border
  $10\frac{3}{4} \times 7\frac{3}{8}$. $(10\frac{5}{8} \times 7\frac{3}{16})$.   27566.

OXFORD, EDWARD HARLEY, 2nd Earl of, 1689–1741, son of
Robert, 1st Earl, educ. at Westminster; M.P., Radnor, 1711–
'14; F.R.S., 1713; M.P. co. Cambr., 1722–'24; suc., 1724;
contin. the collection of MSS. commenced by his father, and
increased his library to more than 40,000 vols.; his MSS.
(Harleian) purchased from his widow and transferred to the
Br. Museum, 1754.
  M. Dahl, 1728.   G. Vertue, 1745.
  Wh. len. to front, in robes, holding his coronet in right hand;
a handsome vase stands in a niche behind him; title, &c., in 3
lines below.
  $14\frac{1}{2} \times 9\frac{1}{8}$. $(13\frac{1}{2} \times 8\frac{1}{2})$.   22524.

OXFORD, EDWARD VERE, Earl of, 1540–1604, Lord High Chamberlain.

 Anon. (G. P. Harding del., from a picture at Welbeck).
              J. Brown.
 Ha. len. to right, looking to front, wearing a cap and feather.
 Published, Jany. 1, 1848.
 $10\frac{1}{4} \times 8\frac{1}{4}$. $(5\frac{3}{4} \times 4\frac{7}{8})$.   24669.

OXFORD, ROBERT HARLEY, 1st Earl of, 1661–1724, Statesman; son of Sir Edward Harley; supported the Prince of Orange on his landing, 1688; Speaker of House of Commons, 1702; Sec. of State, 1704–'8; Chanc. of Exchequer, 1710; cr. Earl of Oxford, and Lord High Treasurer, 1711; dismissed and impeached, 1714; acquitted, after 2 years' imprisonment; commenced the " Harleian " Colln. of MSS.
 Sir G. Kneller.   J. Smith, mez.
 J. C. Smith, 197, 2nd state.   22045.

PACKER, an actor, engaged by Garrick at Drury Lane, where he acted for many years.
 See MOODY.

PACKINGTON, or PAKINGTON (more correctly), SIR JOHN, 1549–1625, a great favourite of Q. Elizabeth, at whose invitation he came to court, where he lived at his own expense, in great state; K.B.; was a celebrated swimmer; of Washwood, Worcester.
 From a drawing, taken from the original picture at Washwood.
              R. Clamp.
 Pubd., Oct. 1, 1794, by Harding.
 $10\frac{1}{4} \times 6\frac{1}{4}$. $(8\frac{1}{4} \times 5\frac{3}{8})$.   15702.

PAGET, WILLIAM, 1st Lord, 1506–1563, statesman in reigns of Henry VIII., Edward VI., and Mary; cr. Baron, 1552; disgraced, together with Protector Somerset; restored to favour by Mary; strict adherent of the Romish Church; K.G., &c.
 H. Holbein.   S. W. Reynolds, mez.
 T. Q. len. to front, wearing the George, and holding a staff in right hand.
 From the picture at Beaudesert; inscribed " 2nd Proof;" a private plate.
 $20 \times 13\frac{1}{4}$.   **22048.**

PAINE, JAMES, and his son, JAMES; the elder, 1717–1789, was an architect in considerable practice; published plates of Mansion House at Doncaster, 1751; edited " Vitruvius Britannicus," and two large vols. of " Mansions," 1783; High Sheriff, Surrey, 1785; d. in France.
 Sir J. Reynolds.   J. Watson, mez.
 J. C. Smith, 111; intermediate state between Mr. J. C. Smith's I. and II.; with the inscription below; but without the writing on the scroll.   22904.

PAINE, THOMAS, 1737–1809, Political and Controversial Writer ; b. at Thetford, Norfolk ; went to America, 1774 ; advocated the cause of the American Colonies in a pamphlet, " Common Sense ;" returned to Europe, 1787 ; wrote " Rights of Man," in answer to Burke's " Reflections ;" sat in French National Convention ; wrote " Age of Reason ;" d. at Baltimore.

G. Romney   W. Sharp.

 Ha. len. to left, looking to front ; papers on left, one of which is inscribed *Rights | of Man ;* April 20, 1793.

 $11\frac{12}{16} \times 9$. $(9\frac{1}{2} \times 7\frac{4}{16}$, inside border).   21993

PAISLEY (*sic*) or (more correctly) PASLEY, SIR THOMAS, 1734–1808, b. at Craig, Dumfriesshire, Scotland ; ent. Navy ; post-captain, 1771 ; present, June 1, 1794, at the victory off Ushant, losing a leg in the action ; Rear-Admiral and Baronet ; d. at his seat, near Alton, Hants.

 See COMMEMORATION (1).

PAKENHAM, SIR THOMAS, 1754–1836, 4th son of Thomas, 1st Lord Longford, ent. Navy, 1770 ; disting. in the American War of Independence ; aftds. in West Ind. waters, under Com. Cornwallis ; commanded the " Invincible," June 1, 1794, under Lord Howe off Ushant ; was a singularly good-natured and jocular man, who could jest even in the midst of a battle ; Vice-Admiral ; G.C.B., &c.

 See COMMEMORATION (1).

PAKINGTON, RT. HON. SIR JOHN SOMERSET. *See* HAMPTON, LORD, and DERBY CABINET.

PALEY, WILLIAM, 1743–1805, b. at Peterborough ; grad. senior wrangler, Chr. Coll., Cambr., 1763 ; took orders ; fellow, 1766, and soon after tutor ; Rector of Musgrove, 1775 ; Vicar of Dalston, Cumberland, 1776, and Appleby ; Preb., Carlisle, 1780 ; Archdeacon, 1782 ; Chancellor of Carlisle, 1785 ; Preb., St. Paul's, 1793 ; Rector of Bishop Wearmouth, 1795 ; wrote " Principles of Moral and Polit. Philosophy," " Horæ Paulinæ," " Evidences of Christianity," &c.

 G. Romney.   J. Jones, mez.

 J C. Smith, 59, 2nd state.   26705.

PALMERSTON, EMILY MARY, Lady, 1787–1869, daughter of the 1st Lord Melbourne (1748–1828) , was. m. first (1805) to 5th Earl Cowper, and second (1839) to 3rd Viscount Palmerston, K.G. (1784–1865), whom she survived four years.

 J. Swinton del.   F. Holl, stipple.

 Bust, to left, a veil over the back of her head and shoulders ; vignette, in oval.

 Ind. proof before all letters, except artists' names.

 $21\frac{3}{4} \times 16\frac{7}{8}$. $(9\frac{1}{4} \times 6)$.   27636.

PALMERSTON, HENRY JOHN TEMPLE, Viscount, 1784–1865, Statesman, ent. Parliament, 1806 ; Lord of the Admiralty, 1807 ; Sec. of State for War, 1809–'28 ; Minister for Foreign

Affairs, 1831-'41, and 1846-'51 ; Home Sec., 1853-'55 ; Prime
Minister, 1855-'58, and 1860-'65.
J. Partridge.   S. Cousins, A.R.A., mixed mez.
Wh. len. to front, wearing the star and riband of a G.C.B. ;
right hand to breast, left resting on a paper on table.
Open letter proof.
(26¼ × 16⅝).   21945.
See ABERDEEN CABINET, and also COMMONS (2).

PANMURE, Fox Maule, 2nd Baron, 1801-1874 ; educ. at
Charterhouse ; ent. the Army, serving as an officer (12 years) in
79th Highlanders ; M.P., 1835-'52 ; held office several times ;
Secretary for War, 1846-'52, and 1855-'58 ; P.C. ; K.T., 1853,
&c. ; suc. (1860) to title of Dalhousie.
T. Duncan.   J. Porter, mez.
T. Q. len. slightly to right, looking to front, right hand resting
on a stick, facs. signature " F. Maule," below.
Ind. proof, Aug. 1, 1838.
21¼ × 16.   (16 × 12⅝).   27271.

PAPWORTH, John Buonarotti,   -1847, architect to the
King of Würtemberg ; author of " Sixty-six select Views of
London," " Rural Residences," " Hints on Ornamental Garden-
ing," &c. ; d. at St. Neots.
James Green.   W. Say, mez.
Ha. len. to front, looking to left, holding a pencil in his right
hand, which rests on a book, lettered on the back with the
name of [J. B.] Alberti, the celebrated Florentine writer on
Architecture, Painting, &c.
Proof before all letters ; a private plate.
13⅞ × 9¹³⁄₁₆.   (12⁹⁄₁₆ × 9¹³⁄₁₆).   27226.

PARIS, John Ayrton, 1785-1856, educ. at Caius Coll., Cambr. ;
M.D. ; F.R.C.P., 1814 ; President, 1844 ; author of " Philo-
sophy in Sport made Science in earnest."
C. Skottowe.   S Bellin, mixed mez.
T. Q. len. to front, seated, holding in left hand a book which
rests on his left knee, right arm resting on arm of chair.
Open letter proof, Jany., 1840.
20 × 15¾.   (17¼ × 13⁷⁄₉).   27089.

PARIS, Matthew. See MATTHEW.

PARKE, R. H., Baron. See WENSLEYDALE.

PARKER, Sir Hyde, c. 1711-1782, Midshipman under Anson,
1739-'40 ; Lieut., c. 1744 ; Post Captain, c. 1747 ; served under
Rodney, at Havre, 1759 ; took the Santissima Trinidad, 1762 ;
commanded, as Admiral, in West Indies, 1778 ; served with
Rodney off St. Lucie ; Vice-Admiral, 1781 ; Comm.-in-chf. in
North Sea, 1781, where he defeated the Dutch, a very strong

fleet; sailed for the E. Indies, 1782, with his flag in the *Cato,* 50, but was never heard of again, after leaving Rio.

J. Northcote.   J. R. Smith, mez.
J. C. Smith, 132, 2nd state.   22047.

PARKER, SIR HYDE, 1739–1807, ontd. navy; rendered great service as Captn. of the Phœnix, 1770–'79, in the American War, and was knighted, 1779; Admiral, 1793; Commander-in-Chf. at Copenhagen, 1801; d. in Grt. Cumberland Place, March 16.

G. Romney   Jas. Walker, mez.
J. C. Smith, 12, a 3rd state, not described by Mr. Smith; the separate plate has in this state a publication-line, "*London Publish'd as the Act directs, by J. Walker, No. 50, Frith Street, Soho, June 1st, 1780;*" this confirms Bromley's statement about the date of the plate.

See also COMMEMORATION (1).   23023.

PARKER, MATTHEW, 1504–1575, b. at Norwich, educ. at Cambr.; took orders; adopted views of Reformers; chaplain to Anne Boleyn; **Dean** of Coll. of Stoke Clare; chaplain to the King, after death of Q. Anne; Master of Corp. Chr. Coll., Camb., 1544; being married, depr. by Q. Mary; app. Archbp. of Canterbury by Q. Elizabeth (1559); the "Bishops' Bible" prepared under his supervision (1568); pubd. some other learned works.

A. vander Werff (copy).   P. à Gunst.
Ha. len. slightly to left, looking to right of front, wearing cap, gown, &c.; arms above, mitre and title with inscription in French, below.

$12\frac{1}{2} \times 7\frac{1}{4}$. $(11\frac{1}{4} \times 6\frac{13}{16})$.   29718. 7.

———

     G. Vertue, 1729.
Ha. len. slightly to right, looking to left, seated at a table, with a large book open, resting on two others, lettered: M PARIS. and FLORILEG.

$12\frac{7}{16} \times 8\frac{1}{2}$. $(10\frac{1}{2} \times 7\frac{1}{2})$.   22522.

PARKER, RICHARD,   –1797, seaman, "*who was executed on board the Sandwich off Sheerness, on Friday June 30th, 1797, | pursuant to the sentence of a Court Martial, for having been the Principal | in a most daring Mutiny on board several of his Majesty's ships at the | Nore, & which created a dreadful alarm through the whole Nation.*"

Bailey delt.   Sansom, stipple.
Sh. ha. len. to front, looking to right, long hair, dark neckcloth, white waistcoat; oval; below, name in open letters and the inscription quoted above; pubd. July 21, 1797.

$6\frac{1}{2} \times 4\frac{3}{8}$. $(3\frac{11}{16} \times 3\frac{7}{16})$.   22905.

PARNELL, REV. THOMAS, 1679–1717, b. in Dublin; educ. at Trin. Coll., Dublin; Archdeacon of Clogher, 1705; D.D.; friend of Addison, Pope, Steele, Swift, and Gay; Pope pubd.

a selected edition of his works, of which the best known is
"The Hermit;" d. at Chester on his way to Ireland.

Anon. Anon., mez.
J. C. Smith, p. 1741, 122. 22525.

PARR, THOMAS, 1483(?)–1635, "*The Olde, Old, very Olde*
"*Man or Thomas Par, the | Sonne of John Parr of Win-*
"*nington in the Parish of Alberbury | In the County of*
"*Shropshire who was Borne in 1483 in | The Raigne of*
"*King Edward the 4th, and is now liuing in | The Strand,*
"*being aged 152 yeares and odd monethes 1635.*"

Anon. Anon.
Sh. ha. len. slightly turned to right, seated; wearing a cap.
He is blind.

$6\frac{3}{16} \times 4\frac{1}{8}$. ($4\frac{1}{8} \times 4$). 27104.
Printed on a broadside, at head of which is the title, "LE
"VRAY PORTRAIT D'VN HOMME | QUI FYT PRE-
"SENTÉ AV SERENISSIME ROY | de la Grand'Bretagne, le
"neufiéme iour d'Octobre dernier," &c., below, an extract from
a letter from London, November 27, 1635, in French, in two
columns of 30 lines each, giving an account of the old man's
life and death.

PARR, SAMUEL, 1747–1825, b. at Harrow, son of a surgeon-
apothecary; released from the distasteful employment of
assistant, entd. Emm. Coll., Cambr., 1765; assist. master,
Harrow, 1767; disappointed at not getting the head-mastership,
kept school at Stanmore, then at Colchester, 1776, and at Norwich, 1778; Rector of Asterby, Lincolnshire, 1780; curate at
Hatton, Warwicks., 1783, and Preb., St. Paul's; Rector of
Wadenhoe, 1790; of Graffham, 1802, and head chapl. to Q.
Caroline, 1820; pubd. many learned and excellent works,
memoirs, sermons, &c.

J. S. Lonsdale. W. Skelton.
Ha. len. slightly to right, seated, looking to front; left hand
in bosom. Aug. 20, 1823.

$15\frac{9}{16} \times 13\frac{1}{4}$. ($13\frac{7}{8} \times 11\frac{4}{8}$). 21848.

PARRY, SIR WILLIAM EDWARD, 1790–1855, Arctic Discoverer,
b. at Bath; ent. the Navy, 1803; accomp. Sir John Ross on
his Polar Expedition, 1818; sailed in command of the "Hecla"
and "Griper," to discover the N. W. Passage, 1819; knt.,
1829; Commiss. in New South Wales, 1830–'35; Rear-
Admiral, 1852; Lieut. Governor of Greenwich Hospital, 1853;
d. at Ems; F.R.S.

W. Haines. S. W. Reynolds, mez.
Ha. len. to right, in Captain's uniform, looking to front,
wearing a cloak with fur collar; March 21, 1827.

14×10. (9×7). 21904.
See also ARCTIC COUNCIL.

PARSONS, WILLIAM, and JOHN MOODY (q. v.), as "Varland"
and "Major O'Flaherty" in "The West Indian," Act IV.,

Scene 9. PARSONS, 1736–1795, was a comedian, chiefly famous for impersonations of old men; b. at Maidstone; first appeared at Edinburgh; engaged by Garrick, and app. as "Filch," 1763, at Drury Lane, his wife playing Mrs. Peachum; his best characters were "Sir Fretful Plagiary," "Crabtree," "Snarl," &c.; d. at Mead Row, Lambeth.

J. Mortimer.   W. Dickinson, mez.

J. C. Smith, 57, 3rd state.   21925.

PARSONS, WILLIAM—*continued*; in the Character of Paul Prig : Prologue to the Spanish Barber.

From a "Collection . . . . of English Prologues," &c., 1779.   28187. 12.

See also BANNISTER, JOHN.

PASLEY. See PAISLEY.

PASQUIN, ANTHONY. See WILLIAMS, JOHN.

PATERSON, JOHN, 1705–1789, son of a Colonel; page to the Earl of Stair, in 1715; clerk to the Barber-Surgeons' Company; City Solicitor; clerk to the Irish Society; to the Commissioners of Land and House Tax for London, 1772; carried out many improvements about London, and projected several which were effected long afterwards.

Sir J. Reynolds.   T. Watson, mez.

J. C. Smith, 29, 2nd state.   27863.

PATTESON, SIR JOHN, Knt., 1790–1861; Justice of the Queen's Bench, 1830–'52.

Mrs. Carpenter.   S. Cousins, A.R.A., mez.

Ha. len. to left, seated, looking to front, with right hand resting on a large book on table, on left.

Open letter proof; Novr. 20, 1837.

$20\frac{7}{8} \times 16$. $(17\frac{1}{8} \times 13\frac{7}{16})$.   24236.

Another, a presented proof before all letters, except the artists' names, from Mrs. Carpenter to John Sheepshanks, Esqre. (Sheepshanks Gift.)   18880.

A companion print to the portrait of Sir John T. Coleridge.

PATTISSON, WILLIAM HENRY EBENEZER, 1801–1832, and JACOB HOWELL, 1803–1874, sons of William Henry Ebenezer Pattisson, of Witham, Essex; the elder, with his wife, was accidentally drowned, during their honeymoon, in the Lac de Gaube, near Cauterets, Hautes Pyrénées; the younger m., and left a family.

Sir T. Lawrence, P.R.A., 1811–'17. J. Bromley, mixed mez.

Nearly wh. len., in a landscape, playing with a young donkey; the elder on the left, looking to front; water and trees in background. The picture is now in possession of Mr.

Naylor, Leyland Hall, Welshpool; it was exhibited at the
R. A., 1817; entitled RURAL AMUSEMENT.
Pub. Jany. 1, 1831, by Colnaghi, Son, & Co., &c.
$18\frac{5}{8} \times 14\frac{1}{4}$. $(15\frac{7}{16} \times 11\frac{3}{4})$.   23557.

PAXTON, Sir Joseph, Kt., 1803-1865, b. at Milton-Bryant,
near Woburn; became gardener to the Duke of Devonshire,
who placed him at Chatsworth, where he effected great and
striking horticultural improvements; designed the building
of the Exhibition, 1851, and the Crystal Palace, Sydenham,
for which he was knighted; organised and superintended the
Army Works Corps in Crimea, 1854; M.P. for Coventry, 1854,
till his death; wrote several horticultural works.
 O. Oakley.   S. W. Reynolds, mixed mez.
 T. Q. len. slightly to right, looking to front; hat in left
hand, stick and gloves in the other; resting against a pillar.
 Ind. proof; May 1, 1851.
 Facs. signature (initials) below, on right.
 $23\frac{3}{4} \times 16\frac{7}{8}$. $(20\frac{1}{2} \times 14\frac{13}{16})$.   22203.

———

               Anon., woodcut.
 Ha. len. slightly to right, looking to front; cut from an
illustrated paper.
 $(4\frac{1}{2} \times 4\frac{1}{2})$.   15220. 1.

PAYE, Richard Morton, c. 1750–1821, subject-painter, b. at
Botley (Kent), first employed in London as a chaser; soon
distinguished, took to painting, and for a time enjoyed popularity; two of his pictures are said to have been sold as works
of Velasquez and Wright of Derby; exhibited in 1773;
patronised by Dr. Wolcot, with whom he soon quarrelled; sank
rapidly into ill-health and indigence; d. in obscurity. Some
of his works were engraved by J. Young, who befriended him,
and V. Green; he himself engraved two, "Puss in durance"
and "No Dance no Supper."
 R. M. Paye del.   R. Dagley, stipple.
 Bust, to front, wearing a fur cap; circular, in border,
with a palm-branch, palette, and scroll below, on which is the
name; 1832.
 $7\frac{1}{16} \times 4\frac{1}{2}$. $(2\frac{13}{16}$ diamr., including border, $\frac{1}{4})$. 28443. 4.

PAYNE, John Willett, –1803, rear-admiral, vice-adm.
of Devon and Cornwall; commanded a ship in Lord Howe's
victory, off Ushant, June 1, 1794; treasurer of Greenwich
Hosp.; Lord Warden of Stannaries, &c.; d. at Greenwich;
bur. at St. Margaret's, Westminster.
 See COMMEMORATION (1).

PEASE, Sir Joseph Whitwell, 1828– , son of Joseph
Pease, a well-known coal and ironstone-mine-owner, of Dar-
lington; educ. privately; M.P., 1865 to present time (1895);
Liberal; J.P.; Bart., 1882; member of Society of Friends;
Pres. Peace and Anti-Opium Societies.

 O 82849.   A A

Wh. len. to front, resting right hand on walking-stick; the
Clock Tower, Westminster, in distance, on right.
A proof on Ind. paper before all letters, except faes. signature.
26¼ × 18⅜. (22¹⁄₁₆ × 15¾).   27240.

PEEL, JULIA, Lady, 1795–1859, b. at Trichinopoly; daughter
of General Sir John Floyd, Bart.; m. (1820) to Rt. Hon. Sir
Robert Peel, Bart., M.P., Premier, &c. (1788–1850).
   Sir T. Lawrence, *late* P.R.A.   S. Cousins, mixed mez.
   Full ha. len., slightly turned towards left, looking to front,
wearing broad-leafed hat with feathers, a fur-trimmed cloak,
and bracelets, &c.
   Open letter proof, before the name of the personage; July 17,
1832.
   15½ × 11½. (10⁹⁄₁₆ × 8¼).   24137.

PEEL, SIR ROBERT, Bart., 1750–1830, M.P., Govr. Christ's
Hospital, &c.
   J. Northcote, R.A.   W. Dickinson, mez.
   J C. Smith, 58.
   May 1, 1818.   24237.

PEEL, SIR ROBERT, 1788–1850, son of Sir Robert Peel; educ.
at Harrow and Oxford; M.P., Cashel, 1809; Chief Sec.
for Ireland, 1812–'18; Home Sec., 1822–'27, and 1828–'30;
M.P., Tamworth, 1830–'50; Premier, 1834–'5, and 1841–'6,
when he abolished the Corn-laws; d. from a fall from his horse
on Constitution Hill.
   Sir T. Lawrence, P.R.A.   H. T. Ryall.
   Ha. len. to front, looking to right, wearing a cloak; 1836.
   13⁵⁄₈ × (?) cut. (8¹⁄₁₆ × 7⁷⁄₁₆).   20637.

   J. Linnell.   J. Scott, mixed mez.
   Full ha. len. to right, looking to front, one button of coat
fastened, right hand on hip; holding in left hand a bundle of
papers, on which is written *Rt. Hon.* | *Peel Bart.* | *Rector* |
City of | *Glasgow.*
   Ind. proof; Jany. 1, 1840.
   22⅛ × 16. (16⁵⁄₁₆ × 12¾).   23763.

   Sir T. Lawrence, P.R.A.
                           S. Cousins, A.R.A., mixed mez., 1850.
   T. Q. len. to front, looking to right, left hand on hip, right
resting on table.
   Ind. proof, with open letters; Decr. 16, 1850.
   22⅜ × 17¼. (18¼ × 14).   22133.
   See also WELLINGTON.

PEEL, CAPTAIN SIR WILLIAM, 1824–1858, third son of Sir
Robert Peel; ent. the Navy; disting. himself as Commander of
Naval Brigade in the Crimea, 1855–'6, and in India during
the Mutiny, 1857–'8; C.B., 1856; K.C.B., 1858; severely

wounded on the march to Lucknow, died of his wounds, at Cawnpore.
 J. Lucas.   J. J. Chant, mixed mez.
 Wh. len. to front, leading an attack, holding his drawn sword in right hand, and waving his hat in left ; a man of the 53rd Regt., on his right, sailors charging a gun on the other side ; facs. signature below.
 Proof on Ind. paper ; July 2, 1860.
 $31\frac{1}{2} \times 21\frac{3}{8}$ (26×17).   **25754.**

PELHAM, RT. HON. HENRY, 1694–1754, Statesman, 2nd son of Thomas, 1st Lord Pelham, and brother of Thomas, Duke of Newcastle ; M.P. for Seaford, 1718 ; Sec. for War, 1724 ; Paymaster General, 1730 ; First Commissioner of the Treasury and Chancellor of the Exchequer, 1743–'54.
 W. Hoare, 1752.   R. Houston, mez.
 J. C. Smith, 86, 2nd state.   **21916.**

PELHAM, THOMAS. *See* CHICHESTER.

PEMBROKE, PHILIP HERBERT, Earl of, –1652, suc. 1630.
 Van Dyck.   P. Lombart.
 When Lord Herbert, but inscribed "Comes Pembrokiæ;" T. Q. len. to right, looking to front.
 Cut. $(12\frac{1}{4} \times 9\frac{1}{8})$.   E. 2121.–'89.

 Van Dyck.   B. Baron, 1740.
 Wh. len. seated with his wife and family.
 $18\frac{3}{8} \times 25\frac{5}{16}$. $(16\frac{1}{2} \times 24\frac{9}{16})$.   **27605.**

PEMBROKE, THOMAS, Earl of. *See* LORDS JUSTICES.

PEMBROKE, W., Earl of. *See* BODLEY.

PENDRILL, RICHARD, –1671, farmer in Staffordshire ; brother of William Pendrill ; aided the escape of Charles, Pr. of Wales (aftds. Charles II.), after the battle of Worcester, by keeping him concealed in his cottage and in the neighbouring wood ; rewarded after the Restoration ; d. in London ; buried at St. Giles's-in-the-Fields, where a monument was erected to his memory.
 Zoust.   R. Houston, mez.
 J. C. Smith, 88, 2nd state.   **22262.**

PENDRILL, WILLIAM, of Boscobel, brother of Richard Pendrill.
 From the very rare print in Suth. Colln.
 [Burghers ?, 1651.]   Anon.
 Æt. 84, an oval suspended in an oak, 22 verses below ; "are to be sold by S. Woodburn," &c.
 Cut. $(10\frac{9}{16} \times 9\frac{3}{8})$.   E. 356.–'90.

PENN, SIR WILLIAM, 1621–1670, b. at Bristol ; Admiral, commanded the fleet at the taking of Jamaica, 1655 ; after the

Restoration, he served under the Duke of York in the successful
battle with the Dutch fleet, 1664, for which he was knighted;
d. at Wanstead, Essex.
See NAVAL HEROES (2).

PENN, WILLIAM, 1644-1718, son of Admiral Sir William Penn,
became early a follower of Quakerism, for which he had to
suffer persecution; obtained, 1681, a grant of the country West
of the Delaware from Charles II.; founded Philadelphia;
Governor of Pennsylvania.
    B. West.   J. Hall.
   Making a "Treaty with the Indians when he founded the
"Province of Pensylvania in North America, 1681;" a composition of many figures; Penn stands on the right, near the
middle, addressing the Indians, one of whom, seated, holding a
pipe, listens attentively, while two of the English sailors show
merchandise to him and his countrymen; June 12, 1775.
    $(16\frac{3}{4} \times 23\frac{1}{4})$.   22006.

PENNANT, THOMAS, 1726-1798, Naturalist and Antiquary;
b. at Downing, Flint; educ. at Wrexham, Fulham, Queen's and
Oriel Colls., Oxf.; early devoted himself to the study of natural
history; corresponded with Linnæus and Buffon; Memb. of
Royal Socy., Upsal; commenced his "British Zoology,"
1784-'7; pub. also "Account of London," various tours, topographical works, &c.
    T. Gainsborough.   J. K. Sherwin, 1778.
   Full ha. len., to left, sitting on a bank, under a tree, holding
a book, lettered "Barrington's Statutes," under his left arm;
hands clasped together; pubd. Jany. 1, 1779.
    $(10\frac{1}{2} \times 8)$.   24089.

PENNINGTON, Sir JOHN. *See* NAVAL HEROES (2).

PEPYS, SAMUEL, 1632-1703, b. in London, where his father was
a tailor; educ. at St. Paul's school and Magd. Coll., Cambridge;
became known to Sir Edward Montagu, naval commander,
aftds. Earl of Sandwich; Clerk of the Acts of the Navy, 1660,
and Sec. to the Admiralty, 1680; P.R.S., 1684; his celebrated
"Diary" was deciphered by Rev. J. Smith, and edited by Lord
Braybrooke; first pubd., 1825, Royal 4to.
    [White.]   R. White.
   Sh. la. len. to right, looking to front; oval; motto above,
"Mens cujusque is est Quisque;" name and title, in two lines
(Latin), below; letterpress on back; retouched, modern, from
the Diary of 1825 (?).
    $(4\frac{13}{16} \times 3\frac{3}{8})$.   26706.

PERCEVAL, SPENCER, 1762-1812; Prime Minister, 1809;
murdered by Bellingham, 1812.
    Sir W. Beechey.   W. Skelton.
   Ha. len. seated, to front, holding in his right hand the
"Regency Bill."

Published, March 1st, 1813. In the left hand lowest corner is the word "PROOF."
$20\frac{1}{8} \times 15\frac{1}{8}$. $(17\frac{5}{8} \times 13\frac{3}{16})$. 23024.

PERCY, THOMAS, Gunpowder Plot conspirator, slain at Holbeach, Staff., 1605.
See CONCILIUM.

PERCY, THOMAS, 1728–1811, educ. at Ch. Ch. Coll., Oxf.; entered the Church; pubd. his celebrated "Reliques of Antient English Poetry," 1765, and afterwards other works; Dean of Carlisle, 1778; Bishop of Dromore, 1782.
Sir J. Reynolds. W. Dickinson, mez.
J. C. Smith, 60, state IV., undescribed by J. C. S.; the words "Dean of Carlisle" are erased, but "Decanus Carliolensis 1778" not yet inserted instead; the address reads "Publish'd by "W. Dickinson at Mrs. Sledge's Henrietta Street Covent Garden LONDON." J. C. Smith's state IV. becomes, therefore, V. The plate is still uncut. 25792.

PETERBOROUGH, CHARLES (MORDAUNT), 3rd Earl of, 1658–1735, General, favoured the accession of William III., by whom he was cr. Earl of Monmouth, 1689; distinguished himself as Commander of the English forces in Spain during the Succession war; took Barcelona.
Sir G. Kneller. J. Houbraken.
Sh. ha. len. to right, looking to front; long wig, plate armour; oval in ornamented border; a battle below, in a panel.
$14\frac{5}{8} \times 9\frac{3}{16}$. $(14\frac{1}{4} \times 8\frac{13}{16})$. 20798.

———

Sir G. Kneller. P. a Gunst.
Sh. ha. len. to left, looking back to right; in armour; wearing long wig; oval in border, the title in 2 lines, on a plinth, below.
$22\frac{1}{2} \times 16\frac{5}{8}$ (?). $(21\frac{7}{8} \times 15\frac{7}{8}$; oval, $14\frac{1}{4} \times 12\frac{1}{2})$. 22263.

PETERS, MATTHEW, b. at Freshwater, I. of Wight; removed to Dublin, where he became a member of the Dublin Society, held an office in the Customs, and published some works on agricultural subjects, 1770–'1, highly commended by Donaldson.
W. Peters, R.A. J. Murphy, mez.
J. C. Smith, 11, 1st state, 1778.
The picture was painted by the son of the personage. 25755.

PETTY, SIR WILLIAM, 1623–1687, son of Anthony Petty, clothier at Rumsey, Hants; stud. mathematics and medicine; went to Ireland, 1652, as physician to the army, and Sec. to Henry Cromwell; Knt. and made Surveyor-General of Ireland after the Restoration; pub. "Political Arithmetic," "Political Anatomy of Ireland," &c.; founder of the Lansdowne family.
J. Closterman. J. Smith, mez.
J. C. Smith, 201, 2nd state. 21871.

PHILIP II., KING OF SPAIN, 1521–1595, Consort of Queen Mary, 1555.

Sir Anton Moro. (G. P. Harding del., 1812.)

Joseph Brown, sculpsit.

With his Queen.

Open letter proof (?), facs, autog. signatures below.

15⅞ × 11⅞. (9 3/16 × 6½).   24639.

Titian.   G. Vertue, 1735.

"From an Excellent Original," at the Duke of Devonshire's.

Ha. len. to left, looking to front, in armour.

11 13/16 × 7⅝. (11 × 7).   14169.

PHILIPS, JOHN, 1676–1708, b. at Bampton, Oxf.; educ. at Winchester, and Chr. Ch. Coll., Oxf.; at Oxf. he wrote "The Splendid Shilling," in imitation of Milton, and "Blenheim," in praise of Marlborough; his chief work was the poem "Cyder," founded on the Georgics; so fond of tobacco that he mentions it in all his pieces, except " Blenheim ; " d. at Hereford.

Anon.   M. vander Gucht.

Sh. ha. len to right, looking to front, wearing long hair, open collar, and cloak; in an oval border of oak leaves; below, on a tablet, JOHANNES PHILIPS and inscription in Latin, 6 lines; at foot.

LONDON. *Printed for Bernard Lintott at the Cross-Keys between the two Temple Gates in Fleet Street, pr. 1s.*

14¼ × 10¼. (13 11/16 × 9⅞).   23161.

PHILLIP, JOHN, 1817–1867, painter of portraits and subjects; b. at Aberdeen, son of an old soldier; came to London, 1836, by the favour of Lord Panmure, and stud. 3 years under T. M. Joy; exhib. at R. A. 1838–'51, having returned meanwhile to Aberdeen; visited Spain, 1852; exhib. 1853–'7; A.R.A., 1857; R.A., 1859, continuing to exhibit portraits and subjects (chiefly Spanish) till 1866; d. at Campden Hill.

Wingfield, photogr.   Maclure & Co., lith.

Bust to front, dark necktie, coat and waistcoat; oval.

(17⅞ × 14½).   23172.

PHILLIPS, MRS., wife of Thomas Phillips, R.A. (1770–1845).

Mrs. Dawson Turner, etched.

Full ha. len. to front, seated, holding an open book on right arm of chair; a private plate, without any inscription, but dated 1814; vignette.

9⅜ × 7⅞. (7 × 6⅞).   E. 1281.–'86.

PHILLIPS, THOMAS, 1770–1845, portrait-painter, b. at Dudley, received a good education, showed early love of art, studied under Eginton, the glass-painter, at Birmingham; came to London, 1790; studied under West; exhibited, 1792, but soon devoted himself to portraiture, in which he rapidly became famous and successful; R.A., 1808; Professor of Painting,

R.A., 1824; visited Italy; wrote several articles on Art for Rees' Encyclopædia.

Mrs. Dawson Turner, etched.

Bust to front, looking to right; vignette.

6⅜ × 5¼. (4½ × 4¼). 28300. 46.

PHILLIPS, WILLIAM, 1773–1828, mineralogist, son of a printer and bookseller; b. in London; author of "Elementary Intro-" duction to the Knowledge of Mineralogy," "Outlines of " Mineralogy and Geology;" &c.; d. at Tottenham.

Bowman delt. M. Gauci, lith.

Sh. ha. len. slightly inclined to right, looking to front, holding a crystal in left hand.

Ind. proof, 1831.

(9¼ × 7¼). 22906.

PHILLPOTTS, HENRY, 1778–1869, b. at Gloucester; educ. at Corp. Xti. Coll., Oxford; fellow of Magd. Coll., 1796; Chapl. to Dr. Barrington, Bishop of Durham, 1806; presd. to the living of Stanhope; Dean of Chester, 1828; Bishop of Exeter, 1830; extreme High-Churchman; pubd. very many charges, sermons, and controversial pamphlets; excommunicated his Metropolitan, in a letter, pubd. 1850.

S. Hodges. S. Bellin, mixed mez.

T. Q. len. to right, seated, looking to front, his right hand resting on the curved handle of a walking-stick.

Open letter proof; Jany. 1, 1867.

20⅛ × 16⅟₁₆. (16 × 12⅟₂). 24223.

PICTON, SIR THOMAS, c. 1758–1815, b. in Wales; Govr., Trinidad; Lt.-Genl.; killed at Waterloo.

M. A. Shee. C. Turner, mixed mez.

Wh. len. to front, sabre over right shoulder; the army advancing to the siege of Badajoz, led by Picton.

Proof before all letters.

(26½ × 18). 22907.

PIGOTT, CAPTAIN, - , commanded a ship in Lord Howe's victory, off Ushant, June 1, 1794.

See COMMEMORATION (1).

PILLANS, JAMES, 1778–1864, b. at Edinburgh; educ. at the High School, with Henry Brougham and F. Horner; became a tutor at Eton, subsequently Rector of the High School, Edinb.; early contributor to the Edinb. Review; pubd. Lectures, Letters, Outlines of Geography, Eclogæ, Rationale of Discipline, and other works; LL.D., &c.

Sir H. Raeburn, R.A. C. Turner, mez.

T. Q. len. to left, seated, looking to front; left hand resting on knee, a book in right hand; other books on table, at left.

Scratch-letter proof (?); Septr. 1, 1823, Edinburgh.

20 × 14. (15⅟₂ × 12½). 22908.

PINCHBECK, Christopher, Senior, -1732, mechanician; lived first in Albion Place, Clerkenwell; aftds. at the sign of the " Astronomico - Musical Clock," Fleet Street; constr. musical automata for exhibition at Bartholomew Fair, musical clocks for "the Grand Monarque," and an organ for the Great Mogul; invented the metallic composition, copper with zinc alloy, imitation gold, which was called after him, " Pinchbeck ; " bur. in St. Dunstan's Church.

I. Whood.   J. Faber, junr., mez.
J. C. Smith, 289, 2nd state, retouched.   27140.

PINCHBECK, Christopher, Junr., 1710–1783, mechanician, and toy-maker ; " well known and ingenious ; zealous and in- " defatigable; strictly just in all his dealings; possessed of a " truly benevolent heart" (Gent. Mag. LIII., 273) ; d. in Cock-spur Stt., Charing Cross.

Cunningham des.   W. Humphrey, mez.
J. C. Smith, 15.   27668.

PINDAR, Peter. See WOLCOT, John, M.D.

PINE, John, 1690–1756, engraver, kept a print-shop in St. Mar-tin's Lane, was the friend of Hogarth, who painted his portrait and introduced him as the friar in his " Calais Gate ; " engraved the ceremonial of the revival of the Order of the Bath, the tapestry in the House of Lords, and a finely-illustrated Horace, some portraits, an etching of himself, and a mezzotint head of Garrick ; appointed Blue-mantle, 1743.

Hogarth.   J. McArdell, mez.
J. C. Smith, 143, 2nd state.   21911.

PIOZZI, Hester Lynch, 1739–1821, b. at Bodvil, Caernarvon-shire ; daughter of J. Salusbury ; married Henry Thrale, an opulent brewer, in Southwark, and M.P. ; became an intimate friend of Dr. Johnson till death of Thrale, 1781 ; went to Bath ; soon after, married Piozzi, an Italian musician ; went to Florence, and founded there a kind of poetical magazine ; pubd., 1786, " Anecdotes of Dr. Johnson," &c.

J. Jackson delin.   H. Meyer, stipple.
Ha. len. to left, seated, looking to front ; wearing large hat and cloak ; vignette.
Open letter proof (?) ; Decr. 21, 1811.
14¾ × 12¾. (10 × 8¾).   27250.

PITCAIRN, William, c. 1711–1791; M.D., F.R.S. ; tutor to James, 6th Duke of Hamilton, at Oxf., where he graduated and obtained his M.D. ; physician of St. Bartholomew's Hospl., by a small majority over Dr. Barrowby, c. 1750; President, 1775–'84, of the Coll. of Physns., where he died, Oct. 25.

Sir J. Reynolds.   J. Jones, mez.
J. C. Smith, 62, 2nd state.   27272.

PITT, Rt. Hon. William, 1759–1806, statesman ; 2nd son of 1st Earl of Chatham ; M.P for Appleby, 1780 ; Chancellor of the

Exch., 1782; Prime Minister, 1783-1801 ; carried the India Bill and Union with Ireland; maintained a warlike policy against France ; Prime Minister again, 1804-'6.

Gahagan.   E. Bell, coarse stipple.
Large bust, to front, looking to left.
Cut. (24¾ × 16⅝).   24725.

S. De Koster.   G. Keating, mez.
J. C. Smith, 9, 2nd state, inscription below cut off.   25579.

T. Gainsborough.   J. K. Sherwin.
T. Q. len. to left, looking to front, holding in left hand a roll of paper, to which he points with his right; inkstand and papers on table, left ; on right, robes lying over a chair.
Proof with scratched letters, the arms, &c., in outline ; June 15, 1789.
20 × 14⁷⁄₁₆.   (16⅛ × 13).   21987.

J. S. Copley.   F. Bartolozzi.
Sh. ha. len. to right, in oval ; Jany. 19, 1789.
Cut. (5 × 4¼).   E. 1468. A.-'85.

J. Hoppner, R.A.   T. Bragg.
Wh. len. to front, looking to left, left hand on hip, right resting on papers on table ; publication-line on a separate slip, pasted on the print, under the engraver's name, but near the lower edge of the plate, *London, Published June 4*, 1810, *by Phœbe Hoppner, No.* 18, *Charles Street, St. James's.*
Her name is written on the back of the print.
28½ × 18.   (26 × 16¾).   22002.

PITT. *See* CHATHAM.

PLAYFAIR, John, 1740-1819, eminent mathematician and natural philosopher, b. at Bervie, near Dundee; educ. at St. Andrews; ent. the Church, but resigned his father's living, to which he had succeeded, went to Edin., where he became Prof. of Mathematics; stud. Geology ; made observations on the Alps ; pub. several learned works.
See SCIENCE.

PLOT, Gunpowder. *See* CONCILIUM.

PLUNKET, Oliver, 1622-1681 ; b. at Rathmore Castle, Meath, Ireland; completed at Rome his studies begun at home ; held a Professor's Chair of Theology ; cr. Archbishop of Armagh, and Primate of Ireland, 1669 ; accused of high treason, and condemned ; executed, July 1, 1681 ; described by Anthony à Wood as "most venerable and religious."
                                                 [Laurie], mez.

J. C. Smith, p. 1406, 1st state, before the publication-line; the inscription ends with "Clogher;" undescribed by J. C. S.
24670.

PLUNKET, WILLIAM CONYNGHAM PLUNKET, Baron, 1764–1854; Solicitor-General (Ireland), 1803; Attorney-General, 1805; again, 1822–'27; Chief Justice of Common Pleas, 1827–30; cr Baron, 1827; Lord Chancellor (Ireland), 1830–'34, 1835–'41.

R. Rothwell. D. Lucas, mixed mez.

Ha. len to right, seated, looking to front, with right hand, holding spectacles, on arm of chair.

Open letter proof; June 24, 1844.

$16\frac{7}{8} \times 13\frac{3}{8}$. ($12\frac{3}{16} \times 9\frac{15}{16}$). 22909.

POCOCK, EDWARD, 1604–1691, b. at Oxford; educ. at Thame School, Mag. Hall, and Corp. Chr. Coll., Oxf.: studied Oriental languages, and obtained a fellowship, 1628; pubd. the Epistles, in Syriac, at Leyden, 1630; went to Aleppo as chaplain to the English factory; collected MSS. for Laud; made professor of Arabic; presented to living of Childrey, Berks.; professor of Hebrew, 1648, with a canonry; pubd. "Specimen Historiæ Arabum," &c.

W. Green. F. Morellan de la Cave.

Sh. ha. len. to left, looking to front, in cap and gown.

Proof before all letters.

$11\frac{13}{16} \times 7\frac{3}{8}$. ($11\frac{9}{16} \times 7$). 25794.

POCOCK, SIR GEORGE, 1706–1792, Admiral; son of Rev. Thomas Pocock, one of the chaplains of Greenwich Hospital; entd. Navy, under Byng, and rendered distinguished services, especially against the French in East Indies, 1754–'60; K.C.B., 1761; M.P., Plymouth; took Havannah, 1762; retired, 1766, on the promotion of his junior, Sir Charles Saunders, to be first lord.

Anon. Aliamet.

Sh. ha. len. slightly to right, wearing the ribbon of the Bath; oval in border ornamented with naval trophies; title in cartouche below.

$7\frac{1}{8} \times 4\frac{5}{8}$. ($6\frac{3}{4} \times 4\frac{7}{16}$). 29718. 9.

See also TRIUMPH OF BRITANNIA.

POCOCK, NICHOLAS, 1741–1821, marine painter, b. at Bristol, son of a merchant of good family; commanded a merchant vessel; sketched on his voyages; left the sea, adopted art, painted portraits, landscapes, sea-pieces, but chiefly the last; exhibited constantly, 1782–1789, when he went to London, and continued to exhibit till 1815; painted chief battles of the war; original member of the Water-colour Society; d. at Maidenhead.

J. Pocock. E. Scriven, stipple.

Ha. len. slightly to left, looking to front, coat buttoned loosely, high collar, white hair.

Ind. proof with open letters.

$9\frac{7}{8} \times 7\frac{3}{8}$. ($6\frac{3}{16} \times 5\frac{1}{8}$, incl. border, $\frac{1}{8}$). 27227.

POLE, POOL, or POLUS, REYNOLD, or REGINALD, 1500–1558,
younger son of Sir Richard Pole, K.G., by Margaret, daughter
of George, Duke of Clarence, brother to Edward IV.; b. at
Stourton Castle, Staff.; educ. at Carth. Monasty. Shene, and
Magd. Coll., Oxf.; preb., Salisbury, 1517, and Dean of Wimborne Minster and Essex, 1519; opposed Henry VIII.'s
divorce; stripped of his preferments; fled to Rome; cr.
Cardinal, 1536; Legate to the Council of Trent, 1545; to
England, 1554; Archbishop of Canterbury, and Chancellor of
Oxf. and Cambr. Universities, 1556; author of a few theolo-
gical treatises.

  Sebastiano Luciani (called S. del Piombo).

N. de Larmessin.

  T. Q. len. to right, seated, in cardinal's robes, looking to front.
The picture, formerly in the Crozat Gallery, is now at the
Hermitage, S. Petersburg.

  13¼ × 9⅓½. (11⅜ × 9⁷⁄₁₆).   24238.

POLLOCK, RT. HON. SIR FREDERICK, 1783–1870, Bart.;
Attorney-General, 1834; Chief Baron of Exchequer, 1844–
1866; cr. baronet, 1866.

  F. Grant, A.R.A.   S. W. Reynolds, mixed mez.

  Wh. len. to front, seated, in robes, with right hand slightly
extended, as though about to speak.

  Open letter proof; June 24, 1850.

  17¼ × 12⅜. (12⅝ × 8¼).   25756.

POLLOCK, SIR GEORGE, 1786–1872, distinguished soldier; ent.
the Bengal Artillery, 1802; Captain, 1805; Major, 1819;
Col. 1829; and General, 1859; having held some staff appointments, commanded army sent to Burmah, under Sir A. Campbell; C.B.; commanded armies on West of Indus, relieved Sir
R. Sale, and took Kabul, 1841; G.C.B., K.S.I., Field-Marshal.

G. H. Ford, lith., 1850.

  T. Q. len. to front, slightly to right, looking to left; in uniform;
oval.

  (15¾ × 12½).   25757.

POND, ARTHUR, c. 1705–1758, painter and engraver, educ. in
London, travelled to Rome with Roubilliac, the sculptor;
worked with the etching-needle, and in the chalk and crayon
manners, and made clever imitations of Poussin, Rosa, and
other Italian masters; painted portraits, and engraved some
fine plates after Raffaelle, Parmegiano, and Caravaggio; F.R.S.,
F.S.A., 1752; his collection of drawings by old masters was
sold for 1,449l.

  A. Pond, 1751 (?).   A. Pond, etched.

  Ha. len. to right, looking to front, holding a paper, on which
is inscribed "Arthur Pond, Painter," in his right hand.

  7¼ × 4¹⁸⁄₁₆. (7 × 4¹⁸⁄₁₆).   26257.

PONSONBY, MISS SARAH, 1757–1831, daughter of Chambre
Brabazon Ponsonby, cousin of the Earl of Bessborough; one of

the " Ladies of Llangollen," who lived a life of seclusion; in
the same print with LADY ELEANOR BUTLER (q. v.).

POOLE, JOHN, 1785–1872, the author of the favourite play of
" Paul Pry;" wrote besides several travesties, burlesques,
interludes, farces, comic sketches, &c.
    H. W. Pickersgill, R.A.   G. Clint, A.R.A., mez.
    Ha. len. to left, looking to front, oval in rectang.; facs.
signature below.
    Proof before all letters, except the artists' names and publi-
cation-line; May 11, 1827
    $13\frac{3}{16} \times 9\frac{5}{16}$. $(10\frac{3}{4} \times 9\frac{1}{4})$.   25793.
    An impression presented by the engraver and publisher to
Mr. W. Cribb, another print-publisher.

POPE, ALEXANDER, 1688–1744, b. in Lombard Street, London;
son of a linendraper; educ. privately, and at Twyford, and
elsewhere; soon began writing poetry; "Pastorals," 1704;
" Essay on Criticism," 1711; " Messiah;" " Rape of the
Lock;" " Iliad;" "Dunciad," 1729; " Essay on Man," 1734.
    Vanloo.   J. Faber, junr., mez.
    J. C. Smith, 294 (all lettering cut off after JOHANNES
FABER); 2nd state.   27108.

[Vanloo].   E. F. Burney delin.   L. Schiavonetti.
    Reversed from the print by Faber, or some similar print.
Turned to the right, the poet leans on his left elbow, with left
hand to head, and looks to left; below is a group of 3 women
with an infant, a lyre, and other emblems.
    Cut. $(4\frac{13}{16} \times 3\frac{1}{4})$.   E. 1707.–'88.

Sir G. Kneller.   J. Smith, mez.
    J. C. Smith, 203, 2nd state.   26707.

Sir G. Kneller.   G. White, mez.
    J. C. Smith, 35, 3rd state, late, the whole address erased.
                                        27562.

                              J. Richardson, etched.
    Head, in profile, to right; oval, inscribed below, *Amicitiæ
Causa*.
    $3\frac{5}{8} \times 3\frac{1}{8}$. $(3\frac{3}{16} \times 3\frac{9}{16})$.   E. 1703.–'88.

POPE, MRS.,   –1733, daughter of William Turner, Esq., of
York; was not the daughter (as stated on the print), but the
sister-in-law, of Samuel Cooper, who in. her sister; was the
mother of Alexander Pope, the poet; d. at Twickenham.
    J. Richardson, Senr., del., 1731.   C. Carter, etched, 1774.
    Bust to front, wearing a linen cloth over her head; vignette.
    $8\frac{1}{4} \times 6\frac{1}{4}$. (6×5).   E. 1708.–'88.

POPE, Sir Thomas, c. 1508–1559, b. at Dedington, Oxf.; educ. at Eton; went to Gray's Inn; called to the bar, became clerk to the Crown in Chancery; favourite of Henry VIII., who knighted him and gave him several lucrative offices and grants of land; under Mary, he had the care of the Princess Elizabeth; founded Trin. Coll., Oxford.

Holbein (at Wroxton Abbey).   W. Skelton.

T. Q. len. to front, in furred robe, holding gloves in right hand; behind is a tablet, on the left, inscribed QVOD TACITVM VELIS | NEMINI DIXERIS.

Ind proof; Oct. 1821

$13\frac{3}{8} \times 11\frac{7}{16}$. $(12\frac{1}{16} \times 9\frac{13}{16})$.   22910.

POPHAM, Sir Home, 1762–1820, b. at Gibraltar, fought in the American War, the Baltic, and the E. Indies; took a prominent part in the conquest of the Cape of Good Hope, 1805; less successful at Buenos Ayres; aftds. Comm.-in-chf., on Jamaica station; d. soon after his return to England, 1820; K.M., F.R.S.

M. Brown.   A. Cardon, stipple.

Ha. len. slightly to right, looking to front, in uniform, wearing the collar and cross of the order of S. John of Malta; 1807.

$17\frac{3}{4} \times 14\frac{5}{16}$. $(14\frac{5}{16} \times 12)$.   22476.

PORSON, Richard, 1759–1808, great classical scholar; son of a parish clerk; rose to be Prof. of Greek at Cambr., 1793; aftds. Librarian of the London Institution; author of "Notes and Emendations of Greek Poets," &c.

T. Kirkby.   C. Turner, mez.

T. Q. len. to left, seated, holding a folded paper in left hand, wearing a gown.

Ind. proof with open letters; Oct. 1, 1812.

$20 \times 13\frac{4}{5}$. $(17\frac{1}{2} \times 13\frac{4}{5})$.   22049.

PORTER, Sir Robert Ker, 1780–1842, b. at Durham, brother of the novelists, Jane and Anna Maria Porter; student in the R. A., c. 1790; painted, c. 1802, large pictures of the Storming of Seringapatam, Siege of Acre, and Agincourt; Capt., Westmr. Militia, 1803; historical painter to Emperor of Russia, 1804; went with Sir J. Moore to Spain; Kn. of S. Joachim of Würtemberg, 1807; travelled through the East, 1817–'20; K.C.H., 1832; Consul at Caracas, 1826; wrote "Travelling Sketches," and other similar works.

G. Harlowe.   W. O. Burgess, mixed mez.

Wh. len. standing, to left, looking to front, wearing orders and sword; leaning with right arm on part of a cliff by the sea. March 11th, 1843.

$18\frac{1}{4} \times 12\frac{3}{4}$. $(14\frac{3}{8} \times 9\frac{3}{4})$.   24239.

PORTER, Sir Robert Ker—*continued*.
  G. Harlowe.   Woolnoth, stipple.
  Ha. len. to left, looking to front; from the same picture;
vignette. July 1, 1822.
  $(4\frac{1}{2} \times 4\frac{1}{4})$.   E. 2206.-'89.

PORTEUS, Beilby, 1745–1825; b. at York; educ. at Cambr.;
  Chaplain to George III., and Dean of Chapel Royal; Bishop
  of Chester, 1776; Bishop of London, 1787; author of "Lent
  Lectures."
  J Hoppner, R.A.   C. Turner, mez.
  T. Q. len. to left, looking to front, seated, in robes, holding
cap on knee; large open book, inkstand, &c. on table, at left.
  Scr. letter proof; May 16, 1807.
  $20 \times 13\frac{3}{8}$. $(17\frac{1}{8} \times 13\frac{3}{4})$.   22265.

PORTLAND, Lady Margaret Cavendish Harley, Duchess
  of,   –1785; only dau. and heir of Edward Harley, 2nd Earl
  of Oxford; Prior's "Peggy;" m., 1734, to William Bentinck,
  2nd Duke of Portland; was a great collector.
  M. Rysbrack.   G. Vertue.
  A bust, from one by Rysbrack, to front, on a richly-
ornamented table; drapery on right; engraved for Waller's
Poems, 1729.
  $(8\frac{3}{16} \times 6\frac{1}{4})$.   27673.
  See also PORTLAND, William, 2nd Duke of.

PORTLAND, William Bentinck, 2nd Duke of, with his
  DUCHESS (Margaret, q. v.), and Lady MARY WORTLEY
  MONTAGU (q. v.). The Duke, 1709–1762, suc. his father,
  1726; m. Lady Margaret Cavendish Harley, 1734; F.R.S.,
  K.G., D.C.L. &c.
  F. Zincke, 1738.   G. Vertue, 1739.
  These are three sh. hn. len., the Duke in the centre, to left,
in a rich dress, looking to front; the Duchess, on the left,
turned to right, wearing a low dress and boa with necklace and
brooch; Lady Mary, on the right, to front, looking to left,
wearing necklace and low dress trimmed with lace and pearls
at the shoulders; three ovals, arms and titles under each,
within a decorated border.
  $9\frac{1}{4} \times 13\frac{1}{4}$. (9×13).   24125.

PORTLAND, William Henry Cavendish Bentinck, 3rd
  Duke of, 1738–1809, statesman; son of William, 2nd Duke;
  suc., 1762; Lord of Treasury, 1783; Home Secretary, 1794–
  1801; Lord President, 1801–'5; Prime Minister, 1807–'9.
  Sir J. Reynolds.   J. Murphy, mez.
  J. C. Smith, 13, 2nd state.   21920.

PORTSMOUTH, Renée de Penencovet de Quérouaille
  (Keroual, Keromaille, or Quérouailles), Duchess of, c. 1650–
  1734, maid of honour to the Duchesse d'Orléans; attracted the
  attention of Charles II. at the celebrated interview (1670) at

Dover with his sister, at whose death she came to London; maid of honour to the Queen; had a son by the King, 1672; cr. Duchess of Portsmouth, 1673; extravagant and shameless; retired to France, 1685.

Lely. R. Tompson, mez.
J. C. Smith, 39. 24126.

POTTINGER, Rt. Hon. Sir Henry, 1789–1856, General and diplomat; went to India, as a cadet, 1804; cr. Bart. after the Affghan war, 1839; envoy to China, and concl. the treaty of 1842; Gov. of Hong Kong, 1843–'4; Gov. of Cape of Good Hope, 1846–'7; Gov. of Madras; Maj. General, G.C.B., &c.; d. at Malta.

F. Grant, A.R.A. J. Burnet, F.R.S., mixed mez.
Wh. len. to left, seated, looking to front, holding open before him a paper, lettered *Draft | of the treaty of | Nankin*; a view of Chinese houses and padoga, through an open window, on left; May 1, 1847.
30 × 20⅞. (25⅜ × 17). 23027.
See NANKING.

POWELL, Harriet, actress and singer, married to Kenneth Mackenzie, who was born, 1744, cr. Visct. Fortrose, 1744, and Earl of Seaforth, 1771, both in Peerage of Ireland; he d. 1781; she was his second wife, but the marriage is not mentioned in the peerages.

C. Read. C. Corbutt [*i.e.*, R. Purcell], mez.
J. C. Smith, 63, probably 2nd state, but cut at bottom.
This is a copy of the original by Houston. 26425

POWELL, speaking the Prologue to the Anniversary of His Majesty's Birth-Day.
From a "Collection . . . of English Prologues," &c., 1799. 28187. 13.

POWER, Tyrone, distinguished comedian, very popular in the U.S. America; lost in the President, steamship, 1841.
N. J. Crowley, R.H.A. C. G. Lewis, mixed mez.
Wh. len., "In the character of Connor O'Gormon, in Mrs. " Carter Hall's Popular Drama of ' The Groves of Blarney.' " Open letter proof.
19¹¹⁄₁₆ × 22⅞. (16¹³⁄₁₆ × 20¼). 25795.

POYNTER, Edward John, R.A., 1836– , b. at Paris, son of Ambrose Poynter, an architect; educ. at Westminster and at Ipswich; stud. art in Engl. schools, 1854–'6, and in Paris, under Gleyre, 1856–'9; A.R.A., 1869; Slade Prof., Lond., 1871 and 1873–'7; exhib. at R.A., 1867 and following years; Art Director and Principal of the Nat. Art Training School at S. K. for several years; Director of the Nat. Gallery, 1894.
Le Gros, etched.
Sh. ha. len. to right, looking to front; body only in outline; without inscription.
10 × 6¼. (8⅜ × 6³⁄₁₆). 27728.

PRAED, WINTHROP MACKWORTH, 1802–1839, Poet and politician; b. in London; educ. at Eton and Cambr.; called to the Bar, 1829; ent. Parliament, 1830; Sec. to the Board of Control, in Sir R. Peel's Ministry, 1835; author of many poems and political verses.
A. Meyer. M. Gauci, lith.
Bust, to front, looking to left; vignette; heightened in places with white, by hand.
(13 × 13¼). 22526.

PRATT, JOHN TIDD, 1797–1869, registrar of Friendly Societies, and author; called to the Bar, 1824; consulting barrister to the Commissrs. for the Reduction of Nat. Debt, 1828, and appointed to certify the rules of Savings Banks, &c.; J.P.; wrote several works on the Turnpike Roads Acts, Friendly Societies, Property Tax Act, &c.
H. Pickersgill, R.A. H. Davis, mez.
Ha. len. seated, to front, looking to right, holding an envelope addressed to himself. Published, June 18th, 1858.
16¼ × 12⅝. (12$\frac{9}{16}$ × 9¾). 27273.

PRATTEN, ROBERT SIDNEY, 1824–1868, very distinguished flute-player, b. at Bristol, son of a musician; played in his 12th year at Bath and Bristol concerts; next at Theatre Royal, Dublin, as first flute; came to London, 1846; first flute at R. Italian Opera, Sacred Harmonic and Philharmonic Societies, &c.; wrote for the flute; had a very powerful tone and remarkable execution.
See MUSICAL UNION.

PRETENDER, OLD. See JAMES FRANCIS EDWARD.

PRETENDER, YOUNG. See CHARLES JAMES EDWARD.

PRICE, RICHARD, 1723–1791, b. at Tynton, Glamorg., stud. at a Dissent. Acad. in London; Minister to various Dissent. Congregations in London, from 1743; wrote in favour of the American Colonies, 1775–'6, for which he received the freedom of the City of London, and was invited by Congress to America; after the war, was consulted, as a financial authority, by Pitt, concerning the liquidation of the National Debt; contr. many papers to "Philosophical Transactions;" a great authority on life assurance, &c.; D.D.; F.R.S.
B. West, R.A. T. Holloway.
T. Q. len. slightly to left, seated, holding glasses and an open paper; on table at his left lies a book, lettered "Butler's Analogy."
Ind. proof.
15½ × 11$\frac{7}{16}$. (12⅛ × 9⅜). 23133.

PRIDEAUX, W., Aëronaut. See GREEN (2).

PRIESTLEY, JOSEPH, 1733–1804, b. near Leeds; educ. at Daventry; became dissenting minister at Needham Market and elsewhere; pubd. "History . of Electricity," which procured him his election as F.R.S. and degree of LL.D., Edinb.; wrote other books on political and scientific subjects; lost his house, library, MSS., and apparatus, by fire, in riots at the time of the French Revolution; went to U.S. America, where he died.

Anon.

Sh. ha. len. to left, in profile; oval, in border, ornamented with flowers; below are artistic and scientific instruments.

$(6\frac{1}{2} \times 3\frac{1}{16})$.　　　　　　　　　　　　　　　　29608.　L.

PRINGLE, Captain,　　　–　　commanded a ship in Lord Howe's Victory, off Ushant, June 1, 1794; rose to flag-rank. *See* COMMEMORATION (1).

PRIOR, Matthew, 1664–1721, b. (probably) at Wimborne, Dorset; educ. at Westminster under Dr. Busby, and at St. John's Coll., Cambr., of which Coll. he became a fellow; wrote, 1687, (with Charles Montagu) "The Country Mouse and the City Mouse," in burlesque of Dryden's "The Hind and the Panther;" served in diplom. posts at the Hague, &c., and was finally, 1711, ambassador at Paris; besides his Poems, he began the "History of his own Time;" d. at Wimpole, Lord Oxford's seat; buried in Westminster Abbey, with a monument to his memory.

J. Richardson.　　　　　　　　　　G. Vertue, 1719.

T Q. len. to front, seated, looking to right, holding a pen in right hand, left thrust into breast of coat; cap on head.

$14\frac{13}{16} \times 10\frac{13}{16}$.　$(12\frac{1}{4} \times 9\frac{7}{8})$.　　　　　　　26708.

PRITCHARD, Hannah Vaughan, Mrs., 1711–1768, distinguished actress, successful alike in Tragedy and Comedy; noted particularly in the characters of "Lady Macbeth" and "The Queen" in "Hamlet;" d. at Bath.

R. E. Pine.　　　　　　　　　　　F. Aliamet.

Wh. len. to front, as "Hermione" in the "Winter's Tale," looking downwards to right, wearing a necklace of pearls, from which hangs a cross; a large vase stands on the left; 1765.

$20 \times 13\frac{7}{8}$.　$(17\frac{3}{4} \times 12\frac{13}{16})$.　　　　　　　22266.

PROUT, Samuel, 1783–1852, water-colour painter, b. at Plymouth, educ. at grammar-school there, and taught drawing by a local master; had a sun-stroke, and suffered from ill-health throughout his life; met John Britton, who befriended him and gave him instruction; exhibited at the R. A.; member of the Water-colour Society, 1820; travelled abroad, painted cathedrals, churches, market-places, in Normandy, Italy, Flanders, Germany and Switzerland; d. at Camberwell.

Anon., woodcut.

Bust, to front, vignette; oval; cut from an illustrated paper.

$(4\frac{1}{4} \times 3\frac{5}{8})$.　　　　　　　　　　　E. 2218.–'89.

PUGIN, Augustus, 1762–1832, architectural draughtsman, b. in France, came to this country; entd. the schools of the R. A.,

where he began exhibiting, 1790, chiefly views of Gothic buildings; worked with Nash for more than 20 years; exhibited,
from 1807, at the Water-colour Society; a member of that
Society, 1821; employed largely by Ackermann; published
several works on Architecture; married an English lady; d. in
Bloomsbury.

J. Green.   E. Scriven, stipple.
Sh. ha. len. to front; for the "Library of the Fine Arts,"
1833; vignette; facs. signature below.
(4 × 3¼).   E. 2203.–'89.

PUGIN, Augustus Welby Northmore, 1812–1852, architect,
b. in London, son of A. Pugin, the elder, by whom he was
educ.; learned to draw with accuracy, designed furniture and
goldsmith's work; painted scenery for theatres; cruised about
the channel, collecting archæological and natural curiosities;
manufactured Gothic ornament; devoted himself finally to
architecture; turned Roman Catholic; designed churches;
became insane; d. at Ramsgate.
J. R. Herbert, R.A.   J. R. Herbert, etched and mez.
Ha. len. to front, looking to front, at a table, on which is a
plan, on which he holds a pair of compasses with his right hand.
Ind. proof before all letters.
17 × 13½.   (10¾ × 8½).   22264.

R. Herbert.   J. H. Lynch, lith.
Ha. len. to left, looking to front, holding a pair of compasses
on a plan, on a table; in an arched frame; his name, divided, at
top and bottom; the motto "En avant," repeated three times,
on each side.
(5½ × 3⅝).   E. 2207.–'89.

PULTENEY, Rt. Hon. William, Earl of Bath.   See BATH.

PURCELL, Henry, 1658–1695, the greatest of English musi-
cians; educ. at Westminster as a chorister; succeeded Dr.
Gibbons there as organist; composed sacred music, operas, odes,
sonatas, &c.; buried in Westminster Abbey.
Closterman.   Zobel, mixed mez.
Ha. len. slightly to right, looking to front, holding up a roll of
music in right hand; wearing long wig, and flowered waistcoat.
Ind. proof; facs. signature.
16⅞ × 12⅛.   (13 × 10).   21953.

PYE, Henry James, 1745–1813, Poet-Laureate; b. in London;
educ. at Oxford; for some time an officer in the Berks. Militia;
appointed Poet-Laureate, 1790; wrote "Alfred," an Epic Poem,
&c.
S. I. Arnold.   B. Pym, mez.
Ha. len. to left, looking to front; white neckcloth; all the
rest very dark; oval in border; Feb. 2, 1801.
14⅛ × 10⅞.   (13 × 10¾).   22527.

PYE, John, 1782–1874, engraver, b. at Birmingham; came to London, 1802, and worked under James Heath; soon obtained reputation for rendering landscapes, especially those of Turner, who was so pleased with his engraving of his "Pope's Villa" that he engaged him to engrave his "Temple of Jupiter at Ægina," which made his fame; spent much of his life in Paris; was one of the founders of the "Artists' Benevolent Fund," was President, 1826–'8, of the "Artists' Annuity Fund;" opposed the R. A. bitterly.

W. M[ulready].   J. H. R[obinson].
Head, to left, in profile; **vignette.**
  3½ × 2¾. (2¼ × 1⅝).   29023.   B.

PYM, John, 1584–1643, Statesman, b. in Somersets.; gained influence as an opponent of James I. in Parlt.; took part in the impeachment of the Duke of Buckingham, 1626, and of the Earl of Strafford, 1640; one of the authors of the "Grand Remonstrance," 1641; one of the Five Members whom Charles I. attempted to have arrested, 1642; Lieut.-Gen. of the Ordnance, 1643.

Anon.   J. Houbraken, 1738.
From a picture "In the possession of Thomas Hales, Esqr."
Sh. ha. len., slightly turned to left, looking to front, with broad collar, own hair, not very long; in Birch's "Lives."
  14½ × 9¼. (14 × 8¾).   21815.

QUICK, John, 1748–1831, distinguished comedian, b. in Whitechapel, London; appeared at the Haymarket Theatre, 1769, and became a great favourite of the King; the original "Tony Lumpkin;" retired, 1798; d. at Islington.
See MATTOCKS.

QUIN, James, 1693–1766, b. in King St., Cov. Garden; grandson of a Lord Mayor of Dublin (1676); son of a lady who supposed her husband dead, not having heard of him for nearly 7 years; prevented, therefore, from inheriting his father's property; became very celebrated as an actor, and also for his sense and wit; d. at Bath.

T. Hudson.   J. Faber, junr., mez.
J. C. Smith, 301, retouched.

RACE, Daniel, 1700–1775, Chief Cashier of the Bank of England; d. at Clapton.

T. Hickey.   J. Watson, mez.
J. C. Smith, 122, 1st state.   E. 1658.–'89.

RADCLIFFE, John, 1650–1714, b. at Wakefield, educ. at Gr. School there, and at Univ. Coll., Oxf.; M.D., settled in London, 1684; soon gained reputation; app. physician to Princess Anne of Denmark, 1686; and, after Revolution, often consulted by William III., whose favour he lost by indiscretion of speech; received large sums of secret service money for his prescriptions for Q. Anne; left 40,000*l.* to Univ., Oxf., for foundation of a

public library of medical science; provided also for purchase of
books, for two travelling fellowships, and Observatory and Infirmary at the same University.

Anon,   M. Burghers.

Sh. hn. len. to right, looking to front, in oval; arms above;
book-shelves and books behind; title and inscription below, in
11 lines; the engraver's name erased.

10⅝ × 7½. (10$\frac{7}{16}$ × 7$\frac{3}{16}$; oval, 5¼ × 4$\frac{1}{2}$).   29718.   10.

RADSTOCK, William, Lord, 1758–1825; admiral; Baron of
Castletown, Ireland; governed Newfoundland; G.C.B.; &c.

G. Hayter.   T. Landseer.

Ha. len. seated, to right, looking to front, in plain clothes,
with star.

Open letter proof, Jany. 1, 1820.

12 × 9⅛. (8$\frac{7}{16}$ × 6$\frac{1}{8}$).   27,111.

RAE, John, L.R.C.S., M.D., LL.D., F.R.S., F.R.G.S, &c.,
1813–1893, b. at the "Hall of Clestrain," in Orkney; educ. at
home, and at Univ. of Edinburgh; grad., 1833; Surg. to
Hudson's Bay Compy.'s ship; accepted, 1845, command of
expedition to Arctic Seas in two small boats; again, in 1846;
made other expeditions for purposes of survey; brought first
information of Franklin's fate; pubd. brief narratives and
reports of his expeditions.

S. Pearce.   J. Scott, mixed mez.

Ha. len to left, wearing fur cloak; facs. signature below.

Ind. proof; Jany. 26, 1858.

15 × 12. (11 × 9).   27274.

RAEBURN, Sir Henry, R.A., P.R.S.A., 1756–1823, portrait-
painter; travelled in Italy; settled in Edinburgh; elected
President of the Socy. of Artists of Edinb., 1812; R.A., 1815;
Knt., and appointed Portrait-painter to the King, 1822.

Sir H. Raeburn, R.A.   W. Walker, stipple.

Ha. len. to left, looking to front, left hand to chin, left elbow
resting on right hand.

Ind. proof with open letters; Jany. 1, 1826.

19 × 13⅞. (13 × 10$\frac{5}{8}$).   21843.

RAFFLES, Thomas, 1788–1863, b. in Spitalfields, D.D., LL.D.,
pastor at Hammersmith Congregational Church, 1808–1811,
succeeding (in 1811) to the pulpit in Great George St. Chapel,
Liverpool, where he remained till 1861; pubd. Memoirs, Poems,
new edn. of Brown's Self-interpreting Bible, Translation of
Klopstock's Messiah, Letters, Lectures, &c.

W. Scott.   C. Turner, A.R.A., mez.

Hn. len. to front, in pulpit, right hand raised, in act of
preaching, left hand on open book.

Ind. open letter proof; June 23, 1835.

19⅞ × 14. (15⅜ × 12).   25839.

RAGLAN, FitzRoy Somerset, Lord, 1788–1855, youngest son of the 5th Duke of Beaufort; ent. army, 1804; disting. himself in Peninsular War and at Waterloo; Mil. Sec. to Duke of Wellington, 1819–'52; raised to the Peerage, 1852; Comm.-in-Chf., Crimea, 1854; d. in camp before Sebastopol, June 28, 1855.

Sir F. Grant, R.A. — H. Cousins, mixed mez.

Wh. len. to front, in uniform, holding his hat in left hand; despatch-box and Army List on table, at left.

Open letter proof, Septr. 20, 1854.

(26 × 16). — 21949.

RAIKES, Robert, 1735–1811, b. at Gloucester; contributed greatly to improvement of prison-discipline and establishment (1781) of Sunday-schools; pubd. an account of his essays in Sunday-school system, Gent.'s Mag. 1784.

Romney. — T. Woolnoth, stipple.

T. Q. len. to left, seated, looking to front, holding a paper folded in right hand, left hand on chair-arm; a table, with inkstand, &c. on his right.

Ind. proof; June 7, 1821.

$14\frac{1}{2} \times 11$. ($11\frac{1}{8} \times 8\frac{7}{8}$). — 23029.

RAIMBACH, Abraham, 1776–1843, engraver; b. n London; son of a Swiss, domiciled here; pupil of J. Hall; student at R. A. schools; worked for the booksellers, and painted miniatures, of which he exhibited many at the R. A., 1797–1805; settled on line-engraving, which he pursued with success, after Reynolds, Wilkie, and other painters; d. at Greenwich.

J. E. Gatteaux. — A. R. Freebairn (Bate's Patent Anaglyptograph).

Bust, to right, in profile; circular; facs. signature below.

$9\frac{6}{8} \times 6\frac{7}{16}$. (4, diamr). — 23031.

RALEGH, Sir Walter, 1552–1618, Statesman, Warrior, and Scholar; b. at Hayes, Devon; ent. at Oxford; served in France and Netherlands; founded a settlement in Virginia, whence he is said to have introduced potatoes and tobacco into Europe; rose high in Queen Elizabeth's favour; impris. 12 years by James I., when he wrote his unfinished "History of the World;" released to undertake an expedition to Guiana; executed after his return, Oct. 1618.

Anon. — J. Houbraken, 1739.

Sh. ha. len. to front; oval in border — In Birch's "Lives."

$14\frac{7}{8} \times 9\frac{3}{8}$. ($14\frac{1}{4} \times 8\frac{7}{8}$). — 21816.

"From an original Picture, 1598. Æta. 44." — R. Bell.

T. Q. len to left, looking to front; in outline.

Ind. proof.

$11 \times 8\frac{7}{8}$. ($8\frac{1}{2} \times 6\frac{5}{8}$). — 22686. 1.

RALEGH, Sir WALTER—*continued*.
Anon. Anon., woodcut.
Bust, slightly inclined to left, looking to front, wearing a hat, and smoking a long pipe, the bowl of which is not seen; within a border ornamented with long pipes, a flagon, &c.
Ind. proof.
$5\frac{3}{4} \times 3\frac{1}{2}$. ($2\frac{6}{16} \times 1\frac{7}{8}$). 29608. **A.**

RALEGH, ELIZABETH THROGMORTON, Lady.
"From an original picture, Ætat. 35." R. Bell.
T. Q. len. to front, dropping a globe from her left hand; in outline. At her left is the motto, "Laisse tomber le monde."
Ind. proof.
$11 \times 8\frac{7}{8}$. ($8\frac{5}{8} \times 7\frac{5}{16}$). 22686. 2,

RAMSAY, ALLAN, 1685–1758, Scottish poet; b. at Leadhills; apprent. to a wigmaker; became a bookseller at Edinburgh, where he published poems, 1721, 4to, favourably received; again a vol., 1728; "The Gentle Shepherd" appeared in the latter; published "The Evergreen," a misc. selection of Scottish poetry, in which two pieces of his own were inserted; d. at Edinburgh.
W. Aikman. G. White, mez.
J. C. Smith, 36, 2nd state. 26718.

RAMESEY, or RAMSEY, WILLIAM D.D., 1626– ; b. in Westminster; physician to Charles, II.; author of "Christian Judicial Theology Vindicated," "Vox Stellarum," 1651; "Astrologia Restaurata," 1653, and some medical and educational works; mentioned in "Spectator," No. 582; pubd. no more after 1672; said to have d. in jail.

T. Cross.
Bust, on pedestal, slightly to right; long hair, classic drapery; a landscape behind; four mottoes; one above, *Homo Quasi vmbra*; another, on left, *Nosce te ipsum*; the third, on right, *Memento Mori*; the fourth, below, *Nemo sine crimine vivit*; "Æ 24: Mar: 13: $16\frac{5}{6}\frac{2}{6}$. | *Sould by T: H: & G: C:*"; prefixed to his "Astrologia Restaurata, 1653."
($4\frac{14}{16} \times 3\frac{3}{16}$). 29718. 1.

RAMSDEN, JESSE, 1735–1800, son of an innkeeper, near Halifax; came to London, 1758, and bound himself to a philos. instrument-maker; m. the dau. of Dollond, about 1765; carried on business in the Haymarket, and aftds. in Piccadilly; invented and improved many instruments; received 1,000*l.* from Board of Longitude, 1777, and Copley medal for his inventions and improvements; F.R.S., 1786; d. at Brighthelmstone.
R. Home. J. Jones, mez.
J. C. Smith, 66, 2nd state. 22051.

RATHBORNE, AARON, 1572–   ; mathematician.

S. van de Pass.

Ha. len. to front, with broad lace collar, holding compasses in right hand; oval in border, the name above and " *Ata. fuæ* 44."; "QUI IN ME VIVIT PRO ME MORTUOS EST. ANNO SALUTIS NOSTRI 1616," on the oval; books above, in the corners, lettered, "Euclid, Ptolomy," &c.; in the lower corners, mathematical instruments, &c.; a white space below the subject. The monogram is in the lower corner on the left.

This portrait is prefixed to the author's " The Surveyor. In four bookes," London, 1616, fol.

$7\frac{9}{16} \times 4\frac{5}{8}$. $(5\frac{0}{16} \times 4\frac{5}{8})$. 26868.

RAY, MARTHA, c. 1747–1779, apprent. to a mantua-maker at Clerkenwell; became Lord Sandwich's mistress; noted as a singer; shot dead, through jealousy, by the Rev. J. Hackman as she was leaving Cov. Garden Theatre, April 7, 1779.

N. Dance, R.A., 1777. V. Green, mez.

J. C. Smith, 106, 1st state. 22531.

RAYMOND, JAMES GRANT, actor, b. at Strathspey; played tragic characters, Macbeth, &c.

W. H. Bate. C. Turner, mez.

Ha. len. to front, looking to right and upwards; wearing a lace collar with tassels, &c.;

Open letter proof; Jany. 14, 1818.

$15\frac{1}{2} \times 12$. $(13\frac{7}{16} \times 11\frac{1}{4}$, including ruled border, $1\frac{5}{8})$. 22911.

REDESDALE, SIR JOHN FREEMAN MITFORD, Lord, 1748–1830; lawyer and statesman; Solicitor-General, 1793; Attorney-general, 1800; Speaker, 1801; cr. Baron, 1802; Lord Chancellor of Ireland, 1802–1806.

T. Lawrence, R.A. G. Clint, mez., 1804.

T. Q. len. to front, seated, looking to left, in robes and wig. Open letter proof.

Cut. $(17\frac{1}{2} \times 13\frac{16}{16})$. 23032.

REED, ISAAC, 1742–1807, b. in London; brought up to the conveyancing business, but left it for literary pursuits; lived in Staple's Inn, where he collected a curious library; pubd. Lady M. W. Montague's Poems; revised Dodsley's "Old Plays;" pubd. "Biographia Dramatica," an edition of Shakspere, European Magazine, &c.

G. Romney. W. Dickinson, mez.

J. C. Smith, 67. 24090.

REES, ABRAHAM, 1743–1825, learned divine; b. in Montgomery-shire; educ. at a dissent. academy at Hoxton; mathemat. and philos. tutor there, and at New Coll., Hackney; edit. "Chambers' Cyclopædia," and "Rees' Cyclopædia;" D.D., Edinb.; F.R.S.

J. Opie, R.A. J. Yeatherd, mez.

J. C. Smith, 3, 2nd state. 22529.

REFORM BANQUET, The, held in the Guildhall, City of London, July 11, 1832, to celebrate the passing of the Reform Bill.

B. R. Haydon.   J. C. Bromley, mixed mez.

A composition of many figures, including the Prime Minister, Earl Grey, K.G., in the chair, and all the most prominent Liberal politicians of that day.

$22\frac{3}{16}$ (?) × 28 (?).   ($20\frac{4}{8}$ × $26\frac{1}{4}$).   25845.

REFORM BILL, The, receiving the Assent of King William IV. by Royal Commission, in the House of Lords, June 7, 1832.

S. W. Reynolds.   W. Walker and S. W. Reynolds, stipple.

A composition of many figures, including those of all the best known and most prominent politicians of the time; on an additional plate at foot are the title and facs. signatures of the King, Lords Grey, Durham, Holland, Brougham, Lansdowne, and Wellesley, the Royal Commissioners.

Proof, 1836.

30 × $24\frac{1}{2}$.   ($28\frac{8}{8}$ × $22\frac{4}{8}$).   Addit. plate, $3\frac{1}{4}$ × $22\frac{6}{8}$.   23050.

REFORMERS, a Group.

                                            Anon.

Bishop Hooper is on the left ; next to him is Ridley ; then Latimer ; next, Cranmer ; J. Bradford and R. Taylor on the right ; hn. len., seated at a table, on which is an open Bible, before Latimer, and a candle, at which blasts are directed by the heads of a cardinal, a pope, a monk, and a demon ; below are 4 verses :

"*Tho' Hell and Rome with all their might, Labour to*
"*put out Gospel Light,*
"*Yet their Attempts are all in vain, God ever will his*
"*Truth maintain.*"

                                    29719.   2.

RELPH, John, c. 1800, M.D., Physician to Guy's Hospital ; &c.
See MEDICAL SOCIETY.

RENDEL, James Meadows, 1799–1856, civil engineer, b. near Dartmoor ; early empl. by Telford ; surv. harbours on S.W. coast of England ; settled in London, 1838 ; built docks at Birkenhead and Great Grimsby, and harbours of refuge at Holyhead and Portland ; Pres. Inst. C. Engineers, 1852–'3 ; member of Intern. Com. to examine the practicability of a canal across the Isthmus of Suez ; &c.

G. Opie.   S. Bellin, mixed mez.

T. Q. len. to front, seated, looking to left, dark cravat, coat, waistcoat, &c., arms resting on arms of chair.

Open letter proof.

$20\frac{3}{8}$(?) × $16\frac{1}{4}$.   (18 × $10\frac{3}{16}$.)   27275.

RENNIE, John, 1757–1821, engineer ; b. in East Lothian ; settled in London, 1783 ; built the Waterloo, Southwark, and

new London, Bridges; the Breakwater at Plymouth, Hull, and
Sheerness Docks, &c.

   Sir F. Chantrey, R.A.   S. W. Reynolds, mez.
Bust, on pedestal, slightly inclined to left, but the head turned
to right; the name of the personage scraped in white on the
plinth, and those of the sculptor and engraver, one on either side,
below.
     20 × 14. (19$\frac{3}{10}$ × 13$\frac{3}{4}$).   21800.
     See also SCIENCE.

REVETT, NICHOLAS, 1721–1804, architect and artist; the fellow-
traveller of James Stuart, and joint-editor of " The Antiquities
and Ruins of Athens;" travelled also with Dr. Chandler through
Asia Minor, and pubd. " Ionian Antiquities;" returned to
England, where he designed some important churches and other
buildings.

   Ramsay.   W. C. Edwards.
Sh. ha. len. to right, looking to front, seated; in a ruled border,
1827.
     13$\frac{3}{8}$ × 10. (6$\frac{1}{4}$ × 5, within the border).   22912.

REYNOLDS, SIR JOSHUA, 1723–1792, b. at Plympton, Devon.;
pupil of Hudson; went to Italy, 1749; on his return, 1752,
became the leading portrait-painter of the day; his works have
maintained their value, though he used fleeting colours too
often; first President R.A., Kt., 1768; a friend of Burke,
Goldsmith, Johnson; d. in Leicester Fields; buried in St.
Paul's Cathedral.

   Sir J. Reynolds.   V. Green, mez.
J. C. Smith, 110, 2nd state; the inscription erased.   21924.

   Sir J. Reynolds.   J. K. Sherwin.
Ha. len. to right, looking to front, wearing Doctor's cap and
gown; left hand to breast; a paper in right hand.
   Ind. proof.
     11$\frac{1}{8}$ × 10. (10$\frac{11}{16}$ × 9).   22532.

   Sir J. Reynolds.   W. Ridley, stipple.
Sh. ha. len. to left, looking to front; wearing a furred robe;
oval. For the " General Magazine and Impartial Review,"
April 1, 1792.
     6$\frac{7}{16}$ × 4$\frac{1}{2}$. (3$\frac{1}{2}$ × 3).   28300. 49

                                Anon.
Bust, to left, in profile; circular.
     4$\frac{3}{4}$ × 4. (3$\frac{5}{16}$ diamr.).   28300. 48.

                          J. Condé, stipple.
Sh. ha. len. to left, looking to front, with curled hair; coat
buttoned, white lappels, and shirt frill; oval.
   Septr. 1, 1793.
     (3$\frac{3}{8}$ × 3).   28300. 47.

REYNOLDS, Sir Joshua—*continued.*

Sir J. Reynolds.　　　　C. Turnor, F.S.A., 1797, stipple.
Sh. ha. len. to left, looking to front, wearing Doctor's cap and gown; oval　An early example of Charles Turner's work, executed only 2 years after he had entd. the R. A. Schools, and while under the influence of Bartolozzi. He then spelled his name as above.
Ind. proof.
$4\frac{9}{16} \times 3\frac{1}{4}$.　$(3\frac{1}{16} \times 2\frac{7}{16})$.　　　　　　E. 2209.–'89.

Sir J. Reynolds.　　　　W. Bond, etched.
Full ha. len. to right, looking to front, wearing Doctor's cap and gown ; a bust on pedestal at right, on which he rests his left hand, in which is a scroll. Etched for J. Britton's " The Fine Arts of the English School," in which publication the finished plate occurs, at p. 39.　Jany. 20, 1811.
$(7\frac{5}{16} \times 6\frac{1}{8})$.　　　　　　　28300.　50.

[Sir J. Reynolds]. A. Hadamard del.　Fontenier (?), woodcut.
Sh. ha. len. to right, looking to front, wearing Doctor's cap and gown ; vignette.
From some illustrated paper ; laid down.
$(4\frac{1}{4} \times 4\frac{1}{2})$.　　　　　　　E. 2210.–'89.
See also ACADEMY.

REYNOLDS, Richard, 1735–1816, b. at Bristol, member of the Soc. of Friends ; noted for business enterprise and active philanthropy ; his virtues commemorated in James Montgomery's lines to " The Memory of the Just ; " his letters, with a memoir, were pubd. by his granddaughter, Hannah Mary Rathbone.
W. Hobday.　　　　　　　W. Sharp.
Ha. len. to right, seated, looking to front, holding a Bible, open at Romans, Chap. V. ; Decr. 1, 1817
$15\frac{1}{2} \times 12$.　$(11\frac{13}{16} \times 9\frac{1}{4},$ excl. ruled border, $\frac{3}{4})$.　　　23028.

RICARDO, David, 1772–1823 ; of a Jewish family ; political economist, member of Stock Exchange ; wrote in the Morning Chronicle on depreciation of currency ; advocated the principles of Malthus ; pubd. a treatise on " Political Economy and Taxation ; " M.P. for Portarlington.
T. Phillips.　　　　　　　T. Hodgetts, mez.
Ha. len. seated, to right, looking to front, holding a paper.
May 6, 1822.
$15\frac{4}{16} \times 12$.　$(12 \times 9\frac{3}{8})$.　　　　　22913.

RICE. *See* MONTEAGLE.

RICE, Captain William, 　–　 , 25th Bombay Native Infantry ; author of " Tiger-shooting in India," 1850–'54.
Anon.　　　　　　　　W. G. M. (?), woodcut.

T. Q. len. to left, seated; within an ornamental border of
grasses, leaves, and arms, with the figure of a tiger below.
Ind. proof.
$(4\frac{5}{16} \times 3\frac{1}{2})$. 29718. 14.

RICHARD I., King, "Cœur de Lion," 1158-1199, suc. 1189.
From the print in Montfaucon's "Antiquities," after the
monument in the Abbey of Font-evraud, where the King was
buried.
Vertue.
Ha. len. to front, with battle-axe in right hand, and crowned.
$11\frac{1}{2} \times 7\frac{3}{4}$. $(11 \times 7\frac{3}{16})$. 27178. 7.

Note.—There is no other original portrait of this King known.

RICHARD II., King, 1366-1400 (or 1419), son of Edward, the
"Black Prince"; suc. his grandfather, Edward III., 1377;
m. 1st, Anne, daughter of the Emp. Charles IV.; 2nd, Isabel,
dau. of Charles VI. of France; deposed, 1399; murdered,
1400, or, according to other accounts, escaped from Pomfret
Castle, and lived in Scotland until 1417, or 1419.
From a very ancient picture in Westminster Abbey
G. Grisoni del. G. Vertue.
Wh. len. to front, enthroned, crowned, holding the orb in
right hand and sceptre in left; inscription (in Latin) in 6 lines
below. The picture, hidden by successive coats of paint, was
cleaned (1866); it is in tempera, in perfect preservation, and
the oldest genuine royal portrait we possess.
$(19\frac{1}{8} \times 10)$. 21804.

RICHARD III., King, 1453-1485, suc. 1483.
From an "Antient Original Painting on Board" at Kensington Palace. G. Vertue.
Ha. len. to left, wearing a jewel in his cap, and a jewelled
collar.
$11\frac{9}{16} \times 7\frac{1}{8}$. $(11 \times 7\frac{1}{2})$. 23142.

RICHARDS, George, 1769-1837, matr. at Trin. Coll., Oxf.,
1785; fellow of Oriel, 1790; Vicar of Bampton, 1796; Rector,
St Martin's-in-the-Fields, 1820; pubd. Poems, Lectures, Sermons, &c.
C. Ross. C. Turner, A.R.A., mez.
T. Q. len. seated, slightly turned to right, looking to front,
right hand open before him, a book in his left.
Open letter proof (?); Novr. 1st, 1832.
$20\frac{1}{16} \times 14\frac{1}{16}$. $(15\frac{3}{16} \times 12)$. 23136.

RICHARDSON, Sir John, 1787-1865, ent. Med. branch of
Navy; served at the blockade of the Tagus, and subseq. in
various parts of the world; joined Franklin's expedition, 1819,
as surgeon and naturalist; again, 1825-'7; Insp. Naval Hospitals, 1838; volunteered to lead an expedition in search of
Franklin, 1848; returned unsuccessful to Haslar; resigned,
1855; wrote a "Memoir of Sir John Franklin."
See ARCTIC COUNCIL.

RICHARDSON, JONATHAN, 1665–1745, portrait-painter; apprent. to his step-father, a scrivener; pupil of J. Riley, four years; married Riley's niece; acquired reputation even in the lifetime of Kneller and Dahl; after that, ranked with Jervas at head of the profession; also etched a few slight portraits; was distinguished as a writer, having pubd. "an essay on the whole Art of Criticism," 1719, and other works; left a collection, sold by auction, at which Hudson, his son-in-law, bought many drawings.

[Bretherton.]   C. Bretherton, etched.
A head, to left, looking to front; vignette (Walpole's "Anecdotes," Vol. IV., p. 15).
(5 × 3⅜).   25461. 18.

RICHMOND AND GORDON, CHARLES HENRY GORDON-LENNOX, 6th Duke of, 1818– ; Major in the Army, retired; formerly A.D.C. to F. M. the Duke of Wellington and to Visct. Hardinge; K.G., P.C., D.C.L., Chancellor of the Univ. of Aberdeen; elder brother of Trinity House; suc. 1860; Dukedom of Gordon added to that of Richmond, 1876; Lord Pres. of Council, &c.
See DERBY CABINET

RICHMOND AND LENNOX, FRANCES THERESA, Duchess of, c. 1648–1702, daughter of Dr. Walter Stuart, third son of Lord Blantyre; maid of honour to Queen Catharine, 1663; captivated Charles II. and many others by her wonderful beauty, as related by Grammont; eloped with, and m. next day (his 3rd wife) to, Charles Stuart, 6th Duke of Lennox and 3rd Duke of Richmond, 1667; her portrait was stamped by Roettiers on his die for the new coinage, as the head of Britannia; disfigured by small pox, 2 years later; passed the latter part of her life between cards and cats.

Sir P. Lely.   T. Watson, mez.
J. C Smith, 5 (III.), 3rd state.   22477.

Sir P. Lely.   I. Thomson, stipple.
See LA BELLE ASSEMBLÉE, 1819.   13867. 26.

RICHMOND, JAMES STUART, 1612–1655, son of Esmé II., Duke of Lennox; suc. as 2nd Earl of March, 1624; 4th Duke of Lennox; K.G., P.C.; cr. Duke of Richmond, 1641; Lord Steward; &c.
A. van Dyck.   J. Houbraken, 1740.
Sh. hn. len. to right, looking to front, wearing the George. In Birch's " Lives."
14¹¹⁄₁₆ × 9¼. (14⅛ × 8¾).   20793.

RIDLEY, NICHOLAS, c. 1500–1555, b. at Wilmontswick, Northumb.; educ. at Pembr. Hall, of which he became fellow and master; studied in the Sorbonne, Paris; Bishop of Rochester, 1547; of London, 1550; supported Lady J. Grey;

on accession of Mary, imprisoned; and, with Latimer, burnt for heresy, Oct. 16, 1555; pubd. theological works.

A. Vander Werff.   P. à Gunst.

Sh. ha. len. to right, looking to front, in robes; circle in border; arms, &c., below.

12½ × 7¼. (11⅓ × 7).   24671.

See also "REFORMERS," and "PROTESTANT MARTYRS," 25736.

RIGAUD, JOHN FRANCIS, 1742–1810, b. at Turin, son of a merchant, and descended from a French Protestant family, early studied art; painter to the King of Sweden; travelled in Italy for improvement; member of Acad. of Bologna, 1766; went to Paris, 1772; thence came to England, where he exhibited in the R. A. that year; A.R.A., same year; R.A., 1784; painted history and portraits; the fresco altar-pieces at Packington, and St. Martin Outwich, London; translated Da Vinci's "Treatise," 1806.

G. Dance, April 1, 1793.   W. Daniell.

Sh. ha. len to right, in profile, seated; July 1, 1812; vignette.

10¹¹⁄₁₆ × 7¹⁵⁄₁₆. (5¾ × 5).   E. 2211.–'89.

RILEY, JOHN, 1646–1691, portrait-painter, b. in London; son of Lancaster Herald, Record-keeper at the Tower; pupil of Soest and Fuller; practised in London; at the death of Kneller, rose in public estimation; painted Charles II., and James II. and his Queen; appointed state-painter; painted William and Mary several times; his portraits are good; several are in the National Portrait Gallery; a good example at Hampton Court.

Anon.   A. Bannerman.

Sh. ha. len. to right, looking to front; oval in border; a small portrait of Egbert van Hemskerk below; this occurs in Walpole's "Anecdotes," 1763, vol. III., p. 122.

(6¾ × 5).   25461. 2.

RIPON, FREDERICK JOHN ROBINSON, 1st Earl of, 1782–1859, 2nd son of Thomas, Lord Grantham; M.A., 1802; M.P., 1806–1827; P.C., Presidt. Board of Trade, Chancr. of Exchequer, cr. Visct. Goderich, 1827, Earl of Ripon, 1833; &c.

Sir T. Lawrence.   C. Turner, mez, 1824.

Ha. len. to left, looking to right, holding a glove in left hand. Open letter proof.

14 × 10¹⁄₁₆. (12 × 9³⁄₁₆).   24127

RIZZIO, RIZZI, or RICCI, DAVID, –1566, b. at Turin, son of a musician and dancing-master; came to Holyrood, 1564, in the suite of the Ambassador of the Grand Duke; soon favoured by Mary, who appointed him her secretary; murdered by Darnley, Ruthven, and others.

Anon., 1564.   C. Wilkin, 1814.

Ha. len. to front, holding and playing on a lute; the face coloured; the body in outline; oval.

10½ × 8½. (5⁷⁄₁₆ × 5⁵⁄₁₆).   24241.

ROBERTS, DAVID, 1796–1864, b. at Edinb.; began as a house-painter; then practised scene-painting; exhib. at the R. A., 1826; R.A.; excelled as an architectural painter, chiefly of Eastern subjects; Pres. Soc. of Br. Artists; d. in London.

C. Baugniet del., 1844.   C. Baugniet, lith.

T. Q. len. to front, seated, looking to right, holding a sketch-book, which rests on his right thigh, and a pencil in right hand; Egyptian carvings in the background, on left; vignette; facs. signature below.

Ind. proof.

(15 × 12¼).   22269.

ROBERTSON, WILLIAM, 1721–1793, Theologian and his-torian; b. at Borthwick, Mid-Lothian; ent. Church of Scotland; Principal of Edinb. Univ.; Author of Histories of Scotland, Charles V., and America; d. at Grange House, near Edin-burgh.

Sir J. Reynolds.   J. Dixon, mez.

J. C. Smith, 30, 2nd state; but the date has been altered by hand, probably that of the publisher, to " *Feby. 1st 1773.*"

                      21944.

ROBINS, GEORGE HENRY, c. 1875–1847, son of Henry Robins, Auctioneer, Covent Garden; pursued his business with success during 50 years, being well-known for his great command of flowery language in his descriptions of property to be sold; d. at Brighton.

Anon. [Madeley (?)].   G. E. Madeley, lith.

Ha. len. to left, seated, looking to front, holding a pen in right hand, which rests on papers on a table; vignette; facs. signature below.

Ind. proof.

(9 × 8¼).   22479.

ROBINSON, MRS. ANASTASIA, c. 1695–1750, daughter of a painter at Bath; stud. music and singing under Dr. Croft, P. G. Sandoni, and "the Baroness;" sang in Handel's "Amadigi," 1715, and afterwards in other operas; quitted the stage, 1723, on being privately married to the Earl of Peterborough, who did not avow the marriage till shortly before his death, 1735.

I. Vanderbank, 1723.   I. Faber (junr.), 1727, mez.

J. C. Smith, 307, intermed. state between 2nd and 3rd; before "*& Son,*" but with "*at the Black Horse in Cornhill.*"

                      24717.

ROBINSON, FREDERICK JOHN, Rt. Hon. *See* RIPON.

ROBINSON, HENRY, 1574–1616, Bishop of Carlisle, where he was born; provost of Queen's Coll., Oxford.

Anon.   Anon., in line and aquatint.

Wh. len. kneeling, to front, his crozier on his left shoulder; in his right hand a candle surrounded with an inscription in Greek and a glory; Carlisle Cathedral in background; an angel in the clouds, and other figures; copied from his monumental brass. Inscription in Latin, 6 lines, below; followed by 4 Latin verses in two columns.

$22(?) \times 16\frac{1}{4}(?)$. $(18\frac{1}{16} \times 15\frac{1}{8})$. 29604. 1.

ROBINSON, MRS. MARY, or MARIA, 1758–1800, b. at Bristol; daughter of an American sea-captain, named Darby; resided in Great Queen St., with Mrs. Worlidge, on site of present Freemasons' Tavern; played Perdita, in the Winter's Tale, at Drury Lane, and so attracted the notice of the Prince of Wales (aftds. George IV), whose mistress she became for two years; she published several vols. of Poetry, Effusions of Love, Lyrical Tales, &c.

G. Engleheart. R. Stanier, stipple.

Full. ha. len. to front, looking to left, wearing broad-leafed hat with feather; oval; Jany. 1, 1788.

$(3\frac{7}{8} \times 3)$. 26957. 3.

ROBISON, JOHN, 1739–1805, educ. at Glasgow Univ.; went to sea as tutor to Admiral Knowles's son, being rated as a midshipman, 1759; aftds. empl. afloat, testing Harrison's chronometers, &c.; succ. Black, at Glasgow, as Prof. of Natural Philosophy, 1767; accomp. Admiral Knowles to St. Petersburg as his Sec.; Insp. Gen. of Coll. of Naval Cadets, Cronstadt, 1770–'4; Prof., Nat. Phil. Edinb., 1774; LL.D.; author of " System of Mech. Philosophy," &c.; d. at Edinburgh.

Sir H. Raeburn. C. Turner, mixed mez.

T. Q. to left, seated, looking to right, in striped gown and white linen cap, his left arm resting on arm of chair near a large open book, his right hanging over the other arm of his chair. Oct. 27, 1805.

$19\frac{3}{16} \times 13\frac{11}{16}$. $(17\frac{3}{8} \times 13\frac{1}{16})$. 27109.

ROCHESTER, JOHN WILMOT, 2nd Earl of, 1647–1680, Poet and Courtier; son of Henry, 1st Earl; educ. at Oxford; personal favourite of the King; noted for his wit and profligacy; wrote satires and songs; d. repentant, according to Bishop Burnet, who ministered to him on his death-bed.

Sir P. Lely. R. White, 1681.

Sh. ha. len., to front, head turned to left, looking to front, long wig, lace handkerchief, oval with bays; arms below; title in 4 lines on plinth at foot; " Sold by R. White in Bloomsbury Market neare the Golden heart."

$15\frac{3}{16} \times 10\frac{11}{16}$. $(13 \times 10\frac{5}{16})$. 22268.

ROCHESTER, LAWRENCE HYDE, Earl of, 1641–1781; 2nd son of Edward, Earl of Clarendon; M.P., 1660–1681; Ambassador; Secret Envoy to the Prince of Orange; First Lord of Treasury; P.C.; cr. Earl, 1682; K.G., Lord High Treasurer; Lord Lieut., Ireland; Lord President of Council; &c.

Sir G. Kneller. J. Houbraken, 1741.

Sh. ha. len. to right, looking to front, wearing chain and
George ; oval in border.
  $14\frac{1}{10}\times 9\frac{1}{4}$. $(14\frac{1}{2}\times 8\frac{1}{2})$.   27120.

ROCHFORD, WILLIAM HENRY ZULESTEIN DE NASSAU, 4th Earl
  of, 1717–1781 ; suc., 1738 ; Ambassador to Turin, Madrid, and
  Paris ; Sec. of State, 1768–1775 ; K.G., 1778.
    Peronneau.   V. Green, mez.
    J. C. Smith, 111, 2nd state.   27660.

ROCKINGHAM, CHARLES WATSON-WENTWORTH, 1730–1782 ;
  suc. 1750 ; F.R.S., K.G., P.C., First Lord of Treasury, 1765,
  and 1782.
    Sir J. Reynolds.   E. Fisher, mez.
    J. C. Smith, 52, an intermediate state between the 3rd and
  4th described by J. C. S. ; with the date, 1775, and still published by E. Fisher.
    From the collection of John Young.   23145.

RODEN, ROBERT JOCELYN, Earl of, 1788–1870 ; Baron Clan-
  brassil, Newport, &c. ; M.P. Louth ; suc. 1820.
    F. R. Say.   T. Lupton, mez.
    T. Q. len. to front, looking to left, wearing ribbon and star.
    Proof before letters ; April 28, 1839.
    $22\frac{1}{8}\times 17\frac{1}{2}$. $(16\frac{3}{4}\times 13\frac{5}{8})$.   27276.

RODNEY, GEORGE BRIDGES, Lord, 1718–1792 ; entd. navy,
  rapidly promoted ; cr. Bart., 1761, for his services ; M.P. for
  Northampton, and aftds. for Westminster ; after his great
  victory, 1782, over De Grasse, off Guadaloupe, was cr. Baron ;
  Vice-Admiral ; K.B. ; &c.
    T. Gainsborough, R.A.   G. Dupont, mez.
    J. C. Smith, 9, 2nd state.   25796.

    Sir J. Reynolds.   W. Dickinson, mez.
    As Sir George Bridges Rodney, Bart., Admiral of the White.
    J. C. Smith, 70.   E. 340.–'90.

ROGERS, SAMUEL, 1763–1855, b. at Stoke Newington ; son of a
  banker ; applied himself to study of art and letters ; travelled ;
  suc. to ample fortune at death of his father, 1793 ; quitted
  business ; pubd. "Pleasures of Memory," 1792 ; "Poems,"
  1798 ; "Italy," 1822, &c. ; patron of art and entertainer of
  literary and other distinguished men.
    [G. Richmond ?]   Anon. chalk and stipple.
    Bust, to right, looking to front ; life-size ; vignette.
    Ind. proof before all letters.
    $(18\frac{1}{2}\times 18)$.   27084.

ROGET, PETER MARK, 1779–1869, physician and physiologist ;
  b. in London ; stud. at Edinb. ; pract. at Manchester, and aftds.
  in London ; M.D. ; F.R.S., Sec. to the R. S. ; Lecturer on

4

Physiology at the Royal Inst.; author of Bridgwater Treatise on " Animal and Vegetable Physiology, considered with reference to Natural Theology," " Treatises on Physiology and Phrenology" and "Thesaurus of English Words and Phrases."

E. U. Eddis. J. Cochran, stipple.

Ha. len. to front, left hand in breast, coat buttoned across chest; facs. signature below; 1839.

11½ × 9. (4½ × 3¾). 27606.

ROMAINE, Rev. William, 1714-1795, b. at Hartlepool, his father being a refugee from France on the Rev. of the Edict of Nantes; educ. at Oxford; Lecturer at St. Botolph's; Morning Preacher at St. George's, Han. Sq.; zealous disciple of Hutchinson; Rector of St. Andrew's, Wardrobe, and St. Anne's, Blackfriars, and a most popular preacher; oppos. the Bill for Naturalization of Jews; author of " Life, Walk, and Triumph of Faith;" d. at Clapham.

F. Cotes. R. Houston, mez.

J. C. Smith, 105, 1st state. 21923.

ROMILLY, Sir Samuel, 1757-1818; lawyer and politician; Solicitor-General, 1806; published "Observations on the Criminal Law of England," 1810; died by his own hand, in a paroxysm of cerebral inflammation.

M. Cregan. S. W. Reynolds, junr., mez.

Ha. len. to front, seated.

Open letter proof, Decr. 1, 1818.

14¼ × 10¼. (11¾ × 9¹⁴⁄₁₆). 22530.

ROMNEY, George, 1734-1802, b. at Dalton-le-Furness, apprent. to a cabinet-maker; acquired some skill in that trade and in wood-carving; showed taste for music, made himself a fiddle, on which he played; took to painting portraits; married, and deserted his wife and two children; travelled to Rome; returned, 1775; became fashionable portrait-painter; painted some subjects; discovered Emma Lyon, afterwards Lady Hamilton; retired, 1798; returned to his wife; became imbecile; d. at Kendal.

Romney. (J. Jackson, R.A., delt.) W. T. Fry, stipple.

Sh. ha. len. to left, looking to front, wearing cloak; vignette.

June 4, 1817.

(7 × 6½). E. 2208.-'89.

M. A. Shee, R.A. W. Bond, stipple.

Full ha. len. to front, looking to right, wearing cloak.

Done for " The Fine Arts of the English School," by J. Britton and W. Bond, March 1, 1810.

11⅝ × 10. (7½ × 6). 27228.

RONALDS, Sir Francis, 1788-1873, b. in London; son of a merchant; educ. at a private school at Cheshunt; early showed taste for orig. expts., for which he made his own apparatus;

excellent draughtsman; stud. electricity; wrote several papers on Electro-Galvanic Agency, &c., pubd. in Phil. Mag., 1814; demonstr. practically the feasibility of the Electric Telegraph, at Hammersmith, 1816; author of "Mechanical Perspective," "Sketches at Carnac, Brittany" (with A. Blair), 1836; first Hon. Director of Kew Observatory; F.R.S., 1844; invented many instruments, including self-registering magnet, and meteorol. insts.; retired from **Kew**, 1852; spent last 10 years of life at Battle, Sussex; Knt. 1870.

See SCIENCE.

ROOKE, Sir George, 1650–1709, b. in Kent; ent. the Navy early; Capt. 1673; took part in the Battles off Beachy Head, 1690, and Cape Harfleur, 1692; burned the French ships off La Hogue; Vice-Admiral of England, 1701; victorious with the Duke of Ormonde, at Vigo, and destroyed the galleons, 1702; took Gibraltar, 1704; M.P for Portsmouth, but, in consequence of his opposition to the Whig party, allowed to spend the rest of his life in retirement.

M. Dahl.   R. Williams, mez.
J. C. Smith, 51, 2nd, or possibly 1st state (?).   22270.
The engraver's name has been scratched out (?), and put in again (?) with a pen and ink.

ROSCOE, William, 1753–1831, historian, b. at Liverpool; articled to an attorney, 1767, commenced practice, 1774; but devoted to literature, wrote poetry, the "Life of Lorenzo de' Medici," 1796, the "History of the Life and Pontificate of Leo X." 1805; M.P. for Liverpool for a short time; banker till 1820, when the firm was bankrupt.

J. Thomson.   J. Thomson, stipple.
Sh. ha. len. to right; vignette; facs. signature below.
This occurs in the European Magazine, Augt. 1, 1822.
Ind. proof.
$9\frac{1}{2} \times 5\frac{1}{2}$. $(4\frac{3}{4} \times 4\frac{1}{4})$.   28298. **7.**

ROSS, Alexander,   –   , Resident Engineer of the Conway District; employed in construction of the famous tubular bridge.

See MENAI STRAITS.

ROSS, Sir James Clark, 1800–1862, Antarctic discoverer, nephew of Sir John Ross; b. in London; ent. the Navy; accomp. his uncle on 5 voyages to the Polar Seas; comm. the "Erebus" on a scientific expedition to the Antarctic Ocean, 1839–'43; knighted on his return; comm. an expedition in search of Sir John Franklin, 1848; F.R.S.

T. H. Maguire.   T. H. Maguire, lith., 1851.
Ha. len. to front, looking to right, in uniform, a globe at his left hand; rectilin. with corners lopped off.
$(10\frac{3}{4} \times 9\frac{1}{2})$.   22533.
See also ARCTIC COUNCIL.

ROSS, Sir William, R.A., Kt., 1794–1860, miniature-painter, b. in London; son of H. Ross, miniature-painter, and Mrs. Maria Ross, portrait-painter; showed precocious talent for drawing; carried off several prizes of the Society of Arts and Academy Schools; exhibited at age of 15; painted in oils; but most successful in miniatures, of which he executed on ivory over 2,200, including the Queen and Royal Family; R.A., 1839.

C. Baugniet.   C. Baugniet, 1844, lith.
T. Q. len. to front, looking to right, holding brush in right hand, miniature in left, resting on table.
(15¾ × 12½).   24242.

ROSSE, William Parsons, Earl of, 1800–1867, Astronomer; educ. at Magd. Coll., Oxon.; suc., 1841; devoted years of labour and experiment to the construction, at great expense, of the largest telescope in the world, which he erected at his family seat, Birr Castle, Parsonstown, Ireland; obtained by this a better knowledge of the moon's surface and of the nebulæ than before; P.R.S., 1849–'54; author of an account of his telescope, "Letters on the State of Ireland," &c.; a statue of him was erected at Parsonstown, 1876.

Claudet daguer.   Bosley, lith.
Ha. len. to front, seated, looking to left; facs. signature below; arched at top.
Proof, Sepr. 1, 1849.
(8¾ × 8⅞).   27637.

ROSSLYN, Alexander Wedderburn, Earl of, 1733–1805, Scottish Judge and Statesman, son of a Lord of Session; Sol.-Gen., 1778; Attorney-Gen., 1778; Lord Chf. Justice of Com. Pleas, 1780; Lord Chancellor of England, 1793; cr. Lord Loughborough, 1780; Earl of Rosslyn, 1801; presided at the Gordon Trials, 1780.

W. Owen.   F. Bartolozzi, line and stipple.
T. Q. to front, slightly inclined to left, looking to front, wearing Chancellor's robes; the mace is by his right hand.
Proof before letters, except artists' names and publication-line, Feb. 1, 1800; arms in centre, with no motto.
20⅛ × 15⅛. (16½ × 13⅜).   21830.

J. Northcote, R.A. (J. Jackson del.).   H. Meyer, stipple.
Ha. len. to left, seated, looking to front, in robes, with mace, &c.; Decr. 7. 1812.
(13½ × 9¾.)   24290.

ROTHSCHILD, Nathan Mayer, 1777–1836, banker, financier, millionnaire, came to England, 1800, as agent for his father (Mayer Anselm, at Frankfort), for buying Manchester goods for the Continent; became agent for the Elector of Hesse Cassel and other German princes; effected loans and transactions in

bullion and foreign exchanges; d. at Frankfort; buried in London.
Anon. W. Walker, mez.
Ha, len. to front, slightly turned and looking to front.
Proof; private plate; facs. signature below; 1837.
$15\frac{7}{16} \times 12$. $(12\frac{1}{16} \times 9\frac{3}{16})$. 23030.

ROUBILLIAC, Louis François, c. 1703–1762, sculptor; b. at Lyons; pupil of Balthazar at Dresden; came to England, where he executed his principal works, some of which are in Westminster Abbey; travelled in Italy with Arthur Pond.
A. Carpantiers. W. Holl.
T. Q. len. to left, designing the statue of Shakspere.
This was engraved for Wivell's Shakspere series; being a duplicate of No. 14 (28836. 15). 28297. 4.

A. Carpentiers. T. Chambars.
T. Q. len. to left, designing the statue of Shakspere. 26266.
This occurs in Walpole's "Anecdotes," Vol. IV., 1771.

ROUTH, Martin Joseph, 1755–1854, b. at South Elmham, near Beccles, where his father was Rector; entd. as a battler at Queen's Coll., Oxf., 1770; elected a demy of Magd. Coll., 1771; M.A. and a fellow, 1776; Coll. Librarian, 1781; Senior Proctor, 1783; junr. Dean of Arts, 1784–'5; B.D., 1786; Coll. Bursar, 1791; President, 1791 till his death; a profound and acute critic; pubd. a few excellent treatises.
T. C. Thompson, R.H.A. D. Lucas, mixed mez.
Full hn. len. slightly to right, standing with hands together, an open book before him, in his stall.
Jany. 2, 1843.
$20\frac{1}{12} \times 15\frac{1}{3}$. $(15\frac{11}{12} \times 12\frac{3}{16})$. 24633.

ROXBURGHE, John Ker, 3rd Duke of, 1740–1804; b. in London; educ. at Eton; suc., 1755; great book-collector; his library sold, 1812, created extraordinary excitement among collectors; commemorated by the foundation of the Roxburghe Club, chiefly for republication of rare books.
Anon. Anon., stipple.
Sh. ha. len. to left, looking to front; vignette.
Ind. proof, May 1, 1816, pubd. by William Clarke, New Bond St.
$14\frac{1}{2} \times 11\frac{7}{16}$. $(6 \times 6\frac{1}{4})$. 22528.

ROXBURGHE, Susanna Stephania, Duchess of, V.A., c. 1814–1895, only child of Lt.-General Sir James Charles Dalbiac, K.C.H., M.P. Ripon; she was m., 1836, to James Henry Robert, 6th Duke, who d. 1879; she was lady of the bedchamber to the Queen so early as 1868, and was appointed Acting-Mistress of the Robes, 1892.
A. Robertson. Cochran, stipple.

Ha. len. to front, looking to left, wearing a low dress; ringlets; an eye-glass in her left hand; rectilin., the corners cut off.

Proof before all letters, except the artists' names, which are scarcely visible; 1836.

$14\frac{1}{16} \times 1\frac{1}{16}$. $(9\frac{1}{2} \times 7\frac{7}{16})$.   E. 1064.-'88.

ROY, ROBERT, schoolmaster, of Burlington-street.

     M. A. Shee, R.A.   J. Heath, A.R.A.

     T. Q. len. to left, seated, holding in right hand a book lettered EUCLID ELEM^s., resting on right thigh; left arm on table.

     Published Feby. 10, 1804, by Messrs. Colnaghi & Co., and others, though Evans calls this a private plate, which would seem a mistake.

$20\frac{1}{8} \times 15\frac{5}{16}$. $(16\frac{3}{4} \times 13\frac{1}{2})$.   29697 c.

RUMFORD, COUNT. See THOMPSON.

     See also SCIENCE.

RUPERT, PRINCE, 1619-1682, 3rd son of Frederick, Elector Palatine of the Rhine, and Princess Elizabeth, and therefore nephew of Charles I., on whose side he fought in the Civil War, with more courage than wisdom; disting. at sieges of Worcester, Cirencester, Birmingham, and Bristol; cr. Duke of Buckingham; K.G.; outgeneralled by Cromwell, and retired abroad; returned after Restoration, held a naval command, defeating the Dutch, 1673; pursued art and study of mathematics and chemistry; practised mezzotinto-scraping, but did not invent it; d. at his house in Spring Gardens.

     W. Dobson.   W. Faithorne.

     L. Fagan, p. 13, 2nd state.   24128.

     Van Dyck.   J. Cochran.

     T. Q. len to front, wearing sword, and holding a staff in right hand; helmet in background.

     This occurs in Lodge's "Portraits," Feb. 1, 1829.

$10 \times 7\frac{9}{16}$ (?). $(4\frac{3}{4} \times 3\frac{1}{16})$.   E. 2213-'89.

RURAL AMUSEMENT. See PATTISSON.

RUSHWORTH, JOHN, c. 1607-1690. b. in Northumberland; educ. at Queen's Coll., Oxford; barrister of Linc. Inn; assist. clerk, H. of Commons, 1640; M.P., Berwick; much employd in negotiations during civil wars; sec. to Ld. Keeper Bridgeman, after Restoration; pubd. "Historical Collections," with trial of Strafford, valuable, though partial; d. in K. Bench Prison.

     [R. White (?)]   R. White.

     Bust, to front, wrapped in a cloak; oval in border; frontispiece to his "Historical Collections," 3rd Part, 1692.

$(9\frac{1}{8} \times 5\frac{15}{16})$.   22914.

RUSSELL, Lord John, aftds. 1st Earl, 1792–1878, 3rd son of John, 6th Duke of Bedford; educ. at Westminster and Edinb. Univ.; M.P., 1813; became a disting. statesman, orator, and writer; held various high offices of State, and was Prime Minister, 1846–'52, Foreign Sec. 1859, and held that office till 1865, when he again became premier; retired, 1866; cr. Earl Russell and Visct. Amberley, 1861.

See COMMONS (2), and ABERDEEN CABINET.

RUSSELL, William, Lord, 1639–1683, politician; 3rd and eldest surviving son of William, 1st Duke of Bedford; M.P. for co. Beds.; P.C., 1679; supported the Exclusion Bill, and presented the Duke of York as a recusant in Westminster Hall; was accused falsely, but convicted, of complicity in the "Rye House Plot," and executed; the proceedings were annulled after the Revolution.

Sir G. Kneller.   P. Vanderbanck.

Sh. ha. len., to right, looking to front, wearing long wig, lace bands, and cloak; oval in border; arms beneath oval; title below, in 2 lines.

$(31\frac{1}{4} \times 10\frac{1}{2})$.   22267.

G. Hayter.   J. Bromley, mixed mez.

Wh. len. in Trial Scene, a purely imaginary composition of many figures.

Proof with scratched letters, 1830.

$19\frac{7}{8} \times 25$. $(13\frac{11}{16} \times 21)$.   15585.

RUTHERFORD, Andrew, Lord, 1792–1854, Judge and Politician; called to the Scottish Bar, 1812; Sol.-Gen. for Scotland, 1837; Lord Advocate, 1839–'41 and 1846–'51; M.P. for Leith Burghs, 1839–'51; d. in St. Colme St., Edinburgh.

J. W. Gordon, A.R.A., R.S.A.   T. Lupton, mixed mez.

T. Q. len. to front, in robes, seated, hands together, books on table on right; crest and motto below, with facs. signature.

Ind. proof; Feb. 1, 1848.

$10\frac{13}{16} \times 15$. $(17 \times 13\frac{3}{4})$.   22915.

RUTHERFORD, Daniel, 1742–1819, natural philosopher and physician, b. at Edinburgh; stud. in the University there; succ. Dr. John Hope as Professor of Botany and Keeper of the Botanic Garden, 1786; discoverer of nitrogen, and first who represented oxygen as the necessary constituent of all acids.

See SCIENCE.

RUTLAND, Edward, Earl of. See NAVAL HEROES (1).

RUTLAND, John J. R. Manners, 6th Duke of. See MANNERS.

RYDER, Sir Dudley, 1691–1756: Attorney-General, and knighted, 1737; chief-justice, 1754; P.C.; &c.

J. Crank.   J. Faber, junr., mez.

J. C. Smith, 313.   27277.

RYLAND, WILLIAM WYNNE, 1738–1783, engraver; b. in London; apprent., c. 1752, to Ravenet; went abroad, c. 1760, and travelled several years, improving himself; returned home, engraved the King and Lord Bute, refused by Strange, and the Queen, after Cotes; engraver to his Majesty; worked first in line; later in imitation of chalk; extravagant and irregular; executed for forgery.

   P. Falconet del., 1768.   D. P. Pariset.

Bust to left, in profile; **medallion in** border; one of the set of artists engraved by Pariset.

   ($6\frac{7}{8} \times 4\frac{15}{16}$; med., $3\frac{7}{16}$ diamr.).   E. 2214.–'89.

RYSBRACK, JOHN MICHAEL, 1693–1770, sculptor, b. at Antwerp, son of a landscape-painter; came to England, 1720; soon found employment in portrait busts; executed many monuments in Westminster Abbey and elsewhere; retired, 1766, and sold his models, casts, &c. by auction; d. in Vere St., Oxford St.

   J. Vanderbanck, 1728.   J. Faber, junr., mez.

   J. C. Smith, 314, 2nd state, retouched.   21860.

See also ARTISTS, A Society of.

SABINE, SIR EDWARD, 1788–1883, served in the Royal Artillery, 1803–'14; explorer under Ross and Parry, 1818–'19; made several voyages; F.R.S.; V.P.R.S., 1850; K.C.B., &c.

See ARCTIC COUNCIL.

SACHEVERELL, HENRY, 1672(?)–1724, educ. at Oxford; D.D., 1708; impeached by the House of Commons, 1709, for sermons preached at St. Saviour's, Southwark, and at St. Paul's, and the two sermons sentenced to be burnt; suspended for three years; the condemnation of the sermons, of which the object was to excite hostility against Dissenters, overthrew the Ministry and made the fortune of the preacher, who was presented to the rectory of St. Andrews, Holborn, 1713.

   A. Russell, 1710.   J. Smith, mez.

   J. C. Smith, 219, 2nd state.   21869.

SACKVILLE, LORD GEORGE GERMAIN, 1st Viscount, 1716–1785, general and statesman; 3rd son of 1st Duke of Dorset; fought at Dettingen, Fontenoy, and Culloden; dismissed from the service for his conduct at Minden, 1769; Colonial Minister, 1775–'82; cr. Viscount, 1782; took the name of Germain on succeeding to the estate of Lady Betty Germain; was one of the many reputed authors of "The Letters of Junius."

   G. Romney.   J. Jacobé, mez.

   J. C. Smith, 3, 2nd state.   22238.

SADLER, JAMES, "first English aëronaut;" made balloon ascents at York, Liverpool, Lincoln, &c.; lectured at Surrey Institution.

   B. Taylor del.   B. Taylor, chalk and dot.

Sh. ha. len. to front, looking to left; vignette; May 1, 1812.

   $9\frac{7}{8} \times 8\frac{13}{16}$.   ($5\frac{1}{2} \times 6\frac{1}{8}$).   23037.

SAINT ALBANS. *See* BACON, Francis.

SAINT-LEONARDS, Edward Burtenshaw Sugden, Lord, 1781–1875; solicitor-general, 1829, Lord Chancellor (Ireland), 1835, again, 1841–'46; Lord High Chancellor, and cr. Baron, 1852.
Anon.   W. Walker, mez.
T. Q. len., to right, seated, looking to left, in robes and wig.
Proof before all letters.
21½ × 16¼.   (18⅜ × 14¼).   27278.

ST. PATRICK, Installation of Knights of the Order of.
J. K. Sherwin.   "Partly engraved by J. K. Sherwin, but finished by others after his decease."
The Installation Banquet, held in St. Patrick's Hall, Dublin Castle, presided over by the Marquess of Buckingham (q. v.), Lord-Lieutenant of Ireland (in 1782, and again in 1787), Grand Master of the Order.
Proof before all letters.
The picture, which, according to Redgrave, was 50 or 60 feet long, " so far as it was carried, was an absolute failure."
(22½ × 31).   27147. A.
With this is a MS. tracing (or sketch) of a key to the names of the personages represented.   27147. B.

SAINT-VINCENT, John Jervis, Earl of, 1735–1823; educ. at Burton-on-Trent free school, and Greenwich; midshipman, 1748; Post-Captain, 1760; K.B., 1782; M.P. 1783–'94; Rear-Admiral, 1787; Vice-Admiral, 1793; Admiral, 1795; cr. Baron Jervis and Earl of St. Vincent, 1797, in which year he gained a victory over the Spanish fleet; cr. Visct. St. Vincent, 1802; Admiral of Red, 1805; Admiral of Fleet, 1821; G.C.B.
Sir W. Beechey, R.A.   C. Turner, mez.
Wh. len. to front, looking to right, in robes; a globe and books on table, on left, behind him, and a picture of naval battle.   Scr. letter proof, Novr. 11, 1816.
24½ × 16¾.   (22⅜ × 16¾)   21898.
See also COMMEMORATION (2).

SALE, Florentia, Lady, daughter of Mr. George Wynch, and wife of Sir Robert Henry Sale, "the hero of Jellalabad," to whom she was m. in 1809; her heroic conduct during the too memorable retreat from Afghanistan will not be soon forgotten
                                                  Anon., mez.
Full ha. len. to front, wearing a turban and low dress, with brooch, bracelet, and rings.
12 × 9⅝.   (9⁹⁄₁₆ × 7⅜).   27956.

SALE, Sir Robert Henry, 1783–1845, "the hero of Jellalabad," ent. army, 1795; served with distinction in India and Burmah; compelled Dost Mahommed to surrender, 1840; successfully defended Jellalabad during the disastrous retreat from

Afghanistan, 1842; recovered Cabul; fell in the Battle of
Moodkee; Maj.-General, G.C.B., &c.

H. Moseley.   T. L. Atkinson, mixed mez.

T. Q. len. to front, holding his sword, in scabbard, across his
chest with both hands; a cannon on the right, a fortress on
left, in distance; Novr. 1, 1845.

$21\frac{3}{8} \times 16\frac{1}{4}$. ($17\frac{3}{8} \times 13\frac{1}{4}$).   21952.

SALISBURY, JAMES CECIL, 7th Earl of, 1748–1823; D.C.L.;
M.P.; Treasurer of Household; suc., 1780; P.C.; Lord
Chamberlain; F.R.S.; cr. Marquis, 1789; K.G., &c.

Sir W. Beechey, 1803.   W. Say, mez.

Wh. len. slightly to left, looking to front, in robes of Garter.
Open letter proof. The inscription is on a separate plate at
foot. Excl. of additional plate, ($26 \times 17\frac{2}{3}$).   24243.

SALISBURY, ROBERT CECIL, 1st Earl of, 1563–1612; M.P.,
1584; Kt., 1591; Sec. of State, 1596; Privy Seal, P.C., cr.
Baron, 1603; Visct., 1604; Earl, 1605; K.G., Lord High
Treasr., &c.

In Birch's "Lives."   Anon., 1747.

Certainly, *not* by Houbraken, as stated by "Bromley."

$14\frac{1}{16} \times 9$. ($13\frac{1}{8} \times 8\frac{3}{8}$).   27279.

SALOMONS, SIR DAVID, 1797–1873, Alderman, Sheriff, 1835;
M.P., 1851; Lord Mayor, 1855; Sheriff of Kent, 1839; author
of works on Banking, Currency, and Persecution of Jews.

Mrs. C. Pearson.   C. Turner, A.R.A., mez.

T. Q. len. to right, looking to front, in robes, with chain, &c.;
March 1, 1837.

$21 \times 15\frac{1}{2}$. ($16\frac{3}{4} \times 12\frac{13}{16}$).   27141.

SANCROFT, WILLIAM, 1616–1693, b. at Fressingfield, Suffolk;
educ. at, and fellow of, Emm. Coll., Cambr.; lost his fellowship,
1649; at Restoration, became Rector of Houghton-le-Spring,
1660; Preb., Durham, 1661–'2; Master, Emm. Coll., 1662;
Dean of York, 1663–'4; Dean of St. Paul's, 1664; Archbishop
of Canterbury, 1677–'8; sent to the Tower, 1688; suspended;
displaced by Tillotson, 1681.

D. Loggan.   D. Loggan, 1689.

Sh. ha. len., slightly to right, looking to front, in robes; oval
in border; arms below, and three lines of Latin inscription.

($13\frac{3}{16} \times 9\frac{3}{4}$).   25801.

See also the SEVEN BISHOPS.   26668.

SANDBY, PAUL, 1725–1809, b. at Nottingham; came to London,
1745; employed by Gen. Watson in the Highlands, and by Sir
Joseph Banks; introduced *aqua-tint* engraving; an original
R.A.; chief drawing-master to Woolwich Academy, 1768;
many plates have been published by him, and after his drawings
in pencil and water-colours.

F. Cotes.   E. Fisher, mez.

J. C. Smith, 55.   22097.

SANDBY, PAUL—*continued.*
G. Dance, Dec. 21, 1794.   W. Daniell.
Sh. ha. len. to right, in profile; vignette; Dec. 15, 1809.
$10\frac{1}{8} \times 7\frac{7}{8}$. $(7 \times 4\frac{1}{2})$.   28299.   4.

────────

P. Jean, miniat.   J. Thomson.
Sh. ha. len. to right, looking to front; Windsor Castle in the
distance; oval.
$(4\frac{1}{4} \times 3\frac{3}{16})$.   28200.   54.

────────

Sir W. Beechey, R.A.   (W. Evans delt.)   H. Landseer,
                                                     stipple.
Sh. ha. len. to right, wearing waistcoat with large rolling
collar; vignette. Decr. 4, 1809.
$(7\frac{1}{4} \times 7\frac{1}{4})$.   E. 2225.-'89.

SANDERSON, NICHOLAS, 1682–1739, Mathematician; b. at
Thurleston, Yorks.; lost his sight, when 12 months old, by
small-pox; in spite of this, acquired great knowledge of Classics
and mathematics; lectured on the Newtonian philosophy at
Cambridge; Lucasian Prof. of Mathematics, 1711; LL.D., &c.
J. Vanderbanck.   J. Faber, junr. mez.
J. C. Smith, 316.   22478.

SANDERSON, SIR WILLIAM, c. 1585–1676, secretary to George
Villiers, Duke of Buckingham; attached to Charles I. during
the civil war; author of "Graphice. The use of the Pen and
Pensil," &c., 1658, and "A compleat History of the Life and
Raigne of King Charles," &c., 1658.
Anon.   W. Faithorne, 1658.
This is prefixed to the first of the two works named above.
L. Fagan, p. 58, 1st state.   24434.

SANDFORD, DANIEL, 1766–1830, b. at Delville, near Dublin;
educ. at Ch. Ch., Oxf.; minister of an Episcopalian Congregn.
(for which a Chapel was built, 1797), at Edinburgh, 1792;
joined Episcl. Ch. of Scotland, 1803; Bishop of Edinb., 1806;
consecrated for his own congregn. the new Chapel of St.
John, 1818; pubd. "Lectures," "Sermons," &c.; D.D. Oxon.
J. W. Gordon.   W. Walker, etched, and S. Cousins, mez.
T. Q., len. to right, seated, holding spectacles in right hand in
his lap.
A private plate.
Open letter proof; March 1, 1829.
$15\frac{1}{2} \times 12$. $(10\frac{5}{8} \times 8\frac{1}{4})$.   27553.

SANDWICH, EDWARD MONTAGU, 1st Earl of, 1625–1672;
Colonel under Cromwell, 1653; Admiral with Blake, 1656;
conveyed Charles II. to England, 1660; cr. Earl, 1660; helped
to defeat the Dutch, 1665; killed in the battle of Southwold
Bay.
Anon.   Maurit. Lang.

Sh. ha. len. to left, looking to front; with long hair, in armour; 2 lines of inscription below, in Italian; numbered 197 at top, on right; probably from an Italian history, or collection of portraits.
($7\frac{5}{8} \times 5\frac{7}{8}$). 20923.

SANDWICH, Edward Montagu—*continued.*
Sir P. Lely. A. Blooteling.
Sh. ha. len. to right, looking to front, in armour, wearing long dark wig, the George, &c.; oval in border; title in 5 lines on a tablet below the oval.
$13\frac{5}{8} \times 10\frac{1}{8}$. ($8\frac{1}{8} \times 7\frac{1}{8}$, inside oval). 21974.

SANDWICH, Edward Montagu, 2nd Earl of, (b. before) 1648–1689; M.P., 1670–'2; suc., 1672; Ambassador Extraord. to Lisbon, 1678; &c.
Sir P. Lely. A. Blooteling.
Full ha. len. to right, looking to front, with hand to breast, in loose robe.
($8\frac{3}{4} \times 7\frac{1}{2}$). 20922.

SANDWICH, John Montagu, 1718–1792, 4th Earl of; Statesman; suc., 1729; Minister Plenipo. at Aix-la-Chapelle, 1746; First Lord of the Admiralty, 1748–'51, and 1771–'82.
J. Zauffely. V. Green, 1774, mez.
J. C. Smith, 117, 3rd state. 22102.

—

T. Gainsborough, R.A. J. K. Sherwin.
Wh. len. to front, looking to left, holding in left hand a paper, on which is the word "INFIRMARY;" Greenwich Hospital partly seen behind him; he is leaning on one of its pillars.
Open letter proof; Jany. 1, 1788.
$25 \times 17\frac{7}{8}$. ($22\frac{1}{8} \times 15\frac{1}{8}$). **21985.**

SASS, Henry, 1788–1844, portrait-painter and teacher; b. in London, son of an undistinguished artist; stud. in R. A. schools; exhibited, 1808, his first work; visited Italy, 1816; continued to exhibit, without success; devoted himself to elementary teaching in art; very successful; painted many portraits; retired from his school, because of ill-health, some time before his death.
Anon. E. Stalker.
T. Q. len. slightly to right, looking to front, holding crayon in right hand; behind, on right, are a bust of Raffaelle, a skull, and a paper inscribed "Elements of Art," on which he rests left hand.
Ind. proof with open letters; March 7th, 1822.
$10\frac{1}{2} \times 8\frac{7}{8}$. ($7\frac{11}{16} \times 6\frac{1}{8}$). 28261.

SAUMAREZ, Sir James (afterwards Lord) de, 1757–1836, Admiral; ent. the Navy, 1772; second in command to Nelson at the battle of the Nile, 1799; gained the victory of Algeciras;

Commanded in Chief in the Baltic, 1814; Vice-Admiral of
England, 1831, General of Marines, and cr. Baron; K.B.
    T. Phillips, R.A.   W. Say, mixed mez.
    Wh. len. to left, looking to front, leaning on his sword; ships
in the distance; ropes and anchor in foreground.
    $24\frac{3}{4} \times 16\frac{7}{10}$. $(23\frac{7}{8} \times 16\frac{1}{4})$.   22095.

SAUNDERS, Sir Charles,   -1775, Admiral, served under
    Anson and Hawke; M.P. for Plymouth, 1750; Admiral, 1759;
    assisted Wolfe in capture of Quebec; K.B., 1761; First Lord,
    1766; bur. in Westminster Abbey, near monument of Wolfe.
    See TRIUMPH OF BRITANNIA.

SAUNDERS, William, 1743-1817, b. in Scotland; stud.
    medicine at Edinb.; settled in London; M.D.; Bart.; physician
    to Guy's Hospital, 1770; physician extraordinary to the Pr.
    of Wales; greatly improved the system of teaching medical
    science; pubd. several learned works.
    See MEDICAL SOCIETY.

SAVILE, Sir George, Bart., 1727-1784; son of Sir George
    Savile of Rufford; suc., 1748; F.R.S.; Vice-president of
    Society of Arts and Sciences; M.P., county York; Colonel, 1st
    battalion, West Riding Militia; d. unmarried.
    B. Wilson.   " Engraved & etched by B. W. and Mr.
                                                  Basire."
    Wh. len. to left, seated, looking to right, resting right hand on
a plan of "The Calder Navigation," which lies on a table; window
in background, on left. Published, Decr. 4, 1770.
    $19\frac{13}{16} \times 13\frac{9}{16}$. $(17\frac{7}{16} \times 12\frac{1}{2})$.
    From the Burleigh James Collection.   E. 1659. '89.

SAWBRIDGE, John,   -1795, Alderman, M.P. for Hythe;
    Lord Mayor, 1776; supported Wilkes.
    B. West.   T. Watson, mez.
    J. C. Smith, 32.   24129.
    See also BECKFORD.

SAXE-COBURG-GOTHA. See EDINBURGH, Duke of.

SCARLETT, James. See ABINGER.

SCARLETT, The Hon. Sir James Yorke, 1799-1871, son of the
    1st Lord Abinger; Lieut.-Genl.; distinguished at the battle of
    Balaklava, 1854; suc. Lord Lucan in command of Cavalry in
    Crimea, 1855; Adj.-Genl., 1860; G.C.B., 1869.
    E. Havell.   V. Brooks, lith.
    Sh. ha. len. to right, looking to front; facs. signature below.
Sep. 22, 1862.
    Vignette. $(10\frac{1}{2} \times 9\frac{1}{2})$.   27229.

SCHIAVONETTI, Lewis, 1765-1810, b. at Bassano; son of a
    poor stationer; pupil of G. Colini, came to England, 1790;
    befriended and instructed by Bartolozzi; executed many plates

after Van Dyck, Michael Angelo, Blake, Loutherbourg, and others; largely employed in book-illustration; worked both in line and in stipple with admirable effect.

H. Edridge.   A. Cardon, stipple.
Sh. ha. len. to front, looking to right; vignette.
Open letter proof, on Ind. paper; Jany. 1, 1811.
$11\frac{3}{8} \times 9\frac{7}{16}$. $(5\frac{3}{4} \times 5\frac{1}{4})$ 22916.

SCHOMBERG, ISAAC, -1813, naval officer and historian; served in American War; disting. himself in the victory gained by Rodney over Count de Grasse; capt. of "Culloden," under Howe, on June 1, 1794; Commissioner of Navy; author of "Naval Chronology," 5 vols.
See COMMEMORATION (1).

SCIENCE, THE DISTINGUISHED MEN OF, of Great Britain, living in the years 1807-8; a group of 51 portrait-figures, viz., Sir William Herschell, Francis Baily, William J. Frodsham, Sir John Leslie, Prof. J. Playfair, Dr. Daniel Rutherford, Dr Nevil Maskelyne, Peter Dollond, Dr. Thomas Young, Robert Brown, Dr. Edward Jenner, Davies Giddy Gilbert, Sir Joseph Banks, Capt. Henry Kater, Dr. William Smith, Edward C. Howard, Hon. Henry Cavendish, Wm. Allen, Dr. William Henry, Dr. W. H. Wollaston, Charles Hatchett, Dr. John Dalton, Sir Humphry Davy, Henry Maudslay, Sir M. I. Brunel, Sir Samuel Bentham, Matthew Boulton, Bishop Watson, Capt. J. Huddart, James Watt, Count Rumford, Thomas Telford, William Murdoch, John Rennie, William Chapman, William Jessop, Robert Mylne, Sir William Congreve, Samuel Crompton, Bryan Donkin, Edward Troughton, Charles Tennant, Rev. Dr. Edmund Cartwright, Dr. Thomas Thomson, William Symington, Patrick Miller (of Dalswinton), Francis Ronalds, Alexander Nasmyth, Charles Earl Stanhope, Joseph Bramah, and Richard Trevithick.
Designed by Gilbert, and Drawn by F. Skill and W. Walker.
W. Walker and G. Zobel, mixed stipple.
The plate is arched at the top; the figures are disposed round a table and otherwise, in groups, "assembled in the Library of the Royal Institution," in the order of the names given above, from the left to the right of the plate.
Open letter proof (?); June 4, 1862.
$26\frac{1}{4} \times 44\frac{1}{4}$. $(20\frac{5}{16} \times 41\frac{5}{8})$ 27678.

——— Key to the above-described group, the outline portraits of the personages numbered; May 20, 1862.
$(10 \times 14\frac{11}{16})$.   27678. A

SCOTT, SIR GEORGE GILBERT, 1811-1878, architect, b. at Gawcott, near Buckingham, where his father was incumbent; showed early taste for church-architecture; was partner with W. B. Moffatt till 1845; erected the "Martyrs' Memorial," Oxford, 1841, followed by churches at Camberwell and elsewhere; was entrusted with the rebuilding of S. Nicholas, at

Hamburg, restoration of Doncaster Church, Cathedral of Ely, Westminster Abbey, &c.; led the movement of Gothic revival; R.A.; Kt.; &c.

Anon., woodcut.
Bust, to left, in profile; done for an illustrated paper; oval. Ind. paper impression.
(6¼ × 5⅛).   28444.   3.

SCOTT, JOHN, 1774–1828, Engraver, b. at Newcastle; chiefly known for his excellent engravings of horses and dogs in "The Sportsman's Cabinet," and for his "Series of Horses and Dogs;" he engraved plates also after Reinagle, A. Cooper, Gainsborough, and Callcott.
    J. Jackson, R.A., 1823.   W. T. Fry, chalk and dot.
    T. Q. len. to left, seated, looking to front; hands folded before him, legs crossed; books, plate, &c., on table, at right.
    Ind proof; Jany., 1825.
    (9¼ × 7 ⁷⁄₁₀).   22534.

SCOTT, SAMUEL, c. 1710–1772, marine painter, b. in London (?); boon companion of Hogarth and his friends, and one of the jovial water-party to Gravesend, 1732; his drawing and colouring were good; was one of the early water-colour painters, but worked chiefly in oils; gained great reputation for his sea-pieces and topographical views; exhibited at Spring Gardens, 1761, and at the R. A., 1771; retired to Bath, where he died of gout.
    T. Hudson.   J. Faber, junr., mez.
    J. C. Smith, 319, 1st state.   21865.
    The same, 2nd state.   29049.

SCOTT, THOMAS, 1747–1821, the Commentator; began as surgeon's apprentice for two months, and as a farm labourer for nine years; acquired an education by private study; deacon, 1772; priest, 1773; Curate of Weston Underwood; suc. Rev. J. Newton at Olney, 1780; lecturer, Lock Hospital, 1785; Rector of Aston Sandford, 1803 till death; author of "The Force of Truth," "Bible, with Expl. notes," &c.
    L. Cossé.   J. Collyer, A.R.A.
    Ha. len. to left, in gown, resting right hand on open book on table, looking to front.
    (16¹⁄₅³ × 12¼). (11¾ × 9½).   27957.

SCOTT, SIR WALTER, 1771–1832, poet, historian, and novelist, b. at Edinburgh, son of a writer to the signet; educ. at Edinb.; wished to be a soldier; called to the Bar, 1792, but devoted himself to literature; sheriff of Selkirkshire, 1799; translated from the German; author of "Minstrelsy of the Scottish Border," 1802, and "Lay of the Last Minstrel," 1805, followed by "Marmion," "Lady of the Lake," "Waverley Novels," "Tales of a Grandfather," &c., &c., ; cr. Bart., 1822.
    E. Landseer.   W. Mayer, etched.
    Bust to left, in profile; vignette; facs. signature below.
    8¾ × 6⅝   (7 × 4½).   18639.

SCOTT, Sir WALTER—*continued.*

Raeburn. C. Turner, mez.

Wh. len. to left, seated, looking to front, holding pencil in right hand, book in left, which rests on his left knee; landscape with river and castle in distance; January (?), 1810.

$21 \times 14\frac{9}{16}$. $(17\frac{7}{8} \times 14\frac{9}{16})$. 22090.

Sir T. Lawrence. J. H. Robinson.

Full ha. len. to front, seated, looking to right, holding pencil in right hand; papers on table, at right.

Unfinished proof before all letters.

$16\frac{5}{8} \times 13\frac{1}{4}$. $(11\frac{5}{8} \times 9\frac{1}{4})$. 18637.

Also, a finished proof before all letters, except the artists' names and publication-line, Oct. 1, 1833.

$16\frac{13}{16} \times 13\frac{1}{2}$. $(11\frac{3}{4} \times 9\frac{3}{4})$. 22149.

W. Allan, R.A. J. Burnet.

Wh. len. to right, seated, reading; right elbow on table; a dog at his feet, by the fire "in his study at Abbotsford."

Ind. proof; March 25, 1835.

$22 \times 16\frac{1}{2}$. $(17 \times 13\frac{1}{4})$. 22148.

Sir D. Wilkie, R.A., 1817. R. Graves, A.E.

Wh. len. to front, seated with his family, "The Abbotsford Family."

Proof before all letters, except the artists' names.

$15\frac{1}{4} \times 18$. $(11\frac{1}{4} \times 14\frac{15}{16})$. 27608.

—"and his Literary Friends at Abbotsford."

T. Faed, A.R.S.A. J. Faed, mixed mez.

Sir Walter, seated, at the right, directed towards the left, looks up from a paper which he is reading to a circle of friends; the friends represented are, beginning on the left, Thomas Thomson, Sir Humphry Davy, standing, James Ballantyne, A. Constable, Sir D. Wilkie and Sir W. Allan, both standing; T. Campbell, T. Moore, Sir Adam Ferguson, Fr. Jeffrey, W. Wordsworth, J. G. Lockhart, G. Crabbe, Prof. J. Wilson, standing, H. Mackenzie, and Jas. Hogg, the "Ettrick Shepherd." A purely imaginary group.

Ind. proof.

$(?) \times 31\frac{1}{2}$. $(20\frac{1}{4} \times 28\frac{1}{4})$. 22481.

SCOTT, WILLIAM. *See* STOWELL, LORD.

SCRIVEN, EDWARD, 1775–1841, engraver, b. at Alcester, in Warwicks.; pupil of R. Thew for 7 or 8 years, at Northall, Herts.; came to London, worked on some of the principal publications of the day, for the Dilettanti Society, "Shakespeare Gallery," "Fine Arts of the English School," &c.; engraved portraits after Lely, West's studies of heads; app. engraver to the

Pr. of Wales; worked in stipple, later in line; founded the
"Artists' Fund."
A. Morton. B. P. Gibbon.
Bust, to front, wearing spectacles; inscription below and
facs. signature; lightly etched; vignette.
6×5⅛. (3⅜×2¾). 29023. C.

SEAFORTH, FRANCIS HUMBERSTON MACKENZIE, 1754–1815,
cr. Lord, Baron Mackenzie of Kintail, co. Ross., 1797; Lieut.-
General in army; d. s. p. m.
See DILETTANTI SOCIETY.

SEATON, JOHN COLBORNE, Lord, 1779–1863; in command of
the 52nd Regt., contributed to the victory of Waterloo; Govr.-
Gen. of Canada, 1838–'39; cr. Baron, 1839; lord high Commissioner, Ionian Islands, 1843–'49; Comr.-in-Chf., Ireland,
1855–'60; field-marshal, 1860; G.C.B., &c.
G. Richmond. W. J. Edwards, stipple.
Bust, to front, looking to right; vignette.
Open letter proof, Sepr. 20, 1855.
21⅛×17. (9¾×8½). 23040.

SECKER, THOMAS, 1693–1768, b. at Sibthorpe, Notts.; studied
medicine for some time; went to Oxford; entd. the Church, 1722;
Rector of Houghton-le-Spring, 1724; Rector of St. James's,
London, 1738; Bishop of Bristol, 1735; of Oxf., 1737; Dean
of St. Paul's, 1750; Archbishop of Canterbury, 1758; pubd.
one medical treatise and many sermons, and theological works.
T. Hudson. J. MacArdell, mez.
J. C. Smith, 164, 2nd state. 26709.

SELBY, PRIDEAUX JOHN, 1789–1867, Naturalist, of Twizell
House, Northumb., and Ightham Mote, Kent; J.P. and Dep.-
Lieut. for Northumb., and High Sheriff, 1821; author of "Illus-
"trations of British Ornithology," "History of Br. Forest
Trees," and the vol. on "Pigeons," in the "Naturalist's
Library;" joint editor of "Illustrations of Ornithology."
T. H. Maguire. T. H. Maguire, lith.
T. Q. len. to front, seated, slightly inclined and looking to
right; left arm on chair-back, a book in right hand; rectilin.,
with corners lopped off; vignette; facs. signature below
Ind. proof.
(10×9½). 16527.

SELDEN, JOHN, 1584–1654, Jurist and Antiquary; b. at
Salvington, Sussex; educ. at Chichester, Oxford, and Inner
Temple; M.P. for Lancaster, 1623, and Bodmin, 1628; opposed
the Court; actively engaged in drawing up Petition of Rights,
and Remonstrance against the Tunnage and Poundage Bill;
M.P. for Univ. Oxf. in Long Parliament, 1640; opposed im-
peachment of Strafford; sat as a Layman in Westminster
Assembly of Divines, 1643; valued friend of Clarendon, author

of " Titles of Honour," " Mare Clausum," " Table Talk," &c.;
d. in London; bur. in Temple Church.

    Sir P. Lely.   G. Vertue, 1725.

    Sh. ha. len. to right, looking to front; oval in border; arms
below; title in Latin.

    $(13\frac{1}{4} \times 7\frac{4}{5})$.   23143.

    See also BODLEY.

SELWYN, GEORGE AUGUSTUS, 1719–1791, surveyor to the
Mint; M.P.; registrar in Chancery, Barbados, &c., with
EDGCUMBE, HON. RICHARD, 1716–1761, afterwards Baron
Edgcumbe of Mount Edgcumbe, &c., and WILLIAMS,
Gilly, Esqr.

    Sir J. Reynolds.   J. Scott, mez.

    Selwyn is T. Q. len., standing, on left; the others seated at
table, on right.

    $8\frac{1}{4} \times 9\frac{3}{4}$. $(4\frac{1}{4} \times 7)$.   27255.

    See also CARLISLE, FRED., Earl of.

SEPPINGS, SIR ROBERT, 1768–1840; eminent naval architect;
contributed several valuable papers on naval architecture to
Phil. Trans., 1814–'18–'20.

    W. Bradley.   R. J. Lane, A.R.A., lith.

    Ha. len. to right, looking downwards, to left; right hand
raised, papers in left; with extract below from paper read
before the R. Socy., March 10, 1814, and facs. signature. A
private plate; so described, and signed, by R. J. Lane.

    $(11\frac{1}{4} \times 10)$.   20681.

SERRES, DOMINIQUE, 1722–1793, marine painter; b. at Auch, in
Gascony; intended for the church, ran away to Spain; became
a sailor; taken prisoner by English frigate, 1752; released on
parole, became an artist; married and settled in England;
original member of the R. A.; exhibited many sea-pieces,
marine battles, &c., of which several are at Greenwich, and
Hampton Court; marine painter to George III.

    O. Humphry delt., 1778.   W C E[dwards?], 1821.

    Sh. ha. len., rather to left, looking to front, head bent forwards;
vignette; slightly etched.

    $4\frac{1}{8} \times 4$. $(2\frac{3}{4} \times 2\frac{1}{2})$.   E. 2215.–'89.

SEWARD, WILLIAM, 1747–1799, b. in London; educ. at
Charterhouse and Oxford, of independent means, followed no
profession; F.R.S., and F.S.A.; intimate with Dr. Johnson
and other eminent men; contributed "Drossiana," a collection
of anecdotes to the European Magazine, 1789, and published
more afterwards in 2 vols., 1794, and "Biographiana," 2 vols.,
1799.

    G. Dance delt. May 5, 1793.   W. Daniell, stipple.

    Sh. ha. len to right, in profile; vignette; Feb. 1, 1809.

    $10\frac{1}{4} \times 7\frac{1}{2}$. $(7 \times 4\frac{3}{4})$.   28299.   5.

SEYMOUR, ARABELLA STUART, Lady. *See* STUART, ARA-
BELLA.

    O 82849.   D D

SEYMOUR, Sir George Francis, 1787-1870; eldest son of Adml. Lord Hugh Seymour; severely wounded on board *Northumberland* at St. Domingo, 1806; commanded *Pallas* frigate, Walcheren, 1809, and other ships, till 1814; Serj. at arms, House of Lords, 1820; lord of Admiralty, Commander in Chf., Pacific, &c.; Vice-Adml.; Adml., 1866; G.C.B.; G.C.H.; &c.

 J. Harrison.   F. Holl, stipple.

 Sh. ha. len. to right, looking to front; wearing stars, &c.

 Ind. proof before all letters, except the artists' names, and publication-line, 1852. Vignette.

 $21\frac{1}{2} \times 17$. $(10 \times 8\frac{1}{2})$.   27638.

SEYMOUR, Lord Hugh, 1759-1801, ent. Navy, c. 1770; Post-Cap., 1779; disting. as captain of the "Latona" frigate, 1782, at relief of Gibralter, and conspicuous for valour, in "Leviathan" (74), in Lord Howe's actions, May 28 and 29, and June 1, 1794; Col. of Marines; Admiral, 1795; served in "Sanspareil" (80), under Lord Bridport, off Ile de Groix; on Board of Admiralty, 1795-'8; Com.-in-chf., Leeward Isles and Jamaica, until his death.

 See COMMEMORATION (1).

SEYMOUR, Jane. *See* JANE SEYMOUR.

SEYMOUR, of Sudeley, Sir Thomas, Lord, -1549, K.G., Lord High Admiral, younger brother of the Protector Somerset; cr. Baron, 1547; mar. the Dowager Queen, Catherine Parr; condemned by Parliament, and executed under a warrant of the Protector.

 Holbein.   W. Hilton del.   T. Cheesman.

 Ha. len. to front, wearing a dark dress and cap, with the George. July 1, 1818. This occurs in Lodge's large series.

 $14\frac{3}{4} \times 10\frac{3}{4}$. $(6\frac{3}{4} \times 5\frac{3}{4})$.   27162.

 See also NAVAL HEROES (1).

SHADWELL, John, M.D., c. 1800, member of the MEDICAL SOCIETY (q. v.).

SHADWELL, Thomas, c. 1640-1692, b. at Stanton Hall, his father's seat, in Norfolk; educ. at Caius College, Cambr.; entered at the Temple; travelled abroad; returned, he wrote several successful plays, and succeeded Dryden as laureate, at the Revolution; attacked by Dryden, in consequence, in his "Mac Flecknoe."

 Kerseboom.   W. Faithorne, mez.

 J. C Smith, 36 (a proof?).   24130.

SHAFTESBURY, Anthony Ashley Cooper, Earl of, 1621-1683; son of Sir John Cooper, Bart; suc., 1631; M.P., 1640; Colonel, 1643; Councillor of State; P.C., Chancr. of Exchequer; F.R.S.; cr. Earl, 1672; Lord High Chancr., &c.

 Sir P. Lely.   J. Houbraken.

 Sh. ha. len. to right, looking to front; wearing long hair, breastplate, &c.

 $(14 \times 8\frac{1}{2})$.   20812.

SHAFTESBURY, Anthony Ashley, Earl of, 1671-1713.
Philosopher, Admiral of co. Dorset, &c.
 J. Closterman.   S. Gribelin.
 Wh. len. in loose robes.
 $6\frac{6}{8} \times 3\frac{7}{8}$. $(6\frac{1}{8} \times 3\frac{9}{16})$.   26678.

SHAKSPERE (or SHAKESPEAR, or SHAKESPEARE,)
William, illustrious poet and dramatist, 1564-1616; b. at
Stratford; educ. at grammar school there; went to London,
and soon entered the Blackfriars Theatre, of which he became
part-owner, 1596, as well as of the Globe; bought New Place
at Stratford, to which he retired, 1611; wrote the Sonnets,
other Poems, tragedies, "histories," and comedies, including
"Hamlet," "Romeo and Juliet," "King Lear," "Merchant of
Venice," &c.
 J. Taylor, or R. Burbage.   G. Vertue, 1719.
 Sh. ha. len. to right, looking to front; oval in border; from the
"Chandos picture," now in the National Portrait Gallery, but
then in the possession of R. Keck, of the Inner Temple, Esqr.
 $14\frac{5}{16} \times 9\frac{1}{2}$. $(13\frac{3}{4} \times 8\frac{7}{8})$.   27865. 3.

 J. Taylor, or R. Burbage. [Walker?], mixed mez.
 Sh. ha. len. slightly to left, looking to front; oval in border;
from the "Chandos Shakspere."
 Ind. proof before all letters.
 $15\frac{1}{2} \times 12\frac{1}{4}$. (10×8).   28770.

 From Ozias Humphry's copy of the "Chandos Shakspere."
 W. Harvey del.   J. Thompson, woodcut.
 Bust, to left, looking to front; square, in a border adorned
with scenes from the plays, in compartments; frontispiece to
C. Whittingham's edition in 10 vols., containing 60 other
illustrations on wood.
 Ind. proof.
 $(4\frac{15}{16} \times 2\frac{13}{16})$.   24005.

 Scheemakers (from the monument in Westminster Abbey).
          A. Miller, mez.
 J. C Smith, 46
 An interesting impression, folded up and sent by post
to "Jas. Warburton Esqr., Somerset Herald of Arms at
Stamford Lincolnshire," by the engraver, who has written that
address on the back, as well as the following note, "Sr. I had
"not an Oppertunity of Sending it the way that I Proposed so
"was obliged to make Use of this Method.
      Yr. Hum. Servt.,
        Andw. Miller
 "P.S. if you are inclind to have yr. own Plate I will let you
"have it for a Guinea & a Half." The last 13 words are all
nearly obliterated with a pen.
        E. 4-1886.

        D D 2

SHAKSPERE—*continued.*

A set of the illustrations to "An Inquiry into the History,
"Authenticity, and Characteristics of the Shakspeare Portraits,
" &c., by Abraham Wivell," and "Supplement,"
London, 8vo, 1827.

Proofs before the inscriptions, except in some cases the artists'
names, on Ind. paper; viz.:—

1. The monument in the church at Stratford, from a
drawing . . . . , the figure of the bust by A. Wivell,
engraved by W. Wallis.
$9\frac{7}{16} \times 6\frac{7}{16}$. ($4\frac{1}{2} \times 3$). 28836. 1.

2. The portrait "the property of George Nicol Esqre."
(the "Felton picture").
R. Burbage.   J. Cochran.
$9\frac{5}{16} \times 7\frac{1}{2}$. ($4\frac{1}{4} \times 3\frac{1}{2}$).   28836. 13.

3. The "Chandos portrait."
A. Wivell delt.   J. Cochran
$9\frac{13}{16} \times 7\frac{3}{8}$. ($5\frac{1}{4} \times 4\frac{1}{2}$).   28836. 6.

4. The "Droeshout portrait."
M. Droeshout.   C. Picart.
$10\frac{1}{8} \times 7\frac{3}{16}$. ($5 \times 4\frac{3}{16}$).   28836. 4.

5. The "Marshall portrait."
W. Marshall, 1640.   Anon.
8 English verses below.
$6\frac{1}{8} \times 4\frac{7}{10}$. ($3\frac{1}{4} \times 2\frac{7}{8}$).   28836. 5.

6. The Duke of Somerset's portrait.
C. Janssens.   T. Wright.
$10\frac{3}{8} \times 7\frac{5}{16}$. ($5\frac{3}{4} \times 4\frac{5}{16}$).   28836. 7.

7. Front and Profile of the Monumental Bust.
E. Blore del.   Thompson.
$9\frac{1}{2} \times 5\frac{11}{16}$. ($6\frac{1}{2} \times 2\frac{1}{2}$).   28836. 2.

8. Head from the Bust by G. Johnson.
A. Wivell delt.   T. A Dean.
$9\frac{1}{8} \times 7\frac{3}{8}$. ($2\frac{1}{2} \times 2\frac{1}{16}$).   28836. 3.

9. Mr. Gilliland's portrait, oval.
A. Wivell delt.   W. Holl.
$8\frac{7}{8} \times 6\frac{7}{8}$. ($3\frac{13}{16} \times 2\frac{16}{16}$).   28836. 19.

10. Mr. C. Auriol's miniature, oval.
Anon.   W. Holl.
$8\frac{7}{8} \times 6\frac{5}{8}$. ($2 \times 1\frac{5}{8}$).   28836. 18.

11. The "Zincke portrait."
W. F. Zincke.   W. Holl.
$7\frac{7}{8} \times 5\frac{11}{16}$. ($6\frac{1}{4} \times 4\frac{5}{16}$).   28836. 20.

12. The Group at the Shakspeare Gallery.
J. Banks, R.A.   B. Holl.
$9\frac{7}{8} \times 7\frac{1}{2}$. ($6\frac{5}{8} \times 4\frac{1}{4}$).   28836. 16.

SHAKSPERE—*continued*.

   13. From the print by J. Simon (mez.).
Soest.   W. Holl.
$8\frac{1}{4} \times 6\frac{1}{4}$. $(4\frac{1}{2} \times 3\frac{3}{4})$.   28836. 11.

   14. Roubilliac designing the Statue.
A. Carpentiers.   W. Holl.
$8\frac{7}{8} \times 6\frac{7}{8}$. $(4\frac{1}{4} \times 3\frac{1}{4})$.   28836. 15.

   15. From a Print by R. Cooper.
Janssens.   W. Holl.
$8\frac{13}{16} \times 6\frac{7}{8}$. $(4 \times 3\frac{1}{8})$.   28836. 14.

   16. The Dunford Portrait, painted by E. Hoder.
                     W. Holl.
$8\frac{15}{16} \times 6\frac{7}{8}$. $(4 \times 3\frac{1}{8})$.   28836. 12.

   17. From Sir J. B. Burges's miniature, oval.
                     B. Holl.
$8\frac{7}{8} \times 6\frac{7}{8}$. $(1\frac{13}{16} \times 1\frac{4}{8})$.   28836. 10.

   18. From R. Cosway's picture.
                     W. Holl.
$8\frac{1}{8} \times 6\frac{7}{8}$. $(4 \times 3\frac{1}{8})$.   28836. 8.

   19. The Monument in Westminster Abbey.
                     B. Holl.
$9\frac{13}{16} \times 7\frac{1}{2}$. $(7\frac{3}{4} \times 4\frac{1}{2})$ 28836. 17.

   20. From the frontispiece to "Rape of Lucrece."
W. Faithorne.   R. Sawyer.
$6\frac{7}{8} \times 5$. $(4\frac{1}{2} \times 3)$.   28836. 9.

*** These have been arranged here in the order in which they appear in the book and its Supplement.

Droeshout.   W. J. Linton, woodcut.
Bust, to left; oval in a border ornamented with views of his house, the church at Stratford, &c.
$(11\frac{7}{8} \times 9\frac{1}{8})$.   29658. A.

W. Harvey del.   W. T. Green, woodcut.
Sh. ha. len. to right, after W. Marshall's print, 1640; frontispiece to C. Knight and Co's. edition; facs. signature below.
$(7 \times 3\frac{7}{8})$.   29658. B.

W. Harvey delt.   J. Thompson, woodcut.
Wh. len. seated, holding pen, surrounded by figures illustrating his works; arched at top.
Ind. proof.
$(4\frac{1}{2} \times 8\frac{3}{4})$.   29658. C.
—— Apotheosis.
M. Retzsch.   M. Retzsch.
Wh. len. seated, supported by an eagle, and crowned with stars by emblematical figures; "FRONTISPIECE. Plate 1."
$(6\frac{5}{8} \times 8\frac{1}{4})$.   29658 D.

SHAKSPERE—*continued.*

Title to the Doubtful Plays of Shakspere, by H. Tyrrell.
T. D. Scott del.   G. Greatbach.
Wh. len. seated, at top of the title, which is surrounded by
figures illustrating the plays.
(8¾ × 6).   29658. E.

Wh. len. sleeping, surrounded by figures illustrating Macbeth,
Hamlet, The Tempest, &c.
Richter del.   Angus.
Proof.
(6⅝ × 4).   29658. F.

Anon.   Anon.
Bust to left, in profile, in a circle of laurel, with wings at
the sides; a scroll below, with keys, pencils, palette, masks, &c.
Proof.
(3⅝ × 2¼).   29658. G.

From the print by Houbraken.   T. Cook, c. 1770.
Sh. ha. len. to left, looking to front.
Published by G. Kearsley.
(6¹⁄₁₆ × 4⅜).   29658. H.

From the portrait by Droeshout.   Day & Son, photo-lith.
Sh. ha. len. to front; 8 verses below, in 2 columns; 1864.
(7½ × 6⁵⁄₁₆).   22480.

"SHAKSPEARE AND HIS FRIENDS."
J. Faed, R.S.A.   J. Faed, mixed mez.
The poet is seated in the middle of the composition, directed
to front, looking to right, his right arm resting on table, his left
hand holding a book, with forefinger between the leaves; all
his most distinguished contemporaries are represented, grouped
about him, their names engraved below; "published exclusively
" for the Members of the Cosmopolitan Art Association," 1859–
'60.
27 × 31½.   (22³⁄₁₆ × 28).   27609.

SHARP, GRANVILLE, 1734–1813, grandson of the Archbp. of
York; b. at Durham; served in Ordnance Office; resigned at beginning of American War, the principle of which he disapproved;
devoted his life to study and philanthropy; instituted Society
for abolition of Slave Trade, advocated parliamentary reform,
and other patriotic and benevolent objects; critical Hebrew
and Greek scholar.
G. Dance delt., July 3, 1794.   W. Daniell, 1809.
Sh. ha. len. to right, in profile, seated; vignette.
(7¾ × 6⅜).   26202.

SHARP, GRANVILLE—*continued.*

L. Abbot (1784, added in pencil). C. Turner, mez.
Ha. len. to right, looking to front, holding in left hand a paper inscribed *The Claims of the People of England*; his left elbow rests on a pile of books, lettered "Bracton de Leg^{bus}," &c., "Fortescue de Laudibus Leg. Angliæ," &c.
Open letter proof, Novr. 2, 1805.
14 × 10. (12$\frac{1}{15}$ × 10). 22482.

SHARP, WILLIAM, 1749–1824, son of a gun-maker in the Minories, London, where he was born; received a premium from the Society of Arts; apprent. to B. Longmate, engraver on plate; engraved from the old masters; executed plates for the "Novelist's Magazine," after Stothard; engraved Guido's "Doctors of the Church disputing," and many other fine plates; was very credulous; believed in Joanna Southcott and other impostors; d. poor; buried at Chiswick.

G. F. Joseph. W. Sharp.
Sh. ha. len. to front, slightly turned, and looking to right, holding roll of paper in right hand.
Proof before all letters.
14$\frac{3}{8}$ × 12$\frac{3}{8}$. (12 × 9$\frac{3}{4}$, including ruled border, 1$\frac{5}{16}$).
E. 216.–'93.

Anon. [Haydon (?)] J. Thomson, stipple.
Sh. ha. len. to front, looking to right; right hand, with fingers closed, rests on a table; vignette; facs. signature below; Oct. 1, 1824. This occurs in the European Magazine.
Ind. proof.
8$\frac{3}{4}$ × 5$\frac{1}{4}$. (4$\frac{1}{2}$ × 4$\frac{3}{4}$). E. 1279.–'86.

B. R. Haydon, 1816. Anon., lith.
Head, to left, looking upwards, with open collar; vignette. Touched up with white by a later hand.
(4 × 4$\frac{1}{2}$). 26278.

SHAW, RT. HON. SIR FREDERICK, 1799–1876, b. in Dublin; educ. at Trin. Coll. Dublin, and at Braz. Coll., Oxford; Irish barrister, 1822; Recorder of Dublin, 1828; M.P. for Dublin, 1830, M.P for Dub. Univ., 1832'48; leader of Irish Cons. party; P.C.

F. Cruickshank. E. Scriven, stipple.
Ha. len. slightly to left, seated, looking to front, wearing dark coat, light waistcoat, &c.; rectilin. with corners lopped off; engraved for Ryall's "Portraits of Eminent Conservatives," &c., 1836.
13$\frac{7}{16}$ × 9$\frac{11}{16}$. (8$\frac{3}{4}$ × 7$\frac{1}{16}$). 20638.

SHEE, SIR MARTIN ARCHER, 1769–1850, b. in Dublin; studied there in the School of Design; gained the chief medal, 1787; came to London, 1788, and entd. R. A. Schools, 1790; began exhibiting, 1789; soon acquired reputation, working very hard,

with great self-denial; A.R.A., 1799; R.A., 1800; painted
some subjects, but his true art was portraiture; pubd.
"Rhymes on Art," 1805, and other pieces; P.R.A., 1830,
and Kt.

J. Jackson, A.R.A., delin.   W. T. Fry, stipple.
Sh. ha. len. to left, looking to front; vignette; Jan. 14, 1817.
   (7 × 6¼).   28298.   8.

SHEE, SIR MARTIN ARCHER—*continued*.

M. A. Shee.   J. Thomson, stipple.
Sh. ha. len. to front, looking to left; coat loosely buttoned;
vignette; facs. signature below.
   (6 × 4½).   28300.   55.

SHEEPSHANKS, JOHN, 1787–1863, son of a cloth-manu-
facturer at Leeds; devoted his leisure to study of fine arts;
formed a fine collection of pictures by British artists; presented
the whole (233 oil paintings, 103 sketches and drawings by
Turner, Stanfield, Chalon, and others) to the nation, 1856;
they are deposited in the Museum at South Kensington.

A. Geddes, A.R.A.   A. Geddes, etched.
Sh. ha. len. to front, looking rather to the left.
In 4 states:—

  1. The head, down to the collar of coat; unfinished; no
     background.   16309.
  2. The body, with furred coat, added; background still
     white. Ind. paper.   16310.
  3. The background put in; the part which touches the
     right shoulder not cross-hatched.   16311.
  4. The background behind the right shoulder cross-
     hatched, more work on face, &c. Ind. paper.   16312.
(Varying from 5¹⁄₆ to 5¼ × 4⅜).

SHEFFIELD, EDMUND, Lord, c. 1564–1646, only s. and h. of
John, 2nd Baron Sheffield; suc. 1568; mtr., Oxon., 1574;
volunteer in Holland, 1568; Capt. of a man-of-war, 1588,
against the Armada; Knt., 1588; K.G., 1593; cr. Earl of
Mulgrave, 1626.

See NAVAL HEROES (1), and NAVAL HEROES (2).

SHEFFIELD, JOHN BAKER, Lord, 1741–1821; soldier and
statesman.

Sir J. Reynolds.   J. Jones, stipple.
Ha. len. to right, in robes; arms below, in Middle; April 6,
1789.
  10¼ × 8⁹⁄₁₀ (?).   (8¼ × 7).   22536.

SHELDON, GILBERT, 1598–1677, b. at Stanton, Staff.; educ. at
Trin. Coll., Oxf.; Warden of All Souls', and Chapl. to
Charles I., 1635; ejected and imprisd., 1647; at Restorn.,
Master of Savoy, the Savoy Conference having been held in his

lodgings; Bishop of London, 1660; Archbishop, Canterbury, 1663; pubd. two sermons, 1660.

Anon.   Anon., mez.

J. C. Smith, 109 ("Engravers not ascertained," p. 1671).

NOTE.—"The picture by Lely is in the Sheldonian Theatre, at Oxford" (J. C. S.).

25800.

SHELLEY, PERCY BYSSHE, 1792–1822, eldest son of Sir Timothy Shelley; b. at Field Place, Sussex; educ. at Eton and Oxford; expelled from the University for his heterodoxy; devoted himself to poetry; wrote "Rosalind and Helen," "Queen Mab," "Alastor," "Revolt of Islam," "Prometheus Unbound," "The Cenci," &c.; friend of Byron; drowned near Via Reggio.

Miss Curran delt.   C. W. Sharpe, stipple.

Sh. ha. len. to front, resting on right elbow; vignette.

March 1st, 1860.

15$\frac{1}{16}$ × 12$\frac{3}{4}$. (5$\frac{3}{4}$ × 5).   27639.

Anon. (Miss Curran).   J. H. Baker, stipple.

Bust, to front; vignette.

Ind. proof before all letters.

10$\frac{1}{4}$ × 6$\frac{3}{4}$. (3$\frac{1}{4}$ × 2$\frac{1}{4}$).   27521.

SHERIDAN, ESTHER (or HESTER) JANE,   –1817, youngest daughter of the very Rev. N. Ogle, D.D., of Kirkley, Northumberland, and Dean of Winchester; second wife, and widow, of the Rt. Hon. Richard Brinsley Sheridan; by the prudence of her father, a settlement of 15,000*l*. was secured, which ensured her independence and produced a provision for her son.

J. Hoppner, R.A.   T. Nugent, chalk and stipple.

Wh. len. with her little son on her back; carrying a pitcher, and approaching water in foreground on left, in a landscape; April 2, 1800.

26 × 16$\frac{1}{8}$. (23$\frac{1}{2}$ × 14$\frac{1}{4}$).   27640.

SHERIDAN, RICHARD BRINSLEY, 1751–1816, Dramatist, Orator, statesman; author of the "School for Scandal," &c.; ent. Parliament as the friend of Burke and Fox, 1780; made his famous speech against Warren Hastings, 1787; favourite of the Prince Regent, and opponent of Pitt; Treasurer of the Navy, 1806.

Sir J. Reynolds.   J. Hall.

Full ha. len. to left, looking to front, leaning with right hand on table; pillar and curtain behind.

Open letter proof, April 30, 1791.

20$\frac{7}{16}$ × 15. (17$\frac{7}{8}$ × 13$\frac{1}{4}$).   21840.

SHERIDAN, Mr., speaking the Prologue to Cato.
Dod del. Cook.
Pubd. by Fielding & Walker, Feby. 3, 1780.

28187. 14.
From a "Collection ; . . of English Prologues," &c.

SHERLOCK, Thomas, 1678–1761, son of Dean Thomas Sherlock, b. in London; educ. at Eton and Cath. Hall, Cambr., of
which he became a fellow; Master of the Temple, 1704; Preb.,
London, 1713; Master of Cath. Hall, 1714; Dean of Chichester, 1715; Preb., Norwich, 1719; Bishop of Bangor, 1728; of
Salisbury, 1734; of London, 1748; declined Archbishopric
of Cant., 1747; pubd. Discourses, &c.
Vanloo, 1740. S. Ravenet, 1756.
T. Q. len. to left, looking to front, in robes, holding in right
hand a book, which rests on his knee; arms below.
(13½ × 10⅜). 24675.

SHIELD, William, 1748–1829, b. at Swallwell, Durham, son
of a singing-master; apprent. to a boat-builder, but stud.
music under C. Avison; led at theatre and concerts at Newcastle; engaged by Giardini as second violin at Opera, London,
1772; played principal viola, 1773–'91; produced comic opera,
"Flitch of Bacon," 1778; composer to Cov. Gar. Theatre, till
1797; wrote many Operas, Songs, "Introduction to Harmony,"
&c.; buried in Westminster Abbey.
J. Opie, R.A. R. Dunkarton, mez.
J. C. Smith, 35, 3rd state. 21928.

SHIPLEY, Jonathan, c. 1714–1788, educ. at Ch. Ch., Oxf.;
Preb., Winchester, 1743; Chapl. to Duke of Cumberland, 1745;
canon, Ch. Ch., Oxf.; Incumbt. Silchester and Chinbolton;
Dean of Winchester, 1760; Bishop of St. Asaph (transld. from
Llandaff), 1769; pubd. sermons, &c.
Sir J. Reynolds. T. Trotter.
Sh. ha. len. to front, in robes; oval in border.
Open letter proof (?); April 2, 1792.
10⅝ × 7⁷⁄₁₆. (7 × 4¹¹⁄₁₆). 23132.

SHIRLEY, Sir Anthony, 1565–1630, traveller, knighted for
services in Ireland; Ambassador from Persia; Admiral of
Levant Seas; &c.
P. Oliver (min.). (Harding del.) Jos. Brown.
Sh. ha. len., slightly to right, looking to front, wearing a
turban; Aug. 1, 1846.
11⅞ × 8. (4¹¹⁄₁₆ × 8⅝). 27557.

SHIRLEY, Sir Robert, c. 1570–1627, traveller, accomp. his
brother, Sir Anthony, on his journey to Persia, where he was
employed by the Shah; ret. to Europe, 1609; cr. a Count
Palatine by Emp. Rodolph; came to Court of James 1, 1612;
d. in Persia.
Anon. (W. Gardiner del.). Birrell, stipple.

Wh. len. to front, wearing a turban and the rest of an Eastern dress, with a quiver, &c.; a curtain behind him.
From a picture at Petworth.
May 1, 1799.
(12¼ × 8¼). 22535.

SHOVEL, Sir Cloudesley, 1650–1707, b. near Cley, Norfolk; served under Sir John Narborough in the Mediterranean, where he destroyed the shipping of the Dey of Tripoli; took a distinguished part in the battles of Bantry Bay, La Hogue, and Malaga; commanded the Mediterranean Fleet, 1707; Admiral; Lt. Colonel of Marines; wrecked and drowned off the Scilly Isles; his body found, and buried in Westminster Abbey.
W. de Ryck. J. Smith, mez.
J. C. Smith, 230, 3rd state (1692). 22274.

SHREWSBURY, Anna Maria, Countess of.
Sir P. Lely. J. Thompson, stipple.
See LA BELLE ASSEMBLÉE, 1819. 13867. 28.

SHREWSBURY, Charles Talbot, Duke of, 1660–1718, Statesman and Scholar; eldest son of the Earl of Shrewsbury; promoted revolution of 1688; Sec. of State, Lord Lieut. of Ireland, Lord Chamberlain, and Lord Treasurer; cr. Duke, 1694; called by Pope "the wise and great;" d. at Isleworth.
Anon. (J. Smith), mez.
J. C. Smith, 187, 4th state; altered from the portrait of John, Earl of Mulgrave. 27536.
See also LORDS JUSTICES.

SHREWSBURY, Elisabeth, Countess of, 1520–1607, "Bess of Hardwick," daughter of John Hardwick, of Hardwick, co. Derby; 4 times married; first, to Robert Barley, of Barley co. Derby; next, to Sir William Cavendish (d. 1557), his third wife; then to Sir William St. Loo, Captain of the Guard to Q. Elizabeth; last, to George, 6th Earl of Shrewsbury, K.G., the richest and most powerful peer of his time; a masterful woman, proud, greedy, unfeeling, furious, and selfish; d. immensely rich.
C. Janssens. G. Vertue.
Full ha. len., slightly to right, looking to front, with ruff and lace cap, a scarf across her left shoulder; oval in border, arms below.
Cut. (12₁₆³ × 7½). 24207.

SHUTER, Edward, c. 1730–1776, b. in a cellar near Cov. Garden, by his own account, son of a sedan-chairman and an oyster-woman; joined a strolling company, by whom he was called "Comical Ned;" brought forward by Garrick at Drury Lane; soon a public favourite; said to have been a devoted follower of Whitfield; buried at St. Paul's, Cov. Garden.
J. Zauffely. J. Finlayson, mez.
Wh. len., with Beard (q. v.) and Dunstall (q. v.).
J. C. Smith, 14, 2nd state. 25799.

SIDDONS, SARAH, 1755–1831, great tragic actress, daughter of Roger Kemble, manager of a travelling company, was b. at Brecknock ; m. to an actor, Siddons, 1772 ; appeared in London as Portia, unsuccessfully, 1775 ; improved at Bath ; completely successful at Drury Lane, 1782 ; remainder of her career one long triumph ; her greatest parts were Lady Macbeth, Constance, and Lady Randolph in "Douglas."

W. Hamilton. J. Caldwall.

Wh. len., with her son, whose left hand she holds with both of hers ; she is dressed in black, wearing a veil ; in the tragedy of "Isabella ;" June 1, 1785.

$26 \times 18\frac{1}{2}$. ($24\frac{5}{8} \times 17\frac{13}{16}$). 25219.

W. Hamilton. J. Caldwall.

Wh. len., in the Tragedy of "The Grecian Daughter," directed to the left, looking back, and with left arm extended upwards, to right.

Open letter proof, March 1, 1791 (?).

$26\frac{1}{8} \times 18\frac{5}{8}$. ($24\frac{3}{8} \times 17\frac{3}{4}$). 21963. A.

Sir J. Reynolds. F. Haward, A.R.A., stipple.

Wh. len., as "The Tragic Muse," seated, looking upwards to left ; two figures with dagger and bowl behind her, clouds at her feet ; pubd. June 4, 1787.

$24\frac{5}{8} \times 17\frac{7}{8}$. ($21\frac{3}{4} \times 15\frac{7}{8}$). 22205.

SIDMOUTH, HENRY ADDINGTON, Viscount, 1757–1844, Barrister, M.P. 1784 ; Recorder of Devizes ; Speaker of the House of Commons, 1789–1801 ; P.C. ; Chancr. of Exchequer ; First Lord of Treasury, 1801–'4 ; cr. Visct., 1805 ; Lord President ; Privy Seal ; Home Sec.

G. Richmond. E. Scriven, stipple.

Hn. len. to front.

Ind. proof, 1836.

$12\frac{7}{8} \times 10\frac{3}{16}$. ($9 \times 7\frac{1}{8}$). 20639.

J. S. Copley, R.A. R. Dunkarton, mez.

J. C. Smith, 1, 2nd state. 22105.

SIDNEY, ALGERNON, c. 1617–1683, second son of Robert, Earl of Leicester ; patriot and republican ; served with distinction during Irish rebellion ; joined parliamentarians, 1643 ; Govr. of Dover ; member of High Court of Justice for trial of Charles I. ; retired during the Commonwealth ; abroad at Restoration ; pardoned, 1677 ; arrested on suspicion of complicity in Rye House Plot ; arraigned before Jeffreys ; found guilty on insuff. and illegal evidence ; executed on Tower Hill.

From a seal by T. Simon. I. B. Cipriani, etched.

Bust, in oval, to left, in profile, carrying a banner with inscription, "Sanctus Amor Patriæ Dat. Animum ;" 19 lines of inscription below ; 1760.

$10\frac{1}{4} \times 6\frac{7}{8}$. ($6\frac{1}{2} \times 5\frac{3}{4}$). 26717.

SIDNEY, Sir Philip, 1554–1586, Soldier, Poet, and Statesman; eld. son of Sir Henry Sidney; educ. at Shrewsbury and Oxf.; a favourite of Q. Elizabeth, who sent him on missions to the Continent; wrote "Defence of Poetry;" Sonnets and Poems, and " Arcadia ; " invited to become a candidate for the crown of Poland; Gen. of Horse, under Leicester, in the Netherlands, 1585 ; d. of a wound received at Zutphen.

Anon. R. Elstracke.
Ha. len. slightly turned to left, looking to front, in armour ; oval in border; Compton Holland excudit.
$7\frac{3}{8} \times 4\frac{3}{4}$. ($7\frac{1}{4} \times 4\frac{4}{8}$). E. 1702.–'88.

1. Oliver. G. Vertue, 1745.
Wh. len. seated, to right, leaning against a tree, looking to front, house and formal garden in background.
From " a curious limning, in the collection of Dr. Richard Mead."
$11\frac{1}{8} \times 7\frac{1}{2}$. ($7\frac{1}{4} \times 5\frac{5}{16}$). 22917.

1. Oliver. G. Vertue, 1741.
Ha. len. to front, wearing a ruff, in arched border ; a wreath and flaming star above ; a sword, serpent, open book, another labelled " Arcadia," and shield below ; from a picture in Lord Chesterfield's collection.
$14\frac{1}{2} \times 9\frac{1}{4}$. ($13\frac{3}{4} \times 8\frac{9}{16}$). 22537.

SIGNING and sealing of the Nanking Treaty of Peace, &c. See NANKING.

SIMS, James, M.D., 1740–1820, President of the Medical Society (q. v.); F.A.S., R.I.A., &c.; d. at Bath.
G. Dance, Sep. 1, 1796. W. Daniell.
Sh. ha. len. seated, profile to right ; vignette.
April 10, 1802.
$10\frac{3}{8} \times 7\frac{7}{8}$. ($6\frac{1}{4} \times 5\frac{1}{4}$).
See also MEDICAL SOCIETY. 28293. 6.

SINCLAIR, Sir John, 1754–1835, b. at Thurso Castle, Caithness ; Memb. Fac. Advocates, 1775 ; M.P., 1780–1810; called to the Engl. Bar, Linc. Inn., 1782 ; travelled in Northern Europe, 1786, and cr. a Bart.; P.C., 1810 ; d. at Edinb.; wrote " History of the Public Revenue," and other valuable works ; founder of the Board of Agriculture ; LL.D., &c.
A. Robertson (min.). W. Bond.
Sh. ha. len. to right, looking to front, in a border.
Ind. proof with open letters ; May, 1833.
$9 \times 5\frac{3}{8}$. ($3\frac{3}{8} \times 2\frac{1}{8}$). E. 1060.–'88.

T. Lawrence. W. Skelton.
Ha. len. to front, seated, looking to right, resting right arm on a vol. lettered " Hist. of the Revenue," one of his works ; arms below.
$9\frac{7}{8} \times 6\frac{7}{8}$. ($7\frac{3}{4} \times 5\frac{5}{16}$). 21984.

SKEGG, EDWARD, 1773-1842, educ. at Christ's Hospital;
went young into a large business-house in the City; entered
Coutts' Bank, c. 1795; confidential clerk nearly 46 years,
retired on pension, 1841; had collected books and prints, sold at
Sotheby's, 1842, 2,500*l.*; d. at Brighton.

    Anon.   R. G[raves ?].
    Sh. ha. len. to right, looking to front; vignette; facs.
signature below.
    Ind. proof; a private plate.
    $9\frac{1}{4} \times 6$. (3×3).   27939.

SLATER, J. W., a native of England; went early to Ireland,
and practised miniature painting in Dublin, where his works
were much esteemed, about 1770; came to London, and exhibited at the R. A., 1786 and '87; his miniatures were good.

    J. Slater.   E. Morton, lith.
    Bust, to right, nearly in profile; vignette; slightly tinted
with red, and touched up with pencil, by a later hand.
    $(6 \times 5\frac{1}{4})$.   E. 2220.-'89.

SLOANE, SIR HANS, 1660-1752, of Scotch extraction, b. at
Killeleagh, co. Down; stud. in London and Paris; M.D.;
physician to the Duke of Albemarle, Govr. of Jamaica, 1687-'9;
cr. a Bart., the first physician so honoured, 1716; Phys.-Genl.
to the Army; Phys. in Ordy. to George II., and Pres. Coll.
Phys.; Pres. R. S., 1727; formed the Botanic Garden at
Chelsea; his collections, bought for the nation for 20,000*l.* (the
sum named in his will), were the nucleus of the Br. Musm;
his chief work was his "History of Jamaica."

    Sir G. Kneller.   J. Faber, junr., mez.
    J. C. Smith, 328, 1st state; from collection of John Young.
                                                         26710

SLOPER, E. H. LINDSAY, 1826-1887, b. in London, a pupil of
Moscheles, and (1840) of Aloys Schmitt, at Frankfort, of Carl
Vollweiler, at Heidelberg, and at Paris, of Boisselot, for composition, 1841; remained there five years, gaining great
reputation as composer and pianist; appeared with success in
London, 1846; and became a successful teacher, performing
occasionally in public.
    See FIRST READING.

SMART, SIR GEORGE THOMAS, 1776-1867, son of a music-seller
and contrabassist; educ., as chorister of Chapel Royal, under
Dr. Ayrton; learned organ-playing from Dr. Dupuis and composition from Dr. Arnold; organist at St. James's, Hampstead
Road, and violinist at Salomon's concerts; taught the harpsichord and singing; knt. at Dublin, where he had conducted
some concerts; conductor of Philharmonic Socy., 1813-'44;
conducted Festivals.

    J. Cawse.   E. Stalker, mez.
    Ha. len. to right, seated, looking to front, wearing glasses,
holding a book in right hand, his fingers between the leaves.
    $11\frac{7}{8} \times 9\frac{7}{8}$. $(9 \times 7\frac{1}{2})$.   22918.

SMIRKE, Robert, 1752–1845, b. at Wigton; brought to London, 1765, by his father, who d. soon after; apprent. to a heraldic painter; entd. R. A. schools, 1772, and exhibited, 1786; A.R.A., 1791; R.A. 1793, presenting, as his diploma picture, "Don Quixote and Sancho;" contributed to the Shakspere Gallery; elected keeper of the Academy, 1804, but the appointment not sanctioned by the King, on account of his revolutionary opinions; continued to paint domestic subjects, and to illustrate books; published a satire on the Directors of the Brit. Institution, 1815.

Miss Smirke pinx.   J. Jackson del.   C. Picart, stipple.
Sh. ha. len. to right, looking to left; vignette; May 2, 1814.
15 × 12⅝.   (7½ × 7½).   E. 2219–'89.

SMIRKE, Robert, Junr., 1780–1867, architect, b. in London, second son of R. Smirke, R.A. (1752–1845); educ. at Apsley School, Beds.; pupil of Sir J. Soane for a year, and student at the R. A., won silver and gold medals, 1799; travelled abroad till 1805; built Lowther Castle; architect to the Mint; A.R.A., 1808; R.A., 1811; built many public edifices, clubs, &c.; Kt., 1831.
G. Dance, 1809.   W. Daniell, stipple.
Sh. ha. len. to left, in profile, seated; Sepr. 15, 1809.
10¾ × 8.   (7 × 6).   28299. 7.

SMITH, Albert, 1816–1860, b. at Chertsey; son of a surgeon; educ. for same profession, which he abandoned for literature; began contributing to magazines in London, 1841; wrote "The Wassail Bowl," "Mr. Ledbury," "Scattergood Family," "Marchioness of Brinvilliers," "Christopher Tadpole," "Pottleton Legacy," "The Gent," "Ballet Girl," "Flirt," &c.; wrote and performed the entertainment, "The Ascent of Mont Blanc," until within two days of his death.
F. Talfourd.   R. J. Lane, A.R.A., lith.
Head, to right, looking to front; vignette.
Presentation-copy, with autograph inscription, on the occasion of the 1000th representation of "Mont Blanc," May 2, 1855.
(5½ × 4⅜).   24091.

SMITH, Benjamin,   –1833, pupil of Bartolozzi; engraver in the stipple manner; employed by Boydell on the Shakspere Gallery; engraved after West, Rigaud, Copley, Romney, and other prominent painters of the day; largely assisted by his pupils in executing his plates; d. at 21, Judd Place, where Mrs. Woollett lived many years.
Anon.   B. Smith, stipple.
Ha. len. to left, seated, leaning against a tree.
Private plate; proof before all letters.
9 × 6¼.   (6¾ × 4½).   E. 2221.–'89.

SMITH, Sir Francis Pettitt, 1808–1874, b. at Hythe; originally a grazing-farmer; in early life made many models of small boats, for which he contrived various modes of propulsion;

patented his "screw-propeller," 1836; the "Archimedes" was fitted with a "Screw," launched and proved successful, 1838; his system generally adopted, in spite of great difficulties; received a pension of 200*l*., 1855; Curator of Patent Museum, S.K., 1861–74; Knt., 1871.

W. Boxall, A.R.A. S. Marks, mixed mez.
Ha. len. to left, looking to front, a model of a ship's stern, with screw-propeller attached, on his right; his right hand resting on the model, while he points to the screw with his left.
17⅞ × 14⅝. (14¼ × 11¼). 27610.

SMITH, FREDERIC COOKE, 1720–1739, a student of architecture, or of sculpture (?).

G. Richmond. F. C. Lewis, stipple.
T. Q. len. to front, seated, looking to right, holding a pair of compasses in his right hand; a private plate.
22 × 17. (14¼ × 11¼). 27233.

SMITH, SIR HENRY GEORGE WAKELYN, 1788–1860, Major-General, afterwards Lt. Gen.; son of a surgeon; b. at Whittlesea; served in S. America, the Peninsula, and at Waterloo, &c.; Adj. Gen. at the battle of Maharajpore; commanded a division at Ferozeshah, Moodkee, &c.; won the battle of Aliwal; cr. baronet, 1846; Govr. of the Cape, 1847; G.C.B.; d., London.

R. Dalton. R. Dalton, lith.
Ha. len. to right, looking to front, in uniform; vignette. In[d. proof.
(10¼ × 9¼). 23034.

SMITH, JAMES, 1775–1839, b. in London, son of Robert Smith, F.R.S., F.S.A., solicitor to the Board of Ordnance; followed his father's profession, and suc. to place of solr. to the Customs; contributed to the "Pic Nic," and prefaces to a new edition of "Bell's Br. Theatre," and to the "Monthly Mirror," 1807–'10, with his brother Horace, with whom he wrote the famous "Rejected Addresses," 1812.

J. Lonsdale. H. Cousins, mixed mez.
Ha. len. to front, looking to right; left hand resting on the handle of a walking-stick.
Open letter proof; December 1st, 1835
15 15/16 × 11 14/16. (10⅞ × 8½). 22136.

SMITH, SIR JAMES EDWARD, 1759–1828, Physician and Botanist; b. Norwich; one of the founders, and first Pres., of Linnæan Society; author of "Flora Britannica," "Introduction to Botany," "The English Flora," and other works; M.D., F.R.S.

W. Lane. F. C. Lewis, chalk and dot.
Full ha. len. to front, looking to left, holding in his left hand a spray with some leaves upon it; March 15, 1816.
(?) × 15. (16½ × 11½). 26711.

SMITH, JOHN, 1654–1720, mezzotinto-engraver; served his apprenticeship under Tillot, or Tillet, a painter, in Moorfields;

studied mezzotinto-scraping under Isaac Becket and J. Vander
Vaart; engaged by Sir G. Kneller to engrave many of his
portraits, which are his best works.

Sir G. Kneller, 1696.   J. Smith, 1716, mez.
J. C. Smith, 232, 2nd state.   22100.

SMITH, John—*continued.*

Sir G. Kneller.   S. Freeman, stipple.
Copy of the mezzotinto plate by J. Smith.
$5\frac{3}{8} \times 5\frac{3}{8}$.   ($4\frac{1}{4} \times 3\frac{1}{2}$).   E. 2216.-'89.

SMITH, John, c. 1690, a writing master.
[W. Faithorne del.]   [P. vander Banck.]
Sh. ha. len. to left, ooking to right; lace collar, long hair, and
cloak; in an oval of laurels, surmounted by a wreath with two
pens; the title on a tablet below.
($11\frac{1}{2} \times 7\frac{1}{2}$).   28857. 1.

SMITH, or SMYTH, Rt. Hon. John, of Heath Hall, co. Yorks.,
1748–1811; M.P., for Pontefract; Lord of Admiralty, of Treasury, Master of Mint, P.C., &c.
See DILETTANTI SOCIETY

SMITH, John Pye, 1774–1851, Independent Divine; b. at
Sheffield; appr. to his father, a bookbinder; entd. Rotherham
Indep. Coll.; classical and aftds. Divinity tutor at Homerton
Coll., 1800–'50; author of "Scripture and Geology," the
"Scripture Testimony to the Messiah," &c.; D.D., F.R.S.,
F.G.S.; d. at Guilford.
C. Baugniet, 1845.   Baugniet, lith.
T. Q. len. to right, in gown; book in right hand; microscope
and books on table, on right.
Ind. proof with open letters.
($13\frac{3}{4} \times 11\frac{1}{4}$).   23089.

SMITH, Robert Henry Soden, 1822–1890, son of Capt. Robert
Smith, of Dirleton, Co. Haddington, of the 44th Regt., Athlone
Pursuivant of Arms; educ. at Trin. Coll., Dublin; for more
than 30 years held office at South Kensington; Keeper of the
Art Library.
Anon.   Meisenbach, process print.
Sh. ha. len. to front, looking to left; vignette; in Illustr.
Lond. News, July 12, 1890.
$3\frac{1}{4} \times 2\frac{1}{4}$.   ($2\frac{1}{2} \times 2$).   E. 674.-'90.

SMITH, Sydney, 1771–1845, b. at Woodford, Essex; educ. at
Winchester and New Coll., Oxf.; fellow, 1790; curate, Nether-
Avon, Wilts., 1794–6; went to Edinb., where he lived 5 years;
minister of Charlotte Episcopal Chapel, and founded the Edinb.
Review; came to London, 1804, preached at the Foundling,
lectured at the Royal Institution; Preb., Bristol, 1828; Canon,
St. Paul's, 1831; publd. Sermons, Letters, &c.
J. Hayter.   W. Sharp, lith.
O 82849.   E E

T. Q. len. to left, seated, with left hand resting on papers
and books on a table.
Ind. proof.
$(17\frac{13}{14} \times 12\frac{1}{16})$.　　　　　　　　　　　　　　　　　　22919.

SMITH, or SMYTH, SIR THOMAS, 1514–1577; b. at Saffron-
Walden; entd. Queen's Coll., Cambr., 1526; fellow, 1531;
Publ. Orator, 1538; went abroad for 2 or 3 years, taking his
degree D.C.L. at Padua; Reg. Profr. Civil Law, Cambr., 1542;
Rector of Leverington; Chancr., Ely; Dean of Carlisle;
knighted; Sec. of State; Ambassr. to Germany, 1548;
Ambassr. to France, 1551, 1559, 1562, 1567, 1572; Prov.,
Eton, 1554; succ. Burleigh as Sec. of State, and Chancr. of
Garter, 1572; pubd. several learned works.
　　Holbein.　　　　　　　　　　　　　　J. Houbraken, 1743.
　　Sh. ha. len. slightly to right, in furred dress, looking to front;
oval in border.
　　This occurs in Birch's " Lives."
　　$14\frac{11}{16} \times 9\frac{1}{4}$.　$(14\frac{1}{8} \times 8\frac{3}{4})$.　　　　　　　　　　　24676.

SMITH, THOMAS, æt. 112.
　　Anon.　　　　　　　　　　　　　　　　　Anon, etching.
　　Ha. len. to front, hair curling at sides of head, beard, wide
open collar, waistcoat showing four buttons, two and two;
vignette; from the collection of John Barnard.
　　Proof.
　　$11\frac{6}{16} \times 8\frac{9}{16}$.　$(8 \times 8\frac{1}{3})$.　　　　　　　　　15575. D.
　　Mentioned by " Bromley," p. 475.

SMITH, THOMAS ASSHETON, 1776–1858, one of the most famous
sportsmen and riders of his time; Master of the Quorn Hounds,
Leicestershire, 1805–'17; of the Burton, Linc., 1817–'26;
and of the Tedworth, Hants., from 1826 to his death; M.P.,
Andover, and aftds. for Carnarvonshire; proprietor of great
and very valuable slate-quarries; d. at Vaenol, near Bangor.
　　W. Sextie.　　　　　　　　　　D. G. Thompson, mixed mez.
　　Wh. len. on horseback, directed to left, looking to front;
three hounds by his horse's head, to which one of them lifts his
nose, another hound behind his horse, on right.
　　Open letter proof, Novr. 1, 1853.
　　$25\frac{3}{4} \times 31\frac{1}{4}$.　$(20\frac{1}{8} \times 27\frac{7}{8})$.　　　　　　　　　25841.
　　See also SUTTON.

SMITHS (" of Chichester "), " the three, Brothers and Painters;"
sons of a Baptist minister.
　　WILLIAM, 1707–1764, b. at Guildford, painted portraits, and
afterwards tried landscape, fruit, and flowers; member of the
Free Society of Artists; d. at Shopwyke, near Chichester.
　　GEORGE, 1714–1776, b. at Chichester; highly distinguished
as a landscape-painter, gaining the first premium of the Society
of Arts, 1760, in competition with R. Wilson; excellent violon-
cello-player; pubd. some poetry; and, with his brother John,

engraved 53 small plates from their landscapes; member of Free Society of Artists.

JOHN, 1717–1764, also painted landscapes, but inferior to George; member of Free Society of Artists.

W. Pether. W. Pether, mez.
J. C. Smith, 32, 2nd state. 25759.

SMITH, WILLIAM, 1769–1839, "the father of English Geology," published "Improvement of boggy land by Irrigation," "Observations on Water-meadows," "Mineral Survey," "Strata Identified," Geological Maps, &c.
See SCIENCE.

SMITH, WILLIAM, 1781–1835, eminent print-seller of Lisle Street, Leicester square, where he died, aged 54.
W. Fisk, S. Freeman, stipple.
Ha. len. to front, seated, holding a paper in right hand, and spectacles in left; facs. signature below, 1836.
Ind. proof; a private plate.
$9 \times 5\frac{3}{4}$. $(4\frac{3}{4} \times 3\frac{1}{2})$. 27940.

SMITH, WILLIAM, 1808–1876, printseller and connoisseur, of Lisle St., son of the eminent printseller who had traded there for many years; suc. to the business, 1835, by which he and his brother realised large fortunes; assembled a magnificent collection of water-colour drawings, which he partly gave, partly bequeathed to the South Kensington Museum; was very active in the formation of the National Portrait Gallery; F.S.A., &c.
[W. Carpenter.] W. Carpenter, etched.
Sh. ha. len. to left, seated; vignette; 1853.
Private plate; Ind. paper proof.
$9 \times 5\frac{1}{5}$. $(5\frac{1}{2} \times 5)$. E. 163.–'91.

SMITH, SIR WILLIAM SIDNEY, 1764–1840, b. at Westminster; entd. the navy, 1776; Commander, in the Mediterranean, 1798; successfully defended Acre against Napoleon, 1799; co-operated with Abercromby in Egypt, 1801; K.C.B., 1815; Admiral, 1821; Lt.-General of Marines, 1830; G.C.B., &c.
J. Eckstein. A. Cardon, stipple.
Wh. len. to front, looking back to left, pointing to right with his sword; Jezzar Pasha and two companions are behind him.
Open letter proof.
$23\frac{1}{4} \times 15\frac{2}{3}$. $(20\frac{7}{8} \times 13\frac{1}{4})$. 22009.

SMITHSON, HENRIETTA; actress; of Irish family; aftds. m. (1833) to H. Berlioz, French composer.
R. E. Drummond. J. Thomson, stipple.
See LA BELLE ASSEMBLÉE, 1819. 13867. 17.

SMOLLETT, TOBIAS, 1721–1771, b. at Cardross, Scotland; educ. at Dumbarton and Glasgow; stud. medicine; became a surgeon's mate on board a King's ship; present at Carthagena; left the service, and returned to London, 1746; pubd. "Roderick

E E 2

Random," 1748; "Peregrine Pickle," 1751; M.D., and tried to
practise at Bath; but returned to London, and pubd. "Ferd.
Count Fathom," and a translation of "Don Quixote;" edited
"Critical Review," for a libel in which he was fined and
imprisoned; wrote other novels, poems, &c.; d. at Leghorn.

 Anon.   J. Collyer.

 Sh. ha. len. to right, looking to front; oval in border;
figures below of Time and the Muse of History; prefixed to his
continuation of Hume's History, 1790. 8vo.

 $7\frac{7}{8} \times 5\frac{7}{15}$. $(6\frac{1}{15} \times 4\frac{1}{8})$.   25803.

SMYTH, WILLIAM, 1765–1849, educ. at Peterhouse, Cambr.,
where he became fellow and tutor; prof. Mod. Hist. in that
University, 1807 till his death; pubd. "Lectures on Mod.
Hist.," and "Lectures on the French Revolution," 1840.

 J. Slater delin.   I. W. Slater, lith.

 Ha. len. to right, looking to front, left arm extended; vignette.
Ind. proof, April 21, 1831.

 $(7\frac{1}{4} \times 8\frac{1}{2})$.   23574.

SNOW, RALPH, 1670–1744, a well-known Writing-master.

 J. Whood.   A. Van Haecken, mez.

 J. C. Smith, 15.   28857. 2.

SOANE, SIR JOHN, 1752–1837, b. at Reading, son of a bricklayer; educ. at a private school; pupil under Dance, 1767, and
then in Holland's office; student at Royal Academy, gained
silver medal, 1772; gold medal, 1776; sent to Rome; architect
and surveyor to Bank of England, 1788; Clerk of the Works,
St. James' Palace, Houses of Parliament, Chelsea Hospital, &c.;
Prof. Architecture, Royal Academy; knt. 1831; F.R.S., F.S.A.;
bequeathed his collection of pictures, books, antiquities, &c., to
the nation.

 Sir T. Lawrence, R.A.   C. Turner, mez.

 T. Q. len. to front, seated, holding spectacles in left hand; an
open window behind, on left.

 Proof before all letters, except the publication-line, Jany. 18,
1830; a private plate (according to Evans).

 $22 \times 15\frac{15}{16}$. $(16\frac{1}{4} \times 12\frac{5}{8})$.   26615.

 S. Drummond, A.R.A.   T. Blood, stipple.

 Sh. ha. len. to front, looking upwards to left; coat buttoned
loosely. Engraved for the European Magazine, Feb. 1, 1813.

 $6\frac{1}{2} \times 4\frac{7}{15}$. $(3\frac{1}{2} \times 2\frac{1}{8})$.   13586.

 F. Chantrey, R.A.   C. Turner, A.R.A., mez.

 A bust, to front, looking to right; inscription on pedestal in
14 lines; dated, 1831.

 The print was published Jany., 1832.

 $14\frac{1}{16} \times 19\frac{1}{16}$. $(9\frac{3}{5} \times 4\frac{1}{4})$.   26616.

SOBIESKI. See CLEMENTINA.

SOMERS, John, Lord, of Evesham; 1650–1716, b. at
Worcester; stud. at Mid. Temple; counsel for the Seven
Bishops, 1688; Attorney-General, 1692; Lord Chancellor and
Baron Somers, 1697; removed, impeached, and acquitted,
1700; Lord Pres. of Council, 1708-'10; Pres. of R. S., 1698–
1703; &c.
 Sir G. Kneller.   J. Faber, junr., mez., 1733.
 J. C. Smith, 208 (26 of Kit-Cat Club).   22101.
 See also LORDS JUSTICES.

SOMERSET, CHARLES SEYMOUR, Duke of, 1662–1748, suc.
1679; K.G.; Colonel, 1685; Speaker of House of Lords; Lord
Justice; Lord President of Council; Master of the Horse; P.C.
 Sir G. Kneller.   J. Faber, junr., mez., 1733.
 J. C. Smith, 208. (In Kit-Cat Club 2.)   25813.

SOMERSET, EDWARD SEYMOUR, Duke of, c. 1500–1552;
known as " The Protector;" eldest son of Sir John Seymour,
Knt., and brother to Queen Jane Seymour; became Protector
of the Realm, Governor of King Edward VI., and Duke of
Somerset, 1547; K.G.; charged with treason; beheaded.
 Holbein.   J. Houbraken, 1738.
 Sh. ha. len. to right, wearing a broad-leafed hat, and cloak;
the George hangs from the fingers of his left hand. Below, the
coronation of Edward VI. is represented; engraved for
Birch's " Lives."
 14⅞ × 9⅝. (14 × 8⅞).   21975.

SOMERSET, ROBERT CAR (or KER), Earl of, c. 1587–1645;
infamous favourite of James I.; Viscount Rochester, etc.;
Knight, 1607; K.G.; P.C.; cr. Earl, 1613; Lord Chamber-
lain of Household, 1614; m. the profligate and divorced
Frances, Countess of Essex; both convicted of murder of Sir
Thomas Overbury; Prisoner in the Tower, 1615-'22; par-
doned, released, and restored, 1624.
 Anon.   Anon.
 Wh. len., at left, with his Countess, at right; frontisp. to
" Truth brought to Light," Lond., 1651, 4to.
 From the Burleigh James Collection.
 (7½ × 5¾).   28076.

SOMERVILLE, MISS, of Drury Lane Theatre.
 Anon.   Alais, stipple.
 See LA BELLE ASSEMBLÉE, 1817. 13867. 16.

SOMERVILLE, MARY, 1780–1872, Astronomer, Geographer,
&c.; daughter of Vice-Admiral Sir W. G. Fairfax; b. in Scotland; m. young to Samuel Greig, of the Russian Navy, from
whom she learned much of her mathem. knowledge; her second
husband was Dr. W. Somerville; in 1826, presented to Royal
Socy. a paper on the " Magnetising Power of the more refran-
gible Solar Rays;" author of several learned works on Astronomical and other subjects; received Gold Medal of Geogr.
Socy., 1869.
 J. R. Swinton del., 1848.   W. Holl, stipple.

Bust, to front, slightly inclined to right, looking to left, wearing a cap; vignette.
Ind. proof; 1848.
9×6. $(3\frac{1}{2} \times 2\frac{7}{8})$. 26570.

SOMERVILLE, MARY—*continued.*
From a bust by Macdonald. E. Finden.
Slightly turned to left, a chaplet on her head, and a veil; 1846. Used as frontispiece to her work "On the Connexion of the Physical Sciences."
Ind. proof before all letters, except the name on the bust.
$11\frac{1}{2} \times 7\frac{3}{16}$. $(4\frac{7}{16} \times 3\frac{3}{16})$. 26569.

SOPHIA, ELECTRICE DOWAGER OF BRUNSWICK, 1630–1714; Wife of Ernest Augustus of Hanover, 1658; Mother of K. George I.
[Weidman (?)] I. Smith, mez., 1706.
Oval, the figure turned to the left.
J. C. Smith, 237, 2nd state. 25039.
Also a duplicate in Genealogical Chart, 553. 1.
26712.

——
Anon. J. Smith, mez.
J. C. Smith, 238, 2nd state. 25438.
In Genealogical Chart, 553. 1.

SOPHIA DOROTHY, 1666–1726; daughter of George William, Duke of Zelle, m. 1682 to George I.; sep. 1694.
S. Harding. A. Birrel, stipple.
Ha. len. looking to front, in oval.
$6\frac{1}{2} \times 5$. $(4\frac{1}{8} \times 3\frac{3}{4})$. 25841.
In Genealogical Chart, 553. 1.
Also, in same, a coloured drawing, portrait of same.
$5\frac{1}{2} \times 4\frac{3}{4}$. 390.

SOPHIA, PRINCESS, daughter of George III., 1777–1848.
H. Ramberg. Ogborne, stipple.
Oval, with flowers.
$(10\frac{7}{8} \times 8\frac{3}{4})$. 26725. 5.
Also, a duplicate, in Genealogical Chart, 553. 1.
Open letter proof.
$14 \times 10\frac{1}{4}$. 25068. 1.

——
Sir W. Beechey. Cheesman, stipple.
T. Q. len. to front, looking to left, seated; oval.
Published by Harding, May 19, 1806.
$10\frac{7}{8} \times 8\frac{7}{8}$. $(7\frac{7}{8} \times 6\frac{3}{8})$. 25059. 2.
In Genealogical Chart, 553. 1.

——
Anon. Anon., lith.
T. Q. len. seated, slightly to left, winding wool(?), "after she became blind" (added in pencil).
Ind. proof before letters.
$(13\frac{1}{4} \times 10\frac{3}{8})$. 25063.
In Genealogical Chart, 553. 1.

SOTHEBY, WILLIAM, 1757–1833, b. in London; educ. at Harrow; joined the 10th Dragoons, 1774; m. and quitted the army, 1780; made a pedestrian tour through Wales, 1788, and pubd. a poetical description of it; came to London, 1791; wrote poems; translated Wieland, the Georgics of Virgil, and Homer; wrote Tragedies, &c.; F.R.S., F.S.A.

Sir T. Lawrence, R.A.   F. C. Lewis, stipple.

Sh. ha. len. to right, looking to left; wearing a frogged coat; vignette.

Ind. proof before all letters, except the artists' names, lightly scratched. A private plate.

10$\frac{1}{16}$ × 8$\frac{1}{4}$.   (6$\frac{1}{4}$ × 6$\frac{1}{2}$).   22154.

SOUTHAMPTON, HENRY WRIOTHESLEY, 3rd Earl of, 1573–1624, 2nd son of Henry, 2nd Earl; suc., 1581; educ. at Cambr.; B.A., 1589; M.A., Oxon., 1592; Captain in Navy, 1597; Vice-Admiral, 1597; Knt., 1597; Lt.-Genl. of the Horse, Ireland, 1599; attainted and impris., 1601–'3; K.G., 1603; rest. Earl of Southampton, 1603; P.C., 1619; friend of Shakspere; d. at Bergen-op-Zoom.

Anon.   Dunkarton, mez.

Wh. len. to front, in a richly-ornamented dress, a helmet with plumes on his right, a breastplate on his left, on the floor.

J. C. Smith, p. 236.

Proof before all letters.

13$\frac{1}{4}$ × 9$\frac{1}{8}$.   (11$\frac{1}{8}$ × 8).   27611.

SOUTHCOTT, JOANNA, 1750–1814, religious impostor; at the age of 40, gave out that she was an inspired prophetess; is said to have led a sect of 100,000 by her blasphemous rhapsodies; described herself as the woman mentioned in the book of Revelation; scribbled a mass of unintelligible nonsense; drove a brisk trade in seals, as passports to heaven; announced herself the destined mother of the promised Shiloh; d. of dropsy.

W. Sharp.   W. Sharp.

Ha. len. to left, seated, looking to front, in white bonnet and dress; a Bible open before her; Jany., 1812.

Proof before publication-line.

14 × 11$\frac{1}{4}$.   (12 × 9$\frac{3}{4}$, incl. ruled border, 1$\frac{1}{16}$).   22483.

SOUTHERNE, THOMAS, 1659–1746; b. in Dublin; educ. at Trin. Coll., Dublin; went young to London, where he devoted himself to writing plays and poetry; served in the army against the Duke of Monmouth; esteemed by Dryden; amassed a considerable sum by the success of his plays, of which the best known are "Oroonoko" and the "Innocent Adultery."

J. Worsdale.   J. Simon, mez.

J. C. Smith, 138, 2nd state; Simon's address nearly obliterated.   26713.

SOUTHEY, ROBERT, 1774–1843, b. at Bristol, where his father was a linendraper; educated privately, at Westminster (1788), and at Bal. Coll., Oxf. (1792–'4); began publishing poems immediately on leaving Oxford; m. in 1795, and pubd. "Joan of Arc;" went abroad; returned, settled near Keswick, 1804; Poet Laureate, 1813; LL.D., 1821; m. again, 1839; author of "Wat Tyler," "Thalaba," "Metrical Tales," "Madoc," "Curse of Kehama," "The Doctor," &c.

    S. Lane.   H. Dawe, mez.

    Sh. ha. len. to left, looking to right; white neckcloth, coat loosely buttoned.

    Proof before letters, except the artists' names, and publication-line, Feb. 20th, 1826.

    $12\frac{8}{16} \times 8\frac{4}{8}$ $(10\frac{1}{8} \times 8\frac{4}{16})$.   **24244.**

SOUTHEY, ROBERT,—*continued.*

    T. Phillips, R.A.   S. W. Reynolds, mixed mez.

    Ha. len. to right, seated, in a furred gown, holding a closed book in both hands; landscape in the distance, on right.

    $(3\frac{7}{8} \times 3)$.   **23580.**

SOUTHWELL, SIR ROBERT. *See* NAVAL HEROES (1).

SPEED, JOHN, c. 1555–1629, b. at Farrington, Cheshire, by trade a tailor, patronised by Sir Fulk Greville, who enabled him to leave his trade and pursue the study of antiquities; pubd. "The Theatre of the Empire of Great Britain," 1606; "The History of Great Britain," 1614; and "The Cloud of Witnesses," a popular work, formerly prefixed to large bibles.

    Anon.   S. Savery.

    T. Q. len. to right, seated, holding a pair of compasses, on a plan on table, at right; his right arm rests on his chair; he wears a hat, and furred robe; below, an inscription in Latin, in 7 lines, signed "D. Georgius Humble."

    $(10\frac{3}{16} \times 7\frac{5}{16})$.   **25798.**

SPELMAN, SIR HENRY, 1562–1641, b. at Congham, Norfolk; educ. at Trin Coll., Cambr., and Linc. Inn; wrote, when very young, a Latin treatise on coat-armour, for which he was admitted a member of the first Society of Antiquaries; high-sheriff, 1604; sent as Commissioner to Ireland, and appointed Comr. to inquire into the exaction of fees, for which he was knighted; compiled "Archæologus" or "Glossarium," a "History of the Civil Wars," "History of Tenures," &c.

    Anon.   W. Faithorne.

    L. Fagan, p. 61; the second plate, 2nd state.   **24131.**

SPENCE, WILLIAM, c. 1780–1860, Entomologist; early showed a disposition for the study of insects; formed a friendship with Rev. W. Kirby, with whom he wrote the popular work, "Introduction to Entomology."

    [T. H. Maguire.]   T. H. Maguire, lith., 1849.

    Full ha. len. to front, seated, looking to right; right hand on thigh, left on arm of chair, coat buttoned; rectilin. with corners lopped off; facs. signature below.

    $(9\frac{3}{4} \times 9\frac{1}{2})$.   **22543.**

SPENCER, GEORGE JOHN SPENCER, 2nd Earl, 1758-1834;
F.R.S., 1780; M.P., 1780; Lord of Treasury, 1782; suc.,
1783; P.C.; Lord Privy Seal, 1794; Ambassador Extraord.
to Vienna, 1794; First Lord of Admiralty; K.G., etc.; great
book-collector.

    J. Hoppner, R.A.   H. Meyer, mez.
    Ha. len. to left, holding a book, which he reads.
    Open letter proof.
    $14 \times 9\frac{7}{8}$. $(12\frac{1}{3} \times 9\frac{2}{9})$.   24092.

———

    J. S. Copley, R.A.   R. Dunkarton, mez.
    J. C. Smith, 37, 2nd state.   22104.

SPENCER. See ALTHORP.

SPENS, NATHANIEL, 1728-1815, 4th son of Thomas Spens,
Esq., of Lathallan; educ. at Edinb., under his uncle, John
Douglas, an eminent surgeon; in earlier years pract. as a
surgeon; aftds. as a physician; P.R.C.P. Edinb., 1794-'6;
redeemed estate of Craig-Sanquhar, 1793, where he died, after
enjoying a prosperous career.

    Sir H. Raeburn.   J. Beugo.
    Wh. len. to front, in archer's dress, drawing a bow; one of
Raeburn's best portraits, and Beugo's masterpiece; the picture
was painted for the Royal Company of Archers, whose property
it is still, and it hangs in the Archers' Hall, Edinb. The
"Spens Anniversary Medal" is annually shot for by the Royal
Company.
    Ind. proof.
    $26\frac{1}{8} \times 17\frac{7}{8}$. $(23\frac{9}{16} \times 15\frac{7}{8})$.   27515.

SPRAGGE, or SPRAGUE, SIR EDWARD,   -1673, a brave
English Admiral; was a captain in the first engagement with
the Dutch, 1665; knighted by the King on board, for his
gallant conduct; disting. in the 4 days' battle, 1666; burned a
number of Dutch fire-ships, in the Thames, throwing their
whole fleet into confusion; destroyed seven Algerine men-of-
war in the Mediterranean, 1671; went down in his boat, in an
engagement with Tromp, 1673, while going from his own sink-
ing ship to another.
    See NAVAL HEROES (2).

SPRAT, THOMAS, 1636-1713, and his son, Thomas SPRAT, 1679-
1720; the father was b. at Tallaton, Devon.; educ. at Wad.
Coll., Oxon.; Canon of Windsor; Chapl. to D. of Buckingham
and Charles I.; one of the first F.R.S.; Dean of Westminster,
1683; Bp. of Rochester, 1684; author of "History of the
Royal Socy.," "Life of Cowley," &c.; distinguished preacher
and controversialist; bur. in Westminster Abbey. The son
was Preb. of Westminster, and Archdeacon of Rochester.

    M. Dahl.   J. Smith, mez., 1712.
    J. C. Smith, 243, 1st state.   22052.

STABLES, EDWARD, Clerk to the House of Commons, during Sir Robert Walpole's Administration.
See COMMONS.

STAFFORD, WILLIAM HOWARD, Viscount, 1612–1680; cr. 1640; F.R.S., 1665; accused by Titus Oates; Prisoner in Tower, 1678–'80; impeached, tried, and condemned, though absolutely innocent; beheaded.
    A. van Dyck. (Wm. Derby del.)   E. Scriven, stipple.
    Published, March 25, 1825. In Lodge's Large Series.
    $14\frac{7}{8} \times 10\frac{11}{16}$. $(7\frac{3}{16} \times 5\frac{11}{16})$.   27153.

STAFFORD, G. G. LEVESON-GOWER, Marquess of.   See SUTHERLAND.

STAIR, JAMES DALRYMPLE, Viscount, 1619–1695 , great lawyer; President of Court of Session, 1671; published "Institutes of Law of Scotland," 1681 ; cr. Viscount, 1690.
    Sir J. Medina.   J. Horsburgh.
    Ha. len. to left, looking to front, in wig and robes.
    Proof with open letters; 1825. Edinburgh.
    $15 \times 10\frac{1}{2}$. $(7\frac{3}{8} \times 5\frac{1}{8})$.   26714.

STANFIELD, WILLIAM CLARKSON, 1794–1867, b. at Sunderland, of Irish parentage ; son of a literary man ; went to sea and sketched marine subjects ; discharged, obtained engagements to paint scenery in London Theatres; exhibited with the Socy. of British Artists, 1823, and at the R. A., 1827; A.R.A., 1831; R.A., 1835 ; travelled in Italy ; painted many seascapes, Italian views, &c.
    J. Simpson.   W. Say, mez.
    Ha. len. to right, looking to front, holding pencil in right hand ; coat buttoned to throat.
    $14\frac{1}{4} \times 12(?)$. 12×10.   23035.
    ────
    Anon.   C. Fox, 1828.
    Ha. len. to front, slightly inclined to left, looking to right ; left hand raised.
    Ind. paper proof before all letters, except the engraver's name and date ; vignette.
    $11\frac{15}{16} \times 9\frac{1}{2}$. $(9\frac{1}{4} \times 8\frac{3}{4})$.   E. 1303.–'88.
    ────
    Anon.   Anon, woodcut.
    Bust to right, looking to front.
    Cut from an illustrated paper, and laid down.
    $(6\frac{3}{4} \times 5\frac{11}{16})$.   E. 2217–'89.

STANHOPE, CHARLES, EARL, 1743–1816, politician and man of Science; educ. at Eton and Geneva; M.P. until 1786, when he suc. to the peerage; avowed republican sentiments ; author of many inventions, a method of rendering buildings safe from fire, an arithmetical machine, a new printing press, &c., &c.
See DILETTANTI SOCIETY. See also SCIENCE.

STANHOPE, JAMES STANHOPE, Earl, 1673–1721; wounded at
siege of Namur, 1695; served in Spain, Commander-in-Chief,
1708; took Mahon, in Minorca, and Madrid, 1710; Premier,
1717.
 Sir G. Kneller. I. Faber, Junr., mez.
 In Kit-Cat Club. J. C. Smith, 208 (20). 22273.

STANLEY, EDWARD, 1770–1849, son of Sir John Thomas
Stanley, Bart., and father of Dean Stanley; educ. at Cambr.;
presented by his father to the rectory of Alderley, Cheshire,
1805; Bishop of Norwich, 1837; Pres. of the Linnæan Society;
author of the "Familiar History of Birds."
 T. H. Maguire. T. H. Maguire, lith., 1840.
 Full ha. len. to left, seated, looking to front, in robes; facs.
signature below ("E. Norwich").
 13½ × 10¾. (10¾ × 10½). 22539.

STANLEY, LORD. See DERBY.

STANLEY, THOMAS, 1625–1678, b. at Leytonstone; educ. at
home and at Pembr. Hall, Cambr.; M.A., 1641; went abroad;
returning, settled in the Temple; pubd. poems and translations,
1649; edited Æschylus; best known by his "History of
Philosophy," 1655, 1687, 1743, to the first of which this port.
was prefixed.
 Sir P. Lely. W. Faithorne.
 L. Fagan, p. 61, where he is incorrectly called "Sir Thomas
Stanley." The picture is in the Nat. Port. Gallery. 27142.

STEELE, SIR RICHARD, 1671–1729, b. in Dublin; educ. at the
Charterhouse and Oxford; ensign in the Guards; printed a
book called "The Christian Hero," dedicated to Lord Cutts,
who made him his Secy., and obtained for him a Captain's
Commission; author of several plays; established Tatler, and
Spectator; M.P., 1713; expelled for a political paper; on ac-
cession of George I., knighted; received various appointments.
 Sir G. Kneller. I. Simon, mez.
 J. C. Smith, 141, 2nd state. E. 2165.–'89.

_____

 Sir G. Kneller. J. Faber, junr., mez.
 J. C. Smith, 208 (31 of Kit-Cat Club). 21866.

STEPHEN, OF BLOIS, King; 1105–1154; suc. 1135.
 G. Vertue. G. Vertue.
 Bust, crowned, profile to right; from a silver coin.
 11⅝ × 7⅟₁₄. (11⅟₁₆ × 7³⁄₁₆). 27178. 6.
 NOTE.—No other original portrait of this King is known.

STEPHENSON, GEORGE, 1781–1848, Engineer; son of an
engine-tenter near Newcastle; began life as a pit-engine boy;
constructed his first locomotive, 1814; planned and executed
the first English Railway, between Stockton and Darlington,
1818–'25; constructed the Liverpool and Manchester Railway;

acted afterwards as engineer to most of the lines built until
1840, when he retired.

J. Lucas. T. L. Atkinson, mixed mez.

Wh. len. to front, holding hat in right hand, railway and
train in distance; water in foreground, on right.

Ind. proof before letters; facs. signature.

$32 \times 20\frac{5}{8}$. $(27\frac{1}{2} \times 17\frac{1}{4})$. 22272.

STEPHENSON, ROBERT, 1803–1859, Engineer; son of George
Stephenson; b. near Newcastle; apprent. to a Coal-Viewer;
helped his father in railway construction; built the "Rocket"
locomotive engine, 1829; invented and first constructed tubular
bridges; made the Lond. and Birmingham R'way; extensively
engaged in railroad works in all parts of the world; M.P. for
Whitby; bur. in Westminster Abbey.

J. Lucas. J. R. Jackson, mixed mez.

T. Q. len. to right, seated, looking to front, his right hand
resting on a paper on which is drawn the side view of a
locomotive engine; facs. signature below; March 1, 1846.

$(16\frac{1}{4} \times 13\frac{1}{2})$. 24735.

G. Richmond, 1849. F. Holl, 1860, chalk and dot.

Bust to front, looking to left, the bust not much more than
indicated; background machine-ruled; vignette.

Proof before letters, except names of artists' and printer, and
the words "Presentation Copy."

$(8 \times 7\frac{3}{4})$. 22202.

See also MENAI STRAITS.

STEPNEY, GEORGE, 1663–1707, poet, diplomatist, and political
writer; member of the Kit-Cat Club.

Sir G. Kneller. J. Faber, junr., mez., 1733.

J. C. Smith, 208 (35). 23131.

STERNE, LAURENCE, 1713–1768, b. at Clonmel, where his
father, a lieut. in the Army, was quartered; educ. at a school
near Halifax, and at Jesus Coll., Cambr.; M.A., 1740; Vicar
of Sutton, prebend of York, rector of Stillington and Curate of
Coxwold; author of "Tristram Shandy," "Sentimental Journey,"
"Sermons," &c.

Sir J. Reynolds. E. Fisher, mez.

J. C. Smith, 56, 4th state. 24721.

STEVENS, GEORGE ALEXANDER, in the character of a Poet.
Epilogue to the Disquisition.

Dod del. Cook.

From a "Collection . . . of English Prologues," &c.

Pubd. by Fielding and Walker, Jany. 1, 1780. 28187. 15.

STEVENSON, SIR JOHN ANDREW, Knt., Mus. Doc., c. 1762–
1833, b. in Dublin, son of John Stevenson, violinist in state
band at Dublin; chorister at St. Patrick's and Ch. Ch. Cathedrals, 1773–'79; vicar choral of both Cathedrals, and member

of choir of Trin. Coll.; Mus. Doc., 1791; Knt, 1803; composed Operas, Services, Anthems, and the Symphonies and accompts. to Moore's "Irish Melodies."

    G. F. Joseph, A.R.A.   E. Scriven, line and stipple.

    Ha. len. to right, seated, looking to front, holding a pencil in right hand, his right arm resting on some MS. music on table.

    Ind. proof, with open letters; March 28, 1822.

    $14\frac{7}{8} \times 10\frac{5}{8}$. $(8 \times 6\frac{1}{2})$.   21850.

STEWART, CHARLES WILLIAM, Lieut.-General, the Hon., K.G.; G.C.B.; &c., 1778–1854, distinguished soldier and diplomatist, one of the ablest Companions in arms of the D. of Wellington during the Peninsular War; Ambassador, Vienna, &c.; afterwards 3rd Marquess of Londonderry.

    Sir T. Lawrence, R.A.   H. Meyer, mez.

    Sh. T. Q. len. to left, looking to right, in hussar uniform, carrying sword in scabbard over right shoulder.

    $(18\frac{1}{16} \times 13\frac{15}{16})$.   23038.

——, when Marquess of Londonderry.

    Bostock.   Jenkins, stipple.

    Ha. len. to left, seated, in ordinary dress. 1837.

    Ind. proof.

    $13 \times 10\frac{1}{4}$. $(8\frac{7}{8} \times 7)$.   20635.

STEWART, DUGALD, 1753–1828, Philosopher; Prof. Mathematics and Moral Philosophy, Edinb., 1785–1810; founded the "Speculative Society"; one of the most popular University lecturers of his time; author of "Philosophy of the Human Mind," "Outlines of Moral Philosophy," &c.

    Sir D. Wilkie, 1824.   S. Cousins, chalk and dot.

    Ha. len. to front, left hand resting on and grasping a large open book on a table by his side; a private plate; vignette.

    Ind proof; facs. signatures of subject and painter.

    $21\frac{1}{4} \times 17$. $(17\frac{1}{4} \times 15\frac{1}{2})$.   21954.

STEWART. See also STUART.

STILL, JOHN, 1543–1607, b. at Grantham; educ. at Cambr.; Lady Marg. Prof. of Divinity, 1570; reputed author of "Gammer Gurton's Needle," a humorous drama, characteristic of the manners of the time, and the first English comedy; Bp. of Bath and Wells, 1593.

    Anon.   W. Say, mez.

    Ha. len. to front, holding a book in right hand, his fingers between the leaves; he wears a white beard, skull-cap, hood, lawn sleeves, &c. The picture (1607) is at Trin. Coll., Cambr. This is a copy of the mez. by Jones, 1789, of which only 20 impressions were taken.

    Proof before the plate was reduced in size; only 25 printed in this state.

    $10\frac{1}{4} \times 7\frac{1}{4}$. $(4\frac{7}{16} \times 2\frac{7}{16})$.   22096.

STILLINGFLEET, EDWARD, 1635–1699, learned divine; b. at
Cranbourne, Dorset; educ. at Cambridge; Preb. of St. Paul's
and Archdeacon of London, 1677; Dean of St. Paul's, 1678;
Bishop of Worcester, 1689; author of "Origines Sacræ,"
"Origines Britannicæ," &c.

 Mary Beale.   A. Blooteling.

 Sh. ha. len. to front; oval in border; title in 3 Latin lines on
tablet below; engraved before Stillingfleet was made a Bishop;
he was still only "Ecclesiæ Cantuariensis et Paulinæ Canonicus."
$13\frac{5}{8} \times 10$. (Inside oval, 8×7).   22271.

STOCK, JOHN,   , "the late, of Poplar, for many years an
"able and conscientious instructor of youth, and a Magistrate of
"the County of Middlesex."

 H. W. Pickersgill, R.A.   C. E. Wagstaff, mixed mez

 Ha. len. to front, seated, looking to right, right hand resting
on an open book on table; coat buttoned; left arm akimbo;
facs. signature below, and also that of the painter, "his
Affectionate Pupil."

 Proof with open letters; July, 1842.

$16\frac{1}{4} \times 11\frac{15}{16}$. ($10\frac{5}{8} \times 8\frac{9}{16}$).   23115.

STOKES, ADRIAN. See SUFFOLK, FRANCES, Countess of.

STOTHARD THOMAS, 1755–1834, b. in Long Acre, London; son
of an inn-keeper; not being strong he was sent to an uncle at
Acomb, near York; educ. at school there, at Tadcaster, and at
Ilford; apprent. to a pattern-draftsman for brocaded silks in
Spitalfields; designed about 4,000 illustrations for magazines
and books, such as "Peregrine Pickle," 1781; "Clarissa," &c.;
exhib. "The Canterbury Pilgrims," "The Four Periods of a
Sailor's Life," &c.; R.A., 1794; Librarian to the Royal
Academy, 1812; designed goldsmith's work.

 J. Jackson del.   H. Meyer, stipple.

 Ha. len. to left, looking to front; vignette.

 Open letter proof (?); March 17, 1815.

$14\frac{11}{16} \times 12\frac{7}{8}$. ($7\frac{1}{4} \times 5\frac{1}{4}$).   E. 222.–'93.

 G. H. Harlow   W. H. Worthington.

 Ha. len. slightly inclined, and looking to right, resting left
arm on table; part of "The Canterbury Pilgrims" seen in
background.

 Ind. proof; May 1, 1818.

$13\frac{1}{8} \times 11\frac{7}{8}$. ($11\frac{1}{8} \times 10\frac{3}{10}$).   21851.

 Anon.   Anon.

 Wh. len. to left, seated in chair; a crayon in his right hand,
which rests on some papers, lying on a table; vignette; facs.
signature below.

 "Published May 1, 1834, by W. B. Tiffin."

$8\frac{1}{4} \times 4\frac{5}{8}$. ($5\frac{1}{4} \times 4\frac{3}{8}$).   15320.

STOW, John, c. 1525–1605, b. in Cornhill, London, bred a tailor, but devoted himself to the study of antiquity, encouraged thereto by Archbishop Parker and the Earl of Leicester; pubd. the "Summary of the Chronicles of England," enlarged as "Flores Historiarum," &c., 1600; "Survey of London," 1598; died a pauper; buried at St. Andrew's, Undershaft.

From the bust on his monument.   G. Vertue.

Bust to right, looking to front; narrow ruff and furred gown. Below, a sketch of the monument, books, deeds, &c.

$13\frac{15}{16} \times 9\frac{1}{8}$ (?).   ($13\frac{3}{8} \times 8\frac{13}{16}$).   25797.

STOWELL, Hugh, 1799–1865, b. at Douglas, Isle of Man; educ. at St. Edm. Hall, Oxf., 1818; grad., 1822; ord., 1823; curate of Shapscombe, Gloucest., and of Trin. Ch., Huddersfield, for two years, and then of St. Stephen's, and aftds. of Chr. Ch., Acton Square, Salford; Hon. Canon of Chester, 1845, and Rural Dean of Salford; pubd. Memoirs, Sermons, Poems, &c.

W. Bradley.   H. Cousins, mixed mez.

Full ha. len. standing, to left, in gown, looking to front; finger-tips of right hand resting on an open book.

Ind. proof, with open letters; Oct. 10, 1838.

$21\frac{1}{2} \times 15\frac{1}{16}$.   ($16\frac{11}{16} \times 12\frac{15}{16}$).   27086.

STOWELL, William Scott, 1st Lord, 1745–1836; son of a merchant at Newcastle, and elder brother of Lord Eldon; b. at Heworth, Durham; educ. at Newcastle and Oxford; Fellow and Tutor, Univ. Coll., Oxon.; Judge, Consist. Court, 1788–1821; Knt., 1788; Judge, High Court of Admiralty, 1798–1828; M.P., Univ. Oxford, 1801–'21; cr. Baron, 1821; d. at Early Court, Berks.

T. Phillips, R.A.   C. Turner, mez.

T. Q. len. to front, seated, in robes, looking to right.

Proof before all letters, except the artists' names and publication-line; June 2, 1828.

20×14.   ($15\frac{1}{2} \times 12\frac{3}{4}$).   22920.

STRAFFORD, Thomas Wentworth, Earl of, 1593–1641; Kt., 1611; M.P., 1621; P.C., 1629; Lord Deputy, Ireland, 1633; despotic and cruel, caused the rebellion of 1641 by his infamous claim of Connaught for the Crown; cr. Earl, 1639; K.G., 1640, Lieut.-General; impeached, sacrificed by the King, and beheaded.

With Sir Philip Mainwaring, Sec. of State.

A. van Dyck.   G. Vertue, 1739.

Ha. len. to right, looking to front, holding a letter in left hand. Scarce (according to Evans).

($10\frac{3}{4} \times 8\frac{1}{2}$).   24677.

STRAHAN, William, 1715–1785, b. at Edinburgh; apprent. to a printer; came to London, where he worked as a journeyman in the same office as Benjamin Franklin; set up for himself;

successful purchaser of copyrights; King's printer, 1770; M.P., 1775–'84.

   Sir J. Reynolds.   J. Jones, mez.

   J. C. Smith, 70.   22538.

STRANGE, Sir John, 1696–1754; Recorder of London; Master of the Rolls, 1750; buried at Leyton, in Essex.

   Anon.   J. Houbraken.

   Sh. ha. len. to right, looking to front, in wig and robes; oval in border. Inscription, with name and date, in three lines below, in the border.

   (9¼ × 6¼).   26716.

STRANGE, Sir Robert, 1721–1792, b. at Pomona, Orkney; educ. at Kirkwall, intended for the law, but, showing talent for drawing, apprent. to R. Cooper, engraver, at Edinburgh; joined in the fighting of '45; escaped from Culloden to Paris, where he studied under Le Bas; returned to London, 1751; refused commission to engrave portraits of the King and Lord Bute; travelled in Italy, spent some years in Paris; engraved many of the finest classical pictures; regained the favour of the Court, 1787; engraved the Apotheosis of the three children of the King; Knt.; elected member of Academies of Rome, Florence, Bologna, Parma, Paris, but not of London.

   J. B. Greuse.   R. Strange Eques.

   Head, in profile to left; medallion; finished proof.

   Prefixed to Strange's " Collection of Historical Pictures."

   6 × 5⅟₁₆. (5¼ diamr.).   24687.

   J. B. Greuse delt.   W. C. Edwards.

   Head, in profile, to left; medallion; copied from the one engraved by Strange himself.

   Ind. proof; Feb. 15th, 1828.

   8⅟₁₆ × 5¼. (3½ diamr.).   26279.

STRUTT, Jedediah, of Belper, 1726–1797; b. at Normanton, near Alfreton; second son of a farmer and maltster; acquired some education and knowledge of science by his own efforts; after perfecting Lee's frame, went to Derby, and established a manufactory of ribbed stockings; entd. into partnership with Arkwright, the promise of whose waterframe he was the first to see; was the founder of an opulent manufacturing family.

   J. Wright (of Derby).   H. Meyer, stipple.

   Ha. len. to front, seated, looking to left, resting head on right hand; vignette; facs. signature below; 1833.

   (5⅝ × 5⅟₁₆).   28298. 9.

STRUTT, Joseph, 1749–1802, b. at Springfield, Essex; apprent. to W. W. Ryland, the engraver, and became a student at the Royal Academy, 1770; employed to make drawings at the Br. Museum; pubd. " Regal and Ecclesiastical Antiquities," 1773; " View of the Manners," &c., " Chronicle of England,'

1777, unfinished; Dict. of Engravers, 1785–'6; "Sports and Pastimes," &c.

O. Humphry, R.A.   J. Ogborne.

Sh. ha. len. to left, looking to front; shirt with frill; coat buttoned loosely across.

Proof before all letters, and before the border-line.

$7\frac{7}{8} \times 5\frac{7}{8}$. $(3\frac{3}{4} \times 3)$.   27556.

Id.—Ind. proof, with the artists' names and border-line added.

E. 2222.–'89.

STRYPE, John, 1643–1737; b. at Stepney; educ. at St. Paul's school, and at Jesus Coll., Cambr.; M.A., 1669; received the benefices of Theydon Boys, Essex; of Low Layton, where he stayed 63 years; and the sinecure of Terring, and Lectureship of Hackney; wrote Lives of the Archbishops Cranmer, Parker, Grindall, and Whitgift; other Memoirs; Ecclesiastical Memorials; Annals of the Reformation; &c.

Anon.   G. Vertue.

T. Q. len. to right, seated, looking to front; left hand on pile of three books; right hand on knee; bookcase on left; arms below; title in three lines of inscription; frontispiece to his Ecclesiastical Memorials.

$(8\frac{3}{16} \times 5\frac{13}{16})$ 22545.

STUART, Arabella, commonly called the Lady Arabella, 1575–1615, b. at Chatsworth, only child of Charles Stuart, Earl of Lennox, the brother of Henry Lord Darnley, father of James VI. of Scotland; privately m., 1610, to William Seymour, grandson of the Earl of Hertford; imprisoned by James I. at Lambeth, and her husband in the Tower; escaped; she was overtaken, and immured in the Tower, where she finally lost her reason and her life.

"*Are to be Sould in Popes head Ally by George Humble. I, W.Se.*(?) *scup.*"

Ha. len. to right, looking to front, in rich dress with collars of pearls, &c.; oval in ornamented border; arms above; below, "*The Pictuer of the most Noble | and, Learned Ladye | Arbella Steuart, &c.*"

Anno 1619, on the scroll which crosses the oval border. Fine, and very rare (see "Bromley," p. 61).

$7\frac{1}{4} \times 4\frac{5}{16}$. $(7 \times 4\frac{3}{16})$.   26715.

STUART, Lord Dudley Coutts, 1803–1854, politician, M.P. for Marylebone, 1847–'54.

Anon.   N. Ploszczynski, lith.

Ha. len. to front, looking to right; vignette; facs. signature below.

Ind. proof, March 1st, 1850.

$(9\frac{1}{4} \times 8\frac{1}{2})$.   27612.

STUART, James, 1713–1788, architect, called *Athenian Stuart*, b. in London; son of poor parents; contributed, when a boy, to his own and his family's support, by painting fans; learned mathematics, Latin, and Greek, by himself; travelled on foot to Italy, was taught architecture at Rome by Mr. Revett, with whom he went to Greece, 1751; served in Hungary as engineer; returned to Greece; author of the "Antiquities of Athens;" surveyor to Greenwich Hospital; F.R.S., F.S.A.

Proben (Romæ).   W. C. Edwards.

Sh. ha. len. to left; white neckcloth; hair tied behind head.

Scratched letter proof; in a ruled border.

$13\frac{7}{16} \times 10\frac{1}{8}$.   (Excl. of border, $6\frac{1}{2} \times 5$).   28297. 2.

Id.—A later proof, with "From a Picture in the possession of Richard Brettingham, Esq., Shotford Hall, Norfolk," added below.   22921.

STUART, James—continued.

Sir J. Reynolds del.   S. W. Reynolds, etched.

Sh. ha. len. to left, looking to front, wearing cap and loose gown; the etcher's name and "Athenian Stuart, From an original sketch by Sir J. Reynolds, publish'd March 30, 1795," lightly etched in the margin below, and difficult to decipher. Undescribed.

Note.—The etcher has added some strokes of the rocker in the shadows of the cap and on the dress.

$9\frac{3}{8} \times 7\frac{1}{2}(?)$. (6×5).   26268.

———

Anon.   Anon. (J. Basire?).

T. Q. len. to left, seated, wearing a fur cap and gown; he is drawing; oval. A vignette in the title to "Rudiments of Architecture," 1789.

Proof before all letters.

$3\frac{1}{2} \times 4\frac{7}{16}$. $(2 \times 2\frac{2}{3})$.   26267.

STUART, Charles James Edward. See CHARLES James Edward ("The Young Pretender").

STUART, James Francis Edward. See JAMES Fr. E. ("The Old Pretender").

STUART, Sir John, 1793–1876, son of a Highland laird, educ. at High School and Univ. Edinb.; called to the bar at Linc. Inn, 1819; Tory M.P. for Newark, 1847–'52, and for Bury, 1852, July till Oct., when he was made a Vice-Chancellor; Bencher of Linc. Inn; resigned in 1871.

Anon.   W Walker, mez.

T. Q. len. to front, with right hand to side, left hand resting on a pedestal.

Proof before all letters.

$20\frac{1}{16} \times 16\frac{1}{2}$. $(17\frac{5}{16} \times 13\frac{1}{2})$.   27958.

"STUART, La Belle." See RICHMOND.

STUBBS, George, 1724–1806, b. at Liverpool, son of a surgeon; studied anatomy; visited Italy; returned to England, and soon became well known and patronised as a painter of horses and other animals; A.R.A., 1780; R.A., 1781, but declined to give the usual picture, and remained A.R.A.; painted the "Fall of Phaeton," which was very successful; executed some enamels on iron.

P. Falconet del, 1769.   D. Pariset, stipple.
Bust to left, in profile; medallion in border; from the set of Artists engraved by Pariset.
$(6\frac{13}{16} \times 4\frac{7}{8})$.   28300. 52.

G. Dance, 1794.   W. Daniell.
Sh. ha. len., in profile to right, seated; published April 10, 1802; vignette.
$10\frac{1}{2} \times 7\frac{11}{16}$. $(8\frac{1}{4} \times 6\frac{3}{4})$.   28299. 8.

Humphry.   W. Nicholls, stipple.
Ha. len to right, looking to front; drapery behind him, and a picture of heads of four racing horses. Decr. 1st, 1800.
$7 \times 4\frac{15}{16}$. $(4\frac{7}{8} \times 3\frac{1}{2})$.   28300. 53.

Anon.   Anon., etched.
T. Q. len. to right, in profile, seated, holding the brush in his left hand, painting a galloping horse.
$(6\frac{3}{4} \times 5\frac{3}{16})$.   18106.

STUKELEY, WILLIAM, 1687–1765, b. at Holbeach, Linc.; entd. of Benet Coll., Cambr., 1703; M.B., 1709; M.D., 1719; pract. at Boston, London (1717), and Grantham (1726); ord., and received the living of All Saints, Stamford, 1729; of Somerby, 1739; Rector of St. George the Martyr, Lond., 1747; wrote many antiquarian works, "Palæographia Britannica," accounts of Abury, Stonehenge, &c.; one of the founders of the Antiquaries', Spalding, and Egyptian Societies.

Sir G. Kneller.   J. Smith, 1721, mez.
J. C. Smith, 248, 2nd state.   25758.

STURGE, JOSEPH, 1793–1859, b. at Elverton, Gloucest.; eminent corn-factor and philanthropist; established, 1820, the firm of J. & C. Sturge at Birmingham, where he died; wrote, with T. Harvey, "The West Indies in 1837," "Visit to the United States in 1841," &c.

[G. Richmond (?)].   W. Holl.
Bust to right, looking to front; vignette.
Ind. proof before all letters.
$22\frac{7}{8} \times 16$. (8×7).   25840.

SUETT, RICHARD, 1758–1805, distinguished comedian, d. at Chelsea.

S. De Wilde.   S. De Wilde, 1811, mez.
Ha. len. slightly to right, seated, looking to front, holding a roll of paper in left hand; inscribed as above, in pencil; Evans attributes this (?) plate to Cawthorn.
$11\frac{1}{2} \times 9\frac{1}{4}$. $(9\frac{7}{16} \times 7\frac{1}{4})$.   27554.

SUFFOLK, CHARLES BRANDON, Duke of, 1484-1545; Captain of a Man-of-War, 1512; Master of the Horse; K.G.; Marshal of the King's Army, 1513; cr. D. 1514; Ambassador to France; P.C.; Earl Marshal; Lord Presidt.; &c.
Anon. J. Thane.
Bust to front, looking to right; facs. signature below.
From an original at Strawberry Hill.
$8\frac{3}{8} \times 5\frac{1}{2}$. $(7\frac{3}{8} \times 4\frac{1}{4})$.   14165.

SUFFOLK, FRANCES BRANDON, Duchess of,   -1559, the elder of the two surviving daughters of Charles Brandon by Mary, Queen of France, youngest sister of Henry VIII.; m., firstly, to Henry Grey, 1533, 3rd Marquess of Dorset (cr. Duke of Suffolk, 1551, d. 1554); secondly, to Adrian Stokes, master of her horse.
L. de la Heere. G. Vertue, 1748.
Ha. len. on the left, turned towards her second husband, Adrian Stokes, who is on the right of the print, both looking to front, richly dressed. The picture was in Hor. Walpole's collection.
$18\frac{1}{2}$ (?) $\times 22\frac{1}{4}$. $(17\frac{7}{8} \times 21\frac{11}{16})$.   24645.

SUFFOLK, HENRY GREY, Duke of, b. before 1510-1554, son of Thomas, 2nd Marquess of Dorset; suc. as 3rd M., 1530; K.C.B., K.G., cr. D. 1551; beheaded.
M. Gerard.   (W. Derby del.)   S. Freeman, stipple.
Ha. len. to right, looking to front, wearing the Collar and George. June 1st, 1825.
$14\frac{1}{2} \times 10\frac{1}{4}$. $(7\frac{1}{2} \times 5\frac{3}{8})$.   27154.

SULLIVAN, SIR HENRY, 1786-1814; Lieut.-Col.; Bart.; M.P.; in Coldstream Guards; killed in the Sortie from Bayonne, 14th April, 1814.
H. Edridge. W. Bond, aquat.
Wh. len. to left, looking to front, resting his hand, with high cap, on a gun, on left; fortifications in the background.
$20\frac{1}{8}$(?) $\times 14\frac{3}{8}$. $(18 \times 12\frac{7}{8})$.   24726.

SUMNER, CHARLES RICHARD, 1790-1874, Bishop; youngest brother of John Bird Sumner (q.v.); b. at Kenilworth; educ. at Eton and Trin. Coll., Cambr.; Rector of Abingdon, and Librarian to George IV.; Preb., Worcester, 1822; Preb., Canterbury, 1825; Dean of St. Paul's, Preb., London, and Bishop of Llandaff, 1826; transld. to Winchester, 1827; resigned, 1869; publd. several theologl. works.
Sir M. A. Shee, P.R.A. S. Cousins, mez.
T. Q. len. to left, seated, in robes of the Garter, looking to front; his cap in his right hand; a cathedral in distance.
Open letter proof.
$20\frac{15}{16} \times 14\frac{9}{16}$. $(17\frac{1}{8} \times 13\frac{3}{4})$.   27085.

SUMNER, JOHN BIRD, 1780-1862, Archbishop; eldest son of Rev. Robert Sumner, Vicar of Kenilworth; b. at Kenilworth;

educ. at Eton and King's Coll., Cambr. ; B.A., 1803 ; M.A., 1807 ; D.D., 1828 ; assist. master and fellow, Eton, and Rector, Mapledurham, Canon of Durham, 1820 ; Bishop of Chester, 1828 ; Archbishop of Canterbury, 1848 ; publd. many Essays, Treatises, Lectures, Sermons, &c.

Mrs. Carpenter.   J. R. Jackson, mixed mez.

T. Q. len., to right, seated, in robes, looking to front ; his left hand rests on a table, near an open book.

$20\frac{1}{4} \times 16$. $(17\frac{3}{4} \times 13\frac{7}{8})$.   27087.

Mrs. Carpenter.   S. Cousins, A.R.A., mixed mez.

T. Q. to left, seated, in black gown, holding in left hand an open book which rests on his knee.

Proof before all letters, except the artists' names, in open letters, and the scratched publication-line, April 20, 1840, Chester and London ; with line of autogr. presentation by Mrs. Carpenter.

$20\frac{3}{4} \times 15\frac{7}{8}$. $(17\frac{5}{16} \times 13\frac{1}{4})$.

In the Sheepshanks Gift.   18909.

SUNDERLAND, CHARLES SPENCER, Earl of, 1675–1722 ; M.P., 1695 ; suc., 1702 ; Envoy Extr. and Plenipo. to Vienna, 1705 ; P.C., 1706 ; Lord Lieut. Ireland, 1714–'5 ; Lord Keeper Privy Seal ; Lord Presidt. ; First Lord, Treasury, 1718–'21 ; K.G., &c.

Anon.   J. Houbraken, 1746.

Sh. ha. len. to left, looking to front, wearing the Collar of the Garter.

In Birch's "Lives."

$14\frac{1}{2} \times 8\frac{11}{16}$. $(13\frac{5}{8} \times 8\frac{1}{4})$.   27121.

SUNDERLAND, LADY DOROTHY SIDNEY, Countess of, 1617–1684, daughter of Robert Sidney, 2nd Earl of Leicester ; m. 1st, 1639, to Henry, Lord Spencer, cr. Earl of Sunderland, 1643 ; 2nd to Richard Smythe, of Bounds, Kent, whom she survived ; celebrated as " Saccharissa " by Waller.

Sir A. van Dyck.   P. Lombart.

T. Q. len. to right, looking to front, resting right hand on vase, in which a plant is growing, to which she points with her left hand ; in decorated border.

$14 \times 9\frac{5}{8}$. $(12\frac{7}{16} \times 9\frac{5}{16}$, including border, $\frac{5}{8})$.   21823.

SUNDERLAND, HENRY SPENCER, 1st Earl of, 1620–1643 ; son of William, 2nd Lord Spencer ; b. at Althorp ; educ. at Oxford ; suc. his father, 1636 ; mar. Lady Dorothy Sidney (q.v.), 1639 ; present at the setting up of the Royal Standard at Nottingham, Aug. 22, 1642 ; disting. himself at Edge Hill, Oct., 1642 ; cr. Earl of Sunderland, 1643 ; fell at Newbury.

" From an original Portrait."   E. Bocquet, 1809.

T. Q. len. to left, looking to front, in armour ; horsemen and tents in distance, on left.

$12 \times 9\frac{3}{4}$. $(7\frac{3}{4} \times 6\frac{1}{4})$.   27613.

SUNDON, Charlotte, Viscountess, -1742, of co. Herts; favourite of Queen Caroline; resid., Sundon House, Bedford; a Life of her was written by Mrs. Thomson, 1847.

"From an Original Picture." E. Harding, stipple.

Ha. len. to front, hair descending on right shoulder; 1 May, 1799. The picture said to be "in the Possession of the Revd. Mr. Jacobs."

$8\frac{1}{4} \times 6\frac{1}{4}$. $(6 \times 5\frac{1}{4})$. 25006.

SURREY, Henry Howard, Earl of, c. 1517–1547, Poet and soldier; son of Thomas, 3rd Duke of Norfolk; served with distinction under his father in France and Scotland; wrote "Songs and Sonnets," highly esteemed by his cotemporaries; tried on a charge of quartering the Arms of Edward the Confessor with his own, and aspiring to the hand of the Princess Mary; beheaded.

Titian. T. A. Dean, stipple.

T. Q. len. in a rich, embroidered dress, leaning with right arm on a pillar, under an arch, over which is the letter H, supported by two amorini.

Ind. proof before all letters.

$15 \times 10\frac{3}{8}$. $(8\frac{3}{16} \times 5\frac{3}{8})$. 22147.

SUSSEX, Anna, Countess of, – , daughter of Robert Wake of Antwerp; m. to James Savile [1649–1671], Earl of Sussex, Baron Savile, of Pontefract, &c.

Sir A. van Dyck P. Clouwet.

Wibiral, 171, 3rd state.

$(9\frac{3}{16} \times 7)$. E. 2303.–'86.

SUSSEX, Augustus Frederick, Duke of, 1773–1843, sixth son of George III.

Sir Wm. Beechey, R.A. Wm. Skelton.

Ha. len. in Scottish dress.

Published, May 1, 1816, by W. Skelton.

With the word PROOF in the lower left corner.

$19\frac{7}{8} \times 15\frac{3}{8}$. $(17\frac{1}{8} \times 13\frac{11}{16})$. 29697. A.

Also, an impression without the word, PROOF. 27252.

And another, in Genealogical Chart, 553. 1. 25056. 7.

———

I. J. Masquerier. T. Hodgetts, mez.

Ha. len. to front, looking to left, wearing star on coat.

Published April 5, 1813, by Edwd. Orme.

The word *Proof* is scratched in the lower right corner.

$13\frac{7}{8} \times 9\frac{7}{8}$. $(11\frac{7}{8} \times 9\frac{7}{8})$. 27944.

See also VICTORIA, Princess Royal, Christening of; and VICTORIA, Queen, CORONATION, MARRIAGE, &c.

SUSSEX, THOMAS RATCLIFFE, Earl of, 1525-1583; M.P.,
1553; Baron Fitzwalter, 1553; Ambassador Extr. to Spain,
1554 ; Lord Deputy, Ireland, 1556-'8; suc. as 3rd Earl, 1557;
P.C., 1570; &c.
  Sir A. More.   H. Meyer, stipple.
  Ha. len. to right, looking to front.
  Ind. proof.
  $14\frac{1}{8} \times 10\frac{3}{8}$. $(7\frac{1}{8} \times 5\frac{1}{4})$.   27614.

SUTHERLAND, GEORGE GRANVILLE LEVESON-GOWER, Duke
of, 1758-1833; son of Granville, 1st Marquess of Stafford,
M.P., 1787; Ambassador Extr. and Plenipo. to Paris, 1790-'2;
P.C.; suc. as Marquess, 1803; cr. D. 1833.
  W. Owen (1811).   [H. Meyer ?] mez.
  As Marquess of Stafford. Ha. len. to left.
  Proof before all letters.
  $(11\frac{7}{8} \times 9\frac{1}{16})$.   20928.

————

  T. Phillips, R.A.   H. Meyer, mez.
  As Marquess of Stafford; sh. ha. len. to front, looking to left.
  Proof with scratched letters.
  $20 \times 14\frac{1}{2}$. $(11\frac{5}{8} \times 10)$.   27615.

SUTTON, CHARLES MANNERS, 1755-1828, 4th son of Lord
George Manners Sutton ; educ. at Emm. Coll., Cambr. ; Dean
of Peterborough, 1791; Bishop of Norwich, 1792; Dean of
Windsor, 1794; Archbishop of Canterbury, 1805; pubd. ser-
mons and an entomological treatise.
  J. Hoppner, R.A.   C. Turner, A.R.A., mez.
  T. Q. len. to left, standing, in robes, looking to front, holding
a roll of paper in right hand ; a view into St. George's Chapel,
Windsor, in background, on left.
  Open letter proof (?); Jany. 1, 1830.
  $10 \times 13\frac{3}{4}$. $(15\frac{1}{4} \times 11\frac{1}{2})$.   27584.

SUTTON, SIR RICHARD, 1799-1855, of Norwood, co. Notts;
sportsman ; country squire ; M.F.H.; &c.
  F. Grant, R.A.   F. Bromley, mixed style.
  Sir Richard, on horseback, directed to the left, is near the
middle of the print, but rather to the right; in the middle is
Mr. T. Assheton Smith (q. v.); around them are other sportsmen,
whips, and the Quorn (?) hounds.
  Open letter proof, Novr. 14, 1855.
  $25\frac{1}{4} \times 38\frac{3}{4}$. $(20\frac{9}{16} \times 34\frac{7}{8})$.   25848.

—— Key to the above, the personages numbered.
  (6×10).   25848. A.

SWIFT, JONATHAN, 1667-1745, son of Jonathan Swift, of
English family ; b. in Dublin; educ. at Kilkenny and Trin.
Coll., Dublin ; Sec. to Sir William Temple; took orders, and
obt. a living in Ireland ; pub. "Tale of a Tub," 1704; joined
Tory party; wrote in "Examiner," and produced many
pamphlets ; Dean of St. Patrick's, 1713; said to have been
privately married to Esther Johnson ("Stella"), 1716; pub.

his "Drapier's Letters" (about "Wood's Halfpence "), 1724; "Gulliver's Travels," 1726; became insane before his death; bur. in St. Patrick's Cathedral.

F. Bindon.   A. Miller, Dub.; 1743, mez.
J. C. Smith, 53.   25802.

SYDENHAM. *See* THOMSON.

SYKES, Sir Tatton, Bart., 1772–1863, of Sledmere, Yorks.; celebrated sportsman, owner of horses, and Master of Foxhounds.

H. Tilbury.   J. A. Vinter, lith.
Wh. len. to right, seated, wearing boots; " in his 87th year."
Ind. proof; 1860.
$(15 \times 11\frac{7}{8})$.   25760.

SYLVESTER, Joshua, 1563–1618, poet; translated Du Bartas into English verse, once a very popular book, praised by Ben Jonson ; also wrote " Tobacco Battered and the Pipes Shattered " about their Eares, that idlely Idolize so base and barbarous " a Weed; or at leastwise over-love so loathsome a Vanity" (c. 1620), and other pieces.

Anon.   C. van Dalen.
Sh. ha. len. to right, looking to front, crowned with laurel, wearing high ruff; oval in rectang. border; title round the oval; below, 6 English verses, " Behould the man . . . . . . a Saint expired," signed " John Vicars."
$9\frac{7}{16} \times 6.$ $(7\frac{1}{2} \times 5\frac{3}{4})$.   27674.

SYMINGTON, William. *See* SCIENCE.

SYMONDS, Sir William, 1782–1856, son of a naval officer, of an old Suffolk family; entd. navy, 1794; served in Lord Bridport's action, 1795, and in many other subsequent engagements; Surveyor to the Navy, 1832–'47, during which time 180 various ships were built; Knt., 1836; C.B., 1848; Rear-Admiral; F.R.S.; d. on a voyage from Malta to Marseilles.

H. W. Phillips.   E. Morton, lith.
T. Q. len. to front, in uniform (as captain), left hand on thigh, pair of compasses in right hand on papers; vignette; Feb. 25, 1850.
$(12\frac{1}{4} \times 10\frac{3}{4})$.   24036.

TABLEY, Sir John Fleming, Baron de. *See* LEICESTER.

TALBOT, Charles Talbot, 1st Baron, 1684–1737, eldest son of Rev. W. Talbot, aftds. Bishop of Durham ; educ. privately, and at Oriel Coll., Oxon.; fellow of All Souls; member of Inner Temple; M.P. for Tregony, and Durham; Solr.-Genl., 1726–1733, when he became Ld. Chancellor ; cr. Baron Talbot; d. suddenly ; bur. in Barrington Ch., Gloucestershire.

J. Vander Banck.   J. Houbraken, 1739.

Ha. len. to left, looking to front, wearing wig and robes; oval, in border; mace, scales, &c., below.

In Birch's "Lives."

$14\frac{3}{4} \times 9\frac{1}{4}$. $(14\frac{1}{4} \times 8\frac{3}{4})$.   27122.

TALBOT, CHARLES CHETWYND CHETWYND-TALBOT, Earl, 1777– 1849; Visct. Ingestre; suc., 1793; Lord Lieut., Ireland, 1817– '21; P.C., K.P., K.G., &c.

T. C. Thompson, R.H.A.   S. W. Reynolds, mez.

Wh. len. to left, looking to right, in robes of the order of S. Patrick.

"Proof sec^d. 50," with inscription in open letters, on a separate plate.

Without separate plate, $25\frac{3}{4} \times 16\frac{1}{4}$.   E. 1571–'88.

TALFOURD, SIR THOMAS NOON, 1795–1854; Sergeant-at-law; Justice of Common Pleas, 1849; published "Ion," a tragedy, 1835; "Vacation Rambles," &c., 1844; "Final Memorials of Charles Lamb," 1848; M.P., &c.

J. Lucas.   W. O. Burgess, mez.

As Sergeant; T. Q. len. to right, seated, looking to front, holding a book on his knee.

Proof with scratched letters, Jany. 1, 1840.

16×12. $(12\frac{3}{4} \times 10)$.   22484.

TALMASH (sic), THOMAS,   –1694; of Helmingham, Suffolk; General; served in Ireland, for William III.; wounded in the attack on Brest, and d. at Portsmouth.

Sir G. Kneller.   J. Houbraken.

Sh. ha. len. to left, looking to front, in armour, with long hair; oval in border. The name is properly TOLLEMACHE.

In Birch's "Lives."

$14\frac{1}{4} \times 9\frac{1}{2}$. $(14 \times 8\frac{1}{4})$.   20801.

TANNER, THOMAS, 1674–1735, b. at Market Lavington; educ. at Queen's Coll., Oxf.; removed to All Souls', 1694, where he became a fellow; Chancr. of Dioc. of Norwich, 1701; Rector of Thorp, 1706; Preb., Ely, 1713; Canon, Ch. Ch., Oxf., 1723; Bishop of St. Asaph's, 1732; wrote "Notitia Monastica," &c.

Anon.   G. Vertue.

Sh. ha. len. slightly to right, looking to front, in robes; oval in border; arms below, in centre; four lines of inscription.

From the Tunno Collection.

$(13\frac{7}{16} \times 10)$.   23141.

TATTERSALL, RICHARD, 1724–1795, of Ridge and Hurstwood, 2nd son of Edmund Tattersall; educ. at Burnley Gram. School; came to London, and set up as a horse-auctioneer, taking a 99 years' lease, 1766, of premises at Hyde Park Corner, where the business was carried on till the end of the lease, when it was removed to Albert Gate; he sold the stud of a former patron, the Duke of Kingston, 1774; entertained George IV., when Prince of Wales, Charles J. Fox, and others, at Highflyer

Hall, near Ely, named after the famous horse, Highflyer, which he had bought of Lord Bolingbroke, 1779, for 2,500*l.*; joint owner, with the Pr. of Wales, of the "Morning Post;" m. Catharine Somerville, gr. dau. of 12th Lord Somerville; "Old Tatt" d. at his house, Hyde Park Corner, Feb. 2, 1795.

T. Beach. J. Jones, mez.
J. C. Smith, 71. 22059.

TATTERSALL, RICHARD, 1785–c. 1858, grandson of Richard, the founder of the firm, and son of Edmund, on whose death, 1810, he became the head of the firm, a very well-known and respected man for 50 years in London.

C. Hancock. W. Giller, mixed mez.
T. Q. len. to right, seated at table, on which he writes, looking to front; the book, on which lies the paper on which he is writing, is labelled "Private Stud-Book."
Proof with open letters; Novr. 15, 1841.
$15\frac{5}{16} \times 12\frac{1}{16}$. $(11\frac{1}{2} \times 9\frac{3}{16})$. 27230.

TAYLOR, EDGAR, 1793–1839, a descendant of John Taylor, the eminent Hebraist, himself a distinguished scholar and solicitor of London; translated the Brothers Grimms' German Popular Stories, illustrated by G. Cruikshank; pubd. "Lays of the Minnesingers," 1825, "Book of Rights," "Master Wace his Chronicle," &c.; F.S.A.

E. W. Eddis. C. Turner, A.R.A., mixed mez.
Full ha. len. to left, seated, holding a closed book in his right hand, resting on his knee.
Ind. proof, August 10th, 1841.
$15\frac{1}{4} \times 11\frac{1}{2}$. $(11\frac{1}{4} \times 9\frac{1}{4})$. 22922.

TAYLOR, SIR HERBERT, 1775–1839; Lieut.-General; private Secretary to the Duke of York, and to George III.; M.P., Windsor; G.C.B., and G.C.H.; Master of St. Katherine's Hospital.

W. I. Newton (min.). W. Ward, [Junr.], mez.
Ha. len. to left, looking to front, in uniform, with star, cloak, &c.
A private plate; scr. letter proof; 1836.
$12 \times 8\frac{1}{2}$. $(6\frac{3}{8} \times 4\frac{13}{16})$. 25762.

TAYLOR, JEREMY, 1613–1667, one of the most illustrious divines of the 17th century; b. at Cambridge; educ. at Cambridge University; a favourite and follower of Laud; settled, with a fellowship, at Oxford; pres. by Juxon, c. 1638, to rectory of Uppingham; Chaplain to Charles I., attended him at Oxford, and through the Civil War; cr. D.D. by the King's command; imprisoned and depr. during Commonwealth, preaching, writing, and keeping a school; went to Ireland, 1658; at Restoration, Bishop of Down and Connor; P.C., Ireland; &c.

Anon. (P. Lombart.)
Wh. len. to front, inclined slightly to right, looking to front, left hand raised; standing on pedestal, inscribed MERCVRIVS

CHRISTIANUS; from title to his "Holy Living and Dying," 1650, 8vo.
$(4\frac{13}{16} \times 2\frac{1}{8})$. 29718. 8.

Anon. P. Lombart.
Sh. ha. len., slightly to right, looking to front; wearing a gown, and holding a book in right hand; oval in border; arms below, and three lines of inscription: NON MAGNA LOQUIMUR. SED VIVIMUS. . . . . FACIAM.
$10\frac{3}{8} \times 6\frac{1}{16}$. $(10\frac{3}{16} \times 5\frac{13}{16})$. 27143.

TAYLOR, JOHN, c. 1580–1654, the *Water Poet*, b. in Gloucestershire; educ. at Gloucester; apprent. to a waterman; served, 1596, in the fleet under the Earl of Essex; present at attack on Cadiz; returning, plied on the Thames, collecting wine-dues for the Lieut. of the Tower; retired to Oxford at Rebellion; kept a public house there, and aftds. another, near Long Acre; his works were published in folio, 1634.
Anon. E. Scriven, stipple.
Sh. ha. len. to right, looking to front, with ruff, and cloak over left side; from the original picture in possession of the Watermen's Company.
Ind. proof, April 30, 1827.
$9\frac{7}{8} \times 7\frac{7}{16}$. $(5 \times 3\frac{7}{8})$. 21747.

TAYLOR, REV. JOHN, 1694–1761, eminent Unitarian divine, born in Lancashire; educ. at Whitehaven; pastor for some years at Norwich; tutor of Divinity at newly-founded Academy at Warrington; pubd. several works, including his "Sketch of Moral Philosophy."
Heins, 1746. J. Houbraken, 1754.
Ha. len. to left, looking to front; oval in border, inscription round oval; "intended as a frontispiece to Dr. Taylor's Hebrew Concordance" (MS. note below portrait).
$13\frac{13}{16} \times 8\frac{5}{8}$. $(13\frac{3}{8} \times 8\frac{1}{4})$. 29722. 13.

TAYLOR, SIR JOHN, –1788, Bart., of Lysson Hall, Jamaica; cr. Bart., 1778; F.R.S., &c.
See DILETTANTI SOCIETY.

TAYLOR, MICHAEL ANGELO, 1758–1834, an active and rather prominent politician; M.P.; became Recorder of Poole.
J. Lonsdale. S. W. Reynolds, mez.
Ha. len. to right, seated; coat buttoned across; one hand, the right, partly seen.
Open letter proof; March 7, 1822.
$14\frac{1}{8} \times 9\frac{3}{4}$. $(12\frac{5}{8} \times 9\frac{13}{16})$. 27535.

TAYLOR, MISS, of the Surrey Theatre.
R. E. Drummond. Anon.
See LA BELLE ASSEMBLÉE, 1817. 13867. 54.

TAYLOR, RICHARD, 1781–1858. eminent printer (of the firm,
R. & J. Taylor), and naturalist, gr.-grandson of John Taylor,
D.D. (author of " Hebrew Concordance ") ; b. at Norwich;
joined Dr. Tilloch (1822) as editor of " Philosophical Maga-
zine ; " pubd. Scientific Memoirs, notes and additions to Tooke's
" Diversions of Purley," to Warton's " History of English
Poetry," &c.; F.R.A.S.; F.S.A.; Under-Sec. to Linn. Socy.;
d. at Richmond.

Maguire.   T. H. Maguire, lith., 1851.
Full ha. len. to front, looking to right, seated, with right hand
on thigh; rectilin., with corners lopped off; facs. signature
below.
(10¼ × 9⅜).   22540.

TAYLOR, ROWLAND, 15..-1555, one of the most learned English
divines of the 16th century, most illustrious in his heroic death
as Protestant martyr ; was chaplain to Archbp. Cranmer; presented to living of Hadleigh, Suff.; opposed restoration of
Romanism at Mary's accession ; imprisoned, deprived, burnt at
stake on Aldham Common, near Hadleigh.
See REFORMERS.

TEESDALE, SIR CHRISTOPHER, 1833–1893, when a Capt. in
the R.A., was A.D.C. to Gen. Sir W. F. Williams, in the
defence of Kars, 1855, where he received the V.C.; returned to
England, as Major, and shared the applause with which his chief
was received ; A.D.C. for 10 years to the Queen ; knighted, 1887 ;
Equerry to the Prince of Wales for many years; Master of the
Ceremonies, 1890.

Baugniet.   Baugniet, 1857, lith.
Ha. len. slightly to left, looking to front; vignette; facs.
signature.
(9¼ × 6⅜).   23616.

TEIGNMOUTH, JOHN SHORE, Lord, 1751–1834, Statesman and
Author ; Govr.-Genl., India, 1793–'8.

H. P. Briggs.   H. Dawe, mez.
T. Q. len. seated, to left, looking to right, fingers of each hand
interlocked with those of the other ; his works (" Life of Sir
W. Jones," etc.) on table, at right.
Scratched letter proof.
(17½ × 13⅒).   27231.

TELFORD, THOMAS, 1757–1831, distinguished civil engineer, b.
in Eskdale, Dumfriesshire ; began life as a shepherd boy;
appr. to a stone-mason, 1771 ; came to London, 1782 ; settled
at Shrewsbury, 1787, and became surveyor for Co. Salop till
his death ; constr. Ellesmere canal; surv. for Caledonian Canal;
built the bridge over the Menai Straits, 1826; St. Catherine's
Docks, &c.; F.R.S.E.; F.R.S.; &c.

S. Lane.   W. Raddon.
T. Q. len. to left, seated, looking to right ; the Menai Straits
and bridge in the distance, on left.

Proof on Ind. paper before all letters, except the artists' names
and publication-line, Jany. 10, 1831.
$16\frac{7}{16} \times 12\frac{7}{8}$. $(13\frac{7}{8} \times 10\frac{7}{8}.)$ 22150.
See also SCIENCE.

TEMPLE, RICHARD GRENVILLE TEMPLE, Earl, 1711–1779,
statesman; son of Richard Grenville and Hester, daughter of
Sir Richard Temple, who inherited (1749) the title and estates
of her brother, Richard Temple, Visct. Cobham, and aftds. was
cr. Countess Temple; her son held the office of Privy Seal, was
an active politician, "Squire Gawky;" Ld. Lieut., Bucks;
K.G., 1760; D.C.L., Oxon., 1771; &c.
    W. Hoare.   R. Houston, mez.
    J. C. Smith, 113, 1st state, before the addition of ribbon, star
and garter.   21917.

    Sir J. Reynolds.   W. Dickinson, 1778, mez.
    J. C. Smith, 82, 2nd state.   24132.

TEMPLE, SIR WILLIAM, 1628–1699, M.P. for Carlow and
Camb. University.
    Sir P. Lely.   Vander Banck.
    Sh. ha. len. to left, looking rather to right than to front; oval
in border, 1679.
    Scarce (according to Evans).
    $13\frac{5}{8} \times 10\frac{4}{16}$. $(13\frac{3}{8} \times 10)$.   23168.

TENISON, THOMAS, 1636–1715, b. at Cottenham, Cambridge-
shire; educ. at Cambr.; Vicar of St. Martin's-in-the-Fields,
1680; Archdeacon of London, 1689; Bishop of Lincoln, 1691;
suc. to Tillotson as Archbp. of Canterbury, 1694; wrote against
Hobbes; author of Sermons, Treatises against Popery, &c.
    R. White.   R. White.
    Sh. ha. len. to right, looking to front, in robes; oval in border;
arms under centre, and title, in 3 lines of Latin inscription
below, fyllowed by the address, "*Printed and Sold by John*
"*King at the Globe against the Church in the Poultry.*"
    $(12\frac{3}{8} \times 9\frac{1}{4})$.   22278.
    See also LORDS JUSTICES.

TENNANT, CHARLES. *See* SCIENCE.

TENNENT, SIR JAMES EMERSON, 1804–1869, Bart.; Author
and Statesman; assumed the name of Tennent, 1831; Sec.
India Board, 1841–5; Poor Law Board, 1852; Bd. Trade. 1862–
67, etc.
    G. Richmond.   R. A. Artlett, stipple.
    Ha. len. to right, seated, looking to left.
    Ind. proof, with scratched letters; 1836.
    $12\frac{3}{4} \times 10\frac{1}{16}$. $(8\frac{3}{4} \times 7)$.   20640.

TENTERDEN, CHARLES ABBOT, 1st Lord, 1762–1832; lawyer; b. at Canterbury; barrister, 1795; Just. of King's Bench, 1816; Lord Chief Justice, 1818; cr. Baron, 1827.

W. Owen, R.A.   S. W. Reynolds, mixed mez.

T. Q. len. to left, seated, looking to front, in robes with the SS collar, &c.

"Proof," April 10, 1820.

20 × 14.   (17¾ × 13½).   22092.

TERRY, DANIEL, 1780–1828, actor, b. at Bath; educ. at Wingfield, Wilts; manager of Edinburgh theatre, and proprietor of the Adelphi, London.

A. Geddes.   J. A. Stewart.

Ha. len. to left, seated; Novr. 1823.

Open letter proof.

10$\frac{7}{16}$ × 8.   (5½ × 4⅝).   22923.

THACKERAY, WILLIAM MAKEPEACE, 1811–1863, b. at Calcutta; educ. at Charterhouse and Trin. Coll., Cambr.; took no degree; inherited small fortune; travelled abroad, studying art; relinquished that study for literature; lost much of his fortune by unlucky speculation; contributed to Fraser's Magazine and Punch; author of "Paris Sketch Book," "Irish Sketch Book," "Vanity Fair," "Pendennis," "Newcomes," "Esmond," "Virginians," Ballads, and many other works.

S. Laurence.   F. Holl, stipple.

Bust to front, looking to right; wearing spectacles; vignette; facs. signature below; March 1, 1853.

(7½ × 7).   27281.

THOMAS, JOHN, 1813–1862, b. at Chalford, Gloucestershire; came to London, to take part in the decoration of the New Houses of Parliament; exhibited sculptures at the R. A., 1838–'62, chiefly busts, with an occasional design for a monument; designed figures and pediment for the Great Western Hotel, the new works at the head of the Serpentine, "Musidora," in marble, "Lady Godiva," "Una and the Lion," &c.

Anon.   Anon., woodcut.

T. Q. len. to front, seated, looking to right; long hair, white waistcoat; right arm thrown over back of chair; arched at top.

Cut from an illustrated paper, and laid down.

(7$\frac{5}{16}$ × 5$\frac{1}{16}$).   E. 2223.–'89.

THOMPSON, SIR BENJAMIN, 1752–1814, afterwards Count RUMFORD; Natural Philosopher, Philanthropist, &c.; b. at Rumford (now Concord), New Hampshire, U.S.A.; educ. at Harvard; served on English side in American War; Knt. at its conclusion, 1784; served in Colonial Office, London; served in Bavarian Army, where he became a General; Count of Holy Roman Empire, 1791; assisted in founding Royal Institution;

improved hospitals, &c., in Ireland; wrote many essays and other papers.

J. R. Smith.   J. R. Smith, mez.

J. C. Smith, 143, 1st state ; from the collection of John Young.   23147.

See also SCIENCE.

THOMPSON, GEORGE, M.P. for Tower Hamlets, 1847 ; pubd. a "Discussion on American Slavery," 1836; Letters and Addresses [on American Negro Slavery] during his mission in the United States, from Oct. 1, 1834, to Novr. 27, 1835.

G. Evans.   C. Turner, A.R.A., mixed mez.

Sh. T. Q. len. to right, looking to front ; arms folded on breast ; on table at left, three folios, lettered " ORIENTAL | HERALD | 14 | 1827," " FRIEND | OF | INDIA | VOL. | III.", and " AMERICAN | ANTISLAVERY | MAGAZINE ; " facs. signature below.

Ind. proof ; Novr. 12th, 1842.

$15\frac{1}{2} \times 11\frac{2}{3}$. $(12 \times 9\frac{3}{16})$.   27959.

THOMPSON, RICHARD. *See* DILETTANTI SOCIETY.

THOMSON, CHARLES POULETT, 1799–1841, M.P., Presidt. Board of Trade; afterwards Lord Sydenham ; Govr.-Genl. of Canada.

S. W. Reynolds.   S. W. Reynolds, senr., mez.

T. Q. to left, looking to front, standing ; the fingers of right hand resting on papers on a table ; facs. signature below.

Proof ; July, 1833. A private plate.

$19\frac{15}{16} \times 15\frac{3}{4}$. $(14\frac{1}{4} \times 11\frac{2}{3})$.   24673.

S. W. Reynolds.   S. W. Reynolds, mixed mez.

Ha. len. (copy of the larger portrait of the same personage) ; facs. signature, *Sydenham*, added below. 1843 (Murray).

$(5\frac{1}{2} \times 3\frac{4}{16})$.   21385.

G. Hayter.   W. H. Mote, stipple.

Ha. len. to right, holding eyeglass in right hand ; facs. signature below.

Ind. proof.

(5×4).   21384.

THOMSON, HENRY, 1773–1843, b. in London ; son of a purser in the Navy ; educ. at Bishop's Waltham ; went to Paris with his father, 1787 ; returned to London, pupil of Opie, entd. R.A. schools, 1790 ; went with his father to Italy, 1793–1798, then to Vienna, Dresden, Berlin, Hamburg ; returned again, contributed to Boydell's " Shakspere ;" exhibited at R. A. ; A.R.A., 1801 ; R.A., 1804 ; Keeper of the R. A., 1825 ; resigned, 1827 ; retired to Portsea, where he died.

J. Jackson, R.A., delin.   R. Cooper, stipple.

Ha. len. to left, seated ; vignette. April 2nd, 1817.

$(8\frac{1}{4} \times 8)$.   28298.   11.

THOMSON, James, 1700–1748, Poet, b. at Ednam, Roxburgh-
shire; educ. at Edinb.; came to London, where he pub. his
"Seasons," 1726–'30; app. Sec. of Briefs by Ld. Chanc.
Talbot, 1733; Surv. Gen. of Leeward Islands, 1744; wrote
"Tancred and Sigismunda," and other tragedies, "Castle of
Indolence," &c.; d. and buried at Richmond.
  W. Aikman.   J. Basire, 1761.
  Sh. ha. len. to right, looking to left, wearing a cap and loose
gown; oval in border, cupids with wreaths below, on each side of
the altar, on which is the inscription, "JAMES THOMSON |
ÆTATIS XXV." The decorations designed by the engraver.
  $10\frac{1}{4} \times 7\frac{7}{8}$. $(9\frac{3}{4} \times 7)$.   22485.

THOMSON, Thomas, 1773–1852, b. at Crieff; Regius Professor
of Chemistry at the University of Glasgow; part editor of
Encyclopædia Britannica; F.R.S., &c.
  See SCIENCE, and also SCOTT, Sir Walter.

THORESBY, Ralph, 1658–1725, b. at Leeds, educ. there, and
at Rotterdam, where he learned Dutch and French, for mercantile purposes; carried on extensive trade at Leeds; cultivated
antiquarian knowledge; F.R.S.; author of "Ducatus Leodiensis,"
"Museum Thoresbianum," "Vicaria Leodiensis," 1724;
"Diary," &c.
  Anon.   G. Vertue.
  Sh. ha. len. to left, looking to front, wearing long wig
and loose robe; oval in border; arms in centre below, and
"RADULPHUS THORESBY | Leodiensis, S.R.S., 1712."
  $(9\frac{3}{8} \times 5\frac{13}{16})$.   27555.

THORNHILL, Sir James, 1676–1734, b. at Melcombe Regis;
came to London; placed under T. Highmore, by his uncle,
Dr. Sydenham; soon made progress; patronised by Q. Anne,
who commissioned him to paint the Dome of St. Paul's, and
appointed him Serj.-Painter; painted great hall at Blenheim,
and at other great houses; Kt., 1720; repurchased his family
estates; M.P. for Melcombe; d. at his mansion near Weymouth.
  J. Highmore.   J. Faber, junr., mez.
  J C. Smith, 345, 1st state.   27232.

  (Highmore)   T. Worlidge, etched.
  Ha. len. to right, looking left, holding palette in left hand,
brush in right; much of the subject, except the figure and
head, is in outline.
  $7\frac{13}{16} \times 6\frac{1}{8}$. $(7\frac{11}{16} \times 6)$.   E. 224.–'89.

  (Highmore).   Anon. stipple
Bust to right, looking to left; vignette; printed in red.
  $7\frac{3}{16} \times 4\frac{1}{7}$ (?). $(4 \times 3\frac{3}{4})$.   26256.
  See also COMMONS.

THORNTON, ROBERT JOHN, c. 1758–1837, botanist, educ. at Camb.; M.D., Lecturer at Guy's Hospital on Medical Botany; physician to Marylebone Dispensary; pubd. a work in support of the Brunonian System, entitled " Philosophy of Medicine," 1788, also the " Temple of Flora," &c.
See MEDICAL SOCIETY.

THORNTON, THOMAS, c. 1753–1823, of Thornville Royal, Yorks.; b. in London; educ. at Charter-house; Lt.-Col. of the West York Militia; famous as a sportsman; author of a "Sporting Tour," 1804–'5 ; " Sporting Tour " in France, 1806 ; d. at Chambord.
Gilpin & Reinagle. M. N. Bate, stipple.
T. Q. len. to front, looking to right, wearing hat and feather, carrying a magazine gun with many barrels ; attended by a keeper with a dog; in a woody landscape ; within a border of emblematical objects, guns, nets, a hawk, a fox, &c. ; arms below.
Proof before all letters.
The title in lettered impressions reads thus: " Lieut. Col. " Thornton, a Roebuck Shooting in the Forest of Glenmore, " with the only 12-barrelled Rifle ever made." Pubd. Novr. 16, 1810.
10½ × 8¼. (5¾ × 4⅞). 26656.

THRALE, MRS. See PIOZZI.

THURLOE, JOHN, 1616–1668, Statesman; b. in Essex; called to the Bar, 1647 ; appointed by Cromwell Secretary to Council of State, 1652 ; Sec. of State to Protector, 1653; cont. to hold office under Richard Cromwell; impris. for a short time for promoting return of Charles II.; retired from public life, though invited by the King to hold office.
Cooper. J. Houbraken.
Sh. ha. len. to front, looking to right, wearing long hair, wide collar, &c.; oval in border.
From Birch's "Lives," 1738.
(14 × 8¾). 20826.

THURLOW, EDWARD, Lord, 1732–1806, called to the Bar, 1754; ent. Parliament, 1768 ; Attorney General, 1771; cr. Baron, 1778 ; Lord Chancellor under Pitt, 1778–'92.
Sir J. Reynolds. F. Bartolozzi, 1782, line and stipple.
T. Q. len. to left, in robes, seated ; the mace and bag on a table, left ; May 25, 1782.
20 × 14¹⁵⁄₁₆. (16¹⁵⁄₁₆ × 13¾). 21833.

THYNNE, THE HON. JAMES, 1701–1705, a younger son of Thomas, 1st Viscount Weymouth; died young, in the lifetime of his father (1640–1714) ; not mentioned by Burke ; but the picture is at Longleat.
I. Kerseboom. W. Faithorne, mez.
J. C. Smith, 40, 2nd state. E. 2125.–'89.

O 82849. G G

TIERNEY, George, 1761–1830, Statesman; ent. Parliament, 1788; an able debater and opponent of Pitt, with whom he fought a duel; Treasurer of the Navy, 1802; Pres. Board of Control, 1806; Master of the Mint, 1827.

L. F. Abbott.   W. Nutter, stipple.

T. Q. len. to left, looking to front, resting his left elbow on an open book on table, and holding in his right hand a roll of a petition from Southwark; a view of the bridge and borough in distance, on left.

Open letter proof; May 7, 1798.

$2\frac{1}{8} \times 16\frac{1}{8}$. $(18\frac{3}{8} \times 14\frac{1}{16})$.   21991.

TILLOTSON, John, 1630–1694, son of a clothier at Sowerby, Yorks.; educ. at Cambr.; Preacher at Linc. Inn; Chaplain to Charles II., 1669; Dean of Canterbury, 1672; Dean of St. Paul's, 1869; Archbp. of Canterbury, 1691; author of controversial works, sermons, &c.

Sir G. Kneller.   J. Faber, junr., mez.

J. C. Smith, 346, 3rd state.   22276.

TILSON, Henry, 1659–1695, b. in Yorks; grandson of the Bishop of Elphin; pupil of Lely; went with Dahl, to Italy; studied there 7 years; at Rome, 1687; returned to England; painted many portraits in oil and crayons; his works are heavy, stiff, and overwrought; shot himself, through disappointment in love; buried at St. Dunstan's in the West.

H. Tilson.   H. Meyer, stipple.

Ha. len. to right, looking to left, holding a palette in left hand; long hair; loose robe, open at throat.

Ind. proof.

$15 \times 11\frac{4}{8}$. $(12\frac{1}{4} \times 10$ full).   25761.

H. Tilson.   T. Chambers.

From the same picture as the print by Meyer (q. v.).

Engraved for Walpole's "Anecdotes" (v. iii., p. 103).

$(5\frac{13}{16} \times 4\frac{13}{16})$.   25461.   10.

TINDAL, or TINDALL, Matthew, c. 1657–1733, b. at Beer-Ferres, Devon; educ. at Linc. Coll., and Exeter Coll. Oxf.; elected to a law fellowship at All Souls; LL.D., 1685; joined the R. C. Church; reverted, 1688; res. chiefly in London; frequently sat as Judge in the Court of Delegates; pubd. a number of discourses, pamphlets, &c.

B. Dandridge, 1733.   J. Faber, Junr., mez.

J. C. Smith, 347, 1st state.   24247.

TINDAL, Nicholas, 1687–1774, nephew of Dr. Matthew Tindal; b. in Devonshire; educ. at Ex. Coll., Oxf.; M.A., 1713; fellow of Trin. Coll.; Vicar of Great Waltham, and Rector of Alverstoke; resigned the former on receiving the living of Colbourne, I. of Wight, 1740; Chapl. of Greenwich Hosp.; pubd. translation of Calmet's History of the Hebrews,

and Cantemir's History of the Ottoman Empire, and wrote
part of a history of Essex, and translated and continued
Rapin's History of England.
    G. Knapton.   B. Picart, 1733.
    Sh. ha. len. to left, looking to right, wearing a cap and loose
gown; a bookcase and drapery behind him; arms in centre,
below.
    $12\frac{7}{8} \times 8\frac{11}{16}$. ($12\frac{3}{8} \times 8\frac{3}{16}$).   24246.

TINDAL, Sir Nicholas Conyngham, 1777–1846, Judge; son
of a solicitor at Chelmsford; educ. at Cambr.; called to the
Bar, 1809; M.P., 1824, for Wigton Burghs, and Univ. of
Cambr., 1827; Sol.-Gen., 1826; L.C.J. Com. Pleas, 1829–'46;
d. at Folkestone; bur. at Kensal Green.
    J. Lucas.   J. Lucas, mixed mez.
    T. Q. len. to right, in robes, seated, his left hand resting on a
table.
    Scr. letter proof; May 1, 1835.
    $19\frac{7}{8} \times 15$. (16×14).   22924.

TOLLEMACHE, Thomas, General. See TALMASH.

TOMLINE, Sir George Pretyman, 1750–1827; son of George
Pretyman, a tradesman at Bury; took the name, Tomline, for
an estate, 1803; educ., Pembr. Hall, Cambr.; B.A., senior
wrangler and first of Smith's Class., 1772; fellow and tutor,
and pri. tutor to W. Pitt, 1773; Rector, Corwen, 1782; Bishop,
Linc., and Dean, St. Paul's, 1787; Bishop, Winchester, 1820;
pubd. various theological works; D.D.; F.R.S.; &c.
    J. Jackson, R.A.   H. Meyer, stipple.
    Sh. ha. len., slightly to right, looking to front, in robes of
the prelate of the Garter; vignette.
    $9\frac{1}{4} \times 6\frac{3}{4}$. ($4\frac{1}{2} \times 5$).   28007.

TOMPION, Thomas, 1638–1713, said to have been originally a
blacksmith; rose to first rank as a maker of clocks and
watches; buried in Westminster Abbey.
    Sir G. Kneller.   J. Smith, mez.
    J. C. Smith, 252, 2nd state.   22277.

TONSON, Jacob, 1656–1736, Bookseller and Publisher; son of
a barber-surgeon in Holborn; pub. Dryden's "Spanish Friar,"
and his translations from the Classics; bought copyright of
"Paradise Lost;" Sec. to Kit-Cat Club, which he is said to
have originated, and which met for some time at Barn Elms,
his country house.
    Sir G. Kneller.   J. Faber, Junr., mez.
    J. C. Smith, 208 (43, Kit-Cat Club).   22060.

TOOKE, John Horne, 1736–1812, Politician and writer;
ent. the Church, but stud. aftds. for the Bar; in politics was a
partisan of Wilkes; opposed the American War; several times

imprisoned for libel; M.P. for Old Sarum, 1801; author of
"Diversions of Purley."
    J. R. Smith.   W. Ward, mez.
    J. C. Smith, 84, 2nd state, undescribed, with the words
FIRST FIFTY in the right corner, at foot; marked, in pencil, 23.
                                                        22068.

    See also GLYNN.

TORRENS, SIR HENRY, 1779–1828; b. at Londonderry; assist.
Adjt.-Genl., co. Kent; Maj.-Genl.; buried at Welwyn, Herts.
    Sir T. Lawrence, P.R.A.   C. Turner, mez.
    Wh. len. to front, in uniform, looking to left, Windsor Castle
in the distance, on left.
    Ser. letter proof; July 1st, 1817
    $27\frac{3}{4} \times 17$. $(24\frac{1}{4} \times 15)$.   22925.

TORRINGTON, ARTHUR HERBERT, 1649–1716; Lieut. R.N.,
1667; Captn., 1668, Vice-Adml., 1676, 1681; Rear-Adml. of
England, 1684–'7, Lord of Admiralty, 1684–'7; M.P., Dover,
1685–'6; Coll., 15th foot, 1686–'7; P.C., cr. Baron Herbert of
Torbay, and Earl of Torrington, 1689; Admiral; &c.
    I. Riley.   R. White.
    Sh. ha. len, slightly to right, looking to front, face turned to
left; in armour; oval in border; ships fighting, on either side,
below; arms in centre; 4 lines of titles; 1689.
    $15\frac{5}{8} \times 11\frac{1}{16}$. $(14\frac{1}{16} \times 10\frac{5}{8})$.   27662.

TORRINGTON, THOMAS NEWPORT, b. before 1650–1719;
M.P., 1699; Commissr. of Customs; cr. Baron Torrington,
1716; Lord of Treasury, P.C., etc.
    Sir G. Kneller.   J. Smith, mez.
    J. C. Smith, 254, 2nd state.   22094.

TOTNES, GEORGE CAREW, Earl of, 1557–1629; subdued rebellion in Ireland, 1602; collector; author; Governor of Jersey.
                                                     Voerst.
    T. Q. len. to right, looking to front, in armour; oval, in
border, 4 Latin verses below.
    $(10\frac{1}{2} \times 7\frac{5}{8})$.   27645.

TOWNLEY MUSEUM, THE.
    Charles Townley (or Towneley), a celebrated antiquary,
1737–1805, collector of the Townley Marbles, now in the Br.
Museum; b. at Townley, Lancashire; lived at Rome, 1768–
1772, and formed a museum of Ancient Art, which he afterwards increased and arranged in his two houses in Park Street,
Westminster, where he died.
    J. Zauffely, R.A.   W. H. Worthington.
    Wh. len. seated, on the right, turned towards the left, a dog
crouched at his feet, in his Museum, surrounded by the famous
marbles, including the Discobolus and the Clytie; by the latter
sits M. d'Hancarville, the French antiquary; behind, on the

left, stands the Hon. Charles Greville; and on the right,
Mr. Thomas Astle, Keeper of the Records in the Tower.
(27½ × 21⅞).   26666.

TOWNSEND, JAMES,   –1787, eldest son of Chauncy
Townsend, a considerable merchant in Austin Friars; married,
1763, Rosa, only child of Henry Hare, last Lord Coleraine;
M.P., and leading democrat; Alderman; Lord Mayor, 1773;
d. at Bruce Castle, Tottenham.
See BECKFORD.

TOWNSEND, JOHN, 1757–1826, minister of an Independent
congregation, at Bermondsey, 1784 till his death; founded the
London Asylum for the Deaf and Dumb children of the poor,
1792; pubd. sermons, &c.
From a marble bust by W. Behnes.   R. H. Dyer, stipple.
Bust, to front, in plain drapery.
Ind. proof; March 12, 1827.
19⅞ × 13⅞   (13¼ × 9¼).   27616.

TOWNSHEND, RT. HON. CHARLES, 1725–1767; 2nd son of
3rd Viscount; M.P. for Yarmouth, 1747, aftds. for Harwich;
held various high political offices; Chancellor of the Exchequer; P.C.
Sir J. Reynolds.   J. Dixon, mez.
J. C. Smith, 34, 3rd state.   26719.

TOWNSHEND, HENRY, 1736–1762; 3rd son of Thomas, who
was 3rd son of Charles, 2nd Viscount Townshend; Lieut.-
Col.; died, June 24, 1762, of the wounds which he received in
the battle fought that day at Wilhelmstahl.
[Sir J. Reynolds ?]   J. McArdell, mez.
J. C. Smith, 177.   23571.

TOWNSHEND, RT. HON. LORD JOHN, 1757–1833; M.P., 1780;
a man of wit and genius, and author of some poetical pieces.
Sir J. Reynolds.   J. Jones, mez., 1789.
J. C. Smith, 74, 2nd state.   27661.

TREATY of Peace, Signing and Sealing of the Nanking, &c.
See NANKING.

TREDGOLD, THOMAS, 1788–1829, civil engineer, and writer on
mechanics; b. at Brandon, Durham; apprnt. to a carpenter
and worked at that trade for some years; came to London,
employed in an architect's office; stud. chemistry, geology,
mathematics, in his leisure; pubd. "Elementary Principles of
Carpentry," "Principles of Warming and Ventilating Publ.
Buildings," &c., " The Steam Engine;" M.I.C.E.
Anon.   Anon.
Sh. ha. len. to front, looking to left, hair brushed back roughly
from forehead; vignette; facs. letter below; and, lower, on an
additional plate, an inscription, from which it appears that 100

impressions were printed and presented to eminent men by
John Weale, the well-known publisher (1791-1862).
12×9   (5¾×4¾.)   Additional plate, 2¾×9.   27144.

TREE, Miss A. M.
   Anon.   Anon., stipple.
   See LA BELLE ASSEMBLÉE.   13867. 18.

TREE, Miss M., actress; sister of Mrs. Charles Kean; m. 1825
to Mr. Bradshaw, some time M.P. for Canterbury, when she
retired from the stage.
   See BLANCHARD.

TRELAWNEY, Sir Jonathan. *See* "BISHOPS, SEVEN,"
a group

TRENCH, Sir Frederick William, 1775-1859; entd. the
army, 1803; Lieut. and 2d Captain, 1807; Major, 1811;
Lt.-Col., 1813; Coll., 1825; Maj.-General, 1837; Lt.-General,
1846; General, 1854; served in Sicily, 1806-7; Walcheren,
1809; Peninsula, 1811; Holland, 1814; K.C.H.; Permanent
Asst. Qr. Master General, 1832; d. at Brighton.
   Robson.   H. Robinson.
   Sh. ha. len. to front, looking to right, in uniform, with star,
   &c.
   Ind. proof with scratched letters, 1839.
   13 1/15 × 10 1/16.   (8 1/1 × 7 1/16).   27617.

TRENCHARD, Sir John, 1650-1694 (or '95), statesman;
M.P. for Taunton, 1678, and 1681; imprisd. on suspicion of
complicity in the Rye-house plot, 1683; supported Monmouth's
rebellion, 1685, but escaped to the Continent; returned at the
Revolution; M.P. for Dorchester, 1688 and 1690; Sec. of
State, 1693.
   Anon.   J. Watson, mez.
   J. C. Smith, 144 (2nd state ?).   27618.

TRESHAM, Henry, c. 1749, or 1756-1814, b. in Dublin; educ.
under West; came to London, 1775; worked at drawing small
portraits; invited by Lord Cawdor to travel with him in Italy,
where he remained, chiefly at Rome, for 14 years; returned to
England, 1789; exhibited at the R.A. that year, and in 1791,
A.R.A.; R.A., 1799; employed in illustrating books, and dealt
in works of art; his drawings in black and white were his best
productions; published poems, &c.
   A. Pope delin.   A. Cardon, stipple.
   Ha. len. to right, looking to front, wearing white neckcloth
   and frill to shirt; vignette. Jan. 27, 1814.
   (8×7½).   28298. 10.

   ────

   J. Opie.   S. Freeman, stipple.
   Sh. ha. len. to right, looking to front; coat buttoned up, with
   high collar, oval.
   5 9/16 × 4 9/16 (?).   (3½×2⅔).   26220.

TREVITHICK, RICHARD, distinguished engineer, took out a patent, 1802, with A. Vivian, for the high-pressure engine; worked at mining enterprises; went to Peru; returned, poor and disappointed.
See SCIENCE.

TRIMMER, MRS. SARAH, 1741–1810, daughter of J. J. Kirby, writer on perspective and architecture; b. at Ipswich, showed early signs of talent; attracted attention of Dr. Johnson; m. to Mr. Trimmer, and resided at Brentford, 1762–1810; devoted herself to the education of her 12 children; actively encouraged Sunday schools, and published a number of educational works for the improvement of the education of the children of the poor.
H. Howard. W. Bond, stipple.
Ha. len. to left, seated, holding pen in right hand, which rests on a paper; spectacles in left hand; books, pens, and inkstand on table before her. Jany. 1, 1799.
$10\frac{7}{16} \times 6\frac{1}{2}$. $(6\frac{9}{16} \times 5\frac{1}{4})$. 28008.

TRIUMPH OF BRITANNIA, THE.
F. Hayman. S. F. Ravenet, 1765.
Britannia, in her chariot, is drawn across the sea from right to left, holding the medallion portrait of George III.; swimming by the side of her chariot are nymphs and tritons, bearing the medallion portraits of ANSON and HAWKE, in the middle; of POCOCK and BOSCAWEN, on the left; and of SAUNDERS, KEPPEL, and HOWE, on the right.
"In the background is represented the defeat of the French Fleet by Sir Edw. Hawke, Nov 20th 1759."
$16\frac{3}{4} \times 21$. $(15\frac{1}{16} \times 20\frac{7}{16})$. 27528.

TROLLOPE, FRANCES, Mrs., 1778–1863, daughter of Rev. W Milton, fellow of New Coll., Oxf.; b. at Stapleton, near Bristol, where her father had a curacy; m. to Thomas Anthony Trollope, 1797; a widow, 1825; resided about 3 years (1829–'32) in the U.S., America, and aftds. travelled in Europe, spending last 10 or 12 years of her life at Florence; author of "Domestic Manners of the Americans," 1831, "Refugee in America," "Abbess," "Paris and the Parisians," "Michael Armstrong," &c., &c.
Miss I. Adams delin. W. Holl, stipple.
Ha. len. to left, seated, looking to front, wearing large cap; facs. signature below; 1845.
$8\frac{3}{4} \times 5\frac{1}{4}$. $(5\frac{5}{16} \times 4\frac{1}{4})$. 22026.

TROUGHTON, EDWARD, 1753–1835, celebrated astronomical instrument-maker, b. in London; his bust by Chantrey is in the Observatory at Greenwich.
See SCIENCE.

TRURO, THOMAS WILDE, Lord, 1782–1855; Solicitor-General, 1839; Attorney-General, 1841, and again, 1846; Chief Justice

of Common Pleas, 1846; cr. Baron, 1850; Lord High Chancellor, 1850-'52.
    F. Grant, R.A.   G. Zobel, mez.,
T. Q. len. seated, to right, in robes; the mace on table, right.
Open letter proof; May 1, 1851 (wrongly engraved, "1581").
(15 × 11⅞).   25804.

TUCKERMAN, Joseph, 1778-1840, b. in Boston; grad. Harv.
Coll., 1798; pastor of a Unitarian church at Chelsea, 1801-
1826; and at Boston, ministering among the poor, 1826 till a
little before his death at Havana; author of many sermons,
letters, Reports as Minister at Large, and other works.
    A. Robertson.   M. Gauci, lith.
Ha. len. to front, looking to right; rectilin. subj., with corners
cut off; facs. signature below.
Ind. proof; July 1, 1834.
(7⅞ × 6⅝).   E. 1059.-'88.

TURNER (or TURNOR, as he spelt it at first), CHARLES, 1773-
1857, engraver. b. at Woodstock; entered R.A. schools, 1795;
influenced by Bartolozzi at first, produced good stippled work,
followed by etched and aquatinted plates; worked for J. M. W.
Turner's "Liber," and engraved some of his pictures with the
greatest success; elected A.E., 1828; engraved also after Lawrence, Jackson, Shee, Owen, Reynolds; his mezzotints, in
which he sometimes employed the needle, are extremely good.
    J. Lonsdale (?).   C. Turner, mez.
Ha. len. to left, looking to front, wearing white neckcloth
and black velvet waistcoat.
Proof before all letters.
14 × 10.   (10 × 8⅜).   22560.

TURNER, FRANCIS, Bishop of Ely. See BISHOPS, Seven,
a group.   26668.

TURNER, SIR GEORGE JAMES, 1798-1867, judge; M.P. for
Coventry, 1847-'51; Vice-Chancellor, 1851; a Lord Justice of
the Court of Appeal in Chancery, 1853.
    G. Richmond.   F. Holl, stipple.
Bust, to front; vignette.
Ind. proof before all letters, except the artists' names.
21¾ × 17.   (8½ × 7¼).   27235.

TURNER, JOSEPH MALLORD WILLIAM, 1775-1851, son of a
hairdresser in Maiden Lane, Covent Garden; admitted to the
R.A. schools, 1789; had already exhibited; learned perspective
under T. Malton; studied at Dr. Monro's house, coloured
prints, and worked in other ways to support himself; soon
attracted notice; A.R.A., 1799; R.A., 1802; travelled; painted
in oils and water-colours some of the finest landscapes in the
world; amassed a fortune; left pictures, and most of his
wealth, to the nation.
    C. Turner, A.R.A.   C. Turner, mez.

T. Q. len. to right, seated, holding a pencil in his right, and a drawing in his left hand; landscape in the distance; facs. signature below.

Ind. proof.

$20\frac{5}{16} \times 16\frac{1}{16}$. $(14\frac{1}{4} \times 11\frac{7}{16})$.   26637.

Also, another impression, with additional work, and publication-line added, July 31, 1856.   22561.

TURNER, JOSEPH MALLORD WILLIAM—*continued.*
J. Linnell.   C. Wentworth Wass, mixed mez.
Sh. ha. len. to front, looking to right; wearing furred coat; oval.

Published by J. Noseda, April 17, 1873.

$19\frac{7}{8} \times 15$. $(16\frac{1}{2} \times 12\frac{1}{2})$.   26720.

J. Gilbert delin.   W. J. Linton, woodcut.
T. Q. len. to right, holding brush and palette; a picture on an easel behind, on right; vignette.

$(7\frac{1}{2} \times 5\frac{3}{8})$.   E. 2227.—'89.

—— entitled "The Fallacy of Hope."
(Count D'Orsay?)   Anon., lith.
Wh. len. to left, in profile, holding a cup of tea which he stirs with a spoon held in his right hand; a pianoforte in the background.

Ind. proof, Jany. 1, 1851; vignette; printed by Hullmandel & Walton; a little colour added on the face.

$(11\frac{1}{4} \times 7\frac{3}{4})$.   E. 2261. A. 1889.

TURNERELLI, PETER, 1774–1839, sculptor, b. at Belfast, son of an Italian modeller; came to London, 1792; studied under Chenu, and at R. A.; soon attracted notice and obtained employment; George III. sat to him for his bust, 1810; sculptor to the Queen and Princess of Wales; executed a bust of Louis XVIII., 1813, being in France; designed many monumental works.
S. Drummond, A.R.A.   J. Thomson, stipple.
Ha. len. to right, looking to front; his bust of George III. by him, on a table on right. "Published (for the Proprietors of the European Magazine), June 1, 1821." Vignette.

$(5\frac{3}{8} \times 4\frac{1}{2})$.   28444. 4.

TYRWHITT, THOMAS, 1730–1786, son of Dr. Tyrwhitt, canon of Windsor; educ. at Eton, Queen's Coll. and Merton Coll., Oxf.; Under Sec. at War, 1756; clerk in the House of Commons, 1762; resigned, 1768, and devoted the rest of his life to literature; pubd. Observations on some Passages in Shakespeare; Fragmenta Duo Plutarchi; Canterbury Tales of Chaucer; exposure of the Chatterton forgeries, &c., Co-curator, with Mr. Cracherode, of the Br. Mm., 1784.
B. Wilson.   J. Jones, mez.
J. C. Smith, 75, 2nd state.   25806.

TYTLER, ALEXANDER FRASER, Lord Woodhouselee.
  See WOODHOUSELEE.

UNION, THE MUSICAL. See MUSICAL.

URE, ANDREW, 1778–1857, Chemist; b. at Glasgow; educ. for
  the Med. Profn.; M.D.; lectured on Chemistry, Natural
  Philosophy, and Mat. Med., in Glasgow; Astronomer there, on
  the founding of an observatory; settled in London, 1830;
  Analytical Chemist to the Board of Customs; Author of
  "Dictionary of Chemistry," "Dictionary of Arts, Manufactures, and Mines," and other works; d. in London.
    H. W. Diamond, M.D., photogr.   C. Cook, line and stipple.
    Ha len., slightly inclined towards, and looking to, right;
  seated; a curtain behind, on left; a landscape seen through an
  open window, on right; facs. signature below.
    $11\frac{7}{16} \times 7\frac{11}{16}$. $(6\frac{1}{16} \times 4\frac{1}{4})$.   27619.

USHER, or USSHER, JAMES, 1580–1656, b. in Dublin; educ.
  at, and fellow of, Trin. Coll., Dublin; Prof. of Divty., 1607–'20;
  Chancr., Cath. of St. Patrick, 1607; Bishop, Meath, 1620; P.C.,
  Ireland, 1623; Archbishop, Armagh, 1624; Preacher, Linc.
  Inn, 1647–'54; pubd. many learned works; buried, Westminster
  Abbey, in Erasmus Chapel.
    Sir P. Lely.   G. Vertue, 1738.
    Sh. hn. len. slightly to right, looking to front, wearing broad
  ruff and robes; oval in border, arms below in centre.
    $14\frac{2}{3} \times 9\frac{2}{3}$. $(13\frac{1}{2} \times 8\frac{3}{4})$.   23160.

UWINS, THOMAS, 1782–1857, subject-painter, b. at Pentonville,
  where he was educ. at a day-school; apprent. to an engraver,
  1797; admitted as a student of the Royal Academy, 1798;
  began drawing portraits and illustrating books; Assoc. Water
  Colr. Socy., 1808; full member, 1809; in ill-health, travelled
  abroad, 1814; went to Edinburgh, and in 1824 to Italy; returned, 1831; exhibited oil paintings at the R. A.; A.R.A.,
  1832; R.A., 1833; Keeper of the National Gallery, 1847.
    T. H. Illidge.   J. Smyth, stipple.
    Full hn. len. to left, seated, looking to right, hands folded
  together; facs. signature below.   Vignette.
    Ind. proof.
    $7\frac{1}{4} \times 5\frac{1}{4}$. $(4\frac{1}{2} \times 3\frac{3}{4})$.   27620.

VANBRUGH, SIR JOHN, 1666–1726; began as a playwright
  and theatrical manager; became an architect; built Blenheim,
  Castle Howard, King's Weston, &c.; Clarencieux King at
  Arms; Surveyor, Greenwich Hospital; knighted at the accession
  of George I.; d. at Whitehall.
    Sir G. Kneller.   J. Simon, mez.
    J. C. Smith, 154, 2nd state.   24625.

VANBRUGH, Sir John—*continued.*

Sir G. Kneller.   W. C. Edwards.
Sh. ha. len. to left, looking to right; long hair and wearing badge. Engraved for Murray's " Lives of British Architects," 1830, Vol. 14 of " Lives of British Painters, Sculptors, &c.," 1830–'1, VI. Vols. 12mo.
(3 × 2½).   E. 2244.–'89.

VANDERBANCK, John, c. 1684–1739, son of Peter Vanderbanck (q. v.), b. in England, where he stud.; much employed as a portrait-painter in the reigns of Anne and George I.; caricaturist, and illustrated " Don Quixote ; " seceded from Thornhill's academy, and himself established a drawing-school, which had a short existence; d. at Holles St., Cavendish Square.
See ARTISTS, A Society of.

VANDERBANCK, Peter, 1649–1697, engraver, of Dutch extraction, b. at Paris; a pupil of Poilly; came to England, c. 1674 ; soon gained reputation for beauty of finish, as well as large size, of his plates, for which he was ill paid; married a lady of good family, at Bradfield, Herts ; executed many fine plates ; supposed to have been interested in manufacture of tapestry ; d. at Bradfield, where he lived when in difficulties.
Sir G. Kneller.   A. W. Warren.
Ha. len. to left, looking to front ; wearing long hair ; oval in border.
Engraved for Walpole's " Anecdotes," 1828 edn., Vol. V.
Ind. proof before all letters.
8¼ × 5¼.   (4 × 3¼).   E. 2231.–'89.

VANE, Sir Henry, 1612–1662, " Regicide ; " M.P., 1640 ; beheaded.
     [W. Faithorne.]
L. Fagan, p. 64.
This portrait was prefixed to " The Life and Death of Sir Henry Vane," 1662. 4to.   26721.

VANSITTART, Rt. Hon. Nicholas. *See* BEXLEY, Lord.

VERE, Sir Francis, 1554–1608 ; General ; defended Ostend, 1600, in the war between Holland and Spain.
     W. Faithorne.
L. Fagan, p. 64.
Prefixed to " The Commentaries of Sir Francis Vere," &c., Camb., 1657, fol.   25807.

VERNEY, Greville 1694(?)–1710(?), younger son of the Hon. John Verney, who obtained the title of Baron Willoughby de Broke, 1695.
Dahl.   R. Williams, mez.
J. C. Smith, 53.   E. 1288.–'88.

VERNON, Edward, 1684–1747 ; educ. under Dr. Busby ; went to sea, and was promoted ; M.P., 1722 ; virulent opponent of Govt. ; declared, 1739, that Porto Bello could be captured by six sail of the line; taken at his word, made an admiral, succeeded within 4 months in capturing the place; aftds. failed in other undertakings; continued to oppose Govt.; struck off list of admirals by the King's command; d. suddenly; buried in Westmr. Abbey.

T. Gainsborough.   J. McArdell, mez.
J. C. Smith, 182, 1st state.   24093.

VERNON, EDWARD VENABLES, 1757-1847, youngest son of George, first Lord Vernon; b. at Sudbury Hall, Derbyshire; educ. at Ch. Ch., Oxf.; preb., Gloucester; Canon, Ch. Ch., 1785; Bishop of Carlisle, 1791; Archbishop of York, 1807; D.C.L.; pubd. three sermons.

W. Owen, R.A.   W. Ward, junr., mez.
T. Q. len. to left, seated, looking to front, in robes, holding with right hand a large book with clasps.
Open letter proof; Sepr., 1828.
$22\frac{7}{8} \times 16\frac{1}{4}$.   ($17\frac{4}{5} \times 13\frac{7}{8}$).   27627

VERNON, ROBERT, 1774-1849, horsedealer; amassed a large fortune; having retired from trade, collected the pictures by modern British Artists which, under the name of the "Vernon Gallery," he gave to the nation, 1847.

H. W. Pickersgill, R.A.   W. H. Mote, stipple.
Ha. len. to front, seated, looking to left, wearing a dressing-gown, and holding a little dog on his lap; oval.
Proof with open letters; pub. for the Proprietors of the Art Journal.
($8\frac{3}{4} \times 7$).   22541.

VERTUE, GEORGE, 1684-1756; b. in St. Martin's-in-the-Fields; pupil of Vander Gucht; collected materials for the history of British Art, which Walpole bought, and used in compiling his "Anecdotes of Painting" and "Catalogue of Engravers;" published "Catalogues," &c.; engraver to the Society of Antiquaries; buried in the Cloisters, Westminster.

G. Vertue.   T. Priscott.
Wh. len. to right, looking to front, and extending the right hand.
From the group in which **Vertue is represented with his wife** (q. v.)
Vignette; facs. signature below; April 1, 1818.
($5\frac{1}{4} \times 3\frac{3}{4}$).   15219, 14.

Anon.   M. Gauci, lithog.
Ha. len. to right, seated, looking to front, with prints, miniatures, &c., on table, on right; "facsimile of a Drawing in the Possession of the Publisher," Dec. 1821.
Ind. proof.
($9\frac{5}{16} \times 5\frac{5}{8}$).   E. 224.-'93.

VERTUE, GEORGE, and MARGARET his wife, with two dogs.
G. Vertue. W. Humphrey, etched.
Wh. len. "in the very Habits they were married ; Feby. 17th,
" Anno Domini 1720. From the Original Drawing in the
" Collection of the Rt. Honble. Lord Cardiff." Vertue, on the
left, gives his right hand to his wife, who takes it with her right
and holds a book in her left hand ; in a room, the wall of which,
behind the figures, is hung with prints, miniatures, &c.
14¾ × 17½(?). (13⅛ × 16⁷⁄₁₀). 22927.

VESTRIS, MADAME, 1797–1856, daughter of Bartolozzi, the
engraver; m. at 16 to A. Vestris, ballet-master at the King's
Theatre, Haymarket; went with him to Paris; became a
successful actress and singer in burlesque, on her return ; widow,
1825 ; lessee of Olympic, 1829 ; m. to Charles James Mathews,
1838; visited America with him ; took Cov. Garden, 1839 ;
engaged afterwards at other theatres.
A. E. Chalon. H. Robinson.
T. Q. len. to front, looking to left, holding a dog on a cushion
with her left hand ; 1838 ; rectilin. subject, but with corners
cut off.
13 × 9½. (7¼ × 5½). 24248.

R. E. Drummond. Alais, stipple.
See LA BELLE ASSEMBLEE, 1820. 13867. 19.

——— See also LISTON.

VICTORIA ALEXANDRINA, QUEEN, 1819– ; only daughter
of H.R.H. Edward, Duke of Kent (4th son of George III.),
and Maria Louisa Victoria (daughter of Francis, Duke of Saxe-
Saalfeld-Coburg, and widow of Emich, Prince of Leiningen) ;
suc. her Uncle, William IV., 20th June 1837 ; crowned June
28, 1838; m. to PrinceAlbert of Saxe-Coburg and Gotha, Feb.
10, 1840, (who d. December 14, 1861).
Represented as an infant, and again as a young girl.
See KENT, DUCHESS OF.

Anon. Anon., stipple.
(As Princess ?) Wh. len. to front, looking to right, wearing
a large bonnet; a little dog running by her side.
(12½ × 7½). 25065.
In Genealogical Chart, 553. 1.

H. Collen. T. Woolnoth.
T. Q. len. to left, looking to front ; a landscape, with cascade,
in the background.
Published, May 24th, 1837.
(5⅞ × 4⅞). 25066.
In Genealogical Chart, 553. 1.

VICTORIA ALEXANDRINA, QUEEN, receiving the Holy Sacrament
at her Coronation in Westminster Abbey, June 28, 1838.
    C. R. Leslie, R.A.   S. Cousins, A.R.A., mixed mez.
    The Archbishop (William Howley), on the left, administers
the Sacrament to the young Queen, who kneels on the steps of
the altar ; a composition of many figures.
    Ind. proof of the plate, originally pubd. May 1, 1848, now
republishd, Feb. 15, 1853.
    $27\frac{1}{4} \times 45\frac{3}{8}$. $(23 \times 40\frac{5}{8})$.   27680.

—— Coronation of Her Gracious Majesty, Queen, 1838.
    Sir G. Hayter.   H. T. Ryall.
    The Queen is enthroned rather to left of centre ; a composi-
tion of many figures.
    Open letter proof.
    $25\frac{1}{4} \times 36\frac{5}{8}$. $(22\frac{7}{16} \times 33\frac{7}{8})$.   25847.
    Key-plate to the above, the personages numbered to correspond
with a list of their names below.
    $(8\frac{3}{8} \times 16\frac{1}{4})$.   25847. A. 1.

—— Marriage of Her Most Gracious Majesty, Queen, 1840.
    Sir G. Hayter.   C. E. Wagstaff, mixed manner.
    The Queen and Prince Albert stand hand in hand before the
Archbishop (William Howley); a composition of many figures.
    $24\frac{7}{8} \times 36\frac{1}{2}$. (22×34).   25847. 8.
    Key-plate to the above, the personages numbered to correspond
with a list of their names below.
                                Day & Haghe, lith.
    $(10\frac{1}{2} \times 17\frac{1}{8})$.   25847. c.

——
    W. Fowler.   B. P. Gibbon, mixed manner.
    In an oval, wearing a crown.
    Published, Feby. 10th, 1840, by Welch and Gwynne.
    $15\frac{7}{8} \times 11\frac{7}{8}$. $(11\frac{3}{8} \times 9\frac{3}{4})$.   18746.

——
    J. Thomson.   A. Wivel, chalk and dotted manner.
    Sh. ha. len. Vignette.
    Published, May 1, 1840, by Henry Brooks.
    $10 \times 7\frac{7}{8}$. $(4\frac{1}{8} \times 3\frac{1}{2})$.   23592.

——
    W. C. Ross, A.R.A.   F. Bacon.
    T. Q. len. seated, inclined slightly to right, looking to front.
    Published May 5, 1841, by Colnaghi and Puckle.
    $(7\frac{5}{8} \times 5\frac{3}{16})$.   25053. 1.
    In Genealogical Chart, 553. 1.

——
    F. Winterhalter.   T. H. Maguire, lith.
    Ha. len. to right, looking to front, wearing a coronet with
black pearls ; facs. signature below.
    $(16\frac{11}{16} \times 12\frac{3}{4})$.   22177.

VICTORIA Alexandrina, Queen—*continued.*
F. Winterhalter. J. A. Vinter, lith.
Bust, in oval, looking to front, and wearing a crown.
($20\frac{7}{8} \times 17\frac{1}{2}$). 22175.

R. Thorburn. H. Robinson.
Ha. len. (for the Art Union Monthly Journal).
($6\frac{7}{8} \times 5\frac{3}{4}$). 26419.

J. Gilbert. J. Williamson, woodcut.
" The Queen opening Parliament," Decr. 3, 1857, seated on
throne, the Prince Consort on her left; a composition of many
figures; from the Illustrd. London News, Decr. 12, 1857.
$19\frac{1}{2} \times 27\frac{1}{2}$. 25069.
In Genealogical Chart, 553. 1.
See also FIRST OF MAY, and
LOUIS PHILIPPE (Foreign).

VICTORIA Adelaide Mary Louisa, Princess Royal, 1840–
; m. (1858) to the Crown Prince Frederick William of
Prussia, afterwards German Emperor.
C. R. Leslie, R.A. H. T. Ryall, mixed manner.
The christening of this Princess, in Buckingham Palace, Feb.
10, 1841. The Archbishop of Canterbury (William Howley)
holds the infant at the font; on the right are the Queen, Prince
Consort, and others; on the left are the Duke of Wellington,
Duke of Sussex, and others.
India proof, with scr. letters; originally pub. Sep. 25, 1849,
now republished Feb. 15, 1853.
$27\frac{3}{4} \times 46\frac{3}{8}$. ($22\frac{7}{8} \times 40\frac{1}{2}$). 27681.

W. C. Ross, A.R.A., min. painter.
H. T. Ryall.
T. Q. len. seated; an infant.
Published Decr. 1, 1841, by Thos. McLean.
15×12. (5×4). 20029.

F. Winterhalter. T. Fairland, lith., 1851.
As a child; in an oval.
($12\frac{1}{2} \times 12$). 22189.

F. Winterhalter. R. J. Lane, A.E.R.A., lith., 1856.
Wh. len. to left, looking to front.
($19\frac{1}{2} \times 14\frac{3}{8}$). 22185.

VICTORIA Adelaide Mary Louisa, Princess Royal—*cont*.
Anon.   J. and A. W., woodcut.
Her Marriage to Prince Fred. William of Prussia, Jan. 25,
1858; from the Illustrd. London News, Jan. 30, 1858.
19⅞ × 13¾.   25071.
In Genealogical Chart, 553.   1.
See also ALBERT EDWARD.

VICTORS OF THE NILE, a number of portraits, medallions, ar-
ranged on an oblong tablet, in two rows, seven in each, as follows:
SAUMAREZ (James, Lord de, 1757–1836); TROU-
BRIDGE (Sir Thomas, c. 1750–1819); DARBY (George, c.
1720–1790); LOUIS (Sir Thomas, Bart., –1783); PEYTON
(   ); BALL (Sir Alexander John, 1757–1809);
HOOD (Sir Samuel, 1762–1814); first row: GOULD (
); FOLEY (Sir Thomas, 1757–1833); WESTCOTT
(George,   –1798); THOMPSON (Sir Thomas,   –
1828); HALLOWELL (Sir Benjamin (Carew), 1760–1834);
MILLER (   ); BERRY (Sir Edward, 1768–1831);
second row.   Above are the figures of Plenty, a Sphinx, and
Fame, the last suspending a medallion portrait of Nelson on a
palm-tree: ships, towers, pyramids, &c., behind.
R. Smirke, R.A.   W. Bromley and I. Landseer. (Por-
                                          traits by Lenney.)
(26¼ × 17).   1803.   15594. A.

VILLIERS, William, Lord (–1721), and Lady Mary
(–1735), children of Edward Villiers, cr. Earl of Jersey,
1697. William suc. 1711
Sir G. Kneller.   J. Smith, mez.
J. C. Smith, 259.   E. 1289.–'88.

VINCE, Rev. Samuel, M.A.,   –1821, Mathemat.; b. at
Fressingfield, Suffolk; Plumian Prof. of Astronomy and Exp.
Philosophy, Cambr.; Rector of Kirby Bidon, Norfolk; Arch-
deacon of Bedford; author of "Principles of Hydrostatics,"
"Complete system of Astronomy," &c.
T. Wageman del.   R. Cooper.
Full ha. len. to left, seated, looking to front, holding eye-
glasses in left hand, wearing gown; vignette.
Ind. proof with scratched letters; Oct. 10, 1821.
12⅝ × 10¼.   (8½ × 7½).   27621.

VINCENT, William, 1739–1815; educ. at Westminster and
Trin. Coll., Cambridge; vicar of Langdon, Worcester; rector
of Allhallows; St. John's, Westminster, and Islip, Oxf.; head-
master, Westminster, 1788; Dean, 1802; published "Voyage
of Nearchus," 1797; "History of the Commerce and Navigation
of the Ancients in the Indian Ocean," 1807.
W. Owen, R.A.   C. Turner, mez.

T. Q. len. to left, seated, with books and plans at his right,
and a globe on his left.
Open letter proof; Septr. 20, 1811.
20 × 13$\frac{1}{16}$. (17$\frac{9}{16}$ × 13$\frac{7}{8}$). E. 2127.–'89.

VIVARES, FRANCIS, 1709–1780, landscape-engraver, b. near
Montpelier, in France; apprent. to a tailor, but fond of drawing;
etched some plates of landscape; came to London, 1727, pupil
of Chatelain, who befriended him; studied assiduously, became
distinguished, and founded a school of landscape-engraving;
executed many fine plates, after Gaspar Poussin, Gainsborough,
Claude, the Smiths of Chichester and Derby; was much admired
by Woollett.
    Anon. (Vivares?).   F. Vivares & Caldwal.
    Sh. ha. len. to front, looking to right; oval, supported by
cupids, on a pedestal among trees, shrubs, and flowers; water at
foot. April 4, 1776.
    From the collection of J. F. Gigoux.
    8$\frac{3}{16}$ × 6$\frac{7}{10}$. (7$\frac{2}{3}$ × 6).   27641.

WADE, GEORGE, 1673–1748; Maj.-Genl., 1709; commanding in
Scotland, made many roads and a bridge over Tay; M.P. for
Hindon, aftds. for Bath; field-marshal, 1743; buried in West-
minster Abbey.
    J. Vanderbank.   A. Vanhaecken, 1736, mez.
    J. C. Smith, 18.   24133.

WAGER, SIR CHARLES, 1666–1743; served under Shovel and
Rooke, and at the taking of Majorca, under Leake; distinguished
in the West Indies; rear-admiral of the White, 1709, and
knighted; served aftds. in Mediterranean, &c.; first lord of
Admiralty, 1733; M.P. for West Loe; buried in Westminster
Abbey
    I. Whood.   J. Faber, junr., mez.
    J. C. Smith, 368, 2nd state.   25808.

WAGHORN, THOMAS, 1800–1850, b. at Chatham; entd. the
navy, 1812; lieut., 1842; originated the Overland Route to
India; pubd. "Overland Guide to India by four Routes,"
1842; Letter on Steam Navigation, 1846, &c.; d. at Pentonville; a monument erected to his memory on the Isthmus of
Suez, 1869.
    C. Baxter.   Day & Haghe, lith.
    Ha. len. seated, to front, holding pen in right hand; on the
table, before him, lies a book or paper, inscribed EGYPT IN
1837 | T. WAGHORN. Vignette.
    Ind. proof; 1837.
    (9 × 9).   23043.

WAITHMAN, ROBERT, 1765–1833; Lord Mayor of London,
1823; M.P. for the City.
    W. Patten, junr., 1818.   E. Scriven, stipple.

Ha. len. to left, seated, looking to front, in Alderman's Gown.
Ind. open letter proof. Jany. 1, 1821.
18⅜ × 13⅞. (13¾ × 11¼). 22928.

WAKE, ANNA. *See* SUSSEX.

WAKEFIELD, GILBERT, 1756–1801 ; educ. at Cambr. ; B.A.,
1776 ; became a distinguished scholar and critic, and theological
controversialist, and finally a politician ; sentenced to two years'
imprisonment, 1799, for remarks on the General Orders of D.
of York ; presented with a sum of 5,000l., subscribed by friends ;
he translated the New Testament ; edited the Georgics,
Lucratius, &c.
W. Artaud. R. Dunkarton, mez.
J. C. Smith, 38. 24249.

WALDEGRAVE, MARIA, Countess, 1739–1807, daughter of
Mr. (afterwards Sir Edward) Walpole and Mrs. Dorothy
Paxton ; m. first, 1759, to James, 2d Earl Waldegrave, who d.
1763 ; second, 1766, to William Henry, Duke of Gloucester,
brother of George III., who was much displeased, sent them
abroad, and did not allow the marriage to be published till 1772,
soon after which the brothers were reconciled ; d. at Brompton ;
buried at Windsor ; a prominent personage in the Walpole
correspondence.
Sir J. Reynolds. J. MacArdell, mez.
J. C. Smith, 184, 3rd state. 27175.

WALKER, GEORGE, –1690, minister of Dungannon ; defender
of Derry ; " The Reverend and Valiant Mr. George Walker
" Governour of London Derry ;" killed at the battle of the
Boyne.
Sir G. Kneller (ad vivum). Vander Banck, 1689.
Sh. ha. len., slightly to left, head slightly to right, looking to
front ; oval in border ornamented with oakleaves and apples ;
arms below in centre.
(15¾ × 11¾). 22287.

WALKER, JAMES, 1781–1862, civil engineer ; b. at Falkirk ;
educ. at Falkirk, and at Glasgow Univ. ; stud. under his uncle,
Ralph Walker, engineer of the W. Ind. Docks ; made the
harbours of Dover, Channel Islands, and Tyne ; Victoria Bridge
over Clyde, at Glasgow ; Middle Level Drain and Sluices ;
many Lighthouses ; was Consult. Engineer to Admiralty ;
Pres. Inst. C. Engineers ; 1835–'45 ; F.R.S.
J. P. Knight, R.A. S. Bellin, mixed mez.
T. Q. len. to right, seated, looking to front, holding eye-glasses
in right hand, left hand resting on thigh.
Facs. signature below ; inscription in open letters ; " Sub-
scriber's Copy."
17⁷⁄₁₀ × 13½. (13 × 10⅜). 23044.

WALKER, Robert, portrait-painter, contemporary with Van Dyck, whose works he studied, but founded a style of his own, aiming at great truth and character; painted the Protector and chief officers of his army; there is a fine portrait of him at Hampton Court, another at Oxford; his pictures are vigorous, truthful, expressive, full of character.

R. Walker. P. Lombart.

Sh. ha. len. to right, looking to front, holding a paper in right hand. Oval in border, with monogram of W. R., between two palm branches, below.

From the picture at Hampton Court.

($10\frac{1}{8} \times 7\frac{9}{16}$; oval, $7\frac{1}{8} \times 6\frac{1}{8}$). 22929.

[Walker.] T. Chambers.

A copy of the print by P. Lombart, in the same direction, engraved for H. Walpole's "Anecdotes of Painting," Vol. II., p. 155, MDCCLXII.

$6\frac{3}{4} \times 5\frac{1}{8}$. ($5\frac{5}{8} \times 4\frac{11}{16}$). 25461. 7.

WALKER, Sayer, c. 1800, M.D., Physician in ordinary to the City of London Lying-in Hospital; Treasurer to the MEDICAL SOCIETY (q. v.).

WALL, Charles, associated with the House of Baring Brothers; m. Harriet, eldest daughter of Sir Francis Baring, 1790.

See BARING, Sir Francis.

WALLER, Edmund, 1605–1687, poet, b. at Coleshill, Herts.; educ. at Eton, and King's Coll., Cambr.; M.P. in Long Parliament, and appointed one of the commissioners to treat with the King; accused of complicity in a plot, 1643; to save his life, made a confession, suffered a year's imprisonment, was fined 10,000*l*., and then liberated; resided in France, till permitted by Cromwell to return; wrote a panegyric on the Protector; was equally servile to Charles II. and James II.; his poems were "light and harmonious."

Sir G. Kneller, 1684. G. Vertue, 1727.

Sh. ha. len. to right, looking to front, with long wig; oval in border. Arms below the oval and motto, "Sed Carmina Major Imago;" name below, with quotation, two lines.

"All but the nymph, ... approve his Song. W."

$14\frac{3}{8} \times 9\frac{5}{8}$. ($13\frac{1}{2} \times 9$). 27107.

WALLER, Sir William, 1597–1668; Parliamentary General; M.P., Andover; reduced Portsmouth; captured Hereford; defeated at Roundway-down, co. Wilts; and at Cropredy bridge, Oxford; M.P., Middlesex; d. at Osterley Park.

Anon. P. Aubry, exc.

Sh. ha. len. to left, looking to front, two lines of inscription below: "William Waller Ritter, General Sergeant Maior Der " Armada des Parlaments in Engellandt, etc." Oval.

It is a reversed copy of the portrait by Hollar, Parthey, 1821.

$5\frac{1}{4} \times 3\frac{7}{8}$. ($4\frac{5}{8} \times 3\frac{3}{8}$). 29758. 6.

WALLICH, NATHANIEL, 1786–1854, celebrated Danish botanist, b. at Copenhagen; educ. for the Med. profn.; studied botany under Vahl; went to East Indies, 1803; stationed at Serampore as surgeon; appointed to temp. charge of Bot. Gardens, Calcutta, 1815; permanent, soon after; zealously prosecuted study of Botany in India; visited Nepaul, Penang, Singapore, &c.; pubd. "Flora of Nepaul," and other excellent works; visited England, 1828; ret. to India, 1833; presided over Sc. Mission to enquire and report on Cultivation of tea in Assam.

A. Robertson.   M. Gauci, lith.
Ha. len. to front, looking to right; vignette; facs. signature. Ind. proof.
(6½ × 5¼).   E. 1058.–'88.

WALLIS, JOHN, D.D., 1616–1703, Mathemat. and Divine; b. at Ashford; educ. at Cambr.; Savilian Prof. of Geometry at Oxford, 1648; inv. the art of decyphering, and probably the method of teaching the deaf and dumb to speak and understand a language; one of the Revisers of the Liturgy, 1661; Pres., Royal Society.

D. Loggan.   D. Loggan.
Sh. ha. len. slightly turned towards right, looking to front, wearing skull-cap, bands, and gown; oval, arms below, in a smaller oval; dated 16 . . . 78.
(9½ × 7¼).   22279.

WALPOLE, HORACE, 1717–1797, Miscellaneous writer and art and antiquity-collector; youngest son of Robert Walpole, 1st Earl of Orford; b. in Arlington St.; M.P. for Callington, Castle Rising, and King's Lynn, 1741–1768; estab. himself at Strawberry Hill, Twickenham, 1747, where he formed his famous collection; author of "The Castle of Otranto," "Catal. of Royal and Noble Authors," "Anecdotes of Painting," "Letters," &c.: suc. his nephew as 4th Earl of Orford; d. unmarried.

Sir J. Reynolds.   J. MacArdell, mez.
J. C. Smith, 186, 2nd state.   22285.

——, as 4th Earl of ORFORD
Sir T. Lawrence, R.A.   T. Evans, stipple.
Bust to right; a sketch.
(10¼ × 8¼).   22903.

WALPOLE, SIR ROBERT, 1676–1745, aftds. 1st Earl of ORFORD, K.G.; Statesman; son of Robert Walpole, Esq.; b. at Houghton, Norfolk; ent. Parliament as a supporter of the Whigs, 1700; Sec. for War, 1708; depr. of his office on the defeat of the Whigs, 1711; Prime Minister under George I., 1715–'17, and under George II., 1721–'42; cr. Earl of Orford, 1742.

Sir G. Kneller.   J. Faber, junr., mez.
J. C. Smith, 208 (28, Kit-Cat Club).   22055.

185

WALPOLE, Sir Robert—continued.
Vanloo.   J. Watson, mez.
J. C. Smith, 149.   21914.
See also COMMONS.

WALPOLE, Rt. Hon. Spencer Horatio, 1806–   , educ. at
Eton and Cambr.; barrister, 1831; Q.C., 1846, and M.P.;
Home Sec., 1852; again in 1858, and 1866–'7; retired, 1882.
See DERBY CABINET.

WALSH, William, 1663(?)–1708, Critic and minor poet; b.
at Abberley, Worcestershire; Gent. commoner, Wad. Coll.,
Oxford; M.P.; friend of Dryden, and early friend and adviser
of Pope (see "Essay on Criticism," 729).
Sir G. Kneller.   J. Faber, junr., mez.
J. C Smith, 208 (39, Kit-Cat Club).   27106.

WALSINGHAM, Sir Francis, 1536–1590; Statesman; b. at
Chiselhurst; educ. at Cambr.; Ambassador to Paris, 1570–'3;
Sec. of State, and Knt., 1573; Chancellor of Duchy of Lancaster;
principal agent of Elizabeth against Mary, Queen of Scots;
K.G., 1587.
F. Zucchero.   J. Houbraken, 1738.
Sh. ha. len. to left, looking to front; oval in border.
In Birch's "Lives."
14¾ × 9¾. (14¼ × 8⅝).   22281.
See also ELIZABETH.

WALTON, Brian, 1600–1661, b. at Cleveland, Yorks; educ. at
Cambr.; Preb. of St. Paul's, and chaplain to Charles I.; fled
to Oxford at the beginning of the Civil War; formed there the
plan of the "Polyglot Bible," his chief work, which he pub. in
6 vols., 1657; Bishop of Chester, 1660; d. in London.
Anon.   P. Lombart.
Full ha. len. seated, turned towards the right, looking to
front, holding a pen in right hand, resting upon the "Biblia
Polyglotta," which lies open on a table, on right; this is the
frontispiece to his Polyglot Bible.
(12 1/16 × 9).   22288.

WALTON, Izaak, 1593–1683, b. at Stafford, kept a linen-
draper's shop in the Royal Exchange, and afterwards at the
corner of Chancery Lane, Fleet Street; left London, c. 1643;
d. at Winchester; the patriarch of anglers; author of the
"Compleat Angler," also of the "Lives of Donne, Wotton,
Hooker, Herbert, and Bishop Sanderson," and, at the age of
90, of a preface to the "Thealma and Clearchus" of J. Chalk-
hill; wrote also some very fair poetry.
J. Huysmans.   (W. Derby delin.)   W. Humphrys.
Ha. len. to right, looking to front, holding stick in right hand
and glove in left hand, crossed over the right. Below, a facs.
quotation, and signature, Iz = Wa. Oct. 1, 1836.
12⅝ × 10. (4¾ × 3¼).   22488.

WANDESFORD, CHRISTOPHER,   –1641, of Kirklington,
Yorks; accompanied his friend, Lord Wentworth, afterwards
Earl of Strafford, to Ireland; master of the rolls there, 1633–'40.
His descendants were cr. Baron Wandesford, Viscount Castle-
comer, and Earl of Wandesford; but these titles became extinct,
1784. He is called erroneously "Lord Chief Baron" on this
print.
 Van Dyck. (G. Farington delint.) **J. Watson, mez.**
 J. C. Smith, 150.   27145.

WANLEY, HUMPHREY, 1672–1726, Bibliographer; b. at
Coventry; educ. at Oxford; under-librarian, Bodl.; Librarian
to Robert Harley, Earl of Oxford, and to his son; formed a
Catal. of Ang.-Saxon MSS. for Dr. Hickes's "Thesaurus;"
began Catal. of Harl. MSS.
 T. Hill.   **J. Smith, mez.**
 J. C. Smith, 263.   21743.

WARBURTON, WILLIAM, 1698–1779, Theological writer and
Controversialist; b. at Newark-on-Trent; preacher at Linc.
Inn, 1746; afterwards, Chaplain to the King, Dean of Bristol,
and, 1759, Bishop of Gloucester; author of a Crit. and Philos.
Inquiry into the causes of Prodigies and Miracles," "The Alliance
between Church and State," "The Divine Legation of Moses
Demonstrated," &c.
 C. Philips.   **T. Burford, mez.**
 J. C. Smith, 19.   21927.

WARD, EDWARD MATTHEW, 1816–1879, b. in Pimlico, son of
the sister of James and Horatio Smith; soon turned to art, and
obtained the silver palette of the Society of Arts, 1830; indebted
to Chantrey and Wilkie for valuable advice, entd. the Academy
schools, 1835; went to Rome, 1836, and obtained the silver medal
for historical composition in the Academy of St. Luke; exhibited at the R. A., 1839, and following years; painted eight
pictures for corridor of House of Commons; A.R.A., 1846;
R.A., 1855; died by his own hand, at Windsor.
 T. Brigstocke.   **J. Smyth.**
 Hn. len. to right, looking to front, leaning his chin on right
hand; vignette; facs. signature below.
 (4¾ × 3⅜).   28300. 57.

WARD, JAMES, 1769–1859, animal painter and engraver, b. in
London; studied engraving under his brother, William, and a
few months under J. R. Smith, and anatomy under Brooks;
soon distinguished himself by his artistic mezzotints; exhibited
some clever rustic pictures, 1792–'93; appointed "Painter and
Mezzotint engraver to the Pr. of Wales," 1794; painted many
pictures of cattle, &c.; A.R.A., 1807; R.A., 1811; exhibited
as late as 1855.
 Anon.   Anon., mez.

Ha. len. to left, looking to front, head inclined to left ; in dark coat with three bright buttons. Evans was unable to name the painter or mezzotinter of this portrait.
Proof before all letters.
$14\frac{1}{16} \times 10\frac{7}{8}$. (10×8). 22290.

WARD, JAMES—continued.
Anon. Anon., stipple.
Full ha. len. seated, to front, looking to left, hands folded together ; vignette ; facs. signature below.
$(7 \times 4\frac{3}{4})$. 15219. 15.

J. H. Wilson. Williamson, woodcut.
Sh. ha. len. slightly to left, looking to front ; oval, cut from " The Illustrated London News," Decemr. 24, 1859.
$(6\frac{5}{8} \times 4\frac{11}{16})$. 15220. 2.

WARD, SETH, 1617–1689, Mathematician and Astronomer ; b. at Buntingford ; educ. at Cambr. ; fellow of Sid. Sus. Coll. ; deprived for refusing to join the " Solemn League and Covenant ;" app. Prof. of Astronomy at Oxford by Parliament, and took oath of Allegiance to Commonwealth, 1649 ; after Restoration, by Clarendon's interest, made Bishop of Exeter, 1662 ; of Salisbury, 1667 ; one of the founders of the Royal Society.
D. Loggan. D. Loggan.
Sh. ha. len. to left, looking to front, in the robes of the Chaplain of the Order of the Garter ; oval in border ; title, under arms, below.
$14\frac{7}{8} \times 10\frac{5}{8}$. (13¼ × 10½). 25811.

WARE, ISAAC, –1766, originally a chimney-sweep's boy, noticed by a patron, who sent him to Italy, where he studied architecture ; designed Chesterfield House, finished, 1749, other mansions, part of Bloomsbury Square, &c. ; one of the Artist Committee, 1755, for planning a Royal Academy, and of the Surveyors of the Board of Works ; edited Palladio, &c.
Anon. Anon., stipple.
Sh. ha. len. to right, wearing spectacles ; oval.
$(3\frac{7}{8} \times 3\frac{1}{16})$. 15219. 16.

WARE, JAMES, 1756-1815, b. at Portsmouth, educ. there at Gram. Sch. ; stud. at Haslar and St. Thomas's Hospitals ; devoted himself to ophthalmic surgery ; pubd. several learned and useful works ; actively promoted the foundation of the School for the Indigent Blind, 1800 ; &c.
See MEDICAL SOCIETY.

WARHAM, WILLIAM, 1460-1532 ; b. at Okeley, Hants ; sent by Henry VII. on an embassy to the Duke of Burgundy, 1493 ; Bishop of London, 1502 ; Archbishop of Canterbury, 1504 ; Chancellor of Oxf. Univ. ; Lord Keeper, 1502–'4 ; Lord High Chancellor, 1504–'15 ; resigned because of Wolsey's ascendancy.
H. Holbein. G. Vertue, 1737.

Hn. len. slightly to left, in robes, both hands resting on a cushion before him; arms and insignia below.
$14\frac{3}{16} \times 8\frac{13}{16}$. $(12\frac{3}{4} \times 8\frac{1}{4})$. 24251.

WARREN, CHARLES TURNER, 1767–1823, engraver, of whose youth little is known, but that he married, 1785; got the better of difficulties, 1802, chiefly by supplying book-illustrations, by which he became widely known; perfected the process of steel-engraving, for which he got the medal of the Society of Arts; illustrated the "British Poets," 1798, &c., and engraved two plates for Boydell's Shakespeare; was too fond of society, and improvident, d. suddenly at Wandsworth.
 W. Behnes, sculptor.   S. W. Reynolds, mixed mez.
 From a bust, to left; June 10th, 1824.
$13\frac{13}{16} \times 9\frac{15}{16}$. $(13\frac{3}{4} \times 9\frac{3}{8})$. 22930.

WARREN, EDMUND THOMAS, c. 1750–1800, musician, author of "Reliques of Ancient Music;" pubd. an annual collection, and also a monthly collection, of Catches and Glees, which were in high repute for many years.
 Roubilliac.   J. Jones, mez.
 J. C. Smith, 78, 2nd state.   26270.

WARREN, SIR JOHN BORLASE, 1754–1822, Bart., Admiral; commanded at Quiberon Bay, 1795; captured 4 French ships, sent to aid the rebellion in Ireland, 1798; Ambassador to Russia, 1802; d. at Greenwich; K.B., &c.
 S. Drummond.   J. Stow, stipple.
 Wh. len. to front, looking to left, in uniform, left arm akimbo; a ship partially seen on the right, in distance.
$26\frac{3}{8} \times 19\frac{1}{4}$. $(24\frac{1}{4} \times 17\frac{3}{4})$. 22007.

WARREN, RICHARD, 1731–1797, son of a clergyman of Cambridge; educ. at Bury St. Edmunds and Jesus Coll., Cambr.; F.C.P., 1763; M.D.; Physician to George III., and the Prince of Wales; a man of much wit and polished manners, behaved with great skill in the delicate and difficult position in which the illness of the king placed him; d. in Dover St., Piccadilly, leaving more than 150,000l. to his widow and children.
 T. Gainsborough, R.A.   J. Jones, mez.
 J. C. Smith, 79, 2nd state.   22286.

WARTON, THOMAS, 1728–1790; b. at Basingstoke; educ. at Trin. Coll., Oxford; fellow, 1751; Professor of Poetry, 1757–'67; instituted to the living of Kiddington, 1771, and presented to the donation of Hill Farrance, 1782; Camden Professor of Ancient History at Oxford, and Poet-Laureate, 1785–'90; pubd. "Observations on the Faerie Queene of Spenser," 1754; "History of English Poetry," 1774–'81; &c.
 Sir J. Reynolds.   C. Hodges, mez.
 J. C. Smith, 33, 3rd state.   28146.

WARWICK, ROBERT RICH, Earl of. *See* NAVAL HEROES (1).

WASHINGTON, GEORGE, 1782–1799, founder of the Independence, and first Pres., of the U.S. America; began as a land-surveyor; Adj.-Genl. in Virginia, 1751, served in his first campaign against the French, 1754; resigned, 1758; m., 1759; member of first Congress, 1774; opposed the British, against whom he was successful; resigned his commission, 1783; first Pres., 1789; re-elected, 1793; took leave of the nation in a dignified proclamation.

J. Trumbull.   T. Cheesman, stipple.

Wh. len. to front, looking to left, holding a spy-glass in right hand; in uniform, as a General; orderly with charger in background.

Open letter proof; June, 1796.

29 × 19½. (25¼ × 17½).   27622.

G. Stuart.   H. S. Sadd, mixed mez.

Wh. len. to front, looking to left, sword in left hand, right extended as in the act of speaking.

Pubd. at the Albion Office, New York, 1844.

30 × 22⅝. (26⅜ × 20½).   27623.

Houdon, cast from life by, 1785.   W. E. Marshall, painted and engraved by (woodcut).

Bust to left, white neckcloth and frill; from Harper's Weekly, March 2, 1878.

(19⅛ × 14).   15739. 1.

WATERLOO BANQUET, THE.

W. Salter.   W. Greatbach.

This annual banquet, in commemoration of the Battle of Waterloo, was given by the 1st Duke of Wellington to the principal officers who fought under him on that occasion. It was held at the Duke's London mansion, Apsley House, Piccadilly, and has been discontinued since his death in 1852. In this print, the Duke is seen, standing, as if in the act of speaking, in the centre; the figures surrounding the table are all portraits.

Proof before all letters, except artists' names and publication-line, June 18, 1846.

28½(?) × 46(?). (24⅝ × 44).   27677.

WATERLOO BANQUET, KEY TO THE.

A copy of the engraving by Greatbach after Salter, in outline, the portraits numbered to correspond with a list, at foot, of the names of personages represented.

(11¼ × 19¾).   27677. A.

WATSON, RICHARD, 1737–1816, b. near Kendal, son of a clergyman; educ. at Cambr.; Fellow of Trin. Coll., 1760; Prof. Chem., 1764; of Divinity, 1778; Bishop of Landaff, 1782; F.R.S.; author of "Chemical Essays," "Apology for

Christianity," &c.; opposed Gibbon and Tom Paine; d. at Calgarth Park, Westmoreland.

G. Romney.   J. Jones, mez.
J. C. Smith, 80, 2nd state.   21886.
See also SCIENCE.

WATT, JAMES, 1786–1819, b. at Greenock; learnt business of a math. instr. maker in London; settled at Glasgow; employed as a civil engineer; began investigating power of steam, c. 1758; patented a steam-engine, 1769; joined Boulton, at Soho Works, Birmingham, as partner, 1774; discovered double-action principle, parallel motion, and the "governor;" invented copying-press, bleaching by chlorine, &c.; retired, 1800; monument by Chantrey to his memory in Westminster Abbey, with inscription by Lord Brougham.

Sir T. Lawrence.   C. Turner, mez.
T. Q. len. seated, slightly inclined to left, looking to front; right hand resting on papers on table; snuff-box in left hand.

Proof before all letters.
$20\frac{7}{8} \times 15\frac{7}{8}$. ($17\frac{3}{4} \times 14$).   27238.
See also SCIENCE.

WATTS, ISAAC, D.D., 1674–1748, Dissenting Divine; b. at Southampton; minister to a congregation in Mark Lane; retired because of failing health, 1712; wrote on "Logic," &c.; became widely known by his metrical version of the Psalms, and by his Hymns.

G. White.   G. White, mez., 1727.
J. C. Smith, 55, 3rd (or 4th) state. "*Sold by E & C Dilley in the Poultry;*" a state not described by J. C. S. 22056.

WAYNFLETE, or WAYNFLEET, WILLIAM PATTEN of, –1486; eldest son of Richard Patten, of Waynflete, Linc.; educ. at Oxf.; head-master, Winchester, c. 1429; first provost of Eton, 1440; Master of St. Mary Magd. Hosp., 1438; bishop of Winchester, 1447; Lord High Chancellor, 1456–'60; founded Magdalen Coll. and Hall, Oxf., 1456.

Anon.   J. Faber, senr., mez.
From the picture at Magd. Coll., Oxford.
J. C. Smith, 34, among the "Founders," 2nd (?) state.
    24719.

————

(From the same Picture as the print described above.)
    J. Houbraken, 1742.
Bust slightly to right, looking to front, wearing mitre, cope, &c.
($14 \times 8\frac{3}{4}$).   20825.

WEBSTER, ANTHONY, c. 1750–1780, actor and singer, performed in London and Dublin; led by his vanity to think that an Irish lady of distinction had fallen in love with him, he incurred much displeasure; d. shortly before the publication of this print.

Wheatley. H. Kingsbury, mez.
J. C. Smith, 15, 2nd state. 26418.

WEBSTER, Joseph Samuel, 1774(?)–1796, portrait-painter, of Loughborough, practised in London; there is a portrait by him in the Drapers' Hall; McArdell and J. Watson scraped several plates from his portraits; he also painted some ideal subjects; according to Evans, he was a pen-and-ink imitator of prints.

Anon. Anon.
Sh. ha. len. to right, looking to front, holding a book in his left hand; wearing long hair; white lappels to coat turned back; oval; name and date of death, July 6th, 1796, above.
(3 × 2¾). E. 2242.–'89.

WEDDERBURN, Alexander. See ROSSLYN.

WEDGWOOD, Josiah, 1730–1805, the younger son of a potter, distinguished himself early by discovering improvements in the manufacture of pottery; invented the " Queen's Ware," 1763; added six other new varieties of ware; built the village Etruria, near Newcastle-under-Line, Staffs.; F.R.S.; F.S.A.; &c.

Sir J. Reynolds. S. W. Reynolds, mixed mez.
Ha. len. to left, looking to front, wearing white neckcloth and frill; facs. signature below. Impression on Ind. paper. May 1, 1841.
16⅟₁₆ × 12½. (11½ × 9⅜). 22931.

WEEVER, John, c. 1576–1632, b. in Lancashire; educ. at Queen's Coll., Cambridge; travelled abroad and through England and Scotland, in search of antiquities; pubd. " Ancient Funeral Monuments of Great Britain," &c., fol., 1631; buried in St. James's, Clerkenwell.

Anon. T Cecill.
Ha. len. slightly turned to right, looking to front, resting left hand on skull; two books by him, on left; oval in border; about the oval, VERA EFFIGIES JOHANNIS WEEVER ÆTATIS SVÆ, 55, Anno 1631. Four lines below, in the white margin,
" Lancashire gaue him breath, | And Cambridge education. |
" His studies are of Death. | Of Heauen his meditation."
6½ × 4⅟₁₆. (5⅞ × 4¼). 27561.

WELD, Thomas, 1773–1837, Cardinal, eldest son of Thomas Weld, founder of Stoneyhurst College, b. at Lulworth Castle, Dorset; took orders, 1815; coadjutor bishop of Canada; cr. Cardinal by Pius VIII., 1829; d. at Rome.

J. Ramsay. C. Turner, mez.
Ha. len. to left, seated, looking to right, in robes, with left hand resting on the leaves of an open book.
Proof before all letters.
14 × 10. (11⅓ × 9½). 22932.

WELLESLEY, RICHARD COLLEY, Marquess, 1760–1842, States-
man, eldest son of 1st Earl of Mornington; Gov.-General of
India, 1797–1805; Sec. of State for Foreign Affairs, 1809–'12;
Lord Lieut. of Ireland, 1821–'8, and 1833; K.G.; &c.

    Sir T. Lawrence, R.A.   C. Turner, mez.

    T. Q. len. to front, seated, wearing the Garter and jewel, left
hand gloved resting on table; curtain and pillars behind; sea and
sky in distance, on left.

    Proof before all letters, except the artists' names and publica-
tion-line, May 13, 1815.

    $21\frac{7}{16} \times 15\frac{13}{16}$. $(16\frac{7}{8} \times 13\frac{11}{16})$.   **21893.**

    A. Robertson.   H. Meyer, stipple.

    Wh. len. to right, looking to front, in robes of the Garter.

    Ind. proof, with scratched lettering.

    $19 \times 13\frac{1}{2}$. $(15\frac{1}{4} \times 10\frac{9}{16})$.   E. 644.–'85.

WELLINGTON, ARTHUR WELLESLEY, Duke of, Field-marshal
and Statesman, 1769–1852; entered the army, 1787; M.P.
(Dublin Parliament), 1790; went to Calcutta, 1797; took
Seringapatam, 1799; gained first victory at Assaye, 1803; after
more successes, retd. to England, 1805; M.P., Rye, 1806; Sec.
Ireland, 1807; served in Danish Expdn., 1807; took command
in Portugal, 1808; cr. Viscount Wellington, 1809; cr. Earl of
Wellington, 1812; took Badajoz, 1812; cr. Marquess; cr.
Duke, 1814; won Waterloo, 1815; Comm.-in-chief, 1827 and
1842; Premier, 1828 and 1834; d. at Walmer.

    A. Aglio.   H. S. Minasi. Stadler, aquat.

    As Marquess, on horseback, towards left, pointing forwards,
but looking back; a church and landscape behind, with troopers.
Feb. 27, 1813.

    $17\frac{1}{2} \times 13\frac{1}{2}$. $(13\frac{7}{8} \times 12)$.   **26203.**

    Sir W. Beechey, R.A.   W. Skelton.

    Ha. len. to front, looking to left.

    The word PROOF is in the left corner at foot: Decr. 1, 1814.

    $(18 \times 14\frac{1}{2})$.   E. 1563.–'85.

——, " Giving orders to his Generals, &c."

    " *Painted and Engraving finished by T. Heaphy.*"

    " *Etched and Engraving began by the late Anker Smith,
A.R.A.*"

    The Duke on horseback, surrounded by general officers and
staff, is directed, and points, to the left; a dying soldier, a
priest, and others, form a group in the left foreground. A composition of many figures, Aug. 8, 1822. The scene is that of
the Battle of the Nivelle.

    $25\frac{3}{4}(?) \times 36$. $(22 \times 33\frac{3}{4})$.   **27115.**

WELLINGTON, ARTHUR WELLESLEY, Duke of—*continued.*
Sir T. Lawrence. W. D. Taylor.
Ha. len. slightly to right, looking to front, wearing a cloak.
Ind. proof, with open letters ; March 15, 1827.
$13\frac{15}{16} \times 11$. $(10\frac{3}{8} \times 8\frac{13}{16})$. 21849.

Sir T. Lawrence, P.R.A. . H. T. Ryall.
Ha. len. in cloak, slightly to right, looking to front, right hand
to breast on left ; white waistcoat, &c. ; facs. signature below.
$13\frac{5}{16} \times 10\frac{1}{4}$. $(9\frac{7}{16} \times 7\frac{5}{16})$. 20930.
Also, an Ind. proof of an earlier state of the plate, much less
worked all over the dress, background, &c. The corners not
filled out, so as to make the plate rectangular. Otherwise the
dimensions are the same. Pubd., 1836. 20641.

Sir T. Lawrence, P.R.A. W. Bromley.
Wh. len. to left, on his charger " Copenhagen," his hat in his
right hand.
Scratched letter proof.
$(24 \times 16\frac{1}{4})$. 15587.

J. Simpson, 1838. B. P. Gibbon, etching.
T. Q. len. slightly to right, wearing cocked hat, cloak, &c.,
and holding a sword in both hands.
Ind. proof., pubd. Decr. 24, 1838. This plate was afterwards finished in mezzotinto.
(Sheepshanks Gift.)
$21\frac{7}{16} \times 15\frac{13}{16}$. $(16\frac{1}{4} \times 12\frac{3}{4})$. 18773.

H. P. Briggs, R.A. J. T. Wedgwood, stipple.
Ha. len. to front, slightly inclined to right ; arms folded ;
vignette.
Open letter proof (?) ; March 20, 1841.
10×8. $(5\frac{1}{4} \times 3\frac{3}{4})$. 29760. B.

T. Phillips, R.A., 1844. T. Lupton.
Sh. ha. len. to right, looking to front, left hand to breast ; in
cloak ; oval in border.
Open letter proof, signed by the painter ; June 1, 1845.
$14 \times 10\frac{11}{16}$. $(11\frac{1}{8} \times 9)$. 23025.

Sir T. Lawrence, P.R.A. S. Cousins, mixed mez.
Wh. len. to front, with arms folded, holding a telescope.
Open letter proof ; June 15, 1848.
$31 \times 19\frac{7}{16}$. $(26\frac{5}{8} \times 16\frac{3}{8})$. 22145.

WELLINGTON, Arthur Wellesley, Duke of, with Sir
Robert PEEL.
   F. Winterhalter.   J. Faed, mixed mez.
   Wh. len., to right; Wellington on the left; Peel, with folded
hands, looking to right; drapery and a pillar behind.
   Ind. proof; March 31, 1851.
   $31 \times 20\frac{1}{2}$. $(27\frac{1}{2} \times 17\frac{1}{3})$.   23764.

———

                               A. Stanesby, lith.
   Hn. len. seated, to left, holding a paper in left hand; vignette,
Oct. ; 1852 ; facs. signature below.
   $(8\frac{1}{2} \times 7\frac{1}{4})$.   29756. 2
———, meeting Blucher, after the battle of Waterloo.
   D. Maclise, R.A.   Lumb Stocks, R.A.
   A composition of many figures; Wellington in the centre, on
horseback, directed towards the left, holds the hand of Blucher;
behind them is a building on which is a sign, "A La Belle
Alliance;" from the picture in the Palace of Westminster; pubd.
by the Art Union of London, 1875.
   Ind. proof.
   $16\frac{1}{4} \times 48$. $(11\frac{3}{4} \times 45\frac{1}{2})$.   27290.
   See also FIRST OF MAY ; "HEROES of the Penin-
sular;" WATERLOO BANQUET; VICTORIA Adelaide,
Princess Royal, Christening of; and VICTORIA, Queen,
CORONATION, and MARRIAGE of.

WELLS, Mrs.   , whose maiden name was Davies; actress;
performed at the Haymarket, c. 1781 ; aftds. at Drury Lane and
Covent Garden ; her portrait, under the name of "Cowslip,"
was done in mez. by J. R. Smith (J. C. S., 191).
   See EDWIN.

WENSLEYDALE, James Parke, Lord, 1782-1868, Justice of
the King's Bench, 1828 ; Baron of Exchequer, 1834-'56; cr.
Baron Wensleydale, 1856.
   T. Phillips, R.A.   W. Walker, mez.
   As Baron Parke. T. Q. len. to left, standing, looking to front,
resting left hand on hip, right hand on draperies.
   Open letter proof; July 5, 1847.
   $20 \times 15\frac{1}{4}$. $(16\frac{5}{16} \times 12\frac{7}{16})$.   23026.

WESLEY, John, 1703-1791, son of the Rector of Epworth,
Linc., b. there; educ. at Charterhouse and Oxf.; fellow of Linc.
Coll. ; ordd. as his father's curate ; returned to Oxf.; originated
"Methodism," with his brother Charles and others, 1730 ; went
to America, preached in Georgia, 1735 ; returned, 1737 ; built
first meeting house, Bristol, 1739 ; sepd. from Moravians, 1740;
author of Journals, hymns, sermons, &c. ; d. in the City Road,
London.
   W. Hamilton.   J. Fittler.

Ha. len. in pulpit, preaching, to left, with an open book before him.
Ind. open letter proof; Novr., 1788.
$15\frac{7}{8} \times 12\frac{1}{2}$. $(12\frac{9}{16} \times 10\frac{3}{8})$. 22933.

WESLEY, JOHN—continued.

J. Jackson, R.A.   J. Thomson.
Hn. len. to left, in pulpit, preaching; right hand slightly raised, left hand on book, with fingers between the leaves.
$13\frac{11}{16} \times 10\frac{1}{2}$. $(9\frac{5}{16} \times 7\frac{1}{4})$. 22020.

WEST, BENJAMIN, 1738-1820, b. in Chester County, Pennsylvania; began, self-instructed, to paint when very young; visited Leghorn and Rome, 1760; arrived in London, 1763; began exhibiting, 1764; member and one of the Directors of the Incorp. Socy. of Artists, 1766; one of the first members of the R.A.; Historical Painter to the King, 1772; Surveyor of the Royal Pictures, 1790; P.R.A., 1792; painted the "Death of Wolfe," "Battle of La Hogue," and many other pictures.

B. West.   G. S. & I. G. Facius, stipple.
Wh. len. as a boy, on the left, in the composition called "Mr. West and Family."
$(19\frac{1}{16} \times 25\frac{3}{8})$. 23051.

P. Falconet.   B. Reading, stipple.
Sh. ha. len., profile to right, 1792.
$7\frac{3}{16} \times 5\frac{1}{2}$. $(4\frac{3}{4} \times 4)$.   '   28330. 61.

G. Dance, 1793.   W. Daniell, 1809, stipple.
Sh. ha. len., profile to right; vignette.
$10\frac{11}{16} \times 8$. $(7 \times 5\frac{1}{4})$ 28299. 9.

B. West, 1793.   W. T. Fry, stipple.
Ha. len. seated, to left, looking to front, holding a paper in his right hand, which rests on a table, on which are books, &c.; July 12th, 1820.
$(5\frac{5}{16} \times 4\frac{1}{16})$ E. 2238.-'89.

Sir T. Lawrence, P.R.A.   C. Rolls.
Wh. len. to front, in his studio, pointing with right hand to a copy of Raffaelle's cartoon of the Death of Ananias.
Ind. proof; Jany. 1, 1842.
$28 \times 18\frac{1}{2}$. $(23\frac{7}{8} \times 15\frac{3}{8})$. 22151.

C. Josi.   C. Josi.
Sh. ha. len. to right, looking to front; oval; for the European Magazine, 1 July, 1794.
$6\frac{9}{16} \times 4\frac{1}{2}$. $(3\frac{7}{8} \times 3\frac{3}{16})$. 28300. 59.

WEST, BENJAMIN—*continued.*

B. West.   J. Hopwood, stipple.
Sh. ha. len. to left, looking to front; oval; June 1, 1805.
$6\frac{5}{16} \times 4\frac{1}{2}$. $(3\frac{1}{2} \times 2\frac{7}{16})$.   28300. 60.

———

                 Anon., stipple.
Bust, profile to right; vignette.
$(3 \times 2\frac{1}{2})$.   28300. 58.

———

T. Lawrence, R.A.   H. Meyer, stipple.
Ha. len. to right, seated, looking to front, glasses in left hand,
on table; a pillar behind; vignette.
For the fourteenth Number of the British Gallery of Con-
temporary Portraits, April 13, 1813.
$14\frac{3}{4} \times 12\frac{7}{8}$. $(11 \times 10\frac{3}{4})$.   E. 2233.–'89.

———

T. Lawrence.   E. Scriven, stipple.
Ha. len. to right, looking to front; a pillar behind; in a ruled
border.
Open letter proof.
$9\frac{7}{8} \times 6\frac{3}{4}$. $(3\frac{9}{16} \times 2\frac{13}{16})$.   28300. 64.

———

T. Lawrence.   Anon.
Sh. ha. len. to right, looking to front; a pillar behind.
Cut out from a larger print.
$(3\frac{5}{16} \times 2\frac{7}{16})$.   15219. 18.

———

W. J. Newton, min.   W. J. White.
T. Q. len. to left, seated, looking to front, holding a book in
left hand and glasses in right; Windsor Castle in the distance.
Ind. proof before all letters, **except** the publication-line,
Decr. 12th, 1817.
$14\frac{3}{4} \times 11\frac{3}{8}$. $(8\frac{1}{4} \times 5\frac{5}{8})$.   E. 2234.–'89.

———

[W. J. Newton.]   H. Grevedon, lith., 1827.
Sh. ha. len. to right, looking to front; vignette.
$(11\frac{1}{2} \times 10\frac{3}{4})$.   E. 2235.–'89.

———

G. H. Harlow.   H. Meyer, stipple.
Ha. len. to front; looking to left; resting left arm on books;
vignette.
(3×4).   28300. 63.

WEST, BENJAMIN—*continued.*
 G. H. Harlow.   J. Jenkins, stipple and line.
 Full ha. len. to front, looking to left; resting left hand on
books; facs. signature below.
 Ind. proof; 1829.
 $8\frac{3}{16} \times 5\frac{11}{16}$. $(4\frac{1}{8} \times 3\frac{1}{2})$.   28300. 62.

———

 Behnes.   Anon, stipple.
 Bust to left; vignette. "No. 50."
 $11\frac{11}{16} \times 9\frac{7}{16}(?)$. $(4\frac{1}{4} \times 3)$.   28300. 12.

 See also ACADEMICIANS.

WEST, RICHARD, −c. 1821, wax-chandler and oilman, of
King Street, Soho, London.
 Anon.   Anon., mez.
 Ha. len. to left, looking to front, within a rectang. border;
wearing curly hair, white waistcoat, dark coat, fastened by
three buttons; name in MS. below. Probably a private plate,
which, perhaps, never had any lettering; not noticed by J. C.
Smith.
 15×11 $(12\frac{3}{4} \times 11)$.   E. 15.-'95.

WEST, MRS. W.
 R. E. Drummond.   J. Alais, stipple.
 See LA BELLE ASSEMBLÉE, 1819. 13867. 21.

WESTCOTT, CAPTAIN GEORGE, −1798; commanded H.M.S.
     , June 1, 1794, under Lord Howe, off Ushant;
killed at the battle of the Nile.
 See COMMEMORATION (1).

WESTMACOTT, SIR RICHARD, 1775-1856, b. in London, son
of a statuary, sent to Italy, 1793; made rapid progress; gained
gold medal for sculpture in Academy of St. Luke at Rome, and
at Florence the premium of first class in sculpture in the
Academy, and the Pope's medal at Rome; visited Germany,
exhibited at the R. A., 1797; executed many statues and busts
for St. Paul's, Lincoln's Inn, &c., the group for the pediment,
Br. Museum, &c.; A.R.A., 1805; R.A., 1815; Prof. Sculp.,
1827; Kt., 1837.
 J. Derby.   J. Thomson, stipple.
 Sh. ha. len. to right, loose shirt collar; vignette; facs. signature
below.
 For the European Magazine, Jany. 1st, 1823.
 $8\frac{3}{4} \times 5\frac{1}{2}$. $(4\frac{1}{4} \times 5)$.   E. 2237.-'89.

WESTMORLAND, JOHN FANE, Earl of, &c., 1685-1762, educ.
at Oxford; M.P. for Kent, 1715-'22; for Buckingham, 1727-'33;
suc. 1736; Lt.-General, 1742; Chanc. of Univ. Oxford, 1759;
D.C.L., 1759; General of the Horse, 1761.
 T. Worlidge del   T. Worlidge, etched.

Ha. len. to right, in robes, as Chancellor of the University of Oxford, at his own installation in the Sheldonian Theatre; a composition consisting of a multitude of heads and figures, mostly portraits, including one of the artist himself; March 28, 1761.

18$\frac{1}{16}$ × 24$\frac{1}{4}$.   (17$\frac{1}{8}$ × 23$\frac{7}{8}$).   26665.

WESTMORLAND, John Fane, Earl of, 1784–1859; diplomat and musical composer.
Sir T. Lawrence.   J. Bull.
As Lord Burghersh. Bust to left, profile. Novr 1, 1838.
Published by Welch and Gwynne.
16 × 12.   (9$\frac{1}{8}$ × 7$\frac{7}{16}$).   22817.

WESTON, Thomas,   –1776, son of the first cook of George III.; became a famous low comedian at the Haymarket and Drury Lane; much addicted to drink.

In the character of Scrub; Prologue to Trip to the Jubilee.
Dod del.   Cook.
Pubd. by Fielding & Walker, Jany. 20, 1780.
From a "Collection . . . of English Prologues," &c.
                                                          28187. 16.
See also FOOTE.

WETHERELL, Sir Charles, 1770–1846; Recorder of Bristol; M.P.; Solicitor and Attorney-General.
Moore.   H. B. Hall, stipple.
Ha. len. to left, seated, looking to front.
Ind. proof; 1837.
13$\frac{1}{4}$ × 10$\frac{1}{4}$.   (8$\frac{7}{8}$ × 7$\frac{1}{8}$).   20642.

WHARNCLIFFE, James Archibald Stuart-Wortley Mackenzie, 1st Baron, 1776–1845, grandson of John, 3rd Earl of Bute; educ. at Charterhouse; ensign, 48th Regt., 1790; Capt., 72nd, 1793; took name of Wortley, 1795; Lt.-Col., 12th Regt.; M.P., 1797–1818; M.P., co. York, 1818, 1820–26; cr. Baron, 1826; Lord Keeper of Privy Seal, P.C., Lord Pres. of Council, &c.
H. P. Briggs, R.A.   F. Holl, stipple.
Ha. len. to left, looking to front.
Ind. proof, with scr. letters; 1836.
12$\frac{7}{8}$ × 10$\frac{1}{8}$.   (8$\frac{3}{4}$ × 7$\frac{1}{8}$).   20643.

——
F. Grant, A.R.A.   H. Cousins, mixed mez.
Wh. len. to front, seated, with left leg crossed over right; a paper in his left hand, glasses in right; a Skye terrier under his chair.
Ind. proof before all letters, except artists' names, facs. signature, and publication-line, March 8, 1846.
31$\frac{1}{8}$ × 19.   (26$\frac{3}{4}$ × 16$\frac{1}{2}$).   27282.

WHARTON, Thomas, Marquess of, 1640–1715, Lord Lieut.,
Ireland; Lord Privy Seal, 1714, &c.
    Sir G. Kneller.   J. Houbraken, 1744.
    Sh. ha. len. to left, looking to front; oval in border.
    In Birch's "Lives."
    $14\frac{3}{4} \times 9\frac{3}{8}$. $(14\frac{1}{4} \times 8\frac{3}{4})$.   27124.

WHATELY, Richard, 1787–1863, Archbishop of Dublin; son
of a clergyman; b. in Cavendish Square; educ. at Oxford;
Principal of St. Alban's Hall, Oxf., 1825; Prof. Pol. Econ.,
1830; Archbp. of Dublin, 1831; author of "Elements of
Logic," "Difficulties in the Writings of St. Paul, &c.," "Errors
of Romanism," &c.; promoted unsectarian education in Ireland;
d. in Dublin.
    C. Smith, R.H.A.   G. Sanders, mez.
    T. Q. len. to front, in gown, wearing the jewel of the order
of St. Patrick, of which he was ex officio Chancellor; his right
hand rests on his girdle, the left on a table.
    Open letter proof.
    $22\frac{15}{16} \times 17\frac{3}{16}$. $(18\frac{1}{8} \times 13\frac{7}{8})$.   23046.

WHEATLEY, Francis. 1747–1801, b. in Wild Court, Covent
Garden, son of a master tailor; studied in Shipley's School,
and at the R. A.; carried off several prizes of the Socy. of Arts;
soon found employment; but fell into theatrical society, extravagance, and debt; went to Dublin; exhibited at R.A., 1771,
portraits, &c.; excelled in rural subjects, and landscapes; A.R.A.,
1790; R.A., 1791; became a pensioner on the Academy.
    G. Dance.   W. Daniell.
    Sh. ha. len., profile to right; vignette.
    Proof before the artists' names.
    $10\frac{3}{4} \times 7\frac{7}{8}$. $(6\frac{3}{4} \times 4\frac{1}{2})$.   E. 2240.–'89.

WHEWELL, William, 1794–1866, son of a mechanic; b. at
Lancaster; educ. at Cambr.; Prof. of Mineralogy, 1828–'32; of
Moral Philosophy, 1838–'55; Master of Trin. Coll., and Presid.
of British Assocn., 1841; author of "History of the Inductive
Sciences," &c.; d. at Cambr.; munificent benefactor of his Coll.
and University.
    S. Lawrence.   W. Walker, mez.
    T. Q. len. to front, in gown, hands clasped together; corners
rounded off, except the lower one on the left.
    Proof before all letters.
    20×15. $(15\frac{3}{4} \times 12)$.   22934.

WHISTON, Rev. William, 1667–1752, Mathematician, Astronomer, &c.; b. at Norton, Leicestershire; educ. at Tamworth,
and Clare Hall, Camb.; suc. Newton as Lucas. Prof. of
Mathematics; depr. of this post and expelled from the University
on account of his Theol. opinions; author of "A New Theory
of the Earth," "Prælectiones Astronomicæ," "Prælectiones
Physico-Mathematicæ," &c.; minister of Lowestoft, Suffolk.
    Anon.   G. Vertue, 1720.

Ha. len. to right, looking to front, holding an open book in left hand, right hand raised, in rectangular frame; inscription in English, Latin, and Greek, in nine lines, in a cartouche, below.

Proof before the introduction of instruments (dipping needle, &c.) in corners.

From John Young's Collection.

(13⅓ × 9½). 24134.

WHITAKER, Thomas Dunham, 1759-1821, antiquary, pubd. "History of Whalley and Clitheroe," 1801; "History and Topography of . . . Leeds," 1816; "History of Richmondshire," 1823; Vicar of Whalley, Rector of Heysham, Lancashire; LL.D, ; F.S.A.; &c.

J. Northcote, R.A. W. Holl, stipple.

Ha. len., slightly to right, looking to left, in gown and bands. Open letter proof; March 1, 1816.

14¹³⁄₁₆ × 10½. (8¾ × 6½). 27628.

WHITBREAD, Samuel Charles, 1796- ; M.P. for Middlesex, 1820 and 1826.

H. W. Pickersgill. W. Ward, A.R.A., mez.

J. C. Smith, 88.

June 27, 1820. 22063.

WHITE, Anthony, M.B.

T. F. Dicksee. W. Walker, mez.

T. Q. len. to front, seated, with right elbow resting on table, and hand supporting head; a pen in his left hand. On the table are a watch, an inkstand, and a book, labelled "A Discourse on Anatomy."

A private plate.

Open letters, before the name, which is written below in pencil. Aug. 20, 1852.

17 × 12¹³⁄₁₆. (14½ × 11¼). 22935.

WHITE, Joseph Blanco, or Don José Maria Blanco y Crespo, as he was called in Spain, 1775-1841; b. at Seville, educ. for the Rom. Cath. Church; ordd. priest, 1799; became an unbeliever, 1800, though retaining his calling till 1810, when he escaped to England, where he passed the remainder of his life; established and carried on a monthly in Spanish till 1814; became a Unitarian, 1834; removed to Liverpool, 1835, where he died; author of "Letters from Spain," and other works.

W. Behnes. F. C. Lewis, stipple.

Ha. len. seated, to front, with open book before him, looking to left; vignette.

Scr. letter proof (?); April 18, 1836.

15 × 11⅞. (10 × 9½). 26204.

WHITE, Thomas, Bishop of Peterboro'.

See BISHOPS, Seven. 26668.

WHITEFIELD, GEORGE, 1714–1770, Methodist preacher; b. at Glo'ster; admitted a servitor at Oxf.; joined the Wesleys, already called "Methodists," from their regular mode of life, 1734; B.A., 1736; went to Georgia, U.S., 1737; began open-air preaching, 1739; Chaplain to the Countess of Huntingdon; his works pubd., 1771; d. at Newbury.

Hone. Greenwood, mez.
J. C. Smith, 6, 2nd state. 25763

WHITEFOORD, CALEB, 1734–1810, b. at Edinburgh; became a wine merchant in London, and remarked for wit and literary attainments; immortalised by Goldsmith in "Retaliation," and Wilkie's picture of "The Letter of Introduction;" wrote "Cross-Readings, or, A new Method of Reading the Newspapers," 1766; F.R.S., London and Edinb., F.S.A., "Sec. to the Brit. Commission, for treating of Peace with America—Anno 1782."

Sir J. Reynolds. T. Jones, mez.
J. C. Smith, 83, 2nd state. 24252.

WHITELOCKE, SIR BULSTRODE, 1605–1676, statesman; b. in Fleet St.; sat in Long Parliament, 1640; took leading part in Strafford's impeachment, and in most of the negotiations between Parliament and Charles I.; one of the Commissioners of the Great Seal, 1648; Ambassador to Sweden, 1653-'4; Speaker in Cromwell's third Parliament; retired after Restoration; wrote "Memorials of English Affairs."

Anon. H. Hulsbergh.
Sh. ha. len. to right, in armour, looking to front; long hair; in oval; arms below, and Latin inscription in 4 lines on either side of the oval in which the shield is suspended.
$10\frac{3}{16} \times 7\frac{3}{16}$. $(10 \times 6\frac{1}{8})$. 22289.

WHITGIFT, JOHN, 1530–1604, b. at Grimsby, Linc.; rector of Faversham, Cambr.; vice-chancellor, Cambr. Univ.; chaplain to Q. Elizabeth; dean of Lincoln, 1571; bishop of Worcester, 1577; transld. to Canterbury, 1583; d. at Lambeth; buried, Croydon.

Anon Anon., woodcut.
On back of title to "Life of the Most Reverend and Religious "prelate, John Whitgift, Lord Archbishop of Canterbury. "Written by Sir George Paule Knight, Comptroller of his "Grace's Householde," 1612. 4to.

Ha. len., to front, in robes; arms in upper corner on left, with motto below, VINCIT QVI PATITUR; and on right OBIIT ANNO ÆTATIS SVÆ 73.
$5 \times 3\frac{7}{8}$. 28828. 12.

WHITTINGTON, SIR RICHARD, 1360(?)–1425, Lord Mayor of London, 1397, 1406, and 1419.

Anon. R. Elstrack.

Ha. len., slightly to left, looking to front, wearing the gold chain and jewel; with his right hand he caresses his cat.
A modern impression.
$7\frac{1}{8} \times 4\frac{4}{8}$. ($5\frac{3}{8} \times 4\frac{1}{4}$). 24135.

WHITWORTH, CHARLES, Earl, 1754–1825, son of Sir Charles Whitworth, knt.; Ensign, Guards, 1772; Lieut. and Capt., 1776; Lieut.-Col., 104th, 1781; Minister Plenip., Warsaw, 1785; Envoy Extr., Petersb., 1788–1800; K.B., 1793; cr. Baron, 1800; P.C.; Ambas. Extr., Paris, 1801–'3; cr. Visct., 1813; G.C.B., and Earl, 1815.
   Sir T. Lawrence.   C. Turner, mez.
   T. Q. len. to right, looking to left, holding a paper with both hands.
   Proof before all letters.
   $22 \times 15\frac{7}{8}$. ($17\frac{7}{8} \times 13\frac{3}{4}$). 22936.

WICKLIFFFE, or WYCLIFFE, JOHN, 1324–1384; reformer, principal of Balliol Coll., Oxf., 1361; ambassador to Bruges, 1374; minister of Lutterworth, Lincoln; denied the doctrine of transubstantiation, 1381; translated the Bible into English; d. at Lutterworth; his remains burnt by order of Council of Constance, 1428.
   (From a picture in King's Coll., Cambr.)
                                        J. Faber, senr., mez.
   J. C. Smith, 58, among the Reformers, 2nd state, with Houston's name substituted for that of Faber. 26722.
   See also REFORMATION, in Foreign Series.

WIGRAM, SIR JAMES, Kt., 1793–1866; Equity Judge; son of Sir R. Wigram, Bt., an eminent London merchant; b. at Walthamstow; educ. at Cambridge; called to the bar, 1819; M.P. for Leominster, 1841; Vice-Chancellor, 1841–'50; Kt., 1841.
   Sir J. W Gordon, R.A.   W. Walker, mez.
   Ind. proof; Jany. 23, 1849
   Sh. ha. len., to left; oval in border.
   $16 \times 12\frac{7}{16}$. ($11\frac{1}{2} \times 9\frac{1}{4}$). 22937.

WILBERFORCE, SAMUEL, 1805–1873, educ. at Oriel Coll., Oxf.; Rector of Brighston, I. of Wight, and Alverstoke, Hants; canon of Windsor; Archdeacon of Surrey; Dean of Westminster, 1845; Bishop of Oxf., 1845; transld. to Winchester, 1869; published "Life and Correspce. of Wm. Wilberforce," 1838; "Agathos," 1840; "Eucharistica," 1852; killed by a fall from his horse.
   G. Richmond.   H. Robinson, stipple.
   As Bishop of Oxford; ha. len. to left, nearly in profile; vignette.
   Scratched letter proof; arms below, in centre.
   ($9 \times 8\frac{1}{2}$). 27088.

WILBERFORCE, Samuel—continued.

G. Richmond.   R. Jackson, mixed mez.
As Bishop of Winchester; ha. len. to right, seated, looking to
left, right hand and arm resting on a large open book; open
window behind, on right, showing trees and sky in distance.
Open letter proof; July 1, 1871.
  16⅞ × 12¾. (11½ × 9⅞).   27237.

WILBERFORCE, William, 1759–1833, philanthropist; famous
for the part he took in the movement for abolition of slave-
trade, and for the emancipation of the slaves in Br. Colonies,
ent. Parliament, 1780; d. soon after the second reading of the
Emancipation Act, 1833.
  G. Richmond.   S. Cousins, mixed mez.
Wh. len., to front, seated, with legs crossed, holding an eye-
glass; an open book, inkstand, &c., on table, left.
Ind. proof; May 20, 1834.
  22 × 15¾. (17¹⁵⁄₁₆ × 13¼).   22135.

H. Edridge.   J. Vendramini, chalk and dotted.
Sh. ha. len., to right, seated, reading; vignette; Oct. 27, 1809.
(9 × 8).   E. 1468. B.–'85.

WILD, Charles H   , Assistant Engineer during the floating of one of the tubes of the Britannia Bridge.
  See MENAI STRAITS.

WILHELMINA CAROLINE, Princess of Brandenburg-
Anspach, 1683–1737, m., 1705, to Prince George, afterwards
George II. of England.
  Kneller   V. Gunst.
As Princess of Wales; sh. ha. len., to left, looking to front.
(13½ × 20⅔).   25040.
In Genealogical Chart, 553. L

WILKES, John, 1727–1797, politician, M.P. for Aylesbury, 1757;
attacked Govt. in his "North Briton;" arrested and comm. to
Tower; liberated by Chf. Justice Pratt; outlawed for publishing "Essay on Woman;" lived in France till 1768; M.P. for
Middlesex; prev. from taking his seat, and comm. to Queen's
Bench Prison; four times re-elected, but still kept in prison;
Lord Mayor of London, 1774; elected again and allowed to
take his seat for Middlesex; resolutions of House of Commons
on his former elections for Middlesex expunged, 1782; Chamberlain, 1779; d in Grosvenor Square.
  See GLYNN.

WILKIE, Sir David, Kt., R.A.. 1785–1841, b. at Cults, Fifeshire,
where his father was the minister; educ. at Trustees' Academy
at Edinburgh, 1799–1803, under John Graham, studying
diligently; painted his first picture in 1804; came to London,
1805; successful from the first; painted and sold "The Rent

Day " for 300 Ggs.; A.R.A., 1809; R.A., 1811; travelled much
abroad; had bad health and pecuniary losses; changed his
style, more than once, after foreign experience; painter-in-
ordinary; knighted by William IV., 1836; d. at sea, off Malta.
    G. H. H[arlow] delt. 1812. [Mrs. Dawson Turner], etched.
    Sh. ha. len., to front, looking to left; vignette.
    $10 \times 6\frac{15}{16}$. $(7\frac{1}{2} \times 6)$.   E. 221.-'93.

WILKIE, Sir DAVID, Kt., R.A.—*continued.*
    A. Geddes.   W. Ward, A.R.A., mez.
    J. C Smith, 90.   23045.

    Sir W. Beechey, R.A.   H. Robinson, line and stipple.
    T. Q. len. to left, seated, looking up to right, holding brushes
and palette, hands clasping knee; sketch of " The blind fiddler "
behind; facs. signature below.
    $(4\frac{9}{16} \times 3\frac{3}{4})$.   28300. 65.

    J. Jackson, R.A.   H. Meyer, stipple.
    Sh. ha. len., to right, looking to front; hair brushed up off
forehead; vignette.
    Proof before all letters.
    (6×5).   28300. 66.

    Wilkie (1818).   Anon., woodcut.
    Sh. ha. len., to front; hair brushed from forehead; cut from
The Illustrated London News, April 9, 1859. The picture is in
the National Portrait Gallery.
    $(5\frac{5}{8} \times 3\frac{1}{4})$.   15220. 3.
    See also SCOTT, Sir WALTER.

WILKINS, JOHN, 1614–1672, mathematician; b. at Fawsley,
Northants.; grad. at Magd. Hall, Oxford; joined the " Solemn
League and Covenant," 1648; Warden of Wad. Coll., Oxf.,
1648; married Robinia Cromwell, sister of the Protector, 1659;
Master of Trin. Coll., Cambr. but lost that post at Restoration;
in favour again, 1663, Bishop of Chester, 1668; wrote " Essay
towards a real Character, and a Philosophical Language," and
other works; one of the founders of the Royal Society.
    Mary Beale.   A. Blooteling.
    Sh. ha. len., slightly turned to left, looking to front, wearing
long hair, bands, hood, surplice, &c.; in ornamented oval;
inscription on plinth below, "Effigies Reverendi . . . . .
Cestriensis," in 3 lines.
    $(15\frac{1}{2} \times 9\frac{1}{4})$.
    From John Young's collection.   24679.

WILLES, Sir JOHN, Kt., 1685–1761, Lord Chief Justice of
Common Pleas, 1737; P.C., &c.
    J. B. Vanloo.   G. Vertue, 1744.

T. Q. len., seated, to right, looking to front, wearing the robes
and chain, &c.
15⅝ × 11¾₁₆. (14¹¹₁₆ × 10¼). 27283.

WILLIAM I., "The Conqueror," 1027–1087 ; suc. 1066.
From three silver coins and a small illumination in Doomsday
Book. G. Vertue.
Ha. len., to front, crowned, and holding sword in right hand.
11½ × 7⁹₁₆. (11₁₁₆ × 7³₁₆). 27178. 3.

WILLIAM II., "Rufus," 1056–1100; suc. 1087.
From two silver coins. G. Vertue.
Bust, to front, crowned, and holding sceptre in right hand.
11½ × 7⁹₁₅. (11₇₈ × 7⁵₁₆). 27178. 4.
   Note.—No other portrait of this King is known.

WILLIAM, III., Prince of Orange, 1650–1702 ; son of
William, Prince of Orange, and Mary, daughter of Charles I. ;
m. Mary, daughter of James II. ; suc. K. of England, 1689.
   [Kneller ?] G. Valck.
   "Imprimé chez Nicolas Visscher, Avec Privil:," etc.
   Sh. ha. len. in armour, with long hair, to left, looking to
front ; oval in border.
   14¹⁵₁₆ × 10⁴₁₆. (14¼ × 10¾). 23124.

——

   Sir G. Kneller. G. Valck exc.
   Sh. ha. len. in armour, with long hair ; oval in border.
   22¼ × 16¼. (21¾ × 15⅞). 25810. 1.
   Note.—Bromley, p. 164, attributes this (?) to P. Vanderbanck, whose
style it resembles ; but it is not signed by him.

——

   Altered from the portrait of Cromwell by W. Faithorne.
   Wh. len., between two pillars.
   "Sold by Joseph Claver at the Black a mores head over
a gainst y⁰ East India hous in Leaden hall street."
   L. Fagan, p. 31, 3rd state.
   22½ × 17½(?). (22⁹₁₆ × 16¹¹₁₆). 25488.

——

   Wyssing pinx. G. Sanders invent. P Tanjé fecit, 1749.
   Sh. ha. len. to right, looking to front, in armour ; oval in
border.
   (13¾ × 8¾).
   In Genealogical Chart, 553. 1. 25018. 2.

——

   Sir G. Kneller. J. Smith, mez.
   J. C. Smith, 271, 2nd state. 21875.

WILLIAM IV., 1765–1837, 3rd son of George III.; ent. Navy ;
   m. Princess Adelaide of Saxe-Meiningen, 1811 ; suc., 1830.
   B. West, P.R.A. F. Bartolozzi, sc., and P. Sandby, aquat.

Wh. len. as a midshipman, on board H.M.S. Prince George; printed in brown ink; ded. to the Navy, and pubd., by A. Poggi, January 15, 1782.
$24\frac{3}{4} \times 18\frac{7}{8}$. $(20\frac{3}{4} \times 16\frac{7}{8})$. 22283.

WILLIAM IV.—*continued.*
M. A. Shee, R.A. Jas. Ward, mez.
As Duke of Clarence; wh. len. in robes.
J. C. Smith, 10, 2nd state; inscription in open letters.
E. 515.-'85.

A. Wivell. W. Ward, junr., mez.
As Duke of Clarence; ha. len. to right, looking to front, holding a telescope; in Admiral's uniform.
Published Oct. 10, 1824, by W. Sams.
Proof, with inscription in scratched letters.
$13\frac{1}{2} \times 9\frac{3}{4}$. $(10\frac{1}{4} \times 8\frac{3}{4})$. 15592. A.

W. Skelton. W. Skelton.
Sh. ha. len. to left, looking to front; in uniform, with star.
Published Jan. 1, 1821.
In lowest left-hand corner is the word "Proof."
$19\frac{7}{8} \times 15\frac{1}{8}$. $(18\frac{1}{4} \times 14)$. 25046. 4.
In Genealogical Chart, 553. 1.

A. M. Huffam. J. Rogers, mez.
Ha. len., to left, turned and looking to right; in uniform, with star, cloak, &c.
Published by J. McCormick, Aug. 1st, 1830.
$(5\frac{3}{8} \times 4\frac{3}{8})$. 15592. B.

Sir Thomas Lawrence. Thomas Hodgetts, mez.
Wh. len. front, looking to left, hat under his left arm.
Proof before the title.
Published by M. Colnaghi, Sepr. 1831.
$(24\frac{7}{8} \times 15\frac{7}{16})$. 27947.

A. Morton. S. W. Reynolds, mixed mez.
Wh. len. to front, looking to right, in admiral's uniform, with orders, &c.; the sea in distance on right.
Open letter proof; August, 1832; the inscription is on a separate plate at foot.
$25\frac{3}{4} \times 17\frac{1}{8}$. $(25\frac{1}{2} \times 16\frac{1}{2})$; the lettered plate, $2\frac{11}{16} \times 17\frac{1}{8}$.
23150.

J. Cochran. Hy. Dawe.
Full ha. len. seated; facs. signature below; a crown above.
$(4\frac{1}{2} \times 3\frac{1}{2})$. 26417.
See also WATERLOO BANQUET.

WILLIAMS, ANNA, 1706–1783, poetess and writer of prose, author of "Miscellanies in prose and verse;" blind; friend, guest, and dependent of Dr. Johnson.

Frances Reynolds.   A. Wivell, 1839.

Ha. len. to front, looking to right; lace cap on head, a narrow ribbon round throat; dark dress, full over shoulders.

9½ × 6⅝.   (3¹¹⁄₁₆ × 3₁⁄₁₆).   27675.

WILLIAMS, GILLY.   *See* SELWYN, GEORGE.

WILLIAMS, DAVID, 1738–1816, b. at Cardigan; preacher at Frome, Exeter, and Highgate; resided in Chelsea; miscellaneous writer, historian of Monmouth; published "Lectures on Political Liberty," 1782; founded the "Literary Fund," 1789; buried at St. Anne's, Soho.

Rigaud.   Thornthwaite.

T. Q. len. to front, holding pen in right hand, left elbow resting on a sloped desk, under a bookcase, partly seen on the right: he wears a long gown, or cloak.

11 × 7⅞.   (8 × 6¹⁰⁄₁₆).   27624.

WILLIAMS, SIR JOHN, Knt.   *See* ALDERMEN.

WILLIAMS, JOHN, c. 1750–1818, studied in the R. Academy schools, and under Matthew Darby, the engraver; chiefly known as an art critic, writing over the signature, "Anthony Pasquin;" emigrated to the U.S., America, and d. at Brooklyn; pubd. a "Liberal Critique on the Exhibition for 1794;" "Lives of English and Irish Artists," 1794; "An Authentic History of the Professors of Painting, &c., in Ireland," Critical Guides, &c.; described by Lord Kenyon, 1797, as "a common libeller;" by Dr. Watt (Bibl. Brit.) as "a literary character of the lowest description;" and by Lord Macaulay as "a malignant and filthy baboon," and "a polecat," Edin. Rev. lxxiv., 250).

M. A. Shee (exhibited, 1792).   I. Wright, stipple.

T. Q. len. to left, seated, looking to front, holding pen in right hand, left hand hanging by his side; books, inkstand, &c., on table, left; printed in colours, the lettering lightly engraved.

(9¹⁵⁄₁₆ × 8).   28921.

WILLIAMS, GEN. SIR WILLIAM FENWICK, 1800–1883, Bart., K.C.B., b. in Nova Scotia, entd. R. Artillery, 1826; 1st Lt., 1827; Captn., 1840; served in Turkey till 1843; took part in conferences preceding treaty of Erzeroum, 1847, Br. Col.; Eng. Comnr. for settling Turco-Persian boundary, 1848; Brig.-Gen., 1854; Br. Comnr. with Turkish Army, victorious over Mouravieff, 1855, and defended Kars; recd. Baronetcy on returning home, and pension, &c.; commanded in Canada, 1859; Govr. of Gibraltar, 1870; resigned, 1875; retired, 1877.

[Baugniet.]   Baugniet, 1857, lith.

Ha. len. slightly to left, looking to front, in uniform, as Maj.-General; vignette; facs. signature below; Oct. 15, 1857.

(9¼ × 7¾).   23613.

WILLIAMS, ——, actor, c. 1828.
  See LISTON.

WILLIS, JOHN, –1760 (according to Bromley), writing-
master.
  Stokes.   E. Fisher, mez.
  J. C. Smith, 60, 1st state.   28857. 3.

WILLIS, THOMAS, M.D., 1621–1675; matr. at Ch. Ch., Oxf.,
  1636, and, with other students, took up arms for Charles I.;
  practised physic at Oxf.; Sedleian Profr., Natural Philos.,
  1660; removed to London, 1666; Physician-in-Ord. to Charles
  II.; more successful in gaining reputation and money than any
  predecessor; author of several learned and acute works on
  Physiology, &c.
    Anon.   G. Vertue, 1742.
    Sh. ha. len. to right, looking to front; oval in border; arms,
  books, a skull, &c., below.
    In Birch's "Lives."
    11⅜ × 9¼.   (13⁹⁄₁₆ × 8¾).   22487.

WILSON, actor, c. 1775; in the Character of a Farmer, in the
  Farmer's Return from London.
    Pubd. by Fielding and Walker, Nov. 5, 1779.
    From a "Collection . . . of English Prologues," &c.
                                                  28187. 17.

WILSON, MRS., speaking the Prologue to Polley Honeycombe.
    From a "Collection . . . of English Prologues," &c., 1779.
                                                  28187. 18.

WILSON, ANTHONY, 1750–   ; b. at Wigan, Lancashire.
  See BROMLEY, HENRY.

WILSON, DANIEL, 1772–1858, b. in Spitalfields; educ. at Eltham,
  Hackney, and Oxford; tutor and vice-principal of St. Edmund
  Hall, Oxf.; curate of Chobham and Bisley, Surrey, and of
  Worton; minister of St. John's, Bedford Row; vicar of Islington; bishop of Calcutta, 1832.
    T. Phillips, R.A.   J. Bromley, mez.
    T. Q. len. in robes, to front, looking to right, holding his cap in
  right hand, and in his left a large bible, which rests upon a
  curved piece of carved woodwork.
    Proof before all letters, except the artists' names and the
  publication-line; Feb. 1, 1833.
    21¹¹⁄₁₆ × 15½. (17¼ × 13¾).   26723.

WILSON, HORACE HAYMAN, 1786–1860, assist. surgeon, Bengal,
  to the E. I. C., 1808; served in the assay office of the Mint,
  Calcutta, and cultivated Sanskrit literature; revived interest in
  that, and introduced European Science and English letters to
  the natives; returned to England, Profr. Sanskrit, at Oxf., 1832,

Librarian to the E. I. C., and Director of the R. Asiatic Socy., &c., until his death.
Sir J. Watson Gordon, R.A.   W. Walker, mez.
T. Q. len. to right, seated, looking to front, holding a paper on his lap.
A private plate, with open letters; June 4, 1851.
20 × 15⅝. (17½ × 13¾).   22938.

WILSON, Rt. Hon. James, 1805–1860, political economist; edited the "Economist;" financial member of Council at Calcutta.
Sir J. W. Gordon, R.A.   F. Stacpoole, mez.
T. Q. len. seated, to front, with crossed legs; facs. signature below.
Scratched letter proof; Sepr. 24th, 1860.
18¾ × 14¾. (13¹⁵⁄₁₆ × 11).   27284.

WILSON, James Arthur, M.D.
Publd.(?) a work, "On Spasm, Languor, Palsy, and other Disorders, termed Nervous, of the Muscular System," Lond. 1843 (see Athenænm, 1843, 711).
Mrs. E. Walker.   W. Walker, mixed mez.
Ha. len. to front, looking to right, seated; right hand resting on table, and holding an eye-glass.
Open letter proof. (Private plate ?) The name in pencil.
12¹³⁄₁₆ × 10. (9⅜ × 6¹³⁄₁₆).   24727.

WILSON, John, 1785–1854, distinguished poet, critic, and prose-writer, best known as the "Christopher North" of Blackwood's Magazine; son of a prosperous manufacturer at Paisley; educ. at Glasgow and Oxford, where he won the Newdigate Prize, 1806; author of an "Elegy on the death of James Grahame," "Isle of Palms," &c.; editor of "Blackwood;" Prof. of Moral Philosophy, Edinb.; &c.
T. Duncan, A.R.A.   C. E. Wagstaff, mixed mez., aquat, &c.
Wh. len. to front, looking to right, holding gun in right hand; "Christopher North in his Sporting Jacket," white trousers, shoes with buckles, &c., Jany. 1, 1844.
27 × 18½. (23¾ × 16¾).   27287.
See also SCOTT, Sir Walter.

WILSON, Richard, 1714–1782, R.A., b. at Pinegas, Montgomeryshire, where his father then had a small living; educ. at home; sent to London, 1729, placed under T. Wright, a portrait painter, and remained 6 years; began painting portraits by which he lived till 1750; travelled in Italy, 1750–'6; returned, began to paint the landscapes by which he has become famous; original member of the R. A., 1768, and Librarian, 1776.
R. Mengs.   W. Bond, stipple.

Ha. len. to right, seated, looking to front, holding a brush in right hand, and other brushes and palette in left.
Ind. proof with open letters; Jan. 20, 1812; for Britton's "Fine Arts of England."
$11\frac{7}{8} \times 10$. $(7\frac{3}{8} \times 6\frac{9}{16})$. 21842.

WILSON, Richard—*continued.*
[R. Mengs.] Anon., stipple.
Similar to the print by W. Bond; but lighter; vignette.
Ind. proof before all letters.
$10\frac{15}{16} \times 8\frac{15}{16}$. $(7\frac{3}{4} \times 6\frac{1}{4})$. E. 225.–'93.

——

R. Mengs. W. Bromley, 1809.
Sh. ha. len. to right, looking to front; oval.
Proof before all letters, except the artists' names.
$(4\frac{1}{4} \times 3\frac{1}{8})$. 28300. 67.

——

R. Mengs. C. Pye.
Bust to right, looking to front.
Ind. proof; Sepr., 1822.
$10\frac{3}{16} \times 9$. $(2\frac{3}{8} \times 1\frac{7}{8})$. 28300. 68.

——

Sir G. Beaumont. T. H[astings], etched.
Sh. ha. len., profile to left, carrying a mahl-stick over left shoulder. On the title to "Etchings from the Works of *Ric. Wilson* (facs. signature), *traced from an original sketch made from life by Sir Geo^r. Beaumont, now in the possession of R. Ford, Esq.*," &c. by Thomas Hastings, 1825; title in red and black.
$4\frac{3}{8} \times 3\frac{1}{2}$. (Vignette, $3\frac{1}{4} \times 3\frac{1}{16}$). 28300. 69.

WILSON, Sir Robert Thomas, 1777–1849; son of Benj. Wilson, the artist, entered the Light Dragoons, 1794; Maj.-Genl., 1813; General, 1814; M.P., Southwark, 1818–'31.
H. W. Pickersgill. W. Ward, A.R.A., mez.
J. C. Smith, 92, 2nd state. 24136.

WILSON, Thomas, 1663–1755; b. at Burton, Cheshire; educ. at Trin. Coll., Dublin; curate, Winwick, Lancashire; bishop, Sodor and Man, 1698; Author of "Sacra Privata," pubd., 1800.
I. Fellowes. G. Vertue, 1726.
Ha. len. in robes, to right, looking to front, wearing his square cap.; oval in border; arms below in centre, with name and title in three lines of inscription.
$18\frac{1}{4} \times 12\frac{5}{16}$. $(17\frac{5}{8} \times 11\frac{13}{16})$. 27537.

WILTON, Joseph, 1722–1803, R.A., b. in London; educ. at Hoddesdon, Herts.; son of a manufacturer of architectural ornaments in plaster; stud. for profession of engineer, but gave up that for sculpture; pupil of Delvaux; went to Paris;

instructed by Pigalle, 1744–'7 ; travelled in Italy ; returned,
1755; original member of Royal Academy; successful in his
profession ; retired, 1790 ; Keeper to the Academy.
G. Dance, R.A. W. Daniell, A.R.A., stipple.
Sh. ha. len., seated, profile to right ; vignette.
(6¼ × 4¾). E. 2239.–'89.

WINDHAM, Rt. Hon. William, 1750–1810, son of Col.
Windham of Felbrigg Hall, Norfolk ; educ. at Eton and Oxford ;
M.P., Norwich, 1782 ; one of the managers of Warren Hastings's
impeachment ; Sec. of State for War, 1794–1801, and 1806–'7 ;
celebrated Parliamentary orator.
Sir J. Reynolds. J. Jones, mez.
J. C. Smith, 86, 2nd state (undescribed by J. C. S.) ; the space
on which the lettering appears is not grounded, but cleared.
21885.

WING, Tycho, 1706–1760 (?), said by Noble to have been a son
of the Astrologer, Vincent Wing, who died, 1668. There is a
calculation of Easter, by Tycho Wing, in Vol. IX of the Gent.'s
Mag., and his portrait is at Stationers' Hall. The Gent.'s Mag.,
1815, gives Pickworth as the place of his birth, and the dates,
as above, on the authority of his tomb, in Great Casterton
Churchyard, near Stamford.
J. Vanderbank G. White, mez.
J. C. Smith, 58. 28262.

WINSLOW, Forbes Benignus, 1810–1874, b. in London ; educ.
in Scotland, near London, and at Manchester ; stud. medicine
in New York, and under Drs. Carpue, Turner, Elliotson,
Quain, &c.; M.D., Aberdeen ; Author of several lectures, and
other treatises ; had a large practice, chiefly in cases of brain-
disease ; D.C.L., M.R.C.P., &c.
J. P. Knight, R.A. W. Carlos, mixed mez.
Wh. len. to front, in Doctor's robes, holding square cap in
right hand.
Open letter proof; Oct. 1, 1859.
31 × 19 (26¼ × 16). 27286.

WINSTANLEY, Hamlet, 1700–1761, son of Henry Winstanley,
architect ; pupil of Kneller, painted several portraits, correct in
drawing, but weak in colour and expression ; travelled in Italy ;
devoted himself to engraving ; etched the " Knowsley Gallery,"
and pictures of the Derby family, &c.
Winstanley. J. Faber, junr., mez.
J. C. Smith, 388, 2nd state.

[Winstanley]. Bannerman.
A copy reversed from the mez. print by J. Faber, junr. ; the
head on the canvas is here that of Dorigny, the engraver.
7⁵⁄₁₆ × 5⅜. (6³⁄₁₆ × 4¹¹⁄₁₆). 29962. c.

WINTER, ROBERT, and
WINTER, THOMAS, Gunpowder Plot conspirators,
    See CONCILIUM.

WISEMAN, NICHOLAS PATRICK STEPHEN, 1802–1865, Cardinal ;
  son of an Irish merchant ; b. at Seville ; educ. at Ushaw and
  Rome ; Rector of the English College, Rome ; Pres., Oscott
  Coll. ; Vicar-apost., London District ; Cardinal and Archbishop,
  Westminster, 1850 ; joint editor, "Dublin Review ;" author
  of "Horæ Syriacæ," numerous letters, lectures, &c. ; d. in
  London
    J. R. Herbert, R.A.   G. R. Ward, mixed mez. and stipple.
    T. Q. len. to left, seated, looking somewhat to right of front,
  holding a book on his lap, with a finger of his right hand
  between the leaves.
    Open letter proof on Ind. paper ; March 1, 1855.
    $20\frac{5}{16} \times 14\frac{7}{8}$. $(16\frac{11}{16} \times 12\frac{5}{16})$.   23047.

WISSING, WILLIAM, 1656–1687, b. at the Hague ; came to
  England, employed by Lely, to whose practice he succeeded ;
  became Court painter ; painted with more elegance than Lely
  or Kneller ; many of his pictures reproduced in contemporary
  mezzotints ; d. at Burleigh, the Earl of Exeter's seat ; buried
  at St. Martin's Church, Stamford.
    W. Wissing.   J. Smith, mez.
    J. C. Smith, 278, 1st state.   24253.

    [Wissing.]   A. Walker.
    A copy, reversed, of the mez. print by J. Smith.
    Oval. $(5\frac{1}{16} \times 4\frac{5}{16})$.   £. 2236.–'89.

WITHER, GEORGE, 1588–1667, b. Bentworth, Hants. ; educ. at
  Magd. Coll., Oxf. ; went to Linc. Inn, where he wrote his
  satires, "Abuses stript and whipt," for which he was imprisoned ;
  publ. "The Shepherd's Hunting," 1615 ; fought on the side of
  the Parliament ; enriched himself out of the Royalists' estates ;
  sent to the Tower, at the Restoration.
    [J. Payne (?)].   I. P (*i.e.*, John Payne).
    Sh. ha. len. to left, looking to front, wearing broad-leafed hat
  and lace collar ; arms in background, on left ; oval in border ;
  name about the oval ; 4 verses below " *What I was,* . . . .
  my Beauties bee."   Prefixed to his " Collection of Emblems,"
  1635, fol. Letter-press on the back.
    Cut. $8\frac{3}{16} \times (?)$. $(7\frac{7}{16} \times 6\frac{3}{16})$.   25210.

WIVELL, ABRAHAM, 1786–1849, portrait-painter, educ. at
  Marylebone School of Industry ; apprent. to a wig-maker, 1799,
  and followed that business himself, as well as that of painting
  water-colour miniatures, which he soon began ; made portraits
  of Cato Street Conspirators, and others ; wrote an " Enquiry

into the history of the Shakspeare portraits;" invented fire-
escapes; painted oil portraits; d. at Birmingham.

A. Wivell.   W. Holl, stipple.
Bust, to right, looking to front; oval.
Ind. proof before all letters.
$8 \times 6\frac{7}{16}$. $(3\frac{3}{16} \times 2\frac{1}{16})$.   28336. 21.

WODSWORTH, CHARLES,   –1844, educ. at Pembr. Coll.,
Cambr.; lecturer at St. John's, Westminster; preacher at St.
George's, Camberwell; vicar of Hardingstone, Northants, and
of Audley, Staffs.; chaplain of St. Ann's Society schools;
preb., St. Paul's; chaplain to Lord Palmerston; d. in South-
wick St., Paddington.

S. Howell.   W. Skelton.
Ha. len. slightly to left, looking to front, in gown and bands.
Open letter proof (?); July, 1831.
$15\frac{1}{2} \times 13\frac{1}{4}$. $(14 \times 11\frac{1}{4})$.   24728.

WOFFINGTON, MARGARET, 1720–1760, comic actress; b. in
Dublin; brought up to the stage by Madame Violante, a rope-
dancer; created sensation at Cov. Garden, in "Sir Harry
Wildair," by her beauty and liveliness; rival of Mrs. Cibber
and Mrs. Bellamy; struck with paralysis on the stage, 1757; d.
at Teddington.

A. Pond.   J. McArdell, mez.
J. C. Smith, 188.   21910.

WOLCOT, JOHN, M.D., 1738–1819, b. at Dodbrooke, Devonshire;
educ. at Kingsbridge, Bodmin, and Fowey, where he was under
the instruction of an uncle, an apothecary, who left him the chief
part of his estate; got an M.D. degree in Scotland, 1767, and
went to Jamaica with Sir William Trelawney; returned, and
settled as physician in Cornwall, instructing Opie, with whom he
went to London, 1870; wrote satirical poems, signed with the
pseudonym "Peter Pindar," against the R. Academy, the King,
and others; became blind some years before his death. He knew
a good deal about painting, and had also a taste for music.

J. Opie.   C. H. Hodges, mez.
J. C. Smith, 35.
The title is in open letters.   22061.

WOLFE, JAMES, 1726–1759, General, killed at the battle of
Quebec, Sept. 13.

Anon.   Engraver not ascertained, mez.
J. C. Smith, 165, p. 1750.   27559.

——, The Death of General.

B. West.   W. Woollett.
A composition of many figures, near the middle of which
Wolfe is seen, dying.
Pubd., Jan. 1st., 1776.
$(16\frac{14}{16} \times 23\frac{3}{4})$.   27189.

WOLFF, Joseph, 1795–1862, converted Jew and curate of High
Hoyland, Yorks; chaplain to Viscount Lorton in Bokhara;
Vicar of Isle Brewers, co. Somers., 1849; missionary to Palestine
and Persia; D.D.
    E. Fancourt.   H. Meyer, mez.
    Ha. len. slightly to left, looking upwards, holding a half-open
book in both hands. Novr. 1, 1827.
    $14\frac{1}{2} \times 10\frac{5}{8}$. $(10\frac{3}{4} \times 9)$.   27558.

WOLLASTON, William, 1659–1724, philosopher; b. at Coton
Stamford, Staff.; educ. at Sidney Sussex Coll., Cambr.; Master,
Birmingham School; resided in Charterhouse Square; author
of several learned works.
    (From the bust at Richmond).   J. Faber, junr., mez.
    J. C. Smith, 125, among " Philosophers of England."
    (*Note.*—The personage is turned to the right, and not to the left, as
erroneously described by J. C. S.)
                                    22939.

WOLLASTON, William Hyde, 1766–1828, Natural Philosopher; M.D.; discovered several new metals; invented the
Camera Lucida, and a sliding scale of chemical equivalents; led
the way to Spectrum Analysis; succeeded Sir Joseph Banks
as Pres. Roy. Socy., 1820.
    J. Jackson, R.A.   W. Ward, A.R.A., mez.
    J. C. Smith, 93.
    Proof before all letters, undescribed by J. C. S.   22064.
    See also SCIENCE.

WOLSEY, Thomas, 1471–1530, b. at Ipswich; rector of
Lymington, Som., and set in the stocks there; dean of Lincoln,
1508; rector of Turrington; canon of Windsor; Chancellor of
the Garter; dean of York; precentor, St. Paul's; bishop of
Lincoln; Archbishop of York, 1514; Cardinal, 1515; built
Hampton Court; had grant of Richmond palace; disgraced,
1529; d. at Leicester Abbey.
    Anon.   P. Fourdrinier.
    T. Q. len. to left, in cardinal's robes, in profile, with right
hand raised, in act of benediction. In the distance, Cathedr.
of Chr. Ch., Oxon., where the picture is.
    $(9\frac{5}{16} \times 6\frac{1}{8})$.   26724.

WOOD, Anthony, 1632–1695, b. at Oxford; educ. at Merton
Coll., Oxf.; M.A., 1655; wrote "Historia et Antiquitates Univ.
Oxoniensis," 1663–'74, and "Athenæ Oxonienses," 1691–'2,
republished twice; the book was burned, and Wood expelled,
because some passages in the first edition, reflecting on Lord
Clarendon, gave offence to the University.
    [M. Burghers.]   *MB* [*i.e.*, Michael Burghers].
    Ha. len. to right, looking to front, holding a book in right hand,
with his thumb between the leaves, on the edges of which
appears the title, *Athen. Oxon. III.*; in an architectural border,
his arms and crest on the pediment above, and H.S.E. | Antonius

WOOD | ANTIQUARIUS | *Ob. 28. Nov. A°.* | *1695 Æt. 64*, on a tablet below. Prefixed to the "Life of Anthony à Wood," Oxford, 1772, 8vo.

$6\frac{1}{6} \times 4\frac{1}{4}$. ($6\frac{5}{8} \times 4$). 25809.

Note.—Burghers lived and worked at Oxford, and scraped also a mezzotint portrait of A. Wood.

WOOD, SIR MATTHEW, 1768–1843, Bart., M.P., son of a serge-manufacturer at Tiverton; in business in the City of London; Sheriff, 1809; twice Lord Mayor, 1815 and 1816; for many years M.P. for the city; friend and supporter of Queen Caroline; cr. Bart., 1837.

A. W. Seirs. W. Say.

Ha. len. to front, in robes, with the collar, &c., looking to right.

Proof before all letters, touched about the face for correction.

$19\frac{3}{16} \times 15\frac{1}{4}$. ($15\frac{1}{16} \times 12\frac{3}{4}$). 23042.

WOOD, ROBERT, 1716–1771, scholar and traveller; made the Tour of Greece and Syria; wrote "The Ruins of Baalbec," "The Ruins of Palmyra," &c.

See DAWKINS, JOHN.

WOODHOUSELEE, ALEXANDER FRASER TYTLER, Lord, 1747–1813, one of the Senators of the College of Justice, and one of the Lords Commissioners of Justiciary in Scotland, F.R.S. Edin.

H. Raeburn, A.R.A. (J. Jackson del.) C. Picart.

Proof with scratched letters; May 10, 1813.

Sh. ha. len. to right, looking to front; a vignette.

$14\frac{3}{4} \times 12\frac{3}{4}$. ($6\frac{3}{4} \times 5\frac{1}{4}$). 27234.

WOODVILLE, WILLIAM, 1752–1805, b. at Cockermouth; M.D. Edinb., 1775; practised 5 or 6 years at Cockermouth; went to London, appointed Physician to Middlesex Dispensary, and in 1792 Physician to the Small-Pox Hospital, where he remained till his death; author of "Medical Botany," &c.; opposed vaccination at first, but afterwards warmly advocated it; d. in St. Pancras Parish.

Abbott. Bond, stipple.

Ha. len. to left, looking to front, arms folded; oval; below, a "View of the Inoculating Hospital at Pancras," designed by Shepherd, and engraved by Woolnoth; vignette.

(Oval, $5\frac{5}{8} \times 4\frac{1}{2}$). 27625.

See also MEDICAL SOCIETY.

WOODWARD, HENRY, 1717–1777, b. in Southwark, acted at age of 14 in a Lilliputian "Beggar's Opera;" went to Dublin, 1747, and had great success there; on his return, engaged by Garrick, but, dissatisfied with his position, speculated as manager of Crow Street Theatre, Dublin, 1758, and failed after 4 years' trial; returned to London, where he was well received.

B. Vander Gucht. J. R. Smith, mez.

J. C. Smith, 177, 1st state ; " *Mr. Woodward in Petruchio* ; " and, in the right lower corner, "*printed by J. Gamble*," these two phrases not observed by Mr. J. C. Smith; they are lightly scratched on the plate.

22284.

WOODWARD, HENRY, in the Character of a Fine Gentleman, Prologue to Barbarossa.
From a " Collection of English Prologues," &c., 1779.

28187. 20.

WOOLLETT, WILLIAM, 1735–1785, b. at Maidstone, of a family originally Dutch ; son of a watchmaker ; apprent. to Tinney, an engraver ; soon distinguished himself in that art ; his " Niobe," after Wilson, and " Death of Wolfe," after West, were the first English prints noticed abroad ; besides these he executed very many beautiful plates.

J. K. Sherwin.   J. K. Sherwin.
Pubd. Aug. 12, 1784.
Ha. len. to right, seated, looking to front, holding a plate and burin, and wearing a cap.
12 × 10.   (10¼ × 9).   22280.

G. Stuart.   C. Watson, mixed stipple.
Ha. len. to left, seated, looking to front, holding a plate ; behind is part of the " Death of Wolfe " picture ; Sepr. 1st, 1785.
(5⅞ × 4⅝).   E. 2241.–'89.

T. Hearne, F.S.A., 1770.   F. Bartolozzi, R.A., 1795.
Sh. ha. len., profile to left, wearing a cap ; oval.
5⅛ × 4⅛.   (3¾ × 3).   26280.

WORCESTER, EDWARD SOMERSET, 2nd Marquess of, 1601–1667, son of Henry, 1st Marquess, whom he suc., 1646 ; like his father, a zealous Royalist ; sent by Charles I. to raise troops in Ireland for service in England ; in France for some years ; on his return imprisoned in the Tower till 1655 ; author of " A Century of Inventions," 1663, in which he describes an engine, constructed by himself, which was really a steam-engine ; unsuccessful in his attempts to bring this invention into notice ; Governor of South Wales ; buried at Raglan.

Anon.   Anon., stipple.
T. Q. len. to left, seated, in classic dress, looking to right.
[Proof (?)].   A private plate, without any inscription.
12 × 10.   (9½ × 8¾).   24094.

WORDSWORTH, WILLIAM, 1770–1850, poet, b. at Cockermouth, educ. at Hawkshead Gr. School, and St. John's Coll., Cambr. ; B.A., 1791 ; visited the Continent ; appointed stamp-distributor for Westmd. and Cumbd. ; pubd. " An Evening Walk," 1793 ; " Lyrical Ballads," 1798 ; Poems, 2 vols., 1807 ; " Excursion," 1814 ; " Peter Bell ; " " The Waggoner," " White Doe of

Rylstone," 1815; "River Duddon," &c.; D.C.L., Oxon. and
Durham; poet-laureate, 1843.

W. Bexall.   J. Bromley, mixed mez.
Ha. len. to front, looking to right; arms folded over breast.
June 10, 1832.
16⅞ × 14.   (12¹¹⁄₁₆ × 9¹⁄₄).   22144.
See also SCOTT, SIR **WALTER.**

WORLIDGE, THOMAS, 1700–1766, painter at first, and draughtsman, at Bath, executing portraits on vellum with pencil or
Indian ink; failing in oils, he took up etching, and used the
dry point freely, imitating Rembrandt; made many drawings of
gems, which were published after his death, and by which he is
best known.
T. Worlidge.   W. H. Worthington.
Sh. ha. len. to left, looking to front, wearing flat cap and furred
robe, and holding a needle in right hand, as in act of etching.
Oct. 15, 1827.
7¹⁵⁄₁₆ × 5⅝.   (4⅝ × 3¾).   26281.

WORSDALE, JAMES,   –1767, a pupil of Kneller, who dismissed him for secretly marrying his wife's niece; he gained
patronage, and was appointed master-painter to Board of
Ordnance; was also a successful actor, author of several
plays, a singer, and mimic; painted portraits.
R. E. Pine.   W. Dickinson, mez.
J. C. Smith, **91.**   E. 1276.–'86.

WORSTER, HENRY, c. 1690.
No particulars of the life of this personage are to be found.
T. Murray.   J. Smith, mez.
J. C. Smith, **282.**   E. 2164.–'89.

WORTLEY, LADY EMMELINE CHARLOTTE ELIZABETH STUART,
1806–1855, 2nd dau. of John Henry, 5th Duke of Rutland; m. to
the Hon. Charles Stuart Wortley (1802–1844), 1831; published
many vols. of Poems, plays, travels, &c., now completely
forgotten; d. at Beyrout, Syria.
F. Grant, R.A.   J. Faed, mixed mez.
Wh. len. to front, seated, right elbow on a pedestal which
supports a vase, right hand to neck, looking to right, left hand
resting on an open book on her knee; landscape in distance, on
right.
Ind. proof with open letters; Grantham, 1859.
26¾ × 20¾.   (21¹⁄₄ × 16⅞).   25842.

WOTTON, SIR HENRY, 1568–1631; Ambassador to Venice;
Provost of Eton, &c.
C. Janssens.   (H. Grease, del.)   T. Cheesman.
Nearly T. Q. len. to right, looking to front, holding a book on
a table with his right hand.
Feb. 1, 1816 (in Lodge).
14⅞ × 10⅜.   (7¹⁄₁₆ × 5⁷⁄₁₀).   27285.

WREN, Sir Christopher, 1632–1723; b. at Knoyle; educ. at Oxford; Prof. Astr., Gresham College, and afterwards at Oxford; F.R.S., 1663; went to France, 1665; architect of Royal Palaces, St. Paul's, and Surveyor-General of Works, 1668; Kt., 1674; rebuilt St. Paul's, and many churches, &c.

  Sir G. Kneller.   J. Smith, mez.
  J. C. Smith, 283, 2nd state.   22057.

  J. B. Cipriani, R.A.   G. Godby, stipple.
  Wh. len. to right, looking to front, holding a view of St. Paul's and compasses with right hand and arm, leaning left hand on a pedestal; vignette. Aug. 1, 1815.
  (18 × 9¼).   28443. 5.

WRIGHT, (Christopher), and
WRIGHT, John, Gunpowder Plot conspirators; schoolfellows of Guy Fawkes, at the Free School at Durham.
  See CONCILIUM.

WRIGHT, Joseph, 1734–1797, b. at Derby, pupil of Hudson, and afterwards of Mortimer; A.R.A., 1781; R.A., 1784; exhibited until 1794; called "Wright of Derby;" his "Experiment with an Air-pump" is in the National Gallery.
  J. Wright.   J. Ward, mez.
  J. C. Smith, 36, 3rd state.   27236.

WRIGHT, Sir Nathan, Kt., 1653–1721; Judge; educ. at Cambridge; called to the bar, 1677; King's Sergeant and Kt., 1697; Lord Keeper, 1700–'5; P.C., 1700; d. at Cancot Hall, Warwickshire, 1721.
  R. White.   R. White.
  "Printed and Sold by John King at the Globe against the Church in the Poultry."
  Sh. ha. len. to right, looking to front, wig and robes, oval in border.
  15⅝ × 11. (13¹⁵⁄₁₆ × 10⁹⁄₁₆).   22940.

WYATT, James, 1748–1813, architect, b. at Burton Constable, son of a farmer and dealer in timber; taken to Italy by Lord Bagot, 1762, and studied under Vincentini; returned to England; A.R.A., 1770; had great success, as architect of several fine mansions, colleges at Oxford, Salisbury and Lincoln Cathedrals; R.A., 1785; Surveyor to the Board of Works, 1796; built Fonthill, the front of White's Club, &c.; F.R.S., F.S.A., &c.
  M. C. Wyatt   C. Turner, mez.
  Ha. len. seated, profile to right. A private plate.
  Open letter proof; May 1, 1809.
  13⅛ × 9⅞. (11¾ × 9½).   22941.

WYATT, Sir Thomas, 1503–1541, Poet and statesman; b. at Allington, Kent; educ. at Camb. and Oxf.; employed by

Henry VIII. in diplomacy; wrote odes and love elegies; translated the Psalms into English verse; friend of the Earl of Surrey.
H. Holbein.   F. Bartolozzi, stipple in colour.
A head, the body only sketched in outline, to right, looking to left, wearing a low cap; from the drawing at Windsor; Oct. 1, 1793.
16⅝ × 12¾.   (13⅝ × 10⅛).   **22542.**

WYATVILLE, Sir Jeffery, 1766–1840, architect, b. at Burton-on-Trent; son of Joseph Wyatt, a surveyor; educ. at the free school; wished to be a sailor; came to London; entered his uncle Samuel's office, where he learned architecture; assisted another uncle, James; joined in a building business; employed on great works at Windsor Castle; A.R.A., 1823; R.A., 1826; received royal license to call himself Wyatville; Kt., &c.
R. Evans.   H. Robinson.
T. Q. len. to front, seated; holding compasses in left hand on a plan; Windsor Castle in distance; facs. signature below; 1834.
8¹⁵⁄₁₆ × 5¾.   (4⅝ × 3¹³⁄₁₆).   28300.   70.

WYCHERLEY, William, 1640(?)–1715, dramatist; b. in Shrops.; gained reputation and the patronage of the Court by his comedy, "Love in a Wood;" wrote also the "Plain Dealer," &c.; disgraced for his clandestine marriage with the Countess of Drogheda; restored to favour and pension by James II.
Sir P. Lely.   J. Smith, 1703, mez.
J. C. Smith, 284, 2nd state.   21874.

WYKEHAM, William of, 1324–1404; b. in Hants; cl. of wks. at Windsor to Edward III; rector of Pulham, Norf.; preb., Flexton, Lichfield; warden of Castles of Leeds, Dover, Hadlam, &c.; dean of Martin-le-Grand, London; bishop of Winchester, 1367, and Lord High Chancellor; founder of New Coll., Oxf.; built, or rebuilt, Winchester Cathedral and College, and Holy Cross, &c.
Anon. ("From the most Ancient Picture of him preserved in Winchester College.")   C. Grignion.
Wh. len. in mitre and cope, holding crozier in left hand, with right raised in act of benediction; 3 lines of inscription below.
21¾ × 14⅞.   (20¹³⁄₁₆ × 14¼).   25812.

From the picture in Winchester College.   W. C. Edwards.
Bust, to front, wearing mitre and cope, 1830.
(3 × 2¼).   E. 2243.–'89.

Anon.   J. K. Sherwin.
Wh. len., recumbent, on his monument, as in the Cathedral Church of Winchester. 4 lines of inscription below.
16⅞ × 18¹³⁄₁₆.   (14¾ × 17¹³⁄₁₆).   27626.

WYNDHAM, Sir William, Bart., 1687-1740, b. at Orchard
Wyndham, Somersets.; educ. at Eton, and Ch. Ch. Col., Oxf.;
M.P. for Somersets.; Tory politician and friend of Bolingbroke;
Sec. for War and Ch. of Exch.; led the opposition against Sir
R. Walpole; retired, 1739; eloquent speaker, described by
Pope as "the master of our passions and his own;" d. at Wells.
    J. Richardson.   J. Houbraken, 1741.
    Sh. ha. len. to front, wearing long wig; oval in a border;
caduceus and coat of arms below.
    $14\frac{3}{4} \times 9\frac{5}{8}$. $(14\frac{9}{16} \times 8\frac{3}{4})$.   27123.

WYNFORD, William Draper, Baron, 1767-1845, Ch. Justice
Com. Pleas, 1824; resigned; cr. Baron, 1829.
    W. Pickersgill, A.R.A.   W. Say, mez.
    T. Q. len. to front, looking to left, seated, in robes, holding
in right hand a book, which rests on his right knee.
    $(17\frac{7}{8} \times 13\frac{1}{2})$.   24107.

WYNN, Sir Watkin Williams, c. 1740-1789, M.P. for co.
Denbigh.
    See DILETTANTI SOCIETY.

WYON, William, 1795-1851, medallist; b. at Birmingham;
came to London, gained two gold medals of the Socy. of Arts;
assistt. to his uncle, Thomas Wyon, 1816, and second engraver
to the Mint; chief engraver, 1828; A.R.A., 1831; R.A., 1838;
designed the Portuguese coins, 1835; produced many fine
medals.
    E. U. Eddis delin.   W. D., litho.
    Sh. ha. len., to left, looking slightly towards right; vignette;
facs. signature below.
    Ind. proof; July 25, 1835.
    $(4\frac{1}{2} \times 4\frac{1}{4})$.   28300. 71.

YARBOROUGH, Henrietta Maria, 1667-1738, eldest daugh-
ter of Sir Thomas Yarborough, of Snaith Hall, Yorks., Maid-of-
Honour to Queens Catharine and Mary; m. to Sir Marmaduke
Wyvill.
    Sir G. Kneller.   J. Beckett, mez.
    J. C. Smith, 100, 2nd state, retouched.   E. 2119.-'89.

YARRELL, William, 1784-1856, naturalist; son of a newspaper agent in London; followed his father's trade, but at same
time devoted much time to rural sports, which led him to study
zoology; pub. "History of British Birds," "History of British
Fishes," &c.
    [Maguire.]   T. H. Maguire, lith.
    Full ha. len., to front, looking to left, seated, with right
arm on arm of chair; coat buttoned; rectilin. with corners cut
off; 1849.
    $11\frac{7}{16} \times 9\frac{7}{16}$. $(9\frac{1}{2} \times 8\frac{3}{4})$.   22544.

YATES, Mrs. Anna Maria, —1787, tragic actress, unsuccessful at first as "Mary Graham;" married to Richard Yates, after which she improved so much that she took complete possession of all the parts left by Mrs. Cibber at her death, 1766, and continued to be the favourite actress; achieved unrivalled success as "Margaret of Anjou," "Lady Macbeth," "Medea," &c.; retired, 1785; d. in Pimlico.

R. E. Pine. W. Dickinson, mez.
J. C. Smith, 92, 2nd state (undescribed by J. C. S.), the following words, at foot, "*Price 10s 6d. Mrs. Yates in the Character of Medea Act I Scene 7*," having been erased.
22292.

——, as the Tragic Muse, Melpomene.
G. Romney. V. Green, mez.
J. C. Smith, 142, cut at foot, owing to which it is impossible to say whether it is 1st state or not; but a fine impression, from John Kemble's collection. 22291.

——, speaking the Epilogue to the "Earl of Warwick."
Dod del. Cook.
Pubd. by Fielding and Walker, Novr. 3, 1779.
From a "Collection of English Prologues," &c. 28187. 10.

YENN, John, —1821, architect; pupil of Sir W. Chambers, and in schools of Royal Academy; gained gold medal, 1771; A.R.A., 1774; R.A., 1791; Treasurer, 1796–1820; suspended with other four members of council, 1803, by General Assembly; reinstated on appeal to the King.
J. F. Rigaud, R.A. I. K. Sherwin, stipple.
Ha. len. seated, to left, looking to front, holding a pair of compasses, over a plan, which lies on table before him; volumes bearing the names of Palladio and Chambers on his right.
A private plate. (10½ × 8¼). E. 2230.–'89.

———
G. Dance, R.A. W. Daniell, A.R.A., stipple.
Sh. ha. len., profile to right; vignette.
Proof before the artists' names.
10⅜ × 7⅛. (6¾ × 5). E. 2246.–'89.

YORK and ALBANY, Prince Edward, Duke of, and Earl of Ulster, 1739–1767, brother of George III.
H. Moreland. R. Houston, mez.
J. C. Smith, 34, 4th state. 27176.

YORK, Frederica Charlotte, Duchess of, 1767–1820; eldest daughter of Frederick William, K. of Prussia, m. 1791.
J. Hoppner. W. Dickinson, mez.
Wh. len.
J. C. Smith, 94. 24716.

YORK, FREDERICA CHARLOTTE, Duchess of —continued.
    H. Villiers.   L. Schiavonetti, stipple.
    Ha. len., to left, looking to front, resting left elbow on a
balustrade; oval. Pubd., 1807, by Colnaghi & Co.
    $9\frac{3}{8} \times 6\frac{7}{8}$. $(4\frac{5}{8} \times 3\frac{5}{8})$.   25050. 2.
    In Genealogical Chart, 553. 1.

YORK AND ALBANY, FREDERICK, Duke of, 1763–1827, 2nd
son of George III.
    Sir J. Reynolds.   J. Jones, stipple.
    Wh. len. to right, looking to front, in robes of the Garter.
Decr. 18th, 1790.
    (24×15).   E. 1647.–'89.

    J. Hoppner, R.A.   W. Dickinson, mez.
    J. C. Smith, 93.   24095.

    H. Villiers.   L. Schiavonetti, stipple.
    Ha len. in uniform, to right, looking to front, in oval. In
Genealogical Chart, 553. 1. Published, 1807, by Colnaghi &
Co.
    $9\frac{3}{8} \times 6\frac{7}{8}$. $(4\frac{5}{8} \times 3\frac{5}{8})$.   25050. 1.

    Sir W. Beechey, R.A.   W. Skelton.
    Ha. len., to front, looking to left. In Genealogical Chart,
553. 1. Published, Oct. 25th, 1812.
    The word "Proof" is in the lowest corner on the left.
    $19\frac{9}{16} \times 15\frac{1}{2}$. $(17\frac{7}{8} \times 13\frac{7}{8})$.   25046. 3.

    J. Jackson, R.A.   J. Wright., chalk and dot style.
    Ha. len. to front, in uniform, looking to right.
    Published, Aug. 16, 1822, by T. Cadell.
    $(12\frac{1}{2} \times 10\frac{3}{16}$ (?)$)$.   27994.

    A. B. van Worrell.   W. Giller, mez.
    On horseback, with two gamekeepers and a dog.
    Open letter proof (?); published, Nov. 1, 1827, by M.
Colnaghi.
    $15 \times 7\frac{7}{8}$. $(11\frac{11}{16} \times 15\frac{1}{2})$.   24724.

    Sir T. Lawrence.   C. Turner, mez.
    T. Q. len. to front, looking to left, in uniform, the badge of
the Garter on his cloak.
    Open letter proof ; Feb. 13, 1821.
    $24\frac{7}{8} \times 20\frac{3}{16}$. $(18 \times 14\frac{1}{2}$, excl. of border, $1\frac{3}{4})$.   22058.

YOUNG, MISS, speaking the Epilogue to "The Runaway."
Dod del.   Cook.
Pub. by Fielding and Walker, Feb. 10, 1780.
From a " Collection . . . of English Prologues," &c.
                                            28187.   21.

YOUNG, MRS., actress, in the character of " Cora," from the
Tragedy of " Pizarro."
W. Hobday.   W. Bond, coarse stipple.
Wh. len. to left, looking upwards to right, her right knee
resting on a bank, on which lies the figure of a sleeping child.
Published, Feb. 15, 1804, by W. Hobday and W. Bond.
$(22\frac{3}{16} \times 15\frac{3}{4})$.   26426.

YOUNG, THOMAS, 1773–1829, Natural philosopher and scholar,
b. at Milverton, Somersets.; educ. at Göttingen and Edinburgh;
Physician to St. George's Hospital; Sec. to the Board of
Longitude, and conductor of " Nautical Almanac ; " Foreign
Sec. to Royal Society.; pub. " Lectures on Natural Philosophy
and the Mechanical Arts," " Hieroglyphics," &c.; d. in Park
Square.
Sir T. Lawrence.   C. Turner, A.R.A., mez.
Ha. len. to front, seated, looking to right, holding spectacles
in right hand ; eye-glass stuck in front of coat, which is buttoned
across chest.
Proof before all letters, except artists' names and publication-
line, April 6, 1830.
$15\frac{1}{4} \times 11\frac{1}{2}$. $(11\frac{7}{8} \times 9\frac{1}{4})$.   22942.
See also SCIENCE.

ZINCKE, CHRISTIAN FREDERICK, 1684–1767, miniature-painter,
b. at Dresden; son of a goldsmith; came to England, 1706,
and studied for a while under Boit, whom he soon surpassed ;
he presently found full employment, especially from the King,
George II., Queen, and Prince of Wales ; he amassed a fair
fortune ; was reckoned the equal of Petitot ; losing his sight,
1746, relinquished his practice ; d. at South Lambeth ; was
twice married ; his second wife, Elizabeth, survived him till
1772.
H. Hysing.   J. Faber, junr., mez.
J. C. Smith, 402, 1st state.   24096.

www.ingramcontent.com/pod-product-compliance
Lightning Source LLC
Chambersburg PA
CBHW022129020426
42334CB00015B/815